Fourth Canadian Edition

Small Business Management

Launching and Growing New Ventures

Justin G. Longenecker
Baylor University

Leo B. Donlevy
Haskayne School of Business
University of Calgary

Victoria A. C. Calvert
Bissett School of Business
Mount Royal College

Carlos W. Moore
Baylor University

J. William Petty
Baylor University

Leslie E. Palich
Baylor University

NELSON / EDUCATION

NELSON / EDUCATION

Small Business Management: Launching and Growing New Ventures, Fourth Canadian Edition

by Justin G. Longenecker, Leo B. Donlevy, Victoria A. C. Calvert, Carlos W. Moore, J. William Petty, and Leslie E. Palich

Associate Vice President, Editorial Director:
Evelyn Veitch

Editor-in-Chief, Higher Education:
Anne Williams

Acquisitions Editor:
Amie Plourde

Marketing Manager:
Kathaleen McCormick

Senior Developmental Editor:
Elke Price

Photo Researcher:
Indu Arora

Permissions Coordinator:
Indu Arora

Senior Content Production Manager:
Anne Nellis

Production Service:
Macmillan Publishing Solutions

Copy Editor:
Karen Rolfe

Proofreader:
Laura Lawrie

Indexer:
Patti Schiendelman

Manufacturing Manager:
Joanne McNeil

Design Director:
Ken Phipps

Managing Designer:
Katherine Strain

Interior Design:
Pre-Press PMG

Cover Design:
Dianna Little

Cover Image:
Tim Robberts/The Image Bank/ Getty Images

Compositor:
Macmillan Publishing Solutions

Printer:
Edwards Brothers

Library and Archives Canada Cataloguing in Publication

Small business management : launching and growing new ventures / Justin G. Longenecker . . . [et al.]. — 4th Canadian ed.

Includes index.
ISBN-13: 978-0-17-650005-4

1. Small business—Management. 2. New business enterprises—Management. I. Longenecker, Justin G. (Justin Gooderl), 1917–

HD62.7.S618 2008   658.02'2
C2008-907396-7

ISBN-13: 978-0-17-650005-4
ISBN-10: 0-17-650005-7

Brief Contents

Contents

Preface

Canadians have been prolific inventors and business creators throughout the history of the country. The list of important Canadian inventions includes many things we take for granted in our everyday life in the early part of the 21st century: the telephone, television, the zipper, frozen foods, plastic garbage bags, the music synthesizer, the IMAX® projection system, and the International Space Station's robotic "Canadarm" were all invented by Canadians. In some cases, very successful companies have been created as a result. The inventor of the Ski-Doo, Joseph Armand Bombardier, started out making tracked vehicles for use on snow, and today the tiny company he founded in 1926 has become a multi–billion dollar high-tech manufacturer of aircraft, recreational sports equipment like the Ski-Doo and Sea-Doo, and light rail vehicles for urban rapid transit systems. All of these ideas and all of the companies that the ideas spawned were the dreams of ordinary Canadians who believed in themselves and their ability to create value by accomplishing their dreams. This edition continues to focus on that large segment of the economy represented by small businesses and on the entrepreneurial process that gives them life and vitality.

This textbook is about turning dreams into reality—dreams that can make a difference by leading to new or better products and/or services, creating jobs, and creating value for owners and investors. Owning and managing a small firm has allowed many people to make their dreams come true. It is our hope that what we present in this book—and the tools and ancillaries that accompany it—will support the varied goals of those seeking independent business careers, either directly or indirectly, through the wise counsel of the instructor who has selected this book.

There has never been a more exciting time to be an entrepreneur! If you are committed strongly enough to your dream, in one creative way or another you will overcome the obstacles that lie ahead. New ventures can create tremendous personal value for both entrepreneurs and the investors who back them with time and money. New ventures can also protect and improve quality of life by creating jobs and providing new services.

OUR GOALS FOR THIS EDITION

In the tradition of earlier editions of *Small Business Management: Launching and Growing New Ventures,* the Fourth Canadian Edition incorporates current theory and practice relating to starting, managing, and growing small firms. We have attempted to provide well-balanced coverage of critical small business issues, and we believe that our diverse backgrounds have contributed to that goal. In developing this book, we kept three primary goals in mind. First, we gave readability a high priority by continuing to write in the same clear and concise style that students appreciated in the last edition. Second, we included numerous real-world examples to help students understand how to apply the concepts discussed in the text. And, finally, we incorporated material to help students explore small business issues in the amazing world of the Internet.

LEARN WHAT'S NEW

We continually strive to present current, relevant content in unique and interesting ways. We found many innovative ideas, trends, companies, and people to write about. This edition offers the following content that's new:

- The new subtitle. We believe "Launching and Growing New Ventures" more accurately reflects the goals of the book and informs the organizational changes and content additions found in the Fourth Canadian Edition.
- Chapter 5, "Developing an Effective Business Plan," continues to highlight the importance of having an effective business plan and contains expanded detail on marketing research, vendor expectations, and business plan content. Chapters 5 through 14 contain material that is integral to learning how to develop workable new venture business plans.
- The discussion of venture capital and criteria (Chapter 5) as a means of financing high-growth businesses has been enhanced. Also, Appendix A is new and contains a Venture Feasibility and Business Plan Checklist.
- Special topics such as family business (Chapter 3) and franchising (Chapter 4) as alternative ways to launch a business are now covered earlier in the book.
- Chapter 6, "Marketing Research and Product Strategy," brings new focus to this edition by highlighting the importance of creating and managing customer relationships. Enriching the discussion is distinct, new content on customer relationship management (CRM), technology and CRM, and on understanding consumer behaviour in order to support a commitment to CRM.
- Chapter 7, "Promotional and Pricing Strategies," contains new and expanded information on Web advertising including direct mail, promotion, sponsorship, linkage, and how to set up a successful corporate website.
- In assessing the implications for small business of an increasingly competitive environment, Chapter 11, "Selecting a Location and Planning the Facilities," demonstrates that size need not limit an entrepreneur's global aspirations. The importance and benefits of locating a business on the Web (eCRM)—including coverage of e-commerce business models, 24/7 e-tailing, and auction sites—and global marketing, including emerging markets such as China, are discussed.
- Two new cases, The Ultimate Garage and Cardio-Core Boot Camp, appear at the end of the text and a new sample business plan, Pulse Dance Inc., is provided in Appendix B.

ACHIEVE YOUR BEST

Small Business Management is organized so as to help students and future entrepreneurs achieve success in whatever field they choose. The wide spectrum of content, applications, cases, graphics, stories, and other details offered in the book has assisted many small business entrepreneurs in making their dreams come true. With a focus on learning, our features emphasize hands-on activities that capture student interest and guarantee practical knowledge.

INTEGRATED LEARNING SYSTEM

Our integrated learning system uses each chapter's learning objectives to give structure and coherence to the text content, study aids, and instructor's ancillaries, all of which are keyed to these objectives. The numbered objectives are introduced in the "Looking Ahead" section, and each is concisely addressed in the "Looking Back" section at the end of each chapter.

The integrated learning system also simplifies lecture and test preparation. The lecture notes in the *Instructor's Manual* are grouped by learning objective and identify the appropriate slides prepared in Microsoft® PowerPoint® presentation software that relate to each objective. Questions in the *Test Bank* are grouped by objective as well. A correlation table at the beginning of each *Test Bank* chapter will help you select questions that cover all objectives or emphasize those objectives you believe are most important.

BUILDING A BUSINESS PLAN

We devote Chapters 5 through 14 to material designed to aid in development of a new venture business plan. A "Venture Feasibility and Business Plan Checklist," in Appendix A, helps students identify important questions to ask in preparing their own business plans. Pulse Dance Inc.'s business plan is available in Appendix B; additional business plans, from the authors' undergraduate classes, are available on the book's website.

In the real world, small business owners-managers often use software specifically designed for business plan writing. To bring this realism into the classroom, we have partnered with JIAN® to offer its commercially successful BizPlan*Builder*® *Express: A Guide to Creating a Business Plan with* BizPlan*Builder* software to your students. BizPlan*Builder* Express is a workbook and CD package that includes the award-winning, best-selling software BizPlan*Builder*. This workbook provides all the essentials for creating winning business plans, with step-by-step instructions for preparing each section of a plan, including ready-to-customize samples, prompts and advice, and detailed marketing analysis with links to demographic and marketing tools to help make it easy, flexible, and straightforward. The software is compatible with both Windows and Macintosh operating systems and may be purchased through your local campus store using ISBN: 0-324-42118-4.

UNIQUE SPOTLIGHT FEATURES

The chapter-opening "In the Spotlight" features profile small business owners whose unique insights into how to start, run, and grow a business will help readers identify and explore the full range of issues facing today's business owners. Much of the material is new to this edition. URLs are included for those firms maintaining a website.

CASES

Cases—including eight new to this edition—are available, providing opportunities for students to apply chapter concepts to realistic entrepreneurial situations. A case grid outlines the chapters and related topics that apply to each of the cases and can be found on page 476 of the book.

IN THE TRENCHES

Practical examples for the world of small business and entrepreneurship carry both instructional and inspirational value. "In the Trenches" boxes appear at critical junctures throughout the chapters, refuelling and refreshing chapter concepts with documented experiences of practising entrepreneurs.

YOU MAKE THE CALL

These appear at the end of each chapter and are very popular with both students and instructors because they present realistic business situations that require examining key operating decisions. By having students take on the role of a small business owner, these exercises give them a leg up in addressing the concerns of small businesses.

EXPLORING THE WEB

To familiarize students with resources on the Internet, we have included at the end of each chapter exercises called "Exploring the Web," which send students to specific locations on the World Wide Web, such as Industry Canada and Dun & Bradstreet. Specific questions require students to search and evaluate the small business–related information found there.

ADDITIONAL KEY FEATURES

Definitions of key terms appear in the margins and in the glossary. A list of each chapter's important terms and concepts appears at the end of the chapter, with corresponding page references.

The "Looking Ahead" learning objectives and "Looking Back" summary in each chapter are designed to keep students focused on the most important points. To simplify review, the summaries are presented as bulleted key points.

At the end of each chapter, "Discussion Questions," "Experiential Exercises," "Exploring the Web," and the real-world decision-making situations in "You Make the Call" offer students practice in applying chapter concepts. Over 40 short cases illustrating realistic business situations are provided.

BOOK SUPPORT SITE http://www.longenecker4e.nelson.com

Small Business Management's website contains student resources such as online chapter quizzes, Microsoft PowerPoint slides, and links to the Internet addresses in the book. Instructors will also find downloadable ancillaries such as the *Instructor's Manual*.

UPDATED TEACHING SUPPLEMENTS

All resources and ancillaries that accompany *Small Business Management*, Fourth Canadian Edition, have been created to support a variety of teaching methods, learning styles, and classroom situations.

INSTRUCTOR'S RESOURCE CD-ROM (0-17-647422-6)

Instructors can get quick access to all of these ancillaries from the easy-to-use Instructor's Resource CD-ROM (IRCD), which lets the user electronically review, edit, and copy what's needed. The CD contains the *Instructor's Manual,* the *Test Bank* in Microsoft Word and in ExamView, and PowerPoint slides.

- **Instructor's Manual** Lecture notes in the *Instructor's Manual* are grouped by learning objective and tied to PowerPoint slides that relate to each objective. The manual also contains answers to the "Discussion Questions," comments on "You Make the Call" situations, and teaching notes for the cases. The *Instructor's Manual* is also available on the password-protected Instructor's Resources link at http://www. longenecker4e.nelson.com.
- **Test Bank** Questions in the *Test Bank* are grouped by learning objectives and include true/false, multiple-choice, and discussion questions. A correlation table at the beginning of each *Test Bank* chapter helps instructors select questions that cover all objectives or that emphasize objectives most important to the instructor's specific course.
- *Computerized Test Bank.* The **ExamView®** computerized testing program contains all of the questions in the printed test bank. **ExamView®** is an easy-to-use test creation software compatible with Microsoft Windows operating systems or Macintosh computers. Instructors can add or edit questions, instructions, and answers, and select questions by previewing them on the screen, selecting them randomly, or selecting them by number. Instructors can also create and administer quizzes on-line, whether over the Internet, a local-area network (LAN), or a wide-area network (WAN).
- **Microsoft® PowerPoint® Presentation** A complete PowerPoint package is available as a lecture presentation aid. Computer-driven projection makes it easy to use these colourful images to add emphasis and interest to lectures. Slides are included on the Instructor's Resource CD-ROM and are also available for instructors to download at http://www.longenecker4e.nelson.com.

VIDEOS (0-17-647421-8)

Available in DVD format, these CBC videos explore many of the issues relevant to small businesses in Canada and bring the real world into the classroom. The videos are also supported by a video guide containing teaching notes and case study questions with solutions.

JoinIn™ on TurningPoint®

JoinIn on TurningPoint is a classroom response software tool that gives instructors true integration with Microsoft PowerPoint slides. Instructors can author, deliver, show, assess, and grade all in Microsoft PowerPoint presentation software without having to toggle back and forth between screens. With JoinIn on TurningPoint, instructors can walk about the classroom as they lecture, showing slides and collecting and displaying responses with ease. It is an effective way to turn the lecture hall into a personal, fully interactive experience for the student.

BIZPLAN*BUILDER* EXPRESS: A GUIDE TO CREATING A BUSINESS PLAN WITH BIZPLAN*BUILDER* (ISBN-10: 0-324-42118-4; ISBN-13: 978-0-324-42118-7)

Now students can learn how to use the award-winning, best-selling, professional software BizPlan*Builder* 10 to create a business plan. This optional workbook/CD package provides all the essentials for creating winning business plans, from the latest BizPlan*Builder* software to step-by-step instructions for preparing each section of a plan. Ready-to-customize samples, advice, a detailed marketing analysis with links to demographic and marketing tools, and helpful financial tools make it easy to create a solid plan. Hands-on exercises and activities throughout the workbook ensure that students fully understand how to maximize BizPlan*Builder*'s dynamic tools. Bundle this text with BizPlan*Builder Express* for a package that will help students get a head start on their path to business success. Contact your Nelson representative for more information.

SPECIAL THANKS AND ACKNOWLEDGMENTS

There are numerous individuals to whom we owe a debt of gratitude for their assistance in making this project a reality. In particular, we thank our friends at Nelson. We are indebted to Elke Price, Amie Plourde, Evelyn Veitch, Kathaleen McCormick, Anne Nellis, and freelance copyeditor Karen Rolfe. They are true professionals!

We would also like to acknowledge many others who assisted in reviewing earlier editions of this textbook: Richard A. Appleby of Okanagan University College, Larry Drew of Conestoga College, Vance Gough of Mount Royal College, Cammie Jaquays of Trent University, Kelly LeCouvie of York University, and Barbara Rice of Conestoga College. For their useful suggestions and thoughtful comments, which helped to shape this edition, we are grateful to the following reviewers and to many others who, for reasons of privacy, chose to remain anonymous:

> Ian Anderson, University of Lethbridge
> Brock V. Cordes, Algonquin College
> Bill Bradburn, University of Manitoba
> Jonathan Kerr, Durham College
> James Douglas Clark, York University

Finally, we express our sincere thanks to the many instructors who use our text in both academic and professional settings. Ultimately, it is your evaluation that is important to us. We want to know what you think. Please contact either of us as questions or needs arise; our e-mail addresses are provided below. We view ourselves as partners with you in this venture, and we wish to be sensitive to your wishes and desires whenever possible. Thank you for letting us serve you.

> Leo B. Donlevy
> E-mail: leo.donlevy@haskayne.ucalgary.ca

> Victoria A. C. Calvert
> E-mail: vcalvert@mtroyal.ca

ABOUT THE AUTHORS

JUSTIN G. LONGENECKER

Justin G. Longenecker's authorship of *Small Business Management* began with the first edition of this book. He authored a number of books and numerous articles in such journals as *Journal of Small Business Management, Academy of Management Review, Business Horizons,* and *Journal of Business Ethics.* He was active in several professional organizations and served as president of the International Council for Small Business. Dr. Longenecker grew up in a family business. After attending Central Christian College of Kansas for two years, he went on to earn his B.A. in political science from Seattle Pacific University, his M.B.A. from Ohio State University, and his Ph.D. from the University of Washington. He taught at Baylor University, where he was Emeritus Chavanne Professor of Christian Ethics in Business until his death in 2005.

LEO B. DONLEVY, HASKAYNE SCHOOL OF BUSINESS, UNIVERSITY OF CALGARY

Mr. Donlevy is a senior instructor in Entrepreneurship and has particular responsibility for the field-experience component of the M.B.A. program. He is also the area chair of the Entrepreneurship and Innovation and Business and Environment Areas of the Haskayne School of Business at the University of Calgary. Mr. Donlevy attained an M.B.A. degree in 1995 following a career in the commercial printing industry as an owner and manager. He has been involved with several other ventures during his career. He has served on several local and national trade and nonprofit boards of directors, including a three-year term as president of the Printing & Graphics Association of Alberta and a four-year term as president of the Calgary & District Soccer Referees' Association. Mr. Donlevy's other teaching responsibilities include co-coaching the team of M.B.A.s who compete every January at the John Molson School of Business International M.B.A. Case Competition, where University of Calgary teams have performed consistently well over the years. Mr. Donlevy holds a private pilot's licence and a Level II Alberta Soccer Referee certification, and counts reading, golf, and wine making among his hobbies. He is a native Calgarian, married, and father of four.

VICTORIA A. C. CALVERT, BISSETT SCHOOL OF BUSINESS, MOUNT ROYAL COLLEGE

Victoria Calvert is a tenured instructor at the Bissett School of Business at Mount Royal College. She teaches and coordinates the New Venture Feasibility and the Consulting Practicum courses offered in the Innovative Bachelor of Applied Business and Entrepreneurship Program. The degree has received national recognition for its small business focus both through the academic curriculum and the Directed Field Studies during which students launch their own ventures with the guidance of faculty mentors.

Mrs. Calvert earned a B.Comm. from Queen's University and an M.B.A. from the University of Western Ontario. She has received an Excellence in Teaching Award (1995), and maintains a consulting practice specializing in feasibility and revitalization.

CARLOS W. MOORE

Carlos W. Moore was the Edwin W. Streetman Professor of Marketing at Baylor University, where he was an instructor for more than 35 years. He was honoured as a Distinguished Professor by the Hankamer School of Business, where he taught both graduate and undergraduate courses in Marketing Research and Consumer Behaviour. Dr. Moore authored articles in such journals as *Journal of Small Business Management, Journal of Business Ethics, Organizational Dynamics, Accounting Horizons,* and *Journal of Accountancy.* His authorship of this textbook began with its sixth U.S. edition. Dr. Moore received an associate arts degree from Navarro Junior College in Corsicana, Texas, where he was later named Ex-Student of the

Year. He earned a B.B.A. degree from the University of Texas at Austin with a major in accounting, an M.B.A. from Baylor University, and a Ph.D. from Texas A&M University. Besides fulfilling his academic commitments, Dr. Moore served as co-owner of a small ranch and a partner in a small business consulting firm until his death in 2007.

J. WILLIAM PETTY

J. William Petty is professor of finance and the W.W. Caruth Chairholder in Entrepreneurship at Baylor University. In 2004, Dr. Petty was designated as a Master Teacher, the highest honour granted to Baylor University Faculty members. He holds a Ph.D. and an M.B.A. from the University of Texas at Austin and a B.S. from Abilene Christian University. He has taught at Virginia Tech University and Texas Tech University, and has served as the dean of the business school at Abilene Christian University. His research interests include corporate restructuring, acquisitions of privately held companies, shareholder value–based management, the financing of small and entrepreneurial firms, and lender–borrower relationships. He has served as co-editor for the *Journal of Financial Research* and editor of the *Journal of Entrepreneurial and Small Business Finance.* He has published articles in a number of finance journals and is the co-author of two leading corporate finance textbooks—*Basic Financial Management* and *Foundations of Finance.* Dr. Petty has worked as a consultant for oil and gas firms and consumer product companies. He also served as a subject matter expert on a best-practices study on shareholder value–based management funded by the American Productivity and Quality Center, and he was part of a research team for the Australian Department of Industry to study the feasibility of establishing a public equity market for small- and medium-size enterprises in Australia. Dr. Petty currently serves on the board of an independent energy company.

LESLIE E. PALICH

Leslie E. Palich is Associate Professor of Management and Entrepreneurship and the Ben H. Williams Professor of Entrepreneurship at Baylor University, where he teaches courses in small business management, international entrepreneurship, strategic management, and international management to undergraduate and graduate students in the Hankamer School of Business. He is also Associate Director of the Entrepreneurship Studies program at Baylor. He holds a Ph.D. and an M.B.A. from Arizona State University and a B.A. from Manhattan Christian College. His research has been published in the *Academy of Management Review, Strategic Management Journal, Journal of Business Venturing, Journal of International Business Studies, Journal of Management, Journal of Organizational Behavior, Journal of Small Business Management,* and several other periodicals. He has taught entrepreneurship and strategic management in a number of overseas settings, including Cuba, France, the Netherlands, the United Kingdom, and the Dominican Republic. His interest in entrepreneurial opportunity and small business management dates back to his grade-school years, when he set up a produce sales business to experiment with small business ownership. That early experience became a springboard for a number of other enterprises. Since that time, he has owned and operated domestic ventures in agribusiness, automobile sales, real estate development, and educational services, as well as an international import business.

TO THE STUDENT

As authors of *Small Business Management: Launching and Growing New Ventures,* Fourth Canadian Edition, we must measure our success by the effectiveness of our presentation to you. Although you may not be involved in selecting this textbook, we consider you our customer and wish to be sensitive to your needs in learning the material presented. For this reason, we have made every effort to make it understandable and relevant. We have also tried to consider your viewpoint in each chapter we have written.

We extend our best wishes to you for a challenging and successful learning experience!

Entrepreneurial

OPPORTUNITY

Entrepreneurs

IN THE SPOTLIGHT

Eco-Friendly Opportunity

Geoff Baker and Laura-Lee Normandeau are the founders of EASYWASH, an eco-friendly carwash franchise based in North Vancouver, British Columbia. They developed the idea in 2002 after they had a hard time finding a good carwash that would clean their truck without scratching the paint. Because they drove 45 minutes to find one, they realized their area was ready for a better carwash. But they were thinking bigger than just a local carwash and started researching the issue. The couple travelled across Canada and the United States studying carwashes and looking for a way to break into the industry with a splash.

It wasn't long before Geoff and Laura-Lee recognized the growing eco trend was their ticket. They created a touch-free carwash that is environmentally responsible, with everything from the soap to the power system being eco-friendly. EASYWASH uses water recycling, on-site filtration, rainwater gathering, and hydrogen fuel cell power. Ninety-seven percent of the construction materials are waste recycled, and the building has high efficiency lighting and eco-friendly paint.

However, it's not just a carwash. You can also clean your pet in the automated touch-free dogwash that was created by a team of animal behaviourists and veterinarians. Dogs or cats can be shampooed and conditioned, freed of fleas and ticks, or even deskunked. The award-winning patented technology has been used in North America for over 10 years. Treatment times vary from 25 to 35 minutes, with a price range of $20 to $40, and no appointments necessary.

Before creating EASYWASH, Geoff owned a web-hosting and marketing company, and Laura-Lee worked with him. While studying at BCIT, Laura-Lee needed a business pitch, and after doing some research they found something they could work on together.

Their ultimate goal? To franchise across Canada. But first, Geoff and Laura-Lee have to get over the start-up phase, which has nearly sunk them with seven-figure debt. They need to come up with a plan to pay the bills or they'll lose their company.

Al Harvey/The Slide Farm

Sources: "Fortune Hunters" (June 1, 2008) at http://www.cbc.ca/news/fortunehunters/hunters/2008/01 (accessed July 18, 2008); and http://www.easywash.com (accessed January 18, 2008).

Would you like to become an entrepreneur, to start and operate a small business of your own? If so, you are not alone. An RBC report indicated that 3.3 million Canadians plan to start a business within the next five years, with almost a million hoping to be their own boss by the end of 2008.[1]

An entrepreneurial fever is also sweeping the nation's campuses, as students take classes to learn how to launch, finance, and run their own companies. In today's world your business courses, whatever your particular specialty or major, should include the study of entrepreneurship. Business students, along with engineers, teachers, artists, pharmacists, lawyers, nurses, and others such as Geoff Baker and Laura-Lee Normandeau of EASYWASH, are hearing the call to own their own businesses. You are living in a world of entrepreneurial opportunity, one that is an immensely more hospitable place for entrepreneurs than it was 20 years ago!

You are about to embark on a course of study that will prove invaluable if you elect to pursue a career in entrepreneurship or small business—or even if you don't. An entrepreneurial career can provide an exciting life and substantial personal rewards, while also contributing to the welfare of society. As a general rule, when you talk to entrepreneurs about what they are currently doing and what their plans are for the future, you can feel their excitement and anticipation—which can be contagious!

Taking a small business or entrepreneurship class is not likely to turn a student who lacks basic business intuition into an opportunity-spotting, money-making genius. Yet there is considerable evidence suggesting that such classes can facilitate the learning curve for those who have the "right stuff." These classes teach many of the basic skills, such as understanding financial statements, writing a business plan, and imposing structure and deadlines on dreams that you might never achieve otherwise.

ENTREPRENEURIAL OPPORTUNITIES

Discuss the availability of entrepreneurial opportunities and give examples of successful businesses started by entrepreneurs.

Entrepreneurial opportunities exist for those who can produce enough products or services desired by customers to make the enterprise economically attractive. A promising entrepreneurial opportunity is more than just an interesting idea. It involves a product or service that is so attractive to customers that they are willing to pay their hard-earned money for it. In other words, an entrepreneur must find a way to create value for customers.

entrepreneurial opportunity
An economically attractive and timely opportunity that creates value

Our working definition of **entrepreneurial opportunity,** as an economically attractive and timely opportunity that creates value for interested buyers or end users, distinguishes between opportunities and ideas. It is important to note, however, that a given opportunity will not be equally attractive to everyone. Because of differences in experiences and perspectives, one person may see an opportunity where others do not. But, in any case, a true opportunity exists only for the entrepreneur who has the interest, resources, and capabilities required to succeed.

Entrepreneurial opportunities exist today in a business world that differs markedly from the business world of yesterday. Refer to the In the Trenches and In the Spotlight to learn about the experiences of Geoff Baker and Laura-Lee Normandeau, and Shanda Jerret.

At any given time, many potentially profitable business opportunities exist. But these opportunities must be recognized and grasped by individuals with abilities and desire strong enough to assure success. The start-ups just presented were quite successful; they were chosen to show the diverse, impressive opportunities that exist. Many individuals achieve success on a more modest level in business endeavours far different from those

IN THE TRENCHES

Entrepreneurial Experiences

Gumdrops

Shanda Jerret could barely wait for Vancouver's infamous yearly rains to begin. While locals got in a last few holes of golf, she was overseeing the final details for a brand new retail store—Gumdrops—Vancouver's first wet-weather boutique. Originally from Australia, where she had experienced a five-year drought and strict water rationing, the wt weather started to affect Jarrett during her second winter on the West Coast. She put on some colourful rubber boots, black with pink swirls, to cheer herself up—and ended up with a business idea.

"I would always see people with a scowl on their face, trudging through their day, carrying their black umbrella". She says, "When I wore my boots, it was like a ray of sunshine hit them. I wore them everywhere and people commented all the time. I would be stopped and asked where I got them. So from there it was, 'there's something in this.'"

Jerrett, a jack-of-all-trades, former restaurateur, and interior designer, went full speed ahead, and, nine months later, Gumdrops opened its doors. Her hard work paid off. Within days, the store had sold out of several items. Popular items include Zeyner nylon backpacks, laptop bags with embroidered flames and chrome skulls on the handles, rock'n'roll-tattoo-patterned gumboots, and dinosaur and firefighter boots for kids.

Designing the store herself, Jerrett infused the welcoming boutique with personality and thoughtful touches. Angled mirrors on the floor give customers a better view of their footwear. Future plans include having Gumdrop's own products in store, then spreading the business. "I'm looking at branding," Jerrett says, "And then I would like to have a store in every rainy city. I just want to spread the fun."

Source: Tamara Komuniecki, "A Puddle Jumper's Paradise," *The Globe and Mail,* Saturday, October 20, 2007, p. L7 and http://www.gumdrops.ca.

---

described here. Others fail, but a failure in business is not a failure in life. Many learn from the experience and go on to start a successful business.

ENTREPRENEURSHIP AND SMALL BUSINESS

> Explain the nature of entrepreneurship and how it is related to small business.
> **2**

Thus far, we have discussed entrepreneurship and small business opportunities in a very general way. However, it is important to note that, despite many similarities, the terms *entrepreneur* and *small business manager* are not synonymous. Some entrepreneurial endeavours, for example, begin as small businesses but quickly grow into large businesses. They may still be entrepreneurial. We need, then, to clarify the meanings of these terms.

WHO ARE THE ENTREPRENEURS?

Entrepreneurs are frequently thought to be individuals who discover market needs and launch new firms to meet those needs. They provide an impetus for change, innovation, and progress in economic life, while trying to mitigate risk in pursuit of a new venture

entrepreneur
a person who
launches, builds,
and/or operates a
business

opportunity. (In contrast, salaried employees receive some specified compensation and do not assume ownership risks.)

For our purposes, we consider all active owner-managers to be **entrepreneurs.** We do not limit the term *entrepreneur* to only founders of business firms; we also apply the term to second-generation operators of family-owned firms, franchisees, and owner-managers who have bought out the founders of existing firms. Our definition, however, does exclude salaried managers of larger corporations, even those sometimes described as entrepreneurial because of their flair for innovation and willingness to accept risk.

To get an idea of the unlimited potential of entrepreneurial ventures, think of the achievements of entrepreneurs Chip Wilson of Lululemon, or Clive Beddoe of WestJet, who founded organizations that developed into industry leaders. It is easy to overestimate the importance of large corporations, because of their high visibility. Small businesses seem dwarfed by such corporate giants as Canadian Tire Corporation Limited (over 455 stores and 48,000 employees), RBC Royal Bank (over 15 million customers in 39 countries and 70,000 staff), and Petro-Canada (over $1.8 billion in profits and 5,000 staff in 2007). Yet almost all companies start as small businesses, and small business remains a vital component of our economy. What is a small business? Definitions vary: Statistics Canada classifies businesses as "small" if they have fewer than 50 employees. Canada Revenue Agency uses profits (less than $400,000) and value of assets as criteria.

Define small business
and identify the
importance of small
business.

3

DEFINITION OF SMALL BUSINESS

CRITERIA USED IN THIS BOOK

In this book we use the following general criteria for defining a small business:

1. Financing of the business is supplied by one individual or a small group. Only in rare cases would the business have more than five owners.
2. Except for its marketing function, the firm's operations are geographically localized.
3. Compared with the biggest firms in the industry, the business is small.
4. The number of employees in the business is usually fewer than 100.

Obviously, some small firms fail to meet *all* of the criteria. For example, a small executive search firm—a firm that helps corporate clients recruit managers from other organizations—may operate in many parts of the country and thereby fail to meet the second criterion. Nevertheless, the discussion of management concepts in this book is aimed primarily at the type of firm that fits the general pattern outlined by these criteria.

WHY IS SMALL BUSINESS IMPORTANT?

As mentioned above, almost all businesses start very small. Few ever reach the size of the major corporations mentioned above, but even WestJet started as a very small company in Calgary in 1996 with three aging aircraft, and offering limited flights in Western Canada. Small businesses dominate the economy of Canada. If we define a business as a commercial entity with at least one employee, Statcan has established there were almost 1,030,000 small businesses, and fewer than 14,000 companies in Canada with more than 100 employees in 2007. Key facts about small business in Canada are as follows:

• Over 97 percent had fewer than 50 employees! There were also over 2.5 million self-employed Canadians.[2]
• Firms with fewer than five employees account for 80 percent of all business entities.

- Two-thirds of those self-employed are male; however, the number of self-employed females is growing at almost twice the rate of males.
- The high-tech, business service, and health and social service sectors are the fastest-growing areas of new business in Canada.
- Fifty-six percent of Canadians work for small and medium-sized businesses.
- Over 80 percent of small business firms provide services.
- New jobs created by small businesses are growing at 2.3 percent per annum, with almost 80 percent of the growth being generated by the newly self-employed.[3]

Refer to the data in the Key Small Business Statistics boxed feature on pages 8–9 for greater insight into the Canadian small business environment.

THE MOTIVATORS OF ENTREPRENEURSHIP

Individuals are pulled toward entrepreneurship by a number of powerful incentives (see Exhibit 1-1). Some are especially attracted by one kind of incentive, while others are drawn by some blend of potential satisfactions. These rewards may be grouped, for the sake of simplicity, into three basic categories: profit, independence, and a satisfying way of life.

THE REWARD OF PROFIT

The financial return of any business must compensate its owner for investing his or her personal time (a salary equivalent) and personal savings (an interest and/or dividend equivalent) before any true profits are realized. Entrepreneurs expect a return that will not only compensate them for the time and money they invest but also reward them well for the risks and initiative they take in operating their own businesses.

THE REWARD OF INDEPENDENCE

Freedom to operate independently is another reward of entrepreneurship. Its importance as an entrepreneurial reward is evidenced by a survey of small business owners.[4] Thirty-eight percent of those who had left jobs at other companies said their main reason for leaving was to be their own boss. Like these entrepreneurs, many of us have a strong desire to make our own decisions, take risks, and reap the rewards. Being one's own boss seems an attractive ideal. A study conducted by the Canadian Federation of Independent Business in 2007 determined the desire for making their own decisions as the primary motivator for Canadians starting their own business. Other motivators, in descending order of importance were, it fit their lifestyle, they wanted to better use their skills, they saw it as a path to financial freedom, they had a great business idea, and they could not find a suitable job.[5]

Some entrepreneurs use their independence to achieve flexibility in their personal lives and work habits. An example would be the owner of a mountain biking tour firm located in Banff. The owner offers tours during the spring and summer season to earn money, then closes the business in September to follow his passion for competitive mountain biking by training and participating in the competitive circuit during the fall and winter.

Obviously, most entrepreneurs don't carry their quest for flexibility to such lengths. But entrepreneurs in general appreciate the independence inherent in entrepreneurial careers. They can do things their own way, reap their own profits, and set their own schedules.

Identify rewards and drawbacks of entrepreneurial careers.

4

IN THE TRENCHES

Entrepreneurial Experiences

Key Small Business Statistics

The Business Register of Statistics Canada maintains a count of business establishments and publishes results twice a year. As of June 2007, there were more than 2.4 million business establishments in Canada. About half of all business establishments are called "employer businesses" because they maintain a payroll of at least one person (possibly the owner). The other half are classified as "indeterminate" because they do not have any employees registered with the CRA. Such businesses may have contract workers, family members and/or only the owners working for them.

Approximately 58 percent of all business establishments in Canada are located in Ontario and Quebec. Virtually all the rest are divided between the western provinces (36 percent) and the Atlantic provinces (6 percent). The Northwest Territories, Yukon, and Nunavut represent only 0.3 percent of Canada's businesses.

Total Number of Business Establishments, and Number of Establishments Relative to Provincial/Territorial Population, June 2007

Provinces/ Territories	No. of Business Establishments			No. of Establishments per 1000 Population
	Total	Employer Businesses	Indeterminate[1]	
Newfoundland and Labrador	26,207	17,051	9,156	51.7
Prince Edward Island	11,152	6,386	4,766	80.3
Nova Scotia	57,070	30,916	26,154	61.2
New Brunswick	44,154	26,387	17,767	59.0
Quebec	482,796	236,584	246,212	62.8
Ontario	904,765	365,417	539,348	70.9
Manitoba	79,149	36,404	42,745	66.9
Saskatchewan	97,990	39,121	58,869	99.0
Alberta	332,931	153,604	179,327	96.4
British Columbia	362,642	170,707	191,935	83.3
Yukon Territory	2,940	1,610	1,330	95.2
Northwest Territories	2,768	1,676	1,092	66.2
Nunavut	891	624	267	28.5
Canada Total	**2,405,455**	**1,086,487**	**1,318,968**	**73.2**

Source: Statistics Canada, Business Register, June 2007; National Income and Expenditure Accounts 2006; Estimates of Population by Age and Gender for Canada, the Provinces and the Territories, June 2007.

Note 1: The "indeterminate" category consists of incorporated or unincorporated businesses that do not have a Canada Revenue Agency payroll deductions account. The workforce of such businesses may consist of contract workers, family members, and/or owners.

Relative to population, the western provinces, Yukon, and Prince Edward Island have more business establishments than elsewhere, with the highest rates in Saskatchewan and Alberta at 99.0 and 96.4 per 1000 population respectively. Nunavut, Newfoundland and Labrador, Nova Scotia, and New Brunswick have the lowest ratios of business establishments per 1000 population. Ontario and Quebec are below the national average of 73.2, with 70.9 and 62.8 business establishments per 1000 population respectively.

About one-quarter of all business establishments produce goods, whereas the remainder provide services. Small firms (those with fewer than 100 employees) make up 97 percent of goods-producing employer businesses and 98 percent of all service-producing employer businesses (see figures below)

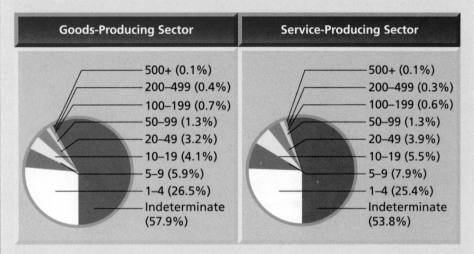

FIGURE **1-1**   *Distribution of Business Establishments in the Goods-Producing and Service-Producing Sectors by Firm Size (Number of Employees), June 2007*

Source: Statistics Canada, *Business Register,* June 2007.

The following table shows the distribution of employer businesses by size of business establishment in each province and territory. Generally speaking, the distribution by size in the provinces is similar to the national average distribution by size. However, there is some variation among the provinces and territories; for example, there is a higher percentage of micro-enterprises (1 to 4 employees) in Quebec (66 percent) and Newfoundland and Labrador (60 percent) than in Ontario (55 percent), Manitoba (52 percent) or the territories (from 30 percent to 52 percent).

Source: Based on "Key Small Business Statistics—January 2008," at
http://www.ic.gc.ca/epic/site/sbrp-rppe.nsf/en/rd02247e.html (accessed July 18, 2008).

(Continued)

TABLE **1-2**   *Employer Businesses by Firm Size (Number of Employees) in the Provinces and Territories, June 2007*

Provinces/ Territories	Total	Employer Businesses — Percent of Total									
		1–4	5–9	10–19	20–49	50–99	*Small* <100	100–199	200–499	*Medium* 100–499	*Large* 500+1
Newfoundland and Labrador	**17,051**	60.3	18.0	10.2	7.3	2.1	98.0	1.0	0.6	1.6	0.3
Prince Edward Island	**6,386**	57.7	18.0	11.9	8.1	2.6	98.2	1.0	0.5	1.6	0.2
Nova Scotia	**30,916**	56.9	17.7	11.7	8.6	2.8	97.7	1.4	0.6	2.0	0.3
New Brunswick	**26,387**	59.8	16.8	11.2	7.8	2.5	98.1	1.2	0.5	1.7	0.2
Quebec	**236,584**	65.8	14.6	9.2	6.3	2.2	98.1	1.1	0.5	1.6	0.3
Ontario	**365,417**	55.2	16.6	12.3	9.4	3.5	97.0	1.7	0.9	2.6	0.4
Manitoba	**36,404**	52.3	18.0	13.5	10.2	3.3	97.3	1.5	0.8	2.4	0.3
Saskatchewan	**39,121**	57.1	17.7	12.4	8.4	2.6	98.2	1.0	0.5	1.6	0.2
Alberta	**153,604**	56.6	16.8	11.9	8.8	3.2	97.2	1.7	0.9	2.5	0.3
British Columbia	**170,707**	58.8	16.8	11.6	8.0	2.7	97.9	1.2	0.6	1.8	0.2
Yukon Territory	**1,610**	52.2	17.9	14.4	10.6	3.1	98.1	0.9	0.8	1.7	0.1
Northwest Territories	**1,676**	38.5	20.4	18.9	14.4	4.8	97.0	2.0	0.9	2.9	0.2
Nunavut	**624**	29.5	21.5	22.3	18.9	5.4	97.6	1.8	0.5	2.2	0.2
Canada Total	**1,086,487**	**58.4**	**16.4**	**11.4**	**8.3**	**2.9**	**97.5**	**1.4**	**0.7**	**2.2**	**0.3**

Source: Statistics Canada, *Business Register,* June 2007.

EXHIBIT **1-1**
Rewards of Entrepreneurship

Of course, independence does not guarantee an easy life. Most entrepreneurs work very hard for long hours. But they do have the satisfaction of making their own decisions within the constraints imposed by economic and other environmental factors. Refer to In the Trenches for a snapshot of the entrepreneur's work life.

THE REWARD OF A SATISFYING WAY OF LIFE

Entrepreneurs frequently speak of the satisfaction they experience in their own businesses; some even refer to the work they do as "fun." Part of their enjoyment may derive from their independence, but some of it reflects an owner's personal fulfillment in working with the firm's products and services—the pleasure, for example, that a ski shop operator gets from talking about skiing and equipment related to it. An entrepreneur may also enjoy being the boss and serving as a civic leader in the community.

At age 26 Tracy Wallace built Natsiq Productions to preserve and to market the Inuit way of life. The firm, based in Nunavut, documents traditional Inuit culture including harvests, hunts, sewing, and storytelling. It creates video documentaries such as eco-tourism travelogues, original drama featuring young local actors, and the stories of Inuit elders. As a winner of the Business Development Bank Young Entrepreneur Award, Tracy is pursuing both a business opportunity and her passion. Additional details on entrepreneurial rewards are outlined the Entrepreneurial boxed feature below.

THE DRAWBACKS OF ENTREPRENEURSHIP

Although the rewards of entrepreneurship are enticing, there are also costs associated with business ownership. Starting and operating one's own business typically demands hard work, long hours, and much emotional energy. Entrepreneurs experience the unpleasantness of personal stress as well as the need to invest much of their own time and labour. Many of them describe their careers as exciting but very demanding. Refer to In the Trenches for additional coverage on why entrepreneurs become small business owners.

The possibility of business failure is a constant threat to entrepreneurs. There is no guarantee of success or even of a bailout for a failing owner. Entrepreneurs must assume a variety of risks related to business failure. While the probability of business failure is often overstated, the 7,519 business bankruptcies reported in Canada in 2005 clearly indicate that the possibility of failure is very real.[6] It is interesting to note that less than 0.3% of the businesses in Canada declare bankruptcy per annum: with the industries most likely to fail being construction, retail, accommodation and food, transportation, and agriculture in descending order. Refer to the federal website http://www.cipo.gc.ca for details regarding bankruptcy per province and industry.

IN THE TRENCHES

Entrepreneurial Experiences

They Work Hard for Their Money

At any gathering of friends, after the requisite talk about Britney and Facebook, inevitably the cocktail-party patter turns to a can't-miss business idea. There's always someone who's sure they have the next must-have widget or thingamajig, a revolutionary new service, a modern twist on an old idea. They're not alone. A new survey finds that 65% of Canadians have thought about becoming entrepreneurs at one time or another.

In conjunction with Small Business Week, Hewlett-Packard Canada and the Canadian Federation of Independent Business commissioned Ipsos Reid to conduct a poll about attitudes toward small businesses in this country—both those who run them and those who use them. According to the CFIB, small and medium-sized enterprises (SMEs) employ more than half of all workers and generate close to half of the Canadian gross domestic product. With the overwhelming majority (95%) falling into the "small" category (fewer than 100 employees), says CFIB president Catherine Swift, "Canada is truly a nation of entrepreneurs."

This despite the many obstacles faced by every startup: bureaucratic paperwork and regulatory compliance, finding workers and markets, securing financing and getting an edge on the competition.

"A lot of people think it's all money, money, money, but actually it's quite the contrary," Ms. Swift says. "[They] do it because they want to make contributions, they want to make their own decisions, they see it as something quite liberating, and so on."

Sure enough, when 900 small business owners were surveyed, throwing off the shackles of gainful but dead-end employment topped the list of reasons these can-do Canadians struck out on their own. Other reasons cited include flexibility of lifestyle, the chance to better apply their skills and knowledge, and financial freedom. Nearly a quarter of them (23%) claim they were prompted by a great business scheme or opportunity—one of those cocktail-party ideas.

However, small business owners are working hard: 15% of them report they put in between 46 and 52 hours a week; 24% say they toil anywhere from 53 to 60 hours a week; and 18% claim to work more than 60 hours a week.

That hard-work ethic has not gone unnoticed. When, in a separate poll, Ipsos Reid questioned 1,842 adult Canadians, nearly all of them (97%) said they view entrepreneurs as highly motivated. Most agree they are innovative, reliable and perform quality work. Overall, respect for small business is high, with a rating of seven on a scale of one to 10, second only to farmers.

Indeed, most citizens surveyed (91%) said they believe running their own business or being self-employed would be a "very" or "somewhat" rewarding experience. However, they should keep in mind another finding of the poll: 44% of business owners were surprised by the workload and reported that the level of effort required was more than they had expected. Something for the rest of us to keep in mind next time we spout off at a cocktail party.

Source: Monday, October 15, 2007 *Financial Post*

IN THE TRENCHES

Entrepreneurial Experiences

Challenges and Rewards

Regardless of the motivations for starting a business small business owners soon find that running a business requires that obstacles be overcome and battles be fought. The biggest hurdle for small business owners is finding new customers and markets, with 59% of respondents reporting this as one of their main challenges. Dealing with finances and paperwork are other challenges. A number of regional differences are also noteworthy, with entrepreneurs from the Prairies being challenged by employment issues and tax obligations. Respondents from Quebec found paperwork most troublesome, while business owners from British Columbia are the least likely to indicate that regulation and red tape are obstacles.

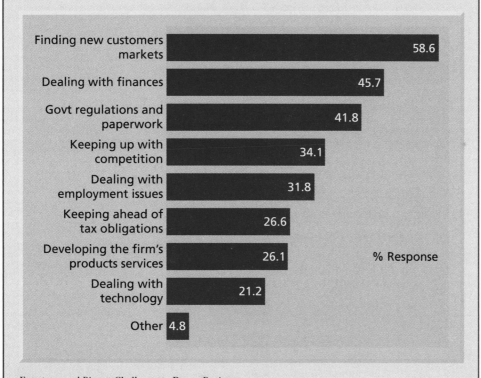

Entrepreneurs' Biggest Challenges to Run a Business

For more than 57 per cent of respondents, a typical work week is more than 45 hours long (see figure below). In fact, about one fifth of respondents say they usually work more than 60 hours per week. Twenty six per cent of business owners work 35 hours or less. Respondents from Atlantic Canada are most likely than others to work less than 35 hours while those from the Prairies are the most likely to work more than 60 hours per week.

(Continued)

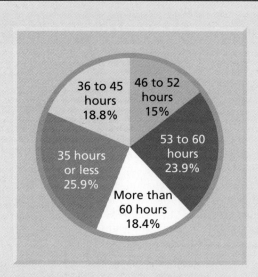

Entrepreneurs Number of Hours of Work per Week

The majority of Canadian entrepreneurs find multiple rewards for running a business, with enjoying the work, the independence and control, and personal drive stated as their key motivators.

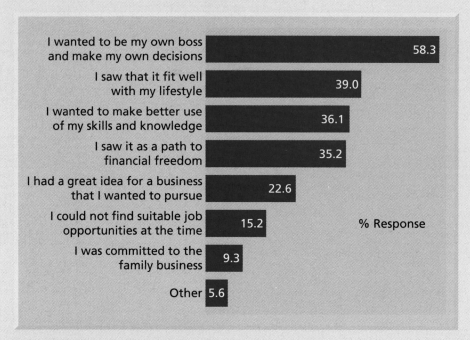

Reasons for Becoming Small Business Owners

Source: "Small Business, Big Value," October 2007, at http://www.cfib.ca/research/reports/rr3040.pdf#xml=http://search.cfib-fcei.ca/texis/search/pdfhi.txt?query=small+business+big+value&pr=default&prox=page&rorder=500&rprox=500&rdfreq=500&rwfreq=500&rlead=500&rdepth=0&sufs=0&order=r&cq=&id=4714617346) (accessed July 18, 2008).

In deciding on an entrepreneurial career, therefore, you should look at both positive and negative aspects. The drawbacks of hard work, emotional stress, and risk require a degree of commitment and some sacrifice on your part if you expect to reap the rewards.

CAUSES OF BUSINESS FAILURE

Extensive research conducted by Stewart Thornhill and Raphael Amit suggests that failure among younger firms in the start-up or post-start-up phases is attributable to lack of managerial and financial abilities. Older firms have developed management procedures but fail because they do not adapt to a competitive environment. Failure also varies by industry, with bankruptcies in the food, construction, transportation and agriculture are mentioned as frequent failures above, and beverages industries typically affecting young firms, while retail and wholesale insolvencies were more common for senior enterprises. The emergence of Internet vendors and "big-box" outlet stores may have eroded the competitive position of established businesses.[7] In a broader study the causes for bankruptcy have been qualified as follows:

- 32 percent because of inadequate research and development
- 23 percent lacked competitive advantage
- 14 percent due to uncontrolled costs
- 13 percent due to poorly developed marketing strategies
- 10 percent because of poor market timing
- 8 percent succumbed to competitor activities[8]

Techniques for reducing the risk of failure will be addressed in Chapter 2.

THE MANY VARIETIES OF ENTREPRENEURSHIP

Entrepreneurship is marked by diversity—that is, there is great variety both in the people and in the firms termed *entrepreneurial*. As a potential entrepreneur, you can be encouraged by this diversity; you do not need to fit some narrow stereotype.

FOUNDER ENTREPRENEURS VERSUS OTHER BUSINESS OWNERS AND FRANCHISEES

Generally considered to be "pure" entrepreneurs, **founders** may be inventors who initiate businesses on the basis of new or improved products or services. They may also be artisans who develop skills and then start their own firms. Or they may be enterprising individuals, often with marketing backgrounds, who draw on the ideas of others in starting new firms. Whether acting as individuals or as part of a group, founders bring firms into existence by surveying the market, raising funds, and arranging for the necessary facilities. The process of starting an entirely new business is discussed in detail in Chapter 2.

The research of J. Robert Baum confirms that successful founders use an entrepreneurial thinking style to cope with uncertainty and opportunities. His three-year study of 122 small businesses indicated that successful founders create a clear vision of their venture, apply their skills from past experience, borrow to overcome insufficient personal funds, adapt goals to manage problems and seize opportunities, and experiment. He suggests a zigzag pattern of quick responses to surprises and shortages contributed to their success.[9]

At some point after a new firm is established, it may be purchased or taken over by a second-generation family member or another entrepreneur who acts as administrator

Describe the various types of entrepreneurs and entrepreneurial ventures. **5**

founder
an entrepreneur who brings a new firm into existence

of the business. These "second-stage" entrepreneurs do not necessarily differ greatly from founding entrepreneurs in the way they manage their businesses. Sometimes, their well-established small firms grow rapidly, and their orientation may be more akin to that of a founder than to that of a manager. Nevertheless, it is helpful to distinguish between entrepreneurs who found or substantially change firms (the "movers and shakers") and those who direct the continuing operations of established firms.

franchisee
an entrepreneur whose power is limited by a contractual relationship with a franchising organization

Another category of entrepreneurs comprises franchisees. **Franchisees** differ from other business owners in the degree of their independence. Because of the constraints and guidance provided by contractual relationships with franchising organizations, franchisees function as limited entrepreneurs. Chapter 4 presents more information about franchisees.

HIGH-POTENTIAL VENTURES VERSUS ATTRACTIVE SMALL FIRMS AND MICROBUSINESSES

Small businesses differ drastically in their growth potential. Amar V. Bhide, who studied the nature of entrepreneurial businesses, distinguished between promising start-ups and marginal start-ups.[10] According to Bhide, promising start-ups are those with the potential for attaining significant size and profitability, while marginal start-ups lack such prospects.

high-potential venture (gazelle)
a small firm that has great prospects for growth

The few businesses that have such glowing prospects for growth are called **high-potential ventures,** or **gazelles.** Even within this group, there is variation in styles of operation and approaches to growth. Some are high-tech start-ups—these success stories often feature a technology wizard with a bright idea, backed by venture capitalists eager to underwrite the next Microsoft. When such companies prosper, they usually grow at blinding speed and make their founders wealthy by being sold or going public.

attractive small firm
a small firm that provides substantial profits to its owner

In contrast to such high-potential ventures, **attractive small firms** offer substantial financial rewards for their owners. Income from these entrepreneurial ventures may easily range from $100,000 to $500,000 or more annually. They represent a strong segment of small businesses—solid, healthy firms that can provide rewarding careers.

microbusiness
a small firm that provides minimal profits to its owner

The least profitable types of firms, including many service firms such as dry cleaners, beauty shops, and appliance repair shops, provide only very modest returns to their owners. They are called **microbusinesses,** and their distinguishing feature is their limited ability to generate significant profits. Entrepreneurs who devote personal effort to such ventures receive a profit that does little more than compensate them for their time. Many businesses of this type are also called **lifestyle businesses** because they permit an owner to follow a desired pattern of living, even though they provide only modest returns. Businesses of this type do not attract investors.

lifestyle business
a microbusiness that permits the owner to follow a desired pattern of living

A major trend in lifestyle businesses in Canada is *mompreneur,* a woman who starts a business because she's been inspired by being a mother, and typically wants more control over her life. A recent competition for best mompreneur in Canada generated more than 400 competitors. An example of a successful mompreneur-type business is Maman Kangourou, launched in 2003 by two women. This business sells baby carriers through stores and distributors around the world. Refer to the company's website at http://www.mamankangourou.com.

ARTISAN VERSUS OPPORTUNISTIC ENTREPRENEURS

Because of their varied backgrounds, entrepreneurs display differences in the degrees of professionalism and in the management styles they bring to their businesses. The ways in which they analyze problems and approach decision making may differ radically. Norman R. Smith has suggested two basic entrepreneurial patterns, exemplified by artisan (or craftsperson) entrepreneurs and opportunistic entrepreneurs.[11]

According to Smith, the education of the **artisan entrepreneur** is limited to technical training. Such entrepreneurs have technical job experience, but they typically lack good communication skills and managerial training. Artisan entrepreneurs' approach to business decision making is often characterized by the following features:

- They are paternalistic—they guide their businesses much as they might guide their own families.
- They are reluctant to delegate authority.
- They use few (usually only one or two) capital sources to create their firms.
- They define marketing strategy in terms of the traditional components of price, quality, and company reputation.
- Their sales efforts are primarily personal.
- Their time orientation is short, with little planning for future growth or change.

A mechanic who starts an independent garage, an esthetician who operates a salon, or a painter who opens a studio is an example of an artisan entrepreneur.

In contrast to the artisan entrepreneur, an **opportunistic entrepreneur** is one who has supplemented his or her technical education by studying such nontechnical subjects as economics, law, or history. Opportunistic entrepreneurs generally avoid paternalism, delegate authority as necessary for growth, employ various marketing strategies and types of sales efforts, obtain original capitalization from more than two sources, and plan for future growth. An example of an opportunistic entrepreneur is a small building contractor and developer who adopts a relatively sophisticated approach to management, including careful record keeping and budgeting, precise bidding, and systematic marketing research.

Smith's description of entrepreneurial styles illustrates two extremes: At one end is a craftsperson in an entrepreneurial position, and at the other end is a well-educated and experienced manager. The former "flies by the seat of the pants," and the latter uses systematic management procedures and something resembling a scientific approach. In practice, of course, the distribution of entrepreneurial styles is less polarized than that suggested by Smith's model, with entrepreneurs scattered along a continuum of managerial sophistication. This book is intended to help you move toward the opportunistic and away from the artisan end of the continuum.

ENTREPRENEURIAL TEAMS

The discussion so far has implied that entrepreneurs always function as individuals, each with his or her own firm. And, of course, this is usually the case. However, entrepreneurial teams are becoming increasingly common, particularly in ventures of substantial size. An **entrepreneurial team** is formed when two or more individuals come together to function as entrepreneurs.

By forming a team, founders can secure a broader range of managerial talents than might otherwise be possible. For example, a person who has manufacturing experience can team up with a person who has marketing experience. The need for such diversified experience is particularly acute in new high-technology businesses.

artisan entrepreneur
a person with primarily technical skills and little business knowledge who starts a business

opportunistic entrepreneur
a person with both sophisticated managerial skills and technical knowledge who starts a business

entrepreneurial team
two or more people who work together as entrepreneurs

Discuss several factors
related to readiness
6 for entrepreneurship
and getting started in
an entrepreneurial
career.

GETTING STARTED IN ENTREPRENEURSHIP

Starting any type of business career is exciting. Launching one's own business, however, can be absolutely breathtaking because of the extreme risk and great potential in such ventures. Before we examine the nuts and bolts of the start-up process, let's think for a moment about start-ups and getting one's feet wet in entrepreneurial waters. There are, in fact, four kinds of entrepreneurial opportunities, or routes to entrepreneurship, and each requires proper preparation.

FOUR ROUTES TO ENTREPRENEURSHIP

As noted earlier, the term *entrepreneur* is sometimes restricted to those who build entirely new businesses, in which case the only real entrepreneurial career opportunity is starting a new firm. If the concept is broadened to include various independent business options, it is apparent that launching an entirely new business is only one of four alternatives:

1. Starting a new business
2. Entering a family business
3. Opening a franchised business
4. Buying an existing business

By following any one of these four paths, an individual can become an independent business owner. Chapters 2, 3, 4, and 5 will discuss these options in greater detail.

AGE, GENDER, AND ENTREPRENEURIAL OPPORTUNITY

One question faced by many prospective entrepreneurs, especially those who are students, is "What is the best age for getting started?" As you might guess, there is no simple answer. Most businesses require some background knowledge. In addition, most prospective entrepreneurs must build their financial resources in order to make the necessary initial investments. A certain amount of time is usually required, therefore, to gain education, experience, and financial resources.

Though there are no hard and fast rules concerning the right age for starting a business, some age deterrents do exist. As Exhibit 1-2 shows, young people are discouraged from entering entrepreneurial careers by inadequacies in their preparation and resources.

EXHIBIT **1-2**

*Age Concerns in
Starting a Business*

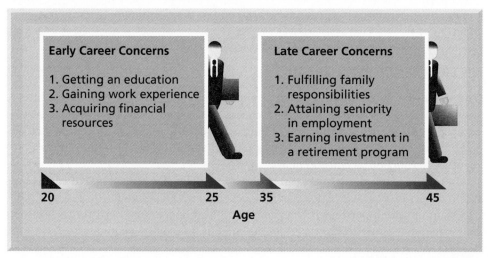

IN THE TRENCHES

Entrepreneurial Experiences

Young Entrepreneurs Quit Corporate Identity

Pablo Salzman is on a fast track: just 23, he and two pals unveiled their second business last month, an online community that aims to be a socially conscious alternative to Facebook, the popular networking website. Inspired by Internet millionaires, disillusioned by the loss of job security in the corporate world and being experts at exploiting technology tools, more 20–30 somethings are starting businesses than ever before. Pablo is a serial entrepreneur.

About three years ago, he and two partners started Blue Horizon Media, a marketing company that devises Internet-based campaigns for clients trying to reach young consumers. Last month the same partners launched Rethos.com, a networking website than connects individuals, companies and non-profits interested in social and environmental issues. Salzman, his partners Alex Salzman (a cousin) and Chris Advansun, and their team or remote employees are based in different cities. They communicate using Skype, a software that lets users talk over the Internet for free, and other technologies.

Bakr Ibrahim is seeing more young people choosing entrepreneurship as a career. He teaches at Concordia University's school of business where it has become a core course. "Young people have realized there's no more guaranteed employment if they join a large company," said Ibrahim. The rising importance of the service and technology sectors is also feeding the growth in entrepreneurship according to Ibrahim. Companies in these sectors "don't require too much capital or physical assets," he said.

Louis Jacques Filion's classes are also filling with students who want to be their own bosses. Many of his students saw relatives let go by big companies and want to know how to go out on their own in case they too are laid off.

Source: Sarah Dougherty, CanWest News Service, "Young Entrepreneurs Quit Corporate Uncertainty," *Calgary Herald*, October 15, 2008, p. B6.

On the other hand, older people develop family, financial, and job commitments that make entrepreneurship seem too risky; they may have acquired interests in retirement programs or achieved promotions to positions of greater responsibility and higher salaries.

The ideal time for entrepreneurship, then, appears to lie somewhere between the mid-20s and the mid-30s, when there is a balance between preparatory experiences on the one hand and family obligations on the other. Research conducted by Paul Reynolds shows that the highest percentage of start-ups is in the 25- to 35-year age group.[12] Obviously, there are exceptions to this generalization: some teenagers start their own firms, and older individuals, even 50 or 60 years of age, walk away from successful careers in big business when they become excited by the prospects of entrepreneurship. While males dominate the entrepreneurial landscape for all age groups, long-term trends indicate a growing female presence.

REFUGEES AS ENTREPRENEURS

Some people, at various ages, "back into" entrepreneurship in a move to escape an undesirable situation. Professor Russell M. Knight of the University of Western Ontario

refugee
a person who becomes an entrepreneur to escape an undesirable situation

has identified a number of factors that serve as external motivators for people who found new firms; he has labelled entrepreneurs affected by such factors **refugees.**[13] Many of these refugees are motivated more by entrepreneurial rewards than by an escapist mind-set. Indeed, it is often a mixture of positive and negative considerations that provides the motivation.

THE FOREIGN REFUGEE

foreign refugee
a person who leaves his or her native country and becomes an entrepreneur in the new country

Many individuals escape the political, religious, or economic constraints of their homeland by crossing national boundaries. Frequently, such **foreign refugees** face discrimination in seeking salaried employment in the new country. As a result, many of them go into business for themselves.

THE CORPORATE REFUGEE

corporate refugee
a person who leaves big business to go into business for him- or herself

Individuals who flee the bureaucratic environment of big (or even medium-sized) firms by going into business for themselves are identified by Knight as **corporate refugees.** Employees of large corporations often find the corporate atmosphere and/or the relocations required by their jobs to be undesirable. Entrepreneurship provides an attractive alternative for many such individuals. Matt Hill and his partner James Kane recently started a second venture installing coin-counting machines in retail outlets. When asked why he quit the corporate world to launch his own company he voiced his disenchantment with the former in five words: "the suits and the culture." "They don't think outside the box—it is very structured. I work the same number of hours for myself, but I have flexibility." After completing an MBA, and working at a financial management firm, Hill quit to start a juice bar called Liquid Nutrition. He and rugby buddy James Kane, who is a chartered accountant, sold the business to launch Change for Change. Coin counters swallow change, read the coins, and provide a receipt users can redeem for cash or spend in stores. Hill and Kane make money on the commission, charged on the amount counted.[14]

PRECIPITATING EVENTS

precipitating event
an event, such as losing a job, that moves an individual to become an entrepreneur

A number of prospective entrepreneurs plan for and seek out independent business opportunities. However, as the types of refugees suggest, many who actually make the move are stimulated by a **precipitating event,** such as job termination, job dissatisfaction, or an unexpected opportunity.

Criticizing management has the potential for creating change—especially in the life of the critic! Many other types of experiences also serve as catalysts, hastening the plunge into entrepreneurship. Some individuals become so disenchanted with formal academic programs that they simply walk away from the classroom and start new lives as entrepreneurs. Others become exasperated with rebuffs or perceived injustices at the hands of superiors in large organizations and leave in disgust to start their own businesses. In a more positive vein, still other entrepreneurs unexpectedly stumble across business opportunities.

It is difficult to say what proportion of new entrepreneurs make their move because of one event. However, many who launch new firms or otherwise go into business for themselves are helped along by precipitating events.

CHARACTERISTICS OF SUCCESSFUL ENTREPRENEURS

Describe some characteristics of successful entrepreneurs.

7

What kinds of people become successful entrepreneurs? As already mentioned, no well-defined entrepreneurial profile exists; individual entrepreneurs differ greatly from each other. Knowing this should encourage you if you wish to start your own business: you do not need to fit some prescribed stereotype.

Some qualities, however, are common among entrepreneurs and probably contribute to their success. One of these characteristics is a strong commitment to or passion for the business. It is an attitude that results in tenacity in the face of difficulty and a willingness to work hard. Entrepreneurs do not give up easily.

Such individuals are typically confident of their ability to meet the challenges confronting them. This factor of self-confidence was described by psychologist J. B. Rotter as an **internal locus of control**—a feeling that success depends on one's own efforts.[15] In contrast, an **external locus of control** reflects an attitude of dependence on luck or fate for success.

internal locus of control
a belief that one's success depends on one's own efforts

external locus of control
a belief that one's life is controlled more by luck or fate than by one's own efforts

Entrepreneurs are often portrayed as risk takers. Certainly, they do assume risk. By investing their own money, they assume financial risk. If they leave secure jobs, they risk their careers. The stress and time required to start and run a business may place their families at risk. Even though entrepreneurs assume risk, they are what we might term moderate risk takers—accepting risks over which they have some control—rather than extreme risk takers, who accept outcomes depending purely on chance.

Jeffry Timmons and Stephen Spinelli have summarized research on entrepreneurial characteristics.[16] They group what they describe as "desirable and acquirable attitudes and behaviours" into the following six categories:

1. *Commitment and determination.* Such entrepreneurs are tenacious, decisive, and persistent in problem solving.
2. *Leadership.* Such entrepreneurs are self-starters and team builders, and focus on honesty in their business relationships.
3. *Opportunity obsession.* Such entrepreneurs are aware of market and customer needs.
4. *Tolerance of risk, ambiguity, and uncertainty.* Such entrepreneurs are risk takers, risk minimizers, and uncertainty tolerators.
5. *Creativity, self-reliance, and adaptability.* Such entrepreneurs are open-minded, flexible, uncomfortable with the status quo, and quick learners.
6. *Motivation to excel.* Such entrepreneurs are goal oriented and aware of their weaknesses and strengths.

GROWING AND MANAGING THE BUSINESS

An airplane pilot not only controls the plane during takeoff but also flies it and lands it. Similarly, entrepreneurs not only launch firms but also "fly" them; that is, they manage their firm's subsequent operation. In this book, you will find a discussion of the entire entrepreneurial process. It begins in the remainder of Part 1 with planning and the various methods of launching a venture including acquisition and franchising. This discussion is followed in Part 2 with a look at a firm's marketing strategy. Part 3 deals with the management of a growing business, including its human resources, operations, and finances. Part 4 addresses special issues such as corporate turnaround and harvesting.

LOOKING BACK

1 **Discuss the availability of entrepreneurial opportunities and give examples of successful businesses started by entrepreneurs.**

- An entrepreneurial opportunity is a desirable and timely innovation that creates value for interested buyers and end users.
- Exciting entrepreneurial opportunities exist for those who recognize them. However, a true opportunity exists only for those who have the interest, resources, and capabilities required to succeed.

2 **Explain the nature of entrepreneurship and how it is related to small business.**

- Entrepreneurs are individuals who discover market needs and launch new firms to meet those needs.
- Owner-managers who buy out founders of existing firms, franchisees, and second-generation operators of family firms may also be considered entrepreneurs.
- Definitions of small business are arbitrary, but this book focuses on firms of fewer than 100 employees that have mostly localized operations and are financed by a small number of individuals.
- Most entrepreneurial firms are small when they begin, but a few grow (some very quickly) into large businesses.

3 **Define small business and identify the importance of small business.**

- Small business definitions are necessarily arbitrary and differ according to purpose.
- Canadian standards vary; Canada Revenue Agency uses profits (less than $200,000), Statistics Canada uses number of employees (fewer than 50 = small; 51–500 = medium-sized).
- This book addresses firms with one or a few investors, situated in one locale, small compared with others in same industry, and having fewer than 100 employees.

4 **Identify rewards and drawbacks of entrepreneurial careers.**

- Entrepreneurial motivators or rewards include profit, independence, freedom (escaping from a bad situation), personal satisfaction, and personal fulfillment.

- Drawbacks to entrepreneurship include hard work, personal stress, and danger of failure.

5 **Describe the various types of entrepreneurs and entrepreneurial ventures.**

- Founders of firms are "pure" entrepreneurs, but those who acquire established businesses and franchisees may also be considered entrepreneurs.
- A few entrepreneurs start high-potential ventures (gazelles); other entrepreneurs operate attractive small firms and microbusinesses.
- Based on their backgrounds and management styles, entrepreneurs may be characterized as artisan entrepreneurs or opportunistic entrepreneurs.
- Entrepreneurial teams consist of two or more individuals who combine their efforts to function as entrepreneurs.

6 **Discuss several factors related to readiness for entrepreneurship and getting started in an entrepreneurial career.**

- The period between the mid-20s and mid-40s appears to be when a person's education, work experience, family situation, and financial resources are most likely to enable him or her to become an entrepreneur.
- Entry into entrepreneurial careers is often triggered by a precipitating event, such as losing a job.
- Entrepreneurs can make no better decision than to develop relationships with mentors who can provide advice.
- Once a business is launched, the entrepreneur must manage growth of the business and issues related to its ongoing operation.

7 **Describe some characteristics of successful entrepreneurs.**

- There is no well-defined entrepreneurial profile, but many entrepreneurs have such helpful characteristics as a passion for their business, strong self-confidence, and a willingness to assume moderate risks.
- Successful entrepreneurs are also thought to possess leadership skills, a strong focus on opportunities, creativity, adaptability, and motivation to excel.

KEY TERMS

DISCUSSION QUESTIONS

1. What is meant by the term *entrepreneur*?
2. Consider an entrepreneur you know personally. What was the most significant reason for his or her deciding to follow an independent business career? If you don't already know the reason, discuss it with that person.
3. Distinguish between an artisan entrepreneur and an opportunistic entrepreneur.
4. Shanda Jerrett, featured "In the Trenches' on page 5 would appear to have many of the features articulated by Robert Baum. Describe them.
5. Why is the period from the mid-20s to the mid-30s considered to be the best time of life for becoming an entrepreneur?
6. Evaluate what your primary motivator would be for starting a venture.
7. What is a precipitating event? Give some examples.

YOU MAKE THE CALL

SITUATION 1

In the following statement, a business owner attempts to explain and justify his preference for slow growth in his business.

I limit my growth pace and make every effort to service my present customers in the manner they deserve. I have some peer pressure to do otherwise by following the advice of experts—that is, to take on partners and debt to facilitate rapid growth in sales and market share. When tempted by such thoughts, I think about what I might gain. Perhaps I could make more money, but I would also expect a lot more problems. Also, I think it might interfere somewhat with my family relationships, which are very important to me.

Question 1 Should this venture be regarded as entrepreneurial? Is the owner a true entrepreneur?

Question 2 Do you agree with the philosophy expressed here? Is the owner really doing what is best for his family?

Question 3 What kinds of problems is this owner trying to avoid?

SITUATION 2

Maria Potenia has just graduated from university. She has developed a new idea for a floating security device that could be used by police agencies or commercial properties to "float" across floors; directed by remote control, the device sends digital messages to a control centre. The device would reduce costs for commercial properties that do not want to install security cameras throughout their building, and would help police to determine the risk of potentially dangerous situations without sending in staff. Maria developed the product while taking a fourth-year engineering course. She has met with several of her professors, as well as the representative of a major security-device manufacturing firm. They have indicated the product has strong potential and that she should work on a venture launch.

Question 1 What type of venture could this potentially be?

Question 2 What type of entrepreneur would she be?

Question 3 What are the benefits that Maria would anticipate by owning her own firm? What are the risks?

EXPERIENTIAL EXERCISES

1. Analyze your own education and experience as qualifications for entrepreneurship. Identify your greatest strengths and weaknesses. Explain your own interest in each type of entrepreneurial reward—profit, independence, and a satisfying way of life. Point out which of these is most significant for you personally and explain why.

2. Interview someone who has started a business, being sure to ask for information regarding the entrepreneur's background and age at the time the business was started. In the report of your interview, indicate whether the entrepreneur was in any sense a refugee and show how the timing of her or his start-up relates to the ideal time for start-up explained in this chapter.

EXPLORING THE WEB

1. There's no time like the present. Go to the textbook Web site at http://www .longenecker4e.nelson.com, if you haven't done so already, to learn what's there and how to navigate the site.

   a. Click on the student resources, and then follow the link to the self assessments. Take at least one of the self-assessments, which will help you learn more about the skills needed to be an entrepreneur. What did you discover about yourself?

Start-up and the Need for Competitive Advantage

IN THE SPOTLIGHT

Brushing Up on Canada's Niche Cosmetic Makers

She calls it "medical chic" but Lee Graff's new cosmetic line is becoming a full-blown fashion statement. Cover FX Skincare Inc., a line of foundations and blushes originally designed for people with skin problems, is getting distribution liftoff. The niche cosmetic brand, which was conceived in the CosMedic Clinic at Toronto's Sunnybrook & Women's College Health Sciences Centre seven years ago, has widespread distribution in Canada and, this month, is being launched in eight U.S. outlets owned by hip cosmetics retailer Sephora after being discovered by Hollywood trend setters. What started as a small line of cover-up and setting powders has morphed into a lineup of 12 product categories and brushes, including bronzers, skin cleansers, and moisturizers, that brings in $10 million a year in retail revenue.

Move over L'Oreal and Estee Lauder: Private label brands are increasingly taking a bigger bite out of the mainstream companies' marketshare. In a global study, ACNielsen reported that total sales for niche cosmetics jumped to 17% in 2005 from 15% a year earlier. In 2007, Holt Renfrew devoted 20% of its new cosmetics counter in Vancouver to the alternative brands and Sephora, the fastest growing cosmetic retailer in the United States, reports 80% of its sales are niche brands.

And whereas Europe once dominated the sector, increasingly, new products are coming from Canada. In addition to launching Cover FX this month, Sephora's U.S. outlets are unveiling [a] new line of lip glosses produced by Toronto-based Balmshell, and is featuring a new line from Toronto-based Cargo Cosmetics Corp.—already a popular brand among Sephora's shoppers. [Sephora owner] Ms. Baber says Canada's proximity to the United States means products reach that large market quicker.

Hana Zalzal, a young civil engineer and MBA graduate, noticed that there was always something new and innovative in fashion, but that wasn't being translated to cosmetics, she says. Ms. Zalzal approached Eaton's department store and offered her vision—a pared-down approach to makeup. "They gave us three stores with prime real estate," she says. Her vision: Cool industrial design (makeup in tin cans) and easy application. Cargo hit home runs with its handy lip gloss travel pouches, colour cards, smoky eyeshadow and frost sticks. This year, Cargo introduced packaging made from recyclable paper and a celebrity designed makeup series.

Competition hasn't stopped other young entrepreneurs from jumping into the fray. Identical twins Fiona and Jennifer Lees, 29, dreamed of owning their own cosmetics company. When the duo came up with the idea of marrying lip gloss with the Retro floating-art pen concept, they cold-called a Hong Kong manufacturer and a Danish engineer to flush out the logistics for a prototype. In addition to rolling out in Holt Renfrew last year, several of Balmshells glosses were just launched in Sephora outlets across the United States. Natalie Penno, vice-president of cosmetics and beauty services at Holt Renfrew, attributes the rise of the Canadian niche brand to the savvy Canadian entertainment industry. The models, the music industry, the film industry, give the products a platform to launch, she says.

Victor Casale, a co-founder of M.A.C. Cosmetics, remains a champion of the private brand: "What happens with international cosmetics brands, is like any business, you try to appeal to as many people as you can, so you don't use a lot of pigment, you make it blah mainstream. [The big brands] don't do any one thing particularly well, whereas the niche companies don't have the marketing muscle but they have a competitive advantage because they can focus."

http://coverfx.com

Photo courtesy of Balmshell

Source: Karen Mazurkewich, "Profits to Make One Blush, Niche Canadian Cosmetic-Makers Thrive," *Financial Post*, October 25, 2007.

start-up
creating a new business from scratch

buyout
purchasing an existing business

Creating a business from scratch—a **start-up**—is the route that usually comes to mind when discussing entrepreneurship. There is no question that start-ups represent a significant opportunity for many entrepreneurs. However, an even greater number of individuals realize their entrepreneurial dreams through other alternatives—by purchasing an existing firm (a **buyout**), by franchising, or by entering a family business. The four different types of small business ownership opportunities include start-ups, buyouts, franchises, and family businesses. Chapter 3 reviews family business, while material pertaining to buyout options is available at the text website; Chapter 4 will explore franchising. In this chapter we will describe opportunity recognition and strategies for start-up.

THE START-UP: CREATING A NEW BUSINESS

1 Give several reasons for starting a new business rather than buying an existing firm or acquiring a franchise.

There are several reasons for starting a business from scratch rather than pursuing other alternatives, such as buying a franchise or an existing business or joining a family business. They include the following:

- To begin a new type of business based on a recently invented or newly developed product or service
- To take advantage of an ideal location, equipment, products or services, employees, suppliers, and bankers
- To avoid undesirable precedents, policies, procedures, and legal commitments of existing firms

Assuming that one of these reasons—or others—exists, you need to address several questions:

- What are the different types of start-up ideas you might consider?
- What are some sources for additional new business ideas?
- How can you identify a genuine opportunity that promises attractive financial rewards?
- How should you refine your business idea?
- What could you do to increase your chances that the start-up business will be successful?
- What competitive advantage could your business have over its rivals?

The entrepreneur's ability to carefully and honestly examine questions such as these will determine the direction she or he will follow. We will examine the issues raised by these questions in the remainder of this chapter.

IDENTIFYING START-UP IDEAS

2 Identify several factors that determine whether an idea for a new venture is a good investment opportunity.

It is critical to determine whether an idea for a business actually represents a good opportunity. Many people have ideas about new products or services that seem like winners but just because something is a good idea does not mean that is a good opportunity.

In fact, a person who becomes infatuated with an idea tends to underestimate the difficulty of developing market interest in that idea. To qualify as a good investment opportunity, a product or service must meet a real market need, and convince consumers of its benefits.

Many criteria exist for judging whether a new business idea is a good investment opportunity. Among the fundamental requirements are the following:

- *Market factors:* The product or service must meet a clearly defined market need, and the timing must be right.

- *Competitive advantage:* A **competitive advantage** exists when a firm offers a product or service that customers perceive to be superior to those of its competitors.
- *Economics:* The venture needs to be financially rewarding, allowing for profit and growth potential.
- *Management capability:* There must be a good fit between the entrepreneur and the opportunity; the entrepreneur must have the appropriate skills and experience to operate the venture.
- *Fatal flaws:* There must be no fatal flaw in the venture.

Exhibit 2-1 presents these five evaluation criteria more fully. Above all, beware of thinking that an idea is a "winner" and cannot miss. The market can deal harshly with those who have not done their homework. However, for those who succeed in identifying a meaningful opportunity, the rewards can be sizable.

competitive advantage
A benefit that exists when a firm has a product or service that is seen by its target market as better than those of competitors

Attractiveness		
Criterion	**Favourable**	**Unfavourable**
Market Factors		
Need for the product	Well identified	Unfocused
Customers	Reachable; receptive	Unreachable; strong loyalty to competitor's product or service
Value created for customers	Significant	Not significant
Market structure	Emerging industry; not highly competitive	Mature or declining industry; highly concentrated competition
Market growth rate	Growing by at least 15% a year	Growing by less than 10% a year
Competitive Advantage		
Control over prices, costs, and distribution	Moderate to strong	Weak to nonexistent
Barriers to entry:		
Proprietary information or regulatory protection	Have or can develop	Not possible
Response/lead time advantage	Competition slow, nonresponsive	Unable to gain an edge
Legal/contractual advantage	Proprietary or exclusive	Nonexistent
Contacts and networks	Well developed; accessible	Poorly developed; limited
Economics		
Return on investment	25% or more; sustainable	Less than 15%; unpredictable
Investment requirements	Small to moderate; easily financed	Large; difficult to finance
Time required to break even or to reach positive cash flows	Under 2 years	More than 4 years
Management Capability	Management team with diverse skills and relevant experience	Solo entrepreneur with no related experience
Fatal Flaws	None	One or more

Source: Adapted from Jeffrey A. Timmons and Stephen Spinelli, *New Venture Creation: Entrepreneurship for the 21st Century* (Boston: McGraw-Hill Irwin, 2007), pp. 128–129.

EXHIBIT **2-1**
Selected Evaluation Criteria for a Start-Up

FINDING START-UP IDEAS

KINDS OF START-UP IDEAS

Business ideas are not all equal, and they originate from different sources. By recognizing the nature and origin of start-up ideas, the founder can broaden the range of new ideas available for consideration. Exhibit 2-2 portrays the three basic categories of new venture ideas: new markets, new technologies, and new benefits.

Many start-ups are developed from **type A ideas**—those providing customers with a product or service that does not exist in their market but already exists somewhere else. For example, Chris Lee owns and manages Crepe It Up! a restaurant that specializes in crepes with a wide range of filling at locations in downtown Toronto. He says "While visiting Quebec City, I stopped at a creperie. Everything was in full view. You could see the cook making the crepes. That moment, I decided I wanted to start my own place." He continues, "My business is something I created. I'm responsible for keeping it going. It is like having a child—it gives you something to nurture."[1]

Some start-ups are based on **type B ideas**—those that involve a technically new process. Jonathan Brett is CEO of MedicLINK Systems Ltd, based in St. John's, Newfoundland. The firm specialized in developing software solutions for eye-care professionals. Established in 2005, it sells its flagship software Eyesistant, to optical stores and optometric practices in Canada and the United States. Named as Emerging Atlantic Entrepreneur of the Year in 2007, 28-year-old founder Brett began developing custom software applications for local companies in 2002. A software application he developed for a friend's optometry practice attracted the interest of others, and within eight months he had delivered the solution to 26 optometrists. His profile rose considerably when he was invited to address more than 2,000 opticians at a tradeshow in 2004. "It just snowballed from there," he says. MedicLINK currently employs 10 staff, and has formed a joint venture to expand the product line into the dermatology field.[2]

Type C ideas probably account for the largest number of all start-ups. They represent concepts for performing old functions in new and improved ways. In fact, most new ventures are founded on "me, too" strategies, differentiating themselves through

type A ideas
start-up ideas concerned with providing customers with an existing product not available in their market

type B ideas
start-up ideas concerned with providing customers with a new product

type C ideas
start-up ideas to provide customers with an improved product

EXHIBIT **2-2**

*Types of Ideas That
Develop into Start-ups*

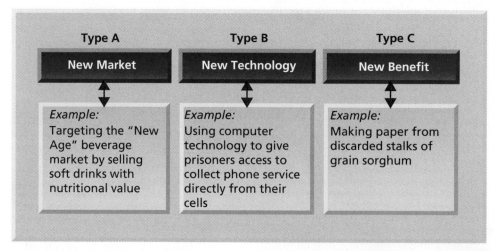

Type A	Type B	Type C
New Market	**New Technology**	**New Benefit**
Example: Targeting the "New Age" beverage market by selling soft drinks with nutritional value	*Example:* Using computer technology to give prisoners access to collect phone service directly from their cells	*Example:* Making paper from discarded stalks of grain sorghum

IN THE TRENCHES

Entrepreneurial Experiences

HeliTours Gets Off the Ground

Julia Henderson, president of the Helicopter Company Inc., loves to fly. In 1999 she and her life partner and co-owner Kevin Smith opened Toronto's first and only heli-tour service, based at the city's Island Airport. Today the company has 40 employees, is booked daily year-round, and is an essential feature of Toronto's tourism industry. However, Henderson and Smith overcame a host of obstacles, from licensing to learning the basics of tourism, to weathering the 9/11 and SARS crises. "There were no helicopters dedicated to tourism in Toronto," Ms. Henderson says of the business premise." We thought we could do well if we were able to share what we love to do—and why not in Toronto; it's gorgeous."

But while the couple knew how to fly helicopters, they knew nothing about tourism. Tourism, an $18 billion industry and one of the top three industries in Toronto and Ontario, is complicated but offers great potential. Due to the high cost of operating a helicopter, the pair had to decide what kind of tours they would offer." Few people can afford a two-hour helicopter ride," Ms. Henderson says. "So we had to break it down into affordable pieces." Tours last 10 to 15 minutes, and entail flying passengers over the city skyline and waterfront at 160 kilometres an hour.

Through networking, they learned their markets were mostly tourists from abroad. So instead of placing brochures in hotels as many tourist businesses do, they direct-market worldwide to tour operators and travel agents in Germany, Hong Kong, Australia, Japan, and the United Kingdom, recognizing that travellers from these regions take trips at different times of the year. They also instituted a reservations system that allowed them to book nearly a year in advance.

Sources: Daryl-Lynn Carlson, "HeliTours Gets off the Ground," *Financial Post*, November 12, 2007, FP6, and http://www.cybf.ca/story-gallery/success-stories/ontario.helicopter.htm

---

superior service, higher quality or performance, or lower cost. The cosmetic companies described "In the Spotlight" have launched products that are successfully competing in a mature marketplace through creative product development, packaging, and promotion. The Helicopter Company Inc., profiled "In the Trenches" offers a new twist for the mature tourism industry, with tourists offered short inner-city flights over Toronto.

SOURCES OF START-UP IDEAS

Since start-ups begin with ideas, let's consider some sources of new ideas. Several studies have sought to discover where new ideas for small business start-ups originate. Exhibit 2-3 illustrates the results of a study by the U.S. National Federation of Independent Business Foundation, which found that "prior work experience" accounts for 45 percent of new ideas. "Personal interest/hobby" represents 16 percent of the total, and a "chance happening" accounts for 11 percent. Another study found that 73 percent of the ideas underlying the top revenue-earning firms came from an in-depth understanding of the industry and the market.[3] Clearly, these studies emphasize the importance of knowledge of the product or service the new firm is to develop and sell.

EXHIBIT **2-3**
Sources of Start-up Ideas

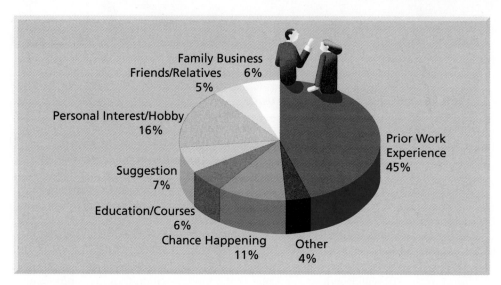

Source: Data developed and provided by the National Federation of Independent Business Foundation and sponsored by the American Express Travel Related Services Company, Inc.

Keep these thoughts about the sources of ideas in mind as we consider in more detail the circumstances that tend to create new ideas. Although numerous possibilities exist—a new idea can come from virtually anywhere—we will focus on four sources: personal experience, hobbies, accidental discovery, and deliberate search.

PERSONAL EXPERIENCE

The primary basis for start-up ideas is personal experience, either at work or at home. The knowledge gleaned from a present or recent job often allows a person to see possibilities for modifying an existing product, improving a service, or duplicating a business concept in a different location.

Louis-Phillippe Arniot, an orthopedic surgeon, developed Navitrack when a fellow surgeon mused how valuable it would be to have a way to get an accurate view of a patient's anatomy during surgery. Arniot founded ORTHOsoft Inc. and developed Navitrack, a navigational tool that gives surgeons a live, three-dimensional image. This allows surgeons to better locate incisions to correctly place implants during knee or hip operations. The result is smaller incisions, less muscle damage, and faster recovery for patients. Arniot still spends some time in the operating room, and this helps him understand how products will be used and what performance parameters surgeons require. Being a surgeon gives Arniot significant credibility when he demonstrates the equipment to fellow surgeons. By 2008 more 35,000 orthopaedic surgeries had been performed using ORTHOsoft's system (http://www.orthosoft.ca).[4]

HOBBIES

Sometimes hobbies grow to become businesses. For instance, a student who loves alpine skiing might start a ski equipment rental business as a way to make income from an activity that she enjoys. Ted Catherwood, a mechanic at Toromount, has been building motorcycles since the '70s. A motorcycling enthusiast, Catherwood has travelled the world on them, including trips to locations such as Afghanistan and India. This experience gave him the impetus to build bikes that are elegant, powerful, and, most importantly, comfortable to ride. Quitting his job, Catherwood created his Niagara-area company TASK Performance, which custom-builds bikes and ships them to customers around the world.[5]

ACCIDENTAL DISCOVERY

Another source of new start-up ideas—accidental discovery—involves something called **serendipity,** or the phenomenon of making desirable discoveries by accident. Anyone may stumble across a useful idea in the course of day-to-day living. Matthew Basan is a carpenter who designs and makes custom handcrafted furniture at his business, *Sound Design,* in Toronto. His Eureka moment came after a terrible storm blew down many trees in his community. He wanted the trees to be recycled, and that prompted him to start his business. "I love making furniture. And if a person has a tree that they'd like to keep in another form I can shape it into furniture, something beautiful that will last." He says working with his hands is gratifying, and his clients take pleasure in owning handmade crafts.[6]

serendipity
the phenomenon of making desirable discoveries by accident

DELIBERATE SEARCH

A start-up idea also may emerge from a prospective entrepreneur's deliberate search—a purposeful exploration to find a new idea. Such a deliberate search may be useful because it stimulates readiness of mind. Prospective entrepreneurs who are thinking seriously about new business ideas will be more receptive to new ideas from any source. Visiting tradeshows and tapping personal contacts with potential customers, suppliers, professors, former coworkers, and the chamber of commerce may generate useful leads.

Magazines and other periodicals are excellent sources of start-up ideas. One way to generate start-up ideas is to read about the creativity of other entrepreneurs. For example, most issues of *Inc.* and *PROFIT* feature many kinds of business opportunities. Visiting the library and looking through the Yellow Pages of other cities for a specific type of business can be productive. Also, travelling to other cities to visit with entrepreneurs in the same line of business is extremely helpful.

Entrepreneurs can evaluate their own capabilities and then look at the new products or services they may be capable of producing, or they can first look for needs in the marketplace and then relate these needs to their own capabilities.

A truly creative person can find useful ideas in many different ways. We encourage you to seek and reflect on new venture ideas in whatever circumstances you find yourself.

USING INTERNAL AND EXTERNAL ANALYSIS TO EVALUATE AN OPPORTUNITY

WHAT IS COMPETITIVE ADVANTAGE?

A competitive advantage exists when a firm offers a product or service that is perceived by customers to be superior to those of competitors, thereby promoting firm profitability. A business opportunity occurs when an enterprise has identified a competitive advantage that has a reasonable chance to succeed. This means that all of the pieces of the puzzle must come together, and in the right order. For example, the entrepreneur

Define competitive advantage and assess features of the environment and organization itself that support competitive advantage.

4

must have a serious interest in the new venture idea, as well as the resources and capabilities to start and operate it.

Perhaps the most critical success factor in business is finding and sustaining an advantage over competing businesses. Entrepreneurs and small business owners who are unable to do this usually are destined to fail. On the other hand, those with a strong, defensible advantage usually enjoy great success. A competitive advantage may just happen, but this edge in the marketplace is more likely to emerge from careful thought about both the mission of the firm and the strategy and positioning that will achieve that mission. Many entrepreneurs and small business owners are not familiar with the kind of systematic analysis that is required to define a real competitive advantage and therefore have difficulty describing their strategy. But a business owner *must*—after examining opportunities, risks, and resources—chart a basic strategy that leads to competitive advantage. And, ideally, this strategy should then be committed to writing in the business plan to ensure follow-through and support future planning.

To establish a competitive advantage, the business owner needs to understand the nature of the environment in which he or she will operate. Studying general trends and the dynamics of competition in an industry may highlight opportunities that match the unique capabilities of the firm, and this knowledge can be used to block the effects of competitive response. In other words, external analysis enables the entrepreneur or business owner to determine *what business potentials exist,* whereas internal analysis reveals *what the firm is able to do.* In combination, assessing environmental opportunities and organizational capabilities can guide a business owner to competitive advantage through a carefully crafted strategy. Exhibit 2-4 presents a model of environmental and organizational analysis, and the relationship between those factors and the opportunity assessment process.

ASSESSING THE ENVIRONMENT

The external environment has a significant impact on the growth and profitability of firms. Thus, entrepreneurs benefit when they analyze the external environment to find opportunities to exploit and threats against which to take protective measures. This analysis should recognize two primary layers within the external environment—the **macroenvironment** and the **industry environment.** The macroenvironment is very broad, comprising general factors that affect all—or at least most—businesses in a society. In comparison, the industry environment is defined more narrowly as the combined forces that directly affect a given firm and all of its relevant competitors.

macroenvironment
the broad environment with its multiple factors that affect most businesses in a society

industry environment
the combined forces that directly affect a given firm and all of its relevant competitors

THE MACROENVIRONMENT
Within the context of the macroenvironment, which encompasses the society as a whole, are a number of critical segments. These can be remembered by the acronym STEP, which stands for *S*ociocultural, *T*echnological, *E*conomic, and *P*olitical/Legal. In the economic segment, for example, forces such as the rate of inflation, interest rates, and even currency exchange rates affect a small business, as they either promote or discourage business growth. In the sociocultural segment are societal trends that may affect consumer demand, opening up new markets and pushing others into decline. The political/legal segment includes governmental trends such as tax laws and safety regulations that may pose a threat to businesses or render an existing or budding entrepreneurial business

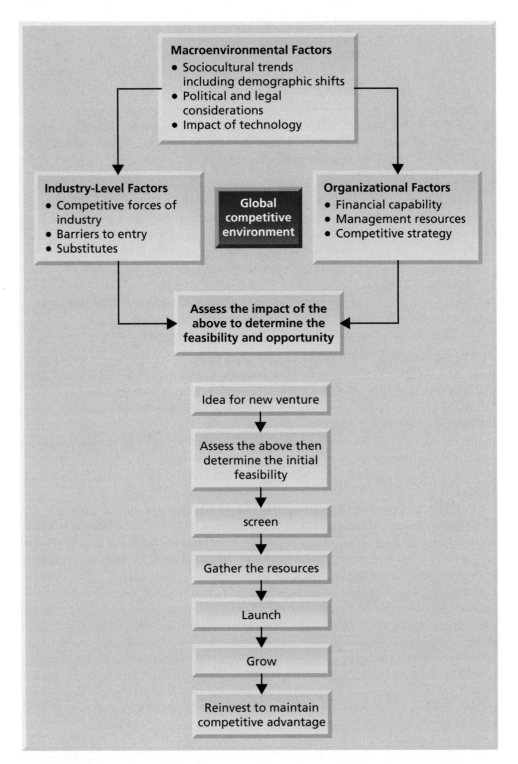

EXHIBIT **2-4**
*A Model of Environ-
mental and Organiza-
tional Impact on
Opportunity Assessment*

concept unviable. Perhaps most relevant to small businesses is the technological segment, since it is this segment that spawns many new ventures—or renders them obsolete. When conducting the analysis, it is useful to consider geopolitical developments that create new opportunities to expand markets, outsource internationally, and invest abroad. The macroenvironment is obviously a two-edged sword, which can open up new opportunities for a small firm—or threaten its existence.

THE INDUSTRY ENVIRONMENT

In addition to macroenvironmental influences, entrepreneurs are also subject to the more direct influences of their industries. A number of factors determine the level of competition within an industry. According to Michael Porter in his book *Competitive Advantage,*[7] five forces determine the nature and degree of competition in an industry:

1. *Bargaining power of buyers:* Are industry customers so powerful that they will force companies to charge low prices, thereby reducing profits?
2. *Threat of substitute products or services:* Can customers turn to other products or services to replace those that the industry offers?
3. *Bargaining power of suppliers:* Are industry suppliers so powerful that they will demand high prices for inputs, thereby increasing the company's costs and reducing its profits?
4. *Rivalry among existing competitors:* How intense is the rivalry among existing competitors in the industry?
5. *Threat of new competitors:* How easy is it for new competitors to enter the industry?

The five factors may offset the attractiveness of a target market. Generally speaking, the profitability of firms in an industry will be inversely related to competitive forces—strong forces yield weak profits, whereas weak forces are likely to spur strong profits.

The more completely entrepreneurs and business owners understand the forces underlying competitive pressure, the better they will be able to assess market opportunities and threats facing their ventures. Obviously, which of these forces dominate industry competition depends on the particular circumstances. Therefore, the challenge is to recognize and understand these forces so that the venture is positioned to make the most of what the industry has to offer.

Once the entrepreneur has identified the opportunities and threats present in the macroenvironment and the industry environment, the competitive foundation begins to form. As strategy expert Gary Hamel sees it, understanding the industry environment and assessing the macroenvironment represent the initial steps in providing a platform for competitive advantage. According to Hamel, first it is important to identify the common practices that tend to guide behaviour in the industry. When combined with knowledge of changes in the macroenvironment—for example, emerging technologies that can be exploited, changes in lifestyle that clear the way for new products or services, and geopolitical shifts that open new market opportunities—these insights can shed light on the path that leads to competitive advantage.[8] Lululemon Athletica is an example of a retail outlet that recognized a trend, and now dominates its market. Founder Chip Wilson recognized that yoga was becoming popular, and that it required flexible and stylish clothing not available in Canada. He created a retail chain that targeted the growing number of yoga practitioners, and created a clothing phenomenon.

Consider the case of Rutter Inc., based in St. John's, Newfoundland, which specializes in marine technology, enhanced radar systems, and engineering consulting. Created in 1998 by Byron Dawe, by 2007 Rutter won an order for a bridge-mounted radar system to track vessel traffic approaching the 18 bridges of the St. Lawrence Seaway. The company's Radar-100S6 system reliably tracks smaller vessels at further distances, day or night, irrespective of weather conditions, providing a safe practical and cost-effective solution to track vessels. Other product lines include control systems for offshore oil platforms, and turnkey engineering procurement.

The superiority of Rutter's radar systems resulted in a 90 percent growth rate, to $2 million in sales for the new product line, and overall company revenues of almost $100 million. The success of Rutter's electronic instruments and engineering consulting is tied directly to expansion of the Canadian East-Coast and international offshore drilling, as well the heightened need for naval security in the post–9/11 era. The company has successfully expanded its services into the international market, with interests in Brazil and France.[9] Refer to http://www.rutter.ca for a detailed description of operations.

Rutter's success illustrates the value of sound environmental assessment: Dawe recognized an emerging need for marine instrumentation technologies. However, the full potential of a business idea is revealed only after the entrepreneur takes another critical step, which Hamel describes as a systematic assessment of the firm's **core competencies** (defined generally as "those things that the firm does best").[10]

ASSESSING THE ORGANIZATION

It is not enough to have a solid grasp of the macroenvironment and the industry context in which the business competes. This understanding must be wedded to insight into internal potential, or what the firm can do. This insight can be gained through systematic analysis of the strengths and weaknesses of the firm, a process called organizational assessment.

In order to assess the organizational potential of a business, entrepreneurs and business owners must understand the difference between resources and capabilities. **Organizational resources** are those basic inputs that a firm uses to conduct its business. They include such factors as capital, technology, equipment, and employees. To be more specific, organizations have **tangible resources,** which are visible and easy to measure. Plants and equipment, cash reserves, and the firm's borrowing capacity all represent tangible resources. These differ fundamentally from **intangible resources,** which are invisible and, therefore, difficult to quantify. Intangible resources include proprietary property rights such as patents and copyrights, as well as assets based on brand recognition and the firm's reputation.

Though the terms are often used interchangeably, resources are not technically the same as capabilities. Whereas resources are singular in nature, **organizational capabilities** are best viewed as the integration of several resources, which are deployed together to the firm's advantage. In reality, resources cannot provide competitive advantage until they are bundled into some useful configuration. Consider this analogy: a keyboard is a resource, but it is of no practical value until it is integrated into a system of computer components that provide the ability to read, store, and analyze data.

This section has introduced the type of analysis required to determine the relative competitive position of an organization. This serves as a starting place from which the entrepreneur can craft a strategy to achieve competitive advantage and superior financial performance.

SCREENING THE POTENTIAL VENTURE

A useful process in selecting a potential venture is the screening of ideas using a go/no-go model. Business ideas are evaluated during a three-stage process that assesses the potential venture with increasing vigor. Exhibit 2-5 outlines the process.

core competencies
value-creating organizational capabilities that are unique to a firm

Evaluate the feasibility of a business. 5

organizational resources
basic inputs that a firm uses to conduct its business

tangible resources
organizational resources that are visible and easy to measure

intangible resources
organizational resources that are invisible and difficult to quantify

organizational capabilities
the integration of several organizational resources that are deployed together to the firm's advantage

EXHIBIT **2-5**
*Venture Feasibility
Screening Model*

Percentage of Ideas in the Pipeline	Stage and Decision
100%	**Stage 1: Back–of-the-Envelope Concept** In one sitting prepare a simple analysis of • Does the product have potential customers? • Can it be done—are core technologies available? • Is it the right business for your skills, goals, and ability? • Is it worthwhile financially—what will sales and costs be? Decision: go or no go based on initial feasibility
20–30%	**Stage 2: Research and Verification** This stage entails extensive market and costing research. • Evaluate the number of potential customers—are there enough? What do they really want? • Evaluate the competition—will you have a competitive advantage? • Evaluate the human resources required—who will you need? • Evaluate the technical feasibility—review to secure product licensing, and costs of designing and producing • Evaluate the financial feasibility—what are the financial dynamics: how much money will be needed, what could potential sales be, at what cost, what are the risks, and is it worthwhile? Decision: go or no go based on the research
10%	**Stage Three: Refining the concept** This stage entails the preparation of a detailed business plan, which will address all the issues and research created in Stage 2 in depth. Decision: go or no go
1%	The Leap of Faith—start the venture[11]

To examine a variety of Canadian ventures that made the "leap of faith" and undertook the necessary steps to move though the concept stage to successful commercialization visit http://www.innovation.gc.ca. A variety of company profiles are available.

Because crafting a strategy for a small, entrepreneurial concern is a complex task, it comes as no surprise that meaningful strategies emerge only when entrepreneurs devote considerable time and energy to the process. Crafting a strategy is best done prior to the business starting up, or when conditions in the marketplace or the environment create opportunities or threats to the ongoing success of the business. The key building blocks for gaining and sustaining a competitive advantage through a well-designed and articulated strategy will be examined.

FACTORS CONTRIBUTING TO COMPETITIVE ADVANTAGE

Though a number of paths can lead to competitive advantage, some of the more common ones include distinctions based on price/value, unique service features, notable product attributes, customer service, and accessibility. The following examples illustrate these platforms for competitive advantage.

- *Price/value:* "If you, as a supplier of a product or service to your customer, can find a way to make them more successful on their terms, why wouldn't they buy from you?" says Paul Britton of Sibson Canada Inc., a management consulting firm. He says companies must supply products and services to customers "at the right time, in the right amount, and at the right value. If you can do that, you've got them hooked."[12]

    One company that understands this is Winnipeg's Corydon Hardware, which uses superior service to increase perceived customer value. This strategy has helped Corydon successfully compete with big-box stores like Revy and Home Depot. Owner Mike Benson says, "Service is a much valued word, but it must be service with knowledge or it doesn't matter if the store staff smile at you or not."[13]

- *Unique service features:* Upside Software Inc. of Edmonton specializes in contract lifestyle management software servicing more than 200 companies worldwide. The firm has been listed as both Alberta's fastest-growing company, and as one of Deloitte's Fast 50 companies. The firm is privately held, with the 130 staff owning more than 90 percent of the shares. President Ashif Mawji attributes the company's high revenue growth to its customer service. Upside offers a competitive pricing structure, invests more than 35 percent of revenues each year to research and development, and structures its pricing to provide customers with a full return on their software investment within one year. Upside maintains its leading edge through both comprehensive product solutions and intense customer focus.[14] Refer to http://www.upsidesoft.com for more information.

- *Notable product attributes:* "It tastes awful. And it works." This famous slogan has helped make Buckley's Mixture Canada's top-selling cough syrup. However, the catchy commercial message is backed by a significant product attribute: it really does work! "You've got to have a product that's significantly different than any other product on the market," says W.K. Buckley Ltd. Chairman Frank Buckley, who is also the star of the company's television commercials. "It also helps to associate an individual with the product, which the big guys can't do."[15]

- *Customer service:* When Wal-Mart came to Canada, Canadian Tire faced a big threat. The company's response was to retool customer service, which had been noticeably lacking in the stores. The company invested millions in retraining staff to ensure top-notch customer service. Now, instead of pointing you to the aisle that has hammers, staff will take you there and find out exactly what kind of hammer you want, helping you to make the right choice.[16]

- *Accessibility:* Greg Brophy came up with a winning formula when he created Shred-it, a mobile document-shredding company in 1989. It was one of a number of ventures Brophy started and ran during his studies at McMaster University in Hamilton. By taking the service to the customer, Shred-it was able to build a very successful business, taking away market share from competitors by saving customers the need to truck documents to a central facility to be shredded and allowing them to oversee the shredding process. The company franchised its business in Canada and other countries, some as far away as Hong Kong and Argentina. Shred-it has grown to more than 140 branches and 900 shredding trucks. Its recycling program saves over 9 million trees a year worldwide. Refer to the company website at http://www.shredit.com.[17]

To the degree that an entrepreneurial venture is able to provide products or services that the customer values, the business achieves competitive advantage and enjoys superior profitability.

Though the importance of competitive advantage is undeniable, entrepreneurs and business owners are often convinced that they cannot achieve this edge in the marketplace. This unfortunate conclusion comes from two prevailing myths. The first is that most of the good business opportunities are already gone. The other is that small firms cannot compete profitably with big companies. Both of these ideas are erroneous! Of course, existing companies, both large and small, do not typically welcome competitors. As well-respected author Karl H. Vesper puts it,

> *Established companies do their best to maintain proprietary shields . . . to ward off prospective as well as existing competitors. Consequently, the entrepreneur who would create a new competitor to attack them needs to have some sort of "entry wedge," or strategic competitive advantage for breaking into the established pattern of commercial activity.*[18]

The selection of an entry wedge must be guided by more than blind instinct or whatever is popular at the time. Good choices result from proper and systematic assessment of the foundations that support solid competitive advantage.

To establish a competitive advantage, the business owner needs to understand the nature of the environment in which he or she will operate. Studying general trends and the dynamics of competition in an industry may highlight opportunities that match the unique capabilities of the firm, and this knowledge can be used to block the effects of competitive response. In other words, external analysis enables the entrepreneur or business owner to determine *what business potentials exist,* whereas internal analysis reveals *what the firm is able to do.* In combination, assessing environmental opportunities and organizational capabilities can guide a business owner to competitive advantage through a carefully crafted strategy.

SELECTING STRATEGIES TO GAIN COMPETITIVE ADVANTAGE

Identify and compare strategy options for building and sustaining competitive advantage.

Generally speaking, a **strategy** is an action plan that guides resource investments to capitalize on potential business opportunities. Wise strategy selections are guided by a solid rationale grounded in the firm's situation, rather than by decisions based on the momentum of past choices, the latest industry fad, or whatever feels right at the moment.

BROAD-BASED STRATEGY OPTIONS

strategy
an action plan that guides resource investments to capitalize on business opportunities

Depending on the situation, many strategies can lead to competitive advantage in the marketplace. However, these strategies can always be traced back to one of two broad-based options—creating a cost advantage or establishing a marketing advantage.

COST-ADVANTAGE STRATEGY

cost-advantage strategy
A plan of action that requires a firm to be the lowest-cost producer within its market

The **cost-advantage strategy** requires a firm to be the lowest-cost producer within the market. The sources of cost advantage are quite varied, ranging from low-cost labour to efficiency in operations. Compared to other strategies, however, competing on cost may be the least sustainable as an advantage. Competitors may respond by finding ways to lower their costs and create conditions for a price war.

Many entrepreneurs and business owners assume that cost-based strategies work only for large corporations; however, cost-advantage factors are so numerous and varied that, in many cases, small businesses may be able to use them with greater success. For example, Calgary-based WestJet Airlines Ltd. began flying in 1996 as a low-fare, no-frills, regional airline. By flying only one type of aircraft, WestJet reduced its training and maintenance costs. The aircraft themselves were all purchased used at about one-third the cost of new ones. The results? WestJet was and is one of few profitable airlines in the world and continues to increase its destinations throughout North America.[19] It should be noted that by 2008 WestJet had dramatically expanded its routes but retained its common aircraft type the Boing 737. The increased competition, from start-up airlines using the WestJet model, combined with the cost of new planes, and increased fuel and maintenance prices, required WestJet to develop operational efficiencies such as sales agents working in their home at company-supplied work stations.

Another example of a firm that uses a cost-advantage strategy is virtual bank ING Direct. A subsidiary of a Dutch bank, the Canadian company has no branches, which significantly reduces its cost of doing business. By reducing costs, ING Direct can offer its customers higher interest on deposits. This is also a good example of how a company can use Internet technology to do business in new ways to gain a competitive advantage.[20]

MARKETING-ADVANTAGE STRATEGY

The second general option for building a competitive advantage is creation of a **marketing-advantage strategy,** an approach that requires differentiation of a firm's product or service along some dimension other than cost. A firm that can create and sustain an attractive differential position will be a successful performer in the marketplace. The consumer must be convinced of the uniqueness and desirability of the product or service—whether real or perceived—if the strategy is to be effective. A wide variety of operational and marketing tactics, ranging from promotion to product design, lead to product or service differentiation.

marketing-advantage strategy
A plan of action designed to provide a product or service with unique attributes that are valued by consumers

Bob Nagy entered the packaged ice market by creating a competitive marketing advantage through product differentiation. Impressed with the success of bottled water, Nagy thought he could do the same for ice by focusing on water quality and brand advertising. Under the Arctic Glacier label, Winnipeg-based The Arctic Group Inc. has become Canada's largest packaged-ice producer, and is one of the largest producers of packaged ice in the United States. The key to this success is state-of-the-art water treatment, which removes 95 percent of the impurities in municipal water, giving Arctic Glacier a key edge over its major competitor, homemade ice, among health-conscious consumers, and making Arctic Glacier harder, clearer, and longer lasting than refrigerator-made ice.[21] This venture relies on product differentiation rather than cost for its competitive advantage.

SUSTAINING COMPETITIVE ADVANTAGE

So far, we have looked at two of the three major components of the competitive advantage model (see Exhibit 2-4). The model highlights the importance of building a solid foundation for competitive advantage through sound environmental

IN THE TRENCHES

Entrepreneurial Experiences

Small Entrepreneurs Against Mega-Retailers

A study released by Barry Cotton and Jean-Charles Cachon of Laurentian University in Sudbury articulates strategies employed by small businesses to successfully compete in the shadow of retail giants such as Wal-Mart, Costco, and Home Depot. The growth of mega-stores has been dramatic, as illustrated by the Toronto-area retailing environment where 93 mega-stores existed in 1990, increasing to 614 by 2002. The study was based upon a sample of 78 smaller retailers during the 1999 to 2003 period.

The study confirmed that small retailers suffered lower sales and clientele upon the arrival of mega-stores with the following results:

- 47.4 percent experienced decreased sales ranging from 6 to 56 percent; the average decrease was 21.3 percent.
- Of the stores experiencing a decrease in sales, profits declined by 12.4 percent on average.
- Staff requirements shrank by one full-time person for these stores.

A key factor raised by the study was the strategies used by the 16 stores, 21.6 percent of the sample, that successfully competed against the mega-stores and achieved an average sales growth of 21 percent. Differentiation and niche marketing were the main aspects of the competitive strategy, with many reflecting superior customer service through time savings, individual customization of service delivery, and problem solving, to create differentiation. For example, a building supplier offered on-roof shingle delivery—a service not offered by the competing mega-retailer.

In addition, some of the strategic moves adopted by successful retailers amounted to a "Vacuum Strategy," which includes the refusal to carry brands or service products available at mega-stores, as well as refusing any alliance with them and making it known to their customers.

Source: Barry Cotton and Jean-Charles Cachon, "Resisting the Giants: Small Retail Entrepreneurs against Mega-Retailers," an empirical study presented in the ICSB World Conference, Washington DC, June 2005.

and organizational assessments. Then, based on that foundation, an entrepreneur must determine which competitive strategy is best for the firm. The third element of the competitive advantage model involves sustaining the performance results derived from competitive advantage foundations.

Entrepreneurs generally choose from a menu of strategy options, selecting the one they believe will lead to desirable outcomes. The considerations may not always be limited to sales revenue and profits. For example, personal interests may dictate a relocation strategy, as in the case of Cindy Burton of iWave, who moved her company from Vancouver to Nelson, B.C. and then to Charlottetown, P.E.I. Such decisions are not as uncommon as you may think.[22] But if the entrepreneur wants to produce results, strategies must be designed to generate outcomes such as superior profitability, increased market share, improved customer satisfaction, and simple survival. These results all contribute to the value of the firm.

No competitive advantage lasts forever. But recent research has emphasized the importance of establishing a **sustainable competitive advantage,** a value-creating industry

sustainable competitive advantage

an established, value-creating industry position that is likely to endure over time

position that is likely to endure over time.[23] From the beginning, the entrepreneur should plan sustainability into strategy by leveraging the unique capabilities of the firm in a way that competitors will find difficult to imitate. However, the entrepreneur must recognize that sooner or later rivals will discover a way to duplicate any value-creating strategy.[24] Therefore, it is also important to think of new ways to invest performance outcomes so that the basis of the competitive advantage can be renewed over the long run.

Competitive advantage clearly has a life cycle. Building a competitive advantage generally requires commitment of considerable resources; a well-planned effort will lead to a performance payoff. However, returns from that competitive advantage will *always* diminish over time. Ian MacMillan describes the competitive advantage life cycle in terms of a three-stage model: launch, exploitation, and erosion. Simply put, firms expend resources in order to gain a competitive advantage that they can later exploit, but that position eventually erodes as rival firms incorporate similar advantages into their own strategies.[25]

In order for a firm to maintain performance over time, it is essential that the business owner be forward-thinking. He or she must maintain a continuous stream of competitive advantages in order to avoid dramatic shifts in performance. The reinvestment of performance results and profits is the foundation of competitive advantage. It is tempting to ride the wave of success, relax, and enjoy the fruits of previous efforts. However, such thinking is nearsighted—tomorrow's performance can be maintained only when supported by today's surplus resources.

Sam Bowman knows how to create a sustainable competitive advantage. His Vancouver-based Pearl Seaproducts Inc. is Canada's largest producer of deepwater cultured oysters, using a unique system of "oyster condominiums" in its three oyster farms to control the depth of the water, and thus the temperature, in which the oysters grow. Temperature can affect the taste and reduce the likelihood of bacterial contamination. This is especially important in the summer months, when most beach-grown oysters lack their usual sweet taste because they are in spawning condition. Lowering the suspension floats of the oyster condos gives the oysters a "cold shower" and causes them to forgo the natural spawning cycle brought on by warmer waters. Knowing this advantage could be easily copied however, Bowman has refocused the company's efforts from production to marketing. Pearl Seaproducts developed innovative packaging that extended the shelf life of oysters to two weeks, helping the company to expand its markets geographically to include Asian and U.S. East Coast markets. It has also developed an oven-ready oyster product called Pearl Bay Oysters Rockefeller, and has several more products in development.[26]

This stage brings the competitive advantage model full circle. Well-planned foundations are more capable of supporting strategies that work, and such strategies ultimately yield desirable results. But the cycle must not be broken. Sustainable competitive advantage can be achieved only when an entrepreneur continuously assesses the firm's external environments and upgrades organizational capabilities. In this way, the entrepreneur will find innovative combinations to support strategies that create value and sustain the firm's competitive position in the industry.

MARKET SEGMENTATION AND ITS VARIABLES

Define market segmentation and its related strategies. **7**

In the previous examples, the cost-advantage and marketing-advantage strategies were applied to marketplaces that were relatively homogeneous, or uniform, in nature. These strategies can also be used to focus on a limited market within an industry.

market segmentation
the division of a market into several smaller groups with similar needs or buying behaviour

Michael Porter refers to this type of competitive strategy—in which cost and marketing advantages are achieved within narrow market segments—as a focus strategy.

A focus strategy depends on market segmentation. Formally defined, **market segmentation** is the process of dividing the total market for a product or service into groups with similar needs or buying behaviour, such that each group is likely to respond favourably to a specific marketing strategy. Developments in the personal computer industry provide a good example of real-world market segmentation. Originally, computer manufacturers aimed at the corporate market and practised very little market segmentation. But as corporate demand declined, the personal computer industry focused on market segments such as small businesses, home offices, and educational institutions.

The need for market segmentation arises from competition. If a business had control of the only known water supply in the world, its sales volume would be huge. This business would not be concerned about personal preferences concerning taste, appearance, or temperature. It would consider its customers to be one market. As long as the water product was wet, it would satisfy everyone. However, if someone else discovered a second water supply, the view of the market would change. The first business might discover that sales were drying up and turn to a modified strategy. In an attempt to be competitive, it would need to segment the market to reflect differences in consumer preferences.

TYPES OF MARKET SEGMENTATION STRATEGIES

There are several types of market segmentation strategies, but the two most common strategies are the multisegmentation approach and the single-segmentation approach.

THE MULTISEGMENTATION STRATEGY

multisegmentation strategy
a strategy that recognizes different preferences of individual market segments and develops a unique marketing mix for each

With a view of the market that recognizes individual segments with different preferences, a firm is in a better position to tailor marketing mixes to various segments. If a firm determines that two or more market segments have the potential to be profitable and then develops a unique marketing mix for each segment, it is following a **multisegmentation strategy.**

Let's assume that Community Writing Company, a pencil manufacturer, has recognized three separate market segments: students, professors, and executives. Following the multisegmentation approach, the company develops a competitive advantage with three marketing mixes, based on differences in pricing, promotion, distribution, or the product itself, as shown in Exhibit 2-6.

Marketing Mix 1 consists of selling felt-tip pens to students through bookstores at the lower-than-normal price of $0.49 and supporting this effort with a promotional campaign in campus newspapers. With Marketing Mix 2, the company markets the same pen to universities for use by professors. Professional magazines are the promotional medium used in this mix, distribution is direct from the factory, and the product price is $1.00. Finally, Marketing Mix 3, which is aimed at corporate executives, consists of selling a gold fountain pen, priced at $50.00, only in exclusive department stores and promoting it by personal selling. Note the distinct differences in these three marketing mixes. Small businesses tend to resist the use of the multisegmentation strategy because of the risk of spreading resources too thinly among several marketing efforts.

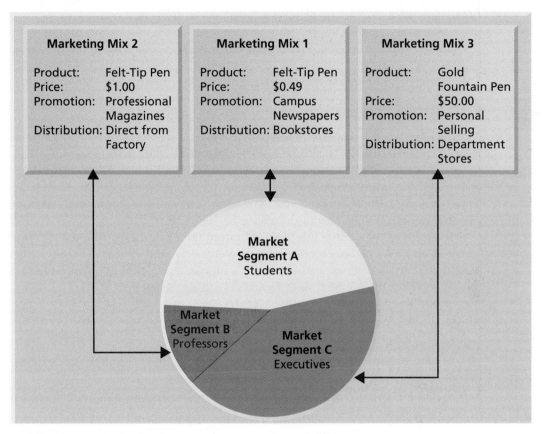

Marketing Mix 2

Product: Felt-Tip Pen
Price: $1.00
Promotion: Professional
              Magazines
Distribution: Direct from
              Factory

Marketing Mix 1

Product: Felt-Tip Pen
Price: $0.49
Promotion: Campus
              Newspapers
Distribution: Bookstores

Marketing Mix 3

Product: Gold
              Fountain Pen
Price: $50.00
Promotion: Personal
              Selling
Distribution: Department
              Stores

**Market
Segment A**
Students

**Market
Segment B**
Professors

**Market
Segment C**
Executives

EXHIBIT **2-6** *A Multisegment Market Strategy*

THE SINGLE-SEGMENTATION STRATEGY

When a firm recognizes that several distinct market segments exist but chooses to concentrate on reaching only one segment, it is following a **single-segmentation strategy**. The segment selected is the one that seems to offer the greatest profitability. Once again, a competitive advantage is achieved through a cost- or marketing-advantage strategy. In this situation the Community Writing Company would decide to pursue a single-segmentation approach and selects the student market segment.

The single-segmentation approach is probably the wisest strategy for small businesses to use during initial marketing efforts. It allows a small firm to specialize and make better use of its limited resources. Once its reputation has been built, the firm will find it easier to enter new markets.

A single-segmentation strategy was followed by Razor Suleman, founder of I Love Rewards, a Toronto-based firm specializing in employee incentive and loyalty programs. Founded in 2002, the firm now employs more than 30 staff and operates from a 6,000 square foot office. The firm targets corporations that want to motivate and reward staff by awarding points for activities such as punctuality or reaching sales targets. Employees redeem the points for a range of brand-name products using a proprietary web-based software supplied by I Love Rewards. The firm has expanded to New York, and is targeting 50 million employee members by 2010. The firm has been recognized as one of Canada's Top 100 Employers, has been ranked as one of the 100 Fastest Growing

single-segmentation strategy
a strategy that recognizes the existence of several distinct market segments but focuses on only the most profitable segment

Companies by *PROFIT Magazine,* and Mr. Suleman received a BDC Young Entrepreneur of the year award. Refer to http://www.iloverewards.com for more information.[27]

A variation of the single-segmentation strategy has become known in recent years as *niche marketing.* Because of its popularity and potential value to a small firm's success, niche marketing will be addressed more fully in the next section.

NICHE MARKETING

Niche marketing is a special type of market segmentation strategy in which entrepreneurs try to isolate their firms from market forces, such as competition, by focusing on a specific target market segment. The strategy can be implemented through any element of the marketing mix—price, product design, service, packaging, and so on. A niche-market strategy is particularly attractive to a small firm that is trying to escape direct competition with industry giants while building a competitive advantage.

Niche marketing can be effective in both domestic and international markets. Noted author John Naisbitt foresees a huge global economy with smaller and smaller niche markets. He believes that success in those markets "has to do with swiftness to market and innovation, which small companies can do so well."[28]

SELECTING A NICHE MARKET

Many new ventures fail because of poor market positioning or lack of a perceived advantage among customers in the target market. To minimize the chance of failure, an entrepreneur should consider the benefits of exploiting gaps in a market rather than going head to head with the competition. Niche marketing can be implemented by using any of the following strategies:

- Restricting focus to a single market segment
- Limiting sales to a single geographical region
- Emphasizing a single product or service
- Concentrating on the superiority of the product or service

A number of entrepreneurs have focused on niche markets, and their creative efforts illustrate just how well these strategies can work. Kerri-Lee Benson launched Kerri'd Treasures Unique Gifts, a wholesale giftware distributor, in 2006. Kerri-Lee sourced a jewellery organizer when she determined customers needed better storage alternatives. The Hidden Treasure Jewellery organizer is both a décor item and a storage solution: it is a black box, approximately two inches deep, which mounts on a wall and has a framed mirror front. Jewellery hangs neatly on brass hooks inside the shallow box. The interior surface, which is black velvet, allows for hanging of rings, bracelets, and earrings on special u-pins. After a successful gift show in August 2006, Kerri'd Treasures secured distribution at over 50 boutique retailers across Canada, including Home Outfitters. Kerri-Lee continues to develop and sources new products, including a recent line of holiday stemware, to service niche opportunities.[29]

Another success story is iWave.com Inc. of Charlottetown, P.E.I. In the early 1990s, founder Cindy Burton had been publishing printed directories of prospective donors for nonprofit fundraisers through her Vancouver-based company, Rainforest Publications. The development of the Internet gave Cindy the idea for an online database. The product gives users a huge advantage over printed directories: faster, more focused searches, plus ongoing updates flagged in each search. The freedom of location the Internet gives also allowed her to move the company to Charlottetown, where it was renamed iWave.

Explain the concept of niche marketing and its importance to small business.

niche marketing
choosing market segments not adequately serviced by competitors

Today, the company's Prospect Research Online service is used by fundraisers throughout North America including Harvard, the Red Cross, and United Way.

Characteristic of a niche player, iWave developed the database in response to a particular need. After the need was identified, the firm differentiated the database in ways that customers value. Because of their flexibility, small companies such as those featured at the beginning of the chapter may actually have an operational advantage over large corporations when it comes to achieving success through niche-oriented strategies.

By selecting a particular niche market, an entrepreneur decides on the basic direction of the firm. Such a choice affects the very nature of the business and is thus referred to as a **strategic decision.** A firm's overall strategy is formulated, therefore, as its leader decides how the firm will relate to its environment—particularly to the customers and competitors in that environment. One small business analyst has a word of caution about selecting a niche market:

> Ventures that seek to capture a market niche, not transform or create an industry, don't need extraordinary ideas. Some ingenuity is necessary to design a product that will draw customers away from mainstream offerings and overcome the cost penalty of serving a small market. But features that are too novel can be a hindrance; a niche market will rarely justify the investment required to educate customers and distributors about the benefits of a radically new product.[30]

Selection of a very specialized market is, of course, not the only possible strategy for a small firm. Nevertheless, finding a niche that can be exploited is a popular strategy. It allows a small firm to operate in the gap between larger competitors. If a small firm chooses to compete head to head with other businesses, particularly large corporations, it must be prepared to distinguish itself in some way—for example, through attention to detail, highly personalized service, or speed of service—in order to make itself a viable competitor.

strategic decision
a decision regarding the direction a firm will take in relating to its customers and competitors

MAINTAINING NICHE-MARKET POTENTIAL

Those firms that adopt a niche-market strategy tread a narrow line between maintaining a protected market and attracting competition. Entrepreneurs must be prepared to encounter competition if their ventures prove profitable. In his book *Competitive Advantage,* Michael Porter cautions that a segmented market can erode under any of four conditions:[31]

1. The focus strategy is imitated.
2. The target segment becomes structurally unattractive because of erosion of the structure or because demand simply disappears.
3. The target segment's differences from other segments narrow.
4. New firms subsegment the industry.

The experience of Minnetonka, a small firm widely recognized as the first to introduce liquid hand soap, provides an example of how a focus strategy can be imitated. The huge success of its brand, Softsoap, quickly attracted several of the industry giants, including Procter & Gamble. Minnetonka's competitive advantage was soon washed away. Some analysts believe that the company focused too much on the advantages of liquid soap in general and not enough on the particular benefits of Softsoap.

Sometimes it is difficult to anticipate the exact source of competition. Before Donald and Maria Pagazani started Dominion Hardware in downtown Whitby, Ontario, in 1992, they felt they had adequately researched the market, including potential competition.

Indeed, business was fine—until Home Depot opened up in the suburbs. Still, the Pagazanis got by, offering personalized service that lured customers back from the big-box store. In 1996, however, Canadian Tire opened up just down the street. Competition from larger competitors forced the Pagazanis out of business in 1999.[32] This is not always the case, however, as shown by the success of companies such as Mountain Equipment Co-op competing with large chains and catalogue retailers by offering competitive pricing, a wide selection, and—most importantly—personalized service. This strategy enables the firm to compete effectively, even against catalogue retailers. Clearly, niche marketing does not guarantee a sustainable competitive advantage. But it does allow small firms to extend their prosperity by developing competitive clout.

LOOKING BACK

1 Give several reasons for starting a new business rather than buying an existing firm or acquiring a franchise.

- A new business can feature a recently invented or newly developed product or service.
- A new business can take advantage of an ideal location, equipment, products or services, employees, suppliers, and bankers.
- A new business avoids undesirable precedents, policies, procedures, and legal commitments of existing firms.

2 Identify several factors that determine whether an idea for a new venture is a good investment opportunity.

- To represent a good investment opportunity, a product or service must meet a real market need with respect to benefits offered and price.
- The fundamental requirements for a good business idea relate to market factors, competitive advantage, economics, management capability, and fatal flaws.

3 Distinguish between the different types and sources of start-up ideas.

- The different types of start-up ideas include existing concepts redirected to new markets, technologically derived ideas, and ideas to perform existing functions in a new and improved manner.

4 Define competitive advantage and assess features of the environment and organization itself that support competitive advantage.

- A firm has a competitive advantage when it offers superior products or services that customers value, which leads to favourable firm performance.
- Competitive advantage usually emphasizes

price/value, unique service features, notable product attributes, customer experience, and accessibility.
- The external environment impacts on the growth and profitability of firms. Entrepreneurs benefit when they analyze the external environment and this analysis should recognize the macroenvironment and the industry environment.

5 Evaluate the feasibility of a business.

- The macroenvironment, the industry, and the organization must be assessed to determine the overall attractiveness of a potential venture.
- A useful process in selecting a potential venture is the screening of ideas using a go/no-go model.
- The venture-feasibility model outlines three stages and decisions: Stage 1: Back-of-the-Envelope Concept, Decision: go or no go based on initial feasibility; Stage 2, Research and Verification, Decision go or no go based on the research; Stage 3, Refining the concept, Decision: go or no go.

6 Identify and compare strategy options for building and sustaining competitive advantage.

- A firm's competitive advantage can be based on a cost or marketing advantage.
- A cost-advantage strategy requires a firm to become the lowest-cost producer in a given market.
- Product differentiation is frequently used as a means to gain a marketing advantage.
- The results of competitive advantage—superior profitability, increased market share, and improved customer satisfaction—should be reinvested for the sake of the firm's future performance.
- Competitive advantages exhibit a life cycle with recognizable phases, including launch, exploitation, and erosion stages.

- Sustainability is achieved when the entrepreneur is forward-thinking and tries to stay one step ahead of rival firms.

7 Define market segmentation and its related strategies.

- A focus strategy relies on market segmentation, which is the process of dividing the total market for a product or service into groups, each of which is likely to respond favourably to a specific marketing strategy.
- Market segmentation strategies include the multisegmentation approach and the single-segmentation approach.

8 Explain the concept of niche marketing and its importance to small business.

- Selecting a niche market is a special segmentation strategy that small firms can use successfully.
- Niche marketing encompasses (1) concentrating on a single market segment, (2) concentrating on a single product, (3) restricting sales to a single geographical region, and (4) emphasizing substantive product/ service superiority.

KEY TERMS

buyout, p. 28
competitive advantage, p. 29
core competencies, p. 37
cost-advantage strategy, p. 40
industry environment, p. 34
intangible resources, p. 37
macroenvironment, p. 34
market segmentation, p. 44

marketing-advantage strategy, p. 41
multisegmentation strategy, p. 44
niche marketing, p. 46
organizational capabilities, p. 37
organizational resources, p. 37
serendipity, p. 33
single-segmentation strategy, p. 45
start-up, p. 28

strategic decision, p. 47
strategy, p. 40
sustainable competitive advantage, p. 42
tangible resources, p. 37
type A ideas, p. 30
type B ideas, p. 30
type C ideas, p. 30

DISCUSSION QUESTIONS

1. Why would an entrepreneur prefer to launch an entirely new venture rather than buy an existing firm?
2. Suggest a product or a service not currently available that might lead to a new small business. How safe would it be to launch a new business depending solely on that one new product or service? Why?
3. If your goal is to start a business with high growth potential, how should you structure the company?
4. What are the five general platforms for achieving competitive advantage? Try to identify a firm in the marketplace that has successfully employed each one.
5. What are the primary factors shaping competition in an industry, according to Porter's

industry-forces model? What is the relationship between the strength of industry forces and trends for prices and profits in the industry? In your opinion, which of these forces will have the greatest impact on industry prices and profits?
6. What are the two basic strategy options for creating competitive advantage discussed in this chapter?
7. What advantages, if any, does a small firm have in creating a competitive advantage?
8. What types of variables are used for market segmentation? Would a small firm use the same variables as a large business? Why or why not?

9. Explain the difference between a multisegmentation strategy and a single-segmentation strategy. Which one is likely to be more appealing to a small firm? Why?
10. Explain what is meant by the term *niche marketing*.
11. Discuss four challenges a firm might face if using a niche marketing strategy.
12. Why is it important to consider sustainability in the development of competitive advantage? What measures can a small business take to ensure sustainability?

YOU MAKE THE CALL

SITUATION 1

After selling his small business, James Sandler set out on an 18-month trip through Europe, China, and Russia with his wife and young children. He had founded the business several years earlier, and it had become a million-dollar enterprise. Now he was looking for a new venture.

While giving his two sons reading lessons on board a train in France, Sandler had an inspiration for a new company. He wondered whether the education materials available in Europe and other countries could be imported, or reproduced, for the North American market to enhance language and science training. He was particularly interested in some of the mechanical toys used to illustrate elementary science in Russia, and the colourful books available in parts of Europe.

Question 1 How would you classify Sandler's start-up idea?
Question 2 What was the source of Sandler's new idea?
Question 3 Do you think Sandler might develop his idea with a start-up or a buyout? Why?

SITUATION 2

Arvin Singh is a retired factory worker who invented a rectangular case with wheels on one end and a retractable handle on the other. The suitcase can hold about four days' worth of clothes and be pulled easily down narrow airplane aisles. It is both light and durable. An integral part of the design is the several internal separators that allow easy storage. Friends and family members who test-drove the bag were enthusiastic about its practicality. Singh researched several potential manufacturers in China, and believed he could bring the luggage to market at a bargain price. Singh exhibited his new product at the luggage industry's annual trade show. The bag created little excitement among buyers. They complained that the suitcase stood on its side, which looked unnatural.

Question 1 What particular niche market, if any, do you think Singh can successfully reach with this product? Why?
Question 2 Do you think he will face an immediate challenge from local or global competitors? If so, how should he react?
Question 3 What type of quality concerns should Singh have regarding the product?

SITUATION 3

Shopping-cart theft is no small problem: Each cart costs about $150, and industry sources estimate that around 100,000 carts are lost yearly. Sue Mei Wong believes that there may be a demand for a firm that recovers stolen carts. She plans to target southern Ontario, where over 38,000 shopping carts were stolen in 2008. Wong estimates her start-up capital will be represented by an old truck and a tank of gas.

Question 1 Do you believe there is adequate demand for Wong's service? Why or why not?
Question 2 If she is successful, what sources of competition should she expect?

EXPERIENTIAL EXERCISES

1. Look through some small business periodicals in your school library or online for profiles of five or six new start-ups. Report to the class, describing the sources of the ideas.

2. Using the databases in your university or college library, as well as search venues such a Proquest, research the stories of some young entrepreneurs from your area. Contact one of them for a personal interview and ask about the special challenges of starting a business as a young person. Report back to the class.

3. Select a start-up with which you are familiar and employ the model show in Exhibit 2-4 to assess the feasibility of the venture given the microenvironment, the industry, and the organization. Apply the screening criteria shown in Exhibit 2-5 to determine if you would have proceeded with the venture.

4. Consult your local newspaper's new business listings and then contact one of the firms to arrange a personal interview. Report to the class on how the idea for the new business originated. Classify the type of idea according to Figure 2-2.

EXPLORING THE WEB

1. Do a word search on the Web for "start-up business." Report on five of the references you found in your search.

2. Find the website of a small business and identify the factors in the external (macroenvironment or industry) and internal (organizational) environments around which the business seems to have been built. Does it appear to you that the firm is more sensitive to internal or external factors? Given your knowledge of the firm's business, do you think the company's sensitivity is good or bad?

Family Enterprise

LOOKING AHEAD

After studying this chapter, you should be able to

1 Discuss the factors that make a family business unique.

2 Explain the forces that can keep a family business moving forward.

3 Outline the complex family roles and relationships involved in a family business.

4 Identify management practices that enable a family business to function effectively.

5 Describe the process of managerial succession in a family business.

IN THE SPOTLIGHT

P.E.I. Business the First Business Ownership Transition Award Winner

The transfer of ownership in any business can be considered a critical point in the life of the business. Doing it well takes time, planning, and a lot of work. Doing it poorly can mean the beginning of the end for the business.

Elmsdale, Prince Edward Island's W.P. Griffin Inc. has been through two such transitions and not only survived, but also won the inaugural business ownership transitions award in 2006 from the Canadian Federation of Independent Business.

Starting out as a family-owned potato farm, the company had expanded into packaging. It managed its award-winning transition from one generation to the next when John Griffin took over the top management role from his mother, Mary Ellen Griffin, in 2001. Mary Ellen had run the business since her husband's death in 1996, and one of her first priorities was planning for the next transition. "A well-executed transition means higher value for a company," according to John. "This has certainly been true in our case as the succession process helped us stay on course with the company's growth plan."

When John became president, he led the business on its largest expansion ever. In an effort to stay ahead of the competition and enhance business opportunities, John expanded and modernized the packaging and processing facilities to a new standard in Canada. W. P. Griffin supplies Sobey's, packages potatoes under the Dole label, and contracts processing to Cavendish and McCain. It has also launched new value-added potato products and has branded its own line of product. John's efforts resulted in a doubling of profits over the next two years.

"W. P. Griffin is a perfect example of how putting the time and energy into creating a well- thought-out succession plan can ensure a business's prosperity into the next generation," said Catherine Swift, president and CEO of the Canadian Federation of Independent Business. "We are very proud to have John and his family as members of CFIB, and it is our hope that, in honouring their achievements, other small business owners will be inspired to start their own succession planning process."

The next phase of growth involves introducing LEAN manufacturing techniques (see Chapter 12), investing in marketing training for staff, and also working on the next generation's succession plan. "Professional legal and tax advice will be needed," said John. "My brother (Peter) and I are both in our early forties and it is time we start planning for the future again. We know how much Griffin's long-term success depends on it."

With such forward thinking and entrepreneurial spirit, it seems Griffin's future is in very good hands.

http://wpgriffin.com

Photo courtesy of W.P. Griffin Inc.

Sources: Adapted from Canada NewsWire, "BDC Names PEI Family as First Recipient of CFIB Business Ownership Transition Award," September 27, 2006, p. 1; and http://wpgriffin.com.

Creating a business from scratch—a start-up—is the route that usually comes to mind when discussing entrepreneurship. There is no question that start-ups represent a significant opportunity for many entrepreneurs. However, an even greater number of individuals realize their entrepreneurial dreams through other alternatives—by purchasing an existing firm (a buyout), franchising, or entering a family business.

There are four different types of business ownership opportunities: start-ups, buyouts, franchises, and family businesses. This chapter examines the issues specifically related to family business. Chapter 4, Franchising Opportunities, explores franchising, and Chapter 16, Buyout Opportunities, available exclusively on the book's website at http://www.longenecker4e.nelson.com, explores the buyout option.

THE FAMILY BUSINESS: A UNIQUE INSTITUTION

Discuss the factors that make a family business unique.

Entrepreneurial life goes beyond start-ups, buyouts, and franchises. Some people get into business by joining an enterprise started by parents, grandparents, or other relatives. Start-ups catch more headlines and generate greater flash and excitement, but don't be deceived: Family businesses are vital to the Canadian economy!

For some people, joining the family business is a "no brainer," especially if they have been groomed for a position in the firm and look forward to its challenges. Others see a job in the family firm as merely one possibility among many career options to be considered during or after their postsecondary years. In any case, the family business offers another doorway to entrepreneurship for those whose families have their own firms. Ideally, the decision to join the family business should be based on an understanding of the unique dynamics of such an enterprise. This chapter examines the distinctive features that characterize the entrepreneurial alternative known as the family business.

A family business is a double-edged sword—it cuts both ways, with unique advantages and potentially frustrating disadvantages. Many advantages arise from the exceptional commitment to the enterprise of family employees, who recognize that the firm's performance has a profound effect on the family, financially and otherwise. On the downside, family businesses sometimes experience severe complications, such as business conflicts that cross over to create problems in the entrepreneur's personal life, and vice versa. There is no question that family firms differ from other types of small businesses in many ways. For example, decision making in a family business is typically more complex since it involves a mixture of family and business values and interests. This section discusses some characteristics of this unique institution.

WHAT IS A FAMILY BUSINESS?

family business
a company that two or more members of the same family own or operate together or in succession

We define a **family business** as a company that two or more members of the same family own or operate together or in succession. The nature and extent of family members' involvement vary. In a number of firms, some family members work part time. In a small restaurant, for example, one spouse may serve as host and manager, the other may keep the books, and the children may work in the kitchen or as servers. Family members most frequently involved in family businesses are spouses, siblings, children, and parents. In-laws participate in some cases, but this is far less common, and the involvement of other relatives, such as aunts, uncles, and cousins, is even more unusual.

Most family businesses, including those we are concerned with in this book, are small. However, family considerations may continue to be important even when such businesses become large corporations. Prominent companies such as Canadian Tire,

McCain Foods, Shaw Cable, Weston's, Irving Oil, Steinberg's, Craig Broadcasting, and Olympia & York are still recognized, to some extent, as family businesses.

FAMILY AND BUSINESS OVERLAP

Any family business is composed of both a family and a business. Although the family and the business are separate institutions—each with its own members, goals, and values—they overlap in the family firm. For many people, these two overlapping institutions represent the most important areas of their lives.

Families and businesses exist for fundamentally different reasons. The family's primary function is the care and nurturing of family members, while the business is concerned with the production and distribution of goods and/or services. The family's goals include the personal development of each member (sometimes with scant concern for limitations in abilities) and the creation of equal opportunities and rewards for each member; the business's goals are profitability and survival.

Individuals involved, directly or indirectly, in a family business have interests and perspectives that differ according to their particular situations. For example, a family member who works in the firm but has no personal or ownership interest might favour more generous employment and advancement opportunities for family members than, say, a family member who owns part of the business but works elsewhere or an employee with neither family nor ownership interest.

Competing interests can complicate the management process, creating tension and sometimes leading to conflict. Relationships among family members in a business are more sensitive than relationships among unrelated employees. For example, disciplining an employee who consistently arrives late is much more problematic if he or she is also a family member. Or, consider a performance review session between a parent-boss and a child-subordinate. Even with nonfamily employees, performance reviews are potential minefields; the existence of a family relationship adds emotional overtones that vastly complicate the review process. As successful entrepreneur and author Lowell J. Spirer observes, no one wants his or her tombstone to read: "Here lies a parent or spouse who fired his own flesh and blood without just cause."[1]

COMPETITION BETWEEN BUSINESS AND FAMILY

Which comes first, the family or the business? In theory, at least, most people opt for the family. Few business owners would knowingly allow the business to destroy their family. In practice, however, the resolution of such tensions becomes difficult. For example, despite being motivated by a sense of family responsibility, a parent may nevertheless become so absorbed in the business that he or she spends insufficient time with the children.

In most cases, families are accustomed to making minor sacrifices for the good of the business. In many family enterprises, the long hours needed in the business can sometimes mean missing dinner with the family or skipping a child's hockey or soccer game. Families usually tolerate some inconveniences and disruptions to family life. Occasionally, however, the clash of business interests and family interests is so persistent or so severe that entrepreneurs must decide which comes first. Even when the stakes are high, some choose business over family. Others declare that their highest loyalty belongs to the family but deny it with their behaviour.

After retiring from his automotive restoration business, David Smith of Penticton, B.C. went into business with his daughter Meika. "I wanted to go into business with my Dad because I didn't get to spend a lot of time with him as a teenager," explains Meika, "and

I just wanted to hang out with him." The Smiths started Smith and Company Beverage Purveyors in 2005 and are still learning to work with each other two years later. "It's not all business with us," says David. "We still have the father/daughter dynamic but now I also respect her as a business woman."[2] Balancing work and other life commitments is discussed in greater detail in Chapter 9.

ADVANTAGES OF A FAMILY BUSINESS

Problems with family firms can easily blind young people to the unique advantages that come with participating in the business. The benefits associated with family involvement should be recognized and discussed when recruiting younger members to work in the family firm.

One primary benefit derives from the strength of family relationships. Family members have a unique motivation because the firm is a family firm. Business success is also family success. Studies have shown that family CEOs possess greater internal motivation than do nonfamily CEOs and have less need to receive additional incentives through compensation.[3] CEOs and other family members are drawn to the business because of family ties, and they tend to stick with the business through thick and thin. A downturn in business fortunes might cause nonfamily employees to seek greener employment pastures elsewhere, but a son or daughter may be reluctant to leave. The family name, its welfare, and possibly its fortune are at stake. In addition, a person's reputation in the

IN THE TRENCHES

Exploring Global Opportunities

Family Business with a Global Reach

Although most family businesses are small, some expand across national borders to reach a global market. One example is McCain Foods Limited in Florenceville, New Brunswick, a family business started by two brothers in 1957. At first, they exported Canadian potatoes to Europe; however, today McCain has 55 production facilities in 13 countries on six continents, including Japan, New Zealand, and Australia, and employs 20 000 people. It churns out frozen French-fries, dinners, vegetables, desserts, pizzas, and juices. Estimates are that Europe generates as much as 45 percent of sales; Canada and the United States generate perhaps 25 percent and 20 percent, respectively. McCain produces one-third of the world's supply of frozen French-fries.

This firm, still wholly owned and managed by the McCain family, is now known as the world's "French-Fry King." However, the firm's attitude toward competitors, described by a former executive as "What's mine is mine, what's yours is mine," also created conflicts in decisions regarding family succession. In a much-publicized struggle for control, Wallace McCain lost out, resigning as CEO when brother Harrison appointed his son, Michael, as CEO of McCain U.S.A. and heir apparent to take over control of the company's worldwide operations. Some of the clan then went to run Maple Leaf Foods, Canada's largest food processor. The succession issue, while nasty, was resolved, and the McCain empire continues to grow. Since 2001, five new production facilities and 4000 employees have been added worldwide.

Source: "McCain Foods Shows Signs of Moving Beyond Feud," Standard (Ste. Catharines), July 21, 1997, p. B4; http://www.thestandard.com and http://www.mccain.com; accessed October 29, 2008.

family and in the business community may hinge on whether she or he can continue the business that Mom or Grandfather built.

Family members may also sacrifice income to keep a business going. Rather than draw large salaries or high dividends, they are likely to permit resources to remain in the business in order to meet current needs. Many families have postponed the purchase of a new car or new furniture long enough to let a business get started or to get through a period of financial stress, thereby greatly increasing the company's chances of survival.

Businesses that are family owned often highlight this feature in their promotional materials to set themselves apart from competitors. For example, a phrase such as "A Family Serving Families" is often placed on signage, websites, and promotional literature where potential customers can't miss it. This is a "high-touch" message, one that resonates with customers who don't want to be treated as "just another number"; as a result, the theme is especially effective for companies that offer highly customized products or very personal services, such as investment planning, chiropractic care, funeral services, and fine dining. Such promotional efforts attempt to convey the fact that family-owned firms have a strong commitment to the business, high ethical standards, and a personal commitment to serving their customers and the local community.

Other features of family involvement in a firm can also contribute to superior business performance. From their study of resource management in family businesses, business professors David Sirmon and Michael Hitt identified the following features of these firms as offering unique advantages (see also Exhibit 3-1):[4]

1. *Firm-specific knowledge:* Family businesses often compete using firm-specific knowledge that is best shared and further developed by individuals who care deeply about the business and who trust one another. These companies are in a unique position to pass this knowledge along from generation to generation, sharpening the edge of that advantage over time.

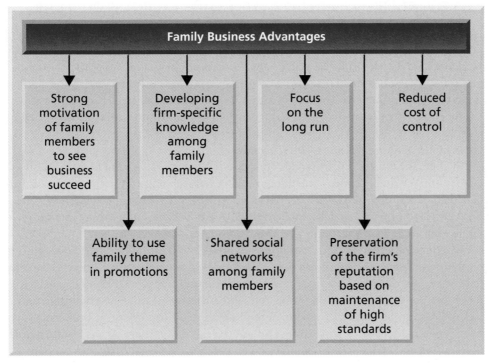

EXHIBIT **3-1**

Advantages of a Family Business

2. *Shared social networks:* Family members bring valuable social capital to the business when they share their networks with younger members of the family and thus help to ensure the firm's future performance.

3. *A focus on the long run:* Most family managers tend to take a long-range perspective of the business, in part because they view it as an asset that must be maintained for the sake of future generations.

4. *Preservation of the firm's reputation:* Because they have a stake in preserving the family's reputation, members of the family are likely to maintain high standards when it comes to honesty in business dealings, such as offering quality and value to the consumer.

5. *Reduced cost of control:* Because key employees in a family business are related and trust one another, the firm can spend less on systems designed to reduce theft and to monitor employees' work habits.

Explain the forces that can keep a family business moving forward.

2

organizational culture

patterns of behaviours and beliefs that characterize a specific firm

FAMILY BUSINESS MOMENTUM

Like other organizations, family businesses develop particular ways of doing things and certain priorities that are unique to each firm. These special patterns of behaviours and beliefs comprise the firm's **organizational culture.** As new employees and family members enter the business, they pick up these unique viewpoints and ways of operating, which create staying power for the company. The culture of the family firm can be a strategic resource that promotes learning, risk taking, and innovation. In fact, family business expert John L. Ward has conducted research that suggests family businesses have an advantage precisely because of their cultures, which tend to emphasize important values like mutual respect, integrity, the wise use of resources, personal responsibility, and "fun" (enthusiasm, adventure, celebration, etc.) in the family business experience.[5]

THE FOUNDER'S IMPRINT ON THE FAMILY BUSINESS CULTURE

Founders leave a deep impression on the family businesses they launch. And the distinctive values that motivate and guide an entrepreneur in the founding of a company may help to create a competitive advantage for the new business. For example, the founder may cater to customer needs in a special way and emphasize customer service as a guiding principle for the company. The new firm may go far beyond normal industry practices to ensure customers are satisfied, even if it means working overtime or making deliveries on a weekend or at odd hours. Those who work in such an enterprise quickly learn that customers must always be handled with special care.

In a family business, the founder's core values may become part of both the business culture and the family code—"the things we believe as a family." Tim Tregunno, a third-generation member of Halifax Seed Company, the country's oldest such business, describes that influence on his father, Warren: "As soon as he could drive, Grandad gave him a map and a list of accounts and said, 'Go do our business.'"[6]

Of course, there is always a darker possibility—that of a founder's negative imprint on the organizational culture. Successful business founders may develop an unhealthy narcissism, or exaggerated sense of self-importance. Such individuals occasionally develop a craving for attention, a fixation with success and public recognition, and a lack of empathy for others. Unfortunately, these attitudes can harm the business by creating a general feeling of superiority and a sense of complacency. While contributions of founders deserve proper acknowledgment, any negative legacy must be avoided.

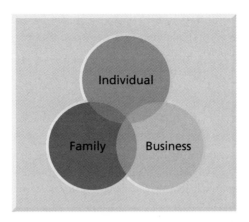

EXHIBIT **3-2**
Competing Interests in the Family Business

Source: Adapted from Tim Barnett and Franz W. Kellermanns, "Are We Family and Are We Treated as Family? Nonfamily Employee' Perceptions of Justice in the Family Firm," *Entrepreneurship Theory and Practice*, vol. 30, no. 6 (November 2006), pp. 837–854.

THE COMMITMENT OF FAMILY MEMBERS

The culture of a particular firm includes numerous distinctive beliefs and behaviours, which help to keep the business moving forward according to the vision of the founder. But sooner or later, the reins of leadership must be turned over to a new generation. The continuity of the business will depend, in large part, on next-generation family members and their level of commitment to the business. Recent research suggests that family members coming into a business do so for a variety of reasons, and these reasons shape the strength and nature of their commitment to the company.

The competing interests model pictured in Exhibit 3-2 is often used to summarize the complexities of dealing with the family firm's interactive components: the business, the family, and the individual. The model is usually applied to founders, since they have an obvious interest in the business, which puts them in the sometimes difficult position of having to balance this interest, their personal aspirations, and the needs of the family. However, if they choose to pursue a career in the business, next-generation family members must deal with some of these same challenges, and their commitment to the company will likely determine the value of their contribution to the business, the financial benefits they bring to the family, and their personal satisfaction with work-related roles.

To explore the connection between commitment and family business involvement, Pramodita Sharma and P. Gregory Irving, two family business experts from Canada studied the research on family enterprises. They found the following four bases of commitment among successors in family businesses: emotional attachment, a sense of obligation, cost considerations, and personal need.[7] In all cases, the outcome was the same—members of the family were persuaded to join the business—but the reasons for joining were very different.

DESIRE-BASED COMMITMENT

When family members join a firm based on a deep-seated, gut-level attraction to the business, it is probably because they believe in and accept the purpose of the enterprise and want to contribute to it. Typically, their personal identity is closely tied to the business, and they believe they have the ability to contribute something to it. In short, these individuals

desire-based commitment

commitment based on a belief in the purpose of a business and a desire to contribute to it

join the company because they genuinely want to. **Desire-based commitment** was clearly the situation for Tim, a young next-generation family member:

> We have an item that we manufacture from scratch, we warehouse it, we wholesale it, and we retail it. I see the business from every angle and I'm involved in it from every angle. It's kind of neat to be able to do that . . . I love being a part of the family business.[8]

OBLIGATION-BASED COMMITMENT

obligation-based commitment

commitment that results from a sense of duty or expectation

Obligation-based commitment drives individuals who feel that they really ought to pursue a career in the family business. Often, the goal is to do what the parent/founder wants, even if that career path is not what the family member had in mind. In many cases, guilt is the primary motivator, as was the case with Polly, who "answered the call" to join the family business:

> [My father] said that the most important thing right now for you as a Stillman is to be visible here because your sister is out . . . We need another family member here. And so with that kind of plea I had no choice in my mind. I couldn't let the family down. So I dropped everything I was doing and . . . went the next day and started working.[9]

COST-BASED COMMITMENT

cost-based commitment

commitment based on the belief that the opportunity for gain from joining a business is too great to pass up

If a family member concludes that there is too much to lose by turning away from a career opportunity within the family business, then his or her decision to join is based on a calculation (**cost-based commitment**), not a sense of obligation or emotional identification. Often, this *have to* response is motivated by the perception that the opportunity for gain is too great to pass up or that the value of the business will fall if somebody doesn't step in to take care of it. In other words, joining the business may be the best way to benefit from what the family firm has to offer or to protect the investment value of what is likely to be inherited in the future. Rob recognized this when he looked more closely at a business that his wife's family owned:

> At that point we really didn't know what [my wife's] involvement was from a shareholder's standpoint. And what we found out was she was heavily involved to the point where it dwarfed what we were doing personally and all of a sudden it did change our perspective . . . It sort of changed our outlook on [the business] . . . and that is when we decided we cannot pass this up.

NEED-BASED COMMITMENT

need-based commitment

commitment based on an individual's self-doubt and belief that he or she lacks career options outside the current business

When family members join the business because of self-doubt or a concern that they might not be able to reach significant career success on their own, their commitment to the family enterprise is based on perceived necessity, or a **need-based commitment.** That is, they need to join the business because they lack options for career success outside it. This reasoning is common among young heirs who leapfrog over nonfamily employees into coveted positions, the demands of which exceed their knowledge and experience. They often feel guilty for their privileged status and are left to wonder if they "have what it takes" to succeed on their own. Ted was 33 years old when he was tapped to run his family's 900-employee business. His self-doubt rings loudly in his reflections:

> I always am a little bit concerned about whether I would have been able to have succeeded and achieved outside of the family's environment . . . That's always something that I think most people in family businesses think about. Whether they believe they would have been as successful outside.

WHY SHOULD ANYONE CARE ABOUT COMMITMENT?

Research shows any form of commitment is better than no commitment at all; however, next-generation family members motivated by desire-based commitment are most likely to pursue long-term careers with the family business. Their deep-seated connection with the enterprise and its alignment with their career interests make for a successful match. And since knowledge and insight passed down from one generation to the next is an advantage that is unique to family businesses, keeping family members in the enterprise can pay in more ways than one.[10]

But commitment is about more than just staying with the company—it also affects what a person does while he or she is on the job. For example, research suggests that people with higher levels of desire- and obligation-based commitment are more likely to support efforts to promote change, which are common in small businesses and very important to their performance and survival. Cost-based commitment may motivate a person to go "beyond the call of duty" to protect or extend his or her financial interests in the company. Obligation-based commitment provides no such motivation, as family members may see their participation in the company as a birthright that provides great job security. However, those with a deep-seated sense of identity with the enterprise (desire-based commitment) are the most likely to work hard, because of their passion for the business. Family members who are committed mostly out of need are often in a perpetual state of self-doubt and lack the confidence to excel; this problem is compounded if they are promoted only because of their last name and honestly lack the capabilities to do the job.

These observations suggest that the type of commitment a person has can significantly impact job performance. Exhibit 3-3 illustrates the forms of commitment and their implications for family businesses.

BREAKING WITH THE PAST

Over time, the sure foundation of the family business—right down to its leadership—has to adjust to a changing environment. But the process of adjustment is almost certain to be complicated by, and interwoven with, changes in the dominant approach of the family business. To appreciate this point, think about the patriarchal culture that is quite common in the early days of a family business. That cultural emphasis may lose its usefulness as business conditions change. For example, as a family business grows, it requires a greater measure of professional expertise. The firm may then be pressured to break from the paternalistic mold, which gives first priority to family authority and less attention to professional abilities. Likewise, the aging of the founder and the maturation of the founder's children tend to weaken the patriarchal family culture with its one dominant source of authority—a parent who "always knows best."

While the values of the founder and the continuity of the culture may give the family firm an edge in the marketplace, these features can also be the ball and chain that keeps it tethered to the past, preventing it from moving forward. As disturbing as it may be, change—at some level—will eventually be necessary. In some cases, a change in leadership may play a role in introducing or bringing about a break with traditional methods of operation. That is, a successor may act as a change agent, as when a founder's son or daughter with a business degree or technical training moves into a leadership position and replaces outdated managerial practices with a more up-to-date professional approach or introduces cutting-edge technology in the company's processes. The topic of leadership succession will be considered in greater detail later in the chapter.

EXHIBIT **3-3**
*Commitment to the
Family Business*

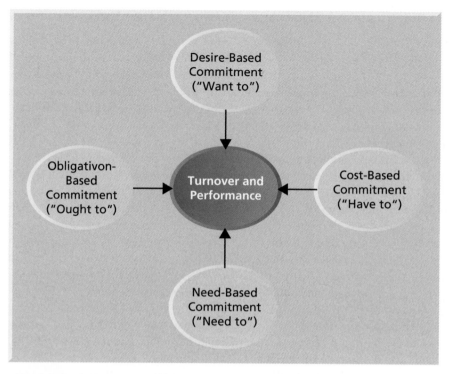

Source: Based on Pramodita Sharma and P. Gregory Irving, "Four Bases of Family Business Successor Commitment: Antecedents and Consequences," *Entrepreneurship Theory and Practice*, vol. 29, no. 1 (January 2005), pp. 13–33.

As you can see, growth of the business and changes in leadership over time will make some cultural adjustments necessary. However, certain values are timeless and should never be altered—the commitment to honesty in dealing with customers and suppliers, for example. While some traditions may embody inefficient business practices and require alteration, others underlie the competitive strength and integrity of the firm.

3 Outline the complex family roles and relationships involved in a family business.

FAMILY ROLES AND RELATIONSHIPS

The overlapping of two institutions—a family and a business—makes the family firm incredibly difficult to manage. "Family business," says the wife of one family business owner, "is an oxymoron. The hope of building something for your kids and passing on traditions is usually thwarted by dynamics within the family."[11] This dim view of the family enterprise is not shared by everyone; however, significant conflicts can result when family roles and business interests collide. Anticipating these challenges and planning for them can really pay off. This section examines a few of the many possible family roles and relationships that contribute to this managerial complexity.

MOM OR DAD, THE FOUNDER

A common figure in family businesses is the man or woman who founded the firm and plans to pass it on to a son or a daughter. In most cases, the business and the family have grown simultaneously. Some founders achieve a delicate balance between their business and family responsibilities. Others must diligently plan time for weekend activities and vacations with the children.

Entrepreneurs who have children typically think in terms of passing the business on to the next generation. Parental concerns associated with this process include the following:

- Does my child possess the temperament and ability necessary for business leadership?
- How can I, the founder, motivate my child to take an interest in the business?
- What type of education and experience will be most helpful in preparing my child for leadership?
- What timetable should I follow in employing and promoting my child?
- How can I avoid favouritism in managing and developing my child?
- Is sibling rivalry likely to be a problem, and can it be avoided?
- How can I prevent the business relationship from damaging or destroying the parent–child relationship?

Of all the relationships in a family business, the parent–child relationship has been recognized for generations as the most troublesome. In recent years, the problems inherent in this relationship have been addressed by counselors, seminars, and books too numerous to count. In spite of all this attention, however, the parent–child relationship continues to perplex many families involved in family businesses.

HUSBAND–WIFE TEAMS

Some family businesses are owned and managed by husband–wife teams. Their roles vary depending on their backgrounds and expertise. In some cases, the husband serves as general manager and the wife runs the office. In others, the wife functions as operations manager and the husband keeps the books. Whatever the arrangement, both individuals are an integral part of the business.

One potential advantage of the husband–wife team is the opportunity to work with someone you really trust and to share more of your lives together. For some couples, however, the benefits can be overshadowed by problems related to the business. Differences of opinion about business matters can carry over into family life. And the energy of both parties may be so spent by working long hours in a struggling company that little zest remains for a strong family life.

Many couples have had to set boundaries and develop routines to cope with the demands of everyday life (like raising children) and still have sufficient time for the business. Ken and Susanne Scott of Kelowna, B.C., were tired of rushing home after a hard day's work, only to have to face the task of putting nutritious food on the table for themselves and their two young children. After 13 years of marriage and lots of discussion, the couple quit their jobs to launch Smart Start Meals, which provides frozen meals for busy families. "I love working with Sue," says Ken. "I could have never imagined what a supportive team we'd make. We try as much as possible to strike a balance between business, personal and family life. We have to make a concerted effort to not burn out or ignore the kids." Susanne adds, "Our business and home life inevitably merge together because of the type of business we are in. All of our recipes and meals are tested by our family before they make the cut to be put on our menu." Testing for the right balance in the meals is sometimes only half as difficult as strengthening the communication and compromise necessary for anyone who works and lives together.[12]

SONS AND DAUGHTERS

Should sons and daughters be groomed for the family business, or should they pursue careers of their own choosing? In the entrepreneurial family, the natural tendency is to think in terms of a family business career and to push a child, either openly or subtly, toward that leadership role. On the other hand, a child's talents may be underestimated by parents merely because there has been little opportunity for the child to develop or demonstrate those talents.

Another issue is personal freedom. Today's society values the right of the individual to choose his or her own career and way of life. If this value is embraced by a son or daughter, that child must be granted the freedom to select a career of his or her own choosing. It's best not to force the issue, because you may be swimming against a strong current of personal interest. Sue Birley, professor of entrepreneurship and director of the Entrepreneurship Centre at Imperial College in London, surveyed 412 children of business owner-managers to see if they planned to enter the family business in the future. Eighty percent of those who were not already working in the business did not intend to join it. And of those who intended to enter the business at some point, 70 percent planned to work somewhere else first.[13]

A son or daughter may feel a need to go outside the family business, for a time at least, to prove that he or she can make it without help from the family. To build self-esteem, he or she may wish to operate independently of the family. Entering the family business immediately after graduation from high school, university, or college may seem stifling, as the child continues to "feel like a little kid with Dad telling me what to do."

Sometimes it is the parent who tells a child that the family business is not for her or him. Michelle Rousseff Kemp has owned or helped launch more than one venture of note, but she has refused to let any of her three grown kids—Jonathan, Katrina, and Natalie—join the family firm. She lays out her reasoning very clearly: "If children go into the business from the get-go, they don't appreciate what they have, and they don't take risks. I don't believe in nepotism. It doesn't create the hunger; it stifles the discovery." Apparently, her logic is sound. Jonathan and Katrina have founded successful companies of their own, and Natalie has gotten into the start-up game.[14] And, who knows? Perhaps some day, one of the kids will be battle-tested and prepared to come back and take the lead of the family business started by Kemp and her husband.

Kemp's attitude is not the norm, though. Many family businesses have been launched with the hope from day 1 that one of the kids would take it over when the time was right. And if the family business is profitable, this can provide substantial rewards. A son or daughter may be well advised to give serious consideration to accepting such an opportunity. But if the business relationship is to be satisfactory, family pressure must be minimized. Both parties must recognize the choice is a business decision as well as a family decision—and a decision that may be reversed, if things do not go well.

SIBLING COOPERATION, SIBLING RIVALRY

In families with a number of children, two or more may become involved in the family business. This depends, of course, on the interests of the individual children. In some cases, parents feel fortunate if even one child elects to stay with the family firm. Nevertheless, it is not unusual for siblings to take positions within the firm. Even those who do not work in the business may be more than casual observers on the sidelines because of their stake as heirs or partial owners.

At best, siblings work as a smoothly functioning team, each contributing services according to his or her respective abilities. Just as families can experience excellent cooperation and unity in their relationships with one another, some family businesses benefit from effective collaboration among brothers and sisters.

However, just as there are sometimes squabbles within a family, there can also be sibling rivalry within a family business. Business issues tend to generate competition, and this affects family, as well as nonfamily, members. Siblings, for example, may disagree about business policy or about their respective roles in the business. And, in some cases, the conflicts can spiral out of control.

Rivalry is a problem between William and David Koh, two brothers who are caught up in a nasty "bean curd war" in Singapore. The family's history in the bean curd business (selling a sort of tofu custard and syrup dessert) goes back to the 1960s, when the Kohs' parents first started selling the sticky delight from a pushcart. The product developed a strong following, and the family business soon became an established and popular enterprise. Sometime after their father died in 1986, their mother turned the ownership of the family store, Rochor Original Beancurd, over to William and his wife. At that point, William, who was the older son, quickly asserted control and edged David out of the business. So David decided there was only one thing to do: open up another bean curd shop right next door to the original location. The two are now competing head to head (and door to door) on the same street in Singapore. Despite being next-door business neighbours, the brothers have not spoken to each other for years, and hopes of a reconciliation are nowhere in sight.[15] As you can see, the family business can do serious damage to the business family.

IN-LAWS IN AND OUT OF THE BUSINESS

As sons and daughters marry, daughters-in-law and sons-in-law become significant actors in the family business drama. Some in-laws become directly involved by accepting positions in the family firm. If a son or daughter is also employed in the firm, rivalry and conflict may develop. For example, family members may disagree about how rewards for performance should compare for an in-law and a son or daughter.

For a time, effective collaboration may be achieved by assigning family members to different branches or roles within the company. But competition for leadership positions eventually will force decisions that distinguish among children and in-laws employed in the business. Being fair and maintaining family loyalty become more difficult as the number of family employees increases.

Sons-in-law and daughters-in-law who are on the sidelines are also participants with an important stake in the business, and their influence on the business and the family can be considerable. They are keenly interested in family business issues that impact their spouses, but, unfortunately, their perspective is typically distorted because they often hear only half of the story when it comes to work-related situations. One highly regarded family business consultant put it this way:

> How many times do brothers and sisters in business together go rushing home or make a phone call home and say, "Dear, I just wanted to let you know that we are so lucky to be in partnership with my brother." Or, "We wouldn't be anywhere near as successful as we are without my sister's leadership skills." I don't think that conversation happens very often.[16]

When family frustrations come up at work, spouses tend to hear all about it at home, often just before the couple goes to bed. The family member vents, then feels better, and goes to sleep. The spouse, on the other hand, is just hearing about the situation and spends the rest of the night worried, angry, or both. Then, when the two siblings sort everything out at the office the next morning and get back to the challenging, satisfying work at hand, neither even thinks about phoning the spouse to let him or her know that the problem was just a silly little matter and that everything is fine. Spouses tend to hear only one side of the story—the bad side—and it shades their view of the business. So, the criticism they receive for having a bad attitude about the family and its enterprise is often undeserved.[17]

When in-laws are employed in the family business, a different set of dynamics can emerge. In some cases, the connections with in-laws can get very complicated. In 2000, Michael Kalinsky cofounded Empyrean Management Group, a recruiting and staffing company. His father-in-law, Bruce Kenworthy, offered to bankroll the start-up with $100,000 of his own money . . . but only if his son, David, could be vice president and a minority shareholder. Kalinsky agreed to the terms, accepted the money, and launched the company. A few years later, however, he discovered that David was neglecting a critical client and had openly criticized Kalinsky and his leadership in front of employees. After thinking about the potential for family fallout, he decided to fire David, which led to a whole new set of problems. After a difficult legal battle, Kalinsky was forced to buy out Bruce's and David's shares of ownership in the company and to pay back the $100,000 he owed Bruce. Empyrean continues to operate, but Kalinsky and David have not spoken since the settlement. David has since opened his own business and wooed away Empyrean's biggest (by far) client. Bruce Kenworthy has concluded that Kalinsky and David will never speak to each other again. "[That] is sad for me," he laments. "It would have been nice if the family and the business had been able to stay together."[18]

THE ENTREPRENEUR'S SPOUSE

One of the most critical roles in the family business is that of the entrepreneur's spouse. Traditionally, this role has been fulfilled by the male entrepreneur's wife and the mother of his children. However, more women are becoming entrepreneurs, and many husbands have now assumed the role of entrepreneur's spouse.

In order for the spouse to play a supporting role in the entrepreneur's career, there must be effective communication between the spouse and the entrepreneur. The spouse needs to hear what's going on in the business; otherwise, she or he may begin to feel detached and respond by competing with the business for attention. The spouse can offer understanding and act as a sounding board for the entrepreneur only if the couple communicates on matters of obvious importance to them, both as individuals and as a family.

It is easy for the spouse to function as worrier for the family business. This is particularly true if there is insufficient communication about business matters. Jeff Dennis, co-founder of Toronto's Secutor Capital Management Corp., observed that the spouse of an entrepreneur is stepping into a crazy adventure, but with limited input or control over the decisions and risks that the whole family then takes on. His wife described the situation in her own way:

> *Being the spouse of an entrepreneur can be the ultimate in risk-taking ventures. When you decide, with or without your spouse's consent, to start a business of your own, you thrust the spouse into the front car of what can be a wild roller-coaster ride . . . [And]*

although your spouse has little control over your business, she suffers all of the conse-quences of ill-advised decision making. "Honey, I lost our fortune. Time to sell the house!" is an experience I know all too well. There's also constant uncertainty. What kind of year will we have? Can we pay our bills? How about retirement?[19]

No wonder so many spouses are worriers!

But the spouse takes on other roles as well. As a parent, he or she helps prepare the children for possible careers in the family business. The spouse may also serve as a mediator in business relationships between the entrepreneur and the children. One wife's comments to her husband, John, and son Terry illustrate the nature of this function:

- "John, don't you think that Terry may have worked long enough as a stockperson in the warehouse?"
- "Terry, your father is going to be very disappointed if you don't come back to the business after your graduation."
- "John, do you really think it is fair to move Stanley into that new office? After all, Terry is older and has been working a year longer."
- "Terry, what did you say to your father today that upset him?"

Ideally, the entrepreneur and her or his spouse form a team committed to the success of both the family and the family business. Such teamwork does not occur automatically—it requires a collaborative effort by both parties to the marriage.

PROFESSIONAL MANAGEMENT OF THE FAMILY FIRM

THE NEED FOR GOOD MANAGEMENT

Good management is necessary for the success of any business, and the family firm is no exception. Significant deviations, for family reasons, from what would be considered good management practices serve only to weaken the firm. Compromising in this way runs counter to the interests of both the firm and the family.

Family business experts and practitioners have proposed a number of "best practices" for family enterprises. Each family and each family business is different, so what is actually "best" will depend on the individual situation; nonetheless, the best practices listed below have helped many family businesses design effective management systems:

- Promote learning to stimulate new thinking and fresh strategic insights.
- Solicit ample input from outsiders to keep things in perspective.
- Establish channels for constructive communication, and use them often.
- Build a culture that accepts continuous change.
- Promote family members only according to their skill levels.
- Attract and retain excellent nonfamily managers.
- Ensure fair compensation for all employees, including those outside the family.
- Establish a solid leadership succession plan.
- Exploit the unique advantages of family ownership.

The family firm is a business—a competitive business. Observing these and other practices of good management will help the business thrive and permit the family to function as a family. Disregarding them will pose a threat to the business and impose strains on family relationships.

Identify management practices that enable a family business to function effectively.   **4**

NONFAMILY EMPLOYEES IN A FAMILY FIRM

Those employees who are not family members are still affected by family considerations.

In some cases, their opportunities for promotion are lessened by the presence of family members who seem to have the inside track. Few parents will promote an outsider over a competent daughter or son who is being groomed for future leadership, and this is understandable. But this limits the potential for advancement of nonfamily employees, which may lead them to become frustrated and to feel cheated.

Consider the case of a young business executive who worked for a family business that operated a chain of restaurants. When hired, he had negotiated a contract that gave him a specified percentage of the business based on performance. Under this arrangement, he was doing extremely well financially—until the owner called on him to say "I am here to buy you out." When the young man asked why, the owner replied, "You are doing too well, and your last name is not the same as mine!"

The extent of limitations on nonfamily employees depends on the number of family members active in the business and the number of managerial or professional positions in the business to which nonfamily employees might aspire. It also depends on the extent to which the owner demands competence in management and maintains an atmosphere of fairness in supervision. To avoid future problems, the owner should make clear, when hiring nonfamily employees, the extent of opportunities available and identify the positions, if any, that are reserved for family members.

Those outside the family may also be caught in the crossfire between family members who are competing with each other. It is difficult for outsiders to maintain strict neutrality in family feuds. If a nonfamily employee is perceived as siding with one of those involved in the feud, he or she may lose the support of other family members. Hardworking employees often feel that they deserve hazard pay for working in a firm plagued by family conflict.

FAMILY RETREATS

family retreat
a gathering of family members, usually at a remote location, to discuss family business matters

Some families hold retreats in order to review family business concerns. A **family retreat** is a meeting of family members (including in-laws), usually held at a remote location, to discuss family business matters. In most cases, the atmosphere is informal to encourage family members to communicate freely and discuss their concerns about the business in an environment that does not feel adversarial. The retreat is not so much an event as it is the beginning of a process of connecting family members. It presents an opportunity to celebrate the founders and their sacrifices, as well as highlight the legacy they wanted to pass down to future generations of the family.

The prospect of sitting down together to discuss family business matters may seem threatening to some family members. As a result, some families avoid extensive communication, fearing it will stir up trouble. They assume that making decisions quietly or secretly will preserve harmony. Unfortunately, this approach often glosses over serious differences that become increasingly troublesome. Family retreats are designed to open lines of communication and to bring about understanding and agreement on family business issues.

Initiating discussion can be difficult, so family leaders often invite an outside expert or facilitator to lead early sessions. The facilitator can help develop an agenda and establish ground rules for discussion. While chairing early sessions, the moderator can establish a positive tone that emphasizes family achievements and encourages rational consideration of sensitive issues. If family members can develop an atmosphere of neutrality, however, they may be able to chair the sessions without using an outsider.

To ensure the success of a family business retreat, Steven White, CEO of a family business consulting firm, suggests that these guidelines be followed:[20]

1. *Set a time and place.* The retreat should be held at a convenient time and in a central location so that everyone can be involved.
2. *Distribute an agenda prior to meeting.* An agenda helps participants organize their thoughts about the issues that are to be discussed.
3. *Plan a schedule in advance.* Details for sessions should be planned ahead of the retreat. Sufficient blocks of time should be provided to deal with important matters and room left in the schedule for refreshment breaks. It's a good idea to set aside one evening for the family to get together and do something fun as a group.
4. *Give everyone a chance to participate.* In sessions, family members should be honest, and they should not interrupt one another. The conversation may be allowed to wander a bit, if this is therapeutic, but the focus should stay on the business.
5. *Keep it professional.* The conversation may become emotional when sensitive topics are discussed, but it should never be allowed to become personal or to spiral out of control. Everyone should leave the retreat feeling good about what was accomplished.

But the talk at family retreats is not always about business. After a retreat, families often speak of the joy of sharing family values and stories of past family experiences. Thus, retreats can strengthen the family as well as the company.

FAMILY COUNCILS

A family retreat could pave the way for creation of a family council, in which family members meet to discuss values, policies, and direction for the future. A **family council** functions as the organizational and strategic planning arm of a family. It provides a forum for the ongoing process of listening to the ideas of all members and discovering what they believe in and want from the business. A family council formalizes the participation of the family in the business to a greater extent than does the family retreat. It can also be a focal point for planning the future of individual family members, the family as a whole, and the business, as well as how each relates to the others.

family council
an organized group of family members who gather periodically to discuss family-related business issues

A council should be a formal organization that holds regular meetings, keeps minutes, and makes suggestions to the firm's board of directors. Experts recommend that it be open to all interested family members and spouses of all generations. During the first several meetings, an acceptable mission statement is usually generated, as well as a family creed.

Family businesses that have such councils find them useful for developing family harmony. The meetings are often fun and informative, and may include speakers who discuss items of interest. Time is often set aside for sharing achievements, milestones, and family history. The younger generation is encouraged to participate because much of the process is designed to increase their understanding of family traditions and business interests, and to prepare them for working effectively in the business.

As with family retreats, an outside facilitator may be useful in getting a council organized and helping with initial meetings. After that, the organization and leadership of meetings can rotate among family members.

CAFE

One organization that specializes in helping family business is CAFE, the Canadian Association of Family Enterprise. CAFE is a national not-for-profit association dedicated to research, education, and assistance for family businesses. CAFE has local chapters in most major Canadian cities, and can be found on the Internet at http://www.cafecanada.ca. CAFE helps family business members through its Personal Advisory Groups (PAGs), which comprise participants from a number of different businesses (only one member from each is allowed) and meet at least monthly in a facilitated problem-solving and group support role. The agenda for each meeting is set by the group and is necessarily a little free form to allow the group to respond to each member's concerns or immediate problems. CAFE also sponsors research on family enterprise, arranges seminars, and publishes a newsletter for members.

FAMILY BUSINESS CONSTITUTIONS

family business constitution

a statement of principles intended to guide a family firm through times of crisis and change

Some experts suggest that families write a **family business constitution,** which is a statement of principles intended to guide a family firm through times of crisis and change, including the succession process. While this is not a legally binding document, it helps preserve the intentions of the founder(s) and ensure that the business survives periods of change largely intact. When a transfer between generations occurs and there is no guiding document, issues such as ownership, performance, and compensation can become flash points for conflict.[21]

A family business constitution cannot foresee every eventuality, but that is not a problem since a family business constitution is a "living, breathing document" that can be amended as needed.[22] The important point is that this document can smooth any transitions—such as a change in leadership, the subject of the next section.

5 Describe the process of managerial succession in a family business.

THE PROCESS OF LEADERSHIP SUCCESSION

The task of preparing family members for careers and, ultimately, leadership within the business is difficult and sometimes frustrating. Professional and managerial requirements tend to become intertwined with family feelings and interests, so the transfer of leadership can quickly run into trouble. And to make the succession process even more challenging, nobody wants to talk about it, for a variety of reasons.

> *The spouse doesn't want to talk about succession because he or she has to face changes at home. The patriarch or the matriarch doesn't want to talk about succession because what are they going to do after retirement? . . . The next generation doesn't want to bring it up. It's inappropriate and painful; it brings on all sorts of very difficult feelings.*[23]

Because everyone is so uncomfortable with the subject, plans for succession often are not well developed or at least are poorly communicated. At a major family business conference at Northwestern University in Chicago, potential leadership successors were asked if they knew the rules and plans for succession at their family firm, and 60 percent said they did not.[24] In other words, a majority of those who may be stepping into the primary role of responsibility for the family business in the future are not really certain they are solidly on that track. This could lead to some very uncomfortable times ahead if things do not turn out as expected, and the health and prosperity of both the family business and the business family could well hang in the balance. According to a survey by Canadian consulting firm Grant Thornton LLP, which specializes in family enterprise, nearly 70 percent of family-owned businesses fail to make the transition from founder to second generation and 90 percent don't reach the third generation.[25]

AVAILABLE FAMILY TALENT

A stream can rise no higher than its source, and the family firm can be no more brilliant than its leader. The business is dependent, therefore, on the quality of leadership talent provided. If the available talent is insufficient, the owner must bring in outside leadership or supplement family talent to avoid a decline under the leadership of second- or third-generation family members.

The question of competency is both a critical and a delicate issue. With experience, individuals can improve their abilities; younger people should not be judged too harshly early on. Furthermore, potential successors may be held back by the reluctance of a parent-owner to delegate realistically to them.

In some cases, a younger family member's skills may actually help to rescue the company, especially when a family business becomes mired in the past and fails to keep up with changing technology and emerging markets. A family firm need not accept the existing level of family talent as an unchangeable given. Instead, the business may offer various types of development programs to teach younger family members and thereby improve their skills. Some businesses include mentoring as a part of such programs. **Mentoring** is the process by which a more experienced person guides and supports the work, progress, and professional relationships of a new or less-experienced employee. In the family business, mentor and protégé have the opportunity to navigate and explore family as well as business-related roles and responsibilities.

mentoring
guiding and supporting the work and development of a new or less-experienced organization member

Perhaps the fairest and most practical approach is to recognize the right of family members to prove themselves. A period of development and testing may occur either in the family business or, preferably, in another organization. If children show themselves to be capable, they earn the right to increased leadership responsibility. If potential successors are found, through a process of fair assessment, to have inadequate leadership abilities, preservation of the family business and the welfare of family members demand that they be passed over for promotion. The appointment of competent outsiders to these jobs, if necessary, increases the value of the firm for all family members who have an ownership interest in it.

STAGES IN THE PROCESS OF SUCCESSION

Sons or daughters do not typically assume leadership of a family firm at a particular moment in time. Instead, a long, drawn-out process of preparation and transition is customary—a process that extends over years and often decades. Exhibit 3-4 portrays this process as a series of **stages in successions**.

stages in succession
phases in the process of transferring leadership of a family business from parent to child

PRE-BUSINESS STAGE

In stage I, a potential successor becomes acquainted with the business as a part of growing up. The young child accompanies a parent to the office, store, or warehouse or plays with equipment related to the business. This early stage does not entail any formal planning to prepare the child for entering the business. It simply forms a foundation for the more deliberate stages of the process that occur in later years. In the latter phases of this stage, the child is introduced to people associated with the firm and, in time, begins to work part-time in various functional areas to get a feel for the business.

EDUCATION AND PERSONAL DEVELOPMENT STAGE

Stage II usually begins when the potential successor goes off to study at a college or university, which is often viewed as a time to "grow up" (the family's perspective) in an environment that facilitates intellectual growth, personal maturity, and network development. This stage provides an opportunity to chart one's own course, but with an eye on

EXHIBIT **3-4**

Stages of Succession in a Family Business

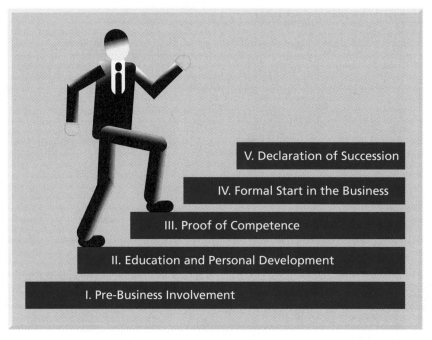

V. Declaration of Succession

IV. Formal Start in the Business

III. Proof of Competence

II. Education and Personal Development

I. Pre-Business Involvement

Source: Adapted from Johan Lambrecht, "Multigenerational Transition in Family Businesses: A New Explanatory Model," *Family Business Review,* vol. 18, no. 4 (2005), pp. 267–282.

the family business and its needs. For example, a business owner who sells pollution control equipment may convince his son or daughter to major in environmental science. Of course, the emphasis placed on a formal education varies with the business. In some cases, the family may not feel that formal studies are necessary; in other cases, earning a diploma is a condition for a career in the business.

PROOF OF COMPETENCE STAGE

One of the difficulties future successors are likely to face when joining a family business is the perception that they are not up to the task, that they have their position only because they are family. Thinking back to his early days with the company owned by his family, Austin Ramirez recalls, "I had the same name as my dad, [so] I was always concerned that there was this presumption that I was not competent unless proved otherwise."[26] No doubt, that thought crossed the minds of some employees, too, underscoring the importance of Stage III, proving competence. One way to do this is for a daughter or son to prove she or he can do the job somewhere else first. Often, mom or dad will push a potential successor to take a position in another company before returning to the family firm, hoping that the independent achievements of the daughter or son will speak for themselves and establish her or his credibility.

FORMAL START IN THE BUSINESS STAGE

Stage IV starts when a son or daughter comes to work at the family business full-time, beginning on a low rung of the corporate ladder. It is common practice for family members to start out by working in various departments in the firm to prove themselves, to win the confidence of employees, and to learn about the business from all perspectives. Handling potential successors wisely involves giving them reasonable freedom to "try their wings," learn from their own mistakes, and gravitate toward business functions that play to their personal strengths and natural capabilities. At this point, succession is not a sure bet, but it is a likely scenario.

DECLARATION OF SUCCESSION STAGE

In Stage V, the son or daughter is named president or general manager of the business and presumably exercises overall direction, although a parent usually is still in the background. The successor has not necessarily mastered the complexities of the role, and the predecessor may be reluctant to give up decision making completely, but all the pieces are now in place. At this stage, it is important to establish a written plan so that there is no doubt about the soon-to-be predecessor's wishes, which could otherwise be questioned in the event of an untimely death or resignation. Establishing the plan in writing will help to minimize political positioning by others who aspire to take the lead, wrangling that can be emotionally explosive and counterproductive to the work of the firm.

RELUCTANT PARENTS AND AMBITIOUS CHILDREN

When the founder of a business is preparing her or his child to take over the firm, the founder's attachment to the business must not be underestimated. Not only is a father, for example, tied to the firm financially—it is probably his primary, if not his only, major investment—but he is also tied to it emotionally. The business is his "baby," and he is understandably reluctant to entrust its future to one whom he sees as immature and unproven. Unfortunately, parents often tend to see their sons and daughters through the lens of their childhood years, even decades after their adolescence.

The child may be ambitious, well educated, and insightful regarding the business. His or her tendency to push ahead—to try something new—often conflicts with the father's caution. As a result, the child may see the father as excessively conservative, stubborn, and unwilling to change.

At the root of many such difficulties is a lack of understanding between parent and child. They work together without a map showing where they are going. Children in the business, and also their spouses, may have expectations about progress that, in terms of the founder's thinking, are totally unrealistic. The successor can easily become hypersensitive to such problems and deal with them in ways that harm the parent–child relationship and actually hinder the progress of the business. But the situation is far from hopeless. In many cases, these problems can be avoided or defused if communication channels are open and all parties come to a better understanding of the development process and how it is to unfold.

TRANSFER OF OWNERSHIP

A final and often complex step in the traditional succession process in the family firm is the **transfer of ownership.** Questions of inheritance affect not only the leadership successor but also other family members having no involvement in the business. In distributing their estate, parent-owners typically wish to treat all their children fairly, both those involved in the business and those on the outside.

One of the most difficult decisions is determining the future ownership of the business. If there are several children, should they all receive equal shares? On the surface, this seems to be the fairest approach. However, such an arrangement may play havoc with the future functioning of the business. Suppose each of five children receives a 20-percent ownership share, even though only one of them is active in the business. The child active in the business—the leadership successor—becomes a minority stockholder completely at the mercy of relatives on the outside. A parent might attempt to resolve such a dilemma by changing the ownership structure of the firm. Those children active in the firm's management, for example, might be given common (voting) shares and others given preferred (nonvoting) shares. However, this is still troublesome because of the relative weaknesses of various ownership securities.

transfer of ownership
passing ownership of a family business to the next generation

Tax considerations are relevant, and they tend to favour gradual transfer of ownership to all heirs. As noted, however, transfer of equal ownership shares to all heirs may be inconsistent with the future efficient operation of the business. Tax advantages should not be allowed to blind one to possible adverse effects on management.

Ideally, the founder has been able to arrange her or his personal holdings to create wealth outside the business as well as within it. In that case, she or he may bequeath comparable shares to all heirs while allowing business control to remain with the child or children active in the business. Planning and discussing the transfer of ownership is not easy, but it is recommended. Over a period of time, the owner must reflect seriously on family talents and interests as they relate to the future of the firm. The plan for transfer of ownership can then be firmed up and modified as necessary when it is discussed with the children or other potential heirs. In discussing exit strategies in Chapter 15, we explain a variety of possible financial arrangements for the transfer of ownership.

Canadian tax laws permit the freezing of the value of a business (or an entire estate) and the establishment of a family trust to aid in minimizing taxes during the transfer of a business to the next generation. This is something best done with professional assistance but the result is the shares in the business being owned by the trust, which is in turn owned by the next generation. Even though the founder may still be operating the business and deriving income out of it, any increase in the value of the business will accrue to the next generation through their ownership of the trust. The main tax advantage is multiplying the lifetime capital gains exemption by the number of shareholders in the trust. A more in-depth discussion of family trusts is beyond the scope of this book.

ENTREPRENEUR

IN THE TRENCHES

Entrepreneurial Experiences

Plan Early

The typical family business seldom matures beyond the second generation. There are many reasons for this, but perhaps the primary reason is that family issues override good business practices. The best of intentions will not prevent this occurrence; only well-thought-out planning and the persistent execution of that plan will ensure success for subsequent generations.

The most important aspect of planning is the timing. Only the planning done early will be effective. Early planning means planning done before it is applicable to any specific individual. Otherwise, business decisions and planning become subject to personalities rather than business wisdom. An example of this was when our partners agreed to a buy-sell agreement. A part of the agreement required the buyout of any partner upon the disability of that partner. The decision was made to fund the disability of the partner with insurance. Ten years later, one of the partners became disabled, and because the decision about what would be done had been made before it applied to a specific individual, the transition occurred seamlessly and without disruption to the continuity or harmony of the family unit. Had the decision been delayed, every nuance of the transaction and every dollar of valuation would have been subject to scrutiny and second-guessing. The decisions on how to value the company, how the buyout would occur, and how the disabled partner would be provided for were all made before they specifically applied to any individual partner. Therefore, no one could reasonably claim the decisions were made to benefit one partner over another.

Tips for Family Business Succession

1. Start planning a minimum of three to five years before succession.

2. Encourage direct communication among family members in a setting where the free exchange of ideas and information is encouraged.

3. Tax considerations are important, but don't let them drive the succession plan.

4. Ensure the family members are qualified for the job.

5. Start a family council if you don't have one; engage objective nonfamily members.

6. Use outsiders to establish fair value for the business and fair compensation for family members.

7. Don't mix active and inactive family members as the next owners of the business.

8. Delegate responsibility and authority to successors.

9. Structure the transfer to protect the value accumulated in and by the business.

10. Make sure the plan is specific, detailed, and written.

LOOKING BACK

1 Discuss the factors that make a family business unique.

- Family members have a special involvement in a family business.
- Business interests (production and profitability) overlap family interests (care and nurturing) in a family business.
- Entrepreneurs face difficult choices in reconciling the competing demands of business and family, and maintaining an appropriate balance between the two is difficult.
- The advantages of a family business include a strong commitment of family members and focus on people, quality, and long-term goals.

2 Explain the forces that can keep a family business moving forward.

- Special patterns of beliefs and behaviours constitute the organizational culture of a family business.
- The founder often leaves a deep imprint on the culture of a family firm.

- Family members may be committed to the family business for different reasons (desire, sense of obligation, calculated costs, and personal needs), and these reasons will likely determine the nature and strength of that commitment.
- Sometimes it is important to change the direction or practices of the family business so that it can keep up with emerging realities, and this often occurs as leadership passes from one generation to the next.

3 Outline the complex family roles and relationships involved in a family business.

- A primary and sensitive relationship is that between founder and son or daughter.
- Some couples in business together find their marriage relationship strengthened, while others find it weakened.
- Sons, daughters, in-laws, and other relatives may either cooperate or squabble with each other as they work together in a family business.
- In-laws play a crucial role in the family business, either as direct participants or as sideline observers.

- The role of the founder's spouse is especially important, as he or she often serves as a mediator in family disputes and helps prepare the children for possible careers in the family business.

4 Identify management practices that enable a family business to function effectively.

- Good management practices are as important as good family relationships in the successful functioning of a family business.
- Family members, as well as all other employees, should be treated fairly and consistently, in accordance with their abilities and performance.
- Following best practices can help family firms design effective management systems.
- Motivation of nonfamily employees can be enhanced by open communication and fairness.
- Family retreats bring all family members together to discuss business and family matters.
- Family councils provide a formal framework for the family's ongoing discussion of family and business issues.

- Family business constitutions can guide a company through times of crisis or change.

5 Describe the process of managerial succession in a family business.

- The quality of leadership talent available in the family determines the extent to which outside managers are needed.
- Succession is a long-term process starting early in the successor's life.
- The succession process begins with the pre-business stage and includes introductions to people associated with the company and part-time jobs in the firm. Later stages involve education and personal development, proof of competence, a formal start in the business, and a declaration of succession.
- Tension often arises between the founder and the potential successor as the latter gains experience.
- Transfer of ownership involves issues of fairness, taxes, and managerial control.

KEY TERMS

cost-based commitment, p. 60
desire-based commitment, p. 60
family business, p. 54
family business
   constitution, p. 70

family council, p. 69
family retreat, p. 68
mentoring, p. 71
need-based
   commitment, p. 60

obligation-based commitment,
   p. 60
organizational culture, p. 58
stages in succession, p. 71
transfer of ownership, p. 73

DISCUSSION QUESTIONS

1. A computer software company began its operation with a three-member management team whose skills were focused in the areas of engineering, finance, and general business. Is this a family business? What might cause it to be classified as a family business or to become a family business?

2. Suppose that you, as founder of a business, have a vacant sales manager position. You realize that sales may suffer somewhat if you promote your son from sales representative to sales manager. However, you would like to see your son make some progress and earn a higher salary to support his wife and young

daughter. How would you go about making this decision? Would you promote your son?

3. As a recent graduate in business administration, you are headed back to the family business. As a result of your education, you have become aware of some outdated business practices in the family firm. In spite of them, the business is showing a good return on investment. Should you rock the boat? If so, how should you proceed in correcting what you see as obsolete traditions?

4. Identify and describe the stages outlined in the model of succession shown in Exhibit 3-4.

YOU MAKE THE CALL
SITUATION 1

Glen Kubota, second-generation president of a family-owned heating and air-conditioning business, was concerned about his 19-year-old daughter, Shannon, who worked as a full-time employee in the firm. Although Shannon had made it through high school, she had not distinguished herself as a student or shown interest in further education. She was somewhat indifferent in her attitude toward her work, although she did reasonably, or at least minimally, satisfactory work. Her father saw Shannon as immature and more interested in riding horses than in building a business.

Kubota wanted to provide his daughter with an opportunity for personal development. This could begin, as he saw it, by learning to work hard. If she liked the work and showed promise, Shannon might eventually be groomed to take over the business. Her father also held a faint hope that hard work might eventually inspire her to get a college or university education.

In trying to achieve these goals, Kubota sensed two problems. First, Shannon obviously lacked proper motivation. The second problem related to her supervision. Supervisors seemed reluctant to be exacting in their demands on Shannon. Possibly because they feared antagonizing the boss by being too hard on his daughter, they allowed Shannon to get by with marginal performance.

Question 1 In view of Shannon's shortcomings, should Glen Kubota seriously consider her as a potential successor?

Question 2 How can Shannon be motivated? Can her father do anything more to improve the situation, or does the responsibility lie with Shannon?

Question 3 How can the quality of Shannon's supervision be improved so that her work experience will be more productive?

EXPERIENTIAL EXERCISES

1. Find a family business that has been transferred between generations. Interview the new leader of the business about how his or her approach to the business is the same or different from the previous generation's.

EXPLORING THE WEB

1. Browse the Internet for information on family businesses. Prepare a one-page report identifying the kinds of data available. Refer to the Canadian Association of Family Enterprise (CAFE) website, http://www.cafecanada.ca to determine the types of services offered to family enterprises.

Franchising Opportunities

IN THE SPOTLIGHT

Changing the Rules of the Real Estate Game: PropertyGuys.com

Business ideas, including franchising ideas, often grow out of astute observation. Such was the situation with Ken Leblanc, the principal founder and President of PropertyGuys.com, winners of the Canada Youth Business Foundation best business award for 2005 for the province of New Brunswick. While a university student, LeBlanc noticed that many "for sale by owner" signs in front of homes quickly converted to real estate agents' signs. "The owners had great intentions of selling their own home, but they seemed to lack the support, supervision, and care to get it done. Then one day, it occurred to me: realtors and brokers have done nothing more than organize the real estate market for agents; why couldn't we do the same thing for the private sale market?" After some careful research, LeBlanc concluded the timing was right to change the rules: a "for sale by owner" approach supported by professionals, an Internet-based marketing method, and no commissions. "The Internet has created a culture of smart, independent people who want to take charge of their own affairs and keep more money in their pockets," notes Leblanc.

From launch in 1998 as a part-time venture with four employees, Moncton-based PropertyGuys.com has grown into a national franchise system with over 100 licensed franchises in Canada, and 100 full- and part-time employees. For a pre-set fee starting at $649, homeowners access all the personal support and marketing material they need to sell their home privately and professionally. The company's industry-leading website—which receives over 55 million hits per month—gives sellers unlimited exposure.

The company continues to add to its franchise network in Canada, while launching in the United States in 2008. Property-Guys.com expanded its online services in 2007 by introducing an international gateway, MTPGU.com, which manages the flow of prospects. According to LeBlanc, "consumers have been telling us they want one-stop shopping for multiple services." At the first Canadian national franchisors' conference in April 2005 the PropertyGuys.com team focused on which new services to roll out and how to do that. The company then added mortgage services to its offering and is planning to add legal and homeowners insurance to its portfolio of services. "This is a great time to get in on the ground floor of a growing industry," says LeBlanc.

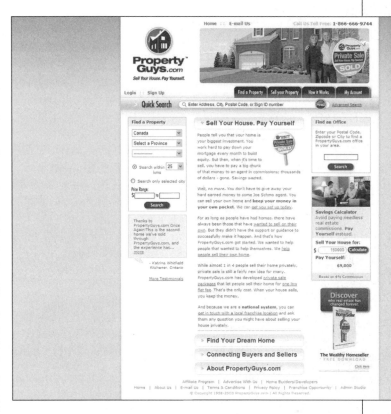

Courtesy of www.propertyguys.com

"PropertyGuys.com is Canada's leading private sale marketing company. We're dedicated to creating a new breed of real estate professional, someone who can guide people and empower them to help themselves regardless of which way they choose to buy or sell." The company was recognized as one of the top 25 Most Successful Canadian Franchise Systems by *Canadian Franchise Magazine*.

http://www.PropertyGuys.com

Source: Canada NewsWire, Ottawa, April 22, 2005, p. 1, and http://www.PropertyGuys.com, accessed January 1, 2008.

Chapter 2 discussed start-up and Chapter 3 discussed family enterprise. This chapter examines beginning a business by franchising. Franchising is an attractive alternative as it offers a proven system with a reduced risk of failure.

Although franchising has existed for decades, rapid growth began during the 1960s with fast-food outlets. Franchising growth has continued with the global expansion of successful franchise concepts. According to Canam Franchise Development Group, a Vancouver-based franchise development firm, Canada is the most franchise-dense economy in the world, with a new franchise outlet opening every two hours, and one franchise unit for every 400 Canadians. Canada has provided the biggest international market for U.S. franchisors, although Europe and Japan have also been extremely receptive. Even China and Russia have extensive franchising from abroad, such as McDonald's, Yogen Fruz, and Kentucky Fried Chicken.

Franchising is a significant economic force as the most common entry point for new business owners. With more than 1.5 million full-time and part-time employees, franchise systems are now Canada's leading employers.[1] Let's look at the language and structure of the franchising industry prior to examining the benefits of the franchising option.

Describe the significance of franchising in Canada.

franchising
a marketing system revolving around a two-party legal agreement, whereby the franchisee conducts business according to terms specified by the franchisor

franchisee
an entrepreneur whose power is limited by a contractual relationship with a franchising organization

franchisor
the party in a franchise contract who specifies the methods to be followed and the terms to be met by the other party

UNDERSTANDING THE FRANCHISE CONCEPT

Franchising provides a unique type of business opportunity; companies with a proven process or retail concept provide turnkey operations to new small business owners in exchange for fees. The franchising system is controlled through formal contracts that govern how the business will operate and what services will be provided to members of the system. Franchise companies usually provide members of the system (franchisees) with names, logos, products, operating procedures, and more. Franchising is the fastest-growing form of retail in Canada, with over 50 percent of all retail sales made by franchise outlets.[2]

Franchise ownership offers entrepreneurs the possibility of reducing the overall risk of starting a business from scratch. The franchise arrangement allows new business operators to benefit from the accumulated business experience of all members of the franchise system.

THE LANGUAGE OF FRANCHISING

The 850 franchising systems in Canada, and their 85,000 outlets, are governed by a wide range of franchise relationships. However, three components exist in all systems. **Franchising** is a marketing system revolving around a two-party legal agreement whereby one party (the **franchisee**) is granted the privilege to conduct business as an individual owner but is required to operate according to methods and terms specified by the other party (the **franchisor**). Franchisees typically pay an initial fee upon signing the franchise agreement, and a royalty fee (percentage of sales) thereafter. Exhibit 4-1 displays selected listings from the Canadian Franchise Association and company websites.

The potential value of any franchising arrangement is defined by the rights contained in an agreement. This legal agreement is known as the **franchise contract**,

EXHIBIT **4-1**
Franchises

Franchisor	Number of Canadian Franchisees	Initial Fee ($ Thousands)	Investment Required ($ Thousands)	Royalty Fee as a Percentage of Sales
Keg Restaurant	50	50	2.5–4 million	n/a
Cap-It Accessory	8	25	185–250	7.0
Dollar/Thrifty Rent a Car	87	15–50	50–300	8.0
Kernels Popcorn	63	25	110–125	9.0
Kwik-Copy Printing	70	29.5	130–1000	9.0
UPS Store	320	30	127–150	6.0
Midas Muffler	1792	25	384.5	10.0
Mini-Tankers Canada	59	45	60	0.0
Mr. Lube	86	50	400	10.0
Mister Transmission	90	25	149	7.0
Orange Julius	134	20	130–205	6.0
Pet Land	17	25	150–250	4.5
Second Cup	400	25	100–140	9.0
Canadian Tire	468	n/a	125+	see below
Dairy Queen	574	30–45	300+	4.0
McDonald's	931	45	300+	17.0
Tim Hortons	2750	50	185+	7.0

Notes

1. The number of franchises does not reflect the number of outlets, as some franchisees have more than one outlet.

2. Details for the top 500 franchises are listed in the *Franchise Handbook* 2008 edition.

3. In some cases, such as Tim Hortons and McDonald's, the cost of real estate and the building is not reflected and, as such, the "required capital" is significantly understated, or a monthly rent fee is incurred.

4. Canadian Tire owns the building and charges rent as a percentage of sales.

5. Some royalty rates include some promotion, advertising, and other fees; in other cases there may be additional fees for this. For example, McDonald's royalty fees include rent, service fees, and advertising.

Source: http://www.cfa.ca, The *Franchise Annual 2008*, and company websites.

franchise contract
the legal agreement between franchisor and franchisee

franchise
the privileges in a franchise contract

product and trade name franchising
a franchise relationship granting the right to use a widely recognized product or name

business-format franchising
an agreement whereby the franchisee obtains an entire marketing system and ongoing guidance from the franchisor

and the rights it conveys are called the **franchise.** The extent and importance of these rights may be quite varied. For example, a potential franchisee may desire the privilege to use a widely recognized product or name. The term commonly used to describe this relationship between franchisor (supplier) and franchisee (buyer) is **product and trade name franchising.** Gasoline service stations, automobile dealerships, and soft-drink bottlers are typical examples.

Alternatively, entrepreneurs may seek an entire marketing system and an ongoing process of assistance and guidance. This broader type of relationship is referred to as **business-format franchising.** Fast-food outlets, hotels and motels, and business services are

master licensee
a firm or individual acting as a sales agent with the responsibility for finding new franchisees within a specified territory

multiple-unit ownership
a situation in which a franchisee owns more than one franchise from the same company

examples of this type of franchising. The volume of sales and the number of franchise units owned through business-format franchising have increased steadily since the early 1970s.

A **master licensee** is a firm or individual having a continuing contractual relationship with a franchisor to sell its franchises. This independent company or businessperson is a type of sales agent. Master licensees are responsible for finding new franchisees within a specified territory. Sometimes they even provide support services such as training and warehousing, which are more traditionally provided by the franchisor. Another franchising strategy gaining widespread usage is **multiple-unit ownership,** in which a single franchisee owns more than one unit of the franchised business. Some of these franchisees are **area developers**—individuals or firms that obtain the legal right to open several outlets in a given area.

Piggyback franchising refers to the operation of a retail franchise within the physical facilities of a host store. Examples of piggyback franchising include a cookie franchise doing business inside an Arby's fast-food outlet and a car-phone franchise within an automobile dealership. This form of franchising benefits both parties. The host store is able to add a new product line, and the franchisee obtains a location near prospective customers.

2 Identify the major advantages and limitations of franchising.

area developers
individuals or firms that obtain the legal right to open several franchised outlets in a given area

piggyback franchising
the operation of a retail franchise within the physical facilities of a host store

THE ADVANTAGES AND LIMITATIONS OF FRANCHISING

"Look before you leap" is an old adage that should be heeded by entrepreneurs considering franchising. Entrepreneurs should not let their enthusiasm cloud their eyes to the realities—both good and bad—of franchising. Weighing the purchase of a franchise against alternative methods of starting a business is an important task, which requires careful consideration of many factors. Exhibit 4-2 illustrates the major factors in this evaluation.

Franchising will not be the ideal choice for all prospective entrepreneurs, because the critical factors are different for different individuals, depending on their personal goals and circumstances. However, many people find a franchise to be the best choice for them. Study carefully the advantages and limitations of franchising presented in this chapter, and remember them when you are evaluating future entrepreneurial opportunities.[3]

ADVANTAGES OF FRANCHISING

Buying a franchise can be attractive for a variety of reasons. The greatest overall advantage by far is its probability of success! Business data on failures of franchises are difficult to find and evaluate. Nevertheless, the success rate for franchises seems to be much

EXHIBIT **4-2**
Major Pluses and Minuses in the Franchising Calculation

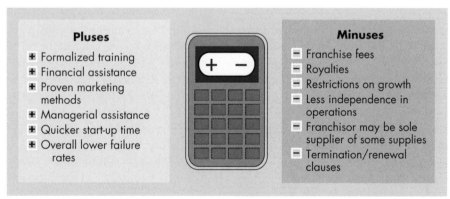

Pluses
+ Formalized training
+ Financial assistance
+ Proven marketing methods
+ Managerial assistance
+ Quicker start-up time
+ Overall lower failure rates

Minuses
− Franchise fees
− Royalties
− Restrictions on growth
− Less independence in operations
− Franchisor may be sole supplier of some supplies
− Termination/renewal clauses

higher than that for nonfranchised businesses, with a failure rate of approximately 5 percent as cited by the Canadian Franchise Association. Of all the franchise opened in Canada within the past five years, 86 percent are under the same ownership, and 97 percent are still in business.[4]

One explanation for the lower failure rate of franchises is that most franchisors are highly selective when granting a franchise. Many potential franchisees who qualify financially are rejected. "You have to be discriminating," says Edward Kushell, president of The Franchise Consulting Group. Many of the large franchisors get 10 applicants for every one they accept.[5]

There are four additional, and more specific, reasons a franchise opportunity is appealing. A franchise is typically attractive because it offers (1) a proven marketing concept and customer base, (2) training, (3) financial assistance, and (4) operating assistance. Naturally, all franchises are not equally strong in all aspects. But such advantages motivate people to consider the franchise arrangement (see Exhibit 4-2).

A PROVEN MARKETING CONCEPT

Most franchised products and services are widely known and accepted. For example, consumers will readily buy McDonald's hamburgers or Baskin-Robbins ice cream, because they know the reputation of these products. Travellers may recognize a restaurant or a motel because of its name or type of roof or some other feature such as the "Golden Arches" of McDonald's. Travellers may turn into a Tim Hortons because of their previous experiences with the chain and the knowledge that they can depend on the food and service that this outlet provides. Thus, franchising offers both a proven line of business and product or service identification.

TRAINING

The training received from the franchisor is valuable because it can help alleviate the weakness in managerial skills typical of many small entrepreneurs. Training by the franchisor often begins with an initial period of a few days or a few weeks at a central training school or at another established location. Major franchisors such as McDonald's, Canadian Tire, and Tim Hortons have centralized training schools or training franchises.

Naturally, the nature of the product and the type of business affect the amount and type of training needed by the franchisee. The Tim Hortons franchise requires an initial training course, which includes such topics as doughnut making, accounting and controls, advertising and merchandising, scheduling of labour and production, and purchasing. In most cases, training constitutes an important advantage of the franchising system, as it permits individuals who have had little training and education to start and succeed in businesses of their own.

Initial training is ordinarily supplemented with subsequent training and guidance. This may involve refresher courses and/or visits by a company representative to the franchisee's location from time to time. The franchisee may also receive manuals and other printed materials that provide guidance in operating the business. Although the franchisor normally places considerable emphasis on observing strict controls, much of the continued training goes far beyond the application of controls. Tim Hortons is an example of a franchisor that offers extensive training and continued support.

Tim Hortons

Ninety-five percent of Tim Hortons stores are franchisee-owned and -operated, the remaining 5 percent being stores that are "in flux or transition," says Patti Jameson, vice-president of corporate communications for TDL Group.

But don't hold your breath if you have your sights set on a Tim Hortons franchise in Ontario, the West, or Atlantic Canada. Franchise applications are being accepted only for Quebec and the United States.

The chance to own a retail operation that is a national icon, at least here in Canada, doesn't come cheap.

According to the Tims Hortons website, a franchise costs anywhere from $185,000, excluding taxes. At least $127,500 of the total cost must be in available cash, on top of another $50,000 in at-hand working capital. The rest can be financed through a bank loan.

That buys a franchisee eight weeks of training at the Tim Hortons Training Centre in Oakville, Ontario, which has classrooms and a fully outfitted store. The cost also covers all store equipment, display equipment, signage, a store opening crew, use of the Tim Hortons manual, the right to use trademarks and trade names, and support from headquarters.

Franchisees are tenants of Tim Hortons, which selects and purchases sites for stores and builds the restaurants.

In addition to rent, franchisees are required to pay a 7 percent royalty and a 4 percent advertising fee based on gross sales.

Kumon

Anxious parents, turning more and more to private tutoring services to supplement their children's education, have sought out Kumon, an arithmetic system created by Toru Kumon, a Japanese high school teacher and also an anxious parent, whose son was struggling with math.

A Kumon franchise licence is comparatively inexpensive—$1000. "We get a lot of publicity as being one of the lowest [cost] franchises," says Sandy Franco, a public relations manager with Kumon's Canadian headquarters.

The fee gives a franchisee the right to open a centre, use the Kumon name, and use the materials and methods, Franco says.

Students are charged from $80–$110 per month per subject. Of that fee, franchisees pay the franchisor a royalty of $28 per month per student per subject.

According to Franco, franchisees are told they need anywhere from 50 to 100 students to break even, depending on the area and operating costs.

Unlike the Tim Hortons and McDonald's of the world, which select locations and own franchise real estate, Kumon franchisees are responsible for renting a location for their centre.

Kumon headquarters will ensure the space meets the requirements for safety, zoning, and parking. However, franchisees aren't allowed to set up an outlet in their home.

Ontario has been the focus of Kumon's franchising efforts in Canada and has 340 centres in the province, half of which are located in the greater Toronto area, with the next largest concentration of franchises in the Vancouver area.

Currently, Kumon is focused on expanding its franchise network in Quebec, specifically in the Montreal and Quebec areas, and has opened a Montreal office.

Source: "Chain Reaction," *Financial Post,* August 31, 2002, p. IN4, and company websites accessed January 1, 2008.

IN THE TRENCHES

Entrepreneurial Experiences

Booster Juice

Booster Juice is a successful Edmonton-based franchise that developed a winning concept in a high-growth market. The Booster Juice concept entails tasty, convenient, nutritious juices, smoothies, and snacks offered in upbeat, fun locations by energetic staff.

The founders built upon the success of their flagship store, and the growth of juice and smoothie market, which is recognized by *Entrepreneur Magazine* as one of the top new business trends for the decade. Whereas the fast-food sector is growing at 3 percent, the smoothie market is increasing at 30 percent annually.

The key feature of the 24 ounce smoothies are the nutritional supplements added to juice, fruit, sorbet, and homemade yogurt. Customers design their drinks, adding such supplements as the Cold Warrior Booster, comprising echinacea and goldenseal, or the Energy Booster, comprising bee pollen and ginseng. The creative ingredients and upbeat atmosphere fit their physically active and youthful target market.

With over 156 franchise locations in Canada, Booster Juice is pursuing an aggressive growth strategy, with an anticipated annual growth rate of 50 percent for the next few years. The company entered the U.S. market in 2003 and has 24 franchises. Booster Juice currently has seven franchises outside the North American market and is expanding into Europe, Central and South America.

Source: http://www.boosterjuice.com; accessed January 1, 2008. Reprinted by permission of Booster Juice.

FINANCIAL ASSISTANCE

The costs of starting an independent business are often high, and the typical entrepreneur's sources of capital are quite limited. The entrepreneur's standing as a prospective borrower is weakest at this time. By teaming up with a franchising organization, the aspiring franchisee may enhance his or her likelihood of obtaining financial assistance.

If the franchising organization considers the applicant to be a suitable prospect with a high probability of success, it frequently extends a helping hand financially. In addition, the franchisee is normally given a payment schedule that can be met through successful operation. Also, the franchisor may permit the franchisee to delay payments for products or supplies obtained from the parent organization, thus increasing the franchisee's working capital.

OPERATING ASSISTANCE

The franchisor will provide a range of operating services including site selection, bulk purchasing of equipment, and inventory. Many franchisors will research traffic flows and consumer trends to determine the optimal location for a new franchise location. Assistance will be provided in determining the store layout, lighting, and decorating.

Franchisors will advise as to the amount of inventory required, the anticipated turnover, and often accounting and inventory systems to track daily inventory turnover.

IN THE TRENCHES

Entrepreneurial Experiences

Franchisee Beware

The lecture on franchising to the author's small business class was going well, until the topic of the support offered by franchisors was introduced. A student voiced his disenchantment by relaying his franchising experience. The prior year he had sent a cheque for $3000 as the initial fee to a Canadian-based car detailing franchisor, having been promised training and marketing support during the start-up of his business. A small cardboard box was delivered shortly thereafter containing the entire training kit, which comprised a 20-minute video, a thin manual, a paint brush, and one small tube of car detailing paint. Phone calls to the head office requesting additional assistance were declined, with the franchisor stating, "Follow the manual and your potential for success is unlimited."

After six futile months of practising on the cars of relatives, and countless unsuccessful sales calls, the student had returned to finish his degree.

Association with a well-established franchisor may improve a new franchisee's credit standing with a bank. The reputation of the franchising organization and the managerial and financial controls that it provides serve to recommend the new franchisee to a banker. Also, the franchisor will frequently cosign a note with a local bank, thus guaranteeing the franchisee's loan.

Ongoing advertising and promotional items offer a key advantage to new franchisees. The entrepreneur who enters a franchising agreement acquires the right to use the franchisor's nationally advertised trademark or brand name. This serves to identify the local enterprise with the widely recognized product or service.

In addition to offering a proven line of business and readily identifiable products or services, franchisors have developed and tested their methods of marketing and management. The operating manuals and procedures supplied to franchisees enable them to operate more efficiently from the start. This is one reason franchisors insist on the observance of quality methods of operation and performance. If a franchise were allowed to operate at a substandard level, it could easily destroy customers' confidence in the entire system.

The existence of proven products and methods, however, does not guarantee that a franchise will succeed. For example, a location that the franchisor's marketing research techniques show to be satisfactory may turn out to be inferior. Or the franchisee may lack ambition or perseverance. However, the fact that a franchisor has a record of successful operation proves that the system can work and has worked elsewhere.

LIMITATIONS OF FRANCHISING

Franchising is like a coin—it has two sides. We have presented the positive side of franchising, but we must also examine the negative side. In particular, three shortcomings permeate the franchise form of business: (1) the costs associated with the franchise, (2) the restrictions on business operations that can accompany a franchise contract, and (3) the loss of entrepreneurial independence.

FRANCHISE COSTS

Franchise costs have several components, *all* of which need to be recognized. Generally speaking, higher fees are charged by well-known franchisors, such as McDonald's.

Following are four typical components of franchising costs.

1. *Initial franchise fee:* The total cost of a franchise begins with an initial franchise fee, which may range from hundreds to thousands of dollars.
2. *Cash investment:* There may be significant costs involved in renting or building an outlet and stocking it with inventory and other equipment. Also, certain insurance premiums, legal fees, and other start-up expenses must be paid. It is often recommended that funds be available to cover personal expenses and emergencies for at least six months.
3. *Royalty payments:* A common practice is for the franchisor to receive continuing royalty payments based on a percentage of the franchise's gross income.
4. *Advertising costs:* Many franchisors require a contribution by franchisees to an advertising fund to promote the franchise. These fees are generally 1 to 2 percent of sales.

If entrepreneurs could generate the same level of sales by setting up an independent business, they would save the franchise fee and some of the other costs. However, if the franchisor provides the benefits previously described, the money franchisees pay for their relationship with the franchisor may prove to be a very good investment. In 2007 the average franchise fee was $25,000, with an average investment requirement of $166,600.[6]

RESTRICTIONS ON BUSINESS OPERATIONS

Franchisors, understandably, are concerned about the image of their franchises. Therefore, they make every effort to control how franchisees conduct certain aspects of the franchise business. Thus, the franchisee is restricted in her or his ability to use personal business judgment. The types of control frequently exercised by a franchisor include

- Restricting sales territories
- Requiring site approval for the retail outlet and imposing requirements regarding outlet appearance
- Restricting goods and services offered for sale
- Restricting the resale of the franchise without the franchisor's permission
- Restricting advertising and hours of operation

LOSS OF INDEPENDENCE

Frequently, individuals leave salaried employment for entrepreneurship because they dislike working under the direct supervision and control of others. Upon entering into a franchise relationship, such individuals may find that a different pattern of supervision has taken over. The franchisee surrenders a considerable amount of independence in signing a franchise agreement.

Even though the franchisor's influence on business operations may be helpful in ensuring success, the level of control exerted may be unpleasant to an entrepreneur who cherishes independence. In addition, some franchise contracts go to extremes, covering unimportant details or specifying practices that are more helpful to others in the chain than to the local operation. As an operator of a franchised business, the entrepreneur frequently occupies the position of a semi-independent businessperson.

Entrepreneurs should recognize that they can lose the right to a franchise if they do not abide by performance standards or fail to pay royalties. Additionally, there is no guarantee that a franchise will be renewed beyond the contracted time, which is typically 15 to 20 years. When the franchise agreement expires, the franchisor may regain control of the franchise, and the franchisee will not be able to recognize any capital gains on the value of the operation. Many major chains, such as Canadian Tire, retain the title to the actual building; the franchisee owns the inventory.

EVALUATING FRANCHISE OPPORTUNITIES

3 Discuss the process for evaluating a franchise opportunity.

After making the initial decision to pursue a franchise opportunity, the prospective franchisee must locate a franchise candidate and investigate it completely. Becoming a franchisee does not guarantee success, even if the franchise system is very successful. The franchisee is a small business owner, and faces all the staffing, financing, and inventory issues all owners encounter. The estimated cost for a typical retail franchise is outlined in Exhibit 4-4.

SELECTING A POTENTIAL FRANCHISE CANDIDATE

With the growth of franchising, the task of initially locating an appropriate franchise has become much easier. Personal observation frequently sparks interest, or awareness may begin with exposure to an advertisement or article in a newspaper or magazine. The headlines of these sources usually appeal to the financial and personal rewards sought by the entrepreneur. *The Globe and Mail*, the *Financial Post, PROFIT*, and local newspapers are examples of publications that include franchisors' advertisements. Numerous websites, such as http://www.betheboss.ca, list franchising opportunities.

GLOBAL FRANCHISING OPPORTUNITIES

Many U.S. franchisors have moved into the Canadian market, but there are also great opportunities for Canadian businesses to franchise in other countries. Traditionally, Canadian franchisors have done most of their international franchising in the United States because of that country's proximity and language similarity. However, this is changing. A combination of events—the structuring of the European Economic Community, the collapse of the Soviet Union, and the passage of the *North American Free Trade Agreement*, to mention only a few—have turned the eyes of Canadian franchisors to other foreign markets. A good example of a Canadian franchisor that has expanded internationally is Yogen Fruz, which has more than 1,580 stores in over 30 countries. Yogen Fruz was started by two brothers, Michael and Aaron Serruya, ages 19 and 20, in 1986. They had originally wanted to buy a franchise, but no one would take a chance on them. So they started their own frozen yogurt shop and began franchising a year later. Now based in Markham, Ontario, the company also owns Swensen's Ice Cream and Java Coast Fine Coffees.[7]

Countries with an expanding middle class, with disposable income to spend on retail items and fast food, are attractive growth prospects. Argentina, Brazil, China, Dubai, India, Indonesia, Mexico, Poland, South Korea, Turkey, and Vietnam, industrializing countries with large populations, are prime franchising locations. "These markets comprise about

EXHIBIT **4-4**
*Estimated Franchise
Cost for a Typical Retail
Franchise*

COST CATEGORY	AMOUNT
Small Retailer, Fast Food	
Franchise fee	$10,000–25,000
First and last months' rent	2500–4000
Leasehold improvements	10,000–15,000
Equipment	10,000–25,000
Furniture and fixtures	1500–4000
Signage	2500–6500
Insurance, licenses, and permits	1000–3500
Training	2000–3000
Initial inventory	5000–6000
Working capital	7500–20,000
	$52,000–112,000

Royalty 5% of sales

Actual costs will vary with geographic area, size and location of the shop, cost of labour and materials, and lease terms.

EXPLANATION OF COSTS

- *Franchise fee:* An individual store franchise gives the rights to a specified geographic area. An area development franchise gives the rights to develop multiple stores in a specified geographic area.
- *First and last months' rent:* Most commercial leases require the payment of rent for the first and last month of the lease at the start of the lease term.
- *Leasehold improvements:* Leasehold improvements are those costs to construct the interior of the store, including building or finishing floors and walls, plumbing, and electrical work.
- *Equipment:* Major equipment consists of computer hardware and software, ovens, and other preparation equipment for a food franchise, as well as installation costs.
- *Furniture and fixtures:* This category includes display cases, shelving, chairs, lighting, pictures and other decorations, as well as the installation costs of the items.
- *Signage:* Installation of storefront and illuminated signs is included in this category.
- *Insurance, licences, and permits:* This category includes property and liability insurance, business licences, and health or other permits required.
- *Training:* Training is usually provided at the franchisor's head office or off-site training facility. These costs are for transportation and room and board while attending the training program.
- *Initial inventory:* An initial inventory of ingredients and supplies is required for the first few weeks of business.
- *Working capital:* About three months' equivalent of operating expenses (wages, rent, supplies) is recommended, as sales will grow over that period to at least a break-even level.
- *Royalty:* The franchisee in this example pays 5 percent of gross sales revenue to the franchisor for ongoing support, cooperative advertising, and ongoing rights to the franchise for the term of the franchise agreement.

half the world's population, and their gross national products are growing more rapidly than those of a number of developed countries," says Fred Elliott, a franchising specialist.[8]

Although the appeal of foreign markets is substantial, the task of franchising there is not easy. One franchisor's manager of international development expressed the challenge this way:

> *In order to successfully franchise overseas, the franchisor must have a sound and successful home base that is sufficiently profitable. The financial position of the*

franchisor must be secure and [the franchisor] must have resources which are surplus to—or can be exclusively diverted from—[its] domestic requirements. [The franchisor] must also have the personnel available to devote solely to international operations, and above all . . . must be patient. On the whole, the development of international markets will always take longer and make greater demands on the resources of the franchisor than first anticipated.[9]

INVESTIGATING THE FRANCHISE CANDIDATE

The nature of the commitment required in franchising justifies careful investigation. Launching a franchised business typically involves a substantial financial investment and entails a business relationship that may be expected to continue over a period of years. Becoming a franchisee does not guarantee success, even if the franchise system is very successful. The franchisee is a small business owner and faces all the staffing, financing, and inventory issues all owners encounter.

The evaluation process is a two-way effort. The franchisor wishes to investigate the franchisee, and the franchisee obviously wishes to evaluate the franchisor and the type of opportunity being offered. Time is required for this kind of analysis. You should be skeptical of a franchisor who pressures franchisees to sign at once, without allowing for proper investigation.

The prospective entrepreneur's first step in evaluating a franchising opportunity should be to tap into sources of information: (1) the franchisors themselves, (2) independent, third-party sources, and (3) existing and former franchisees.

THE FRANCHISOR AS A SOURCE OF INFORMATION

Evaluate franchising from the franchisor's perspective.

The franchisor being evaluated should be the primary source of information about a franchise. Obviously, information provided by a franchisor must be viewed in light of its purpose—to promote a franchise. However, there is no quicker source of information.

There are several ways to obtain information from a franchisor. One way is to correspond directly with the franchisor. Another method is to contact the franchisor indirectly by responding on reader service cards that are provided by most business magazines. Today most preliminary information and details about how to go about applying for a franchise are provided by franchisors through their websites. A good example of this is The UPS Store, formerly Mail Boxes Etc. Exhibit 4-5 shows some of the information available on the company's website, http://www.theupsstore.ca.

Financial data are sometimes provided in the information packet sent initially by the franchisor. However, it is important for potential franchisees to remember that many of the financial figures are only estimates. Profit claims are becoming more common, partly because tough economic times make it difficult to sell a franchise without giving potential franchisees some idea of what they can earn.[10] Reputable franchisors are careful not to misrepresent what a franchisee can expect to attain in terms of sales, gross income, or profits. The importance of earnings to a prospective franchisee makes the subject of earnings claims a particularly sensitive one. In Alberta and Ontario, the only provinces that regulate franchising, a franchisor making earning claims must have a

MAILBOX FRANCHISE

Mail Boxes Etc. Canada (MBEC) is now a wholly owned subsidiary of UPS and operates The UPS Store franchises in Canada. MBEC was founded in 1988 and operates the second-largest number of franchises after the United States.

Contact: MBEC Corporate Office
Address: 505 Iroquois Shore Road, Unit 4
Oakville, Ontario L6H 2R3
Canada
Phone: 800-661-6232
Fax: 905-338-7491

E-mail: Visit the Franchise Sales area of this site or contact the 800 number above
Website: http://www.theupsstore.ca

RESOURCES ON THE WEBSITE

The site contains a downloadable brochure and a number of links including:

☐ Why the UPS Store
☐ Information on seminars
☐ FAQs
☐ News
☐ Process to Being Awarded a Franchise

Other features of the site include an online shipping tracker linked to the UPS system and information on business and document services available at The UPS Store locations and online.

READY TO TAKE THE NEXT STEP?

An online franchisee application form can be filled out. Filling out the application does not obligate the applicant in any way.

STORE LOCATOR

Use the Locations tab at www.theupsstore.ca to find Canadian locations, searchable by city and province, by postal code, or by store number. Use the Locations tab at www.theupsstore.com to find international locations.

reasonable basis, include assumptions underlying the claim, and indicate where substantiating information may be inspected by the potential franchisee.

After an entrepreneur has expressed further interest in a franchise by completing the application form and the franchisor has tentatively qualified the potential franchisee, a meeting is usually arranged to discuss the **disclosure document.** A disclosure document is a detailed statement of such information as the franchisor's finances, experience, size, and involvement in litigation. The document must inform potential franchisees of any restrictions, costs, and provisions for renewal or cancellation of the franchise. Important considerations related to this document are examined more fully in Exhibit 4-6.

EXISTING AND PREVIOUS FRANCHISEES AS SOURCES OF INFORMATION

There may be no better source of franchise facts than existing franchisees. Sometimes, the location of a franchise may preclude a visit to the business site. However, a simple telephone call can provide you with the viewpoint of someone in the position you are considering. If possible, also talk with franchisees who have left the business—they can offer valuable input about their decisions.

**disclosure
document**

a detailed statement of information such as the franchisor's finances, experience, size, and involvement in litigation

EXHIBIT **4-6**
Checklist for Franchisees

Franchise opportunities require careful evaluation prior to investment. Refer to the following checklist to frame the research required to determine whether or not the franchise opportunity fits your training, financial, and growth opportunity requirements. The package provided by the franchisor should be carefully reviewed, and current franchisees should be interviewed.

☐ Does the franchisor provide a complete information package including recent financial statements?

☐ What is the franchisor's standing with the Better Business Bureau, the Canadian Franchise Association, and the local Chamber of Commerce?

☐ Does the franchisor have a comprehensive system for evaluating the performance of franchisees, including computerized inventory and sales programs?

☐ Does the franchisor have a proven success record?

☐ Does the franchisor have a reputation for dealing honestly with its franchisees and customers?

☐ Does the franchisor provide a comprehensive outline as to its growth forecasts?

☐ What innovations has the franchisor introduced recently? Are the products/services offered through the franchise upgraded?

☐ How selective is the franchisor when choosing its franchisees? Does it accept everyone, or require extensive screening for financial capability and managerial involvement?

☐ Is the advertising and promotional program operated effectively, and will it apply to your potential location?

☐ Does the franchisor provide significant service during the start-up phase with regards to store design, layout, equipment purchasing, grand opening, and control systems?

THE PRODUCT OR SERVICE

☐ Is the product or service unique, and does it fit the needs of your target market?

☐ Is the product in the introductory, growth, or mature stage of the product life cycle? Is there still growth opportunity, or has the industry matured and the market been saturated?

☐ Could you create or provide the product or service more effectively than the franchisor?

☐ Would you be able to secure adequate market share without the customer recognition of the franchise?

☐ What is the competitive position for the product or service, or is there a window of opportunity for another provider?

☐ Is the product or service a fad, or will there be long-term growth opportunity?

☐ Who controls the price? Does the franchise price fit the competitive pricing for your target market?

☐ If the product requires repairs, who is responsible, you or the franchisee?

☐ If there is a celebrity involved with selling the product or service, what would the effect be of him or her withdrawing support?

☐ Is the product or process patented or patentable?

LOCATION AND SALES TERRITORY

☐ Will you have an exclusive trading area? If not, what level of franchise or company-owned franchises will be built within your customer base? Will there be enough demand to warrant the number of franchises in your trading area?

☐ What are the conditions and level of flexibility regarding your ability to expand your trading area, or open more outlets within your territory?

☐ What is the present population of target customers currently in the trading area? What is the forecasted number of customers in the trading area five years from now?

☐ For retail outlets, what is the traffic pattern for the location that has been selected? Is the volume of traffic adequate to support the location?

☐ What are the zoning laws for the territory? Are there any licences or zoning issues that could be problematic?

☐ Do the demographics of the territory fit their defined target market for the product or service?

EXHIBIT **4-6**
(*Continued*)

THE FRANCHISE CONTRACT
- ☐ Are the rights and responsibilities of both the franchisee and the franchisor clearly outlined in the contract?
- ☐ Are the payments to the franchisor specific with regards to the initial fee, the royalty, advertising fees, and fees for continued services?
- ☐ Do you have the rights to transfer or assign the franchise?
- ☐ Does the franchisor have the right to terminate the contract, and, if so, what are the conditions that would lead to termination? For example, is there a sales quota that must be attained?
- ☐ Is the level, content, and frequency of the reporting clearly outlined in the contract?
- ☐ What is the level of on-site involvement required of you? Are you allowed other business interests?
- ☐ What is the minimum and maximum quantity of inventory purchases required annually?
- ☐ Must all purchases be through the franchisor, or are you allowed multiple sources of product?
- ☐ What is the term of the contract? Do you have the right to renew?

CURRENT FRANCHISEES
- ☐ Are current franchisees satisfied with the quality and level of service provided by the franchisor?
- ☐ Have franchisees experienced the level of success in sales and customer base indicated by the franchisor?
- ☐ Has the relationship proved equitable? Did the franchisor provide the level of assistance in training, processes, and product that had been promised?
- ☐ Has the advertising and promotional material provided by the franchisor been adequate?
- ☐ Has the financial performance provided an attractive return for the investment?
- ☐ Were there any unanticipated costs or fees?
- ☐ Was the total investment reasonable for the product and service provided by the franchisor?
- ☐ Does the franchisor provide the level of ongoing support that was promised?
- ☐ Is the level of reporting required by the franchisor reasonable, or very time consuming?

Sources: Canadian Business Franchise Handbook (5th ed.); *So You Want to Buy a Franchise* by Douglas Gray and Norman Friend, McGraw-Hill, 1998; and http://www.cfa.ca.

INDEPENDENT, THIRD-PARTY SOURCES OF INFORMATION

Provincial and federal governments are valuable sources of franchising information. Since most provinces do not require registration of franchises, a prospective franchisee must seek other sources of assistance. A comprehensive listing of over 5000 franchisees can be found in the *Franchise Opportunities Guide,* published by the International Franchise Association (IFA). The IFA, which refers to itself as "The Voice of Franchising," is a nonprofit trade association whose membership comprises more than 1300 franchisors, accounting for nearly 400 000 establishments. *Canadian Business Franchise* and *Opportunities Canada* magazines have information on Canadian franchisors and articles about franchising. The Canadian Franchise Association (CFA), begun in 1967, has over 400 franchisor members. The CFA has a number of publications to assist prospective franchisees, including the Investigate before Investing kit, which contains the *Guide to Buying a Franchise Business,* and *Canadian Business Franchise* magazine. The CFA also sponsors workshops, seminars, and trade shows. The CFA is highly selective, and not all companies applying for membership to the association are accepted.

Business publications are also excellent sources of data on specific franchisors, and several include regular features on franchising. *The Globe and Mail,* the *Financial Post,*

PROFIT, Canadian Business, Entrepreneur, and *Inc.,* to name a few, can be found in most libraries or online.

For our hypothetical evaluation of The UPS Store franchise, we researched several business publications and, in the process, located two informative articles on The UPS Store, one in *Success* and the other in *The Globe and Mail.* Frequently, material provided in these kinds of articles is not available from the franchisor or other sources. Articles in business publications often give an extensive profile of franchise problems and strategy changes. The third-party coverage adds credibility to the information in these articles.

Potential franchisees encounter a plethora of alternatives. Opportunities are advertised through tradeshows, magazines, and directories such as the *Franchise Annual,* which lists hundreds of franchises. Numerous websites operate as posting boards for franchise opportunities:

- http://www.cfa.ca
- http://www.franchisemarketplace.com
- http://www.franchisedirectory.com
- http://www.franchise-conxions.com
- http://www.betheboss.ca
- http://www.franchise.org

Another useful source of franchise information is the *Franchise Annual,* which is published by Info Press., an independent business publisher. This publication lists business-format franchisors. The 2008 edition contains over 5000 listings, including more than 1000 Canadian listings.

In recent years, franchise consultants have appeared in the marketplace to assist individuals seeking franchise opportunities. Some consulting firms present seminars on choosing the right franchise; a look through the *Yellow Pages* of any major Canadian city under "Franchising" will yield the names of firms that specialize in franchise consulting. Of course, the prospective franchisee needs to be careful in selecting a reputable consultant. Since franchise consultants are not necessarily attorneys, an experienced franchise attorney should evaluate all legal documents.

SELLING A FRANCHISE

Franchising contains opportunities for both the buyer and the seller. We have already presented the franchising story from the viewpoint of buying a franchise. Now let's briefly consider the franchising option from the perspective of a potential franchisor.

Why would a businessperson wish to become a franchisor? At least three general benefits can be identified:

1. *Reduction of capital requirements:* Franchising allows an owner to expand without diluting capital. The firm involved in franchising in effect borrows capital through fee and royalty arrangements from the franchisee for channel development and thus has lower capital requirements than a wholly owned chain.
2. *Increase in management motivation:* Franchisees, as independent businesspeople, are probably more highly motivated than salaried employees because of profit incentives and their vested interest in the business. Since franchising is decentralized, the franchisor is less susceptible to labour-organizing efforts than centralized organizations.

3. *Speed of expansion:* Franchising lets a business enter many more markets much faster than it could using only its own resources.

There are also distinct drawbacks associated with franchising from the franchisor's perspective. At least three drawbacks can be isolated:

1. *Reduction in control:* A franchisor's right of control is greatly reduced in the franchising form of business because the franchisees are not employees. This is a major concern for most franchisors.
2. *Sharing of profits:* Only part of the profits from the franchise operation belongs to the franchisor.
3. *Increase in operating support:* There is generally more expense associated with nurturing the ongoing franchise relationships—providing accounting and legal services—than there is with a centralized organization.

In addition to the high-profile and hugely successful large franchisors, such as McDonald's, are many less well-known businesses. For example, Doreen Braverman founded the first Flag Shop in Vancouver in 1975. It was probably the first flag shop of its kind in the word. The product line has expanded to include custom flags for over 70 countries, pins, crests, and decals. The franchise will also design new flags as well as install and rent flags, poles, and stands.

With coast-to-coast distribution through 13 outlets from Victoria to Dartmouth, the franchise chain has over 10,000 regular corporate and individual consumer buyers.

Refer to the *Checklist for Franchisees* in Exhibit 4-6, which contains the major questions to be considered prior to acquiring a franchise.

UNDERSTANDING THE FRANCHISOR/ FRANCHISEE RELATIONSHIP

Describe the critical franchisor/franchisee relationship. **5**

The basic features of the relationship between the franchisor and the franchisee are embodied in the franchise contract. This contract is typically a complex document, running to many pages. Because of its importance as the legal basis for the franchised business, the franchise contract should never be signed by the franchisee without legal counsel. In fact, reputable franchisors insist that the franchisee have legal counsel before signing the agreement. An attorney may anticipate trouble spots and note any objectionable features of the contract.

In addition to consulting an attorney, a prospective franchisee should use as many other sources of help as practical. In particular, she or he should discuss the franchise proposal with a banker, going over it in as much detail as possible. The prospective franchisee should also obtain the services of a professional accounting firm in examining the franchisor's statements of projected sales, operating expenses, and net income. An accountant can help in evaluating the quality of these estimates and in discovering projections that may be unlikely to be realized. The most important feature of the franchise contract is the provision relating to termination and transfer of the franchise. Some franchisors have been accused of devising agreements that permit arbitrary cancellation. Of course, it is reasonable for the franchisor to have legal protection in the event that a franchisee fails to obtain a satisfactory level of operation or to maintain satisfactory quality standards. However, the prospective franchisee should be wary of contract provisions that contain overly strict cancellation policies. Similarly, the rights of the franchisee

EXHIBIT **4-7**

Highlights of Franchise Disclosure in Ontario

1. The franchise agreement imposes a duty on each party to act fairly.
2. Franchisees are given the right to form a franchisee association, so that they may communicate.
3. Franchisors are required to provide franchisees with a disclosure document 14 days prior to signing or paying any fees.
4. The disclosure document must contain all material facts contained in the financial statements and the franchise agreement, and will include data on territorial rights, fees, civil litigation, initial investments required, and financing terms and conditions.
5. A franchisee is entitled to damages for misrepresentation or failure of the franchisor to deliver a disclosure document.

Source: Arthur Wishart Act (Franchise Disclosure).

to sell the business to a third party should be clearly stipulated. A franchisor who can restrict the sale of the business to a third party could potentially assume ownership of the business at an unreasonably low price. The right of the franchisee to renew the contract after the business has been built up to a successful operating level should also be clearly stated in the contract.

FRANCHISE REGULATION

Understand issues related to franchise regulation in Canada and know the warning signs of franchise fraud.

In Canada, only Ontario and Alberta require franchisors to report on an accurate basis the actual sales and profit statistics. As such, in international franchising material Canada is referred to as "the Wild West of franchising." Outside Alberta and Ontario, franchisors are under no legal obligation to tell potential franchisees financial information based on actual sales expenses and profits. The lack of legislation has resulted in franchisors misrepresenting or omitting material information, which led to many franchisees making poor investment decisions. Due to continued lobbying by franchisees and the Canadian Franchise Association, enhanced reporting and franchising disclosure legislation will likely be introduced during the next decade in the remaining provinces.

Ontario, home to almost half the franchising systems in Canada, enacted *Bill 33, the Arthur Wishart Act (Franchise Disclosure) 2000,* on January 1, 2001. The act clearly states the responsibilities of the franchisor to provide pre-sale disclosure of all materials and financial statements. Highlights of the act are shown in Exhibit 4-7. The *Alberta Franchise Act* of 1995 "assists prospective franchisees in making informed investment decisions by requiring the timely disclosure of necessary information." Franchisors are required to provide a franchise prospectus that includes a copy of the franchise agreement, the financial statements of the franchisor, and a statement of obligations of both the franchisee and franchisor.

FRANCHISING FRAUDS

Every industry has its share of shady operators, and franchising is no exception. Unscrupulous franchisors offer a wide variety of fraudulent schemes to attract unsuspecting investors. The franchisor in such cases is interested merely in obtaining the capital investment of the franchisee and not in a nurturing relationship. *Entrepreneur* magazine has suggested the following warning signs of a franchise scam:

1. *The rented Rolls-Royce scam:* The overdressed, jewellery-laden sales representative is designed to impress you with an appearance of success. These people reek of money—and you hope, quite naturally, that it will rub off on you. *Motto:* "Don't you want to be like me?" *Antidote:* Check the financial statements in the offering document; they must be audited.

2. *The hustle:* The giveaway sales pitch is "Territories are going fast . . . Act now or you'll be shut out" or "I'm leaving town on Monday afternoon, so make your decision now." The hustler makes you feel like a worthless, indecisive dreamer if you do not take immediate action. *Motto:* "Wimps need not apply." *Antidote:* Take your time, and recognize The Hustle for the crude closing technique that it is.

3. *The cash-only transaction:* An obvious clue that the company is running its program on the fly is that it wants cash, which is untraceable, so that you can't stop payment if things crash and burn. *Motto:* "In God we trust; all others pay cash." *Antidote:* Insist on a cheque—made out to the company, not to an individual. Better yet, walk away.

4. *The boast:* "Our dealers are pulling in six figures. We're not interested in small thinkers. If you think big, you can join the ranks of the really big money earners in our system. The sky's the limit." This statement was in answer to your straightforward question about the names of purchasers in your area. *Motto:* "We never met an exaggeration we didn't like." *Antidote:* Write your own business plan, and make it realistic. Don't try to be a big thinker—just a smart one.

5. *The big-money claim:* Most authorities point to exaggerated profit claims as the biggest problem in business opportunity and franchise sales. "Earn $10,000 a month in your spare time" sounds great, doesn't it? If it is a franchise, any statement about earnings (regarding others in the system or your potential earnings) must appear in the prospectus for franchisors located in Alberta or Ontario. *Antidote:* Read the prospectus carefully to verify sales claims, and if the franchisor is not headquartered in Alberta or Ontario, conduct additional research.

6. *The disclosure dance:* "Disclosure? Well, we're, uh, exempt from disclosure because we're, uh, not a public corporation. Yeah, that's it." No ethical franchisor would fail to deliver a disclosure document at your first serious meeting, whether required to do so by Alberta or Ontario law, or in other parts of Canada. *Motto:* "Trust me, kid." *Antidote:* Disclosure: Don't let your money leave your pocket without it.

The possibility of fraudulent schemes requires alertness on the part of prospective franchisees. Only careful investigation of the company and the product can distinguish between fraudulent operators and legitimate franchising opportunities. In conclusion, we want to emphasize that franchising has made business ownership possible for many individuals who were unable to enter a family business or otherwise would never have escaped salaried employment. In this way, franchising has contributed to the success of many entrepreneurs.

LOOKING BACK

1 Describe the significance of franchising in Canada.

- Franchising is a formalized arrangement that describes a specific way of operating a small business.
- The potential value of any franchising arrangement is determined by the rights contained in the franchise contract.
- Product and trade name franchising and business-format franchising are the two types of franchising.
- Piggyback franchising, master licensees, multiple-unit ownership, and area developers are special approaches to franchising.
- Three levels of franchising systems offer various relationships between franchisor and franchisee.

2 Identify the major advantages and limitations of franchising.

- The overall attraction of franchising is its potential for a high rate of success.
- A franchise may be favoured over other alternatives because it offers training, financial assistance, and operating benefits.
- The major limitations of franchising are its costs, restrictions on business operations, and loss of independence.

3 Discuss the process for evaluating a franchise opportunity.

- The substantial investment required by most franchises justifies careful investigation by a potential franchisee.
- The most logical source of the greatest amount of information about a franchise is the franchisor.
- Existing and former franchisees are good sources of information for evaluating a franchise.
- Independent third parties, such as the government and the Canadian Franchise Association, can be valuable sources of franchise information.

4 Evaluate franchising from the franchisor's perspective.

- The major benefits of becoming a franchisor are reduced capital requirements, increased management motivation, and rapid expansion.
- The major drawbacks to franchising are reduced control, shared profits, and increased operating support costs.

5 Describe the critical franchisor/franchisee relationship.

- The basic features of the relationship between the franchisor and the franchisee are embodied in the franchise contract.
- A franchise contract is a complex document and should be referred to an attorney for evaluation.
- An important feature of the franchise contract is the provision relating to termination and transfer.
- Franchising legislation is in effect in Alberta and Ontario.
- Prospective franchisees should be alert to possible franchising frauds.

6 Understand issues related to franchise regulation in Canada and know the warning signs of franchise fraud.

- Ontario and Alberta are the only provinces that require franchisors to report on an accurate basis the actual sales and profit statistics.
- Ontario enacted *The Arthur Wishart Act (Franchise Disclosure)*, which states the responsibilities of the franchisor to provide pre-sale disclosure of all materials and financial statements. The *Alberta Franchise Act* of 1995 "assists prospective franchisees in making informed investment decisions by requiring the timely disclosure of necessary information."
- Prospective franchisees should be alert and aware of possible fraudulent schemes.

KEY TERMS

DISCUSSION QUESTIONS

1. What makes franchising different from other forms of business? Be specific.
2. What forms of payment are required of franchisees?
3. How significant is franchising in Canada?
4. Discuss the advantages and limitations of franchising from the viewpoints of the potential franchisee and the potential franchisor.
5. Should franchise information provided by a franchisor be discounted? Why or why not?
6. Do you believe the government-required disclosure documents required by Alberta and Ontario are useful for franchise evaluation? Defend your position.
7. Evaluate loss of control as a disadvantage of franchising from the franchisor's perspective.
8. What types of restrictions on franchisee independence might be included in a typical franchise contract?
9. What problems might arise in consulting previous franchisees in the process of evaluating a franchise?
10. What types of franchise information could you expect to obtain from business periodicals that you could not secure from the franchisor?

YOU MAKE THE CALL

SITUATION 1

While still a student in college in 2007, Adrian Johnson began his first business venture. He took his idea for a laundromat to a local bank and qualified for a $90,000 loan. After finding a suitable site close to his campus, he signed a 10-year lease and opened for business. During the first three days, the business averaged over 100 customers per day. The attraction of Johnson's laundromat was its unique atmosphere. The business was carpeted, with oak panelling and brass fittings. There was a snack bar and a big-screen television for patrons to enjoy while waiting for their laundry. Within a week of opening day, Johnson received an offer to sell his business at twice his investment. He rejected the offer because he was considering the possibility of franchising his business concept.

Question 1 What major considerations should Johnson evaluate before he decides to franchise?

Question 2 Would piggyback franchising have potential for this type of business?

Question 3 If Johnson does indeed franchise his business, what types of training and support systems would you recommend that he provide to franchisees?

SITUATION 2

Hard times in the agricultural commodities market led broker Bill Landers to consider leaving his independent business and looking for new opportunities. This time around, Landers was committed to going into business with his wife, Mary, and their teenage son and daughter. His goal was to keep the family close and reduce the stress in their lives. In his previous job as a broker, Landers would leave home early and return late, with little time for his wife or children. Before leaving his job, Landers looked at several franchise opportunities. One possibility that he and Mary were seriously considering was a custom-framing franchise that had been in existence for over 10 years and had almost 100 stores nationwide. However, the Landers were concerned about their lack of experience in this area and also about how long it would take to get the business going.

Question 1 How important should their lack of prior experience be to the Landers' decision?

Question 2 What other characteristics of the franchise should they investigate? What sources would you recommend for this information?

Question 3 Can they reasonably expect to change their lifestyle as owners of a franchise? Explain.

SITUATION 3

One night, Charles Dunn saw an infomercial on television that advertised a franchise for a gourmet-coffee store. One month later, he signed a franchise agreement and paid the initial $20,000 fee. He quit his job and took a second mortgage on his home to raise the $100,000 of capital required by the franchisor. Dunn did no market research; he didn't look at other franchises. His store was the first of its kind in the area, and it had no name recognition.

Shortly after Dunn opened his doors, another store from the same franchisor opened a few miles away. After another year, Dunn shut down his business.

Question 1 What types of research should Dunn have conducted prior to buying the franchise?
Question 2 What kinds of training should this franchisor have provided to Dunn?
Question 3 What types of contractual issues should Dunn have considered in order to get a better deal?

EXPERIENTIAL EXERCISES

1. Interview a local owner-manager of a widely recognized retail franchise such as McDonald's. Ask him or her to explain the process of obtaining the franchise and the advantages of franchising over starting a business from scratch.
2. Find a franchise advertisement in a recent issue of a business magazine. Research the franchise and report back to class with your findings. Determine the following:
   a. The financial costs (including initial fee, investment, and royalty)
   b. The competitive advantages offered by the franchisor (this will entail an evaluation of the competitive environment to determine if there is an opportunity in the proposed market)
   c. Any restrictions, including geographic, that might reduce the attractiveness of the franchise
   d. A detailed listing of the support and training offered by the franchisor
   e. An assessment of the overall feasibility of the franchise opportunity
3. Consider the potential for locating a hypothetical new fast-food restaurant next to your campus. (Be as specific about the assumed location as you can.) Divide into two groups, one of which should support buying a franchised operation and the other an independent nonfranchised business. Plan a debate on the merits of each operation for the next class.
4. Research articles that discuss current fraudulent franchisors and report on your findings.

EXPLORING THE WEB

Locate one of the following websites: http://www.franchise-conxions.com, http://www.betheboss.ca, or http://www.franchise.org.

1. Write a one-page summary describing three different franchisors you find listed at the site. For each franchisor be sure to include the head office location, current franchise locations, support offered by the franchisor, and the required investment level.
2. Go to the Canadian Franchise Association site: http://www.cfa.ca. Write a one-page report on how the Code of Ethics and Mandatory Disclosure Document protect franchisees.
3. Identify three potential franchisors and visit their websites. Evaluate them using the following criteria:
   a. Which franchisor provides the most complete information on its website? Provide support for your opinion.
   b. What types of information about franchise costs are provided on each site?
   c. How could the sites be improved to be more helpful to a prospective franchisee? Be specific.

Planning

AND MARKETING NEW VENTURES

CHAPTER 5

Developing an Effective Business Plan

LOOKING AHEAD

After studying this chapter, you should be able to

1 Answer the question, "What is a business plan?"

2 Explain the need for a business plan from the perspectives of the entrepreneur, the investor, and the lenders.

3 Describe what determines how much planning an entrepreneur and a management team are likely to do.

4 List practical suggestions to follow in writing a business plan, and outline the key sections of a business plan.

5 Identify available sources of assistance in preparing a business plan.

IN THE SPOTLIGHT

Sisters Take Love of Baking to Next Step

When the three sisters decided to open a store selling homemade cupcakes, there were many naysayers wondering how it could be possible to make any money on the delectable delights. The owners of Crave Cookies and Cupcakes today have a business that is thriving and growing each year, with a recognizable name throughout Calgary—and [are] selling scrumptious cupcakes by the hundreds of thousands. Actually, the initial enterprise really started in their mother's kitchen as the three young girls—Carolyne McIntyre Jackson, Jodi Willoughby and Antoinette Knight—grew up on a ranch outside of High River. There were always buckets of cookies in the freezer. Baking was a way of life for the family.

Now, those recipes their mom Helen McIntyre used are the ones baked at Crave.

"We always grew up with home-baked goods and had a real appreciation for quality. So we all went to university and kind of did our own thing for about four or five years; we were all in different careers," says Willoughby. "And Carolyne and I were ready for a change. Antoinette, as well." The company today has a 1,900-square-foot storeIn Hillhurst, which it opened in September 2004, and a 520-square-foot location on 17th Avenue S.W. near Mount Royal Village which opened in May of 2007. Crave has 28 employees.

The genesis for taking a passion for baking to a retail enterprise came when a cousin told McIntyre Jackson: "You need to sell your cookies. Your cookies are so good." "We found this space (on Kensington Road) and then we started doing a business plan and we started finding all the cupcake shops. And we decided we were going to do cupcakes. We knew we had the recipe. We had this fabulous recipe . . . I kind of always thought if I won a million dollars I would open up my own bake shop . . . We kind of discovered it doesn't take a million dollars, it just takes some hard work and some organization."

"People thought we were crazy," says McIntyre Jackson of when Crave opened for business. "They said, 'So you're going to pay the rent just making cupcakes?' So, of course, we were freaked out. We didn't take salaries for over a year. We had the luxury of being able to do something like that so we kept all the money in the business. And we really kind of grew as we needed to."

In their business plan, they thought they might be able to hire a pastry chef in their third year. They hired a pastry chef after about five months. That's how successful the baked goods had become to customers throughout the city. "Everything is baked from scratch every morning," says Willoughby. Crave sells hundreds of thousands of goodies each year with sales increasing by 30 to 40 per cent in each of the last three years. "This year's numbers we're still up from last year and we didn't think we could hardly get any busier from last year," says McIntyre Jackson.

About two-thirds of the sales are from customers who come into the two store locations. The other third is from orders. Crave also has a van that makes deliveries throughout the city. Ninety per cent of the sales are cupcakes. There are 11 regular flavours and one flavour of the month. Crave also bakes and sells cakes and cookies.

Courtesy of www.cravecupcakes.ca

The company is looking at the possibility of expansion outside of Calgary. "We want to give people a true indulgence," says Mcintyre Jackson. "Really, the idea of having a cupcake is to give yourself a treat and that it's a true, honest-to-goodness, good, real, wholesome treat. That it's worth the calories. That it's worth eating because it tastes fabulous. And it's made with real ingredients. There's no preservatives. There's no fillers. It's all real food. Real butter. Real whipping cream. Real icing sugar. Real eggs. It's real everything."[1]

http://www.crave.com

Source: Mario Toneguzzi, Calgary Herald October 01, 2007, mtoneguzzi@theherald.canwest.com © *The Calgary Herald* 2007.

Think back to the last term paper you wrote. Did you experience the frustration of not knowing what to write about and difficulty in getting started? The all-too-frequent result of such frustration and difficulty is procrastination. Many times, students begin the writing process only when they are faced with an impending deadline.

In some ways, preparing a business plan is similar to writing a term paper. Getting started may be agonizing, and you may find it difficult to decide what to say, especially if you lack experience and aren't sure what issues need to be addressed. Even when you know the issues, you may have difficulty expressing your goals and the strategies you plan to use for achieving those goals. But just as you learn from writing a term paper, you increase your understanding of a business opportunity as you write your business plan. Carried out correctly, the process of researching and preparing the plan will clarify what you want to accomplish in a new business and, equally important, what factors might determine your success or failure in the venture.

If you have felt pride on completing a term paper, you will feel exhilaration after writing an effective business plan, in anticipation of what may prove to be the most exciting—and possibly terrifying—experience of your professional career. The business plan—its preparation, content, and organization—will serve as the thread that weaves a common purpose through the following chapters.

WHAT IS A BUSINESS PLAN?

Answer the question, "What is a business plan?"

business plan
a document that sets out the basic idea underlying a business and related start-up considerations

A start-up **business plan** is a written document that sets out the basic idea underlying a business and related start-up considerations. For the entrepreneur starting a new venture, a business plan has four basic objectives. First, it identifies the nature and the context of the business opportunity—why does such an opportunity exist? Second, it presents the approach the entrepreneur plans to take to exploit the opportunity. Third, it identifies the factors that will most likely determine whether the venture will be successful. Finally, it serves as a tool for raising financial capital as mentioned in discussed in the Craves Cookies and Cupcakes "In the Spotlight." To obtain financing to start their venture, the sisters used a business plan that emphasizes the practical implementation of a plan for long-term success.

A business plan can be viewed as an entrepreneur's game plan; it crystallizes the dreams and hopes that motivated the entrepreneur to attempt to start the business. Your business plan should lay out your basic idea for the venture, describe where you are now, indicate where you want to go, and outline how you propose to get there. Above all, your business plan should explain the key variables for success or failure, thereby helping you prepare for different situations that may occur by thinking about what could go right and what could go wrong. In fact, this is a business plan's most important function. While your business plan will represent your vision and goals for the firm, it will rarely reflect what actually happens. Within the context of a start-up, there are just too many unexpected things that can affect the final outcome. Thus, a business plan is in large part an opportunity for an entrepreneur and a management team to think about the key drivers of a venture's success or failure. In some respects, the business plan also acts as a checklist, ensuring that the management team has considered all pertinent factors that affect the business.

As the entrepreneur's blueprint for creating a new venture, the business plan is, in essence, a bridge between an idea and reality. Without first mentally visualizing the desired end result, the entrepreneur is not likely to see the venture become a physical reality. For anything that is built—a house or a business—there is always a need for a written plan. The role of the business plan is to provide a clear visualization of what the entrepreneur intends to do.

The focus in this book is on business plans that propose the launching of a new business. In such plans, the entrepreneur makes projections about the marketing, operational, and financial aspects of the proposed business for the first three to five years. However, a business plan is not a one-time-only or single-purpose document: it should be a "living" plan and updated on a regular basis based on new information. It is also important to revise the business plan in anticipation of new activities such as major expansion of an existing firm. For example, an entrepreneur who has started a small local business may propose opening additional branches or extending the business's success in other ways. Or a business plan may be a response to some change in the external environment (such as the government, demographics, or industry) that presents new opportunities. In today's fast-changing world, revisiting the business plan should be done at least once per year. Therefore, writing a business plan should be thought of as an ongoing process and not as the means to an end product. This last point is very important and deserves to be repeated: *Writing a business plan is primarily an ongoing process and only secondarily the means to an end product or outcome.*

Writing or updating a business plan for an existing business is generally easier than doing so for a new venture, and the expected financial performance is usually more accurate. Existing businesses have a history to draw upon in making projections, and data about everything from historic costs to expected sales revenues is easily available. Many business owners concentrate more on reassessing the external environment than on internal analysis when revisiting their business plans.

THE NEED FOR A BUSINESS PLAN

Most entrepreneurs are results oriented, and for good reason. A "can do" attitude is essential in starting a new business. Without it, entrepreneurs run the risk of becoming paralyzed by inaction. Getting the business operational should be a high priority. However, entrepreneurs who use the need for action as an excuse to neglect planning are making a big mistake. A well-researched business plan helps focus the entrepreneur in identifying the optimal business opportunity, as well as secure financing for launch and growth.

USERS OF A BUSINESS PLAN

A business plan has two primary functions: (1) to provide a clearly articulated statement of goals and strategies for internal use and (2) to serve as a selling document to be shared with outsiders. Exhibit 5-1 provides an overview of those who might have an interest in a business plan for a new venture. One main group of users comprises outsiders who are critical to the firm's success: customers, suppliers, investors, and bankers or other lenders. The other major group is the internal users of the business plan: the new firm's management and its employees. Let's consider the internal users first.

INTERNAL USERS OF THE BUSINESS PLAN

Any activity begun without adequate preparation tends to be haphazard. This is particularly true of such a complex process as initiating a new business. Although planning is a mental process, it must go beyond the realm of speculation. Thinking about a proposed new business must become more rigorous as rough ideas crystallize and are quantified.

Explain the need for a business plan from the perspectives of the entrepreneur, the investor, and the lenders.

2

EXHIBIT **5-1**
Users of Business Plans

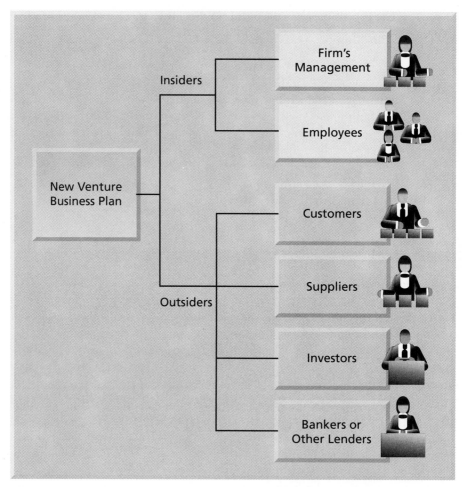

A written plan is essential to ensure systematic coverage of all the important features of a new business. By identifying the variables that can affect the success or failure of the business, the business plan becomes a model that helps the entrepreneur focus on important issues and activities for the new venture.

Preparing a formal written plan imposes needed discipline on the entrepreneur and the management team. In order to prepare a written statement about marketing strategy, for example, the entrepreneur and the team must perform extensive market research. The marketing research would include the environmental analysis introduced in Chapter 2, as well as the customer and competitive research discussed in Chapter 6. Likewise, a study of financial needs requires a review of projected receipts and expenditures, month by month. Otherwise, even a good opportunity is likely to fail because of negative cash flows. In short, business plan preparation forces an entrepreneur to exercise the discipline that managers must possess if their venture is to succeed. Furthermore, because the business plan typically includes at least three years of financial forecasting, it may be used as a control factor. Actual sales should be compared to the business plan forecast to determine how promotional, costing, or purchasing should be modified if projections are not met.

A business plan should also be effective in selling the new venture to those within the company. It provides a structure for communicating the entrepreneur's mission to current—and prospective—employees of the firm.

THE BUSINESS PLAN AND OUTSIDERS

By enhancing a firm's credibility, the business plan can serve as an effective selling tool to use with prospective customers and suppliers, as well as investors and lenders. Suppliers, for example, extend trade credit, which is often an important part of a new firm's financial plan. A well-prepared business plan may be helpful in gaining a supplier's trust and securing favourable credit terms. Occasionally, a business plan can improve sales prospects. For example, by convincing prospective customers of a firm's potential for longevity, the plan may reassure those customers that the new firm is likely to be around to service a product or to continue as a procurement source.

Whether it's for a new business looking for seed money, a growing business looking for bank financing, or even an established business with no need for added capital, a business plan can make all the difference between failure and success. The problem, experts say, is not just convincing business owners that they need a plan; it's getting them to understand all that's involved in putting one together—and the degree to which the quality of the plan affects the future of their organization.

When you're starting a new venture, the business plan is just like a game plan for a sports team: it sets out your goals, how you intend to achieve them, and who is responsible for executing each section of the plan. Of course, a lot changes when the company is actually launched, but a well-thought-out and researched business plan increases the odds of success pretty dramatically. It ensure the entrepreneur has thought about all the issues involved in planning and operating a business.[1]

Entrepreneurs don't need a business school background to put together an effective business plan. Many colleges and universities have assistance programs where students, and sometimes even faculty members, give advice and assistance to entrepreneurs. A word of caution, however: traditional wisdom is that the entrepreneur needs to "own" the plan, and having it written by a third party runs the risk of this not happening. The entrepreneur needs to have a solid understanding of how the business works, and this means being very involved in the development of the plan. People who advise business owners stress the importance of solid research and a sense of realism. Some common business plan flaws include

- Overly optimistic financial projections send up a red flag to lenders, as do inadequate assessments of the competition and the market environment.
- Vague marketing strategies that fail to clearly state product differentiation or the size of the target market(s), or provide a detailed communication strategy for the target market create doubt of venture feasibility.
- A poorly prepared document that looks unprofessional or lacks research material implies lack of commitment or research on the part of the potential entrepreneur.
- Poor organization descriptions, such as limited comments on the management team, hazy timelines, or a vague risk assessment reduce the perception of competency.

When writing a business plan, prepare the financial section last, following careful analysis of the prospective firm's day-to-day operations and sales and marketing strategies. Almost anyone starting a business faces the task of raising financial resources to supplement personal savings. Unless an entrepreneur has a rich relative or friend who will supply funds, he or she must appeal to bankers, individual investors, or venture capitalists. The business plan serves as the entrepreneur's calling card when he or she is approaching these sources of financing.

Both investors and lenders use the business plan to better understand the new venture, the type of product or service it offers, the nature of the market, and the qualifications of the entrepreneur and the management team. A venture capital firm or other sophisticated investor will not consider investing in a new business before reviewing a properly prepared business plan. And the plan can be extremely helpful for a new firm establishing a good relationship with a commercial bank.

The significance of the business plan in dealing with outsiders is aptly expressed by Mark Stevens:

> *If you are inclined to view the business plan as just another piece of useless paperwork, it's time for an attitude change. When you are starting out, investors will justifiably want to know a lot about you and your qualifications for running a business and will want to see a step-by-step plan for how you intend to make it a success. If you are already running a business and plan to expand or diversify, investors and lenders will want to know a good deal about the company's current status, where it is headed and how you intend to get it there. You must provide them with a plan that makes all of this clear.[2]*

prospectus
a marketing document used to solicit investors' monies

While family, friends, and banks will refer to a "business plan," a legal document called a **prospectus,** or offering memorandum, is frequently required for raising capital from venture capitalists or the general public. This document contains all the information necessary to satisfy federal and provincial requirements for warning potential investors about the possible risks of the investment. But the prospectus alone is not an effective marketing document with which to sell a concept. An entrepreneur must first use the business plan to create interest in the start-up, and then follow up with a formal offering memorandum, perhaps several years later, when pursuing additional financing for large capital expansion. Typically investors or lenders who are shown a business plan with key competitive features are required to sign a **confidentiality agreement,** so that they cannot use the ideas or leak information. A copy of a confidentiality agreement is available at http://www.longenecker4e.nelson.com.

confidentiality agreement
a document used to ensure investors keep information confidential

THE INVESTOR'S PERSPECTIVE

If you intend to use a business plan to raise capital, it is important that you understand the investor's basic perspective. You must see the world as the investor sees it—that is, you must think as the investor thinks. For most entrepreneurs, this is more easily said than done, as an entrepreneur generally perceives a new venture very differently than an investor does. The entrepreneur characteristically focuses on the positive potential of the start-up—what will happen if everything goes right. The prospective investor, on the other hand, plays the role of the skeptic, thinking more about what could go wrong. An entrepreneur's failure to not only understand but also appreciate this difference in perspectives almost certainly ensures rejection by an investor. At the most basic level, a prospective investor has a single goal: to maximize potential return on an investment through the cash flows that will be received, while minimizing personal risk exposure. Even venture capitalists, who are thought to be great risk takers, want to minimize their risk. Like any informed investor, they will look for ways to shift risk to the entrepreneur.

As noted by William Sahlman at the Harvard Business School,

> *What's wrong with most business plans? The answer is relatively straightforward. Most waste too much ink on numbers and devote too little to the information that really matters to intelligent investors. As every seasoned investor knows,*

financial projections for a new company—especially detailed, month-by-month projections that stretch out for more than a year—are an act of imagination.

    An entrepreneurial venture faces far too many unknowns to predict revenues, let alone profits. Moreover, few if any entrepreneurs correctly anticipate how much capital and time will be required to accomplish their objectives. Typically, they are wildly optimistic, padding their projections. Investors know about the padding effect and therefore discount the figures in business plans. These maneuvers create a vicious circle of inaccuracy that benefits no one.[3]

The skepticism voiced by William Sahlman clearly indicates that financial forecasting is credible only when based upon extensive market research and prepared in a logical and reasonable manner.

Given the fundamental differences in perspective between the investor and the entrepreneur, the important question becomes "How do I write a business plan that will capture a prospective investor's interest?" There is no easy answer, but two things are certain: (1) investors have a short attention span, and (2) certain features appeal to investors, while others are distinctly unappealing.

THE INVESTOR'S SHORT ATTENTION SPAN

In the 1980s, Kenneth Blanchard and Spencer Johnson wrote a popular book about being a one-minute manager—a manager who practises principles that can be applied quickly but produce significant results.[4] Investors in start-up and early-stage companies are, in a sense, one-minute investors. Because they receive many business plans, they cannot read them in any detailed fashion. Ed Rygiel of MDS Health Group Ltd, a Toronto-based consortium of companies that invests in medical technology companies, receives about 350 business plans per year but invests in only two or three firms. As with most investors, Rygiel simply doesn't have the luxury of time to analyze every plan thoroughly. Conventional wisdom says the business plan should be as brief as possible to tell the story. It's not written to show how much the entrepreneur knows but to highlight the financial opportunity for the investor.[5] The speed with which business plans are initially reviewed requires that they be designed to communicate effectively and quickly to prospective investors. They must not sacrifice thoroughness, however, or substitute a few snappy phrases for basic factual information. After all, someone will eventually read the plan carefully. To get that careful reading though, the plan must first gain the interest of the investor, and the plan must be formulated with that purpose in mind. While many factors may stimulate interest, some basic elements of a business plan that tend to attract or repel prospective investors deserve consideration. Furthermore, a plan may be tailored to fit the reader, with a comprehensive plan used for operational guidance, and a partial plan for investors or suppliers.

BUSINESS PLAN FEATURES THAT ATTRACT OR REPEL INVESTORS

In order to raise capital from outside investors, the business plan must be the "right" plan—that is, it must speak the investors' language. You must know what is important and what is not important to investors and how to present your idea or concept in a way that is meaningful to them. Otherwise, you will immediately lose credibility—and a potential source of financing.

Based on their experience with the MIT Enterprise Forum, Stanley R. Rich and David E. Gumpert identified the characteristics of a business plan that enhance the probability

EXHIBIT **5-2**

Features of a Successful Business Plan

- It must be arranged appropriately, with an executive summary, a table of contents, and chapters in the right order.
- It must be the right length and have the right appearance—not too long and not too short, not too fancy and not too plain.
- It must give a sense of what the founders and the company expects to accomplish three to seven years into the future.
- It must explain in quantitative and qualitative terms the benefit to the user of the company's products or services.
- It must present hard evidence of the marketability of the products or services.
- It must justify financially the means chosen to sell the products or services.
- It must explain and justify the level of product development which has been achieved and describe in appropriate detail the manufacturing process and associated costs.
- It must portray the partners as a team of experienced managers with complementary business skills.
- It must suggest as high an overall "rating" as possible of the venture's product development and team sophistication.
- It must contain believable financial projections, with the key data explained and documented.
- It must show how investors can cash out in three to seven years, with appropriate capital appreciation.
- It must be presented to the most potentially receptive financiers possible to avoid wasting precious time as company funds dwindle.
- It must be easily and concisely explainable in a well-orchestrated oral presentation.

Source: "Plans That Succeed," *Business Plans That Win $$$: Lessons from the MIT Enterprise Forum* by Stanley R. Rich and David E. Gumpert, pp. 126–27. Reprinted by permission of SLL Sterling Lord Literistic, Inc. Copyright © 1985 by David Gumpert.

---

of receiving funding from an investor. Exhibit 5-2 lists some of those features. For instance, to be effective, the plan cannot be extremely long or encyclopedic in detail. It should seldom exceed 40 pages in length, as investors generally will look at brief reports and avoid those that take too long to read. Also, the overall appearance of the report should be attractive, and the report should be well organized, with numbered pages and a table of contents.

Investors are more *market oriented* than *product oriented,* realizing that most patented inventions never earn a dime for the inventors. The essence of the entrepreneurial process is to identify new products, but only if they meet an identifiable customer need. Thus, it is essential for the entrepreneur to appreciate investors' market orientation and, more importantly, to join investors in their concern about market prospects.

Additional features that interest investors include the following:

- Evidence of customer acceptance of the venture's product or service
- An appreciation of investors' needs, through recognition of their particular financial goals, as evidenced in their required rates of return
- Evidence of focus, through concentration on only a limited number of products or services
- Proprietary position, as represented by patents, copyrights, and trademarks[6]

The following are some features that create unfavourable reactions among prospective investors:

- Infatuation with the product or service rather than familiarity with and awareness of marketplace needs
- Financial projections at odds with accepted industry norms

- Unrealistic growth projections
- Need for custom or applications engineering, which makes substantial growth difficult[7]

Investors are also quickly disillusioned by plans that contain page after page of detailed computer-generated financial projections, indicating—intentionally or unintentionally—that the entrepreneur can predict with great accuracy what will happen. Refer to Appendix A for a comprehensive investor's evaluation checklist for business plans.

THE LENDER'S PERSPECTIVE

Entrepreneurs seeking bank financing need to customize their funding proposal according to the type of financing they are pursuing. Research published by Matthew Stark and Colin Mason of the University of Strathclyde indicates that different types of funders analyze business plans differently, have different funding criteria, and place emphasis on different kinds of information. Their research shows that the primary concern of the banker is the risk that the loan will not be repaid. Accordingly, the banker is most interested in the finances of the business in order to judge whether the business can service the debt, and whether assets are available from either the business or the entrepreneur to secure the loan in the event the business fails. The banker will also compare the financial information in the business plan against industry averages. Unlike an investor, the lender is not focused on capital gains, but rather loan repayment. As such, the banker gives less consideration to the nature of the opportunity or the entrepreneurial team. The following is a list of banking criterion for business plan evaluation.

- The availability and quality of collateral
- The strength of cash flow—the ability to cover interest and repay the loan
- The competence and commitment of the founder(s); do they have the skills to operate the venture and have they committed time and money
- The reputation of the founder(s), and their credit rating
- The overall risk of the industry[8]

Hanson Ho and Greg Lam, founders of Sliced Tomatoes, launched their business after participating in a business plan competition in university. Refer to In the Trenches for their experience.

HOW MUCH BUSINESS PLAN IS NEEDED?

To this point, we have presented the process of writing a business plan in either/or terms—either you do it or you don't. We have done so in an effort to make a compelling case for writing a plan, to persuade you that a plan is important both as a guide for future action and as a selling document. In making a decision regarding the extent of planning, an entrepreneur must deal with tradeoffs. Preparing a business plan requires both time and money, two resources that are always in limited supply. Other considerations include

- *Preferences of the management team:* The amount of planning also depends on the management team's personal preferences. Some management teams want to participate in the planning process; others do not. Lack of interest on the part of management is likely to lead to insufficient planning.
- *Complexity of the business:* The level of complexity of a business affects how much planning is appropriate.

Describe what determines how much planning an entrepreneur and a management team are likely to do. 3

IN THE TRENCHES

Entrepreneurial Experiences

A Slice of Success

Vancouver-based *Sliced Tomatoes* started as an entry in a business plan contest at Simon Fraser University, dreamed up by two pals who never thought they would actually take it to the market. But the response from classmates was so enthusiastic they believed should run with it. Neither [Greg] Lam nor his business-plan partner, Hanson Ho, knew much about the food-service industry. "I worked in the restaurant industry for a few years doing everything from dishwashing to bartending, and Hanson's a computer guy, a software developer, and has no clue about food."

Their idea was to provide ingredients and cooking instructions for healthy, gourmet meals that would be delivered to people's homes. They came up with the slogan "home-cookin without the shoppin' or choppin,'" and touted the meal service as a nutritious alternative to fast food.

Through their personal connections they found Ian Lai, a full-time instructor at the Northwest Culinary Academy of Vancouver, who after a glance at the Sliced Tomatoes business plan knew the pair had a winner. "There's a niche market for what they're trying to accomplish," Mr. Lai said. "In today's really busy lifestyle, people still want to eat healthily. It's a little bit on the pricier side, but you're offsetting those costs by saving time." Mr. Lai mentored the team during start-up with all aspects of meal preparation, ingredients, suppliers and kitchen work-flow.

The team secured financing through CYBF [Canadian Youth Business Federation] and two other investors, and is a thriving venture with upward of 700 customers who order frequently, and many more who use the service for special occasions or when they're in a pinch. The menu differs daily, and some entrees come with Weight Watchers points. Orders are submitted on-line, and customers have the option of paying through PayPal. Ingredients are delivered in coolers that are picked up the next day or next order.

Last summer Sliced Tomatoes announced it was going green by recycling, composting and delivering in smaller vehicles. It also focuses on Vancouver-area produce, meats and organics. As with most business start-ups their success came with some pitfalls, including the training and motivation of employees. They also work to stay true to their plan. "We feel we're unique and focused on our niche market. We focus our efforts on just a few projects as opposed to doing everything," Mr. Lam said.

Source: Daryl-Lynn Carlson, A Slice of Sucess: Young Entrepreneurs, *National Post,* November 19, 2007, p. FP10.

- *Competitive environment:* If the firm will be operating in a highly competitive environment, where it must be scrupulously managed in order to survive, a significant amount of planning will be needed.
- *Level of uncertainty:* Ideally, ventures facing a volatile, rapidly changing environment would prepare for all eventualities through extensive planning. In reality, however, entrepreneurs are more inclined to plan when there is less uncertainty because they can better anticipate future events—which is the opposite of what they should be thinking.[9]

So the issue goes beyond the question "Do I plan?" It includes the decision as to *how much* to plan, which, in turn, involves difficult tradeoffs.

PREPARING A BUSINESS PLAN

List practical suggestions to follow in writing a business plan, and outline the key sections of a business plan.

4

Two issues are of primary concern in preparing a business plan: (1) the basic format and effectiveness of the written presentation and (2) the content of the plan.

FORMATTING AND WRITING A BUSINESS PLAN

The quality of a completed business plan ultimately depends on the quality of the underlying business concept. A poorly conceived new venture idea cannot be rescued by good writing. A good concept may be destroyed, however, by writing that fails to effectively communicate.

Clear writing gives credibility to the ideas presented in a business plan; factual support must be supplied for any claims or promises made. When promising to provide superior service or explaining the attractiveness of the market, for example, the entrepreneur must include strong supporting evidence. In short, the plan must be believable.

Skill in written communication is necessary to present the business concept in an accurate, comprehensible, and enthusiastic way. The following are practical suggestions specifically related to writing a business plan:

- Provide a table of contents and individual section tabs for easy reference.
- Use a word-processed 8½×11-inch format and photocopy the plan to minimize costs.
- Package the plan in a loose-leaf binder to facilitate future revisions.
- To add interest and aid readers' comprehension, use charts, graphs, diagrams, tabular summaries, maps, and other visual aids.
- To ensure that the business plan is treated in a confidential manner, indicate on the cover and again on the title page of the plan that all information is proprietary and confidential. Number each copy of the plan and account for each outstanding copy by requiring each recipient of the plan to acknowledge receipt in writing.
- If your start-up is of a particularly sensitive nature because it is based on advanced technology, consider whether you should divulge certain information—details of a technological design, for example, or the highly sensitive specifics of a marketing strategy—even to a prospective investor. You might want to develop an in-depth plan for internal purposes and then use appropriate extracts from it to put together a highly effective document to support your funding proposal.
- As you complete major sections of the plan, ask carefully chosen third parties who have themselves raised capital successfully—including accountants, lawyers, and other entrepreneurs—to give their perspectives on the quality, clarity, reasonableness, and thoroughness of the plan. Once the business plan is in close-to-final form, ask these independent reviewers for final comments before you reproduce and distribute the plan.[10]
- Retain all of your research including articles, competitor data and promotional material, traffic volume maps for retail outlets, interviews, surveys of potential clients, and supplier quotes.

DECIDING ON THE CONTENT OF A BUSINESS PLAN

Four interdependent factors should be given thorough consideration in deciding on the content of a business plan for a start-up company:

- *The people:* Biographies of the men and women starting and running the venture, as well as any outside parties, such as lawyers, accountants, and suppliers providing key services or important resources.

- *The opportunity:* A profile of the business itself—what it will sell and to whom, how much and how rapidly it can grow, what its financial outlook is, and who and what may stand in the way of its success.
- *The context:* The big picture—the regulatory environment, interest rates, demographic trends, inflation, and other factors that inevitably change but cannot be controlled by the entrepreneur.
- *Risk and reward:* An assessment of everything that can go wrong or right, with a discussion of how the entrepreneurial team can respond to the various challenges.[11]

Keep these general factors in mind as you compose the specific content of your business plan.

Although the business plan for each new venture is unique and no single format or formula can guarantee success, there are guidelines a prospective entrepreneur can follow in preparing a plan. Most business plans exhibit considerable similarity in basic content.

Exhibit 5-3 summarizes the major sections common to most business plans, providing a bird's-eye view of the overall content. We will now briefly consider each of these sections. Other chapters look at some sections of the business plan in more detail.

TITLE PAGE The title page is the first page of the business plan and should contain the following information:

- Company name, address, phone number, fax number, and website
- Company logo, if available
- Names, titles, addresses, and phone numbers of the owners and key executives
- Date on which the business plan was issued
- Number of the copy (to help keep track of how many copies are outstanding)
- Name of the contact person, if other than the owners and key executives

TABLE OF CONTENTS The table of contents provides a sequential listing of the sections of the plan, with page numbers.

EXECUTIVE SUMMARY The **executive summary** is crucial for getting the attention of the one-minute investor. It must convey a clear and concise picture of the proposed venture and, at the same time, create a sense of excitement regarding its prospects. This means that it must be written—and, if necessary, rewritten—to achieve clarity and create interest. If the plan is to be presented to a funder, it should clearly state the amount of money being sought, and the capital structure. Even though the executive summary comes at the beginning of the business plan, it provides an overview of the whole plan and should be written last.

Depending on the situation and the preference of the entrepreneur, an executive summary may be in the form of a synopsis or a narrative.

executive summary
a section of the business plan that conveys a clear and concise overall picture of the proposed venture

Synopsis The synopsis is the more straightforward of the two summary formats. A synopsis briefly covers all aspects of the business plan, giving each topic relatively equal treatment. It simply relates, in abbreviated fashion, the conclusions of each section of the completed business plan. Although it is relatively easy to prepare, the synopsis can be rather dry reading for the prospective investor.

Narrative Because the narrative tells the reader a story, it can convey greater excitement than the synopsis. However, composing an effective narrative requires a gifted writer who can communicate the necessary information and engender enthusiasm without crossing the line into hyperbole. A narrative is more appropriate for businesses that are breaking

EXHIBIT **5-3**
*Abbreviated Business
Plan Outline*

Title Page: Provides names, addresses, and phone numbers of the venture and its owners and management personnel; date prepared; copy number; and contact person.

Table of Contents: Provides page numbers for the key sections of the business plan.

Executive Summary: Provides a one- to three-page overview of the total business plan. Written after the other sections are completed, it highlights their significant points and, ideally, creates enough excitement to motivate the reader to continue reading.

Mission Statement and Goals: Concisely describes the intended strategy and business philosophy for making the vision happen. Clearly states start-up and operating goals.

Company Overview: Explains the type of company, such as manufacturing, retail, or service; provides background information on the company if it already exists; describes the proposed form of organization—sole proprietorship, partnership, or corporation. This section should be organized as follows: company name and location; company objectives; nature and primary product or service of the business; current status (start-up, buyout, or expansion) and history (if applicable); and legal form of organization.

Products and/or Services Plan: Describes the product and/or service and points out any unique features; explains why people will buy the product or service. This section should offer the following descriptions: products and/or services; features of the product or service providing a competitive advantage; available legal protection (patents, copyrights, trademarks); and dangers of technical or style obsolescence.

Marketing Plan: Shows who the firm's customers will be and what type of competition it will face; outlines the marketing strategy and specifies the firm's competitive edge. This section should offer the following descriptions: analysis of target market and profile of target customer; methods of identifying and attracting customers; selling approach, type of sales force and distribution channels; types of sales promotions and advertising; and credit and pricing policies.

Management Plan: Identifies the key players—active investors, management team, and directors—citing the experience and competence they possess. This section should offer the following descriptions: management team; outside investors and/or directors and their qualifications; outside resource people and their qualifications; and a human resource plan for recruiting, training, and compensating employees.

Operating Plan: Explains the type of manufacturing or operating system to be used, and describes the facilities, labour, raw materials, and product processing requirements. This section should offer the following descriptions: operating or manufacturing methods; operating facilities (location, space, and equipment); quality-control methods; procedures to control inventory and operations; sources of supply; and purchasing procedures.

Financial Plan: Specifies financial needs and contemplated sources of financing; presents projections of revenues, costs, and profits. This section should offer the following descriptions: historical financial statements for the last three to five years or as available; pro forma financial statements for three to five years, including income statements, balance sheets, cash flow statements, and cash budgets (monthly for first year and quarterly for second year); break-even analysis of profits and cash flows; and planned sources of financing. Detailed notes for the forecasting assumptions should be included.

Appendix of Supporting Documents: Provides materials supplementary to the plan. This section should offer the following descriptions: management team biographies, any other important data that support the information in the business plan, and the firm's ethics code.

new ground, with a new product, a new market, or new operational techniques. It is also a better format for businesses that have one dominant advantage, such as holding an important patent or being run by a well-known entrepreneur. Finally, the narrative works well for companies with interesting or impressive backgrounds or histories.[12]

A sample executive summary from the business plan of a holistic retail store is shown in Exhibit 5-4. Would you consider the example to be a synopsis- or narrative-style executive summary?

EXHIBIT **5-4**

An Example of an Executive Summary for a Holistic Retail Outlet

EXECUTIVE SUMMARY

The Balance Zone will service the growing market niche of those seeking a holistic approach to treat illness and enhance health. The founders, Christine Rose and Tazmina Olio, are experienced industry practitioners with thriving practices. They intend to create an attractive retail space, close to their client base, that will complement their practice. The Balance Zone will address a specific client niche that is currently underserviced and will offer several key differentiating features, including

- A feng shui–designed 350 sq. metre retail and consultation space, in a restored house. Two consultation rooms will allow on-site integrated holistic treatments.
- A wide range of herbal and vitamin supplements including exclusive distribution of several European and aboriginal lines. Refrigeration units will ensure quality for select lines.
- The large vitamin collection will be supplemented with a collection of alternative health reading material for purchase, and a cozy waiting area. Tranquil music and water will ensure relaxation.
- The floor layout has been constructed to optimize natural lighting and air circulation.

The customer demand has been carefully researched regarding both usage patterns and demographics. The target market clusters have been selected to reflect statistical research including the results of the *Complementary and Alternative Medicine in Canada: Trends in Use and Public Attitudes, 1997–2006* report by the Fraser Institute published in May 2007, which found the proportion of Canadians using one or more holistic services to have increased to 74 percent, with 54 percent of the population annual users. The report also indicated that the most commonly used complementary and alternative medicines and therapies were massage (19 percent), chiropractic (15 percent), relaxation techniques (14 percent), and herbal therapies (10 percent).[13] The primary target market will comprise families in the neighbouring community, with household income greater than $75,000, age 30 to 55. It is recognized that secondary target markets will emerge; Health Canada, in a Health and Policy Research Bulletin indicated that specific user groups include

- The well-educated "concerned" well who seek to maintain and enhance their health for the long term
- People with specific health concerns, such as injury, and chronic diseases such as asthma, osteoporosis, diabetes etc.
- The terminally ill or those with life-threatening disease

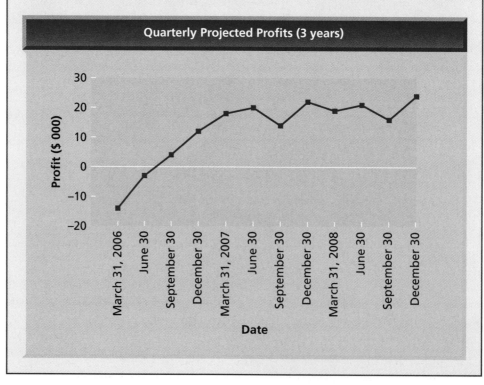

EXHIBIT **5-4**

(Continued)

The management team has sound operational practice, and will rely upon mentors from BDC and the Canadian Youth Business Foundation, as well as an experienced angel investor. Projected financial statements indicate break-even within the first year and a sound profit by the second year of operation.

Fact Sheet—The Balance Zone Inc.

Business Description:	A unique integrated holistic centre, located in a refurbished historical building
Products and Services:	The centre will provide both unique vitamins and herbal remedies, primarily from Germany and the Far East, as well as the booking of holistic professionals for on-site consultation in specially designed feng shui rooms
Location and Zoning:	Cabbagetown, Toronto, commercial zoned building; City of Toronto business licence has been obtained
Legal Structure and Logo:	The venture will be provincially incorporated in Ontario, and a logo trademark has been designed. The private company will issue Class A and B voting shares, and Class C and D non-voting shares
Number of Founders:	Christine Rose and Tazmina Olio
Significant Background:	Christine is a doctor of holistic medicine, has practised for three years, and is recognized for her practice in aboriginal healing. Tazmina is a specialist in herbal remedies, and has operated a cranial sacrum practice for four years.
Staffing:	Founders working full-time, three part-time employees until second year of operation
Projected Sales Potential:	$480,000 in the first year, $750,000 by year three
Projected Share of Market:	4.5% of the local market of 23,000 households after 3 years; at least 20% of clientele will be people travelling through the area for work
Invested to Date:	$2,500 for market research and logo design
Collateral Value:	The inventory and office equipment has a collateral value of $25,000. Two cars, valued at $16,000, have also been offered for collateral.

Estimated Financing Needed:		
	$42,000	Inventory and office equipment
	$11,000	Leasehold improvements
	$ 2500	Legal and accounting expenses
	$22,000	Operating capital (2 months)
	$77,500	

Projected Sources of Financing:		
	$20,000	Equity (Class A shares)
	$25,000	Equity (Class B Shares)
	$15,000	Debt: loan CYBF
	$17,500	Debt: operating line of credit BDC
	$77,500	

Investment Units:	$5000 for each Class B voting share.
Terms and Payback Period:	Shares are nontransferable. Class B shares offer a buy-back provision after three years for $7500. The estimated return for Class A shares is 18% for a three-year period. The loan from the Canadian Youth Business Foundation (CYBF) is payable over a three-year term, prime rate plus 1.5%, no principal paid during the first year. The operating line of credit from BDC is prime plus 3%.
Legal Counsel:	Mohamed Zarah LLB
Financial Counsel and Mentor:	Susanna Quinn, Canadian Youth Business Foundation

MISSION STATEMENT AND GOALS   The firm's **mission statement** concisely describes, in writing, the intended strategy and business philosophy for making the entrepreneur's vision a reality. In a few sentences, it should convey how combined efforts in all areas of the business will move it toward its goal. In addition, it should distinguish the firm from all others. Mission statements can and do vary in length, content, format, and specificity. However, it is essential that a mission statement remain simple, believable, and achievable. A mission statement

- Will tend to be two to four sentences long
- Does not copy other companies
- States your key competencies and your unique features
- Is believed in, by the founders, customers, and employees
- Shows your values

While a good mission statement provides strategic vision and direction, goals are the short-term measure used to accomplish them. Goals are typically developed for functional areas, such as marketing, finance, and operations, and are developed annually. A common guideline for goal development employs the SMART acronym:

- **S**pecific: state exactly what you want to accomplish
- **M**easurable: base the goal upon quantifiable outcomes
- **A**ction oriented: list the steps to be taken to reach the goal
- **R**ealistic: the goal has to be realistic to you, and take into consideration other factors such as the level of competition and customer trends
- **T**imely: the goal must have a target date

Clarity of vision, an important element in any business plan, should be an expression of a company's highest aspirations. The "In the Trenches" feature illustrates how one successful entrepreneur used visioning to successfully expand his venture.

COMPANY OVERVIEW   The main body of the business plan begins with a brief description of the firm. If the firm is already in existence, its history is included. This section informs the reader of the type of business being proposed, the firm's objectives, the firm's location, and whether it will serve a local or international market. In many cases, legal issues—especially those concerning the firm's form of organization—are addressed in this section of the plan. (Legal issues regarding the form of organization are discussed in Chapter 10.) In writing this section, the entrepreneur should answer the following questions:

- What are the basic nature and activity of the business?
- When and where was this business started?
- What has been achieved to date?
- What changes have been made in structure and/or ownership?
- In what stage of development is the firm—for example, seed stage or full product line?
- What are the firm's objectives?
- What is its primary product or service?
- What customers will be served?
- What is the firm's distinctive competence?
- What are the current and projected economic states of the industry?
- What is the firm's form of organization—sole proprietorship, partnership, or corporation?
- Does the firm intend to become a publicly traded company or an acquisition candidate?

IN THE TRENCHES

Entrepreneurial Experiences

Steering Toward Success

It seemed like a good idea at the time. You had a good product or service, the passion and drive to sell it and, having done the proper "homework," knew it would fulfill a need in the marketplace. So what could go wrong?

Well, if you're like many other new small-business entrepreneurs, plenty. "Luck's part of it, but you need to focus on what you do best," says Rob Pittman, who together with partner Johan Rothzen have been running a small business success story at Urban Lighthouse, a software development company in Calgary that helps businesses stream-line management tools in a user-friendly manner.

The company, now in its fifth year, was nominated for the Bennett Jones Emerging Enterprise of the Year Award in 2006. The two men admit their company could have ended up on the scrap heap had they not realized early on they were trying to do too many things. "You have to find a niche and work at it," says Rothzen. "We tried networking at the beginning and found out we weren't very good at it. So we focused on our strengths." Adds Pittman: "It's better to do a couple things really, really well and have clients say 'hey, these guys are good,' than to do a bunch of things half-assed."

It all goes to having a good business plan—a written description of what you are going to do, and how you are going to do it—and using benchmarks, says Tom Thurmeier, a lawyer with the Small Business Legal Centre. "Too many small businesses don't succeed because they fail to plan," he says. "That may sound like a boy-scout phrase, but it's true." Thurmeier says successful businesses like Urban Lighthouse make good business plans, then adapt and adjust as they move forward.

"Having a great idea is not enough," he says. "A good business plan is critical, but it's like a box of chocolates—you never know what you're going to get. "Successful entrepreneurs are smart enough to look at benchmarks along the way to see where their business should be . . . Projections are just that—projections. "At some point reality must set in. Maybe that 'great idea' is not as viable as they thought. And that's when they should be prepared to be flexible and adapt."

Source: Jim Johnson, "Steering Toward Success; Owners Walk a Fine Line Between Success, Failure" *Calgary Herald*, October 16, 2007, p. SB10.

PRODUCT AND/OR SERVICES PLAN As its title reveals, the **products and/or services plan** discusses those products and/or services to be offered to the firm's customers. If a new or unique physical product is to be offered and a working model or prototype is available, a photograph of it should be included in this section of the business plan. Investors will naturally show the greatest interest in products that have been developed, tested, and found to be functional. Any innovative features should be identified and any patent protection explained. Although, in many instances, the product or service may be similar to those offered by competitors—electrical contracting, for example—any special features should be clearly identified.

MARKETING PLAN As stated earlier, prospective investors and lenders attach a high priority to market considerations. They do not want to invest in a product that is well

products and/or services plan
a section of the business plan that describes the product and/or service to be provided and explains the merits of the product and/or service

marketing plan
a section of the business plan that describes the user benefits of the product or service

engineered but unwanted by customers. The **marketing plan,** therefore, must identify user benefits and the type of market that exists. Depending on the type of product or service being offered, the marketing plan may be able to not only identify but also quantify the financial benefit to the user—for example, by showing how quickly a user can recover the cost of the product or service through savings in operating costs. Of course, benefits may also take such forms as savings in time or improvements in attractiveness, safety, or health.

The marketing plan should document customer interest by showing that a market exists and that customers are ready to buy the product or service. This market analysis must be detailed enough to provide a reasonable estimate of demand. An estimate of demand must be analytically sound and based on more than assumptions if it is to be accepted as credible by prospective investors. Most business plans include a market analysis section, which provides a detailed evaluation of the competitive environment, including industry trends. The research processes described in Chapter 6 outline the customer and competitive research upon which the analysis in the business plan is based. Elements of the proposed marketing strategy, for example, the type of sales force and the methods of promotion and advertising that will be used, will be structured to address the customer opportunity and the competitive position. (Chapters 1, 5, 6, and 7 provide additional coverage of the marketing plan.)

management plan
a section of the business plan that describes a new firm's organizational structure and the backgrounds of its key players

MANAGEMENT PLAN Prospective investors look for well-managed companies. Of all the factors they consider, the quality of the management team is paramount; it is even more important than the nature of the product or service. Investors frequently say that they would rather have an "A" management team and a "B" product or service than a "B" team and an "A" product. Unfortunately, an entrepreneur's ability to conceive an idea for a new venture is no guarantee of his or her managerial ability. The **management plan,** therefore, must detail the proposed firm's organizational structure and the backgrounds of those who will fill its key positions. Details regarding the human resource plans for the company should be included, with the skill and number of staff, as well as the hiring, training, and compensation processes outlined. Chapter 9 provides coverage of human resources for small businesses.

operating plan
a section of the business plan that offers information on how a product will be produced or a service provided, including descriptions of the firm's facilities, labour, raw materials, and processing requirements

Ideally, investors desire a well-balanced management team—one that includes financial and marketing expertise as well as production experience and innovative talent. Managerial experience in related enterprises and in other start-up situations is particularly valuable in the eyes of prospective investors.

OPERATING PLAN The **operating plan** offers information on how the product will be produced or the service provided; its importance varies from venture to venture. This plan discusses such items as location and facilities: how much space the business will need and what type of equipment it will require. (These aspects of the operating plan are discussed at length in Chapter 11.) The operating plan should also explain the firm's proposed approach to assuring quality, controlling inventory, and using subcontractors or obtaining raw materials.

financial plan
a section of the business plan that provides an account of the new firm's financial needs and sources of financing as well as a projection of its revenues, costs, and profits

FINANCIAL PLAN Financial analysis constitutes another crucial piece of the business plan; it is contained in the **financial plan** section of the business plan. **Pro forma statements,** which are projections of the company's financial statements, are presented here for the next five years (or longer). The forecasts include income statements, balance sheets, and cash flow statements on an annual basis for five years, as well as cash budgets on a monthly basis for the first year, on a quarterly basis for the second and

pro forma statements
reports that project a firm's financial condition

third years, and on an annual basis for the fourth and fifth years. It is vital that the financial projections be supported by well-substantiated assumptions and explanations of how the figures have been determined.

While all the financial statements are important, statements of cash flows deserve special attention, because a business can be profitable but fail to produce positive cash flows. A statement of cash flows identifies the sources of cash—how much will be raised from investors and how much will be generated from operations. It also shows how much money will be devoted to investments in such areas as inventories and equipment. The statement of cash flows should clearly indicate how much cash is needed from prospective investors and for what purpose. Since experience tells them that the eventual return on their investment will depend largely on their ability to cash out, most investors want to invest in a privately held company for only a limited period and want to be told how and when they may expect to cash out of the investment. Therefore, the plan should outline the mechanism available to investors for exiting the firm. (The preparation of pro forma statements and the process of raising the needed capital are discussed in Chapters 13 and 14.)

APPENDIX OF SUPPORTING DOCUMENTS The appendix should contain various supplementary materials and attachments to expand the reader's understanding of the plan. These supporting documents include any items referenced in the text of the business plan, such as the résumés of the key investors and owners/managers; photographs of products, facilities, and buildings; professional references; marketing research studies; pertinent published research; and signed contracts of sale.

RESOURCES FOR BUSINESS PLAN PREPARATION

> **Identify available sources of assistance in preparing a business plan.**   **5**

We have just presented an overview of the business plan. More extensive descriptions are provided in books on the subject, and computer software is available to guide you step by step through the preparation of a business plan. (A listing of some helpful computer software packages appears at the end of this chapter.) While such resources can be invaluable, we advise that you resist the temptation to adapt an existing business plan to your own use. Changing the numbers and some of the verbiage of another firm's business plan is simply not effective.

COMPUTER-AIDED BUSINESS PLANNING

A computer facilitates preparation of a business plan. Its word-processing capabilities, for example, can speed the writing of narrative sections of the report, such as the description of the product and the review of key management personnel. Working from the original word-processing file in which the narrative was composed, the entrepreneur can correct and refine a series of drafts and then print out the final plan in the form in which it will be presented to investors or others.

The computer is even more helpful for preparing the financial statements needed in the plan. Since the various numbers in a financial plan are interwoven in many ways, a change in one item—such as sales volume, interest rate, or cost of goods sold—will cause a ripple effect throughout the entire plan. A long, tedious set of calculations is required if the entrepreneur wishes to check various assumptions by hand. With a computer spreadsheet, an entrepreneur can accomplish this task easily, experimenting with best-case and worst-case scenarios and quickly ascertaining their effects on the firm's balance sheet, operating profits, and cash flows.

IN THE TRENCHES

Entrepreneurial Experiences

The Elevator Pitch

Entrepreneurs seeking financing often employ an "elevator pitch" to create interest. The pitch can be given anywhere, and is based upon the research and concept gathered for preparation of the business plan. The pitch consists of a three-minute summary of the business that creates a clear vision of the venture and states the opportunity for investors. It essentially is a "door-opening" device. The pitch typically covers the following points:

- Who is the target customer
- What is the concept—clear statement of product or service
- The compelling reason this venture should work; should state how the product is differentiated
- What the investment opportunity is, and the potential payout

The pitch should be practised, and entrepreneurs should be prepared to present on street corners, or anywhere the opportunity presents itself. Keep business cards available to hand to prospective investors at the end of your pitch.

There are many business plan software packages whose basic objective is to help an entrepreneur think through the important issues in beginning a new company and organize his or her thoughts to create an effective presentation. Most of Canada's major banks, as well as government centres, offer clients some form of free business planning software. While the software has broad headings and some hints about what to put in each section, and comes complete with spreadsheets already set up, the output from most of these packages looks more like a loan application than a business plan. The danger in using these tools or any other software is that they make it very easy to gloss over important aspects of the plan. Using them to write the plan may be useful and time saving, but the tools are no substitute for the research and investigation that are the foundation of any good business plan. If you recognize their limitations, however, you can use business plan software packages as useful tools to facilitate the process.

Two of the better software plans available include software created by the Canada Business Service Centre, a federal government agency with offices across Canada, and the BizPlan*Builder*® you received with this text. BizPlan*Builder*® Express is a business plan software package that is available for purchase as a supplement to this text. We chose BizPlan*Builder*® because it does a good job of illustrating some of the capabilities that software brings to business planning. Developed by JIAN, a firm that specializes in time-saving software tools for business, BizPlan*Builder*® takes you through the process of writing each step of a business plan, using flexible templates that work with your computer's word-processing and spreadsheet applications.

Throughout the book, selected chapters end with a special set of exercises to take you through the process of writing a business plan. The exercises comprise questions to be thoughtfully considered and answered. These exercise sets are entitled "The Business Plan: Laying the Foundation" because they deal with issues that are important to starting a new venture and provide guidelines for preparing different sections of a business plan. They also identify parts of BizPlan*Builder*® Express that will help you work through the templates developed by JIAN to complete the major components of a plan (such as the executive summary, vision and mission statement, product strategy, marketing plan, and financial plan) and to format the plan for professional results.

PROFESSIONAL ASSISTANCE IN BUSINESS PLANNING

The founder of any company is most notably a doer. This type of person often lacks the breadth of experience and know-how, as well as the inclination, needed for planning. Consequently, she or he must supplement personal knowledge and skills by obtaining the assistance of outsiders or by adding individuals with planning skills to the management team.

Securing help in plan preparation does not relieve an entrepreneur of direct involvement. The entrepreneur must be the primary planner, as her or his basic ideas are essential to producing a plan that is realistic. Furthermore, eventually the plan will have to be interpreted for and defended to outsiders; to be effective in such a presentation, the entrepreneur must have complete familiarity with the plan.

However, after the entrepreneur has clarified the basic ideas, other individuals may be able to render assistance in preparing the business plan. Calling on outside help, such as business plan consultants, to finish and polish the plan is both appropriate and wise. Other outside sources of assistance include the following:

- Marketing specialists, who can perform market analyses and evaluate market acceptance of a new product.
- Engineering and production experts, who can perform product development, determine technical feasibility of products, and assist in plant layout and production planning.
- Accounting firms, which can guide the development of the written plan, assist in making financial projections, and advise on establishing a system of financial control.
- Incubator organizations, which offer space for fledgling companies and can advise on structuring new businesses (incubators are discussed in detail in Chapter 15).
- Lawyers, who can ensure that the company has the necessary patent protection, review contracts, consult on liability and environmental concerns, and advise on the best form of organization.
- Business Service Centres, which provide assistance to start-up and growing businesses. Refer to http://www.canadabusiness.ca for a complete listing of the centres, as well as other government services.

Now that this chapter has made you more aware of the importance and fundamentals of the business plan, the chapters that follow will examine more closely each of the plan's components.

A BUSINESS PLAN CHECKLIST

Now that you have learned the main concepts of business plan preparation, you can begin the process of creating a business plan by writing a general company description. You also should be able to evaluate a business plan by reviewing the major components and determining the quality of the research and the logic of the product and marketing strategy. In thinking about the key issues in starting a new business, as described though a business plan, the factors listed in Exhibit 5-5 should be articulated.

EXHIBIT **5-5**
Business Plan Checklist

The business plan should be reviewed to ensure clarity and completeness. Refer to the following checklist during the review process. Ignore the items that are irrelevant to your venture.

EXECUTIVE SUMMARY
- Describes the business, and its products or services
- Key features of the business, the owners, location and financing required
- Less than two pages long

MARKETING SECTION
- Description of the venture including its competitive features
- The patents, trademarks, or copyrights obtained
- A detailed description of the industry, major players, and trends
- A competitive analysis showing the position of the venture relative to the industry; may include a competitive matrix
- A detailed description of the target market, its size, and the company's purchasing criteria
- The pricing strategy; includes industry data and supplies information
- The advertising and promotion strategy; sample may be included in the appendix

OPERATIONS SECTION
- Description and cost of equipment to be purchased or leased
- Rationale and cost of the location
- Inventory levels required for retail outlets
- Production volumes and schedule for manufacturing operations
- Description of suppliers or subcontractors
- Detailed outline of the staff required, their compensation, and the hiring and training process
- A list of the licenses, permits, legal agreements required (which could include a business license, a partnership agreement, a GST number, filing for employees with Canada Revenue Agency, and completed forms for a legal structure such as sole proprietorship)
- The features of the computer system selected
- The accounting records and quality controls selected

THE MANAGEMENT TEAM
- A description of the team and their qualifications
- A timeline for business start-up
- A mission and goal statement
- The ownership structure for the venture
- A statement of harvesting or growth expectations

THE FINANCIAL SECTION
- A calculation for start-up costs, and the amount to be contributed in equity
- An estimate of the amount required for operating capital
- The amount and type of loan required, and repayment schedule
- A collateral calculation for lenders
- A sales forecast with an explanation of the rationale
- A three-year pro forma of the financial statements
- A break-even calculation, with analysis showing at what point profits are anticipated
- A risk management analysis including insurance costing

APPENDIXES
- Résumé for the management team
- A list of potential customers (business to business)
- A list of committed or contracted sales
- Price lists for inventory
- Consulting reports regarding marketing feasibility
- Demographic or statistical information on the target market
- Articles regarding the target market or the industry
- Copies of legal agreements or contracts

THE IMPORTANCE OF RESEARCH TO SUPPORT THE PLAN

One of the major weaknesses of many business plans is the lack of good research upon which they are built. The most important kind of research is market research—providing solid evidence that a market exists for the business's product or service, and that customers are likely to buy it. However, it is also important to do other kinds of research, including research into laws and regulations that will affect the business, trends in the industry, competitor information, suppliers, operations process in the industry, costs, insurance etc. There are two types of information: secondary and primary.

Secondary research is the kind we do most often. It is research that comes from secondary sources such as books, published reports, newspaper and journal articles, statistics databases, and Internet sites. Secondary research is generally very good at describing markets and other aspects of the business. Think of secondary research as mainly answering the questions of who, what, when, and how.

Primary research is information derived directly from people: experts in the field, professionals such as lawyers and accountants, industry contacts such as trade association representatives or suppliers, and, most important, potential customers. There are two main ways of gathering primary research: interviews and surveys. More information on conducting market research can be found in Chapter 6.

LOOKING BACK

1 Answer the question, "What is a business plan?"

- A business plan identifies the nature and context of the business opportunity and describes why the opportunity exists.
- A business plan presents the approach the entrepreneur will take to exploit the opportunity.

2 Explain the need for a business plan from the perspectives of the entrepreneur, the investor, and the lenders.

- The business plan provides a clearly articulated statement of the firm's goals and strategies, helping the entrepreneur focus on important issues.
- The business plan helps identify the important variables that will determine the success or failure of the firm.
- The business plan is used as a selling document to outsiders.
- The business plan tells a prospective investor how the business will help achieve the investor's personal goal—to maximize potential return on investment through cash flows received from the investment, while minimizing personal risk exposure.

- The business plan shows an investor how he or she can cash out of the investment with appropriate capital appreciation.

3 Describe what determines how much planning an entrepreneur and a management team are likely to do.

- The allocation of time and money, two scarce resources, affects how much planning will be done.
- Other factors that affect the extent of planning include (1) the entrepreneur's management style and ability, (2) management team preferences, (3) the complexity of the business, (4) the competitive environment, and (5) the level of uncertainty in the environment.

4 List practical suggestions to follow in writing a business plan, and outline the key sections of a business plan.

- To maximize the effectiveness of a business plan, you should (1) provide a table of contents and section tabs for easy reference, (2) package the plan in a loose-leaf binder to facilitate revisions, (3) use charts, graphs, diagrams, tabular summaries, and other visual aids to create interest and make the presentation easy to follow, (4) consider withholding highly sensitive specifics, and (5) ask carefully chosen third parties to give their assessment of the quality of the plan.

- Key sections of a business plan are the (1) title page, (2) table of contents, (3) executive summary, (4) mission statement and goals, (5) company overview, (6) products and/or services plan, (7) marketing plan, (8) management plan, (9) operating plan, (10) financial plan, and (11) appendix of supporting documents.

5 Identify available sources of assistance in preparing a business plan.

- A variety of books and computer software packages are available to assist in the preparation of a business plan.
- Professionals with planning expertise, such as lawyers, accountants, and other entrepreneurs, can provide useful suggestions and assistance in the preparation of a business plan.

KEY TERMS

business plan, p. 104
confidentiality agreement, p. 108
executive summary, p. 114
financial plan, p. 120

management plan, p. 120
marketing plan, p. 120
mission statement, p. 118
operating plan, p. 120

pro forma statements, p. 120
products and/or services plan, p. 119
prospectus, p. 108

DISCUSSION QUESTIONS

1. What benefits are associated with the preparation of a written business plan for a new venture? Who uses such a plan?
2. Why do entrepreneurs tend to neglect initial planning? Why would you personally be tempted to neglect it?
3. In what way might a business plan be helpful in recruiting key management personnel?
4. How might an entrepreneur's perspective differ from an investor's in terms of the business plan?
5. Would an intelligent investor really make a decision based on a one-minute review of a business plan? Discuss.
6. Investors are said to be more market oriented than product oriented. What does this mean? What is the logic behind this orientation?
7. Why is a shorter business plan better than a longer one, especially since a more lengthy plan could include more supporting data?
8. What advantages are realized by using a computer in preparing the narrative sections of a business plan? In preparing the financial plan?
9. How might you quantify the user benefits for a new type of production tool?
10. If the income statement of a financial plan shows that the business will be profitable, why is there a need for a statement of cash flows?

YOU MAKE THE CALL

SITUATION 1

New ventures are occasionally more successful than their initial business plans projected.

In the 1980s Ben Rosen and L. J. Sevin invested in a company then called Gateway Technology, Inc., even though they had reservations about its projected sales volume. Gateway's plan stated that the company would make a portable computer compatible with IBM's personal computer and would sell 20,000 machines for a total of $35 million in its first year—"which we didn't believe for a moment," says Rosen. The sales projection for the second year was even more outrageous: $198 million. "Can you imagine seeing a business plan like this for a company going head-on against IBM, and projecting $198 million?" Rosen asks. He and Sevin told the fledgling company to scale down its projections.

Gateway later changed its name to Compaq Computer Corporation. In its first year, the company sold an estimated 50,000 machines, more than twice the plan's forecast, for $111 million. In the second year, Compaq's sales were $329 million. Rosen and Sevin were astonished by the excellent returns.

Question 1 In view of the significant underestimation of Compaq's projected sales, what benefits, if any, may have been realized through initial planning?

Question 2 What are the implications of the investors' skepticism concerning sales projections for the preparation of a business plan?

Question 3 In general, do you think that entrepreneurs or investors are likely to be more accurate and realistic in making projections for business plans? Why?

SITUATION 2

A young journalist is contemplating launching a new magazine that will feature wildlife, plant life, and the beauty of nature around the world. The prospective entrepreneur intends each issue to contain several feature articles—for example, the dangers and benefits of forest fires, features of Banff National Park, wildflowers found at high altitudes, and the danger of acid rain. The magazine will make extensive use of colour photographs, and its articles will be technically accurate and interestingly written. Unlike *Canadian Geographic*, the proposed publication will avoid articles dealing with the general culture and confine itself to topics closely related to the natural world. Suppose you are a venture capitalist examining a business plan prepared by this journalist.

Question 1 What are the most urgent questions you would want the marketing plan to answer?

Question 2 What details would you look for in the management plan?

Question 3 Do you think this entrepreneur would need to raise closer to $100,000 or $1 million in start-up capital? Why?

Question 4 At first glance, are you inclined to accept or reject the proposal? Why?

SITUATION 3

Ed Jones and John Rose decided to start a new business to manufacture noncarbonated soft drinks. They believed that their location in central British Columbia, close to high-quality water, would give them a competitive edge. Although Jones and Rose had never worked together, Jones had 17 years of experience in the soft-drink industry. Rose had recently sold his own firm and had funds to help finance the venture; however, the partners needed to raise additional money from outside investors. Both men were excited about the opportunity and spent almost 18 months developing their business plan. The first paragraph of their executive summary reflected their excitement:

> The "New Age" beverage market is the result of a spectacular boom in demand for drinks with nutritional value from environmentally safe ingredients and waters that come from deep, clear springs free of chemicals and pollutants. Argon Beverage Corporation will produce and market a full line of sparkling fruit drinks, flavoured waters, and sports drinks that are of the highest quality and purity. These drinks have the same delicious taste appeal as soft drinks while using the most healthful fruit juices, natural sugars, and the purest spring water, the hallmark of the "New Age" drink market.

With the help of a well-developed plan, the two men were successful in raising the necessary capital to begin their business. They leased facilities and started production. However, after almost two years, the plan's goals were not being met. There were cost overruns, and profits were not nearly up to expectations.

Question 1 What problems might have contributed to the firm's poor performance?

Question 2 Although several problems were encountered in implementing the business plan, the primary reason for the low profits turned out to be embezzlement. Jones was diverting company resources for personal use, even taking some of the construction material purchased by the company and using it to build his own house. What could Rose have done to avoid this situation? What are his options after the fact?

EXPERIENTIAL EXERCISES

1. Suppose that you wish to start a business to produce and sell a product designed to hold down a tablecloth on a picnic table so that the wind will not blow it off. Prepare a one-page outline of the marketing plan for this product. Be as specific and comprehensive as possible. Prepare an "elevator pitch" for the product.

2. A former chef wishes to start a business to supply temporary kitchen help (such as chefs, sauce cooks, bakers, and meat cutters) to restaurants in need of staff during busy periods. Prepare a one-page report explaining which section or sections of the business plan are most crucial to this new business and why.

3. Refer to the business plans at http://www.longenecker4e.nelson.com, as well as the sample plan in Appendix A. Referring to the detailed investor checklist on the website, analyze one of the plans. Using the criteria, determine if you think the venture would appeal to an investor.

4. Interview a person who has started a business within the past five years. Prepare a report describing the extent to which the entrepreneur engaged in preliminary planning and his or her views about the value of business plans.

EXPLORING THE WEB

1. In this chapter and others to follow, we reference BizPlan*Builder*® Express, computer software that can be used to help write a business plan.
   a. What are the key features and benefits of using this software to create a business plan?
   b. Examine one or more sample business plans, either on the "Sample Plans" page or by jumping to http://www.bplans.com, a related site. How does the content of these business plans compare with the information given in this textbook?

2. Several industries display sample business plans online. Examine sample "Business Plans" at http://www.virtualrestaurant.com and http://www.bplans.com in order to answer the following questions:
   a. How important to the effectiveness of a business plan is the appearance of the document? What role do charts, illustrations, pictures, and clip art play in enhancing a business plan?
   b. Compare sample plans in service industries to those in manufacturing. What are the main differences? Why would different industries need different types of business plans?
   c. Find a sample business plan on the Internet for a given industry, using a search engine if necessary. Print the plan. Compare its structure to the outline given in this chapter and note the differences.

3. Many software packages designed to assist in the writing of a business plan can be tried online. Use the Web to try out two different software applications. Which do you prefer? Why?

THE BUSINESS PLAN: LAYING THE FOUNDATION

INTRODUCTION

Recognizing that learning is facilitated when you apply what you study, we have designed a feature called "The Business Plan: Laying the Foundation" to conclude selected chapters. This feature provides guidelines for preparing the different segments of a business plan. In "Asking the Right Questions," it presents important questions that need to be addressed, and, in "Using BizPlan*Builder*® Express," it identifies material in a popular software package that can be used to prepare the plan.

USING BIZPLANBUILDER® EXPRESS

As indicated earlier, BizPlan*Builder*® Express provides a framework for writing a business plan. For assistance in answering some of the questions just posed, see parts 1 and 2 of BizPlan*Builder*® Express. This text will provide guidance regarding the executive summary, the firm's objectives, and the present business situation—good starting points for writing your business plan.

Marketing Research and Product Strategy

IN THE SPOTLIGHT

The Best-Laid Plans

It started as such a simple idea: create an online meal-planning service for families too busy to plan diverse and nutritious meals of their own. It's the sort of creative yet earnest idea you might expect from four businesswomen who wanted to stay home for their kids but also keep their hand in business.

But in the year since its launch, Wovenfare International Inc. has taken on a life of its own: underperforming in some measures, but hinting at unexpected opportunities. Wovenfare started as a response to the evening crunch familiar to all working families: what shall I make for dinner/what's in the fridge/if only Tommy ate broccoli. Jodi Maxwell and Michelle Shaw Williams, two 30-something parents, decided to save families from the banality that is SpaghettiOs by launching a Web-based service offering healthy weekly meal plans, with detailed recipes anyone can follow. To round out their skill set, in fall 2005 they teamed up with Cecilia de la Rocha, a professional engineer with marketing experience, and Justine Brown, a Web designer. Together, they fine-tuned the idea of selling subscribers customized meal plans that reflect their lifestyles. They also decided the site should generate weekly grocery lists to ensure the required ingredients—slivered almonds, basmati rice, goat cheese—are in the cupboard when needed.

While all four partners believe in meal planning, they weren't sure how many others did. So de la Rocha oversaw a Web-based survey of prospective customers. Of 480 respondents, 25 percent said they plan their meals in a formalized way. Better still, 75 percent of the rest said they see value in meal planning and would be willing to engage in it. That convinced the partners that a meal-planning service that stresses health could be a winner. In May 2006, they "turned the lights on" at Wovenfare. The plan was to sell "credits" for weekly meal plans, for $3 to $5 a week, depending on how many credits you buy at one time. To get people started, everyone would receive two weeks of free credits.

Working toward a launch date of January 2007, Wovenfare acquired the rights to more than 5000 recipes, including recipes from The Best of Bridge, a cookbook series that has sold more than 3 million volumes in 30 years.

After focusing on launch day for six months, the partners found it raised more problems. A computer glitch resulted in many confirmation emails to new registrants being labelled as spam, which was fixed only two months later when the firm got its own server. Worse, free-trial sign-ups came in at half the projected rate of 50 per day. The detailed registration process required for the personal meal plans seemed to scare prospects away.

In March Wovenfare started cooking, thanks to local news coverage and a Canadian Press story. Briefly, sign-ups hit 200 a week, with Wovenfare ranking near the top in a Google search for "healthy meal plans." Still, fewer than 10 percent of those who registered stepped up to pay for meal planning once their free trial expired. By October the site had been overhauled, and two of the founders had been bought out. With 3016 registered members by November, the company met its year-end target; however, still only 10 percent of those clients have upgraded to paying status.

Wovenfare faces a classic dot-com dilemma. Opportunities abound, but the company has only two people to chase them. They're hoping to boost traffic and revenue, and ultimately raise $500,000 for a U.S. marketing campaign. To really build their client base, Wovenfare must clarify why clients are not signing up after the trial period.

http://www.wovenfare.com

Courtesy of www.woverfare.com

Source: Adapted from Rick Spence, *"Wovenfare International: The Best-laid Plans,"* Canadian Business Online, December 17, 2007.

Describe small business marketing.

small business marketing
those business activities that identify a target market; determine that market's potential; and prepare, communicate, and deliver a bundle of satisfaction to that market

market analysis
an evaluation process that encompasses market segmentation, marketing research, and sales forecasting

marketing mix
the combination of product, pricing, promotion, and distribution activities

WHAT IS SMALL BUSINESS MARKETING?

Marketing was once viewed simply as activities that direct the flow of goods and services from producer to consumer or user. Definitions portrayed marketing as little more than selling. Unfortunately, some entrepreneurs still view marketing in this simplistic manner. In reality, small business marketing consists of numerous activities, many of which occur even before a product is produced and ready for distribution and sale. Wovenfare, featured above, illustrates the research required for service development, as well as the time and effort required to develop a product and take it to market.

In order to portray the scope of small business marketing more accurately, we use a comprehensive definition. **Small business marketing** consists of those business activities that relate directly to (1) identifying a target market; (2) determining target market potential through a detailed analysis of the industry, competition, and potential customers as discussed in Chapter 1; and (3) preparing, communicating, and delivering a bundle of satisfaction to the target market.

This task-oriented definition identifies key marketing activities essential to every small business (see Exhibit 6-1). Market segmentation, marketing research, and sales forecasting are the activities that comprise what is commonly called **market analysis.** Product, pricing, promotion, and distribution activities combine to form the **marketing mix.**

MARKETING PHILOSOPHIES

An individual's personal philosophy about life influences the methods that person uses to achieve personal goals. For example, a person who believes that others should be treated with respect will not cheat or defraud another person. Likewise, a firm's marketing philosophy shapes its marketing activities.

EXHIBIT **6-1**

Small Business Marketing Activities

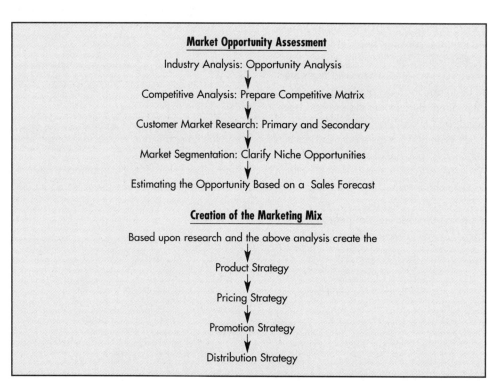

Historically, three distinct marketing philosophies—production oriented, sales oriented, and consumer oriented—have been dominant among small businesses. A production-oriented philosophy emphasizes the product as the most important part of the business. The firm concentrates on producing the product in the most efficient manner, even if this means slighting promotion, distribution, and other marketing activities. A sales-oriented philosophy de-emphasizes production efficiencies and customer preferences in favour of making sales. Finally, a consumer-oriented philosophy expresses the firm's belief that everything, including production and sales, depends on consumer needs. Top priority is assigned to the customer, meaning that all marketing efforts begin and end with the consumer.

A CONSUMER ORIENTATION

Businesses have gradually shifted their marketing emphasis from production to sales and, more recently, to the consumer. The production- and sales-oriented philosophies may each occasionally permit short-term success, but a consumer orientation is preferable. It not only recognizes production efficiency goals and professional selling but also adds concern for customer satisfaction. In effect, a firm that adopts a consumer orientation incorporates the best of each marketing philosophy. Due to competitive or orientation-based reasons, some small firms fail to adopt a consumer orientation even when the benefits seem obvious. The state of competition always affects a firm's orientation; if there is little or no competition and if demand exceeds supply, a firm is likely to emphasize production efficiency. This is usually a short-term situation, however, and one that can lead to disaster.

In addition, some managers are simply too focused on the present. Adopting a sales-oriented philosophy, for example, is a shortsighted approach to marketing. Putting emphasis on moving merchandise often creates customer dissatisfaction, especially if high-pressure selling is used with little regard for customers' needs. On the other hand, a consumer orientation contributes to a firm's long-term survival by emphasizing customer satisfaction.

MARKETING RESEARCH FOR THE NEW VENTURE

Discuss the nature of the marketing research process.   **2**

Every business owner or manager needs to supplement his or her enthusiasm and a hands-on feel for the market with sound market information, both of the customer and the competition. The owners of Wovenfare International, featured above, conducted research to determine their concept was feasible; however, they need a greater understanding of the customer to turn visitors to the site into purchasers.

THE NATURE OF MARKETING RESEARCH

Marketing research may be defined as the gathering, processing, reporting, and interpreting of market information. A small business typically conducts marketing research prior to start-up, and then on an ongoing basis to ensure it maintains its competitive position. Our discussion of marketing research will emphasize the widely used practical techniques that small business firms can employ, cost-effectively, as they analyze their target market and make other operating decisions.

A manager should always compare the costs and time requirements of marketing research with the expected benefits. Although marketing research can be conducted without the assistance of an expert, the cost of hiring such an expert is often money well

marketing research
the gathering, processing, reporting, and interpreting of market information

spent, especially if the expert's advice helps increase revenues or cut costs. The prices for research services reflect the fact that marketing researchers are trained, experienced professionals, not unlike attorneys or architects. For example, focus groups run about $3000 to $10,000 each, and a telephone survey may range anywhere from $5000 to $25,000 or more, depending on the number of interviews and the length of the questionnaire.

Because such large costs represent a substantial investment for most small businesses, owners should ask themselves the following questions before contacting a research firm:

- Is the research really necessary?
- Will data obtained justify the expense?
- Can I do the research myself?

STEPS IN THE MARKETING RESEARCH PROCESS

An understanding of research methodology helps an owner evaluate the validity of any research effort. Typical steps in the marketing research process are identifying the informational need, searching for secondary data, collecting primary data, and interpreting the data.

STEP 1: IDENTIFYING THE INFORMATIONAL NEED

The first step in marketing research is to identify and define the informational need. While Chapter 2 outlined the type of industry and competitive information that is required to determine market demand, additional customer-based research is needed to fully develop the product strategy. Although this step may seem too obvious to mention, the fact is that small business owners sometimes conduct research, including surveys, without pinpointing the specific information that is relevant to their venture. For example, someone contemplating a location for a restaurant may conduct a survey to ascertain customer menu preferences and reasons for eating out. In fact, the more relevant information would be how often residents of the target area eat out and how far they are willing to drive to eat in a restaurant.

When the informational need has been correctly defined, a survey can be designed to concentrate on that specific need. Later in this chapter you will see a survey questionnaire developed by a car wash owner to ascertain customer satisfaction. The informational need that had been identified was determining customers' satisfaction with the manner in which their car had been cleaned.

STEP 2: SEARCHING FOR SECONDARY DATA

secondary data
market information that has been previously compiled

Information that has already been compiled is known as secondary data. Generally, gathering **secondary data** is less expensive than gathering new, or primary, data. Therefore, a small business should exhaust available sources of secondary data before going further into the research process. Marketing decisions can often be made on the basis of secondary data. "It's a myth that only the big guys have the wherewithal to do market research," says Mary Beth Campau, assistant vice president for reference services at Dun & Bradstreet Information Services. There is a wealth of timely information from a variety of sources available in public and university and college libraries throughout

Canada, and from centres and web databases established by federal and provincial governments to assist small business owners. Databases commonly used for research typically available at libraries and universities include

- Business Source Complete: (Ebsco) 4000 full-text magazines and journals covering business, management, economics, banking, finance, and accounting. This database includes country profiles
- Business and Company Resource Center: (Gale) business intelligence on countries, consumers, and industries
- Global Market Information Database: (Euromonitor) business intelligence on countries, consumers, and industries
- Canadian Business and Current Affairs: (Proquest) close to 700 full-text Canadian magazines and newspapers
- Canadian Social Investment Database: (Jantzi) social and environmental profiles of companies in the TSX composite index
- Regional Business News: (Proquest) offers 75 business newspapers, and journals from the United States with corporate data on over 15 000 companies
- Hospitality and Tourism Complete: (Ebsco) scholarly research and industry data from 350 full-text trade and industry periodicals

Secondary data may be internal or external. Internal secondary data consists of information that exists within the firm. External secondary data abounds in industry periodicals, trade association publications, private information services, and government publications. Particularly helpful sources of external data for the small business starting out are federal and provincial bodies such as Statistics Canada, Industry Canada, and the various provincial, regional, and municipal economic development agencies. Industry Canada, for example, is a federal department that brings together responsibilities for international competitiveness and economic development, market and consumer policy activities, telecommunications policy and programs, and investment research and review. Industry Canada's website makes available useful information, including statistics on a number of industries, along with links to a wide range of other sites, including Aboriginal Business Canada, the Atlantic Canada Opportunity Agency, the Community Access Program (CAP), and Western Economic Diversification Canada. With the continuing growth of electronic access to data on the Internet, sites such as these will continue to appear and develop, providing an expanding source of online information to complement published handbooks and bibliographies. However, much non-government-based electronic data is posted without verification, so it is the task of the businessperson to investigate the accuracy of the information before using it as the basis for action. Refer to Exhibit 6-2 for online sources.

STEP 3: COLLECTING PRIMARY DATA

While secondary research may provide excellent trend analysis and an insight into the market opportunity, a search for new information, or **primary data,** is crucial to obtaining competitive and detailed customer information. The sources of primary data range from local government experts, to suppliers, to experts in the marketplace, such as competitors. The techniques used in accumulating primary data are often classified as observational methods and questioning methods. Observational methods avoid interpersonal contact between respondents and the researcher, while questioning methods involve some type of interaction with respondents.

primary data
new market information that is gathered by the firm conducting the research

EXHIBIT **6-2**
Web Sources for
Secondary Research

Although the first stop for secondary data is usually a university or the main branch of the municipal library, key websites offer easy access updated information. The most popular Canadian reference sites are

Statistics Canada: http://www.statcan.ca
Provides demographic and industry data on a local, provincial, and federal level. Complex but comprehensive.

Industry Canada   http://www.ic.gc.ca
One of the largest websites in Canada, it offers industry analysis that can be accessed by using the SIC or NAICS Code.

GD Sourcing   http://www.gdsourcing.com
This site provides excellent industry data and sources of industry data. This site also offers a primer in marketing research that list 1,200 industry links.

Performance Plus   http://sme.ic.gc.ca
A resource by the federal government. This site offers industry trends and data.

Tax information for small business   http://www.ccra-adrc.gc.ca
A tax guide published by Canada Revenue Agency.

Canada Business   http://www.businessgateway.ca
This site lists the government services available to small businesses.

The following sites are worth pursuing for general as well as industry-specific information and assistance to entrepreneurs:

Atlantic Canada Opportunities Agency	http://www.acoa.ca
Canadian Business Service Centres	http://www.cbsc.org
PROFIT Magazine	http://www.profitguide.com
Canadian Council for Small Business and Entrepreneurship	http://www.ccsbe.org
Canadian Federation of Independent Business	http://www.cfib.ca
Canadian Innovation Centre	www.innovationcentre.ca
Canadian Youth Business Foundation	http://www.cybf.ca/
Export Development Corporation	http://www.edc.ca
Guerrilla Marketing	http://www.gmarketing.com
Women Entrepreneurs of Canada	http://www.wec.ca

OBSERVATIONAL METHODS Observation is probably the oldest form of research in existence. Indeed, learning by observing is quite common. Thus, it is hardly surprising that observation can provide useful information for small businesses. An excellent method of observational research has been devised by Jean Sullivan, who experiments with new soup ideas for her Soup Company. She arranges tastings in most of the supermarkets where her soups are sold and closely observes shoppers' reactions to the samples she cooks for them.[1]

Observational methods can be economical. Furthermore, they avoid the potential bias that can result from a respondent's contact with an interviewer during questioning. Observation—for example, counting customers going into a store—can be conducted by a person or by mechanical devices, such as hidden video cameras. The cost of mechanical observation devices is rapidly declining, bringing them within the budget of many small businesses.

FOCUS GROUPS Focus groups bring a number of potential or current customers together to discuss a specific topic or product. A moderator, possibly from a marketing research firm, will guide the group through a series of topics. Focus groups are used to gain insights into customer needs and product recognition, and are useful for both product development and market opportunity assessment.

Focus groups can be conducted cheaply and effectively, depending on the moderator's fee and the compensation for the participants. In some cases participants are given gift certificates or company products for compensation.

Lululemon, referred to "In the Trenches," is an example of how a sportswear manufacturer and retailer fine-tunes its product line based upon country-wide regular customer focus groups.

TEST MARKETING Test marketing is a form of practical research. An existing business may test the potential for a new product or service to determine customer reaction. An inventor may test market the invention by having a number of individuals, or businesses, try it. This is a common technique in the software industry, where "alpha" versions are tested by potential clients. Any problems or issues with the software are identified and fixed by the business prior to mass distribution.

It should be re-emphasized that marketing research is always necessary in launching a new venture. However, test marketing may also be required to ensure the product or service fits the target market. Bill Madway, founder and president of Madway Business Research, says, "Sometimes, you cannot answer all the questions with research . . . you just have to test it. Then the question is whether you can afford to test something that might not work. If there's very little risk involved, or you can test it on a very small scale, you might decide to jump in. But the bigger the risk, the more valuable advance information becomes."[2]

QUESTIONING METHODS Surveys and experimentation are both examples of questioning methods that involve contact with respondents. Surveys can be conducted by mail, telephone, or personal interviews. Mail surveys are often used when target respondents are widely dispersed; however, they usually yield low response rates. Telephone surveys and personal interview surveys achieve higher response rates. However, personal interview surveys are expensive. Moreover, individuals are often reluctant to grant personal interviews because they suspect that a sales pitch is forthcoming. Some marketing researchers offer firms a new way to survey customers— through an online questionnaire. A recent *Inc.* article favourably reviewed this Internet service.[3] However, Internet surveying is so new that credible data is lacking on response rates. Some websites do claim that online surveys have better response rates than paper surveys.[4]

A questionnaire is the basic instrument for guiding the researcher and the respondent when a survey is being taken. A questionnaire should be developed carefully and pretested before it is used in the market. Several major considerations should be kept in mind in designing and testing a questionnaire:

- Ask questions that relate to the issue under consideration. An interesting question may be irrelevant. A good test of relevance is to assume an answer to each question and then ask yourself how you would use that information.

IN THE TRENCHES

Entrepreneurial Experiences

Focus Group Puts Fitness Wear Through a Workout

For workout wear, do you chose fashion over function, only to regret it later as your shorts hike up your butt at the gym? And when you're struggling to yank your sports bra over your head, do you prefer a pack-it-all-in, monoboob style, or a more feminine, lift-and-separate model? These and other dilemmas were discussed candidly at a women's-only focus group at a Calgary Lululemon Athletica store.

The retailers of this insanely popular yoga-inspired athletic wear brought in separate groups of men and women—athletes and loyal customers—to grill them on how well Lululemon apparel works in action. Their feedback is given to designers looking for input on clothing lines debuting next fall and winter. Since Lululemon was founded in 1998 in Vancouver, the line has branched out worldwide, established a cult-like following and expanded into other sports like cycling, climbing, and running.

The secret to its success? Listening to what customers are looking for. That means holding focus groups like these twice a year in each city in which Lululemon is located, from Edmonton and San Francisco to Tokyo and Melbourne. Participants are thanked for their feedback with healthy snacks of sushi and mineral water and $100 gift certificates to the store. Product manager Deanne Schweitzer, who oversees five designers, attends most of these meetings around the world. She's found men and women are looking for quality, fashion, and a variety of cuts.

The ongoing expansion by Lululemon into the United States entails continued product development and local customer involvement. For example, before opening its doors in Honolulu in 2007 the company recruited ambassadors and assembled local yoga enthusiasts for design meetings to gauge what Hawaii's yoga community wanted. After start-up the showroom manager arrange a 10 member design meeting to continue the dialogue which generated ideas such as complementary streetware and accessories that will take customers from the yoga studio to the supermarket without looking like they just came from class.

Deb Leung, a Calgary focus group participant who is also a fitness model and owner of In-Home Physiotherapy & Acupuncture, loves Lululemon's signature style. She wears the company's shorts for photo shoots and its pants for the gym or as casual wear. "I like the quality of the fabric. It moves with you, and the stitching is good—it doesn't fall apart," she says. But she wishes the tops would flatter pear-shaped women like herself more. For now, the bra tops fits her too tightly in the rib cage, and she finds the tank tops flare out needlessly at the waist.

The women's group points out other improvements that need to be made: gym bags that fit into a standard size locker, and more padding in sports bras and the crotch so additional underwear isn't needed for modesty's sake. And they'd love to see the addition of belts and baseball caps to the company's line of accessories.

Schweitzer, along with store owners Sue and Russ Parker, listens attentively to the concerns. It takes six to right months to incorporate any changes, but the responsiveness is good. Based on previous feedback, the company has increased the number of change rooms in stores, added care content tags to clothing and is expanding into golf and cycling apparel for spring. "We've also increased our sizes for women up to a size 14, and we brought in both high- and low-rise pants in different lengths," says Schweitzer.

Source: Barbara Balfour, "One Lulu of a Design: Focus Group Puts Fitness Wear through a Workout," *Calgary Herald*, Thursday, March 24, 2005. Reprinted with permission of the *Calgary Herald*; and http://www.starbulletin.com accessed January 29, 2008.

- Select the form of question that is most appropriate for the subject and the conditions of the survey. Open-ended and multiple-choice questions are two popular forms.
- Carefully consider the order of the questions. Asking questions in the wrong sequence can produce biased answers to later questions.
- Ask the more sensitive questions near the end of the questionnaire. Age and income, for example, are usually sensitive topics.
- Carefully select the words in each question. They should be as simple, clear, and objective as possible.
- Pretest the questionnaire by administering it to a small sample of respondents who are representative of the group to be surveyed.

STEP 4: INTERPRETING THE DATA

After the necessary data have been gathered, they must be transformed into usable information. Without interpretation, large quantities of data are only facts. Methods of summarizing and simplifying information for users include tables, charts, and other graphic methods. Descriptive statistics such as the mean, mode, and median are most helpful during this step in the research procedure. Inexpensive personal computer software is now available to perform statistical calculations and generate report-quality graphics.

Research is necessary for successful businesses, as well as new ventures. Frank Curraro conducted test marketing to determine the market potential for his venture, and continues to conduct product development and research for his expanding product line. Refer to "In the Trenches" for more details.

Market research is invaluable, both to entrepreneurs assessing the venture opportunity, and to small business owner/managers who collect research to modify their marketing mix to fit the evolving customer needs.

ESTIMATING MARKET POTENTIAL

Explain the term *market* and the different methods of forecasting sales.

3

A small business can be successful only if an adequate market exists for its product or service. The sales forecast is the typical indicator of market adequacy. Forecasting is particularly important prior to starting a business. An entrepreneur who enters the marketplace without it is much like a high diver who leaves the board without checking the depth of the water. Many types of information from numerous sources are required to determine market potential. This section examines market components and the forecasting process.

INGREDIENTS OF A MARKET

The term *market* means different things to different people. Sometimes, it refers to a location where buying and selling take place, as in "They went to the market." On other occasions, the term is used to describe selling efforts, as when business managers say "We must market this product aggressively." Still another meaning is the one we emphasize in this chapter: A **market** is a group of customers or potential customers who have purchasing power and unsatisfied needs. Note carefully the three ingredients in this definition of a market.

First, a market must have buying units, or *customers*. These units may be individuals or business entities. Consumer products are sold to individuals, and industrial products

market
a group of customers or potential customers who have purchasing power and unsatisfied needs

IN THE TRENCHES

Entrepreneurial Experiences

Bag of Beans Started Coffee Empire

Frank Cuffaro's coffee business didn't amount to a hill of beans at first. It was, literally, one bag. "My start-up budget was about $300. I bought a 132 pound bag of coffee beans for $1/pound, paid a friend of mine $60 for an hour of roasting time, bought 100 plastic bags to put the coffee in, and a machine to seal the bags, and spent $11 on business cards. That was it. I worked out of my Dad's garage," Cuffaro, recalled at his Montreal headquarters of Adelia Coffee, his now eight-year old company.

Cuffaro figures Adelia will have about $2 million in revenue this year, mostly in its espresso niche. It has its own coffee products, with more in the pipeline, and a retail store on St. Laurent Boulevard. Within two years they intend to expand into Ontario, and create a line of coffee-flavoured desserts and beverages. He has an employee working full-time on research and product development, with espresso concentrate as a main ingredient.

By the late 1990s, Cuffaro sensed that espresso was catching on. He talked to a friend who owned a supermarket into letting him test market his product for one weekend at a stand in the store. "I sold it in see-through plastic bags for $10 a kilo; my profit was $8. We sold about 50 kilos," he says. With revenue from the first bag he bought another and did the same thing the following weekend; when it became evident that there was ongoing demand, he set his sights on a prominent local distributor, Faema. "I brought them a sample, and went back six days a week for a month before they finally ordered a hundred pounds." Adelia moved out of the garage and gradually took over the current 8,000 square foot facility which employees 18 staff. "We're having a fantastic time building this company. It's an entrepreneur's dream," he said.

Source: Paul Delean, "Bag of Beans Started Coffee Empire," Calgary Herald, November 19, 2007, p. B10.

are sold to business users. Thus, a market is more than a geographic area; it must contain potential customers.

Second, customers in a market must have *purchasing power*. Assessing the level of purchasing power in a potential market is very important. Customers who have unsatisfied needs but who lack money and/or credit do not constitute a viable market because they have nothing to offer in exchange for a product or service. In such a situation, no transactions can occur.

Third, a market must contain buying units with *unsatisfied needs*. Consumers, for instance, will not buy unless they are motivated to do so—and motivation can occur only when a customer recognizes his or her unsatisfied needs. It would be difficult, for example, to sell luxury urban apartments to desert nomads!

Determining market potential is the process of locating and investigating buying units that have both purchasing power and needs that can be satisfied with the product or service that is being offered. Segmentation variables are often used to define the buyer markets.

As stated above, a market is a group of customers or potential customers who have purchasing power and unsatisfied needs. Although a firm's target market could be defined simply as "anyone who is alive" in that market, clearly this definition is too broad to be useful. In order to divide the total market into appropriate segments, an entrepreneur must consider **segmentation variables,** which are labels that identify the particular dimensions that distinguish one form of market behaviour from another. Four broad sets of segmentation variables that represent major dimensions of a market are benefit variables, geographic variables, demographic variables, and psychographic variables.

BENEFIT VARIABLES

The definition of a market highlights the unsatisfied needs of customers. **Benefit variables** are related to customer needs since they are used to identify segments of a market based on the benefits sought by customers. For example, the toothpaste market has several benefit segments. The principal benefit to parents might be cavity prevention for their young children, while the principal benefit to teenagers might be fresh breath. Toothpaste is the product in both cases, but it has two different market segments.

GEOGRAPHIC VARIABLES

Usually used in combination with other variables to define a target market segment, typical **geographic variables** might be postal code zone; quadrant of a city; western, central, or Atlantic Canada; country "A" versus country "B"; or even rural versus urban.

Benefit variables alone are insufficient for market analysis; it is impossible to implement forecasting and marketing strategy without defining the market further. Therefore, small businesses commonly use demographic variables as part of market segmentation. Typical demographic variables for a consumer market are age, marital status, gender, occupation, education level, ethnic origin, and income. For a business market it may be company size, purchasing budget, and industry type. Recall the definition of a market—customers with purchasing power and unsatisfied needs. **Demographic variables** refer to certain characteristics that describe customers and their purchasing power.

PSYCHOGRAPHIC VARIABLES

Some markets can be segmented by variables that reflect how people think and behave. Examples of **psychographic variables** are lifestyle trends such as fitness, diet, political orientation, and sexual orientation. These are usually used in combination with other variables to identify market segments.

THE SALES FORECAST

Formally defined, a **sales forecast** estimates how much of a product or service can be sold within a given market in a defined time period. The forecast can be stated in terms of dollars and/or units.

Because a sales forecast revolves around a specific target market, the market should be defined as precisely as possible. The market description forms the forecasting boundary. If the market for a local coffee shop is described as "all drinkers of coffee," the sales forecast will be extremely large. A more precise definition, such as "adults between the age of 18 and 45 who live in a one-mile radius of the coffee shop and who drink specialty coffees" will result in a smaller but possibly more useful forecast.

It is also important to note that a sales forecast implies a specified time period. One sales forecast may cover a year or less, while another may extend over several years. Both short-term and long-term forecasts are needed in a well-constructed business plan.

segmentation variables
The parameters used to distinguish one form of market behaviour from another

benefit variables
specific characteristics that distinguish market segments according to the benefits sought by customers

geographic variables
defining a market by its location, size, or extent

demographic variables
specific characteristics that describe customers and their purchasing power

psychographic variables
variables related to how people think and behave

sales forecast
a prediction of how much of a product or service will be purchased within a market during a specified time period

A sales forecast is a critical component of the business plan because it is critical to assessing the feasibility of a new venture. If the market is insufficient, the business is destined for failure. A sales forecast is also useful in other areas of business planning. Production schedules, inventory policies, and personnel decisions all start with a sales forecast. Obviously, a forecast can never be perfect; entrepreneurs should remember that a forecast can be wrong in either direction—underestimating potential sales or overestimating potential sales.

LIMITATIONS TO FORECASTING

For a number of practical reasons, forecasting is used less frequently by small firms than by large firms. First, for any new business, forecasting circumstances are unique. Entrepreneurial inexperience, coupled with a new idea, represents the most difficult forecasting situation, as illustrated in Exhibit 6-3. An ongoing business that requires only an updated forecast for its existing product is in the most favourable forecasting position.

Second, a small business manager may be unfamiliar with methods of quantitative analysis. While not all forecasting must be quantitatively oriented—qualitative forecasting is helpful and may be sufficient—quantitative methods have repeatedly proven their value in forecasting.

Third, the typical small business entrepreneur lacks familiarity with the forecasting process and/or personnel with such skills. To overcome these deficiencies, some small firms attempt to keep in touch with industry trends through contacts with appropriate trade associations. Because it has professional staff members, a trade association is frequently better qualified to engage in business forecasting, and a listing of all the Canadian associations is provided by the *Canadian Association Handbook*. Two other important reference guides found in many libraries are the *Directory of Business, Trade and Professional Associations in Canada* and the *National Reference Book*, which can offer information on many of these groups. Entrepreneurs can also provide themselves with current information about business trends by regularly reading trade and business publications such as *The Globe and Mail*, *The Globe and Mail Report on Business*, the *Financial Post*, and *Canadian Business*. There are also numerous regional periodicals that survey in greater

EXHIBIT **6-3**
Dimensions of Forecasting Difficulty

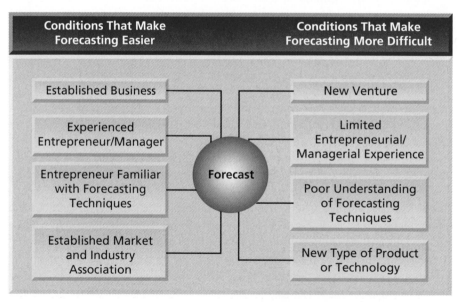

detail the business trends of particular geographical areas. Federal and provincial government publications can also provide valuable general information. Finally, subscriptions to professional or industry-focused forecasting services can supply forecasts of general business conditions or specific forecasts for given industries.

Despite the limitations, a small business entrepreneur should not slight the forecasting task. Instead, he or she should remember how important the sales outlook is to the business plan when obtaining financing. The statement "We can sell as many as we can produce" does not satisfy the information requirements of potential investors.

THE FORECASTING PROCESS

Estimating market demand with a sales forecast is a multistep process. Typically, the sales forecast is a composite of several individual forecasts for different products or locations, so the process involves merging these individual forecasts properly.

The **buildup process** calls for identifying all potential buyers in a target market's submarkets and then totalling the estimated demand. The market share for the business is then calculated, based upon a variety of factors including the competitive environment and the production or service capacity. Next, the sales forecast is calculated by multiplying the potential buyers by the potential market share. The process of calculating the market potential varies between consumer-, manufacturing-, and service-based businesses. Refer to Exhibit 6-4 for a sales forecast calculation for a shoe sales retailer.

The buildup method is especially helpful for industrial goods forecasting. Data on manufacturing from Statistics Canada and from private financial investment firms can be used to estimate potential. The data is often broken down according to the new North American Industry Classification System (NAICS). NAICS was introduced in 1998, but some data is still classified by the former Standard Industrial Classification (SIC) code that was in use until the introduction of NAICS. Both classification systems present

buildup process
a forecasting method in which all potential buyers in the various submarkets are identified; then the estimated demand is totalled and a market share estimate applied

EXHIBIT **6-4**
Sample Sales Forecast

Consumer Product Example: Retail Shoe Store

Step One: **Calculate the Market Size**

City size: 100,000 households

Target market area, within 2 km of the store: 10,000 households

Annual spending for shoes per household: $125

Market potential calculation: $125 \times 10,000 = \$1\ 250,000$

Step Two: **Calculate the potential market share**

$$\frac{\text{Size in square metres of your store}}{\text{Total competitor space (including yours)}} = \frac{200 \text{ sq metres}}{1,000 \text{ (your competition)} + 200} = 16.67\%$$

Step Three: **Calculate the forecasted sales by multiplying the market potential by your market share**

$$\$1,250,000 \times 16.67 = \$208,375$$

Step Four: **Modify the sales forecast to reflect either your competitive advantage or disadvantage. For example,** a new store might decrease its sales forecast in the first year to reflect lack of customer loyalty. The estimate may reflect contingency estimates, with an optimistic and "down-side" projection, as well as the "most-likely" calculation.

information according to the type of industry. The classification systems identify potential industrial customers by code, allowing the forecaster to obtain information on the number of establishments and their geographic location, number of employees, and annual sales. By summing this information for several relevant SIC/NAICS codes, a sales forecast can be constructed. If the SIC codes are being used, there are some differences that should be recognized between Canadian and U.S. codes. Statistics Canada has produced a Concordance between the Standard Industrial Classifications of Canada and the United States, which identifies these differences and provides a framework for relating statistical data from one country to data from the other. The new NAICS system will facilitate comparisons of statistics among industries in Canada, the United States, and Mexico.

4 Identify the components of a formal marketing plan.

THE FORMAL MARKETING PLAN

After the market analysis is completed, the small business manager is ready to write the formal marketing plan. Each business venture is different, and, therefore, each marketing plan will be unique. A manager should not feel that he or she must develop a cloned version of a plan created by someone else. The marketing plan should include sections on market analysis, the competition, and marketing strategy. This section describes these major elements of the formal marketing plan.

MARKET ANALYSIS

customer profile
a description of potential customers in a target market

In the market analysis section of the marketing plan, the entrepreneur should describe the customers in the target market. This description of potential customers is commonly called a **customer profile.** Marketing research information, compiled from both secondary and primary data, can be used to construct this profile. A detailed discussion of the major benefits to customers provided by the new product or service should be included. Obviously, these benefits must be reasonable and consistent with statements in the "Products and/or Services" section of the business plan.

If a manager envisions several target markets, each segment must have a corresponding customer profile. Likewise, different target markets may necessitate an equal number of related marketing strategies.

Another major element of market analysis is the actual sales forecast. It is usually desirable to include several sales forecasts covering the three sales scenarios: "most likely," "pessimistic," and "optimistic." These scenarios provide investors and the entrepreneur with different forecasts on which to base their evaluations.

THE COMPETITION

Frequently, entrepreneurs ignore the reality of competition for their new ventures, believing that the marketplace contains no close substitutes or that their success will not attract other entrepreneurs. This is simply not realistic.

Existing competitors should be studied carefully, the industry leader identified, and the key success factors for the industry clarified. Related products or services currently being marketed or tested by competitors should be noted. A clear picture of the competitive environment can be created through the following process:

1. Gather newspaper and periodical articles regarding trends in the industry.
2. Refer to Statistics Canada for concrete data on the size of the industry, revenues, the number of participants, growth trends, etc.

3. Identify leaders in the industry through conversations to determine which have characteristics that give them the leading edge.

4. Gather information on trends from phone books, directories, trade associations, the Statistics Canada report on household spending, and Dun and Bradstreet industry reports.

5. Research individual competitors through multiple sources: their websites, on-site visits, tradeshows, and a detailed review of their advertising and promotional materials.

6. Create a competitive matrix that lists the key competitive factors and the main players in the market (refer to Exhibit 6-5 for an example of a competitive matrix created by a restaurant owner analyzing the competition).

7. Identify the ideas or characteristics from the competition that would enhance the business. Ensure that the business has built upon the key success factors and has developed a competitive edge. Refer to the factors discussed in Chapter 2 that would contribute to a competitive advantage to clarify the key success factors.

MARKETING STRATEGY

A well-prepared market analysis and a discussion of the competition are important, both as part of the business plan and for ongoing success. Four areas of marketing strategy should be addressed:

1. *Marketing* decisions that will transform the basic product or service idea into a total product or service; refer to Chapters 2 and 6.

2. *Promotional* decisions that will communicate the necessary information to target markets (refer to Chapter 7).

3. *Distribution* decisions regarding the delivery of the product to customers (refer to Chapter 8).

4. *Pricing* decisions that will set an acceptable exchange value on the total product or service (refer to Chapter 7).

Recall that these four areas of marketing strategy are referred to collectively as a firm's marketing mix.

BUILDING CUSTOMER RELATIONSHIPS

Chapters 1 and 2 identified a number of strategies for creating a competitive advantage and getting a new venture started. To be successful in the long term, however, a firm must develop and maintain customer loyalty; it costs a business far more to replace a customer than to keep one. Remember that the customer (consumer) is the heartbeat of every firm. A better understanding of consumers and the transactional relationships a firm has with them will lead to a healthier small business.

Define customer relationship management (CRM) and explain its importance to a small firm.

5

WHAT IS CUSTOMER RELATIONSHIP MANAGEMENT?

Customer relationship management (CRM) means different things to different firms. To some, it is symbolized by simple smiles or comments such as "thank you" communicated by employees to customers who have just made a purchase. For others, CRM embodies a much broader marketing effort, leading to nothing short of complete customization of products and/or services to fit individual customer needs. The goals of a CRM program for most small companies fall somewhere between these two perspectives.

DIRECT COMPETITORS				
Key Competitive Factors	**The Noodle House**	**Fettuccini Palace**	**The Roman Garden**	**Little Italian Grill**
Quality and Presentation of Food and Beverage	Mixture of traditional and vegan dishes. Excellent coffee and desserts	Wide selection of simple tasty dishes. Standard items for both food and beverage	Award-winning fusion cuisine; limited selection of wine, but excellent quality	Modern European menu, small elegant portions. Excellent wine selection
Level of Service	Varies—some staff are unskilled	Friendly staff—service is slow at peak hours	Friendly and knowledgeable staff	Superior service. Friendly but not obtrusive
Price Range of Dinner Entrée	$8–$14	$11–$16	$14–$24	$13–$26
Interior Design Ambiance	Simple, older furniture but cozy	Warm and cozy	Upscale but fun. Stone fireplace.	White tablecloth. Fresh flowers. Formal
Exterior Design and Signage	Restored older building with patio. Small neon sign	National chain franchise; easily recognized from main road	Pleasant stucco exterior; small patio in summer	European stone frontage Small menu display
Reputation	Fun and friendly	Friendly and reliable	Gaining recognition	Well established
Reservations	Not taken	Available but not required	Recommended but not necessary	Required for Friday and Saturday evenings
Availability of Parking	Limited; many clientele walk	Large lot at the side	Yes, at back	Attendant will park car at back
Demographics of Clientele	Campus crowd; university four blocks away	Families	Young professionals	Age 35–55 professionals.

EXHIBIT **6-5** *Competitive Matrix: Italian Restaurants in a 10-Block Radius*

Regardless of the level of a firm's commitment to customer relationship management, the central message of every CRM program is "Court customers for more than a one-time sale." A firm that strongly commits to this idea will appreciate the many benefits a CRM program can offer.

Formally defined, **customer relationship management (CRM)** is a "company-wide business strategy designed to optimize profitability and customer satisfaction by focusing on highly defined and precise customer groups."[5] In a way, CRM is a mind-set—the implementation of customer-centric strategies, which put customers first so that the firm can succeed. The central theme of CRM isn't new. For decades, entrepreneurs have recognized the importance of treating customers well; "the customer is king" is an old adage. What is new is giving this idea a name and using technology to implement many of its techniques. Modern CRM focuses on (1) customers rather than products; (2) changes in company processes, Systems, and culture; and (3) all channels and media involved in the marketing effort, from the Internet to field sales.

customer relationship management (CRM) a company-wide business strategy designed to optimize profitability and customer satisfaction by focusing on highly defined and precise customer groups

THE IMPORTANCE OF CRM TO THE SMALL FIRM

A firm's next sale comes from one of two sources—a current customer or a new customer. Obviously, both current and potential customers are valued by a small firm, but sometimes current customers are taken for granted and ignored. While marketing efforts devoted to bringing new customers into the fold are obviously important, keeping existing customers happy should be an even higher priority. A CRM program addresses this priority. Brian Vellmure of Initium Technology, a provider of CRM solutions to small firms, has identified five economic benefits of maintaining relationships with current customers:[6]

1. Acquisition costs for new customers are huge.
2. Long-time customers spend more money than new ones.
3. Happy customers refer their friends and colleagues.
4. Order-processing costs are higher for new customers.
5. Old customers will pay more for products.

ESSENTIAL MATERIALS FOR A CRM PROGRAM

Assembling a CRM program requires a plan so that the entrepreneur knows what people, processes, and so on (parts) she or he needs—and there are many parts in a successful CRM program. In the remainder of this chapter, we consider two vital building blocks of any CRM program: (1) outstanding relationships with customers and (2) knowledge of consumer behaviour. These blocks may be constructed with a variety of "materials," as depicted in Exhibit 6-6. In the sections that follow, we examine those materials we believe to be tremendously important in constructing these two building blocks.

COMPONENTS OF CUSTOMER SATISFACTION

Discuss the significance of providing extraordinary customer service.

A number of factors under a firm's control contribute to customer satisfaction. One classic article identifies the following four elements as keys to customer satisfaction:[7]

1. Providing the most basic benefits of the product and/or service—the elements that customers expect all competitors to deliver
2. Offering general support services, such as customer assistance

EXHIBIT **6-6** *Essential Materials of a Successful CRM Program*

3. Setting up a system to counteract any bad experiences customers may experience
4. Delivering extraordinary services that excel in meeting customers' preferences and make the product and/or service seem customized

Small firms are in a unique position to offer extraordinary service. Relationship marketing advocate Patrick Daly suggests the following ways to provide extraordinary service:[8]

- *Naming names:* In today's detached, "just give me your account number" world, nothing is more well received than individual, personalized attention. Even though you may already be courteous and friendly to customers, greeting them by name is valued 10 times more on the "worthy of loyalty" scale.

- *Custom care:* Customers pretty much know what they do and don't want from your company. If you remember what they want on an individual basis—even if it's something as simple as knowing a dry cleaning customer likes light starch in his collars—then you have mastered one of the key elements of a strong loyalty program.

- *Keeping in touch:* You can't communicate enough on a me-to-you basis with your customers. And don't just connect to make a pitch. Clip out a newspaper or magazine article that pertains to a customer's business and send it to him or her with a note saying "FYI—thought you'd be interested." When customers know that you're taking time to think about them, they don't forget it.

- *"Boo-boo research":* Part of any customer loyalty program is taking the time to reach out to lost customers to learn why they went elsewhere. In many cases, just contacting them and showing them that you really care about getting their business will win them back—along with their contribution to your profits.

EVALUATING A FIRM'S CUSTOMER SERVICE HEALTH

Establishing an effective customer service program begins with determining the firm's "customer service quotient," which indicates how well the firm is currently providing service to its customers. Then strategies can be developed to improve the effectiveness of customer service efforts. Exhibit 6-7 shows some popular approaches to creating customer service strategies; it also provides a space for evaluating how well your firm is currently performing in each area.

Which of the following can be used to support your marketing objectives	For each strategy, comment below on: marketing objectives? 1. How well your company is doing. 2. Improvements to pursue further.
Provide an exceptional experience throughout every transaction by ensuring that customers are acknowledged, appreciated, and find it easy to do business with you. Note that this requires you to (1) make a list of the typical chain of contacts between you and your customers—from when they first see your advertisement until you send them a customer survey after the sale and (2) evaluate your company"s performance on each contact point.	
Provide sales materials that are clear and easy to understand, including website, marketing materials, retail displays, and sales conversations.	
Respond promptly to customers' requests and concerns by acting with urgency and responsibility in customer inquiries, transactions, and complaints. Have a service recovery plan in place.	
Listen to customers and respond accordingly by soliciting feedback, encouraging interaction, staying engaged throughout transactions, and taking the appropriate action necessary to please the customer.	
Stand behind products/services by providing guarantees and warranties and ensuring customers that you deliver on your promises. Also, create products and deliver services that exceed expectations.	
Treat customers as family members and best friends by valuing them the same way you honor those you care most about.	
Stay in the hearts and minds of customers by not taking customers for granted and finding ways to let them know you hold their best interests.	
Other initiatives? List them here.	

Source: "Exceptional Customer Experiences," *FastTrac*, Ewing Marion Kauffman Foundation, 2006.

EXHIBIT 6-7
Customer Service Strategies

How good or bad is the quality of customer service? One survey of consumers described the situation this way.[9]

- *On the phone:* Some 80 percent of companies still haven't figured out how to get customers the assistance they need.
- *Online:* Some 35 percent of all email inquiries to companies don't get a response within seven days, and about 25 percent don't get a response at all.
- *In "IVR" hell:* To save on labour costs, many of America's largest companies have installed software that the industry calls Interactive Voice Response (IVR) systems. Yet more than 90 percent of financial service consumers say they don't like these systems.

- *In a rage:* Nearly one in three customers say they have raised their voices at customer service reps and nearly one in 10 say they have cursed at them over the past year, according to a phone survey by Customer Care Measurement & Consulting.
- *In response:* Two-thirds of the estimated 800,000 consumer complaints that have been passed along over the past three years to PlanetFeedback.com's trouble shooting website share the same theme: not getting a response from a company, says Sue MacDonald, marketing director.

Although customer service issues may be identified through a formal review process within the small firm, they often surface via customer complaints in the course of normal daily business operations. (Later in this chapter, we will show how complaint activity is part of the overall consumer behaviour process.) Every firm strives to eliminate customer complaints. When they occur, however, they should be analyzed carefully to uncover possible weaknesses in product quality and/or customer service.

Managers can also learn about customer service concerns through personal observation and other research techniques. By talking directly to customers or by playing the customer's role anonymously—for example, by making a telephone call to one's own business—a manager can evaluate service quality. Some restaurants and motels invite feedback on customer service by providing comment cards to customers.

USING TECHNOLOGY TO SUPPORT CUSTOMER RELATIONSHIP MANAGEMENT

7 Illustrate how technology, such as the Internet, can improve customer relationships.

Long-term transactional relationships with customers are fostered by good information. A logical time to gather such data is during direct customer contacts, such as when a product is being sold. Customers may be contacted in many ways, including phone calls, letters, faxes, personal interactions, and e-mail. The ability to enjoy one-on-one contact with customers has always been a competitive advantage for small firms. Numerous software CRM software programs are designed to help companies gather all customer contact information into a single data management program. Web-based marketers, in particular, are attracted to CRM technology. Online shoppers expect excellent customer service, which is supported by such CRM tools as live chat. Overall, customer-service experts report positive perceptions by consumers of most company websites.[10]

Deciding which marketing activity should get initial CRM support is not always easy. However, the sales department is a popular place to start, because sales endeavours generate the greatest amount of customer contact. CRM focuses on such sales activities as accurate and prompt order filling, follow-up contacts to ensure customer satisfaction, and providing a user-friendly call centre to handle all inquiries, including complaints.

Using products such as Enterprise Miner, a business can sift through data looking for patterns that can be used to increase response rates of site visitors and tag the most profitable customers. For example, consider a customer who shops only once a year to purchase, say, roses on Valentine's Day; chances are that such a customer wouldn't appreciate repetitive marketing contacts. But another customer whose history shows purchases for occasions throughout the year might be responsive to more frequent contact and special offers. The SAS CRM software makes it possible to email selected customers once a month to remind them of upcoming dates that the customers have pre-registered, thereby increasing the chance that they will make a purchase.

Having ample support resources for CRM information technology can be a concern for a small firm. This concern has led some entrepreneurs to outsource certain applications. For example, hosted call centres, which handle email and Web communications for clients, may be more cost-effective than comparable in-house centres, a crucial consideration for many cash-strapped small firms. In addition to cost, lack of in-house expertise is a major justification for using these outside services.

UNDERSTANDING THE CUSTOMER

Identify the key characteristics of consumer behaviour.   **8**

Customer satisfaction results from a customer's interaction with the firm. Therefore, better understanding of consumers should lead to higher levels of customer satisfaction and loyalty. The concepts of consumer behaviour presented here can help a marketing manager achieve this important goal. Exhibit 6-8 presents a model of consumer behaviour structured around three major aspects: decision-making process, psychological factors, and sociological factors.

STAGES IN CONSUMER DECISION MAKING

One theory about consumer information processing holds that consumers are problem solvers. According to this theory, consumer decision making has four stages.

Let's use this widely accepted theory to examine consumer decision making among small business customers.

STAGE 1: PROBLEM RECOGNITION

Problem recognition occurs when a consumer realizes that her or his current state of affairs differs significantly from some ideal state. Some problems are routine conditions of depletion, such as a lack of food when lunchtime arrives. Other problems arise less frequently and may evolve slowly. A decision to replace the family dining table, for example, may take years to develop.

A consumer must recognize a problem before purchase behaviour can begin. Thus, the problem recognition stage cannot be avoided. Many small firms develop their product strategy as if consumers were in later stages of the decision-making process, when in reality consumers have not yet recognized a problem!

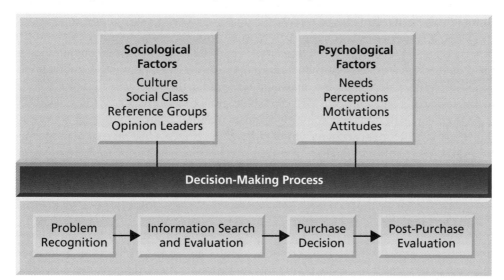

EXHIBIT **6-8**
Simplified Model of Consumer Behaviour

Many factors influence consumers' recognition of a problem—either by changing the actual state of affairs or by affecting the desired state. Here are a few examples:

- Change in financial status (a job promotion with a salary increase)
- Change in household characteristics (the birth of a baby)
- Normal depletion (using up the last tube of toothpaste)
- Product or service performance (breakdown of the iPod)
- Past decisions (poor repair service on car)
- Availability of products (introduction of a new product or service)

Small business managers must understand the problem recognition stage in order to select the appropriate marketing strategy to use. In some situations, they may need to *influence* problem recognition through advertising or promotion to trigger recognition by consumers.

STAGE 2: INFORMATION SEARCH AND EVALUATION

The second stage in consumer decision making involves consumers' collection and evaluation of appropriate information from both internal and external sources. The consumer's principal objective is to establish **evaluative criteria**—the features or characteristics of the product or service that the consumer will use to compare brands.

Small business owners should understand which evaluative criteria consumers use to formulate their evoked set. An **evoked set** is a group of brands that a consumer is both aware of and willing to consider as a solution to a purchase problem. Thus, the initial challenge for a new firm is to gain *market awareness* for its product or service. Only then will the brand have the opportunity to become part of consumers' evoked sets.

The information search and evaluation process is critical in competitive markets where consumer needs change quickly. The survival of Chaussures Régence Inc., a Canadian footwear manufacturer, is based upon the company's ability to produce high-quality boots to order with a quicker turnaround than other North American companies. Chaussures Régence constantly surveys the market to determine new trends and concepts.

STAGE 3: PURCHASE DECISION

Once consumers have evaluated brands in their evoked set and made their choice, they must still decide how and where to make the purchase. A substantial volume of retail sales now comes from nonstore settings such as catalogues, TV shopping channels, and the Internet. These outlets have created a complex and challenging environment in which to develop marketing strategy. Consumers attribute many different advantages and disadvantages to various shopping outlets, making it difficult for the small firm to devise a single correct strategy. Sometimes, however, simple recognition of the factors can be helpful.

Of course, not every purchase decision is planned prior to entering a store or looking at a mail-order catalogue. Studies have shown that over 50 percent of most types of purchases from traditional retail outlets are not intended prior to the customers' entering the store.[11] This fact places tremendous importance on such features as store layout, sales personnel, and point-of-purchase displays.

STAGE 4: POST-PURCHASE EVALUATION

The consumer decision-making process does not end with a purchase. Small firms that desire repeat purchases from customers (and they all should) need to understand post-purchase behaviour. Exhibit 6-9 illustrates several consumer activities that occur

evaluative criteria
the features of a product that customers use to compare brands

evoked set
a group of brands that a customer is both aware of and willing to consider as a solution to a purchase problem

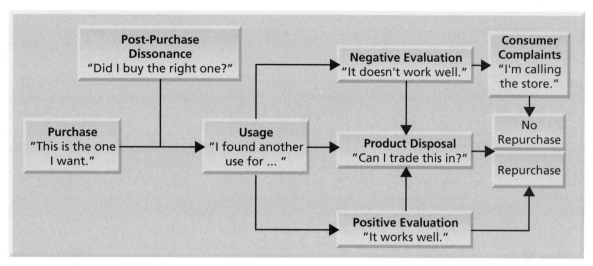

EXHIBIT **6-9** *Post-Purchase Activities of Consumers*

during post-purchase evaluation. Two of these activities—post-purchase dissonance and consumer complaints—are directly related to customer satisfaction.

Post-purchase dissonance is a type of **cognitive dissonance,** a tension that occurs immediately following a purchase decision when consumers have second thoughts as to the wisdom of their purchase. This anxiety is obviously uncomfortable for consumers and can negatively influence product evaluation and customer satisfaction. Small firms need to find effective ways to manage cognitive dissonance among their customers.

What do these consumers do when they are displeased? Consumers have several options for dealing with their dissatisfaction, and most of these options threaten repeat sales. Only one—a private inquiry to the offending business—is desirable to the business. These odds are not encouraging; once again, they indicate the importance of quality customer service—both before and after a sale. Studies have shown that over 50 percent of dissatisfied customers will not deal again with the offending business and that almost all of them will tell other people about their bad experience.[12]

PSYCHOLOGICAL FACTORS

The next major component of the consumer behaviour model, psychological factors, is intangible, as such factors can be identified only by the process of inference. The four psychological factors that have the greatest relevance to small businesses are needs, perceptions, motivations, and attitudes.

NEEDS

Needs are often described as the starting point for all behaviour. Without needs, there would be no behaviour. Although consumer needs are innumerable, they can be identified as falling into four categories—physiological, social, psychological, and spiritual.

Consumers' needs are rarely completely satisfied, thereby ensuring the continued existence of business. Careful assessment of the needs–behaviour connection can be very helpful in developing marketing strategy. Different purchases of the same product satisfy different needs. For example, consumers purchase food products in supermarkets to satisfy physiological needs. But they also purchase food in status restaurants to satisfy their social and/or psychological needs. Also, certain foods are demanded by specific market

cognitive dissonance
the anxiety that occurs when a customer has second thoughts immediately following a purchase

needs
the starting point for all behaviour

segments to satisfy those consumers' religious, or spiritual, needs. A needs-based strategy would result in a different marketing approach in each of these situations.

PERCEPTIONS

perception
the individual processes that give meaning to the stimuli confronting consumers

A second psychological factor, **perception,** encompasses those individual processes that ultimately give meaning to the stimuli confronting consumers. When this meaning is severely distorted or entirely blocked, consumer perception can cloud a small firm's marketing effort and make it ineffective.

Perception is a two-sided coin; it depends on the characteristics of both the stimulus and the perceiver. Consumers attempt to manage huge quantities of incoming stimuli through **perceptual categorization,** a process by which things that are similar are perceived as belonging together. Therefore, if a small business wishes to position its product alongside an existing brand and have it accepted as comparable, the marketing mix should reflect an awareness of perceptual categorization. Similar quality can be communicated through similar prices or through a package design with a colour scheme similar to that of an existing brand. These techniques will help a consumer fit the new product into the desired product category.

perceptual categorization
the process of grouping similar things so as to manage huge quantities of incoming stimuli

Small firms that use their existing brand name for a new product are relying on perceptual categorization to pre-sell the new product. If, on the other hand, the new product is generically different or of a different quality, a unique brand name should be selected to avoid perceptual categorization by the consumer.

If a consumer has strong brand loyalty to a product, it is difficult for other brands to penetrate his or her perceptual barriers. That individual is likely to have distorted images of competing brands because of a pre-existing attitude. Consumers' perceptions thus present a unique communication challenge.

MOTIVATIONS

Unsatisfied needs create tension within an individual. When this tension reaches a certain level, the individual becomes uncomfortable and is motivated to reduce the tension.

motivations
forces that organize and give direction to the tension caused by unsatisfied needs

Everyone is familiar with hunger pains, which are manifestations of the tension created by an unsatisfied physiological need. What directs a person to obtain food so that the hunger pains can be relieved? The answer is motivation. **Motivations** are goal-directed forces that organize and give direction to tension caused by unsatisfied needs. Marketers cannot create needs, but they can offer unique motivations to consumers. If an acceptable reason for purchasing a product or service is provided, it will probably be internalized by the consumer as a motivating force. The key for the marketer is to determine which motivations the consumer will perceive as acceptable in a given situation. The answer is found through an analysis of other consumer behaviour variables.

Like physiological needs, the other three classes of needs—social, psychological, and spiritual—can be similarly connected to behaviour through motivations. For example, when incomplete satisfaction of a person's social needs is creating tension, a firm may show how its product can fulfill those social needs by providing acceptable motivations to that person. A campus clothing store might promote styles that communicate that the student wearing those clothes has obtained membership in a group. Understanding motivations is not easy. Several motivations may be present in any situation, and they are often subconscious. However, they must be investigated if the marketing effort's chance for success is to be improved.

ATTITUDES

Like the other psychological variables, attitudes cannot be observed, but everyone has them. Do attitudes imply knowledge? Do they imply feelings of good or bad, favourable or unfavourable? Does an attitude have a direct impact on behaviour? The answer to each of these questions is a resounding yes. An **attitude** is an enduring opinion, based on a combination of knowledge, feeling, and behavioural tendency.

An attitude may act as an obstacle or a catalyst in bringing a customer to a product. For example, consumers with the attitude that a local, family-run grocery store has higher prices than a national supermarket chain may avoid the local store. Armed with an understanding of the structure of an attitude, a marketer can approach the consumer more intelligently.

SOCIOLOGICAL FACTORS

Sociological factors comprise the last component of the consumer behaviour model. Among these influences are culture, social class, reference groups, and opinion leaders. Note that each of these sociological factors represents a different degree of group aggregation: Culture involves large masses of people; social classes and reference groups are smaller groups of people; and opinion leaders are lone individuals who exert influence.

CULTURE

In this chapter, **culture** refers to the behavioural patterns and values that characterize a group of customers in a target market. These patterns and beliefs have a tremendous impact on the purchase and use of products. Marketing managers often overlook the cultural variable because its influences are so deeply embedded within the society. Culture is somewhat like air; you do not think about its function until you are in water over your head! International marketers who have experienced more than one culture can readily attest to the reality of cultural influence.

The prescriptive nature of culture should most concern the marketing manager. Cultural norms create a range of product-related acceptable behaviours that influence what consumers buy. However, because culture does change by adapting slowly to new situations, what works well as a marketing strategy today may not work a few years from now.

An investigation of culture within a narrower boundary—defined by age, religious preference, ethnic orientation, or geographical location—is called *subcultural analysis*. Here, too, unique patterns of behaviour and social relationships must concern the marketing manager. For example, the needs and motivations of the youth subculture are far different from those of the senior citizen subculture, and certain food preferences are unique to particular ethnic cultures. Small business managers who familiarize themselves with cultures and subcultures are able to create better marketing mixes.

REFERENCE GROUPS

Small groups such as families, work groups, neighbourhood groups, or recreational groups influence behaviour. The existence of group influence is well established. The challenge to the marketer is to understand why this influence occurs and how it can be used to promote the sale of a product. Individuals tend to accept group influence because of the perceived benefits, such as a sense of belonging.

attitude
an enduring opinion based on knowledge, feeling, and behavioural tendency

culture
behavioural patterns and values that characterize a group of consumers in a target market

reference groups
groups that an individual allows to influence his or her behaviour

NEL

opinion leader
a group leader who plays a key communications role

product strategy
the way the product component of the marketing mix is used to achieve a firm's objectives

9 Explain product strategy and related concepts.

product item
the lowest common denominator in a product mix—the individual item

product line
the sum of related individual product items

product mix
the collection of a firm's total product lines

product mix consistency
the similarity of product lines in a product mix

OPINION LEADERS

According to widely accepted communication principles, consumers receive a significant amount of information through individuals called **opinion leaders,** who are group members playing a key communications role.

Generally speaking, opinion leaders are knowledgeable, visible, and exposed to the mass media. A small business firm can enhance its own image by identifying with such leaders. For example, a farm-supply dealer may promote its products in an agricultural community by holding demonstrations of these products on the farms of outstanding local farmers, who are the community's opinion leaders. Similarly, department stores may use attractive students as models when showing campus fashions.

DEVELOPING PRODUCT STRATEGY

PRODUCT STRATEGY

Product strategy includes decisions related to the product mix. It covers choices involving branding, packaging, labelling, and other elements comprising the core component of the bundle of satisfaction, whether product or service.

Specifically, **product strategy** describes the manner in which the product component of the marketing mix is used to achieve the objectives of a firm. A **product item** is the lowest common denominator in a product mix. It is the individual item, such as one brand of bar soap. A **product line** is the sum of the related individual product items. The relationship is usually defined generically. Two brands of bar soap are two product items in one product line. A **product mix** is the collection of product lines within a firm's ownership and control. A firm's product mix might consist of a line of bar soaps and a line of shoe polishes. **Product mix consistency** refers to the closeness, or similarity, of the product lines. The more items in a product line, the greater its depth. The more product lines in a product mix, the greater its breadth. Exhibit 6-10 shows the product lines and product mix of a company that sells a wide range of ear muffs.

PRODUCT MARKETING VERSUS SERVICE MARKETING

Traditionally, marketers have used the word *product* as a generic term describing both goods and services. However, whether goods marketing and services marketing strategies are the same is questionable. As shown in Exhibit 6-11, certain characteristics—

EXHIBIT **6-10**
Product Lines and Product Mix for an Ear Muff Company

		Breadth of the Product Mix			
		Ear Warmers	Ear Wear	Gloves	Traning Apparel
Depth of the Product Lines	Training	3 styles		4 styles	• Zone base shirt • Zone base pant • Quantum jacket • Catalyst shirt
	Snow Sport	1 style		7 styles	
		• Tec fleece • Tec fleece w/headphones • Tec fleece kids	• Oovetall • Mortise • Integral • Festo	1 style	
	Casual	9 styles		6 styles	

Source: http://www.180s.com, assessed January 23, 2007.

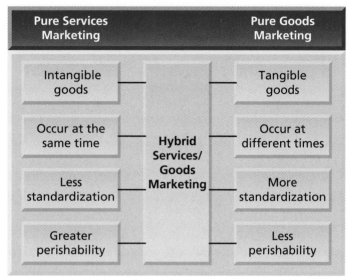

EXHIBIT **6-11**
*Services Marketing
versus Goods Marketing*

tangibility, amount of time separating production and consumption, standardization, and perishability—lead to a number of differences between the two strategies. Based on these characteristics, for example, the marketing of a pencil fits the pure goods end of the scale and the marketing of a haircut fits the pure services end. The major implication of this distinction is that marketing services presents unique challenges that are not faced in product strategy development.

Although we recognize the benefit of examining the marketing of services as a unique form, space limitations require that it be subsumed under the umbrella category of product marketing. Therefore, from this point on, a **product** will be considered to include the total bundle of satisfaction offered to customers in an exchange transaction—whether a service, a good, or a combination of the two. In addition to the physical product or core service, a product also includes complementary components, such as packaging or a warranty. Of course, the physical product or core service is usually the most important to consumers in an element in the total bundle of satisfaction. But sometimes that main element is perceived by customers to be similar for a variety of products. In that case, complementary components become the most important features of the product. For example, a particular brand of cake mix may be preferred by consumers not because it is a better mix, but because of the unique toll-free telephone number on the package that can be called for baking hints. Or a certain dry cleaner may be chosen over others because it treats customers with respect, not because it cleans clothes exceptionally well.

product
a total bundle
of satisfaction—
including a service,
a good, or both—
offered to consumers
in an exchange
transaction

PRODUCT STRATEGY OPTIONS

Failure to clearly understand product strategy options will lead to ineffectiveness and conflict in the marketing effort. The major product strategy alternatives of a small business can be condensed into six categories, based on the nature of the firm's product offering and the number of target markets:

1. One product/one market
2. One product/multiple markets
3. Modified product/one market

4. Modified product/multiple markets
5. Multiple products/one market
6. Multiple products/multiple markets

Each alternative represents a distinct strategy, although two or more of these strategies can be pursued concurrently. A small firm, however, will usually pursue the alternatives in the order listed. Also, keep in mind that once any product strategy has been implemented, sales can be increased through certain additional growth tactics. For example, within any market, a small firm can try to increase sales of an existing product by doing any or all of the following:

• Convincing nonusers in the targeted market to become customers
• Persuading current customers to use more of the product
• Alerting current customers to new uses for the product

When small firms add products to their product mix, they generally select related products. An example would be Greenlite, featured "In the Trenches," which specializes in energy-saving light bulbs. When Nina Gupta adds a new product, by adding another type of light bulb, she expands the product line. But there are, of course, strategies that involve unrelated products. For example, a local dealer selling Italian sewing machines might add a line of microwave ovens, a generically unrelated product. A product strategy that includes a new product quite different from existing products can be very risky. However, this strategy is occasionally used by small businesses, especially when the new product fits existing distribution and sales systems, or requires similar marketing knowledge.

Adding a new unrelated product to the product mix to target a new market is an even higher-risk strategy, as a business is attempting to market an unfamiliar product in an unfamiliar market. However, if well planned, this approach can offer significant advantages. One electrical equipment service business recently added a private employment agency. If successful, this product strategy could provide a hedge against volatile shifts in market demand. A business that sells both snowshoes and suntan lotion expects that demand will be high in one market or the other at all times, evening out the sales curve and maintaining a steady cash flow throughout the year.

BUSINESS ANALYSIS

Business analysis should be conducted for every new product introduced to a retail outlet or manufacturing line. Every new product or service idea must be carefully studied in relation to several financial considerations. Costs and revenues are estimated and analyzed with techniques such as break-even analysis. Any idea failing to show that it can be profitable is discarded during the business analysis stage. Four key factors need to be considered in conducting a business analysis:

1. PRODUCT'S RELATIONSHIP TO THE EXISTING PRODUCT LINE

Some firms intentionally add very different products to their product mix. However, in most cases, any product item or product line added should be consistent with—or somehow related to—the existing product mix. For example, a new product may be designed to fill a gap in a firm's product line or in the price range of the products it currently sells. If the product is completely new, it should have at least a family relationship to existing products. Otherwise, the new product may call for drastic and costly changes in manufacturing methods, distribution channels, type of promotion, and/or manner of personal selling.

IN THE TRENCHES

Entrepreneurial Experiences

Shades of Green Guide Montreal Bulb Maker

A couple of years back, a light bulb clicked on in Nina Gupta's brain. Gupta, the CEO of Greenlite, a small Montreal company that sells compact fluorescent light bulbs, decided she wanted to play in the big leagues and, to do that, she'd have to advertise like a big multinational. So, in fall 2007, Greenlite launched a $1 million advertising campaign that put the company on billboards in New York City's Times Square as well as on Sunset Boulevard in Hollywood.

It's a bold strategy to brand her company's energy-saving light bulbs so that consumers will come to call her product by its branded name, Greenlite, rather than by the generic term, compact fluorescent light bulbs, or CFLs. "I want Greenlite to be as synonymous with CFLs as Kleenex is to tissue," she said. "I want people to say, 'Give me a Greenlite, please.'"

Gupta says she knows she's in the right business at the right time. "Coming from Asia, I'm acutely aware of the energy crisis," she said. "India has power outages regularly." Add the fact that countries are banning the sale of incandescent light bulbs and the market for compact fluorescents is poised to explode.

Gupta was recognized in 2007 in the RBC Canadian Woman Entrepreneur Awards, which recognizes female entrepreneurs who have made significant contributions to the Canadian and global economies. Gupta began running the Canadian division of Greenlite in 1993, when her father, who operated a lighting company in Delhi, put her to work on Canadian sales and distribution for the family manufacturing facility. They decided that CFLs were the future, and wanted a product with growth potential.

Greenlite's bulbs are now sold in large stores including supermarkets. The company's research into the growth of "green" products was accurate, and revenues of $12 million in 2005 grew to $30 million in 2007. "We anticipate $50 million in sales in 2008," Gupta said. She plans to take the company public in 2008. "I'm at a stage at which I'm ready to let it fly," she said.

Sources: Adapted from *Calgary Herald* December 17, 2007, p. B7 and http://www.greenlite.ca, accessed on January 29, 2008.

2. COST OF DEVELOPMENT AND INTRODUCTION

One problem in adding new products is the cost of their development and introduction. Considerable capital outlays may be necessary, including expenditures for design and development, market research to establish sales potential and volume potential, advertising and sales promotion, patents, and additional equipment. One to three years may pass before profits are realized on the sale of a new product.

3. AVAILABLE PERSONNEL AND FACILITIES

Obviously having adequate skilled personnel and production equipment is preferable to having to add employees and buy equipment. Thus, introducing new products is typically more appealing if the personnel and the required equipment are already available.

4. COMPETITION AND MARKET ACCEPTANCE

Still another factor to be considered in a business analysis is the potential competition facing a proposed product in its target market. Competition must not be too severe. Some studies, for example, suggest that new products can be introduced successfully only if 5 percent of the total market can be secured. The ideal solution, of course, is to offer a product that is sufficiently different from existing products or that is in a cost and price bracket where it avoids direct competition.

BUILDING THE TOTAL PRODUCT OFFERING

Describe the
components of a
firm's total product
offering.

A major responsibility of marketing is to transform a basic product into a total product offering. Even when an idea for a unique new pen has been developed into physical reality in the form of the basic product, it is still not ready for the marketplace. The total product offering must be more than the materials moulded into the shape of the new pen. To be marketable, the basic product must be named, have a package, perhaps have a warranty, and be supported by other product components. Let's now examine a few of the components of a total product offering.

BRANDING

brand
a verbal and/or
symbolic means of
identifying a product

An essential element of a total product offering is a brand. A **brand** is a means of identifying the product—verbally and/or symbolically. The name Canadian Tire is a brand, as are the golden arches of McDonald's. Since a product's brand name is so important to the image of the business and its products, considerable attention should be given to the selection of a name.

In general, five rules apply in naming a product:

SELECT A NAME THAT IS EASY TO PRONOUNCE AND REMEMBER

You want customers to remember your product. Help them do so with a name that can be spoken easily—for example, Two Small Men with Big Hearts (a moving service) or Nutralawn (a lawn fertilizer business). Ed McNally used "Big Rock" for his specialty brewery, knowing that ice-clear mountain water would provide a positive connotation for the specialty beers. The name also had a personal meaning for him, and reflected the name of a large rock left by the glaciers near his hometown.

CHOOSE A DESCRIPTIVE NAME

A name that is suggestive of the major benefit of the product can be extremely helpful. As a name for a sign shop, Sign Language correctly suggests a desirable benefit. Blind Doctor is a creative name for a window-blind repair business. However, Rocky Road would be a poor name for a mattress!

USE A NAME THAT CAN HAVE LEGAL PROTECTION

Be careful to select a name that can be defended successfully. Do not risk litigation by copying someone else's brand name. A new soft drink named Professor Pepper would likely be contested by the Dr. Pepper company.

SELECT A NAME WITH PROMOTIONAL POSSIBILITIES

Exceedingly long names are not, for example, compatible with good copy design on billboards, where space is at a premium. A competitor of the McDonald's hamburger chain is called Pete's, a name that will easily fit on any billboard.

SELECT A NAME THAT CAN BE USED ON SEVERAL PRODUCT LINES OF A SIMILAR NATURE

Customer goodwill is often lost when a name doesn't fit a new line. The name Just Brakes is excellent for an auto service shop that repairs brakes—unless the shop later plans to expand into muffler repair.

Trademark and **service mark** are legal terms indicating the exclusive right to use a brand. Once an entrepreneur has found a name or symbol that is unique, easy to remember, and related to the product or service, an attorney who specializes in trademarks and service marks should be hired to run a name or symbol search and then to register the trade name or symbol.

PACKAGING

Packaging is another important part of the total product offering. In addition to protecting the basic product, packaging is a significant tool for increasing the value of the total product.

Gen-X siblings Manjit and Ravinder Minhas, profiled in Chapter 7, understand the importance of both labelling and branding. The pair founded Mountain Crest Classic Lager, a preservative-free authentic lager, to go head to head with the major breweries. The local brew has high spirits, with 5.6 percent alcohol, but a low price, approximately $5.50 per six-pack. The label shows a clear mountain stream, and clearly reflects the name and product quality. Consider for a moment some of the products you purchase. How many do you buy mainly because of a preference for package design and/or colour? Innovative packaging is frequently the deciding factor for consumers. If a product is otherwise very similar to competitive products, its package may create the distinctive impression that makes the sale. For example, biodegradable packaging or reusable containers may distinguish a firm from its competition.

LABELLING

Another part of the total product is its label. Labelling serves several important purposes for manufacturers, who apply most labels. One of its purposes is to show the brand, particularly when branding the basic product would be undesirable. For example, a furniture brand is typically shown on a label and not on the basic product. On some products, brand visibility is highly desirable; Roots sweatshirts would probably not sell as well with the name label only inside the clothing. A label is also an important informative tool for consumers. It often includes information on product care and use, and may even provide information on how to dispose of the product.

Laws concerning labelling requirements should be reviewed carefully. Be innovative in your labelling information, and consider including information that goes beyond the specified minimum legal requirements.

WARRANTIES

A **warranty** is simply a promise, written or unwritten, that a product will do certain things or meet certain standards. All sellers make an implied warranty that the seller's title to the product is good. A retailer that deals in goods of a particular kind makes the additional implied warranty that those goods are fit for the ordinary purposes for which they are sold. A written warranty on a product is not always necessary. In fact, many firms operate without written warranties, as they are concerned that a written warranty will serve only to confuse customers or make them suspicious.

trademark
an identifying feature used to distinguish a manufacturer's product

service mark
a legal term indicating the exclusive right to use a brand to identify a service

warranty
a promise that a product will perform at a certain level or meet certain standards

The federal *Consumer Protection Act* is the overriding legislation governing warranties in Canada; however, most provinces have supplementary legislation covering various aspects of warranties. Some of the most notable aspects of the act cover terminology, including the use of the terms *full, limited, express,* and *implied.* In order for a product to get a full warranty designation, the warranty must state certain minimum standards such as replacement or full refund after reasonable attempts at repair.

Warranties not meeting all the minimum standards must carry the limited warranty designation.

Warranties are important for products that are innovative, relatively expensive, purchased infrequently, relatively complex to repair, and positioned as high-quality goods. A business should consider the following factors in rating the merits of a proposed warranty policy:

- Cost
- Service capability
- Competitive practices
- Customer perceptions
- Legal implications

A successful product offering will consist of a concept that has a comprehensive package that includes the core features to meet the needs of the consumer, and additional secondary features that ensure an overall enhanced consumer experience.

BUSINESS MARKETS

There are many differences between purchasing by organizations and consumer purchasing. Both the market research process, and the product design process, must be modified to reflect the differences. The nature of business buying is varied and could include

- Companies that consume, such as manufacturers
- Government agencies—local, provincial, and federal
- Service institutions such as hospitals, schools, medical clinics
- Resellers such as wholesalers or brokers

Business marketing typically has shorter distribution channels, and places a greater emphasis on personal selling. Some of the business marketing characteristics that should be considered when creating the marketing mix are as follows:

- *Greater reliance on promotion:* Trade shows are commonly used to increase exposure to a wider range of industrial buyers.
- *Shorter distribution channels:* The manufacturer-to-user relationship is much closer, and may not entail any middlemen. Consequently the buyer–seller relationship relies upon a sales force to create awareness and close deals.
- *Greater web integration:* Website support, and even ordering tied directly to daily production, is used by many business to provide comprehensive integrated service to key business clients.

LOOKING BACK

1 Describe small business marketing.

- Small business marketing consists of numerous activities, including market analysis and determining the marketing mix.
- Three distinct marketing philosophies are the production-, sales-, and consumer-oriented philosophies.
- A small business should adopt a consumer orientation to marketing.

2 Discuss the nature of the marketing research process.

- Marketing research is the gathering, processing, reporting, and interpreting of marketing information.
- The cost of marketing research should be evaluated against its benefits.
- The steps in marketing research are identifying the informational need, searching for secondary and primary data, and interpreting the data.

3 Explain the term _market_ and the different methods of forecasting sales.

- A sales forecast is an estimation of how much of a product or service will be purchased within a market during a defined time period.
- The forecasting process may be either a breakdown or a buildup process and may be either direct or indirect, depending on the predicting variable.

4 Identify the components of a formal marketing plan.

- The marketing plan should include sections on market analysis, the competition, and marketing strategy.
- The market analysis should include a customer profile.
- Four areas of marketing strategy that should be discussed in the marketing plan are decisions affecting the total product or service, pricing decisions, promotional decisions, and distribution decisions.

5 Define customer relationship management (CRM) and explain its importance to a small firm.

- Customer relationship management (CRM) encompasses the strategies used by companies to manage their relationships with customers, including the capture, storage, and analysis of consumer information.
- The central message of every CRM program is "Court customers for more than a one-time sale."

- CRM is primarily a mind-set—the implementation of customer-centric strategies, which put customers first so that the firm can increase profits.
- A CRM program recognizes the importance of keeping current customers satisfied to ensure their loyalty, given the high costs associated with attracting a new customer.
- Constructing a CRM program requires a plan so that the entrepreneur will know what people, processes, and so on he or she needs.
- Two vital building blocks of any CRM program are outstanding transactional relationships with customers and knowledge of consumer behaviour.

6 Discuss the significance of providing extraordinary customer service.

- To be successful in the long run, small firms must provide outstanding service in order to develop and build customer relationships and maintain loyal customers, as it costs far more to replace a customer than to keep one.
- Extraordinary service is the factor that small firms are in a unique position to offer.
- Providing exceptional customer service can give small firms a competitive edge, regardless of the nature of the business.
- Establishing an effective customer service program begins with determining the firm's "customer service quotient," which indicates how well the firm is currently providing service to its customers.
- Customer service problems are most commonly recognized through customer complaints.
- Managers can also learn about customer service problems through personal observation and other research techniques.
- Although many types of customer service cost very little, there are definite costs associated with superior levels of customer service.

7 Illustrate how technology, such as the Internet, can improve customer relationships.

- Long-term transactional relationships are built with information gathered from positive customer contacts.
- CRM technology helps companies gather all customer contact information into a single data management program.
- Web-based marketers, in particular, are attracted to CRM technology.
- CRM focuses on such sales functions as accurate and prompt order filling, follow-up contacts to ensure

customer satisfaction, and the use of a user-friendly call centre to handle all inquiries, including complaints.
- Having ample support resources for CRM information technology can be a concern for a small firm, and this concern has led some entrepreneurs to outsource certain applications.
- Hosted call centres require lower deployment costs than do comparable in-house centres, a crucial consideration for many cash-strapped small firms.

8 Identify the key characteristics of consumer behaviour.
- It is helpful to view consumers as problem solvers who are going through several stages, from problem recognition to post-purchase behaviour.
- Psychological factors affecting consumer behaviour include needs, perceptions, motivations, and attitudes.
- Sociological factors affecting consumer behaviour encompass culture, social class, reference groups, and opinion leaders.

9 Explain product strategy and related concepts.
- Product strategy describes how a product is used to achieve a firm's goals.
- There are six major product strategy alternatives; they are based on the nature of the firm's product offering and the number of target markets.

10 Describe the components of a firm's total product offering.
- The name is a critical component of a product; it should be easy to pronounce and remember, descriptive, eligible for legal protection, full of promotional possibilities, and suitable for use on several products.
- Packaging is a significant tool for increasing total product value.
- A label is an important informative tool, providing instructions on product use, care, and disposal.
- A warranty can be valuable for achieving customer satisfaction.

KEY TERMS

attitude, p. 155
benefit variables, p. 141
brand, p. 160
buildup process, p. 143
cognitive dissonance, p. 153
culture, p. 155
customer profile, p. 144
customer relationship management (CRM), p. 147
demographic variables, p. 141
evaluative criteria, p. 152
evoked set, p. 152
geographic variables, p. 141

market, p. 139
market analysis, p. 132
marketing mix, p. 132
marketing research, p. 133
motivations, p. 154
needs, p. 153
opinion leader, p. 156
perception, p. 154
perceptual categorization, p. 154
primary data, p. 135
product, p. 157
product item, p. 156
product line, p. 156

product mix, p. 156
product mix consistency, p. 156
product strategy, p. 156
psychographic variables, p. 141
reference groups, p. 155
sales forecast, p. 141
secondary data, p. 134
segmentation variables, p. 141
service mark, p. 161
small business marketing, p. 132
trademark, p. 161
warranty, p. 161

DISCUSSION QUESTIONS

1. What is the scope of small business marketing? Has it always been as broad as it is now? Why or why not?
2. What are the obstacles to adopting a consumer orientation in a small firm?
3. What are the steps in the marketing research process?
4. What are the major considerations in designing a questionnaire?
5. Why is it so important to understand the target market? Referring to Greenlite from "In the Trenches," define the target market(s) for the venture.
6. Think of a recent experience you had with exceptionally good or exceptionally poor customer service. What do you think made the service exceptional?

7. Define CRM, and identify the two essential building blocks of a successful program. How does technology support CRM?
8. Briefly describe the four stages of the consumer decision-making process. Why is the first stage vital to consumer behaviour?
9. List the four psychological factors discussed in this chapter. What is their relevance to consumer behaviour?
10. Describe a competitive matrix. Why is it used when developing a product strategy?
11. Describe business marketing. How is it different than consumer marketing?

YOU MAKE THE CALL

SITUATION 1

Brothers Josh and Seth Frey were driving an ice cream truck. After buying a former postal vehicle and converting it into a dessert-mobile, they operated it between semesters at the university. Seth, a senior, planned to join the corporate world after graduating, but Josh was enjoying being his own boss. The art history major felt he had finally figured out his future. Still, he didn't want to be the neighbourhood ice cream guy for the rest of his life. What else could he sell? Care packages. Josh was impressed that a few dorms at his university offered care packages for parents to send to their kids. How could Josh improve on the product? The care packages should be offered campus-wide, he thought.

Question 1 What type of research could Josh use to estimate demand for the care packages?
Question 2 How could he develop a sales forecast for his product?
Question 3 Would the Internet be helpful to his marketing plan?

Source: Geoff Williams, "Staying Power," *Entrepreneur,* Vol. 26, No. 6 (June 1998), p. 154.

SITUATION 2

Carson Smith is an employee of a small family-owned manufacturing plant located in his hometown of Halifax. One day, while waiting to see someone at a competitor's business, he noticed a memo tacked to a bulletin board and read it. The memo described a forthcoming promotional campaign and details of a new pricing strategy. Upon leaving the plant, Smith returned to his office and informed management of the details of the memo.

Question 1 Is this a legitimate form of marketing research? Why or why not?
Question 2 Do you consider Smith's behaviour to constitute spying?
Question 3 What would you have done in his situation?

SITUATION 3

Mary Wilson is a 31-year-old who wants to start her own company. She has no previous business experience but has an idea for marketing an animal-grooming service, using an approach similar to that used for pizza delivery. When a customer calls, she will arrive in a van in less than 30 minutes and provide the grooming service. Many of her friends think the idea has promise but dismiss her efforts to seriously discuss the venture. However, Wilson is not discouraged; she plans to purchase the van and the necessary grooming equipment.

Question 1 What target market or markets can you identify for Wilson? How could she forecast sales for her service in each market?
Question 2 What advantage does her business have over existing grooming businesses?
Question 3 How would a competitive matrix be useful when determining her product mix?

EXPERIENTIAL EXERCISES

1. Interview a local small business owner to determine the type of marketing research, if any, he or she has used.
2. Visit a local small retailer and observe its marketing efforts—salesperson style, store atmosphere, and warranty policies, for example. Report your observations to the class, and make recommendations for improving these efforts to increase customer satisfaction.
3. For several days, make notes on your own shopping experiences. Summarize what you consider to be the best customer service you received.
4. Visit a local retail store and observe brand names, package designs, labels, and warranties. Choose good and bad examples of each, and report back to the class.
5. Consider your most recent meaningful purchase. Compare the decision-making process you used to the four stages of decision making presented in this chapter. Report your conclusions.

EXPLORING THE WEB

1. Go to http:// www.rbcroyalbank.com. Review the three sample business plans on this text's website at http://www.longenecker4e.nelson. com. Evaluate one of the plans using the criteria for effective business plans outlined in this chapter.

THE BUSINESS PLAN: LAYING THE FOUNDATION

ASKING THE RIGHT QUESTIONS

As part of laying the foundation for your own business plan, respond to the following questions regarding marketing research, sales forecasting, and the marketing plan.

MARKETING RESEARCH QUESTIONS

1. What types of research should be conducted to collect the information you need?
2. How much will this research cost?
3. What sources of secondary data will address your informational needs?
4. What sources of relevant data are available in your local library?
5. What sources of outside professional assistance have you considered using to help with marketing research?

FORECASTING QUESTIONS

1. How do you plan to forecast sales for your product or service?
2. What sources of forecasting assistance have you consulted?
3. What sales forecasting techniques are most appropriate to your needs?
4. What is the sales forecast for your product or service?

MARKETING PLAN QUESTIONS

1. What is the customer profile for your product or service?
2. How will you identify prospective customers?
3. What geographical area will you serve?

4. What are the distinguishing characteristics of your product or service?
5. What steps have already been taken to develop your product or service?
6. What do you plan to name your product or service?
7. Will there be a warranty?
8. How will you set the price for your product or service?
9. What type of distribution plan will you use?
10. Will you export to other countries?
11. What type of selling effort will you use?
12. What special selling skills will be required?
13. What types of advertising and sales promotion will you use?

USING BIZPLANBUILDER® EXPRESS

If you are using BizPlan*Builder*® Express, refer to Part 2 for guidelines on how information about products and services, market analysis, and marketing strategy should be reflected.

Promotional and Pricing Strategies

IN THE SPOTLIGHT

Steam Whistle Brewing

The Steam Whistle story began in the spring of 1998 when three friends were on a canoe trip in the Ontario heartland. Greg Taylor, Cam Heaps, and Greg Cromwell had been colleagues at one of Canada's premier microbreweries in the late 1980s and 1990s before it was bought out by a national brewer and closed down. As they sat around the campfire, the self-named "three Fired Guys" dreamed of running their own brewery. They wanted to make a Pilsner that would compete with the best in the world.

They wrote a plan, attracted investors, started their brewery, and in 2005 and 2007 the Ontario brewing Awards named Steam Whistle the province's Best Pilsner. In May 2007 Cam Heaps was named one of the Top 40 Under 40 young business leaders in Canada.

Steam Whistle is a success not only because of the quality of its beer, but also due to its creative promotions. The company uses vintage trucks, such as a 1949 International Stake Truck painted bright green and sporting shiny chrome wheels, and a 1957 Chevy Pickup that has been fully restored and painted metallic blue. The branding of the brewery is based upon the sounds of steam rushing from factory whistles, signalling the end of a workday and time for personal reward. The whistles were icons of a golden era of prosperity, when things were built to last and the marketing of goods relied on a relationship of trust between manufacturers who produced quality goods and their consumers. The Beer Folks at Steam Whistle use unique vehicles to reflect their unique character and quality craftsmanship. With customers across the country, and awards such as the 2007 Liquor Control Board of Ontario's "Best Special Event" award, the Steam Whistle team has found their niche.

http://www.steamwhistle.ca

Photo courtesy of Steam Whistle Founders

Source: http://www.steamwhistle.ca (accessed January 20, 2008).

The old adage "Build a better mousetrap and the world will beat a path to your door" highlights the importance of innovation in building a successful marketing program but ignores the roles of other vital marketing activities. Promotion, for example, is essential for informing customers about any new, improved "mousetrap" and how they can get to the "door." A solid pricing strategy is required to ensure that customers perceive the new mousetrap as offering better value than their old one. Understanding the decision-making process and customer needs including price sensitivity is basic to developing effective promotional and pricing strategies.

Steam Whistle has created a competitive advantage though its premier product in conjunction with an effective promotional strategy.

Promotion consists of marketing communications that inform consumers about a firm's product and persuade them to use it. Small businesses use promotion in varying degrees, with most firms using a mixture of promotional strategies. The promotional techniques discussed in this chapter are personal selling, advertising, and using sales promotional tools.

promotion
marketing communications that inform and persuade consumers

THE COMMUNICATION PROCESS IN PROMOTION

Promotion is based on communication. In fact, promotion is worthless unless it effectively communicates a firm's message. Therefore, let's begin by looking at the connection between the communication process and promotional strategy.

Communication is a process with identifiable components. The challenge is twofold: (1) to create the promotions that will be most effective in creating awareness and motivation to buy in the target market, and (2) creating a cost-effective promotion program. Most small businesses cannot afford the sophisticated and expensive marketing campaigns pursued by large companies. The communication process is most effective when it integrates key marketing goals, such as percentage of market share, a cohesive promotion mix, and a follow-up evaluation of the promotions to determine their effectiveness. Refer to Exhibit 7-1 for an overview of the communications process.

A **promotional mix** involves a combination of the various promotional methods—personal selling, advertising, and using promotional tools. The composition is determined by four major factors. The first factor is the geographical nature of the market to be reached. A widely dispersed market generally requires mass coverage through advertising, in contrast to the more costly individual contacts of personal selling. On the other hand, if the market is local, with a relatively small number of customers, personal selling is more feasible.

The second factor is the firm's target customers. Shotgun promotion, which "hits" potential customers and nonpotential customers alike, is expensive. An advertising program can be fine-tuned to some extent through consumer analysis, and the media can provide helpful profiles of their audiences. But first a small business has to carefully determine its target market.

The third factor that influences the promotional mix is the product's characteristics. If a product is of high unit value, such as a mobile home, personal selling will be a vital ingredient in the mix. Personal selling is also an effective method for promoting highly technical products, such as automobiles or street-sweeping machinery. On the other hand, advertising is more effective for a relatively inexpensive item, like razor blades.

The fourth consideration in developing a promotional mix is budget. For example, the high total cost of the optimum promotional mix, which could include expensive

promotional mix
a blend of selling, advertising, and promotional tools aimed at a target market

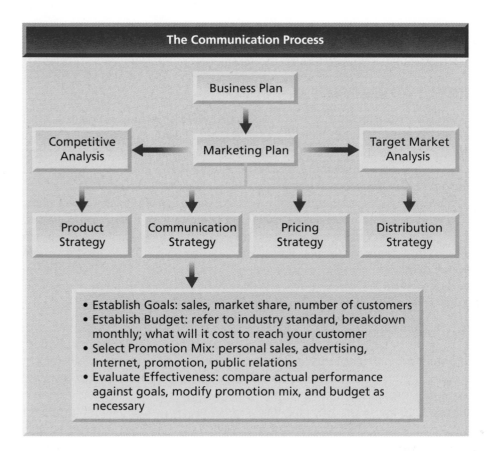

EXHIBIT **7-1**
*Overview of the
Communication Process*

television advertising, may necessitate substitution of a less expensive alternative. The small business owner should identify the promotional mix that will reach the target market, then allocate the budget accordingly.

ADVERTISING PRACTICES FOR SMALL FIRMS

A vital part of small business promotion, **advertising** is the impersonal presentation of an idea that is identified with a business sponsor. This idea is projected through mass media, including television, radio, magazines, newspapers, and billboards.

ADVERTISING OBJECTIVES

As its primary goal, advertising seeks to sell by informing, persuading, and reminding customers of the existence or superiority of a firm's product or service. To be successful, it must rest on a foundation of product quality and efficient service; advertising can bring no more than temporary success to an inferior product. It must always be viewed as a complement to a good product and never as a replacement for a bad product.

The business owner must avoid creating false expectations with advertising, as such expectations can effectively reduce customer satisfaction. Advertising can accentuate a trend in the sale of an item or product line, but it seldom has the power to reverse a trend. It must, consequently, be able to reflect changes in customer needs and preferences.

Identify advertising options for a small business.   **2**

advertising
the impersonal presentation of a business idea through mass media

At times, advertising may seem to be a waste of money. It is expensive and adds little utility to the product. But the primary alternative to advertising is personal selling, which is often more expensive and time consuming.

TYPES OF ADVERTISING

product advertising
the presentation of a business idea designed to make potential customers aware of a specific product or service and their need for it

institutional advertising
the presentation of information about a particular firm, designed to enhance the firm's image

The two basic types of advertising are product advertising and institutional advertising. **Product advertising** is designed to make potential customers aware of a particular product or service and their need for it. **Institutional advertising,** on the other hand, conveys information about the business itself. It is intended to keep the public conscious of the company and enhance its image.

The majority of small business advertising is of the product type. Small retailers' advertisements stress products almost exclusively—weekend specials in a supermarket, for example. It is important to note, however, that the same advertisement can convey both product and institutional themes. Furthermore, a firm may stress its product in online advertisements, while using institutional advertising in the Yellow Pages. Decisions regarding the type of advertising to be used should be based on the nature of the business, industry practice, available media, and the objectives of the firm.

FREQUENCY OF ADVERTISING

Determining how often to advertise is an important and highly complex issue for a small business. Obviously, advertising should be done regularly, and attempts to stimulate interest in a firm's products or services should be part of an ongoing promotional program. One-shot advertisements that are not part of a well-planned promotional effort lose much of their effectiveness in a short period. Some noncontinuous, or seasonal, advertising may be justified, such as advertising to prepare consumers for acceptance of a new product or a Boxing Day sale.

WHERE TO ADVERTISE

Most small firms restrict their advertising, either geographically or by customer type. Advertising media should reach—but not overreach—a firm's present or desired target market. From among the many media available, a small business entrepreneur must choose those that will provide the greatest return for the advertising dollar.

The most appropriate combination of advertising media depends on the type of business and its current circumstances. A real estate sales firm, for example, may rely almost exclusively on classified advertisements in the local newspaper, supplemented by institutional advertising in the Yellow Pages. A transfer-and-storage firm may use a combination of radio, billboard, website, and Yellow Pages advertising to reach individuals planning to move household furniture. A small toy manufacturer may use television advertisements and participation in trade fairs. A local retail store may concentrate on display advertisements in the local newspaper. The selection of media should be based on not only tradition but also a careful evaluation of the various ways that are available to cover a firm's particular market. Trudeau Corporation uses a variety of media to create awareness. See "In the Trenches."

A good way to build a media mix is to talk with representatives from each medium to determine if their "audience" fits the target market. Advertising firms are required to identify the demographics of their audience and the frequency with which the audience

IN THE TRENCHES

Entrepreneurial Experiences

Clicks for Chicks—E Commerce and Social Networking

After the 90s bubble burst, the web was a dangerous place to invest. Now online money-making is on the rise again and from Facebook to YouTube, savvy entrepreneurs know that the next big thing could just be a click away. Alex and Ali de Bold recognized the explosive potential in social networking and created ChickAdvisor.com in late 2006. Modelled after tripadvisor.com ChickAdvisor lets women from all over the country log on to rate and find out what others think about different products and services—from local restaurants to the best new boutiques, lipstick to liposuction.

The idea came suddenly when Ali was planning their 2005 wedding. She was trying to find the perfect salon for the perfect hairdo on her special day, but couldn't find any Canadian reviews online. Then Alex brought up the idea of building their own website with service ratings to fill the gap.

Ali and Alex began doing research on possible competitors. They found that other websites were very generic and not specifically for women.

ChickAdvisor combines social networking and e-commerce, focusing on beauty, shopping, wellness, and restaurants. Users can rate products and services, or join ChickChat and share stories about romantic marriage proposals. The website has about 3,500 members across North America, and editions for cities across Canada including Toronto, Vancouver, and Montreal.

Sources: http://www.cbc.ca/news/fortunehunters/hunters/2008/01 ali_and alex_de_bold.php, and http://www.chickadvisor.com, January 31, 2008.

reads, watches, or listens to the medium. The Media Information Network, and CARD online, provide advertising rates and information for hundreds of advertising venues at http://www.cardonline.ca and http://www.sources.com. The entrepreneur should learn about the weaknesses and the strengths of each medium, carefully considering both the cost and the level of effectiveness for his or her particular client base. Exhibit 7-2 summarizes important facts about several traditional advertising media. Study this information carefully, noting the particular advantages and disadvantages of each medium.

THE MESSAGE

Most small businesses rely on others' expertise to create their promotional messages. Fortunately, there are several sources for this specialized assistance: advertising agencies, suppliers, trade associations, and advertising media.

Advertising agencies can provide the following services:

- Furnish design, artwork, and copy for specific advertisements and/or commercials.
- Evaluate and recommend the advertising media with the greatest "pulling power."
- Evaluate the effectiveness of different advertising appeals.
- Advise on sales promotions and merchandise displays.

EXHIBIT **7-2**
Advantages and Disadvantages of Traditional Advertising Media

Medium	Advantages	Disadvantages
Newspapers	Geographic selectivity and flexibility; short-term advertiser commitments; news value and immediacy; year-round readership; high individual market coverage; co-op and local tie-in availability; short lead time	Little demographic selectivity; limited colour capabilities; low pass-along rate; may be expensive
Magazines	Good reproduction, especially for colour; demographic selectivity; regional selectivity; local market selectivity; relatively long advertising life; high pass-along rate	Long-term advertiser commitments; slow audience buildup; limited demonstration capabilities; lack of urgency; long lead time
Radio	Low cost; immediacy of message; can be scheduled on short notice; relatively no seasonal change in audience; highly portable; short-term advertiser commitments; entertainment carryover	No visual treatment; short advertising life of message; high frequency required to generate comprehension and retention; distractions from background sound; commercial clutter
Television	Ability to reach a wide, diverse audience; low cost per thousand; creative opportunities for demonstration; immediacy of messages; entertainment carryover; demographic selectivity with cable stations	Short life of messages; some consumer skepticism about claims; high campaign cost; little demographic selectivity with network stations; long-term advertiser commitments; long lead times required for production; commercial clutter
Outdoor	Repetition; moderate cost; flexibility; geographic selectivity	Short message; lack of media demographic selectivity; high "noise" level distracting audience
Internet	Fastest-growing medium; ability to reach a narrow target audience; relatively short lead time required for creating Web-based advertising; moderate cost	Difficult to measure ad effectiveness and return on investment; ad exposure relies on click-through from banner ads; not all consumers have access to the Internet.

Source: Charles W. Lamb Jr., Joseph F. Hair Jr., and Carl McDaniel, *Marketing* 9th ed. (Cincinnati: South-Western, 2008), p. 475.

- Conduct market sampling studies to evaluate product acceptance or determine the sales potential of a specific geographic area.
- Provide mailing lists.

Since advertising agencies generally charge fees for their services, an entrepreneur must ensure that the return from those services will be greater than the fees paid. Quality advertising assistance can best be provided by a competent agency. Of course, with the high level of technology currently available, creating print advertising in-house is becoming increasingly common among small firms.

Other outside sources may assist in formulating and carrying out promotional programs. Suppliers often furnish display aids and even entire advertising programs to their dealers. Trade associations are also active in this area. In addition, the advertising media can provide some of the same services offered by an ad agency.

WEB ADVERTISING

The Internet has provided an entirely new way for small firms to advertise. With colour graphics, two-way information exchanges, streaming video, and 24-hour availability, online advertising is challenging traditional media for promotional dollars. Web advertising allows advertisers to reach large numbers of global buyers in a timely manner, at less expense, and with more impact than many alternative forms of advertising. Canadians in particular are digitally connected; with 23 million users in June 2007, the average Canadian consumes 4,000 web views per month, more than users from any other country.[1]

Estimates provided by the Interactive Advertising Bureau, http://www.iabcanada.com, indicate Canadian online advertising revenues of $1.3 billion in 2007, a 32 percent percent increase over the 2006 annual revenue.

Advertisers of all types have flocked to the Internet, hoping (with good reason) that the information superhighway will be the next great mass medium. Most large businesses have a presence on the Web, and many small firms are using Internet technology. The basic methods of Web advertising are (1) banner ads and pop-ups, (2) direct email promotion, (3) sponsorships and linkages, and (4) a corporate website.

BANNER ADS AND POP-UPS **Banner ads** are advertisements that appear across a web page, most often as moving rectangular strips. In contrast, **pop-up ads** burst open on web pages but do not move. When viewers respond by clicking on an ad, they are automatically linked to the site providing the product or sales activity. Both banner and pop-up ads can be placed on search engine sites or on related web pages.

These types of Web advertising are often carried out through an affiliate program. In an affiliate program, a website carries a banner ad or a link for another company in exchange for a commission on any sales generated by the traffic sent to the sponsoring website. Affiliate programs have become quite popular among Web retailers, with one of the most lucrative being eBay's program. A primary reason for the success of eBay's affiliate program is the sheer volume of visitors to its website every day. The millions of items for sale at any given time on eBay provide ample advertising opportunities for affiliates. eBay pays an affiliate a commission not only on sales generated by the users it sends, but also on each already-registered eBay user it sends back to eBay and on each bid and qualified Buy it Now transaction.

These commissions have allowed many affiliates to profit handsomely from their relationship with eBay. The top 50 of the approximately 10,000 affiliates in the eBay program generate more than $1 million annually in commissions. Affiliates can choose from an array of eBay banners, buttons, and logos to feature on their websites. A cookie identifying the affiliate is attached to anyone sent to eBay. Affiliates can also add real-time listings to their sites. For example, if your website reviews musical releases, it can provide up-to-date listings of the CDs for sale on eBay.[2]

Price comparison pop-ups are an effective way to lure surfers from competitive websites. Here's how they work: When a shopper who is browsing in an online store clicks on a specific product, comparison-shopping software generates a pop-up ad that features

banner ads
advertisements that appear across a web page, most often as moving rectangular strips

pop-up ads
advertisements that burst open on computer screens

links to other vendors selling the same item at a lower price. This software works much the same way as a bargain-hunting website like Shopping.com, but it offers competitive prices wherever consumers shop on the Web. Comparison-shopping software has helped Steve Hafner, founder of the travel website Kayak.com, to compete with online giants such as Expedia and Travelocity. Buying keywords on Google and putting banner ads on travel websites were not working for Hafner, but as soon as he started his comparison-shopping ads, he could see the results. The ads generated a click-through rate of 8 to 10 percent, compared with 1 percent for his search engine ads. The icing on the cake was that shoppers who clicked on the new ads were 50 percent more likely to book a trip than those arriving at the website via banner ads or search engines.[3]

e-mail promotion
advertising delivered by means of electronic mail

DIRECT EMAIL PROMOTION E-mail promotion, in which electronic mail is used to deliver a firm's message, provides a low-cost way to pinpoint customers and achieve response rates higher than those for banner ads. However, as more and more businesses use email for this purpose, customer inboxes are becoming cluttered. And users are reluctant to open some email messages, fearing they may contain computer viruses.

Despite their limitations, email promotions can be very effective. Larry and Charlene Woodward own an independent bookstore. When new books are published, Dogwise sends personalized emails to people who have previously purchased books on similar subjects. "Customers love it, and we sell lots of books every time we send a batch of emails," says Larry. Before using email to promote new books, the company sent postcards to its customers.[4] Obstacles to email promotion have risen, as the volume of unsolicited emails (better known as spam) has turned many customers against this type of advertising.

Web sponsorship
A type of advertising in which a firm pays another organization for the right to be part of that organization's web page

linkage
A type of advertising agreement in which one firm pays another to include a click-on link on its site

SPONSORSHIPS AND LINKAGES In Web sponsorship, a firm pays to be part of another organization's web page. When the web page includes a click-on link to the paying firm's site, a linkage has been established. Research shows that a significant number of online purchases originate from online links. Unfortunately for many firms that choose to advertise through Web sponsorship, blocking software from such companies as Web-Washer can be used to prevent ads from appearing on a viewer's web page.[5]

CORPORATE WEBSITES The fourth form of Web advertising involves a more serious commitment by a small firm—launching a corporate website. Numerous decisions must be made prior to launching a site. Three critical startup tasks are related to the promotional success of a corporate website: (1) creating and registering a site name, (2) building a user-friendly site, and (3) promoting the site.

Creating and registering a site: Name the Domain Name System (DNS) allows users to find their way around the Internet. Selecting the best domain name for a corporate website is an important promotional decision and, contrary to general opinion, plenty of website names remain available. Domain names can have up to 63 characters preceding the domain designation. The three most popular domain designations are .com, .net, and .org.[6]

Since a domain name gives a small business its online identity, it's desirable to select a descriptive and appealing name. Obviously, some of the shorter, more creative names have already been taken. But, like real estate, website names can be bought and sold. In the first month of 2007, 10 domain names sold for $35,000 or more. Tied for ninth, the domain name Frisbee.com sold for $35,000; in sixth place was Joystick.com, which sold for $65,250; and in first place, Sportsbook.mobi sold for $129,000.[7]

Once a desired name has been selected, it should be checked for availability and then registered. The Internet Corporation for Assigned Names and Numbers (ICANN) is a nonprofit corporation currently overseeing the global Internet. ICANN, however, does not register names; this must be done through a domain registration firm. Several domain registrars allow a search of the Internet to see if a proposed name is already taken.

Building a user-friendly website: First impressions are important, and high-quality Web design gives a small e-commerce business the opportunity to make a good first impression on each visitor. The technical aspects of developing a website are beyond the scope of this chapter. Fortunately, there are many technical specialists available to help design and build a site. Our purpose here is simply to provide some useful tips about website design. Exhibit 7-3 shows 10 design tips for e-commerce websites.

There are many reasons that websites fail to retain customers. One of the most frequent problems is slow downloading. Online shoppers are a fickle bunch, and the slightest inconvenience sends them away. If your business is conducting a considerable amount of online business, a slow website translates into lost sales revenue. Lost revenue can be direct—missed sales if you're selling online—or indirect—loss of customer trust if you're providing Web-based solutions to clients. The more important a website is to your business, the less you can afford to have it perform slowly or, worse, experience downtime.[8]

Believe it or not, studies show that first-time visitors to your website spend as little as 10 seconds there before deciding whether or not to stay. Web entrepreneurs cannot afford to squander any of these precious seconds with slow downloads. Whenever possible, reduce the number and size of files on your web pages. The more files a page contains and the larger they are, the longer it will take to load.[9]

IN THE TRENCHES

Utilizing New Technology

Trudeau Corporation—Kitchen and Table Products

Trudeau, whose head office is located in Boucherville, Quebec, is a leading Canadian supplier of kitchen and bartending supplies and accessories. Since 1889 four generations have managed the business. As a top supplier of quality kitchen tools and gadgets in North America, Trudeau is known throughout the world for its quality products, and excellent import and distribution logistics.

In the mid-1990s, after a century in the luxury import business, Trudeau decided to start manufacturing its own kitchen products, and innovate in the research and design of new products. A team of Canadian, American, and European designers create the products, which are distributed to retailers in over 40 countries.

A key to the company's continued expansion has been the updating and expansion of its website, http://www.trudeau.ca, unveiled in 2007. The website offers more than 2000 products, and provides a locator for the nearest store location. The website also highlights the media coverage Trudeau has received from popular cooking shows, such as *Every Day with Rachael Ray.*

Source: http://www.trudeau.ca (accessed January 31, 2008).

EXHIBIT **7-3**

Focusing on the Customer: Marketing Growth Strategies

Website Design Tips

TIP 1: MAKE IT EASY TO BUY

This tip may seem vague and ambiguous, but it truly is the most important recommendation. Put yourself in your customer's shoes and test your designs. Isolate issues that might block users from making a successful purchase. Ask questions, such as:

- How many pages and clicks does it take to make a purchase?
- How much information do users have to fill out initially, versus when they make a second-time purchase?
- Can a quick purchase be made directly from the home page?
- Does the site provide clear instructions on how to store selected items before completing a transaction?
- How well does the site communicate with a user?
- Does the site acknowledge users' actions and provide clear, concise feedback as users progress through the purchasing process?
- Can users collect multiple items before checking out?

TIP 2: MAKE A STRONG FIRST IMPRESSION

The e-commerce home page must make a strong first impression. This is where users are grounded to your company and persuaded to start shopping. It is first and foremost important to provide branding for your store. Next, it is important to provide a clear visual definition of your store's categories or departments. This can be accomplished with tabs or within the navigation bar.

TIP 3: MINIMIZE DISTRACTIONS: ADVERTISING ISN'T ALWAYS NECESSARY

You may consider not providing any advertisements on the home page or in other places throughout the purchase process. Remember that the goal of your home page is to encourage shopping and purchasing. You don't want to deter or lose users by having them click on another company's advertisement.

TIP 4: MAKE IT PERSONAL

Looking for a way to build a strong rapport with your shoppers? Provide personalization for the user, after the user registers as a shopper or member. Use this information to provide a personalized greeting to the home page or various department pages. Welcome, Najia, enjoy your shopping experience. Provide a private place that requires a password, where each user can check past orders, order status, wish lists, gift certificates, and so forth.

TIP 5: AVOID LONG INSTRUCTIONS

If you need to include long instructions on how to use the site or make a purchase, it is time to redesign! To complete a quick purchase, a user needs minimal-to-no instructions. Most users will not read long instructions, and may turn away in confusion.

TIP 6: PROVIDE VISUAL CLUES TO LOCATION

For stores that have multiple departments, it is important to create a sense of varying location. This can be accomplished by changing colours on the navigation bar or the background page, and by providing different titles with text or graphics.

TIP 7: SHOW OFF PRODUCTS

If at all possible, provide photographs of individual products. Process the photos in three sizes: thumbnail, medium, and large. A thumbnail photo is best used in a list of several products. At the individual product level, provide a medium-sized image and the ability to click to view the enlarged version of the product. The larger view is not necessary but worth considering if your product has details that are not reflected in the medium-sized or thumbnail photograph. The more details you can provide about the product the better. If you have a long page about the product, be sure to provide the option to purchase or add to your basket or cart from both the top and the bottom of the informational text.

EXHIBIT **7-3**
(*Continued*)

TIP 8: ENCOURAGE SPONTANEOUS PURCHASES

This can be accomplished in various ways. If a product is mentioned on the home page, place product images and details, the sale price, and a direct link to purchase the item there. In a news or feature article, include direct links to purchase products discussed within the article. Or on the side column, where advertisements for other companies traditionally would go, create intimate, focused advertisements for your products, with a direct link to purchase the items from the advertisements.

TIP 9: ALTERNATE BACKGROUND COLOURS IN LONG LISTS

One good visual trick to make a long table of items easier to read is to alternate a light colour background for each row or item. You can see an example of this if you search on an author's name at http://barnesandnoble.com. The search results return in alternate item background colours of gray and white.

TIP 10: ALLOW USERS TO COLLECT ITEMS

Provide a shopping basket or a place for users to collect items before checking out. Never make the user fill out the lengthy payment, shipping, and other forms more than once in a transaction! At the product level, provide a link to check out and a link to add that product to the shopping cart while continuing to shop. One item-storage feature that is currently becoming popular is called a wish list. This feature is similar to a shopping cart, but it does not provide purchasing features. Think of it as a place to store items as you are shopping. When items in your wish list go on sale, the site may notify you.

Source: Nadja Vol Ochs, "Easy-to-Buy E-Commerce Site Design Tips," http://www.microsoft .com/technet/prodtechnol/sscomm/reskit/sitedes.mspx, accessed July 13, 2007. © 1999 Microsoft Corporation. All rights reserved.

Promoting the website: How do customers learn about a website? You have to tell them—and there are many ways to do this. A Web address can be promoted both to existing customers and prospects by including the URL on print promotions, business cards, letterhead, and packaging. Special direct mail and radio campaigns can also be designed for this purpose. Additionally, a website can be promoted by placing banner advertisements on other websites, where a quick click will send users to the advertised site.

The advantage of banner advertisements is that they are placed in front of thousands of visitors to other websites. Payment for banner advertising is usually based on the number of people who actually click on the banner.

Probably the most direct approach to website promotion is making sure that the site is listed on Internet search engines. Search engines are databases, available on the Internet, that allow users to find websites based on keywords included in the site's pages. If a popular search engine does not list a firm's website, many potential visitors will undoubtedly miss it. Registering a site with a search engine is free. However, to get a position at or near the top of a search listing, you may have to pay. Search engine optimization (SEO) is the process of increasing the volume and quality of traffic to a particular website. The sooner your small business is presented in search engine results (i.e., the higher it ranks), the more visitors it will attract. An important goal is to make your website as search engine–friendly as possible. Obviously, your website should include keywords that someone looking for that particular subject might use. Many businesses try to get to the top of a search engine's results by designing their websites to match a particular search engine's ranking index. There are several ways of submitting a website to search engines. A description of submission options appears in Exhibit 7-4.

1. USE A FREE SUBMISSION SERVICE

Free submission services offer to submit your website to as many as 500 of the top search engines for free. And while that may sound like a great deal to the inexperienced site owner, the truth is that using a free submission service will cost you traffic and sales. Every search engine has a different "rule book" that it uses to decide where your website will rank. Because they submit the same information to every single engine, free submission services are useless in achieving top-ranking positions for your firm.

2. USE A LOW-COST, AUTOMATED SUBMISSION SERVICE

Low-cost, automated submission services offer to submit your website to as many as 900+ search engines for a minimal fee (usually between $40 and $80). Much like the free submission services, automated submission services automatically submit the same set of information to *all* of the search engines. Once again, your website is being submitted to multiple search engines without being optimized to meet their individual requirements.

3. DO IT YOURSELF BY MANUALLY SUBMITTING YOUR WEBSITE TO INDIVIDUAL SEARCH ENGINES

This is one of the best ways to submit your website to the search engines. Visit each search engine separately, and manually submit the information for each Web page you wish to have listed. On the downside, submitting your website this way can be very time consuming and labour intensive. Also, there are no professionals to help you.

4. USE A PROFESSIONAL SEARCH ENGINE CONSULTANT

Search engine consultants will educate you and work with you to maximize your site's exposure in each search engine. They know all of the latest tricks and techniques for securing a top spot and will show you exactly what you need to do to optimize your website for the best possible ranking.

5. USE SUBMISSION SOFTWARE

Most of the software out there does exactly what the free and low-cost automated submission services do—it submits the same set of information to all of the search engines. So, your site is never optimized, and you never secure the top ranking you need. Final thoughts: However you decide to submit your website to the search engines, take your time. Don't rush in and make mistakes that could destroy your chances of securing a top ranking. Remember that search engines receive thousands of requests every day from people who want to make changes to their listing!

Source: Adapted from the Internet Marketing Center's website, http://www.marketingtips .com/newsletters/search-engines/search-engine-strategies.html, accessed July 13, 2007.

SALES PROMOTION FOR SMALL FIRMS

Sales promotion serves as an inducement to buy a certain product while typically offering value to prospective customers. Generally, sales promotion includes any promotional technique, other than personal selling or advertising, that stimulates the purchase of a particular good or service.

Sales promotion should seldom comprise all the promotional efforts of a small business. Typically, it should be used in combination with personal selling and advertising. Popular sales promotional tools include specialties, contests, premiums, trade show exhibits, point-of-purchase displays, free merchandise, sampling, and coupons.

SPECIALTIES The most widely used specialty item is a calendar. Other popular specialty items are pens, mouse pads, coffee mugs, and ball caps. Almost anything can be used as a specialty promotion, as long as each item is imprinted with the firm's name or other identifying slogan. In Alberta, many firms servicing the oil and gas industry distribute belt buckles or ball caps with their company logo during Stampede or Gold Rush days.

The distinguishing characteristic of specialties is their enduring nature and tangible value. Specialties are referred to as the "lasting medium." As functional products, they are worth something to recipients. Specialties can be used to promote a product directly or to create goodwill for a firm. Specialties are excellent reminders of a firm's existence.

Finally, specialties are personal. They are distributed directly to the customer in a personal way, they can be used personally, and they have a personal message. A small business needs to retain its personal image, and entrepreneurs often use specialties to achieve this objective. More information on specialties is available on the website of the Promotional Products Association International at http://www.ppa.org.

Bell Canada's "Un été tout léger" promotional campaign won the national PROMO! Award because of its targeted success. Bell Canada's research teams determined that 42 percent of homes in Quebec used traditional answering machines with outdated technology. A promotional campaign was designed to encourage subscription to the call answer service, and abandonment of old answering machines. A budget of almost $850,000 was approved with a goal of 30,000 new customers.

Consumers who subscribed to the call answer service and brought in their old answering machine received a new 35 mm camera and a case worth $60. Those who subscribed but did not turn in their answering machines received a Famous Players movie pass worth $10 in the mail. The offer was presented through telephone solicitors and at the Bell website. What created the outstanding success of generating over 96,000 new subscribers and a consumer recall rate of 72 percent? Bell made the campaign personal to Quebeckers by using Françoise Vallee on all visuals. Françoise had been the voice behind voice mail for 10 years and was a well-known voice in Quebec; however, nobody knew what she looked like. The unveiling of her identity and appearance created interest, and built upon the trust already felt for her. She was presented as a person who watches out for Quebeckers, and she offered to relieve them of their old machines. The campaign was a success due to both the promotional items offered and the personal level at which the key figure reached potential clients.

TRADE SHOW EXHIBITS Advertising often cannot substitute for trial experiences with a product, and a customer's place of business is not always the best environment for product demonstrations. Trade show exhibits allow potential customers to get hands-on experience with a product.

Trade show exhibits are of particular value to manufacturers. The greatest benefit of these exhibits is the potential cost savings over personal selling. Trade show groups claim that the cost of an exhibit is less than one-quarter the cost of sales calls. Many small manufacturers agree that exhibits are more cost-effective than advertising. One leading trade publication, *Sales & Marketing Management,* offers some helpful tips regarding trade shows:[10]

- *Create moving billboards:* Smart exhibitors try to capture attendees' attention all over the trade show and the trade show city—not just at their booth. Give booth visitors handouts that amount to moving billboards. The most popular is a tote bag with your company name and logo that is then carried around the show. Also try sponsoring bus boards and cab boards that cruise the city during the trade show.

- *Make the booth interactive:* Games, contests, tests of skill, trivia challenges, and other interactive activities are effective ways of getting people into your booth. Make sure the prizes are worth winning; otherwise, the encounter may create a lasting negative impression.
- *Qualify leads immediately:* Ask all booth visitors to fill out a qualification card that includes questions on their interest in your product. If they stopped by the booth out of curiosity or simply to enter a draw, that's fine. You just don't want to waste time following up on those who have no real interest in your product.
- *Create a presence on the show floor:* While this may be easier said than done, standing out in the crowd is a must. Some exhibitors hire celebrities, while others run exciting games, or offer samples or prizes. Whatever technique you decide to use, work hard at being extraordinary.
- *Plan ahead:* Just showing up isn't enough. Use the trade show as an opportunity to spend time with particularly important customers or prospects. This means planning well in advance to have the customer or prospect meet you at the booth for a special presentation or demonstration. Since major trade shows attract a large number of interested prospects, book as many meetings and make as many contacts as possible.
- *Recruit customers:* Make sure your marketing staff and salespeople don't stand around the booth talking to each other. Get them out in the aisles. Have them roam the convention hall passing out tote bags, buttons, or other premiums. Have them bring people to the booth for a serious demonstration.

The locations and dates of both Canadian and international trade shows are available through industry associations.

LOYALTY PROGRAMS Many Canadian retailers such as drugstores, grocery stores, and airlines offer loyalty programs. For example, in the Petro-Canada program, points accumulated with gas purchases are redeemable on feature items. Canadian Tire is another example of a long-running program. "Canadian Tire money" is rewarded for purchases, to be redeemed during the next shopping trip to Canadian Tire. Refer to Exhibit 7-5 for the relative effectiveness of various promotional tools.

WHEN TO USE SALES PROMOTION A small firm can use sales promotion to accomplish various objectives. For example, small manufacturers can use it to stimulate channel

EXHIBIT **7-5**
Promotional Tools

Tools	Getting Customer to Try New Product	Increase Seasonal Sales	Increase Effectiveness of Advertising	Encourage Repeat Purchases	Gather Information about Customer
Trade shows	X		X		
Coupon	X	X	X	X	
Mail-in refunds	X		X	X	X
Contests	X	X	X	X	X
Loyalty programs				X	

IN THE TRENCHES

Entrepreneurial Experiences

Trade Shows Work

Trade and consumer shows offer tremendous opportunity to make sales, network and scope out competition, although most entrepreneurs don't know how to achieve these objectives, says a leading expert. Many exhibitors can't articulate precisely why they are there, says Barry Siskind, a trade show and exhibiting specialist and president of International Training and Management Company in Toronto.

To illustrate this point, Mr. Siskind kicks off his book, *Powerful Exhibit Marketing*, with the old song lyrics, "We're here because we're here because we're here because we're here" suggesting this can serve as a theme song for 80 percent of trade show exhibitors. "Planning and organizing for a show is so much more than logistics," Mr. Siskind says. "It's a science."

Mr. Siskind helps companies develop strategies and train booth staff to ensure a return on investment at shows. He says shows are ideal for entrepreneurs just starting out. "For a brand-new company just getting into a business, this is an opportunity to do face-to-face marketing, get out there, talk to people, build relationships and create the experience."

"There's a growing need for returns on investments so it's important to carefully choose which shows to attend," he says, noting there are 13,120 registered trade shows across North American each year, along with smaller regional events. He suggests exhibitors define their target audience. Booth staff often have only 30 seconds or less to make an impression, prompting Mr. Siskind to declare a trade show "a harsh, hostile, unfriendly environment to work in."

Data gathered from formal audits of trade shows offer potential participants detailed information about the type of people who typically patronize the event. "Exhibitors are not impressed with just the quantity of people, what they need to know is the quality of people," he says. "So, more shows are being audited to provide exhibitors with that information. Then you can see if the people you're looking for [are] going to that show in sufficient numbers."

Many exhibitors hold a draw for a prize and ask passersby to simply leave their business card as an entry ballot. Mr. Siskind says, instead, entrants should be required to fill out a ballot and have it "validated" by booth staff to provide opportunity to talk to the person about their business or product interests. The prize should be tied to the business. As examples, Mr. Siskind cites a consulting firm targeting engineers that purchased a $1,000 collection of books of interest to engineers, narrowing down the entrants to the firm's audience. In another instance, a mutual fund company raffled off lunch with one of its top fund managers. "Those are the kinds of prizes that make sense," he says.

Once the show is over, following up leads while the event is still fresh is integral. However, 80 percent of exhibitors don't do this, reports the Texas-based Centre Exhibition Industry Research (CEIR), which tracks trade show data internationally.

It concludes 43 percent of prospective customers who attended a show are contacted far too long after the event, while 18 percent aren't contacted at all. Yet the organization reports in a recent study that on average, one-third of trade show attendees patronize only one such event each year and of those, "an overwhelming 79% of all qualified attendees represent a new potential customer for exhibiting companies, with more than 80% of whom have purchasing influence."

(Continued)

Daniel Somers, president of CTM Exhibits booth design company in Vancouver, agrees "marketing is becoming more sophisticated" at trade shows, prompting some companies to spend more on a booth. Yet, "there are marketing managers who realize that tradeshows can really shift volumes of business their way," but only if they also invest in "intellectual capital" so staff know how to channel sales.

Tina Vedovat, president of Nimlok Canada, which designs and builds trade show booths, affirms such events can be gold mines if used properly. The shows offer startup businesses an ideal opportunity to tap their market and a booth need not be expensive. "You can look like you're playing with the big boys without the big boy prices," she says.

But there is more to the experience than a flashy booth, standing behind it and collecting business cards. "You can go a trade show and have the best booth there, but if you're not working the booth the way you're supposed to be working the booth, you might as well not show up," she says.

Perhaps you have heard this destructive yet pervasive business advice, "Find a need and fill it." In today's competitive marketplace this is a prescription for disaster. Do not make the mistake of marketing to those who "need" your product. Instead, market to those who "want" it. Successful marketing and selling is based on understanding behaviours because business is about dealing with people. No one needs an iPod. No one needs coffee from a drive-thru. No one needs to watch *Survivor*. You could define wants as emotional needs. That means you need to understand consumers' emotional needs and offer them the emotional rewards they crave. Do that and you will have a steady stream of eager customers.

Source: Daryl-Lynn Carlson, "Trade Shows a 'Hostile' Environment," *Financial Post*, October 12, 2007.

members—retailers and wholesalers—to market their product. Wholesalers can use sales promotion to induce retailers to buy inventories earlier than they normally would, and retailers, with similar promotional tools, may be able to persuade customers to make a purchase.

STRATEGIC ALLIANCES AND SALES PROMOTION Joining with another firm to promote products is a form of a strategic alliance. For example, if a local dry cleaner and a nearby independent tailor had similar customers, they might share the cost of a coupon program, increasing the visibility of both firms without taking away each other's business. Small firms, however, are traditionally very independent and only recently have begun to recognize the benefits of cross-promotion.

PUBLIC RELATIONS Public relations refers to a range of activities that may influence the attitudes and awareness of the general public as well as potential customers. Whereas advertising is paid, publicity, one aspect of public relations, is controlled by the media and is not paid for. Publicity is particularly important to retailers because of its high visibility. Publicity can be used to promote both a product and a firm's image; it is a vital part of public relations for the small business. A good publicity program requires regular contact with the news media.

publicity
information about a firm and its products or services that appears as a news item, free of charge

Although **publicity** is considered to be free advertising, this type of promotion is not always free. Examples of publicity efforts that entail some expense include involvement with athletic programs and sponsorship of local sports teams. While the benefits are difficult to measure, publicity is nevertheless important to a small business and should be considered.

A high-tech spin on publicity can be found in the phenomenon of social shopping websites. A social shopping website results from the merging of a search engine, such as Google, with a social networking element, such as MySpace. Although the power of Google can't be contested, Google can't tell shoppers what is cool or what their friends or other consumers recommend. Social shopping websites like Crowdstorm, Kaboodle, StyleChic, and ThisNext do just that. A search on a typical search engine yields the most prominent brands and retailers on its first few pages. A similar search on a social shopping site, such as the ChickAdvisor site featured earlier, displays a wider array of smaller and arguably "cooler" brands. It also includes the recommendations of the site's most fashion-conscious and influential users. Marketing on such sites must be done carefully, as they are geared toward consumers, not marketers. A forward-thinking entrepreneur, however, can post his or her own favorite products on such sites and potentially influence other users' buying decisions.

PERSONAL SELLING TECHNIQUES FOR SMALL FIRMS

Many products require **personal selling**—promotion delivered in a one-on-one environment. Personal selling includes the activities of both the inside salespeople of retail, wholesale, and service establishments and the outside sales representatives who call on business customers and final consumers.

personal selling
a sales presentation delivered in a one-on-one manner

THE IMPORTANCE OF PRODUCT KNOWLEDGE

Effective selling is built on a foundation of product knowledge. If a salesperson is well acquainted with a product's advantages, uses, and limitations, she or he can educate customers by successfully answering their questions and countering their objections. Most customers expect a salesperson to provide knowledgeable answers—whether the product is a camera, a coat, an automobile, paint, a machine tool, or office equipment. Customers are seldom experts on the products they buy; however, they can immediately sense a salesperson's knowledge or ignorance. Personal selling degenerates into mere order-taking when a salesperson lacks product knowledge, and is usually not effective.

THE SALES PRESENTATION

The heart of personal selling is the sales presentation to a prospective customer. At this crucial point, an order is either secured or lost. A preliminary step leading to an effective sales presentation is **prospecting,** a systematic process of continually looking for new customers.[11]

prospecting
a systematic process of continually looking for new customers

USING PROSPECTING TECHNIQUES

One of the most efficient prospecting techniques is obtaining *personal referrals*. Such referrals come from friends, customers, and other businesses. Initial contact with a potential customer is greatly facilitated when the salesperson is able to say, "You were referred to me by . . ."

Another source of prospects is *impersonal referrals* from media publications, public records, and directories. Newspapers and magazines, particularly trade magazines, often identify prospects by reporting on new companies and new products. Engagement announcements in a newspaper can serve as impersonal referrals for a local bridal shop. Public records of property transactions and building permits can be impersonal referrals for, say, a garbage pick-up service, which might find prospective customers among those planning to build houses or apartment buildings.

Prospects can also be identified without referrals through *marketer-initiated* contacts. Telephone calls or mail surveys, for example, isolate prospects. In a market survey conducted to identify prospects for a small business, an author of this book used a mail questionnaire. The questionnaire, which asked technical questions about a service, concluded with the following statement: "If you would be interested in a service of this nature, please check the appropriate space below and your name will be added to the mailing list."

Finally, prospects can be identified by recording *customer-initiated contacts*. Inquiries by a potential customer that do not lead to a sale can still create a "hot prospect." Small furniture stores often require their salespeople to create a card for each person visiting the store. These prospects are then systematically contacted over the telephone. Records of these contacts are updated periodically.

PRACTISING THE SALES PRESENTATION

Practising always improves a salesperson's success rate; after all, "practice makes perfect." Prior to making a sales presentation, a salesperson should give his or her presentation in front of a spouse, a mirror, or a recording device.

The salesperson should be aware of possible customer objections to the product and be prepared to handle them. Most objections can be categorized as relating to (1) price, (2) product, (3) timing, (4) source, (5) service, or (6) need. Although there is no substitute for actual selling experience, salespeople find training helpful in learning how to deal with customers' objections. The first two responses are appropriate when a potential buyer states an objection that is factually untrue; the remaining suggestions can be used when a buyer raises a valid objection.

> Direct denial: Deny the prospect's objection and give facts to back up the denial.
>
> Indirect denial: Express concern about the prospect's objection and follow with a denial.
>
> Boomerang technique: Turn the valid objection into a valid reason to buy.
>
> Compensation method: Admit to agreeing with the objection and then proceed to show compensating advantages.
>
> Pass-up method: Acknowledge the concern expressed by the prospect and then move on.

MAKING THE SALES PRESENTATION

Salespeople must adapt their sales approach to customers' needs. A "canned" sales talk will not succeed with most buyers. For example, a person selling personal computers must demonstrate the capacity of the equipment to fill a customer's particular needs. Similarly, a boat salesperson must understand the special interests of particular customers and "speak their language." Every sales objection must be answered explicitly and adequately.

Successful selling involves a number of psychological elements. Personal enthusiasm, friendliness, and persistence are required. Approximately 20 percent of all salespeople secure as much as 80 percent of all sales because they bring these elements to the task of selling.

Some salespeople have special sales techniques that they use with success. One automobile salesperson, for example, offered free driving lessons to people who had never taken a driver's training course or who needed a few more lessons before they felt confident enough to take the required driving tests. When such customers were ready to take the driving tests, this salesperson would accompany them to the examination grounds to provide moral support. Needless to say, these special efforts were greatly appreciated by new drivers who were in the market for cars.

How you handle objections during a sales presentation is also critical. Following are some examples of how Dann Ilicic, of Wow! A Branding Company, responds to potential roadblocks to a successful sales presentation.[12]

1. **"We can't afford your price."** Dann's response: We present three price options in our proposals. If they still say we're too expensive, that means we haven't demonstrated the value of what we're doing. Nothing's expensive if it provides you a return greater than the cost.
2. **"You guys are too small."** Dann's response: "Those guys are too big. You're a small piece of business to them; to us, you'd be huge."
3. **"We can't do it now. Come back in a year."** Dann's response: I ask, "What would it take for you to make a decision right now?" If it's "We don't have the money, "I say,"Okay, what if you could pay us in six months?" You can tell if they're just hedging.

COST CONTROL IN PERSONAL SELLING

Both economical and wasteful methods exist for achieving the same volume of sales. For example, routing travelling salespeople economically and making appointments prior to arrival can conserve time and transportation expenses. The cost of an outside sales call on a customer is likely to be considerable—perhaps hundreds of dollars—so efficient scheduling is crucial. Moreover, a salesperson for a manufacturing firm, say, can contribute to cost economy by stressing products whose increased sales would give the factory a more balanced production run. Similarly, a salesperson can increase profits by emphasizing high-margin products.

CUSTOMER GOODWILL AND RELATIONSHIP SELLING

A salesperson must look beyond the immediate sale to building customer goodwill and creating satisfied customers who will patronize the company in the future. *Relationship selling* is enhanced when a salesperson displays a good appearance, has a pleasant personality, and uses professional etiquette in all contacts with customers. A salesperson can also build goodwill by understanding the customer's point of view. Courtesy, attention to details, and genuine friendliness will help gain the customer's acceptance.

THE COMPENSATION PROGRAM FOR SALESPEOPLE

Salespeople are compensated in two ways for their efforts—financially and nonfinancially. A good compensation program allows its participants to work for both forms of reward, while recognizing that salespeople's goals may be different from entrepreneurs' goals.

NONFINANCIAL REWARDS
Personal recognition and the satisfaction of reaching a sales quota are examples of nonfinancial rewards recognized by salespeople. Small retail businesses sometimes post the photograph of the top salesperson of the week or the month for all to see. Engraved plaques are also given as a more permanent record of sales achievements.

FINANCIAL REWARDS

Typically, financial compensation is the more critical factor for salespeople. Two basic plans used for financial compensation are commissions and straight salary. Each plan has specific advantages and limitations for the small firm.

Most small businesses would prefer to use commissions as compensation, because such an approach is simple and directly related to productivity. Usually, a certain percentage of the sales generated by the salesperson will be allocated to her or his commission. A commission plan thereby incorporates a strong incentive into the selling activities—no sale, no commission! Also, with this type of plan, there is less drain on the firm's cash flow until a sale is made. Billy Ross, who owns a recreational vehicle (RV) dealership replaced a weekly salary plan for his salespeople with a compensation plan that is more motivational. Salespeople earn cash (up to a certain maximum amount) for each customer whose information is captured for a marketing database, plus a generous 20 percent commission on any RVs sold.[13]

The straight salary form of compensation provides salespeople with more security because their level of compensation is ensured, regardless of sales made. However, working for a straight salary can potentially reduce a salesperson's motivation.

Combining the two forms of compensation creates the most attractive plan for a small business. It is a common practice to structure combination plans so that salary represents the larger part of compensation for a new salesperson. As the salesperson gains experience, the ratio is adjusted to provide more money from commissions and less from salary.

PROMOTIONAL SPENDING

4 Discuss methods of determining the appropriate level of promotional expenditure.

Unfortunately, no mathematical formula can answer the question "How much should a small business spend on promotion?" There are, however, helpful common-sense approaches to budgeting funds for small business promotion:

- Allocating a percentage of sales
- Deciding how much can be spared
- Spending as much as the competition does
- Determining what it will take to do the job

ALLOCATING A PERCENTAGE OF SALES

A simple method of determining how much to budget for promotion is to earmark promotional dollars based on a percentage of sales. A firm's own past experiences should be evaluated to establish a promotion-to-sales ratio. If 2 percent of sales, for example, has historically been spent on promotion, the firm should budget 2 percent of forecasted sales for promotion. Secondary data on industry averages can be used for comparison. One source that reports what firms are doing with their advertising dollars is *Advertising Age*. The *Financial Performance Indicators* (FPI), published by Statistics Canada, are available at most campus libraries, and large public libraries. The FPI provide a breakdown of expenses as a percentage of sales, and are compiled into several categories including firms with sales of $25 million and less and those with sales of $5 million and less. Performance Plus, available online at http://www.sme.ic.gc.ca, provides financial and employment data on 600 small business sectors.

A major shortcoming of this method is an inherent tendency to spend more on promotion when sales are increasing and less when they are declining. If promotion stimulates sales, then reducing promotional spending when sales are down can be disastrous. New firms, or those moving to a new location, should also increase their budget as a percentage of sales.

DECIDING HOW MUCH CAN BE SPARED

Another piecemeal approach to promotional budgeting widely used by small firms is to spend whatever is left over when all other activities have been funded. The decision about promotional spending might be made only when a media representative sells an owner on a special deal that the business can afford. Such an approach to promotional spending should be avoided because it ignores promotional goals.

SPENDING AS MUCH AS THE COMPETITION DOES

Sometimes a small firm builds a promotional budget based on that of the competition. If the business can duplicate the promotional mix of close competitors, it will at least be reaching the same customers and be spending as much as the competition. Obviously, if a competitor is a large business, this approach is not feasible. However, it can be used to react to short-run promotional tactics by small competitors. Unfortunately, this approach results in the copying of competitors' mistakes as well as their successes, although it may enable a firm to remain competitive.

DETERMINING WHAT IT WILL TAKE TO DO THE JOB

The preferred approach to estimating promotional expenditures is to decide what it will take to do the job. This method requires a comprehensive analysis of the market and the promotional alternatives. If reasonably accurate estimates are used, the amount that needs to be spent can be determined.

The best way for a small business to estimate promotional costs incorporates all four approaches, as represented by Exhibit 7-6. Start with an estimate of what it will take to do the job, and then compare this amount with a predetermined percentage of forecasted sales. Next, estimate what can be spared before examining what the competition is spending. Finally, make a decision regarding how much money the firm will budget for promotional purposes.

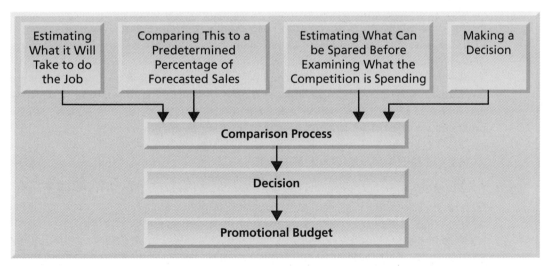

EXHIBIT **7-6** *Four-Step Method for Determining a Promotional Budget*

CREATING A PRICING STRATEGY

Because a product or service must be priced before it can be sold, deciding on pricing is a necessary task in small business marketing. The **price** of a product or service specifies what the seller requires for transferring ownership or use of that product or service. Often, the seller must extend credit to make the product or service more competitive. **Credit** involves an agreement between buyer and seller that payment for a product or service will be received at some later date.

Pricing and credit decisions are vital, because they affect both revenue and cash flow. Care must always be exercised in making such decisions, because customers dislike price increases and restrictive credit policies.

SETTING A PRICE

In setting a price, the seller decides the most appropriate price for a product. Setting a price would be easy if it weren't so important to do it systematically. Because total sales revenue depends on just two components—sales volume and price—even a small change in price can drastically influence revenue. Consider the following situations (where, to emphasize the point, we assume no change in demand):

Situation A

Quantity Sold	×	Price per Unit	=	Gross Revenue
250,000	×	$3.00	=	$750,000

Situation B

Quantity Sold	×	Price per Unit	=	Gross Revenue
250,000	×	$2.80	=	$700,000

The price per unit in Situation B is only $0.20 lower than that in Situation A. However, the total reduction in revenue is $50,000! Clearly, a small business can lose significant revenues if a price is set too low.

Pricing is also important because it indirectly affects sales quantity. In the above example, quantity sold was assumed to be independent of price—and it very well may be for a change in price from $3.00 to $2.80. However, a larger decrease or increase might substantially affect the quantity sold. Pricing, therefore, has a dual influence on total sales revenue. It is important *directly* as one part of the gross revenue equation and *indirectly* through its impact on quantity demanded.

Before beginning a more detailed analysis of pricing, we should note that services are more difficult to price than products because of the intangible nature of services. Estimating the cost of providing a service and the demand for that service can be problematic at best. Thus, the discussions in this chapter focus on product pricing.

COST DETERMINATION FOR PRICING

For a business to be successful, its pricing must cover total cost plus some profit margin. Pricing, therefore, must be based on an understanding of the basic behaviour of costs. As illustrated in Exhibit 7-7 **total cost** includes three components. The first is the cost of goods offered for sale. An appliance retailer, for example, must include in the selling price the cost of the appliance and related freight charges. The second component is the selling cost, which includes the direct cost of the salesperson's time (salary plus

price
a specification of what a seller requires in exchange for transferring ownership or use of a product or service

credit
an agreement between a buyer and seller that provides for a delayed payment for a product or service

total cost
the sum of cost of goods sold, selling expenses, and overhead costs

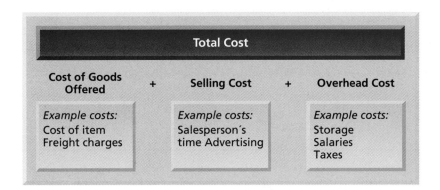

commissions), as well as the cost of other selling activities such as advertising and sales promotion. The third component is the overhead cost applicable to the given product. Included in this cost are warehouse storage, office supplies, utilities, taxes, and salaries. *All* of these cost classifications must be incorporated into the pricing process.

Costs behave differently as the quantity produced or sold increases or decreases. **Total variable costs** are those that increase in total as the quantity of product increases. Material costs and sales commissions are typical variable costs incurred as a product is made and sold. **Total fixed costs** are those that remain constant at different levels of quantity sold. For example, advertising campaign expenditures, factory equipment costs, and salaries of office personnel are fixed costs.

An understanding of the behaviour of different kinds of costs can help a seller minimize pricing mistakes. Although fixed and variable costs do not behave in the same way, small businesses often treat them identically. An approach called **average pricing** exemplifies this dangerous practice. With average pricing, you divide the total cost over a previous period by the quantity sold in that period to arrive at an average cost, which is then used to set the current price. For example, consider the cost structure of a firm selling 25,000 units of a product in 2009 at a sales price of $8.00 each (see Exhibit 7-8). The average unit cost at the sales volume of 25,000 units is $5.00 (that is, $125 000/25,000). The $3.00 markup provides a satisfactory profit at this sales volume (25,000 × $3 = $75,000).

However, consider the impact on profit if sales in 2010 reach only 10,000 units and the selling price has been set at the same $3.00 markup, based on 2009's average cost (see Exhibit 7-9). At the lower sales volume (10,000 units), the average unit cost increases to $9.50 (that is, 95,000/10,000). This increase is, of course, attributable to the need to spread the constant fixed cost over fewer units. The business has lost money. *Average pricing overlooks the reality of higher average costs at lower sales levels.*

total variable costs
costs that vary with the quantity produced or sold

total fixed costs
costs that remain constant as the quantity produced or sold varies

average pricing
an approach in which total cost for a given period is divided by quantity sold in that period to set a price

EXHIBIT **7-8**
*Cost Structure of a
Hypothetical Firm,
2009*

Sales revenue (25,000 units @ $8)		$200,000
Total costs:		
Fixed costs	$75,000	
Variable costs ($2 per unit)	50,000	
		125,000
Gross margin		$75,000

Average cost $= \dfrac{\$125,000}{25,000} = \$5$

EXHIBIT **7-9**

Cost Structure of a
Hypothetical Firm, 2010

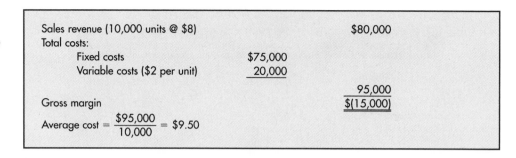

Sales revenue (10,000 units @ $8) $80,000
Total costs:
     Fixed costs $75,000
     Variable costs ($2 per unit)   20,000

                                                95,000
Gross margin $(15,000)

Average cost $= \dfrac{\$95,000}{10,000} = \$9.50$

Under certain circumstances, pricing at less than total cost can be used as a special short-term strategy. Suppose some fixed costs are ongoing even if part of the production facility is idle. In this situation, pricing should cover all marginal or incremental costs—that is, those costs incurred specifically to get additional business. In the long run, however, all costs must be covered.

6 Apply break-even analysis and markup pricing.

APPLYING A PRICING SYSTEM

BREAK-EVEN ANALYSIS

Break-even analysis involves comparing alternative cost and revenue estimates in order to determine the acceptability of each price. A comprehensive break-even analysis has two phases: (1) examining revenue–cost relationships and (2) incorporating actual sales forecasts into the analysis. Break-even analysis is typically presented by means of formulas or graphs; this discussion uses a graphic presentation.

EXAMINING COST AND REVENUE RELATIONSHIPS

The objective of the first phase of break-even analysis is to determine the quantity at which the product, at an assumed price, will generate enough revenue to start earning a profit. Exhibit 7-10a presents a simple break-even chart reflecting this comparison.

EXHIBIT **7-10**

Break-Even Graphs
for Pricing

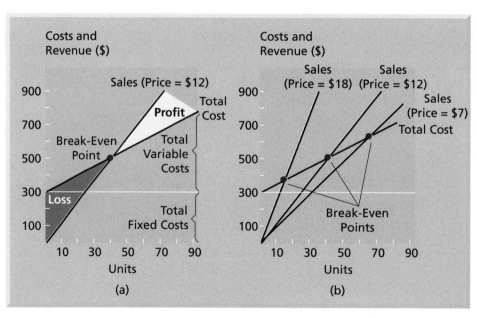

Total fixed costs are represented by a horizontal section at the bottom of the graph, indicating that they do not change with the volume of production. The section for total variable costs is a triangle that slants upward, depicting the direct relationship of total variable costs to output. The entire area between the upward-slanting total cost line and the horizontal base line thus represents the combination of fixed and variable costs. The distance between the sales and total cost lines gives the profit or loss position of the company at any level of sales. The point of intersection of these two lines is called the **break-even point,** because sales revenue equals total cost at this sales volume.

To evaluate other break-even points, additional sales lines for other prices can be plotted on the chart. On the flexible break-even chart shown in Exhibit 7-10b, the assumed higher price of $18 yields a more steeply sloped sales line, resulting in an earlier break-even point. Similarly, the lower price of $7 produces a flatter revenue line, delaying the break-even point. Additional sales lines could be plotted to evaluate other proposed prices.

Because it shows the profit area growing larger and larger to the right, the break-even chart implies that quantity sold can increase continually. This assumption is unrealistic and should be clarified by modifying the break-even analysis with demand information.

break-even point
sales volume at which total sales revenue equals total costs

BREAK-EVEN CALCULATION

$$\text{Break-Even Point (in units)} = \frac{\text{Total Fixed Costs}}{\text{Per-Unit Contribution to Fixed Costs}}$$

$$= \frac{\text{Total Fixed Costs}}{\text{Price per Unit} - \text{Variable Costs Per Unit}}$$

and

$$\text{Break-Even Point (in dollars)} = \frac{\text{Total Fixed Costs}}{\left(1 - \dfrac{\text{Variable Cost per Unit}}{\text{Selling Price per Unit}}\right)}$$

To put these equations in short form, let BP = the break-even point, TFC = the total fixed costs, VC = variable costs per unit, and P = price per unit. Then,

$$BP \text{ (units)} = \frac{TFC}{P - VC}$$

$$BP \text{ (\$)} = \frac{TFC}{\left(1 - \dfrac{VC}{P}\right)}$$

EXAMPLE

Your company will make and sell gift baskets from a retail location. Annual fixed costs (rent, phone, fax, accounting fees, insurance, etc.) are $40,000. You sell the gift baskets for $25 each, and the variable costs per basket (your cost for the basket, contents) and wages of the person who puts them together for you) are $14.00. What is your break-even point in units and dollars?

$$BP \text{ units} = \frac{TFC}{P - VC} = \frac{40,000}{25 - 14} = 3,636.36 \text{ (rounded up to 3,637)}$$

gift baskets you must sell each year to break even (not lose money)

$$BP\ (\$) = \frac{TFC}{\left(1 - \dfrac{VC}{P}\right)} = \frac{40,000}{\left(1 - \dfrac{14}{25}\right)} = \frac{40,000}{1 - .56} = \frac{40,000}{.44}$$

$$= \$90,909.09 \text{ of revenues you must earn to break even}$$

Proof: 3,637 units $\times$ \$25.00 = \$90,925 (difference due to rounding)

If you can't calculate the per unit costs, you have to use total revenues and cost of goods sold from the income statement to calculate break-even in dollars.

INCORPORATING SALES FORECASTS

The indirect impact of price on quantity sold complicates pricing decisions. Demand for a product typically decreases as price increases. However, in certain cases, price may influence demand in the opposite direction, resulting in increased demand for a product at higher prices. Therefore, estimated demand for a product at various prices, as determined through marketing research, should be incorporated into the break-even analysis.

An adjusted break-even chart that incorporates estimated demand is developed by using the initial break-even data and adding a demand curve. A schedule showing the estimated number of units demanded and total revenue at three prices is shown in Exhibit 7-11, along with a break-even chart on which a demand curve is plotted from these data. This graph allows a more realistic profit area to be identified. The break-even point for a unit price of \$18 corresponds to a quantity sold that appears impossible to reach at the assumed price, leaving \$7 and \$12 as feasible prices. Clearly, the preferred price is \$12. The potential for profit at this price is indicated by the shaded area in the graph.

MARKUP PRICING

Up to this point, we have made no distinction between pricing by manufacturers and pricing by intermediaries such as wholesalers and retailers, since break-even concepts apply to all small businesses, regardless of their position in the distribution channel. Now, however, we briefly present some of the pricing formulas used by wholesalers and retailers.

EXHIBIT **7-11**

A Break-Even Graph Adjusted for Estimated Demand

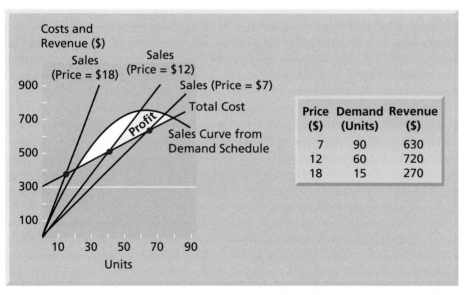

Price ($)	Demand (Units)	Revenue ($)
7	90	630
12	60	720
18	15	270

In the retailing industry, where businesses often carry many different products, markup pricing has emerged as a manageable pricing system. With this cost-plus approach to pricing, retailers are able to price hundreds of products much more quickly than they could using individual break-even analyses. In calculating the selling price for a particular item, a retailer adds a markup percentage (sometimes referred to as a markup rate) to cover the following:

- Operating expenses
- Subsequent price reductions—for example, markdowns and employee discounts
- Desired profit

It is important to have a clear understanding of markup pricing computations. Markups may be expressed as a percentage of either the *selling price* or the *cost*. For example, if an item costs $6 and sells for $10, the markup of $4 represents a 40 percent markup on the selling price:

$$\frac{\$4\ (markup)}{\$10\ (selling\ price)} \times 100$$

or $66\frac{2}{3}$ *percent of the cost:*

$$\frac{\$4\ (markup)}{\$6\ (cost)} \times 100.$$ *Two simple formulas are commonly used per markup calculations:*

$$\frac{Markup}{Selling\ Price} \times 100 = Markup\ expressed\ as\ a\ percentage\ of\ selling\ price$$

$$\frac{Markup}{Cost} \times 100 = Markup\ expressed\ as\ a\ percentage\ of\ cost$$

To convert markup as a percentage of selling price to markup as a percentage of cost, use the following formula:

$$\frac{Markup\ as\ a\ percentage\ of\ selling\ price}{100\%} - Markup\ as\ a\ percentage\ of\ selling\ price \times 100$$

$$= Markup\ as\ a\ percentage\ of\ cost$$

To convert the other way, use this formula:

$$\frac{Markup\ as\ a\ percentage\ of\ cost}{100\%} - Markup\ as\ a\ percentage\ of\ cost \times 100$$

$$= Markup\ as\ a\ percentage\ of\ selling\ price$$

SELECTING A PRICING STRATEGY

Identify specific pricing strategies and create a price quality grid. **7**

Although techniques such as break-even analysis yield a good idea of a feasible price for a specific product, their seemingly precise nature is potentially misleading. Such analyses are only one kind of tool for pricing and should not by themselves determine the final price. Price determination must also include consideration of market characteristics and the firm's current marketing strategy. Pricing strategies that reflect these additional considerations include penetration pricing, skimming pricing, follow-the-leader pricing, variable pricing, flexible pricing, bundling, price lining, and what the market will bear.[14]

PENETRATION PRICING

penetration pricing strategy
a marketing approach that sets lower than normal prices to hasten market acceptance of a product or service, or to increase market share

A firm that uses a **penetration pricing strategy** prices a product or service at less than its normal, long-range market price in order to gain more rapid market acceptance or to increase existing market share. This strategy can sometimes discourage new competitors from entering a market niche if they mistakenly view the penetration price as a long-range price. Obviously, a firm that uses this strategy sacrifices some profit margin to achieve market penetration. Mountain Crest is an example of a firm that has grown dramatically during the past five years by pursuing an aggressive penetration pricing strategy.

SKIMMING PRICING

skimming price strategy
a marketing approach that sets very high prices for a limited period before reducing them to more competitive levels

A **skimming price strategy** sets prices for products or services at high levels for a limited period of time before reducing prices to lower, more competitive levels. This strategy assumes that certain customers will pay a higher price because they view a product or service as a prestige item. Use of a skimming price is most practical when there is little threat of short-term competition or when start-up costs must be recovered rapidly.

FOLLOW-THE-LEADER PRICING

follow-the-leader pricing strategy
a marketing approach that uses a particular competitor as a model in setting prices

A **follow-the-leader pricing strategy** uses a particular competitor as a model in setting a price for a product or service. The probable reaction of competitors is a critical factor in determining whether to cut prices below a prevailing level. A small business in competition with larger firms is seldom in a position to consider itself the price leader. If competitors view a small firm's pricing as relatively unimportant, they may permit a price differential to exist. On the other hand, some competitors may view a smaller price-cutter as a direct threat and counter with reductions of their own. In such a case, the use of a follow-the-leader pricing strategy accomplishes very little.

prestige pricing
setting a high price to convey an image of high quality or uniqueness

Prestige pricing entails setting a high price to convey an image of high quality or uniqueness. Its influence varies from market to market and product to product. Because higher-income markets are less sensitive to price variations than lower-income ones, prestige pricing typically works better in these markets. Products sold in markets with low levels of product knowledge are good candidates for prestige pricing. When customers know very little about product characteristics, they often use price as an indicator of quality. An example of pricing based on competitive advantage is found in the microwave popcorn market. In this market niche, customers are willing to pay a premium price for the convenience of microwave packaging—up to six times the price of conventional popcorn.[15]

IN THE TRENCHES

Entrepreneurial Experiences

Crafting Success: Minhas Craft Brewery

Just more than a decade ago, flat sales and a heavy debt load forced Huber Brewing into Chapter 11 bankruptcy protection. Today, the oldest brewery in this state known for its prominent role in the U.S. beer industry is rapidly expanding thanks mainly to the unquenchable thirst among Canadians for cheap, cleverly marketed beer.

Now known as Minhas Craft Brewery, the former Huber brewery recently marked its first anniversary under the control of Ravinder and Manjit Minhas, two young Canadian siblings of Indian descent. The Minhases operate Calgary, Alberta-based Mountain Crest Brewing Corp., which brews its beer in Monroe before exporting most of it to Canada. Ravinder, 25, and his sister, Manjit, 27, launched Mountain Crest Brewing in 2002. Their company has stirred the Canadian brewing industry by under-pricing the country's two dominant players, Molson Coors Brewing Co. and Labatt Breweries of Canada.

Monroe, with a population of less than 11,000, has played a key part in that story. Mountain Crest Brewing hired Huber in 2003 to brew its beer. By contracting out production, the Minhases saved money. Within a few years, the Minhases decided to buy the Monroe brewery to ensure a long-term production source. Mountain Crest in September 2006 announced its impending purchase of the brewery, and some of the Huber Brewing brands, including Huber, Rhinelander and Wisconsin Club. The price was not disclosed, but the cost of building a similar brewery would have been just less than $100 million, Manjit said.

Under new ownership, the relabeled Minhas Craft Brewery has undergone $2 million in improvements, including a new warehouse, additional production equipment and a revamped tap room that opened in September. The brewery is launching new products, including iEnergy, an energy drink, and Lazy Mutt, aimed at the craft beer market.

Minhas Craft Brewery also does contract brewing. Much of the brewery's production still is devoted to Mountain Crest beer and other low-cost brands. The company's sales are expected to grow when Mountain Crest, now sold mainly in Alberta and other Western provinces, makes its long-delayed entry by 2008 into Ontario which accounts for 38 percent of Canada's population. For years, provincial regulators have blocked Mountain Crest Brewing attempts to sell beer in Ontario. Manjit said the reasons have varied, including the company's outsourcing of its beer production. Buying the Monroe brewery solved that problem, she said.

Building the new warehouse allows Minhas Craft Brewery to more efficiently produce, store and ship beer, including overseas exports, Manjit Minhas said. The company hopes to begin shipping Mountain Crest beer to Japan in November, she said.

Annual production at Minhas Craft Brewery, with around 75 employees, could reach 250,000 barrels by the end of 2007 and soar to 350,000 barrels by the end of 2008, Ravinder said. The Monroe facility has more than doubled its work force since the Minhases came to town four years ago.

The Minhases started Mountain Crest Liquors when Manjit saw an opportunity to import inexpensive spirits into Canada. A few years later, they entered the beer business with a similar low-cost model. After hiring a brewmaster to create formulas for Mountain Crest and other brands, the Minhases began searching for a brewery. Rebuffed by Canadian brewers, who didn't want to help a competitor, they hired Huber. Mountain Crest Brewing ran local TV ads protesting high beer prices. The Minhases also played up the David vs. Goliath theme in their highly publicized clashes with Molson and Labatt. Mountain Crest Brewing, with annual revenue of $55 million, has irritated its competitors. Molson sued in 2002, claiming the label for the Mountain Crest brand copied the label for its Molson Pilsner brand. The dispute was settled out of court.

Source: McClatchy-Tribune "Crafting Success: Duo Hops to Service in Old Brewery" (October 20, 2007) at http://www.GazetteXtra.com/news/2007/oct/20/crafting-success-duo-hops-service-old-brewery (accessed August 8, 2008).

VARIABLE PRICING

variable pricing strategy
a marketing approach that sets more than one price for a good or service in order to offer price concessions to certain customers

Some businesses use a **variable pricing strategy** to offer price concessions to certain customers, even though they may advertise a uniform price. Concessions are made for various reasons, including a customer's knowledge and bargaining strength. In some fields of business, therefore, firms make two-part pricing decisions: they both set a standard list price and offer a range of price concessions to particular buyers.

FLEXIBLE PRICING

flexible pricing strategy
a marketing approach that offers different prices to reflect differences in customer demand

Instead of using total cost as the basis for their pricing decisions, firms with a **flexible pricing strategy** take into consideration special market conditions and the pricing practices of competitors. The following example illustrates this point:

> The owner of a high-speed ferry service always charged $10 for a round-trip ticket between any two destinations. But the ferry was losing money due to low ridership during off-peak hours. The owner decided to differentiate her prices depending on the time of day, the type of rider, and the competing modes of transportation in each of the ferry's destinations, such as cars, buses and commuter trains.
>
> She raised her round-trip price to an average of $12 during commuter and weekend hours—the ferry's busiest times. . . . For frequent users who couldn't afford the higher rate, she sold monthly passes that resulted in a round-trip price of less than $10. Off-peak riders, however, tended to view the ferry as simply a convenient way to get from one place to another. Thus, the owner lowered the price to an average of $8 during off-peak hours. As a result, ridership and revenues rose considerably and an annual loss became an annual profit.[16]

BUNDLING

A bundling strategy involves offering several products for one combined price. Commonly used in the spa or software/hardware industries, the strategy is useful for moving higher volumes. For example, a spa may combine a facial, manicure, pedicure, and massage session to create a "Mother's Day Special" package. Bundling is a useful pricing strategy when

- There are economics of scale in either production or distribution.
- Customers appreciate a simplified purchase decision, for example a "Valentine's Day" package.
- The marginal costs of bundling are low.
- High-volume, high-margin products are being sold.

PRICE LINING

price-lining strategy
a marketing approach that sets a range of several distinct merchandise price levels

A **price-lining strategy** determines several distinct prices at which similar items of retail merchandise are offered for sale. For example, men's suits (of differing quality) might be sold at $250, $450, and $800. The inventory level of the different lines depends on the income level and buying desires of a store's customers. A price-lining strategy has the advantage of simplifying choice for the customer and reducing the necessary minimum inventory.

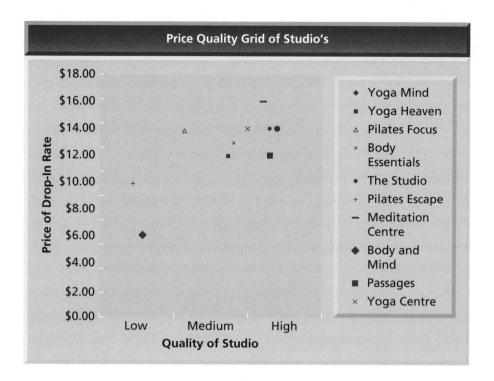

EXHIBIT **7-12**
*Price Quality Grid for a
Yoga and Pilates Studio*

FINAL NOTES ON PRICE STRATEGIES

The relative competitive position of products or services can be depicted using a **price quality grid,** which indicates which items may be "overpriced" or "underpriced" relative to their quality and the competition. The grid requires an assessment of the relative quality of direct competitors. See Exhibit 7-12 for an example of a price quality grid for Yoga and Pilates studios. Note that the studios were evaluated for quality using the following criteria: range of classes available, quality of instruction, atmosphere, ease of location for customers, availability of parking, specialty classes provided, ease of registration, and overall service. Price was based upon the drop-in rate for one class, but could also have been evaluated upon a monthly rate.

It should be noted that companies or products that want to be perceived as offering "value" should be on line with the competition, or to the right of the "value" line. Products higher, or to the left of the "value line," would be perceived as charging too much relative to their quality.

In some situations, local and federal laws must also be considered in setting prices. For example, the federal *Competition Act* generally prohibits price fixing. Most federal pricing legislation is intended to benefit small firms as well as consumers by keeping large businesses from conspiring to set prices that stifle competition. When a small business markets a line of products, some of which may compete with each other, pricing decisions must take into account the effects of a single product price on the rest of the line. For example, the introduction of a cheese-flavoured chip will likely affect sales of an existing flavoured chip. Pricing can become extremely complex in these situations.

price quality grid
A grid that displays the relative positions of competitive products and the value they deliver

LOOKING BACK

1 Describe the communication process and the factors determining a promotional mix.

- Every communication involves a source, a message, a channel, and a receiver.
- A promotional mix is a blend of personal and nonpersonal communication techniques.
- A promotional mix is influenced by three important factors: the geographical nature of the market, target customers, and the product's characteristics.

2 Identify advertising options for a small business.

- Common advertising media include television, radio, magazines, newspapers, billboards, and the Internet.
- Product advertising is designed to promote a product or service, while institutional advertising conveys an idea regarding the business itself.
- A small firm must decide how often to advertise, where to advertise, and what the message will be.
- A firm's Web advertising generally takes the form of banner ads and pop-ups, email campaigns, sponsorships and linkages, and a corporate website.

3 Discuss the use of sales promotion tools and describe personal selling activities.

- Sales promotion includes all promotional techniques other than personal selling and advertising.
- Typically, sales promotional tools should be used along with advertising and personal selling.
- Widely used sales promotional tools are specialties, contests, premiums, trade show exhibits, point-of-purchase displays, free merchandise, sampling, and coupons.
- A sales presentation is a process involving prospecting, practising the presentation, and then making the presentation.
- Salespeople are compensated for their efforts in two ways—financially and nonfinancially.
- The two basic plans for financial compensation are commissions and straight salary, but the most attractive plan for a small firm combines the two.

4 Discuss methods of determining the appropriate level of promotional expenditure.

- Earmarking promotional dollars based on a percentage of sales is a simple method for determining expenditures.

- Spending only what can be spared is a widely used approach to promotional budgeting.
- Spending as much as the competition does is a way to react to short-term promotional tactics of competitors.
- The preferred approach to determining promotional expenditures is to decide what it will take to do the job, while factoring in elements used in the other methods.

5 Discuss the role of cost and demand factors in setting a price.

- The revenue of a firm is a direct reflection of two components: sales volume and price.
- When setting a price, a firm should examine the relationship of price and quality demanded.

6 Apply break-even analysis and markup pricing.

- Analyzing costs and revenue under different price assumptions identifies the break-even point: the quantity sold so that total costs equal total revenue.
- Markup pricing is a generalized cost-plus system of pricing used by intermediaries with many products.

7 Identify specific pricing strategies and create a price quality grid

- Penetration pricing and skimming pricing are short-term strategies used when new products are first introduced into the market.
- Follow-the-leader, variable, and flexible pricing are special strategies that reflect the nature of the competition's pricing and concessions to customers.
- A price-lining strategy simplifies choices for customers by offering a range of several distinct prices.
- Provincial and federal laws must be considered in setting prices, as well as any impact that a price may have on other product-line items.
- A price quality grid can be created to illustrate the relative competitive position of your product to your competitors.

KEY TERMS

advertising, p. 171
average pricing, p. 191
banner ads, p. 175
break-even point, p. 193
credit, p. 190
e-mail promotion, p. 176
flexible pricing strategy, p. 198
follow-the-leader pricing
  strategy, p. 196
institutional advertising, p. 172
linkage, p. 176

penetration pricing
  strategy, p. 196
personal selling, p. 185
pop-up ads, p. 175
prestige pricing, p. 196
price, p. 190
price quality grid, p. 199
price-lining strategy, p. 198
product advertising, p. 172
promotion, p. 170
promotional mix, p. 170

prospecting, p. 185
publicity, p. 184
sales promotion, p. 180
skimming price strategy, p. 196
total cost, p. 190
total fixed costs, p. 191
total variable costs, p. 191
variable pricing strategy, p. 198
Web sponsorship, p. 176

DISCUSSION QUESTIONS

1. Discuss the advantages and disadvantages of different approaches to budgeting funds for promotion.

2. Outline a system of prospecting that could be used by a small camera store. Incorporate all the techniques presented in this chapter.

3. Why are a salesperson's techniques for handling objections so important to a successful sales presentation?

4. Assume you have the opportunity to "sell" your course instructor on the idea of eliminating final examinations. Make a list of the objections you expect to hear from your instructor, and describe how you will handle each objection, using some of the techniques on page 187 of this chapter.

5. What are some nonfinancial rewards that could be offered to salespeople?

6. What are the advantages and disadvantages of compensating salespeople by salary? By commissions? What do you think is an acceptable compromise?

7. What are the four basic approaches to advertising on the Internet?

8. How can the concept of a strategic alliance be used in promotional strategy?

9. How do specialties differ from trade show exhibits and publicity? Be specific.

10. If a firm has fixed costs of $100,000 and variable costs per unit of $1, what is the break-even point in units, assuming a selling price of $5 per unit?

11. What is the difference between a penetration pricing strategy and a skimming price strategy? Under what circumstances would each be used?

12. If a small business has conducted its break-even analysis properly and finds break-even volume at a price of $10 to be 10,000 units, should it price its product at $10? Why or why not?

13. What is a price quality grid, and why would preparing one help in selecting a price?

YOU MAKE THE CALL

SITUATION 1

The driving force behind Cannon Arp's new business was several bad experiences with his car—two speeding tickets and four minor fender-benders. Consequently, his insurance rates more than doubled, which resulted in Arp's idea to design and sell a bumper sticker that read "To Report Bad Driving, Call My Parents at . . ." With a $200 investment, Arp printed 15,000 of the stickers, which contain space to write in the appropriate telephone number. He is now planning a promotion to support his strategy of distribution through auto parts stores.

Question 1 What role, if any, should personal selling have in Arp's total promotional plan?

Question 2 Arp is considering advertising in magazines. What do you think about this medium for promoting his product?

Question 3 How might publicity be useful for selling Arp's stickers? Be specific.

SITUATION 2

Cheree Moore owns and operates a small business that supplies delicatessens with bulk containers of ready-made salads. When displayed in cases, the salads appear to have been freshly prepared at the delicatessen. Moore wants additional promotional exposure for her products and is considering using her fleet of trucks as rolling billboards. If the strategy is successful, she may even attempt to lease space on other trucks. Moore is concerned about the cost-effectiveness of the idea and whether the public will even notice the advertisements. She also wonders whether the image of her salad products might be hurt by this advertising medium.

Question 1 What suggestions can you offer that would help Moore make this decision?

Question 2 How could Moore go about determining the cost-effectiveness of this strategy?

Question 3 What additional factors should Moore evaluate before advertising on trucks?

SITUATION 3

If people are willing to pay to have groceries delivered to their home, why not high-fashion clothing? This type of thinking is what led Claudine Gumbel and her husband, Brian, to develop Caravan, a boutique-on-wheels that brings the latest in high fashion to people all over New York City. Their mobile "caravan" is stocked with merchandise from the trendiest designers. "People like the convenience of a shop that comes to them," comments Brian. "If an area doesn't work, we move on," he adds. Plans are to expand into Toronto and Vancouver soon. Sales for the NYC Caravan were expected to top $700,000 in 2006. It appears that the Gumbels' business has been given the green light.

Source: Karen Edwards, "Shop and Go," *Entrepreneur,* June 2006, p. 97.

Question 1 What might be the best ways for the Gumbels to promote their business in Canada?

Question 2 How can the Gumbels prospect for new customers?

Question 3 In what ways, if any, could the Gumbels use the Internet to promote their business?

EXPERIENTIAL EXERCISES

1. Interview the owners of one or more small businesses to determine how they develop their promotional budget. Classify the owners' methods into one or more of the approaches described in this chapter. Has the firm clearly tied their promotional activities to their targeted customers? Is every aspect of their promotional campaign effective? Report your findings to the class.

2. Plan a sales presentation. With a classmate role-playing a potential buyer, make the presentation in class. Ask the other students to critique your technique.

3. Create an ad for your favourite retail outlet. Select the media that would best fit its target market.

4. Find three ads competing for the same target market and analyze their relative effectiveness. Identify which media would be most effective in reaching the target market.

5. Evaluate the effectiveness of a public relations campaign of a local company.

6. Prepare a price quality grid by referring to three or four fast-food outlets at your college or university. Use the grid to determine if any of the outlets are not providing a good value, and which is providing the best value.

EXPLORING THE WEB

1. Find the website of a small Canadian firm in the adventure travel or information technology industries.
   a. What is unique about each firm's website?
   b. What criticisms can you offer regarding each site?

2. Refer to http://www.cardmedia.com. Select three advertising media, and compare their cost and reach.

Distribution Channels and Global Marketing

IN THE SPOTLIGHT

Guru Drinks March into the Big Apple

Craig Margulies is hoping to strike it rich in the grab-and-go beverage cases on the Upper East Side of Manhattan. A 36-year-old with a master's degree in industrial psychology, Mr. Margulies left a corporate career to become a sales representative for Guru Energy Drink, a new company started by a bunch of old Canadian high school pals.

Guru, which is already selling in Canada, is trying to crack the New York market by zipping around the city in electric minicars painted like Guru cans and hiring cheerful, attractive young women to offer samples at convenience stores, health clubs, supermarkets, and delis. But most of all, it is relying on the skills of salesmen like Mr. Margulies, who in three months on the job has received a quick education on how to win coveted shelf space in beverage cases around the city. It requires a gift for schmoozing, a comfortable pair of shoes and armour-like skin.

The nonalcoholic beverage market, in New York City and elsewhere, is tough. For decades, it was dominated by soft-drink giants Coke and Pepsi, with a few other brands scrambling for the leftovers. But the industry has radically changed in the past decade, as consumers have turned away from soft drinks amid concerns about their impact on health. An enormous variety of drinks, 100 or more even in small delis, have picked up the slack. Bottled water and Gatorade are big sellers, but there's also a rainbow of teas, flavoured waters, sparkling waters, carbonated juices, and yogurt smoothies. And energy drinks, where Guru contends it has found an opening by offering products with all natural and organic ingredients.

The four founders of the Guru beverage have a good story, but the ending remains far from certain. While creating a drink in a blender and finding a bottler is relatively easy and inexpensive, making it a successful brand is difficult. Guru's founders met in high school in Montreal and became close as their paths crossed again in later years. Eric Graveline became an investment banker and moved to New York, where he roomed with François Bazinet, a fashion model. Raymond Jolicoeur worked in Canada for several food and beverage companies, including Kraft and Allied Domecq, now part of Pernod Ricard. (A fifth partner, Eric Tomeo, joined later.)

In the late 1990s, Bazinet noticed energy drinks for sale in his travels in Europe and Japan and suggested to Jolicoeur that they introduce one in Canada. They began experimenting with drinks by mixing in botanical ingredients, including ginseng and guarana, that Bazinet had discovered during his travels. The inspiration for the name came from an article on Bill Gates, which described him as "the guru of technology."

"It was like, wow, you know, this should be the guru of all drinks, as strong as we can make it, as healthy as we can make it," Bazinet said. The company sold its first can of Guru at a small deli in Montreal in 2000. By the end of the first year of production, nearly one million cans had been sold, mostly in Montreal. By 2005, Guru was being sold across Canada, and the company was looking to sell in the United States. New York City was selected because it was the largest market, it was fairly similar to Montreal in terms of its many independent retailers, and Graveline was living there and preparing to retire from Wall Street.

The company's strategy in New York was similar to what worked in Montreal: trying to get the product into as many retail locations and company cafeterias as possible

Photo courtesy of GURU

in a small area to create buzz, and then expanding. That kind of small-scale approach works to a point, but eventually you need to have a good distributor. In New York, apart from the soda companies, much of that business is controlled by one company, Big Geyser. Guru chose Exclusive Beverage as its distributor, hoping Guru would receive more attention with a smaller company.

http://www.guruenergy.com

Source: Adapted from © 2007 CanWest Interactive, a division of CanWest MediaWorks Publications, Inc. and Andrew Martin, *The New York Times*, February 25, 2008.

As part of the marketing process, every product or service must be delivered to a customer. Until this physical exchange has been completed, purchasers cannot derive the benefits they seek. Therefore, a small firm's marketing system requires a distribution strategy to ensure that products arrive at the proper place at the correct moment for maximum customer satisfaction. Also, given today's global marketplace, small businesses may find opportunities in international marketing as they look beyond the domestic markets that have nurtured and sustained them. Guru, featured "In the Spotlight" highlights the role of distribution, as well as export opportunities. The key to success in New York, and other markets thereafter, is securing shelf space in retail outlets. This chapter examines distribution channels as well as several aspects of global marketing.

THE ROLE OF DISTRIBUTION ACTIVITIES IN MARKETING

Explain the role of distribution in marketing.

Entrepreneurs frequently consider distribution to be less glamorous than other marketing activities such as packaging, name selection, and promotion. Nevertheless, an effective distribution system is just as important to a small firm as a unique package, a clever name, or a creative promotional campaign. Prior to formalizing a distribution plan, a small business manager should understand and appreciate certain underlying principles of distribution, which apply to both domestic and international distribution.

DISTRIBUTION DEFINED

distribution
physically moving products and establishing intermediary channels to support such movement

physical distribution (logistics)
the activities involved in the physical movement of products

channel of distribution
a system of intermediaries that distribute a product

breaking bulk
an intermediary process that makes large quantities of product available in smaller amounts

In marketing, **distribution** encompasses both the physical movement of products and the establishment of intermediary (middleman) relationships to guide and support such product movement. The activities involved in the physical movement form a special field called **physical distribution,** or **logistics.** The intermediary relationships are called **channels of distribution.**

Distribution is essential for both tangible and intangible goods. Since distribution activities are more visible for tangible goods (products), our discussion will focus on them. Most intangible goods (services) are delivered directly to the user. An income tax preparer and a barber, for example, serve clients directly. However, marketing a person's labour can involve channel intermediaries, as when, for example, an employment agency is used to provide temporary employees for an employer.

FUNCTIONS OF INTERMEDIARIES
Intermediaries exist to carry out necessary marketing functions and can often perform these functions better than the producer or the user of a product. Let's consider a producer of fruitcakes as an example illustrating the need for intermediaries. This producer can perform its own distribution functions—such as delivery—if the geographic market is extremely small, if customers' needs are highly specialized, and if risk levels are low. However, intermediaries may be a more efficient means of distribution if, for example, customers are widely dispersed or a need exists for special packaging and storage. Of course, many types of small firms, such as retail stores, also function as intermediaries. Four main functions of intermediaries are breaking bulk, assorting, providing information, and shifting risks.

BREAKING BULK Few individual customers demand quantities that are equal to the amounts manufacturers produce. Therefore, channel activities known as **breaking bulk**

take the larger quantities produced and prepare them for individual customers. Wholesalers and retailers purchase large quantities from manufacturers, store these inventories, and then break bulk (sell them to customers in the quantities they desire).

ASSORTING Customers' needs are diverse, requiring many different products. Intermediaries facilitate shopping for a wide variety of goods through the assorting process. **Assorting** consists of bringing together homogeneous lines of goods into a heterogeneous assortment. For example, a small business that produces a special golf club can benefit from an intermediary that carries many other golf-related products and sells to retail pro shops. It is much more convenient for a pro shop manager to buy from one supplier than from dozens of individual producers.

PROVIDING INFORMATION One of the major benefits of using an intermediary is information. Intermediaries can provide a producer with helpful data on market size and pricing considerations, as well as information about other channel members. Intermediaries may even provide credit to final purchasers.

SHIFTING RISKS By using intermediaries called **merchant middlemen,** who take title to the goods they distribute, a small firm can often share or totally shift business risks. Other intermediaries, such as **agents and brokers,** do not take title to the goods.

TYPES OF CHANNELS OF DISTRIBUTION

A channel of distribution can be either direct or indirect. In a **direct channel** of distribution, there are no intermediaries; the product goes directly from producer to user. In an **indirect channel** of distribution, there may be one or more intermediaries between producer and user.

Exhibit 8-1 depicts the various options available for structuring a channel of distribution. Door-to-door retailing and web-based marketing are familiar forms of the direct channel system for distributing consumer goods. A growing trend in the in the past decade has been the growth of home parties to sell a wide range of consumer goods. The Pampered Chef offers high-end kitchen tools at in-home parties hosted by its independent kitchen consultants. A similar distribution system is used by Usborne Books Company, a supplier of educational children's books that has dramatically expanded, by offering home-based consultants commissions of 20 to 27% of sales in addition to "free" products. Refer to http://www.pamperedchef.com and http://www.usbornebooks.com. The remaining channels shown in Exhibit 8-1 are indirect channels involving one, two, or three levels of intermediaries. As a final consumer, you are naturally familiar with retailers. Likewise, industrial purchasers are equally familiar with industrial distributors. Channels with two or three stages of intermediaries are probably the most typical channels used by small firms that have large geographic markets. Note that a small firm may use more than one channel of distribution—a practice called **dual distribution.**

Firms that successfully employ a single distribution channel may switch to dual distribution if an additional channel will improve overall profitability. For example, Rayne Longboards symbolizes a standard manufacturer retail distribution by selling through retail outlets in North America and Europe. However, the company pursues multiple channels of distribution by also selling over the Internet. Refer to "In the Trenches." Many retailers have addressed the need for faster and easier-to-access shopping by offering online ordering of their products and services.

assorting
bringing together homogeneous lines of goods into a heterogeneous assortment

merchant middlemen
intermediaries that take title to the goods they distribute

agents and brokers
intermediaries that do not take title to the goods they distribute

direct channel
a distribution channel without intermediaries

indirect channel
a distribution channel with one or more intermediaries

dual distribution
a distribution system that involves more than one channel

EXHIBIT **8-1**
Alternative Channels
of Distribution

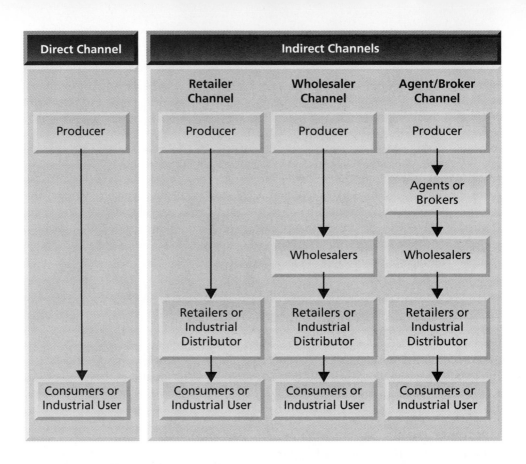

IN THE TRENCHES

Entrepreneurial Experiences

Effective Distribution

Rayne Longboards is an exporting success story. Although owner Graham Buksa launched the Vancouver-based manufacturing venture in April 2004, his dream began in 2002 with a new longboard (a longboard is a skateboard used for transportation cruising, and downhill racing) design sketch on a scrap of paper. Burke had planned to make a single longboard, but soon discovered software and machinery that would enable him to professionally prototype longboards.

In 2003, after making a number of skateboards, Buksa decided he loved doing it. He ordered wood, quit his job, and spent two months making 65 longboards. After enjoying a reasonably successful summer and receiving great industry reviews in the United States, he prepared a business plan and pursued his dream.

Rayne Longboards began by selling through 11 shops in Alberta and B.C. in 2004. By spring 2005, however, the company had secured worldwide distribution deals across Canada, Austria, Germany, Switzerland, the United States, and Japan.

Burke says his original business has led to other opportunities, such as a series of wheels. The company's long-term goals are to develop longboards using sustainable materials and to expand into ski and snowboard technology. For information about Rayne Longboards go to http://www.raynelongboards.com.

Source: http://www.raynelongboards.com, accessed March 15, 2008.

STRUCTURING A DISTRIBUTION SYSTEM

Describe the major considerations in structuring a distribution system. **2**

A firm that is starting from scratch and wants to shape its own distribution system needs to give attention to several important considerations.

BUILDING A CHANNEL OF DISTRIBUTION

There are three main factors in building a channel of distribution: costs, coverage, and control.

COSTS

Business managers should not think that a direct channel is inherently less expensive than an indirect channel just because there are no intermediaries. A small firm may well be in a situation in which the least expensive channel is indirect. For example, a firm producing handmade dolls will probably not own trucks and warehouses for distributing its product directly to customers but will rely on established intermediaries because of the lesser total cost of distribution. Small firms should also look at distribution costs as an investment—spending money in order to make money. They should ask themselves whether the money they "invest" in intermediaries (by selling the product to them at a reduced price) would get the job done if they used direct distribution.

COVERAGE

Small firms often use indirect channels of distribution to increase market coverage. Let's consider a small manufacturer whose sales force can make 10 contacts a week. This direct channel provides 10 contacts a week with the final users of the product. Now consider an indirect channel involving 10 industrial distributors, each making 10 contacts a week with the final users of the product. With this indirect channel, and no increase in the sales force, the small manufacturer is able to expose its product to 100 final users a week.

CONTROL

A third consideration in choosing a distribution channel is control. A direct channel of distribution provides more control. For example, Bernard Callebaut retains tight control over the manufacturing and distribution of his internationally recognized chocolates. The chocolates are created at a modern facility then shipped to retailers across North America. Control is maintained through a detailed distributorship agreement, as well as the use of mystery shoppers who ensure that product display and service complies with the Bernard Callebaut operating standards. Refer to http://www.bernardcallebaut.com for more information. With an indirect channel, a product may not be marketed as intended. As such, a small firm must select intermediaries that provide the desired support.

THE SCOPE OF PHYSICAL DISTRIBUTION

In addition to the intermediary relationships that make up a channel, there must also be a system of physical distribution. The main component of physical distribution is transportation. Additional components are storage, materials handling, delivery terms, and inventory management. The following sections briefly examine all these topics except inventory management, which is discussed in Chapter 12.

TRANSPORTATION

The major decision regarding transportation concerns what mode to use. Available modes of transportation are traditionally classified as airplanes, trucks, railroads, pipelines, and waterways. Each mode has unique advantages and disadvantages. The choice of a specific mode of transportation is based on several criteria: relative cost, transit time, reliability, capability, accessibility, and traceability.[1]

Transportation intermediaries are legally classified as common carriers, contract carriers, and private carriers. **Common carriers,** which are available for hire to the general public, and **contract carriers,** which engage in individual contracts with shippers, are subject to regulation by federal and/or provincial agencies. Shippers that own their means of transport are called **private carriers.**

common carriers
transportation intermediaries available for hire to the general public

contract carriers
transportation intermediaries that contract with individual shippers

private carriers
shippers that own their means of transport

STORAGE

Lack of space is a problem common to many small businesses. When a channel system uses merchant middlemen or wholesalers, for example, title to the goods is transferred, as is responsibility for the storage function. On other occasions, the small business must plan for its own warehousing. If a firm is too small to own a private warehouse, it can rent space in public warehouses. If storage requirements are simple and do not involve much special handling equipment, a public warehouse can provide economical storage.

MATERIALS HANDLING

A product is worth little if it is in the right place at the right time but is damaged. Therefore, a physical distribution system must arrange for materials-handling methods and equipment. Forklifts as well as special containers and packaging are part of a materials-handling system.

DELIVERY TERMS

A small but important part of a physical distribution system is the terms of delivery. Delivery terms specify which party is responsible for several aspects of physical distribution:

- Paying the freight costs
- Selecting the carriers
- Bearing the risk of damage in transit
- Selecting the modes of transport

The simplest delivery term and the one most advantageous to a small business as seller is FOB (free on board) origin, freight collect. These terms shift all the responsibility for freight costs to the buyer. Title to the goods and risk of loss also pass to the buyer at the time the goods are shipped.

GLOBAL MARKETING

3 **Discuss global marketing.**

Given the difficulty of international business, why would anybody want to get involved? One small business international trade expert describes the motivations to go global as follows:

> *Certainly the overall motivation is increased sales, but that is the simple answer. A more complex analysis opens the door to the real fun—the larger game. Ultimately the goal of global trade is to expand the scope and reach of your company so that the tools and resources available to fight your competition give your company an unbeatable edge—an edge that renews and transforms itself faster than the competition can keep up.*[2]

In other words, many small firms are looking to do more than simply expand a profitable market when they get involved in international business. No longer insulated from global challengers, they must consider the dynamics of the new competitive environment. The rival on the other side of the street may be a minor threat compared to an online competitor on the other side of the globe!

One way to adjust to these emerging realities is through innovation. In many industries, innovation is essential to competitiveness, giving a small company an advantage over its large-firm counterparts. Small businesses that invest heavily in research and development often outperform their large competitors. But as R&D costs rise, they often cannot be recovered from domestic sales alone. Increasing sales in international markets may be the only viable way to recover the firm's investment. In some cases, this may require identifying dynamic markets that are beginning to open around the world and locating in or near those markets.[3]

EXPANDING THE MARKET

Today, global marketing by small Canadian firms is becoming more commonplace. Certain opportunities abroad are simply more profitable than those at home. Some 45,737 Canadian businesses exported $401 billion in 2005, with over 2000 new exporters in that year. Establishments exporting more than $25 million annually continue to account for the majority of merchandise exports, with the top 4 percent of exporting firms accounting for 83 percent of total export value. Many small businesses are pursuing an export strategy to expand, with 72 percent of exporters generating less than $1 million from export activities. Ventures with fewer than 50 employees accounted for 70 percent of exporters, and 25 percent of the total value of merchandise.[4]

COUNTRIES TARGETED

Because the primary motivation for going global is to develop market opportunities outside the home country, the focus of globalization strategies tends to be on those countries with the greatest commercial potential. In the past, these were the developed countries (those with high levels of widely distributed wealth). Today, companies are paying greater attention to emerging markets, where income and buying power are growing rapidly, particularly those listed in Exhibit 8-2. Because of their immense

EXHIBIT **8-2**
Emerging Markets

Country	2005 Population (in millions)	2005 Wealth (GNI per capita)	2004–2005 Economic Growth (GDP growth, %)
Argentina	38.7	4470	9.2
Brazil	186.4	3460	2.3
China	1304.5	1740	9.9
India	1094.6	720	8.5
Indonesia	220.6	1280	5.6
Mexico	103.1	7310	3.0
Poland	38.2	7110	3.2
South Africa	48.2	4960	4.9
South Korea	48.3	15830	4.0
Turkey	72.6	4710	7.4
World	**6437.8**	**6987**	**3.6**

Source: Adapted from The World Bank Group, "World Development Indicators, 2007," http://www.worldbank.org/data/countrydata-query.html, accessed February 9, 2007.

populations and potential market demand, countries such as China and India have attracted the greatest attention from international firms. Combined, these two nations account for nearly 40 percent of the world's 6 billion inhabitants, thus providing fertile ground for international expansion. Small companies are among the competitors battling for position in these emerging markets. Refer to the "In the Trenches" for additional information on opportunities in the Chinese market.

PRODUCTS PROMOTED

In the mid-1960s, international business authority Raymond Vernon observed that firms tend to introduce new products in their home market first and then sell them in less-developed countries later, as demand in the home market declines.[5] In other words, they use international expansion to extend a product's life cycle.

Although this approach is effective under some circumstances, it has become less viable as customer preferences, income levels, and delivery systems have become more similar and product life cycles have contracted. Products that sell at home are now more likely to be introduced very quickly abroad, with little or no adaptation in many cases. The role of television programs, movies, the Internet, and print media in shaping cultural tastes throughout the world has eased the entry of small businesses into international markets. By informing consumers about the lifestyles of others, globalization is leading the world toward common consumer preferences.

In addition to the trendy products associated with popular culture, another type of product well suited to international markets is the highly specialized product. As technology makes possible increasingly sophisticated goods, this allows markets to demand more differentiated products that satisfy their unique needs and interests. Fewer consumers in the home market are likely to be interested in a highly differentiated (and often more expensive) product, so it may become necessary to search for international markets with the same unique demand in order to increase sales enough to recover product development costs. Because small companies often follow focused business strategies (with limited domestic market potential) and aspire to grow rapidly, efforts to exploit the competitive advantage of specialized products across international markets may be even more important to them than to their larger counterparts.[6]

The challenges facing a small firm interested in global marketing can be better appreciated by considering the experiences and major obstacles encountered by entrepreneurs in international markets. The next section examines these challenges.

IN THE TRENCHES

Exploring Global Opportunities

Trading with China

While Canada's burgeoning imports from China are frequently in the spotlight, Canada's exports to China are often overlooked. From 2002 to 2006 Canada's exports nearly doubled to $8 billion, and in the first seven months of 2007 they soared 43 percent over the same period in 2006. The gain was the largest posted by any G7 country, and put China neck and neck with Japan as Canada's third-largest export market. While the level of imports by July 2007 remained well above exports, at $21.7 billion versus $5.5 billion, imports grew at a smaller margin of 17 percent.

Resources dominate Canada's exports to China. However, industrial goods have registered significant gains as China's economy builds its economic base by expanding factory production, building logistical networks, and developing infra- structure such as ports and roads. Preparations for the 2008 Olympic Games have been a driving force, with China's import values now the third-highest in the world behind the United State and Germany. A breakdown of Canada's exports to China, as detailed in a recent report by the *Canadian Economic Observer* is displayed below.

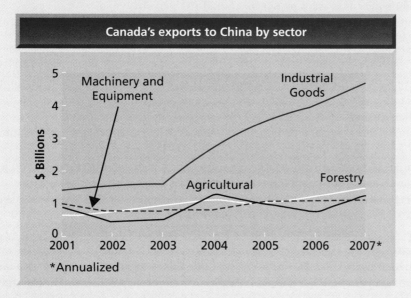

EXHIBIT **8-3** *Canada's Exports to China by Sector*

Source: Statistics Canada, "Trading with a Giant: An Update on Canada-China Trade" (Figure 4), *Canadian Observer* (November 2007) at http://www.statcan.ca/english/freepub/11-010-XIB/ 01107/feature.htm (accessed July 24, 2008).

Canadian firms wanting to crack the Chinese, or other, market, should refer to http://www.export.ca, a site maintained by the Canadian government that lists foreign companies seeking Canadian imports. A review of the site indicates export requests as small as $1000, which could provide sales opportunities to even small firms.

Specialized reports, such as *The Wine Market in China: Opportunities for Canadian Wine Exporters,* published in February 2008 by Agri-Food Canada, describe the opportunities for specific industries. This report provides insight into the export opportunities for Canadian wine producers to the China market. While wine consumption in China is nor- mally reserved for special occasions, imported premium wines have moved from being sold only at restaurants catering to foreigners, to an item used both for gift items and special occasions. White wine and icewine have proven popular, with overall sales increasing to 9.5 billion in 2006. The estimated annual growth is estimated to be 6 per- cent. National tradeshows, such as the Shanghai China International Wine Exposition, host hundreds of exhibitors, and provide opportunities for smaller firms to secure sales.

Sources: Adapted from Diana Wyman, "Trading with a Giant: An Update on Canada–China Trade," *Canadian Economic Observer* (November 2007), http://www.statcan.ca/english/freepub/11-010-XIB/ 01107/feature.htm (accessed August 8, 2008) and Agri-Food Trade Service, "The Wine Market in China: Opportunities for Canadian Wine Exporters" (February 2008) at http://www.ats .agr.gc.ca/asia/4398_e.htm (accessed August 8, 2008)

GLOBAL CHALLENGES

A basic human characteristic is a tendency to shy away from the complex and shun the unfamiliar. Entrepreneurs have traditionally held this attitude regarding foreign markets. One survey of more than 5000 independent businesses found the following factors to be major obstacles in exploring or expanding exports:

- Obtaining adequate, initial knowledge about exporting (72 percent)
- Identifying viable sales prospects abroad (61 percent)
- Understanding business protocols in other countries (57 percent)
- Selecting suitable target markets on the basis of the available information (57 percent)[7]

Nevertheless, the Profile of Canadian Exporters indicates that Canadian entrepreneurs are pursuing international trade opportunities in increasing numbers. While most Canadian businesses don't export, 60 percent of those that do export to the United States only, with Europe at 23 percent of exports the next most significant region.[8]

Evidently, more small firms are accepting the international challenge. Many small companies use government services in conjunction with other strategies to build their international exposure on a limited budget.

For example, In Motion Technology of New Westminister B.C. is a market leader in vehicle area networks. The company's patent pending link acceleration technology provides users with network management software, and is utilized by emergency organizations such as police and fire departments across Canada. In Motion Technology participated in the "Partners in Security" trade mission led by Canada's Department of Foreign Affairs in March 2008. Canada's industry leaders participated in the trade mission to meet potential clients and government contractors in Washington.[9]

Clearly, small firms can be just as successful as large firms in international markets. The idea that global marketing is for big business only is extremely damaging to small firms' efforts to market abroad. Data regarding big business versus small business involvement in international markets is at best inconclusive.[10]

The post–9/11 period has increased difficulty and expense in transportation. Security inspections at border crossings have caused delays, and consequently squeezed margins, for trucking companies transporting merchandise from Canada to the United States. Higher fuel expenses for all distribution methods, truck, rail, and aircraft, in conjunction with the rising Canadian currency, has caused some Canadian products to be less attractive in the international marketplace.

As early as possible in global marketing efforts, an entrepreneur needs to study the cultural, political, and economic forces in foreign markets to determine which adjustments to domestic marketing strategies are required. It is important to remember that what may be acceptable in one culture may be considered unethical or morally wrong in another. When cultural lines are being crossed, even something as simple as a daily "Good morning" accompanied by a handshake may be misunderstood. The entrepreneur must evaluate the proper use of names and titles and be aware of different styles of doing business.

When a foreign market is not studied carefully, costly mistakes may be made. For example, a mail-order concern offering products to the Japanese didn't realize that the North American custom of asking customers for a credit card number before taking their order would insult the Japanese. Later, a Japanese consultant told the company that people in Japan think that such an approach shows a lack of trust.[11]

The following examples further highlight the importance of understanding cultural differences:

- A Canadian firm received its first international contract for a major project in South East Asia. The project was to last two years, and would require a major financial commitment by the company. The firm sent a large contingent of staff, and shipped a significant amount of equipment to Bangkok, anticipating a timely start to the project. An agent had outlined all the local regulations and operating concerns. All the major issues had been addressed; however, the project manager had declined a suggestion by the agent that several government officials would be expecting gifts of significant value. The project suffered significant delays caused by a series of permits that were not approved by the local government officials. After a delay of six weeks, and concern that the project would be a financial disaster, the project manager smoothed the situation by holding a lavish party for local officials and suppliers. Relationships improved, and the permits were granted within two days.

- An hour before an American company was to sign a contract with a Middle Eastern nation, the American executive met for tea with the responsible government official. The American propped his feet on a table with the soles facing his Arab host. The official became angry and left the room. Such an act is a grave insult in the Arab's culture. The contract was finally signed one year later.[12]

TRADE AGREEMENTS

Differences in trading systems and import requirements of each country can make international trade difficult. To appreciate the problems that these differences create, let's consider the situation of Mentor O & O, Inc., a small manufacturer of diagnostic and surgical eye care equipment, which it markets internationally. Mentor regularly modifies its products to meet rigid design specifications that vary from country to country. For example, an alarm bell on Mentor's testing device has an on/off switch that must be removed before it is acceptable in Germany.[13] This is typical of barriers to trade that exist throughout the world.

    The global market has entered a period of positive change with regard to trade barriers. In 1989, Canada and the United States signed the ***Free Trade Agreement*** (FTA), which called for the elimination of most tariffs and other trade restrictions by January 1, 1998. The result is an environment more conducive to trade between these two countries. This is especially important for Canada, since the United States is our largest trading partner.[14]

    In 1993, Canada, the United States, and Mexico signed the ***North American Free Trade Agreement*** (NAFTA).[15] Under NAFTA, all Mexican tariffs on products made in Canada and the United States will be phased out over a period of 15 years; almost half of these tariffs were removed on the agreement's effective date of January 1, 1994.

    November 1993 marked the official beginning of the 27-nation European Union (EU). For the last 15 years, businesses of all sizes have observed the preparations made for a unified Europe including the introduction of a common currency, the euro, in 2002. The breakup of the Soviet bloc created a more complex world and has put pressure on the EU to admit Eastern European nations, with Turkey potentially joining. The exact impact of the EU on small exporters is still unknown; however, with a population of half a billion, the EU is an attractive market. Many small Canadian producers, such as Rayne Longboards featured in "In the Trenches" have successfully entered the EU.

***Free Trade Agreement* (FTA)** an accord that eases trade restrictions between Canada and the United States

***North American Free Trade Agreement* (NAFTA)** an accord that eases trade restrictions among Canada, the United States, and Mexico

General Agreement on Tariffs and Trade (GATT)
an international agreement that aims to reduce tariffs and other trade barriers among countries

4 Describe the initial steps of a global marketing effort.

World Trade Organization (WTO)
an international organization that administers GATT and works to lower tariffs and trade barriers worldwide

Canada is also a signatory to the *General Agreement on Tariffs and Trade* (GATT), which attempts to reduce tariffs and other protectionist barriers to trade among countries. Administration of GATT was taken over in 1996 by the newly created **World Trade Organization** (WTO), which has the general mandate of lowering tariffs and trade barriers worldwide. While there is increasing pressure to reduce barriers, significant issues remain to be resolved. Business owners should review the potential for export on a country-by-country basis.

INITIAL PREPARATIONS FOR GLOBAL MARKETING

Many activities prepare a small firm for a global marketing effort. Two, in particular, are vital for almost every international venture: researching the foreign market and setting up a sales and distribution plan.

RESEARCHING A FOREIGN MARKET

Foreign-market research should begin by exhausting as many secondary sources of information as possible. The federal government offers an array of services to assist firms in locating and exploiting global marketing opportunities. The Department of Foreign Affairs and International Trade (DFAIT) is the primary Canadian government agency responsible for assisting exporters. Probably the best direct assistance comes from the department's trade commissioners, located in over 13 trade centres across Canada and at over 100 Canadian embassies abroad.

There are many other government programs specific to particular industry sectors or other criteria. Information on these can be found through DFAIT's website at http://www.dfait-maeci.gc.ca, which includes

- The Export Information Kit
- A free subscription to *CanadaExport,* a government news site
- Publications such as *So You Want to Export? A Resource Book for Canadian Exporters*
- Geographic, economic, and market data in the series of books called *A Guide for Canadian Exporters*
- Referrals to other federal and provincial government departments and other export organizations
- A business agenda listing seminars, meetings, conferences, and courses offered across the country to anyone currently exporting or who is interested in exporting

Other services offered through DFAIT include

- *Export counselling:* Trade commissioners are available at DFAIT trade centres for individualized export counselling.
- *World Information Network for Exporters (WINS):* This is a list of over 30,000 Canadian exporters and businesses that would like to export. Foreign importers can access WINS to find firms and products that interest them.
- *International Trade Data Bank:* This is a data bank of information about international trade from the United Nations and various trading blocs around the world.
- *Overseas Trade fairs:* Officials of Canadian firms are given financial assistance to participate in a foreign trade fair. This is one service provided under the Program for Export Market Development (PEMD). Other services include assistance with

visiting foreign markets, putting together export consortia, project bidding, and establishing a permanent sales office abroad.

- *Trade leads:* Trade leads are essential in identifying potential customers in target markets.
- *Trade missions:* Assistance is provided to businesses that wish to participate in a trade mission with other businesses and representatives of the federal and provincial governments. It is becoming common for the prime minister and several provincial premiers to be part of these missions. This adds a considerable degree of credibility to any business that is part of the mission, at least in some parts of the world. Trade missions are an excellent way to make government and business contacts in other countries.

Being a member of a trade mission sponsored by the federal government is another means of evaluating a foreign market. A trade mission is a planned visit to a potential foreign market to introduce Canadian firms to appropriate foreign buyers and government officials, and to establish exporting relationships. There have been several of these high-profile "Team Canada" missions in recent years, resulting in several billion dollars' worth of sales and investment for Canadian companies. These missions usually involve a group of several hundred business executives, the prime minister, several provincial premiers, and other government officials, and are organized and planned to achieve maximum results in expanding exports. Members of the group may pay their own expenses or receive some government assistance, and the government picks up the operating costs of the mission.

Survival Systems Limited President Albert Bohemier participated in trade missions to India and Pakistan, Korea, the Philippines, Thailand, Mexico, Brazil, and Argentina over a three-year period. The company benefited not only during the missions but also in the long term. For example, a $400,000 contract for delivery of a system to Malaysia was negotiated, four years after the initial contact during a trade mission.

Located in Dartmouth, the producer of safety training products and services has spent millions developing and manufacturing mobile and fixed-base emergency training simulators. Recognized as the most realistic escape trainer in the world, the firm services both military and commercial organizations. The 60-employee company generates over 50 percent of its sales from exports to a dozen countries. It anticipates that almost all of its growth will be derived from export opportunities.

Bohemier credits government services such as Export Development Corporation, which provides insurance, and Canadian trade commissioners, which facilitate client contacts, with easing his company's entry into the international arena.

Not all experiences have been easy. Brazil, says Bohemier was an administrative nightmare. "It took us an entire year to get a licence for our product. We had to pay huge customs and duty costs that we had not been told of." The difficulty has not put him off; his recommendation to other Canadian exporters? "Pack your bags and go do it. You don't sell internationally without persistence and presence."[16]

In addition to DFAIT, many other federal government departments and programs provide assistance or information to those wishing to export.

- The Canadian Commercial Corporation (CCC) is a Crown corporation that may act as the main contractor when foreign governments wish to purchase goods and services from Canadian companies. The CCC also provides loans to Canadian companies for the purchase of raw materials. The loans do not require repayment until the client pays for the finished goods. The advantage to the foreign government is access to suppliers that have already been reviewed by the Canadian government. Refer to http://www.ccc.ca.

- Export Development Canada provides financial services in the form of insuring or guaranteeing foreign accounts receivable of Canadian exporters. Refer to http://www.edc.ca.
- Canadian International Development Agency (CIDA) is the main international assistance agency of the Canadian government, and it assists Canadian exporters attempting to penetrate new markets in developing countries. Refer to http://www.acdi-cida.gc.ca.
- Canada Revenue Agency, through the Excise and Taxation division, regulates the flow of goods imported to and exported from Canada. Information and assistance is available from any regional office. Refer to http://www.cra-arc.gc.ca/menu-e.html.
- Statistics Canada publishes a variety of data on exports and imports. In addition to published reports such as *Exports by Commodity*, customized data retrieval is available to businesses for a nominal fee. Refer to http://www.statcan.ca.
- The Canadian Trade Commissioner Services provides assistance to small and medium-sized Canadian enterprises through its regional offices. It assists in export financing, market research, and one-on-one export help. Hundreds of foreign markets by industry sector are also available. Refer to http://www.infoexport.gc.ca.
- Industry Canada's website has a number of *Doing Business in . . .* publications for various countries around the world. Refer to http://www.ic.gc.ca.
- The Business Development Bank has several programs to assist exporters, including NEXPRO, a series of in-depth training workshops, on-site counselling, and trade-mission participation for new exporters. The bank also offers seminars, matchmaking services to help firms link up for joint ventures or licensing, and the newsletter *Profits*, which lists export opportunities. Refer to http://www.bdc.ca.

All provincial governments have programs, information, and assistance to support businesses wishing to export. Programs vary by province, and they range from export financing or insurance to making contacts in foreign countries. For example, Ontario and Alberta maintain trade offices in some foreign countries. According to Ted Haney, executive director of the Canadian Beef Export Federation, the addition of a provincial government's presence is important. "If we can get both levels of government speaking on our behalf, it does help," Haney says. "Within trade, it builds awareness, and within foreign government regulators, it improves access."[17]

Banks, universities, and other private organizations also provide information on exporting. The major banks play a key role in transfers of funds. They also may provide some credit information on prospective foreign customers through their relationship with banks in other countries. Information is also available from Canadian Manufacturers and Exporters, the Canadian Bankers' Association, and many local chambers of commerce or boards of trade. Two useful publications available in local and university libraries include Dun & Bradstreet's *Exporter's Encyclopedia* and the *Canadian Export Guide,* published by Mississauga, Ontario's Migra International Ltd.

Prepared by the Canadian Trade Commissioner Services, a simple questionnaire to determine the readiness of companies to export is summarized in Exhibit 8-4.

Talking with a citizen of a foreign country or even someone who has visited a potential foreign market can be a valuable way to learn something about it. International students studying at many universities can be contacted through faculty members who teach courses in the international disciplines.

MARKETING
- Has an export plan been prepared? Has each potential market been researched?
- How will entering the foreign market impact the current marketing strategy? Will your current tools, such as the website, product videos, promotional literature etc. need to be modified?
- Will your product require any design changes or packaging modifications to comply with foreign selling or packaging laws?
- What distinguishes your product or service from the competition; is it still competitive from a pricing viewpoint after shipping and financing costs have been included?

FINANCIAL
- Can your organization allocate funds to the global activity?
- Will the expansion into foreign markets decrease your ability to expand or operate domestically?
- Are you aware of currency risks and alternative forms of export financing?

PRODUCTION
- What extent of your production do you wish to export; can your facilities handle the increased demand?
- How does your quality control standard fit the potential global market; are you deficient?

HUMAN RESOURCES
- Does your organization understand the long-term commitment that exporting or foreign expansion entails?
- Have SMART goals been established for the export initiative?
- Does your staff have the skills to handle foreign operations? What training is needed?

Source: Team Canada Inc., ExportSource.ca.

One of the best ways to study a foreign market is to visit that market personally. Representatives of small firms can do this either individually or in organized groups such as the trade missions addressed earlier.

HOW ORGANIZATIONS EXPAND INTERNATIONALLY

Before establishing foreign operations, small business owners and managers need to analyze not only the marketing potential but also the risks inherent in each country's environment. Typically, small firms begin the international process using a lower-risk approach, and as they become more experienced they consider broader and riskier levels of involvement. Typically there are five methods to operate in the global environment: importing and exporting, foreign distributors, licensing/franchising, strategic alliances, and foreign subsidiary. Each will be addressed briefly. Exhibit 8-5 illustrates how the risk level increases with the level of involvement.

SALES AND DISTRIBUTION CHANNELS

Exporting and importing tend to be the primary method of entering global activities. A company makes products and sells them abroad, typically incurring little risk by requiring payment prior to shipment, or upon point of arrival. Many small Canadian businesses, such as clothing, sporting goods, and home furnishing stores import goods for their retail operations. However, some Canadian manufacturers expand

EXHIBIT **8-5**
Risk Levels and Levels of Involvement

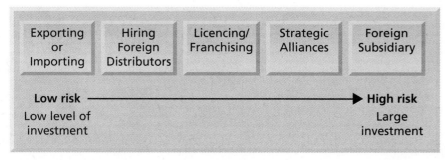

Source: Richard E. Caves, *Multinational Enterprise and Economic Analysis* 1st edition, 1982, Cambridge University Press.

licensing

legal arrangement allowing another manufacturer to use the property of the licenser in return for royalties

not by exporting directly, but by allowing foreign firms to produce their product overseas through licensing arrangements. In fact, licensing is the simplest strategy for conducting international trade. With only a small investment, a firm can penetrate a foreign market. **Licensing** is an arrangement that allows a foreign manufacturer to use the designs, patents, or trademarks of the licenser in exchange for royalties. The practice of licensing helps overcome trade barriers surrounding exporting because the product is produced in the foreign country. Michael Koss, CEO of Koss Corporation, used licensing to diversify his stereo-headphone manufacturing company because "this seemed a good way to generate royalty income in the short run and cement a strategic partnership that could lead, over the long run, to joint ventures." His foreign licensee is the Dutch trading company Hagemeyer, which pays royalties to use Koss's brand name and logo. To ensure quality, Koss has "veto power over all product drawings, engineering specifications, first-product samples, and final products."[18]

A small firm can also participate in foreign-market sales via joint ventures and wholly owned subsidiaries in foreign markets. International joint ventures offer a greater presence abroad at less cost than establishing a firm's own operation or office in foreign markets. For example, Arctic Spas, voted for several years as one of Canada's 50 best-managed companies, manufactures world-class hot tubs. Located near Edmonton, Alberta, Arctic Spas distributes its award-winning designs through over 250 retailers in 30 countries. Refer to the company's website http://www.arcticspas.com for details. While most of the distribution involves shipping products made in western Canada to domestic and international retailers, Arctic Spas has expanded in Australia through a joint venture.[19] Some host countries may require that a certain percentage of manufacturing facilities be owned by nationals of that country, thereby forcing Canadian firms to operate through joint ventures. Other options for foreign distribution channels are identified in Exhibit 8-6.

Many firms find that foreign distributors, by first buying the product and then finding customers, offer a low-cost way to market products overseas. However, some foreign distributors are not strongly committed to selling an individual manufacturer's products. If a small firm mistakenly picks one of these distributors, sales may not grow as quickly as they could. When B.D. Baggies, a men's shirt maker, first began marketing internationally, it contracted with the first foreign distributor that offered to sell its shirts in Europe. "Later, we found that the distributor wasn't right. They were selling our shirts to women's stores as a unisex product," explains Charles M. McConnell, president

EXHIBIT **8-6**

*Additional Foreign
Market Channels
of Distribution*

SALES REPRESENTATIVES OR AGENTS

A sales representative is the equivalent of a manufacturer's representative at home. Product literature and samples are used to present the product to the potential buyer. The representative usually works on a commission basis, assumes no risk or responsibility, and is under contract for a definite period of time (renewable by mutual agreement). This contract defines territory, terms of sale, method of compensation, and other details. The sales representative may operate on either an exclusive or a nonexclusive basis.

FOREIGN DISTRIBUTOR

A foreign distributor is a merchant who purchases merchandise from the domestic manufacturer at the greatest possible discount and resells it for a profit. This would be the preferred arrangement if the product being sold requires periodic servicing. The prospective distributor should be willing to carry a sufficient supply of spare parts and maintain adequate facilities and personnel to perform all normal servicing operations. The manufacturer should establish a credit pattern so that flexible or convenient payment terms can be offered. As with a sales representative, the length of association is established by contract, which is renewable if the arrangement proves mutually satisfactory.

FOREIGN RETAILER

Generally limited to the consumer product line, the foreign retailer relies mainly on direct contact by travelling sales representatives, although catalogues, brochures, and other literature can achieve the same purpose. However, even though direct mail would eliminate commissions and travelling expenses, a Canadian manufacturer's direct mail proposal may not receive proper consideration.

SELLING DIRECT TO THE END-USER

Selling direct is quite limited, and its success depends on the product. Opportunities often arise from advertisements in magazines receiving overseas distribution. This can often create difficulties because casual inquirers may not be fully cognizant of their country's foreign trade regulations. For several reasons, they may not be able to receive the merchandise upon arrival, thus causing it to be impounded and possibly sold at public auction, or returned on a freight-collect basis that could prove costly.

STATE-CONTROLLED TRADING COMPANIES

State-controlled trading companies exist in countries that have state trading monopolies, where business is conducted by a few government-sanctioned and controlled trading entities. Because of worldwide changes in foreign policy and their effect on trade between countries, these companies can become important future markets. For the time being, however, most opportunities will be limited to such items as raw materials, agricultural machinery, manufacturing equipment, and technical instruments, rather than consumer or household goods. This is due to the shortage of foreign exchange facilities and the emphasis on self-sufficiency.

COMMISSION AGENTS

Commission, or buying, agents are "finders" for foreign firms wanting to purchase domestic products. These purchasing agents obtain the desired equipment at the lowest possible price and are paid a commission by their foreign clients.

COUNTRY-CONTROLLED BUYING AGENTS

Foreign government agencies or quasi-governmental firms, called country-controlled buying agents, are empowered to locate and purchase desired goods.

EXPORT MANAGEMENT COMPANIES

EMCs, as they are called, act as the export department for several manufacturers of noncompetitive products. They solicit and transact business in the name of the manufacturers they represent for a commission, salary, or retainer plus commission. Many EMCs carry the financing for export sales,

(Continued)

ensuring immediate payment for the manufacturer's products. This can be an exceptionally good arrangement for small firms that do not have the time, personnel, or money to develop foreign markets but wish to establish a corporate and product identity internationally.

EXPORT MERCHANTS

Export merchants purchase products directly from the manufacturer and have them packed and marked to their specifications. They then sell overseas through their contacts, in their own names, and assume all risk for their accounts.

EXPORT AGENTS

Export agents operate in the same manner as manufacturer's representatives, but the risk of loss remains with the manufacturer.

In transactions with export merchants and export agents, a seller is faced with the possible disadvantage of giving up control over the marketing and promotion of the product. This could have an adverse effect on future success.

Source: Adapted from *A Basic Guide to Exporting*, U.S. Department of Commerce (Washington, DC: U.S. Government Printing Office, 1992). Reprinted by permission of U.S. Department of Commerce, International Trade Administration.

of B.D. Baggies. Subsequently, the firm carefully screened all distributors, and it is now doing good business in more than 40 countries.[20]

SOURCES OF TRADE AND FINANCING ASSISTANCE

Identify sources of trade and financing assistance.

Difficulty in getting trade information and arranging financing is often considered the biggest barrier to small business exporting. In reality, a number of direct and indirect sources of trade and financing information can help a small firm view foreign markets more favourably.

PRIVATE BANKS

Chartered banks typically have a loan officer who is responsible for handling foreign transactions. Large banks may have a separate international department. Exporters use banks to issue commercial letters of credit and perform other financial activities associated with exporting.

letter of credit

an agreement to honour a demand for payment under certain conditions

A **letter of credit** is an agreement to honour a draft or other demand for payment when specified conditions are met. It helps assure a seller of prompt payment and may be revocable or irrevocable. An irrevocable letter of credit cannot be changed unless both the buyer and the seller agree to make the change. The procedure typically followed when payment is made by an irrevocable letter of credit confirmed by a Canadian bank comprises these steps:

1. After exporter and buyer agree on the terms of sale, the buyer arranges for its bank to open a letter of credit. (Delays may be encountered if, for example, the buyer has insufficient funds.)
2. The buyer's bank prepares an irrevocable letter of credit, including all instructions to the seller concerning the shipment.

3. The buyer's bank sends the irrevocable letter of credit to a Canadian bank, requesting confirmation. The exporter may request that a particular Canadian bank be the confirming bank, or the buyer's bank will select one of its Canadian correspondent banks.

4. The Canadian bank prepares a letter of confirmation to forward to the exporter along with the irrevocable letter of credit.

5. The exporter carefully reviews all conditions in the letter of credit. The exporter's freight forwarder is generally contacted to make sure that the shipping date can be met. If the exporter cannot comply with one or more of the conditions, the buyer should be alerted at once.

6. The exporter arranges with the freight forwarder to deliver the goods to the appropriate port or airport.

7. When the goods are loaded, the freight forwarder completes the necessary documents.

8. The exporter (or the freight forwarder) presents to the Canadian bank documents indicating full compliance.

9. The bank reviews the documents. If they are in order, the documents are forwarded to the buyer's bank for review and transmitted to the buyer.

10. The buyer (or agent) gets the documents that may be needed to claim the goods.

11. A draft, which may accompany the letter of credit, is paid by the exporter's bank at the time specified or may be discounted if paid earlier.[21]

A letter of credit, as important as it is, is not an absolute guarantee of payment. Consider the experience of bottled-water exporter Vivant in Japan. Vivant obtained a letter of credit to back an export order for a container-load of bottled water. The buyer's bank cancelled the irrevocable letter of credit on the instruction of the importer, claiming the goods could not be removed from customs due to some errors with the labelling.[22]

FACTORING HOUSES

A factoring house, or factor, buys clients' accounts receivable and advances money to these clients. The factor assumes the risk of collection of the accounts. The Factors Chain International is an association representing 232 factors from more than 63 countries.[23] Its efforts have helped make factoring services available on an international basis. Refer to its website at http://www.factors-chain.com.

The Forum for International Trade Training (FITT) is a nationwide organization that offers an eight-course program through many universities and colleges. The program, which may be viewed at http://www.FITT.ca, serves as a cornerstone in preparing Canadians for international trade.

THE EXPORT DEVELOPMENT CORPORATION (EDC)

To encourage Canadian businesses to sell overseas, the federal government created the Export Development Corporation (EDC) in 1969. Although historically of greatest use to large firms, in recent years EDC has overhauled its programs in order to benefit small firms. The following offerings are particularly helpful to small business exporters:

- *Export credit insurance:* An exporter may reduce its financing risks up to 90 percent by purchasing export credit insurance. Policies include short-term insurance (up to 180 days) and medium-term insurance (up to five years). Risks covered include commercial risks of insolvency of the foreign buyer or bank, unilateral termination of the contract, and repudiation or default by the foreign buyer. Political risks covered include cancellation of import permit, cancellation of export permit by the Canadian government, war and insurrection, and inconvertibility of currency.

- *Bonding facilities:* EDC can directly issue a surety bond to an exporter that needs one or guarantee one to a surety company. EDC also insures bid bonds, advance-payment bonds, supply bonds, and performance bonds.
- *Export financing:* EDC provides two types of loans: (1) direct loans to foreign buyers of Canadian exports and (2) loans to supplier-exporters. Both programs cover up to 85 percent of the Canadian export value, with repayment terms of one year or more.
- *Foreign investment insurance:* EDC will insure foreign investments by Canadian companies for the political risks above, plus transfer and expropriation risk.

LOOKING BACK

1 Explain the role of distribution in marketing.

- Distribution encompasses both the physical movement of products and the establishment of intermediary relationships to guide the movement of products from producer to user.
- Four main functions of channel intermediaries are breaking bulk, assorting, providing information, and shifting risks.
- A distribution channel can be either direct or indirect. Some firms may successfully employ more than one channel of distribution.

2 Describe the major considerations in structuring a distribution system.

- Costs, coverage, and control are the three main considerations in building a channel of distribution.
- Transportation, storage, materials handling, delivery terms, and inventory management are the main components of a physical distribution system.

3 Discuss global marketing.

- A recent survey indicates that Canadian entrepreneurs are breaking new ground in foreign markets.
- Small firms can be just as successful as large firms in international markets.
- An entrepreneur needs to study cultural, political, and economic forces in a foreign market in order to understand why adjustments to domestic marketing strategies are needed.

- Differences among host countries in trading systems and import requirements make international trade challenging.

4 Describe the initial steps of a global marketing effort.

- Researching a foreign market should begin with a look at secondary data sources, such as the export information package and publications available through the Department of Foreign Affairs and International Trade's.
- One of the best ways to study a foreign market is to visit it, either individually or as part of a trade mission.
- Licensing is the simplest and least costly strategy for conducting international business.
- A small firm can also participate in foreign-market sales via joint ventures or through foreign distributors.

5 Identify sources of trade and financing assistance.

- Private banks are a good source of assistance for financial matters associated with small business exporting.
- Increasingly, provinces are developing and implementing their own programs to help small firms in their efforts to export.
- The Export Development Corporation (EDC) has several programs that are particularly helpful to small exporters.

KEY TERMS

agents and brokers, p. 207
assorting, p. 207
breaking bulk, p. 206
channel of distribution, p. 206
common carriers, p. 210
contract carriers, p. 210
direct channel, p. 207
distribution, p. 206

dual distribution, p. 207
Free Trade Agreement (FTA), p. 215
General Agreement on Tariffs and Trade (GATT), p. 216
indirect channel, p. 207
letter of credit, p. 222
licensing, p. 220
merchant middlemen, p. 207

North American Free Trade Agreement (NAFTA), p. 215
physical distribution (logistics), p. 206
private carriers, p. 210
World Trade Organization (WTO), p. 216

DISCUSSION QUESTIONS

1. How does physical distribution differ from channels of distribution?
2. Why do small firms need to consider indirect channels of distribution for their products? Why involve intermediaries in distribution at all?
3. Discuss the major considerations in structuring a channel of distribution.
4. What are the major components of a physical distribution system?
5. Comment on the statement "Channel intermediaries are not necessary and only increase the final price of a product."
6. How have trade agreements helped reduce trade barriers? Do you believe these efforts will continue?
7. Discuss the importance of a careful cultural analysis to a small firm that wishes to enter an international market.
8. What changes in a firm's marketing plan, if any, may be required when selling to foreign markets? Be specific.
9. What are some alternatives to exporting that provide involvement for small businesses in international markets? Which one(s) do you find most consistent with a small firm's situation? Why?
10. Explain the exporting assistance programs of the EDC.

YOU MAKE THE CALL

SITUATION 1

Miriam Gordon owns MG Sport, a custom clothing firm in Toronto. MG Sport makes unique promotional wear out of Tyvek, a very durable Dupont product used for everything from envelopes to wrapping new buildings. Gordon has kept overheads down by remaining the company's only employee—she contracts out all manufacturing and targets major corporations with large advertising budgets, such as breweries and major chains. Miriam is the only salesperson for the company, which has seen revenues jump from zero to over

$1 million in three years. She attributes her success to unique designs, super customer service, and a unique product.

Source: Ted Wakefield, "Surprise Packager," *Canadian Business* (December 1987), pp. 23–24.

Question 1 What do you see as the strong and weak points of the distribution channels the company is currently using?
Question 2 What additional channels would you recommend to Gordon for consideration?
Question 3 Do you think exporting is a feasible alternative for Gordon at this time? Why or why not?

SITUATION 2

Many Canadian small businesses have considered, and seized, the export possibilities occurring in China. Developing the Olympic site entailed billions of dollars for infrastructure, for not only buildings but also telecommunications systems and mass transit for the transportation of athletes, medeia, and spectators. Canadian firms specializing in water purification systems, engineering consulting, and translation software were able to export during the buildup to the Olympics. It is anticipated that the Chinese economy will surpass that of the United States by 2020. The possibilities for exporting Canadian resources, industrial goods, and specialized retail items seems endless—though not without difficulties.

Question 1 What programs offered by federal and provincial governments could assist companies exporting for the first time?
Question 2 What factors, including cultural, should exporters take into consideration for the Chinese market?
Question 3 What sources should firms use to identify potential opportunities?
Question 4 What are the distribution channels and alternatives available to entering the Chinese market?

SITUATION 3

Researching a foreign market does not necessarily have to be an expensive effort. One economical source of good information is the pool of companies that sell related products abroad.

Hugh Dantzer, president of Edmonton's All Complete Roaster, completed a deal to create a company in Japan to build and market his patented machine. The deal happened quite by accident, when the Japanese partner came to Edmonton to buy patio furniture from Dantzer's import–export business. "I introduced him to the roaster business at that time . . . he liked it so much, he wanted to have dibs on the Japanese market," says Dantzer. The Japanese partner already knows the market and has the distribution system set up, so it's a very economical way to get into the market.

Source: Ted Wakefield, "Surprise Packager," *Canadian Business* (December 1987), pp. 23–24.

Question 1 Do you see any risk in having so much business with one firm under these circumstances?
Question 2 What other sources of global marketing information could Dantzer consider?

EXPERIENTIAL EXERCISES

1. Conduct a search of a Canadian industry, using both Google and databases available at your library, such as Euromonitor or Datamonitor. Identify the domestic versus international volume of business in the industry. Then identify a company in the industry using search engines. Reviewing its site, determine if the company is pursuing international opportunities, and if it is, the methods and distribution channels it is using.
2. Interview two different types of local retail merchants to determine how the merchandise in their stores was distributed to them. Determine whether the retail outlets have expanded their distribution capabilities by selling online. Contrast the channels of distribution and report your findings.
3. Review recent issues *of Canadian Business, PROFIT*, or *Inc.*, and report on articles that discuss international marketing.
4. Interview a local distributor concerning how it stores and handles the merchandise it distributes. Report your findings.

EXPLORING THE WEB

Search the Internet for information regarding exporting. Visit Dun & Bradstreet's site at http://www.dnb.com. Summarize the information available at this and any other site you may find.

Managing
NEW VENTURE OPERATIONS

CHAPTER 9

Selecting the Management Team and Managing Human Resources

IN THE SPOTLIGHT

Great People, Great Packaging Solutions

That's the vision statement of the Great Little Box Company (GLBC), a Richmond, B.C.–based manufacturer of cardboard boxes and other packaging materials. It seems many companies struggle to live up to their vision statement but this certainly hasn't been the case for GLBC. From a start-up bought out of receivership in 1982 the company has grown to a staff of over 200, a state-of-the art warehouse and factory in Richmond, and four branches in British Columbia and Washington State. Along the way the company has become a perennial winner of awards such as one of Canada's Top 100 Employers and 50 Best-Managed Companies.

In response to being awarded the 50 Best-Managed Companies award for the 4th consecutive year in 2008, President Robert Meggy said, "As the manufacturing landscape continues to change, it is a daily challenge to successfully meet the stringent financial and operating requirements of this award; this achievement is a testament to the people at Great Little Box Company. Whether in production, administration or sales, all of the employees at Great Little Box Company make this company better every day. They work together to decrease costs, increase efficiencies and ultimately provide an excellent product with superior customer service to our clients."

Scheduler Carrie Dawson first arrived at GLBC as a pregnant temporary worker in 1999, and she quickly sensed she was onto a good thing. "As a temp you get to see how people relate to each other, how friendly the

Photo courtesy of Great Little Box Company

atmosphere is—all that kind of stuff. And when I left, I was like, 'I wanna work here.' After the baby I kept in touch with lots of people in the office and as soon as a job posting came up, I didn't really care where it was in the company."

Why do people love to work for GLBC? Almost everyone mentions the river view from every office (the plans for the new building were deliberately reversed to achieve this) and the 2006 company-wide trip to Cabo San Lucas. There is the on-site gym, and of course the pay is pretty good too. Cash incentives include a monthly bonus based on a percentage of profits that is the same for every employee, regardless of seniority. There's cash for ideas and a percentage of the savings if an idea is used, tuition for work-related classes, and cash to give up smoking. Everyone is above minimum wage and each employee's child under the age of 13 gets a $60 Christmas gift every year. Is it any wonder people love to work for GLBC?

Robert Meggy is rightfully proud to have created a company that is as serious about its people as it is about profit. "Most of your waking hours are spent with a company, so you better enjoy it," Meggy says. "When everybody's drinking margaritas together in a hot tub in Mexico, you can't get better bonding in a company."

http://www.greatlittlebox.com

Source: Press Release posted to the company website on February 12, 2008 and Yolanda Brooks, "Handle With Care," *BC Business*, December 2006. Used by permission.

LEADING AND MOTIVATING

Like any endeavour involving people, a small firm needs an atmosphere of cooperation and teamwork among all participants. Fortunately, employees in small firms can collaborate effectively. In fact, the potential for good teamwork is enhanced in some ways by the smallness of the enterprise. Conversely, a poorly motivated employee in a small company of five to 10 people can result in a 10 to 20 percent loss in productivity, severely impacting the bottom line.

PERSONAL INVOLVEMENT AND INFLUENCE OF THE ENTREPRENEUR

In most small firms, employees get to know the owner-manager personally. This person is not a faceless unknown, but an individual whom employees see and relate to in the course of their normal work schedules. This situation is entirely different from that of large corporations, where most employees may never even see the chief executive. If the employer–employee relationship is good, employees in small firms develop strong feelings of personal loyalty to their employer.

In very small firms—those with 20 or fewer employees—extensive interaction is typical. As a firm grows, the amount of personal contact an employee may have with the owner naturally declines. Nevertheless, a significant personal relationship between the owner and employees is characteristic of most small businesses.

In a large corporation, the values of top-level executives must be filtered through many layers of management before they reach those who produce and sell the products. As a result, the influence of those at the top may be diluted by the process of going through channels. In contrast, personnel in a small firm receive the leader's messages directly. This face-to-face contact facilitates their understanding of the leader's stand on integrity, customer service, and other important issues.

By creating an environment that encourages personal interaction, the leader of a small firm can get the best from his or her employees and also offer a strong inducement to prospective employees. For example, most professional managers prefer an organizational setting that minimizes office politics as a factor in getting ahead. By creating a friendly atmosphere that avoids the intrigue common in some organizations, an entrepreneur can build an environment that is very attractive to most employees.

LEADERSHIP THAT BUILDS ENTHUSIASM

Several decades ago, many managers were hard-nosed autocrats, giving orders and showing little concern for those who worked under them. Over the years, this style of leadership has given way to a gentler and more effective variety that emphasizes respect for all members of the organization and shows an appreciation of their potential. Progressive managers now seek some degree of employee participation in decisions affecting personnel and work processes.

empowerment
increasing employees'
authority to take
action on their own
or make decisions

In many cases, managers carry this leadership approach to a level called **empowerment.** The manager who uses empowerment goes beyond soliciting employees' opinions and ideas by increasing their authority to act on their own and to decide things for themselves. For Brick Brewing Company, one key to its success is staff empowerment. New products are introduced quickly due to effective decision making by staff teams. Management listens to staff ideas and research, and the team is able to move more quickly than the competition because of a high level of staff involvement. Refer to "In the Trenches" for more details.

IN THE TRENCHES

Entrepreneurial Experiences

Philanthropy as a Way of Doing Business

In 1983 Ben Sawatzky started Acheson, Alberta's Spruceland Millworks, determined to be a different kind of employer. According to the company, "Our first social responsibility is to look after the well being, the safety, the health and the comfort of our staff. Together we realize, however, the world is home to many who are less fortunate than we are. For this reason we, the Spruceland Family seek out opportunities to lighten the burdens of the fatherless, the homeless and the hungry." This commitment to making a difference as a company has become the spirit of the workplace at Spruceland. Through voluntary payroll deductions the 130 employees raised $186 000 for charity in 2006 and Sawatzky matched it dollar for dollar. But this is only part of the story.

In 2007 a crew of 16 employees flew to the Dominican Republic to help build the foundations for a new town that will house poor families and give them a fresh start. In 2008 they went back to build 30 homes in the new town. The employees paid for their own tickets, while Spruceland covered all of the costs including wages. "Charity work gives employees an overall sense of community through the workplace and gets a good attitude out there," said Josh Sawatzky, son of Ben, who oversees the HR department.

Money plays a part as well. When the company received a windfall rebate on softwood lumber duties it gave employees a one-time "prosperity bonus" of between $2,500 and $5,000 rather than pocket the cash itself. "It gets employees excited and shows them they are appreciated," said Sawatzky. At the 2006 Christmas party the company hosted its own Deal or No Deal game, where 10 employees had a chance to win $10,000 each. But money isn't everything. Every couple of years, if the company hits its financial targets, Spruceland takes everyone on a fully paid, all-inclusive vacation. It pays for between one and four airline tickets depending on length of time with the company. "When I tell people that when I'm hiring, it's a pretty good sell," said Sawatzky. In the company's more than 25 years there have been 19 trips, including Puerto Vallarta, Mexico, in 2008.

Another key retention strategy is the legacy shareholders plan, which gives employees the opportunity to buy into the company. "This was not done out of necessity," said Sawatzky. "It's the owner's way of taking care of those employees who step up and see a long-term career at Spruceland. The company also markets itself to employees as a family-oriented company by hosting picnics and barbecues. This is a big draw when the company is trying to compete with the province's high-paying oil and construction industry jobs. In fact, until the Alberta economy overheated in 2006 the company had never had to advertise for employees. Another example of this family-oriented approach is that employees are able to end their workdays when they meet daily production targets, allowing them to spend more time with family—and receive a $20 bonus for the day on top of a full day's wage. "Time and again we've been reminded that the people are the key to our success," said Josh Sawatzky. "If you have the staff buy-in, you can make money even if the market slumps or times are hard."

This sincere belief in the importance of its people and the key role of philanthropy have won the company several awards including its third consecutive Canada's Top 100 Employers award in 2008. It has also made the company consistently profitable in a competitive manufacturing business.

Sources: Adapted from Lesley Young, "Spruceland Millworks Benefits for Generosity," *Canadian HR Reporter,* Vol. 20, Iss. 18, October 22, 2007, p. 12. Used by permission, and http:// www.spruceland .net (accessed February 27, 2008).

work team
employee team managing a task without direct supervision

Some companies carry employee participation a step further by creating self-managed **work teams.** In these groups, employees are assigned to a given task or operation, manage the task or operation without direct supervision, and assume responsibility for results. When work teams function properly, the number of supervisors needed decreases sharply.

As referred to in "In the Trenches," the staff of Spruceland are treated very well with the expectation that satisfied employees are more productive, enhancing business profits. To be effective, therefore, small firms must see employees as more than hired hands. Instead, they should regard them as valuable business resources.

Although small businesses may find it difficult to duplicate the personnel programs of such business giants as Bell Canada and Air Canada, they can develop approaches suitable for the 10, 50, or 100 employees on their payrolls. This chapter deals with the type of human resources management that works best for small firms.

In all but the simplest businesses, the entrepreneur's personal talents must be supplemented with the experience and abilities of other individuals. The prospects for any venture are most promising when a firm's leadership is composed of competent, resourceful, and tenacious individuals. As a first step, therefore, an entrepreneur needs to identify and attract a strong management team. A business plan that provides for strong leadership is appealing to prospective investors and attractive to prospective managerial personnel.

2 Discuss the evolving features of small firm management.

DISTINCTIVE FEATURES OF SMALL FIRM MANAGEMENT

Start-up ventures, as discussed above, are managed by the entrepreneur. Most entrepreneurs are not trained or educated in business methods and usually come from either the operations side of the business or the sales side. This leads to three significant issues as a firm grows: the need for business training for the entrepreneur, the need to address organizational issues and the need to formalize management. These issues will be discussed in more detail below.

professional manager
a manager who uses systematic, analytical methods of management

Even though managers in both large and small companies play similar managerial roles, their jobs differ in a number of ways. This is readily recognized by managers who move from large corporations to small firms and encounter an entirely different business atmosphere. Furthermore, a small firm experiences constant change in its organizational and managerial needs as it moves from point zero—its launching—to the point where it can employ a full staff of **professional managers.** Professional managers use more systematic and analytical methods, in contrast to the more haphazard techniques of those who lack their training and experience. In this section, we examine a number of distinctive features that challenge managers of small firms.

PREVALENT MANAGEMENT WEAKNESSES IN SMALL FIRMS

Although some large corporations experience poor management, small businesses seem particularly vulnerable to this weakness. Managerial inefficiency exists in tens (or even hundreds) of thousands of small firms. Many small firms are marginal or unprofitable businesses, struggling to survive from day to day. At best, they earn only a bare living for their owners. The reason for their condition is at once apparent to anyone who examines their operation. They operate, but it is an exaggeration to say that they are managed.

One successful entrepreneur who started several businesses candidly admitted his own inadequacies as a manager:

> *You name the mistake, and I made it during those years. I didn't pay enough attention to detail. I wasn't clear about responsibilities. I didn't hold people accountable. I was terrible at hiring. We had three chief financial officers in 10 years. We didn't start tracking cash flow until we were up to about $12 million in sales, and we went all the way to $25 million without developing an inventory system that worked. As a company, we lacked focus. Once, I brought in a consultant who asked our eight key people about the company's goals, and everyone gave a different answer.*[1]

Weaknesses of this nature are all too typical of small firms. The good news, however, is that poor management is neither universal nor inevitable.

CONSTRAINTS ON MANAGEMENT IN SMALL FIRMS

Managers of small firms, particularly new and growing companies, are constrained by conditions that do not trouble the average corporate executive: They must face the grim reality of small bank accounts and limited staff. A small firm often lacks the money for slick sales brochures. It cannot afford much in the way of market research. The shortage of cash even makes it difficult to employ an adequate number of secretaries and office assistants. Such limitations are painfully apparent to large firm managers who move into management positions in small firms.

Small firms typically lack an adequate specialized professional staff. Most small business managers are generalists who lack the support of experienced professional specialists in market research, financial analysis, advertising, human resources management, and other areas. The manager in a small business must make decisions in these areas without the expertise that is available in a larger business. This limitation may be partially overcome by using outside management assistance. Nevertheless, the shortage of internal professional talent is a part of the reality of managing entrepreneurial firms.

STAGES OF GROWTH AND IMPLICATIONS FOR MANAGEMENT

As a newly formed business becomes established and grows, its organization and pattern of management change. To some extent, management must adapt to growth and change in any organization. However, the changes involved as a business moves through periods of "childhood" and "adolescence" are much more extensive than those that occur with the growth of a relatively mature business.

A number of experts have proposed models related to the growth stages of business firms.[2] These models typically describe four or five stages of growth and identify various management issues related to each of the stages. Exhibit 9-1 shows four stages in the organizational life of many small businesses. As firms progress from the minimum size of Stage 1 to the larger size of Stage 4, they add layers of management and increase the formality of operations. Even though some firms skip the first one or two stages by starting as larger businesses, thousands of small firms make their way through each of the stages pictured here.

In Stage 1, the firm is simply a one-person operation. Even though some firms begin with a larger organization, the one-person start-up is by no means rare.

In Stage 2, the entrepreneur becomes a player-coach, which implies extensive participation in the operations of the business. In addition to performing the basic

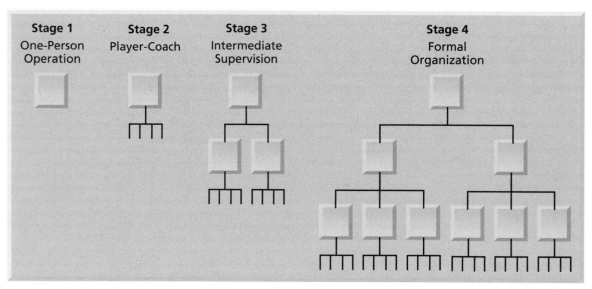

Stage 1
One-Person
Operation

Stage 2
Player-Coach

Stage 3
Intermediate
Supervision

Stage 4
Formal
Organization

EXHIBIT **9-1** *Organizational Stages of Small Business Growth*

work—whether production, sales, writing cheques, or record keeping—the entrepreneur must also coordinate the efforts of others.

In Stage 3, a major milestone is reached when an intermediate level of supervision is added. In many ways, this is a difficult and dangerous point for the small firm, because the entrepreneur must rise above direct, hands-on management and work through an intervening layer of management.

Stage 4, the stage of formal organization, involves more than increased size and multilayered organization. The formalization of management involves the adoption of written policies, preparation of plans and budgets, standardization of personnel practices, computerization of records, preparation of organization charts and job descriptions, scheduling of training conferences, institution of control procedures, and so on. While some formal management practices may be adopted prior to Stage 4 of a firm's growth, the stages outline a typical pattern of development for successful firms. Flexibility and informality may be helpful when a firm is first started, but its growth necessitates greater formality in planning and control. Tension often develops as the traditional easygoing patterns of management become dysfunctional. Great managerial skill is required to preserve a "family" atmosphere while introducing professional management.

As a firm moves from Stage 1 to Stage 4, the pattern of entrepreneurial activities changes. The entrepreneur becomes less of a doer and more of a manager, as shown in Exhibit 9-2.

Managers who are strong on "doing" skills are often weak on "managing" skills. For example, an owner who successfully starts one retail outlet may not be successful in expanding the operation to multiple locations. Firms experience growing pains during expansion due to lack of planning and financing problems.

USE OF MANAGERIAL TIME AT VARIOUS STAGES OF BUSINESS GROWTH

Firms that are too hesitant to move through these organizational stages and to acquire the necessary professional management limit their rate of growth. On the other hand, a

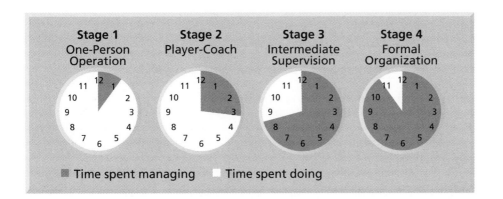

EXHIBIT **9-2**

Use of Managerial Time at Various Stages of Business Growth

small business may attempt to become a big business too quickly. The entrepreneur's primary strength may lie in product development or selling, for example, and a quick move into Stage 4 may saddle the entrepreneur with managerial duties and rob the organization of his or her valuable entrepreneurial talents.

The need for effective management becomes more acute as the business expands. Very small firms often survive in spite of weak management. To some extent, the quality of their products or services may offset deficiencies in their management. In the early days of business life, therefore, the firm may survive and grow even though its management is less than professional. Even in a very small business, however, defects in management place strains on the business and retard its development in some way.

FOUNDERS AS MANAGERS

Founders of new firms are not always good organization members. As we explained in Chapter 1, they are creative, innovative, risk-taking individuals who have the courage to strike out on their own. Indeed, they are often propelled into entrepreneurship by precipitating events, sometimes involving difficulty in fitting into conventional organizational roles. As a consequence, founders may fail to appreciate the value of good management practices. One implication of this is they may be reluctant to change the organization's structure (who reports to whom and has responsibility for what) and to add professional managers as the company's growth requires them. One long-standing truism illustrates this: in many growing companies the need for a sales manager is recognized and the mistake is made to promote the best salesperson, regardless of management ability. Too often, the result is that the company loses their best salesperson and ends up with a bad sales manager. The orientation of the founder frequently differs from that of professional managers. These differences, as outlined in Exhibit 9-3, show the founder as more of a mover and shaker, and the professional manager, in contrast, as more of an administrator.

EXHIBIT **9-3**

Typical Characteristics of Founders and Professional Managers

Founders	Professional Managers
Innovative	Administrative
Intuitive	Analytical
Action-oriented	Planning-oriented
Focused on the long term	Focused on the short term
Bold	Cautious

IN THE TRENCHES

Entrepreneurial Experiences

Young Entrepreneurs Look for Balance

In their definition of success young entrepreneurs reflect a broader trend that has emerged over the past few years. Now entering the workforce, this group of 19–35-year-olds includes the children who were raised in the 1980s by career-obsessed parents who often paid a steep personal price to climb the corporate ladder. They don't want to work for large companies and they don't want to be middle managers, and while they are willing to work hard, they aren't willing to forfeit family life.

"A lot of people used to assume that being self-employed, starting your own business was working 18 hours a day every day," says Steve Edwards, a music school and store owner from St. John's Nfld. "It's not about building a job, it's about building a life. You can only sustain what you really love: one feeds the other."

Another example is Bathurst, New Brunswick's TSi Auto Solutions, an automotive industry software firm that has built about a 30 percent Canadian market share and is aggressively moving into the United States. Founded by Dan Hill and Dino Karatzios, the company has a strategic marketing alliance with multinational accounting and consulting company PriceWaterhouseCoopers, which makes growing the business while remaining in Bathurst possible. According to Hill, "We've had no problem expanding the company or recruiting talent in Bathurst.

Sean Frisky, founder of Regina, Saskatchewan–based Ground Effects Environmental Services says that his business is well positioned in the centre of the continent to reach into the U.S. as well as across Canada. "Saskatchewan is all about quality of life and an excellent culture for work ethic," Frisky observes. "It's also about relationships: my initial financing came from the Nipawin Credit Union. They took a real chance giving me seed capital and no loan payments for a year. The advantage was that they knew me, knew my dad. That matters."

Source: Deirdre McMurdy, "Young Entrepreneurs Seek Work-Life Balance," *CanWest News,* October 21, 2004, p. 1.

Some entrepreneurs are professional in their approach to management, and some corporate managers are entrepreneurial in the sense of being innovative and willing to take risks. Nevertheless, a founder's less than professional management style often acts as a drag on business growth. Ideally, the founder adds a measure of professional management without sacrificing the entrepreneurial spirit and the basic values that gave the business a successful start. Many entrepreneurs recognize the need to upgrade their business skills as the venture grows and the complexity of managing grows with it. There are many sources of education and training: privately offered management training, executive education or continuing education programs offered by colleges and universities, or degree programs in business.

THE MANAGEMENT TEAM

3 Describe the characteristics and value of a strong management team.

If a firm is extremely small, the founder will probably be the key manager and perhaps the only manager. In most firms, however, others share leadership roles with the owner or owners. The concept of a management team, therefore, is relevant to small business.

In general, the **management team,** as we envision it here, includes both managers and other professionals or key persons who help give a new firm its general direction. The key contributors may include advisers or a board of directors, as well as professionals such as an accountant or lawyer. While most new ventures are started with just the founder or founders, the most successful will build a management team that includes advisers during the pre-start-up phase, and will hire managers responsible for accounting and finance, and sales and marketing as the business grows.

THE VALUE OF A STRONG MANAGEMENT TEAM

Strong management can make the best of a good business idea by securing the resources needed to make it work. Of course, even a highly competent management team cannot rescue a firm that is based on a weak business concept or that lacks adequate resources. The importance of strong management to start-ups is evident in the attitudes of prospective investors, who consider the quality of a new venture's management to be the single most important factor in decisions to invest or not to invest.

A management team brings greater strength to many ventures than does an individual entrepreneur. A new or small business requires expertise in three key areas: finance and accounting, sales and marketing, and technology and operations. Most entrepreneurs have skills in one area, usually sales and marketing or technology and operations. A few will have some skill or expertise in two of the areas; almost no one will have sufficient skill and expertise in all three areas to be able to grow the business for long. For this reason, a team can provide a diversity of talent to meet various staffing needs. The range of technical experts, mentors, and internal resources is displayed in Exhibit 9-4. This is particularly true for high-tech start-ups, and it may also be true for other ventures. In addition, a team can provide greater assurance of continuity since the departure of one member of a team would be less devastating than the departure of a

management team

managers and other key persons who give a company its general direction

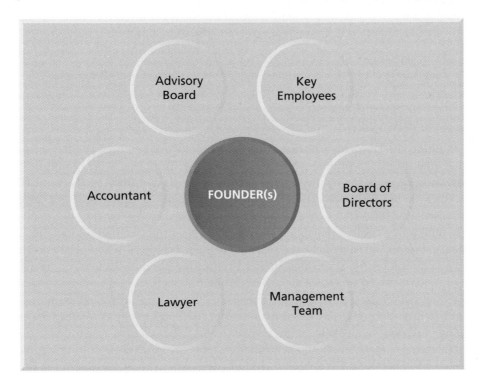

EXHIBIT **9-4**

The Venture Team

sole entrepreneur. Ability or skill is not the only attribute investors look for, however. Experience in management and a "track record" of building successful businesses are highly valued by investors and increase the chance of success of the venture.

BUILDING A COMPLEMENTARY MANAGEMENT TEAM

The management team includes individuals with supervisory responsibilities—for example, a financial manager who supervises a small office staff—as well as non-supervisory personnel who play key roles in the business. A new firm, for example, might begin with one individual who directs its marketing effort. Because of the importance of the marketing function, that person would be a key member of the management team.

The competence required in a management team depends on the type of business and the nature of its operations. For example, a software development firm and a restaurant call for drastically different types of business experience. Whatever the business, a small firm needs managers with an appropriate combination of educational background and experience. In evaluating the qualifications of applicants for key positions, an entrepreneur needs to know whether they have experience in a related type of business, whether the experience included managerial responsibilities, and whether they were ever entrepreneurs.

Not all members of a management team need competence in all areas—the key is balance. If one member has expertise in finance, another should have an adequate marketing background. And there should be someone who can supervise employees effectively.

Even when entrepreneurs recognize the need for team members with varying expertise, they frequently seek to duplicate their own personalities and management styles. While personal compatibility and cooperation of team members are necessary for effective collaboration, a healthy situation exists when the qualifications of team members are diverse. Dr. Stephen R. Covey, a management consultant, puts it this way:

> *In my opinion, the No. 1 mistake that most entrepreneurs make is that they never know how to develop a complementary team. They're always kind of cloning themselves, that is, trying to turn their employees into duplicates of themselves . . . You have to empower other people and build on their strengths to make your own weaknesses irrelevant.*[3]

Planning the company's leadership, then, should produce a management team that is able to give competent direction to the new firm. The team should be balanced in terms of covering the various functional areas and offering the right combination of education and experience. It may comprise both insiders and outside specialists.

In addition to selecting members of the management team, an entrepreneur must design an internal management structure that defines relationships among all members of the organization. Relationships among the various positions—such as advertising manager, marketing director, financial officer, and human resources manager—need to be understood. Although they need not be worked out in great detail, planning should be sufficient to permit an orderly functioning of the enterprise and to avoid an overlapping of responsibilities that invites conflict.

The management plan should be drafted in a way that provides for business growth. Unfilled positions should be specified, and job descriptions should spell out the duties

EXHIBIT **9-5**
*Creating and
Compensating the
Management Team*

STAGE ONE
During the pre-start-up stage key issues regarding skills base, responsibility, and financial rewards should be clarified for the founders. As such, the founders must agree to the following:

- Their title
- How much money they are each contributing
- What their key responsibilities will be, and how much time they are willing to commit to the venture
- The specific skills they bring to the venture
- The salary (or other compensation such as dividends) and shares that each will receive
- How much holiday they expect, for the first year and thereafter
- Their harvesting expectations: how soon they expect to sell and what return they are seeking

STAGE TWO
When the key points such as risk, return, and responsibility factors have been resolved for the founders a similar process should be established for members of the Advisory Board:

- How many and what type of advisers are needed
- The specific skills they should bring to the table
- Their expectations for compensation (in many cases they do not expect compensation but are acting as mentors)

STAGE THREE
The next stage entails determining the type and number of staff required, starting with the management team, and professionals. This stage may occur at start-up, or after several years of growth.

- What type of skills are needed; do they address gaps in the skill base of the founder/founders and the advisers?
- What type of compensation is common in the industry; should they be offered shares or profit sharing?
- What are the expectations regarding performance and the method of evaluation?

of and necessary qualifications for such positions. Methods for selecting key employees should also be explained. When the business is organized as a partnership, the partners need to consider the possible breakup of the partnership—ownership shares need to be thought out carefully. Similarly, compensation arrangements, including bonus or other incentive plans for key organization members, warrant detailed planning. Refer to Exhibit 9-5 for a three-stage process in the formation and compensations of a management team.

THE NATURE OF MANAGERIAL WORK

Thus far, we have treated the management process in a general way. Now it is time to look more closely at what managers do—how they plan, how they exercise leadership, how they organize, and how they control operations. These activities are called **management functions.**

Identify the various kinds of plans and approaches to planning.

4

management functions
the activities of planning, leading, organizing, and controlling

PLANNING

The preparation of a formal business plan for a new business, as discussed in Chapter 5, is only the first phase of an ongoing process of planning that guides production, marketing, and other activities on a month-to-month and year-to-year basis. This section focuses on the ongoing planning process.

IN THE TRENCHES

Utilizing New Technology

Podcasting for Engagement

Nycomed Canada, one of Canada's pharmaceutical success stories and a 2008 Best Workplaces in Canada award winner, uses many conventional and some unconventional ways of attracting and keeping its people. Founded in 1997 as Byk Canada with three employees, today the company is part of Zurich-based Nycomed, and has 265 employees and annual revenues of $219 million in Canada.

One of the unique ways it keeps employees informed about company happenings is monthly "podcasts" or broadcasts over the web. Whether working at its Oakville, Ontario, head office or remotely, the podcasts keep everyone in the loop and have increased employee engagement.

On the financial side, Nycomed offers employees several benefits including topping up (to 100%) maternity leave payments, a generous compassionate-leave program, tuition subsidies up to $5000 and very competitive salaries, which it maintains by doing an external salary survey every six months.

Other initiatives include individual performance reviews every six months, employee referral bonuses of up to $1500, a share-purchase plan, profit sharing, discounts on home computers, and paid time off to volunteer with an employee's favourite charitable organization.

"Culture trumps strategy," said John Suk, founder of Byk in 1997 and now CEO of Nycomed Canada. "Throughout our . . . history we have always found that investing in our people means we are investing our company's success—one cannot thrive without the other. This is especially true in today's rapidly changing pharmaceutical environment. It is the dedication of our employees and their commitment to being a preferred company which instills confidence in our customers and partners."

Source: http://www.canadastop100.com and http://www.nycomed.ca/en/Menu/About+us, accessed June 12, 2008.

NEED FOR FORMAL PLANNING

Most small business managers plan to some degree. However, the amount of planning is typically less than ideal. Also, what little planning there is tends to be spotty and unsystematic—dealing with how much inventory to purchase, whether to buy a new piece of equipment, and other questions of this type. Specific circumstances affect the degree to which formal planning is needed, but most businesses would function more profitably by increasing their planning and making it more systematic.

The payoff from planning comes in several ways. First, the process of thinking through the issues confronting a firm and developing a plan can improve productivity. Second, planning provides a focus for a firm: managerial decisions during a year can be guided by the annual plan, and employees can work consistently toward the same goal. Third, evidence of planning provides credibility with bankers, suppliers, and other outsiders.

long-range plan (strategic plan)
a firm's overall plan for the future

KINDS OF PLANS

A firm's basic path to the future is spelled out in its **long-range plan,** also called a **strategic plan.** As previously noted, strategy decisions are concerned with such issues as market niche and/or features that differentiate the firm from its competitors. A long-range plan provides a foundation for the more specific plans explained below.

Short-range plans are action plans for one year or less that govern activities in production, marketing, and other areas. An important part of short-range operating plans is the **budget**—a document that expresses future plans in monetary terms that is usually prepared one year in advance, with a breakdown by quarters or months.

Other types of plans are less connected to the calendar and more concerned with the way things are done. **Business policies,** for example, are basic statements that serve as guides for managerial decision making. They include financial policies, personnel policies, and so on. A personnel policy may state, for example, that no employee may accept a gift from a supplier unless it is of nominal value.

Procedures are more specific and deal primarily with methodology—how something is to be done. In a furniture store, for example, a procedure might require the sale of furniture on credit to be approved by a credit manager prior to delivery to the customer. Once a work method is established, it may be standardized and referred to as a **standard operating procedure.**

MAKING TIME FOR PLANNING

Small business managers all too often succumb to the "tyranny of the urgent." Because they are busy putting out fires, they never get around to planning. Planning is easy to postpone and therefore easy for managers to ignore while concentrating on the more urgent issues of production and sales. And, like a centre skating with his head down, such managers may be bowled over by competitors.

Some discipline is necessary in order to reap the benefits of planning. Time and a degree of seclusion must be provided if significant progress is to be made. Planning is primarily a mental process. It is seldom done effectively in an atmosphere of ringing telephones, rush orders, and urgent demands for decision making.

The owners of Krave's Candy (see "In the Trenches") were successful in expanding their business due more to their luck and their relentless efforts rather than structured planning. Their continued success has required the introduction of detailed planning and a quality control process.

GOAL SETTING

Setting clear goals is a key aspect of the planning process. Goals are created for critical performance areas, such as manufacturing, quality, sales and profit, customer service, and number of distribution outlets. As mentioned in Chapter 5, clear goals can be established using the SMART criteria.

The owners of Krave's Candy had several SMART long-term goals, including increasing production to 20 million pounds within four years of initial operations, which they achieved.

Objectives are short-term targets, typically for one year or less, that are consistent with long-term goals. They are quantifiable and are frequently used in preparing business plans to provide performance benchmarks for owners, investors, and bankers.

EMPLOYEE PARTICIPATION IN PLANNING

Although a small business owner should personally spend time planning, this responsibility may be delegated to some extent, because some planning is required of all members of the enterprise. The larger the organization, the more important it is to delegate some planning; the owner can hardly specify in detail the program

short-range plans
plans that govern a firm's operations for one year or less

budget
a document that expresses future plans in monetary terms

business policies
basic statements that serve as guides for managerial decision making

procedures
specific methods followed in business activities

standard operating procedure
an established method of conducting a business activity

IN THE TRENCHES

Entrepreneurial Experiences

Krave's Candy Co.: Building a Company Step by Step

Larry Finnson and Chris Emery have been buddies since they met in Grade 10. Now, instead of just hanging around most of the day, they do business in the cutthroat world of candy. In the $24 billion North American market, multinationals such as Hershey Foods dominate, with prime shelf space and expensive advertising. Against all odds, Chris and Larry's Krave's Candy is thriving. The Winnipeg-based manufacturing plant produces 2,500 pounds of candy per hour, including their main product, Clodhoppers.

No one is more surprised by the venture's success than Chris and Larry. The company suffered several near-death experiences brought on by the strains of uneven seasonal demand, flawed packaging, inadequate financing, and spurts of rapid growth. Neither partner had any business experience or a plan when they decided to commercialize a recipe developed by Chris's grandmother, Edith Baker. As a university student, Chris received packages of homemade candy that were such a hit he had to hide them from his roommates. With Chris's marketing skills and Larry's technical background, they scraped together $20 000 from savings, friends, and family, rented industrial space, and transformed a couple of old kettle cookers and packaging equipment into a makeshift production line.

Chris offers some advice: "We didn't do a business plan, and I would definitely recommend to anyone wanting to start their own business to do that. We just jumped right in and learned as we went, and what we learned was you should clearly define who your competition is and what your market is."

Within two years Chris and Larry had to scramble to keep up to the demand generated by seasonal sales to Zellers and Wal-Mart. They had to upgrade their ancient equipment, build inventory levels, and finance the expansion. Financing was patchwork, with a line of credit from a bank, a loan from BDC, and even a loan from a lender of last resort, which charged an interest rate of 30 percent.

Ensis Management of Winnipeg, a venture capital firm, provided $500,000 and administrative and planning skills to the team, and with strong planning and solid marketing the company had increased sales to $10 million by 2004 and was distributing in the United Kingdom, Australia, Japan, and the United States.

The company has moved from a no-plan start-up mode to a highly organized manufacturer selling to over 400 Blockbuster and 274 Rogers Video outlets, Wal-Mart, Zellers, and convenience stores across Canada. Larry Finnson illustrates the thoughtful planning process now used when expanding by referring to the rebranding of one of their biggest sellers in Canada—the chocolate Clodhopper—to "Hip-Hoppers" for the U.S. market. He says, "The No. 1 selling musical genre in the U.S. is hip hop; the No. 1 consumer of hip hop is 12- to 30-year-olds, and the No. 1 consumer of candy is 12- to 30-year-olds. We're looking for an angle. We can't dump $10 million into an advertising campaign; we have to be creative. We are offering hip hop kids their own candy; our competitors don't do that. Our strategy was to test-market though the 10 busiest Blockbuster outlets and 1000 convenience stores in the U.S. to determine demand." The positive results gave them an extra boost in their negotiations to have Hip-hoppers on the shelves of Blockbuster outlets across the United States.

> Krave's success didn't go unnoticed in the industry, and in 2006 the founders sold it to Abbotsford, B.C.'s Brookside Foods, a privately owned confection maker, where Chris Emery is now the marketing director. Larry Finnson has launched another Winnipeg-based company, 24K Water Co. According to Finnson, it was just time to get out. "It was a ten-year run and 24/7, so I thought, 'What else can I do? I'm getting sick of this.' The other shareholders weren't buying into the Chris and Larry vision. So, when the vision is lost and the two founders lose direction of the company, it's time to let it go."
>
> *Sources:* Adapted from Dierdre McMurdy, "Building Future on Sweet Idea," *Financial Post*, February 11, 2002, p. FP1; http://www.clodhoppers.tv/about.html (accessed June 2, 2005); Jack Kohne, "Sounds Like Sweet Success," *Food in Canada*, May 2007, pp. 40–43 and; "The Candy Man Can," *PROFIT*, October 2006, p. 14.

for each department, and the involvement by staff will increase their commitment to the plan.

The concept that the boss does the thinking and the employee does the work is misleading. Progressive managers have discovered that employees' ideas are often helpful in developing solutions to company problems. A salesperson, for example, is closer than her or his manager to the firm's customers and is usually better able to evaluate their needs and reactions.

EFFECTIVE COMMUNICATION

Another key to a healthy organization is effective communication—that is, getting managers and employees to talk with each other and openly share problems and ideas. To some extent, the management hierarchy must be set aside so that personnel at all levels can speak freely with those higher up. The result is two-way communication—a far cry from the old-fashioned idea that managers give orders and employees simply carry them out.

To communicate effectively, managers must tell employees where they stand, how the business is doing, and what the company's plans for the future are. Negative feedback to employees may be necessary at times, but positive feedback is the primary tool for establishing good human relations. Perhaps the most fundamental concept managers need to keep in mind is that employees are people: they quickly detect insincerity but respond to honest efforts to treat them as mature, responsible individuals. In short, an atmosphere of trust and respect contributes greatly to good communication.

To go beyond having good intentions, a small firm manager can adopt any of the following practical techniques for stimulating two-way communication:

- Periodic performance review sessions to discuss employees' ideas, questions, complaints, and job expectations, both on a group and individual basis
- "Notice of the day" emails to keep employees informed about developments affecting them and/or the company
- Open communication with staff by exchanging email or dropping by the owner/manager's office to discuss ideas
- Staff meetings to discuss problems and matters of general concern

The key to open communication is for both participants to listen, a practice that not all business owners or founders find easy to adopt.

Explain the importance of employee recruitment and list some sources that can be useful for finding suitable applicants.

5

RECRUITING PERSONNEL

When recruiting employees, a small firm competes with both large and small businesses, and it cannot afford to let competitors take the cream of the crop. Aggressive recruitment requires the small firm to take the initiative in locating applicants and to search until enough applicants are available to permit wise choices.

IMPORTANCE OF PEOPLE

Hiring the right people and eliciting their enthusiastic performance are essential factors of any business hoping to reach its potential. As Ellyn Spragins has suggested, "With every person you hire, you determine how great your potential successes may be—or how awful your failures."[4]

Employees affect profitability in many ways. In most small firms, the attitudes of salespeople and their ability to serve customer needs directly affect sales revenue. Also, payroll is one of the largest expense categories for most businesses, having a direct impact on the bottom line. By recruiting outstanding personnel, therefore, a firm can improve its return on each payroll dollar.

Recruiting and selecting employees establishes a foundation for a firm's ongoing human relationships. In a sense, the quality of employees determines the human potential of an organization. If talented, ambitious recruits can be attracted, the business, through good management, should be able to build a strong human organization.

ATTRACTING APPLICANTS TO SMALL FIRMS

Competition in recruiting well-qualified business talent requires small firms to identify their distinctive advantages when making an appeal to outstanding prospects, especially to those seeking managerial and professional positions. Fortunately, small firm recruiters can advance some good arguments in favour of small business careers.

The opportunity for general management experience at a decision-making level is attractive to many prospects. Rather than toiling in obscure, low-level, specialized positions during their early years, capable newcomers can quickly move into positions of responsibility in well-managed small businesses. In such positions, they can see that their work makes a difference in the success of the company.

Small firms can structure the work environment to offer professional, managerial, and technical personnel greater freedom than they would normally have in big businesses. One example of a small company that created an atmosphere of this type is Avcorp Industries Inc., an aircraft-parts manufacturer based in Laval, Quebec. This firm introduced "Red Flag," a system that allows production workers to stop production when they encounter a production snag or technology-related issue that could hinder (or help) a delivery commitment. When an employee raises a flag, an alarm sounds at 30-second intervals until a supervisor comes and offers assistance. Then a brief report is drafted and logged into the computer system so that those likely to come up with the solution—including the customer—are notified immediately. Problem contracts no longer get lost in the shuffle, costs have been reduced, and the overall flow of production has been enhanced. Avcorp turned from being a money-losing operation to a profitable one through this type of employee decision making.[5]

In this type of environment, individual contributions can be recognized rather than hidden under the numerous layers of a bureaucratic organization. In addition, compensation arrangements can be designed to create a powerful incentive. Flexibility in work scheduling and job-sharing arrangements are other possible lures. The value of any incentive as a recruiting advantage depends to some degree on the circumstances of the particular firm. From the standpoint of an applicant, ideally the firm should be growing and profitable. It should also have a degree of professionalism in its management that can be readily recognized by prospective employees.

SOURCES OF EMPLOYEES

To recruit effectively, the small business manager must know where and how to find qualified applicants. Sources are numerous, and it is impossible to generalize about the best source in view of variations in personnel requirements and quality of sources from one locality to another.

WALK-INS

A firm may receive unsolicited applications from individuals who walk into the place of business to seek employment. This is an inexpensive source for clerical and production jobs, but the quality of applicants may be mixed. If qualified applicants cannot be hired immediately, their applications should be kept on file for future reference, preferably on an easy-to-find "hot-list." In the interest of good public relations, all applicants should be treated courteously, whether or not they are offered jobs.

ELECTRONIC EMPLOYMENT SITES

Several electronic sites, such as http://www.workopolis.com, are available for job postings. Unfortunately, although the cost to post the job opening on the sites is usually nominal, the number of responses may be quite high, often by unqualified applicants. When using the sites, time should be allocated to screen the applications extensively.

SCHOOLS

Secondary schools, trade schools, colleges, and universities are desirable sources for certain classes of employees, particularly those who need no specific work experience. Some secondary schools and colleges have internship programs involving periods of work in business firms. These programs enable students to gain a measure of practical experience. Secondary and trade schools provide applicants with a limited but useful educational background. Colleges and universities can supply candidates for positions in management and in various technical and scientific fields. In addition, many colleges and universities are excellent sources of part-time employees.

PUBLIC EMPLOYMENT OFFICES

Human Resources and Social Development Canada, a department of the federal government, has Employment Centres in all major cities and in most larger towns that offer—at no cost to small businesses—a supply of applicants who are actively seeking employment. These offices are for the most part a source of clerical workers, unskilled labourers, production workers, and technicians.

PRIVATE EMPLOYMENT AGENCIES

Numerous private agencies offer their services as employment offices. In some cases, employers receive their services without cost because the applicants pay a fee to the agency. However, most firms pay the agency fee if the applicant is highly qualified. Such agencies tend to specialize in people with specific skills, such as accountants, computer operators, or managers. Many agencies solicit applications through employment Internet sites, ensuring a wide range of applicants.

When filling key positions, small firms sometimes turn to executive search firms, called **headhunters,** to locate qualified candidates. Professional recruiters research the skills required for the position, create advertisements, screen applicants, and assist in the interviewing and selection process. Many small businesses use recruiters for key positions such as financial or operations managers. Headhunters, who are paid by the company they represent, can make a wide-ranging search for individuals who possess the right combination of talents, and reduce the pressure on small business operators caused by time constraints.

headhunter
a search firm that locates qualified candidates for executive positions

EMPLOYEE REFERRALS

If current employees are good employees, their recommendations of suitable candidates may provide excellent prospects. Ordinarily, employees will hesitate to recommend applicants unless they believe in their ability to do the job. Many small business owners say that this source provides more of their employees than any other. A few employers go so far as to offer financial rewards for successful employee referrals.

HELP-WANTED ADVERTISING

The "Help Wanted" sign in the window is one form of recruiting used by small firms. A similar but more aggressive form of recruiting consists of advertisements in the classified pages of local newspapers. Although the effectiveness of these forms has been questioned by some, many well-managed organizations recruit in this way.

TEMPORARY-HELP AGENCIES

The temporary-help industry, which is growing rapidly, supplies temporary employees (or temps) such as word processors, clerks, accountants, engineers, nurses, and sales clerks for short periods of time. By using agencies such as Kelly Services, small firms can deal with seasonal fluctuations and absences caused by vacation or illness. As an example, a temporary replacement might be obtained to fill the position of an employee who is on maternity leave. In addition, using temporary employees provides an introduction to individuals whose performance may justify an offer of permanent employment. At such time a commission would be paid to the agency. Staffing with temporary employees is less practical, however, when extensive training is required or continuity is important.

DESCRIBING JOBS TO BE FILLED

A small business manager should analyze the activities or work to be performed and determine the number and kinds of jobs to be filled. Knowing the job requirements permits a more intelligent selection of applicants for specific jobs, based on their individual capacities and characteristics.

Certainly the owner-manager should not select personnel simply to fit a rigid specification of education, experience, or personal background. Rather, she or he must concentrate on the ability of an individual to fill a particular position in the business. Making this determination requires an outline or summary of the work to be performed. A written summary of this type, as shown in Exhibit 9-6, is called a **job description.**

job description
a written summary of duties required by a specific job

Title:	Stock Clerk
Primary Function:	To stock shelves with food products and other items
Supervision Received:	Works under direct supervision of store manager
Supervision Exercised:	None

Duties:
1. Receive and store products in storage area.
2. Take products from storage, open outer wrapping, and place contents on store shelves.
3. Provide information and/or direction to customers seeking particular products or having other questions.
4. Monitor quantity of products on shelves and add products when supplies are low.
5. Perform housekeeping duties when special need arises—for example, when container is broken or products fall on the floor.
6. Assist cashiers in bagging products as needed during rush periods.
7. Assist in other areas or perform special assignments as directed by the store manager.

EXHIBIT **9-6**
Job Description for Stock Clerk in Retail Food Store

Preparing job descriptions need not be a highly sophisticated process. One business-owner simply asked employees to jot down what they did over a period of a few days.[6] The managers then looked for duplication of duties and for tasks that might have fallen through the cracks. In this relatively informal manner, they created job descriptions that spelled out duties recognized by the employees as well as the employer.

Duties listed in job descriptions should not be defined too narrowly. Job descriptions should minimize unnecessary overlap but avoid creating a "that's-not-my-job" mentality. Technical competence is as necessary in small firms as it is in a large business, but versatility and flexibility may be even more important. Engineers may occasionally need to make sales calls, and marketing people may need to pinch-hit in production.

In the process of studying a job, an analyst should list the knowledge, skills, abilities, or other characteristics that an individual must have to perform the job. This statement of requirements is called a **job specification.** A job specification for the position of stock clerk might state that the person must be able to lift 20 kg and must have completed 10 to 12 years of school.

Job descriptions are mainly an aid in recruiting personnel but they also have other uses. For example, they can give employees a focus in their work, provide direction in training, and supply a framework for performance review.

job specification
a list of knowledge, skills, abilities, or other characteristics needed by a job applicant to perform a specific job

EVALUATING PROSPECTS AND SELECTING EMPLOYEES

Identify the steps in evaluating job applicants.

6

An employer's recruitment activities merely locate prospects for employment. Subsequent steps are needed to evaluate these candidates and to select some as employees. An employer can minimize the danger of taking a blind, uninformed gamble on applicants of unknown quality by following the steps described in the next sections.

STEP 1: USING APPLICATION FORMS

The value of having prospective employees complete an application form lies in the form's systematic collection of background data that might otherwise be overlooked.

The information recorded on an application form is useful in sizing up an applicant and serves as a guide in making a more detailed investigation of the applicant's experience and character. Key selection criteria may be used to short list the applicants with the best fit to the job. Key criteria typically address the specific skills and experiences that have the greatest impact on performance.

An application form need not be elaborate or lengthy. However, care must be taken to avoid questions that may conflict with laws concerning unfair job discrimination. Provincial and federal laws limit the use of many questions formerly found on application forms. Questions about race, colour, national origin, religion, age, marital status, disabilities, or arrests are either prohibited or considered unwise unless the employer can prove they are related to the job.

STEP 2: INTERVIEWING THE APPLICANT

An interview permits the employer to get some idea of the applicant's personality, intelligence, and job knowledge. Any of these factors may be significant for the job to be filled. Although the interview is an important step in the selection process, it should not be the only step. Some managers have the mistaken idea that they are infallible judges of human nature and can choose good employees on the basis of interviews alone without confirmation from references. Care must be taken in the interview process, as in designing application forms, to avoid questions that conflict with the law. If possible, applicants should be interviewed by two or more individuals in order to minimize errors in judgment.

Time spent interviewing, as well as in other phases of the selection process, can save time and money later on. High employee turnover, caused partially by poor employee selection, has numerous costs including advertising for the position, time spent interviewing and training, and loss of customers due to reduced staff levels or level of competence. In today's litigious society, firing an employee has become quite difficult. A dismissed employee can bring suit even when an employer had justifiable reasons for dismissal.

The value of the interview depends on the interviewer's skill and methods. Any interviewer can improve his or her interviewing by following these generally accepted principles:

- Determine the job-related questions you want to ask the applicant before beginning the interview.
- Conduct the interview in a quiet atmosphere.
- Give your entire attention to the applicant.
- Put the applicant at ease.
- Never argue.
- Keep the conversation at a level suited to the applicant.
- Listen attentively.
- Observe closely the applicant's speech, mannerisms, and attire if these characteristics are important to the job.
- Try to avoid being unduly influenced by the applicant's trivial mannerisms or superficial resemblance to other people you know.

Employment interviews should be seen as a two-way process. The applicant is evaluating the employer while the employer is evaluating the applicant. In order for the applicant to make an informed decision, he or she needs a clear idea of what the job entails and an opportunity to ask questions.

STEP 3: CHECKING REFERENCES AND OTHER BACKGROUND INFORMATION

Careful checking with former employers, school authorities, and other references can help avoid hiring mistakes, which can have serious consequences later. Suppose, for example, that you hired an appliance technician who later burglarized a customer's home. Checking the applicant's background for a criminal record might have prevented this unfortunate occurrence.

It is becoming increasingly difficult to obtain more than the basic facts concerning a person's background because of the potential for lawsuits brought against former employers by disappointed applicants. However, reference checks on a prior employment record do not constitute infringements on privacy. A written letter of inquiry to these references is probably the weakest form of checking because most people will not put damaging statements in writing. Often, former employers or supervisors will speak more frankly when approached by telephone or in person.

For a fee, an applicant's history (financial, criminal, employment, and so on) may be supplied by private investigation agencies or credit bureaus. If an employer needs a credit report to establish an applicant's eligibility for employment, the federal *Privacy Act* requires that the applicant be notified in writing that such a report is being requested. Refer to the Office of the Privacy Commissioner of Canada site http://www.privcom.gc.ca for more detail.

STEP 4: TESTING THE APPLICANT

Many kinds of jobs lend themselves to performance testing. For example, an applicant may be given a data-entry test to verify speed and accuracy of keyboarding skills. With a little ingenuity, employers can improvise practical tests that are pertinent to many positions. Outside firms, including placement agencies, also provide testing as part of the screening process.

Psychological examinations may also be used by small businesses, but the results can be misleading because of difficulty in interpreting the tests or in adapting them to a particular business. In addition, federal government regulations require that any test used in making employment decisions must be job related.

Useful tests of any kind must meet the criteria of **validity** and **reliability.** If a test is valid, its results should correspond well with job performance; that is, the applicants with the best test scores should generally be the best employees. If a test is reliable, it should provide consistent results when used at different times or by various individuals.

validity
the extent to which a test assesses true job performance ability

reliability
the extent to which a test is consistent in measuring job performance ability

STEP 5: PHYSICAL EXAMINATIONS

A primary purpose of physical examinations is to evaluate the ability of applicants to meet the physical demands of specific jobs. Care must be taken, however, to avoid discriminating against those who are physically disabled. The law permits drug screening of applicants and this can be included as part of the physical examination process. Since few small firms have staff physicians, most of them must make arrangements with a local doctor or clinic to perform physical examinations.

TRAINING AND DEVELOPMENT

Once an employee has been recruited and added to the payroll, the process of training and development must begin. For this process, a new recruit is raw material, while the well-trained technician, salesperson, manager, or other employee represents a finished product.

PURPOSES OF TRAINING AND DEVELOPMENT

One obvious purpose of training is to prepare a new recruit to perform the duties for which he or she has been hired. There are very few positions for which no training is required. If an employer fails to provide training, the new employee must learn by trial and error, which frequently wastes time, materials, and money.

Training to improve skills and knowledge is not limited to newcomers; the performance of current employees can often be improved through additional training. In view of the constant change in products, technology, policies, and procedures in the world of business, continual training is necessary to update knowledge and skills—even in a small firm. Only with such training can employees meet the changing demands placed on them.

Many small businesses also access formal training through government programs, cooperative programs through academic institutions, the local Chamber of Commerce, and seminars through training firms, particularly for computer skills. The Canadian Jobs Strategy Program, sponsored by the federal government, provides a range of training including the Skill Shortage and Investment Program for the upgrading of staff skills due to technological change; the Job Entry Program, which pays for the training of unemployed or undertrained people; and the Community Futures Program, which funds training in areas with economic hardship. Refer to the Human Resources and Social Development Canada website http://www.hrsdc.gc.ca for more details.

Both employers and employees have a stake in the advancement of qualified personnel to higher-level positions. Preparation for advancement usually involves developmental efforts, possibly of a different type than those needed to sharpen skills for current duties. Because personal development and advancement are prime concerns of able employees, a small business can profit from careful attention to this phase of the personnel program. The opportunity to grow and move up in an organization not only improves the morale of current employees but also offers an inducement for potential applicants.

ORIENTATION FOR NEW PERSONNEL

The developmental process begins with an employee's first two or three days on the job. It is at this point that a new person tends to feel lost and confused when confronted with a new physical layout, different job title, unknown fellow employees, different type of supervision, changed hours or work schedule, and/or a unique set of personnel policies and procedures. Any events that conflict with the newcomer's expectations are interpreted in light of his or her previous work experience, and these interpretations can foster a strong commitment to the new employer or lead to feelings of alienation.

Recognizing the new employee's sensitivity at this point, the employer can contribute to a positive outcome by proper orientation. Steps can be taken to help the newcomer adjust and to minimize feelings of uneasiness in the new setting.

In addition to explaining specific job duties, supervisors can outline the firm's policies and procedures in as much detail as possible. A clear explanation of performance criteria and the way in which an employee's work will be evaluated should be included in the discussion. The new employee should be encouraged to ask questions, and time should be taken to provide careful answers. The firm may facilitate the orientation process by providing the recruit with a written list of company practices and procedures in the form of an employee handbook. The handbook may include information about work hours, paydays, breaks, lunch hours, absences, holidays, names of supervisors, employee benefits, and so on. Since new employees are faced with information overload at first, it is a good idea to schedule a follow-up orientation after a week or two.

RETAINING EMPLOYEES

In some parts of Canada, attracting and retaining employees is a huge problem for businesses. Whether it's the hot Alberta economy or the construction boom leading up to the 2010 Winter Olympics in Vancouver, companies are having difficulty attracting and keeping staff. For many, the option is to shorten the hours of operation—even closing on days they were previously open. The local Tim Horton's in Canmore, Alberta, is one example of a company that faced this problem. According to owner Caroline Barham, the younger workforce in Canmore is mostly made up transients—people staying for only a few months as they visit this beautiful part of the country. Barham's response to this chronic shortage of employees was to shorten hours so the staff she could find could give the appropriate level of customer service.[7]

This problem of worker shortages will only intensify as the "baby boom" generation continues to leave the workforce. Some companies have hired back retirees on contract or part-time work, or eased mandatory retirement policies as a way of dealing with the issue. Others have resorted to "signing bonuses," referral fees for finding new employees, and even offering yoga and PlayStation breaks to help keep staff happy. Scott Plastics Ltd. in Sydney, B.C., gives its staff twice-weekly yoga classes. "We started doing it just for a small group of office staff, really for a bit of break," according to Robin Richardson, Scott's vice president of operations. "They seem to really enjoy it and . . . after a while a number of male office staff asked if they could join as well." Richardson says it has been good for employees—and good for business. "We were basically looking for something that was going to be beneficial to them and at the same time basically probably improve the work performance. I think they'd say that it does both."[8]

TRAINING TO IMPROVE QUALITY

Employee training is an integral part of comprehensive quality management programs. Although quality management is concerned with machines, materials, and measurement, it also focuses attention on human performance. Thus, training programs can be designed to promote higher-quality workmanship.

To a considerable extent, training for quality performance is part of the ongoing supervisory role of all managers. In addition, special classes and seminars can be used to teach employees about the importance of quality and ways in which to produce high-quality work.

For Waltec Plastics, a custom injection moulder in Midland, Ontario, on-site training became more a necessity than an option. A pool of trained personnel just hasn't been available from the local area. The company tried hiring employees outside the Georgian Bay area, but that hasn't been successful. "People . . . tend to leave after three to five years," says President Antone Mudde. "Those hired locally tend to stay." Waltec's solution has been to hire mechanically inclined Grade 12 graduates and train them. Aside from skills programs specific to plastics technology, Waltec employees participate in awareness programs geared to the company's corporate culture. They also receive extensive on-site and off-site total quality management (TQM) training.[9]

TRAINING NONMANAGERIAL EMPLOYEES

Job descriptions or job specifications, if they exist, may identify abilities or skills needed for particular jobs. To a large extent, such requirements regulate the type of training that is appropriate.

For all classes of employees, more training is accomplished on the job than through any other method. However, on-the-job training may not be very effective if it depends on haphazard learning rather than planned, controlled training programs. A system designed to make on-the-job training more effective is known as Job Instruction Training. The steps of this program are intended to help supervisors become more effective in training nonmanagerial employees.

1. *Prepare employees:* Put employees at ease. Place them in appropriate jobs. Find out what they already know about the job. Get them interested in learning it.
2. *Present the operations:* Tell, show, illustrate, and question carefully and patiently. Stress key points. Instruct clearly and completely, taking up one point at a time—but no more than the employees can master.
3. *Try out performance:* Test the employees by having them perform the jobs. Have the employees tell, show, and explain key points. Ask questions and correct errors. Continue until the employees know that they know how to do the job.
4. *Follow up:* Check on employees frequently. Designate the people to whom the employees should go for help. Encourage questions. Get the employees to look for the key points as they progress. Taper off extra coaching and close follow-up.

DEVELOPING MANAGERIAL AND PROFESSIONAL EMPLOYEES

A small business has a particularly strong need to develop managerial and professional employees. Depending on its size, the firm may have few or many key positions. To function most effectively, the business must develop individuals who can hold these key positions. Incumbents should be developed to the point that they can adequately carry out the responsibilities assigned to them. Ideally, potential replacements should also be available for key individuals who may retire or leave for other reasons. The entrepreneur often postpones grooming a personal replacement, but this step is also important in ensuring a smooth transition in the firm's management.

Establishing a management training program requires serious consideration of the following factors:

* *Determine the need for training:* What vacancies are expected? Who needs to be trained? What type of training and how much training are needed to meet the demands of the job description?
* *Develop a plan for training:* How can the individuals be trained? Do they currently have enough responsibility to permit them to learn? Can they be assigned additional duties? Should they be given temporary assignments in other areas—for example, should they be shifted from production to sales? Would additional schooling be beneficial?

- *Establish a timetable:* When should training begin? How much can be accomplished in the next six months or one year?
- *Counsel employees:* Do the individuals understand their need for training? Are they aware of their prospects within the firm? Have they been asked about their work goals? Has an understanding been reached as to the nature of training? Have the employees been consulted regularly about progress in their work and the problems confronting them? Have they been given the benefit of the owner's experience and insights without having decisions made for them?

COMPENSATION AND INCENTIVES FOR SMALL BUSINESS EMPLOYEES

Explain the various kinds of compensation plans and the differences between daywork and incentives.

8

Compensation and financial incentives are important to all employees, and the small firm must acknowledge the central role of the paycheque and other monetary rewards in attracting and motivating personnel. In addition, small firms can offer several nonfinancial incentives that appeal to both managerial and nonmanagerial employees.

WAGE OR SALARY LEVELS

In general, small firms find that they must be roughly competitive in wage or salary levels in order to attract well-qualified personnel. Wages or salaries paid to employees either are based on increments of time—such as an hour, a day, a month—or vary directly with their output. A compensation system based on increments of time is commonly referred to as **daywork.** Daywork is most appropriate for types of jobs in which performance is not easily measurable. It is the most common compensation system and is easy to understand and administer.

daywork
a compensation system based on increments of time

FINANCIAL INCENTIVES

Incentive systems have been devised to motivate employees, particularly nonmanagerial employees, to increase their productivity. Incentive wages may constitute an employee's entire earnings or may supplement her or his regular wages or salary. The commission system often used to compensate salespeople is one type of incentive plan. In manufacturing, employees are sometimes paid according to the number of units they produce. While many incentive programs apply to employees as individuals, these programs may also involve the use of group incentives and team awards.

General bonus or **profit-sharing plans** are especially important for managerial or other key personnel, although such plans sometimes include lower-level personnel. These plans provide employees with a piece of the action, which may or may not involve assignment of shares of stock. A profit-sharing plan may simply entail a distribution of a specified share of the profits or a share of profits that exceed a target amount. As illustrated by many examples in this chapter profit sharing provides a more direct work incentive in small companies than in large companies because the connection between individual performance and company success can be more easily appreciated.

profit-sharing plans
a percentage of profits is distributed to employees

Performance-based compensation systems must be designed carefully if they are to work successfully. Such plans should be devised with the aid of a consultant and/or

IN THE TRENCHES

Entrepreneurial Experiences

Employees Are the Assets at Sybase iAnywhere Solution, Inc.

A subsidiary of California's Sybase, Waterloo, Ontario's Sybase iAnywhere Solutions Inc. offers the industry-leading software for web-based and wireless secure offsite access to customers' office computer networks. Founded in Waterloo in 1980 by three University of Waterloo graduates, the company was bought by Sybase in 1995 and is now a major research centre for the larger company. Its efforts have won it a Canada's Top 100 Employers award for 2008.

In order to attract and retain people, Sybase iAnywhere provides three weeks vacation after one year, where most companies offer two, and four weeks after two years; it matches RRSP contributions up to $200 per year, provides up to $6000 in tuition subsidies, hosts onsite ESL classes for employees who are new to Canada, and tops up maternity payments. The company also strongly encourages employees to bring "a piece of themselves" to the workplace by bringing personal items such as children's crafts and artwork, photos of family and other mementos.

Within a relaxed atmosphere that includes a casual dress code, the company provides an employee lounge and rest areas that feature comfortable couches, free beverages, music, television and video games to "promote employee interaction and idea generation (and) bring the employees together as a team," says Sybase president Terry Stepien.

"We're in a high-tech community that is very competitive for the resources we're looking for. Our employees are our greatest asset and while that is a cliché we truly believe it to be true. For the amount of time our employees spend at work, we understand that it is important for us to do the little things that go a long way toward achieving that dynamic and interactive environment we're striving for."

In many businesses that require a lot of creativity and ideas, such as advertising agencies and research and development-dependent technology companies like Sybase iAnywhere, providing alternative ways of stimulating that creativity and collaboration is as important as the financial incentives and other attractions.

Sources: Adapted from Gary Nyp, "The 100 Best Places to Work," *The Record (Kitchener),* October 13, 2007, p. E.1. Used by permission; and http://www.sybase.com/about_sybase, accessed June 2008.

---

accounting firm. Some distinctive features of good bonus plans are identified in the following list:

1. *Set attainable goals:* Incentive pay works best when workers feel they can meet the targets. Tying pay to broad measures such as company-wide results leaves workers feeling frustrated and helpless.
2. *Set meaningful goals:* You can neither motivate nor reward by setting targets employees can't comprehend. Complex financial measures or jargon-heavy benchmarks mean nothing to most workers.
3. *Bring workers in:* Give them a say in developing performance measures and listen to their advice on ways to change work systems. Phase in pay plans gradually so employees have a chance to absorb them.

4. *Keep targets moving:* Performance-pay plans must be constantly adjusted to meet the changing needs of workers and customers. The life expectancy of a plan may be no more than three or four years.
5. *Aim carefully:* Know what message you want to send. Make sure that the new scheme doesn't reward the wrong behaviour. Linking bonuses to plant safety, for example, could encourage cover-ups.[10]

FRINGE BENEFITS

Fringe benefits, which include payments for such items as the employer's share of Canada Pension Plan (CPP) contributions and Employment Insurance premiums, vacations, holidays, health insurance, dental plans, and workers' compensation are expensive. The annual increases in the company contribution to CCP and EI is one of the primary reasons many small businesses use part-time staff and contractors who are not eligible for benefits. The cost of fringe benefits is a substantial part of total labour costs for most small firms, with estimates ranging from 20 percent to 40 percent of base pay.

Even though **fringe benefits** are expensive, a small firm cannot ignore them if it is to compete effectively for good employees. A small but growing number of small firms now use **flexible benefits programs** (or **cafeteria plans**) that allow employees to choose the types of benefits they want to receive.[11] All employees may receive a core level of coverage, such as basic dental and prescription drug coverage, and then are allowed to choose how some amount specified by the employer is to be divided among additional options—for example, child-care reimbursement, extended dental care, pension fund contributions, and additional health insurance.

Outside help in administering cafeteria plans is available to small firms that wish to avoid the detailed paperwork associated with them. Many small companies—including some with fewer than 25 employees—turn over the administration of their flexible benefits plans to outside consulting, payroll accounting, or insurance companies that provide such services for a monthly fee, such as Johnston Group Inc. In view of the increasing popularity of these plans and the wide availability of administrative services, it seems only a matter of time until many small firms will be offering flexible benefits.

fringe benefits
supplements to compensation, designed to be attractive and beneficial to employees

cafeteria plans (or flexible benefits programs)
plans that allow staff to choose their benefits within a set budget

EMPLOYEE STOCK OWNERSHIP PLANS

Some small firms have created **employee stock ownership plans (ESOPs)**, by which they give employees a share of ownership in the business.[12] These plans may be structured in a variety of ways. For example, a share of annual profits may be designated for the benefit of employees and used to buy company stock, which is then placed in a trust for the employees.

ESOPs also provide a way for owners to cash out and withdraw from a business without selling the firm to outsiders. The owner might sell equity to the firm's employees, who can borrow funds for this purpose. In fact, tax advantages for both owners and employees make ESOPs an increasingly popular option.

employee stock ownership plans (ESOPs)
plans that give employees a share of ownership in the business

FACTORS THAT CONTRIBUTE TO QUALITY OF WORK LIFE

A major research project sponsored by the Canadian Policy Research Network, published in 2007, generated data from across Canada from employees who clearly felt that emphasis should be placed by business owners on working relationships and job structure, as well as on salary. The seven top factors that employees in Canada felt contributed to

EXHIBIT **9-7**
What Employees Consider "Very Important" in a Job

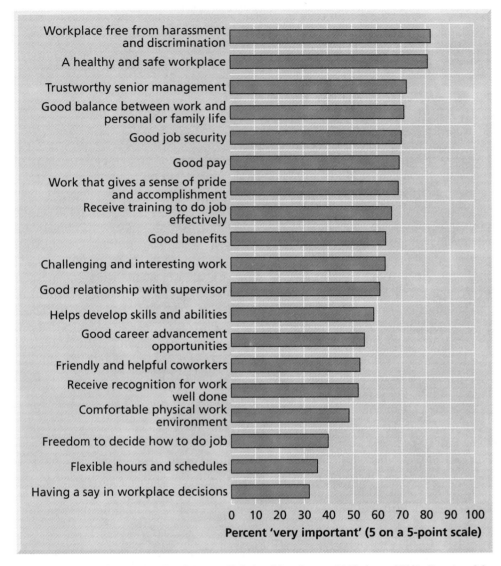

Percent 'very important' (5 on a 5-point scale)

Source: CPRN-Ekos Changing Employment Relationships Survey 2000 (n = 2000). Reprinted by permission of Canadian Policy Research Networks Inc.

a work environment were (1) freedom from harassment and discrimination, (2) a healthy and safe workplace, (3) trustworthy senior management, (4) balance between work and life, (5) job security, (6) good pay and (7) a sense of pride and accomplishment in what both the employee and the company do. Job security, a well-paying job, and good benefits were near the bottom of the factors that motivate employees. Refer to Exhibit 9-7 for a breakdown and ranking of the factors that employees felt were important in their job.

TIME MANAGEMENT

9 Describe the problem of time pressure and suggest solutions.

An owner-manager of a small firm spends much of the working day on the front line—meeting customers, solving problems, listening to employee complaints, talking with suppliers, and the like. She or he tackles such problems with the assistance of only a

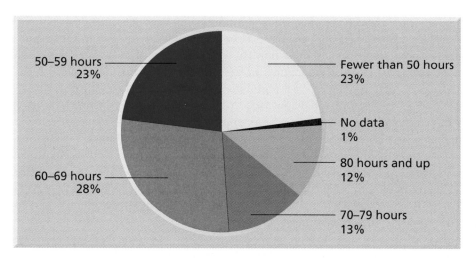

EXHIBIT **9-8**
*Hours per Week Worked
by New Business Owners*

Data developed and provided by the NFIB Foundation and sponsored by American Express Travel-Related Services Company.

small staff. As a result, the owner-manager's energies and activities are diffused, and time is often her or his scarcest resource.

THE PROBLEM OF TIME PRESSURE

Many managers in small firms work from 60 to 80 hours per week. The hours worked by most new business owners are particularly long, as shown in Exhibit 9-8. A frequent and unfortunate result of such a schedule is inefficient work performance. Managers are too busy to see sales representatives who can supply market information on new products and processes. They are too busy to read technical or trade literature to discover what others are doing and what improvements might be adapted to their own use, too busy to listen carefully to employees' opinions and grievances, and too busy to give instructions properly and to teach employees how to do their jobs correctly.

Getting away for a vacation also seems impossible for some small business owners. In an extremely small firm, the owner may find it necessary to close the business during the period of his or her absence. Even in somewhat larger businesses, the owner may fear that the firm will not function properly if he or she is not there. Unfortunately, keeping his or her nose to the grindstone in this way may cost the entrepreneur dearly in terms of personal health, family relationships, and effectiveness in business leadership.

TIME-SAVERS FOR BUSY MANAGERS

Part of the solution to the problem of time pressure is good organization. When possible, the manager should assign duties to subordinates who can work without close supervision. For such delegation to work, of course, a manager must first select and train qualified employees.

The greatest time-saver is effective use of time. Little will be accomplished if an individual flits from one task to another and back again. The first step in planning the use of time should be a survey of how much time is normally spent on various activities. Relying on general impressions is unscientific and likely to involve error. For a period of several days, or preferably several weeks, the manager should record the amounts of time spent on various types of activities during the day. An analysis of these figures will reveal the pattern of activities, the projects and tasks that use up the most time, and the factors responsible for wasted time. It will also reveal chronic time wasting due to excessive socializing, work on trivial matters, coffee breaks, and so on.

After eliminating practices that waste time, a manager can carefully plan his or her use of available time. A planned approach to a day's or week's work is much more effective than a haphazard do-whatever-comes-up-first approach. This is true even for small firm managers whose schedules are interrupted in unanticipated ways.

Many time management specialists recommend the use of a daily written plan of work activities. This plan may be a list of activities scribbled on a note pad or a formal schedule entered into a laptop computer, but it should reflect priorities. By classifying duties as first, second, or third level of priority, the manager can identify and focus attention on the most crucial tasks.

Effective time management requires self-discipline. An individual may easily begin with good intentions and later lapse into habitual practices of devoting time to whatever he or she finds to do at the moment. Procrastination is a frequent thief of time. Many managers delay unpleasant and difficult tasks, retreating to trivial and less-threatening activities and rationalizing that they are getting those items out of the way first in order to be able to concentrate better on the important tasks.

Some managers devote much time to meeting with subordinates. The meetings often just happen and drag on without any serious attempt by the manager to control them. The manager should prepare an agenda for these meetings, set starting and ending times, limit discussion to key issues, and assign any necessary follow-up to specific individuals. In this way, the effectiveness of business meetings may be maximized and the manager's own time conserved, along with that of other staff members.

10

Discuss contract employees, labour unions, the formalizing of human resources management, and legislation pertaining to employee protection.

SPECIAL ISSUES IN HUMAN RESOURCES MANAGEMENT

So far in this chapter, we have dealt with recruitment, selection, training, and compensation of employees. In addition to these primary activities, human resources management can involve a number of other general issues. These issues—contract employees, dealing with labour unions, formalizing employer–employee relationships, hiring a human resources manager, and government legislation pertaining to employment issues—are the focus of this concluding section.

CONTRACT EMPLOYEES

contract employees
independent contractors hired for fixed periods of time or for specific projects

As larger companies have downsized during the past decade, many have met their variable personnel needs by hiring independent contractors, often their former employees, for fixed periods of time or for specific projects. Under this arrangement, **contract employees** are not deemed to be employees of the company, so the contractors invoice the company for work performed. This means the company does not have to withhold taxes, CPP, and EI from the contractor's paycheques, nor does it have to pay its share of those or other benefits. The contractor is responsible for remitting taxes, CPP, and (if applicable) EI deductions to Canada Revenue Agency, and is responsible for his or her own benefits.

Contracting is less expensive for employers than hiring employees since the company does not have to pay benefits, and contracting gives the company a great deal of flexibility since the contractor does not continue with the firm once the terms of the contract have been completed. The arrangement is more expensive for employee-contractors, as they must pay the government both the employer and the employee share of CPP contributions and EI premiums. However, it may be possible for the contractor to deduct from income for income tax purposes such expenses as travel to and from work as well as a home office, which employees cannot do.

Caution must be taken with contracting employees. If all or most of a contractor's revenue comes from one company, Canada Revenue Agency is likely to rule that the contractor is an employee and not a contractor, and expect the company to deduct and remit taxes as well as pay for other benefits.

DEALING WITH LABOUR UNIONS

Most entrepreneurs prefer to operate independently and to avoid unionization. Indeed, most small businesses are not unionized. To some extent, this results from the predominance of small business in services, where unionization is less common than in manufacturing. Also, unions typically concentrate their primary attention on large companies.

However, labour unions are not unknown in small firms. Many types of small firms—building and electrical contractors, for example—negotiate labour contracts and employ unionized personnel. The need to work with a union formalizes and, to some extent, complicates the relationship between the small firm and its employees. One small company whose employees joined a union is a Hamilton, Ontario a mill-service business with eight employees. Owner Russ Cameron says he was paying a good wage for what he calls "pretty low-skilled labour." He believes the workers thought that joining the union would bring their wages in line with skilled trades, but in the end they won only cost-of-living increases, "which they would have gotten anyway," says Cameron. They also have to pay union dues and management now has a "zero tolerance" policy for employees having flexibility to set their own work hours and overtime.[13]

According to Statistics Canada's Labour Force Survey for the first half of 2007, only 13 percent of employees in workplaces with fewer than 20 employees were union members, and in the 20–99 employee category that number rose to 30 percent. "It's common for small business owners to be wary of unionization," says John Weir, director of organizing for the B.C. Federation of Labour. "People react on stereotypes. They think the union won't understand the nature of their business, but unions have economists. We understand the dynamics of private enterprise and what it takes to be successful." After all, Mr. Weir says, workers won't benefit from a business in trouble. "We want to make sure that work works for everybody."[14]

If employees wish to bargain collectively, the law requires the employer to participate in such bargaining. The demand for labour union representation may arise from employees' dissatisfaction with the work environment and employment relationships. By following enlightened human resources policies, the small firm can minimize the likelihood of labour organization or improve the relationship between management and union.

FORMALIZING EMPLOYER–EMPLOYEE RELATIONSHIPS

As we explained earlier in this chapter, the management system of small firms is typically less formal than that of larger ones. A degree of informality can, in fact, constitute a virtue in small organizations. As personnel are added, however, the benefits of informality decline and its costs increase. Large numbers of employees cannot be managed effectively without some system for regulating employer–employee relationships. This situation has been portrayed in terms of a family relationship: "House rules are hardly necessary where only two people are living. But add several children, and before long Mom starts sounding like a government regulatory agency."[15]

Growth, then, produces pressures to formalize personnel policies and procedures. The primary question is how much formality and how soon—a decision that involves judgment. Some matters should be formalized from the very beginning; on the other hand, excessive regulation can become paralyzing.

One way to formalize employer–employee relationships is to prepare a personnel policy manual, or employee handbook, which can meet a communication need by letting employees know the firm's basic ground rules. It can also provide a basis for fairness and consistency of management decisions affecting employees. The content of a policy manual may be as broad or as narrow as desired. It may include a statement of company philosophy—an overall view of what the company considers important, such as standards of excellence or quality considerations. More specifically, personnel policies usually cover such topics as recruitment, selection, training, compensation, vacations, grievances, and discipline. Such policies should be written carefully, however, to avoid misunderstandings. In some provinces an employee handbook is considered part of the employment contract.

Procedures relating to management of personnel may also be standardized. For example, a performance review system may be established and a timetable set up for reviews—perhaps an initial review after six months and subsequent reviews on an annual basis. A firm with only a few employees cannot afford a full-time specialist to deal with personnel problems. Some of the more involved human resources tools and techniques that are required in large businesses may be unnecessarily complicated for small businesses. As it grows in size, however, the small firm's personnel problems will increase in both number and complexity.

HIRING A HUMAN RESOURCE MANAGER

The point at which it becomes logical to hire a human resources manager cannot be specified precisely. In view of the increased overhead cost, the owner-manager of a growing business must decide whether the situation of the business would make it profitable to employ a personnel specialist. Hiring a part-time human resources manager—a retired personnel manager, for example—might be a logical first step in some instances.

Some conditions favour the appointment of a human resources manager in a small business:

- There are a substantial number of employees (100 or more is suggested as a guide).
- Employees are represented by a union.

- The labour turnover rate is high.
- The need for skilled or professional personnel creates problems in recruitment or selection.
- Supervisors or operative employees require considerable training.
- Employee morale is unsatisfactory.
- Competition for personnel is keen.

Until a human resources manager is hired, however, the owner-manager typically functions in that capacity. Her or his decisions regarding selection, compensation, and other personnel issues will have a direct impact on the operating success of the firm.

PROTECTING EMPLOYEE RIGHTS

Employees are people first and employees second. Therefore, employees are afforded protection from robbery, assault, and other crime at work just as they are at home. In addition, some laws—for example, the federal and provincial occupational health and safety acts, employment standards codes, and workers' compensation acts—have been designed primarily for employees and potential employees. In recent years managers of small firms have been introducing **harassment policies** to protect the rights of all staff. Effective implementation usually entails including the policies in the Standard Operating Procedures, and staff training pertaining to appropriate behaviour.

All jurisdictions have an occupational health and safety act, which is administered by a public agency such as the Workers Compensation Board of the Department of Public Health. The purpose of this legislation is to ensure safe workplaces and work practices. These administrative bodies continue, through a structured procedure and by working with industry, to establish additional health and safety standards as they deem necessary.

Federal and provincial employment standards codes set out required working conditions, such as maximum work hours, overtime pay, meal breaks, minimum wages, and parental and maternity leaves. For example, in Alberta, a pregnant woman is entitled to take leave at any time within 12 weeks of her delivery date and for a period after the birth or adoption of a child for a total of up to 15 weeks plus 37 additional weeks of parental leave. The father is allowed 37 weeks of parental leave upon the birth or adoption of a child. The prerequisite is 12 months' continuous employment. Women on maternity leave are entitled to **Employment Insurance** (EI) benefits for a portion of this time.

Workers' compensation was established to compensate employees for injuries, illnesses, and deaths that occur in the course of employment. In the past, many employees could not afford to sue their employers for work-related injuries, and numerous factors, including contributory negligence, made it difficult for them to win in court. Provincial workers' compensation acts require employers to make contributions to a fund to compensate workers for loss or injury. In return, employees may not sue their employers for these losses or injuries.

harassment policies
policies that ensure all employees are treated equitably

Employment Insurance (EI)
benefits paid to workers who become unemployed provided they meet certain requirements, such as having been employed for a minimum number of weeks

LOOKING BACK

1 Discuss the entrepreneur's leadership role.

- An entrepreneur exerts strong personal influence in a small firm.
- Progressive managers use participative management approaches such as empowerment and work teams.
- Effective communication is an important factor in building a healthy organization.

2 Discuss the evolving features of small firm management.

- Management weakness is prevalent in small firms.
- Small firm managers face special financial and personnel constraints.
- As a new firm grows, it adds layers of supervision and increases formality of management.
- As a firm grows, the entrepreneur must become more of a manager and less of a doer.
- Founders tend to be more action oriented and less analytical than professional managers.

3 Describe the characteristics and value of a strong management team.

- The skills of management team members should complement each other, forming an optimal combination of education and experience.
- An entrepreneur should create a management structure that defines relationships among employees.
- A small firm can enhance its management by drawing on the expertise of outside professional groups.

4 Identify the various kinds of plans and approaches to planning.

- Types of plans include strategic plans, short-range plans, budgets, policies, and procedures.
- Planning is easily neglected, and managers must exercise discipline to make time for it.
- A manager may improve planning by drawing on the ideas of employees.

5 Explain the importance of employee recruitment and list some sources that can be useful for finding suitable applicants.

- Recruitment of good employees contributes to customer service and to profitability.
- Small firms can attract applicants by stressing unique work features and opportunities.

- Recruitment sources include walk-ins, schools, public and private employment agencies, employee referrals, advertising, and temporary help agencies.
- Job descriptions outline the duties of the job; job specifications identify the skills needed by applicants.

6 Identify the steps in evaluating job applicants.

- Application forms help obtain background information from applicants.
- Evaluation steps include interviewing, checking references, and administering tests.
- The final evaluation step may be a physical examination or performance test.

7 Describe the role of training for both managerial and nonmanagerial employees in the small firm.

- Training enables employees to perform their jobs and also prepares them for advancement.
- An orientation program helps introduce new employees to the firm and the work environment.
- Training is one component of a firm's quality management program.
- Training and development programs are applicable to both managerial and nonmanagerial employees.

8 Explain the various kinds of compensation plans and the differences between daywork and incentives.

- Small firms must be competitive in salary and wage levels.
- Daywork systems base compensation on increments of time.
- Incentive systems relate compensation to various measures of performance.
- Fringe benefits make up a substantial portion of personnel costs.
- Employee stock ownership plans enable employees to own a share of the business.

9 Describe the problem of time pressure and suggest solutions.

- Time pressure tends to create inefficiencies in the management of small firms.
- The greatest time-saver is effective use of time.
- A manager can reduce time pressure by such practices as eliminating wasteful activities and planning work carefully.

10 Discuss contract employees, labour unions, the formalizing of human resources management, and legislation pertaining to employee protection.
- Some small businesses must work with labour unions.
- As small firms grow, they must adopt more formal methods of human resources management.

- Employing a human resources manager becomes necessary at some point as a firm continues to add employees.
- Business owners and managers should be aware of provincial and federal legislation that protects employees.

KEY TERMS

budget, p. 241
business policies, p. 241
cafeteria plans (flexible benefits), p. 255
contract employees, p. 258
daywork, p. 253
employee stock ownership plans (ESOPs), p. 255
Employment Insurance (EI), p. 261

empowerment, p. 230
fringe benefits, p. 255
harassment policies, p. 261
headhunter, p. 246
job description, p. 246
job specification, p. 247
long-range plan, p. 240
management functions, p. 239
management team, p. 237

procedures, p. 241
professional manager, p. 232
profit-sharing plans, p. 253
reliability, p. 249
short-range plan, p. 241
standard operating procedures, p. 241
validity, p. 249
work team, p. 232

DISCUSSION QUESTIONS

1. As a customer of small businesses, you can appreciate the importance of employees to their success. Describe an experience you've had in which an employee's behaviour was positive and one in which it was negative.
2. What four stages of small business growth are outlined in this chapter? How do management requirements change as the firm moves through these stages?
3. Some hockey coaches have written game plans that they consult from time to time during games. If coaches need formal plans, does it follow that small business owners need them as they engage in their type of competition? Why or why not?
4. Why would investors tend to favour a new business led by a management team over one headed by a lone entrepreneur? Is this preference justified?
5. What practices can a small business manager use to conserve time?

6. What factor or factors would make you cautious about going to work for a small business? Could these reasons for hesitation be overcome by a really good small firm? If so, how? If not, why not?
7. What are the key factors of employment for you; are you more motivated by a high salary or such factors as a flexible workweek and the opportunity to be creative?
8. Based on your own experience as an interviewee, what do you think is the most serious weakness in the interviewing process? How could this be remedied?
9. What steps and/or topics would you recommend for the orientation program of a printing firm with 65 employees?
10. Consider a small business with which you are well acquainted. Have adequate provisions been made to replace key management personnel when it becomes necessary? Is the firm using any form of executive development?

11. What problems are involved in using incentive pay systems in a small firm? How would the nature of the work affect management's decision concerning the use of such incentives?
12. Is the use of a profit-sharing system desirable in a small business? What major difficulties might lessen its effectiveness in providing greater employee motivation?
13. How does contracting employees differ from using a temporary help agency? What are the greatest benefits of contracting?
14. List the factors in small business operation that favour the appointment of a human resources manager. Should such a manager always be hired on a full-time basis? Why or why not?

YOU MAKE THE CALL

SITUATION 1

The following is an account of one employee's introduction to a new job:

> It was my first job out of high school. After receiving a physical exam and a pamphlet on benefits, I was told by the manager about the dangers involved in the job. But it was the old-timers who explained what was really expected of me.
>
> The company management never told me about the work environment or the unspoken rules. The old-timers let me know where to sleep and which supervisors to avoid. They told me how much work I was supposed to do and which shop steward to see if I had a problem.

Question 1 To what extent should a small firm use "old-timers" to help introduce new employees to the workplace? Is it inevitable that newcomers will always look to old-timers to find out how things really work?

Question 2 How would you rate this firm's orientation efforts? What are its strengths and weaknesses?

Question 3 Assuming that this firm has fewer than 75 employees and no human resources manager, could it possibly provide any more extensive orientation than that described here? If so, how? What low-cost improvements, if any, would you recommend?

SITUATION 2

Technical Products, Inc. distributes 15 percent of its profits quarterly to its eight employees. This money is invested for their benefit in a retirement plan and is fully vested after five years. An employee, therefore, has a claim to the retirement fund even if he or she leaves the company after five years of service.

The employees range in age from 25 to 59 and have worked for the company from 3 to 27 years. They seem to have recognized the value of the program. However, younger employees sometimes express a stronger preference for cash than for retirement benefits.

Question 1 What are the most important reasons for structuring the profit-sharing plan as a retirement program?

Question 2 What is the probable motivational impact of this compensation system?

Question 3 How will an employee's age affect the appeal of this plan? What other factors are likely to strengthen or lessen its motivational value? Should it be changed in any way?

SITUATION 3

Nadia Vasilevich, a small business owner, is concerned about increasing costs for the supplementary health and dental plan (which covers the cost of prescription drugs, and dental work, among other things) she provides for her five employees. Vasilevich currently pays 100 percent of the cost, but the insurance company has proposed a large increase in the renewal premium, due to the high number of claims received in the past year. She wonders if she can afford the extra $150 per month in operating expenses. On the other hand,

Vasilevich worries about cancelling the coverage and leaving the employees unprotected. Three of them have families, and a serious illness or expensive dental work would create major problems. "I think we should have protection for everyone," said Vasilevich, "but I don't know if I can afford it."

Question 1 What options does Vasilevich have to keep the coverage in place?

Question 2 Should Vasilevich accept the proposed increase in premium? What options does she have?

Question 3 Should Vasilevich provide the dental and health coverage, even though she is not legally required to?

EXPERIENTIAL EXERCISES

1. Interview a management consultant, CASE counsellor, or representative of a CA firm to discuss small business management weaknesses and the willingness or reluctance of small firms to use consultants. Prepare a report on your findings.

2. Interview the director of the placement office for your university to determine the extent to which small firms use the office's services and to obtain the director's recommendations for improving campus recruiting by small firms. Prepare a one-page summary of your findings.

3. Examine and evaluate the help-wanted section of a local newspaper. Summarize your conclusions and formulate some generalizations about small business advertising for personnel.

4. Select an unstructured block of one to four hours in your schedule—that is, hours that are not regularly devoted to classes, sleeping, and so on. Carefully record your use of that time period for several days. Prepare a report summarizing your use of the time and outlining a plan to use it more effectively.

5. With another student, form an interviewer–interviewee team. Take turns interviewing each other as job applicants for a selected type of job vacancy. Critique each other's performance by using the interviewing principles outlined in this chapter.

6. With another student, take turns role-playing trainer and trainee using the Job Instruction Training method outlined in this chapter. Each student-trainer should select a simple task and teach it to the student-trainee. Jointly critique the teaching performance after each episode.

7. Interview an entrepreneur. Ask him or her about the management and advisory teams, as well as professional advisers. How have the advisory team or outside professionals helped?

8. Search the Internet for job openings. Evaluate the emphasis placed on salary versus the lifestyle the companies are offering.

9. Interview an entrepreneur regarding her or his time management. How many hours a week does the entrepreneur work? Does the individual feel rushed for time? Could he or she delegate or reallocate time to be more effective?

EXPLORING THE WEB

1. Search websites for firms that mention their staff and the compensation programs that are offered.

CHAPTER 10

Form of Organization and Legal Issues

LOOKING AHEAD

After studying this chapter, you should be able to

1 Identify the common forms of legal organization used by small businesses and describe the characteristics of each.

2 Identify factors to consider in choosing among the primary legal forms of organization.

3 Describe the effective use of boards of directors and advisory councils.

4 Explain how different forms of organization are taxed by the federal government.

5 Understand the major legal and regulatory issues businesses face.

IN THE SPOTLIGHT

Powerhouse International: Helping Independent Business Find Advice

Owners of small growing businesses sometimes strengthen their management teams by creating boards of directors or boards of advisers. Directors are hard to attract because of potential liability, so most resort to advisory boards, but even then it can be difficult to find capable and willing board members.

To solve this problem Taunya Woods Richardson created Powerhouse International, a company that builds peer advisory boards for business owners—primarily for businesses under $2 million in annual revenue. It is the first and only member-owned organization of its kind and has been very successful: from its Calgary start-up it now has branches in Edmonton, Vancouver and Kelowna, with planned expansion to Ottawa and Toronto in 2008. According to Woods Richardson, "we group six small business owners together and obviously they're non-competing, complementary communication styles, complementary stages of business. . . . The most important thing we're looking for is subject matter expertise." A facilitator also works with the board, which meets every second week for a year to provide strategic advice, direction, motivation and accountability.

Powerhouse has over 200 members on over 30 boards, with plans to build a base of 4,500 members and $9.5 million in revenue by 2009. The cost for a business to join Powerhouse is $1,495 per year and according to

Woods Richardson, "80 percent of our members renew, so we're doing something right and we believe the biggest thing we can give these business owners is that place to have the conversations that need to be had and get the support to move forward."

Keith Pederson, owner of KBC Electric in Calgary, a three year Powerhouse member says, "I'm a strong believer in the board-type structure of small business because you talk to other people that are not related to your business but are entrepreneurs and small business people alike. There's also some accountability there that a board brings to your business. That's what's really important."

Dan Kelly, the western Canada vice-president for the Canadian Federation of Independent Business, said being a small business owner "can be a lonely job for an entrepreneur, and for small businesses

Ryan McVay/Photodisc/Getty Images

that basically have very few supports, having a group of advisors—sort of a board structure, if you will—can be a real helpful addition." He says Powerhouse's success "shows that there is a real need for entrepreneurs to have some people they can reach out to for strategic advice."

For Woods Richardson, it's about "small business owners coming together to help one another. There are definitely significant challenges people are going through when they're building their business and it . . . always boils down to resources: time, people and money." With Powerhouse, "we're growing this entrepreneurial community."

http://www.powerhouseinc.ca

Source: Mario Toneguzzi, "Organization Helps Small Business Overcome Entrepreneurial Isolation," *Edmonton Journal,* January 8, 2007, p.E3.

FORMS OF LEGAL ORGANIZATION

In launching a new business, an entrepreneur must choose a form of legal orgatniza-tion. The most common options are sole proprietorship, partnership, and corporation. More specialized forms of organization exist, but the vast number of small businesses find one of these common forms suitable for their needs. Therefore, our discussion focuses primarily on these options, although explanations are also given of three less typical forms. Exhibit 10-1 shows the three major forms of organization and also four specialized forms.

THE SOLE PROPRIETORSHIP OPTION

sole proprietorship
a business owned and operated by one person

A **sole proprietorship,** the most rudimentary business form, is a business owned by one person. An individual proprietor has title to all business assets, subject to the claims of creditors. He or she receives all of the firm's profits but must also assume all losses, bear all risks, and pay all debts. Forming a sole proprietorship is the simplest and cheapest way to start an operation and is usually most appropriate for a new small business.

In a sole proprietorship, an owner is free from interference by partners, share-holders, and directors. However, a sole proprietorship lacks some of the advantages of other legal forms. For example, there are no limits on the owner's personal liability—that is, the owner of the business has **unlimited liability** and thus her or his personal assets can be taken by creditors if the business fails. For this reason, the sole propri-etorship form is a practical choice for only very small businesses. In addition, sole pro-prietors are not employees and cannot receive the advantage of tax-free fringe benefits such as insurance and dental plans, which are customarily provided by corporations for their employees.

unlimited liability
liability on the part of an owner that extends beyond the owner's investment in the business

All forms of business, including sole proprietorships, are able to deduct normal business expenses from income for tax purposes. The proprietorship reports its taxes as part of the personal tax return of the proprietor. Proprietorships have a taxation (or fiscal) year-end of December 31.

EXHIBIT **10-1**
*Forms of Legal
Organization for Small
Businesses*

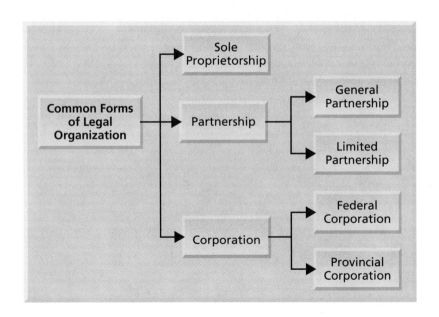

The death of the owner terminates the legal existence of a business that is organized as a sole proprietorship. Therefore, the possibility of the sole proprietor's death may cloud relationships between a business and its creditors and employees. It is important that the owner have a will, because the assets of the business minus its liabilities belong to the heirs. In a will, a sole proprietor can give an executor the power to run the business for the heirs until they can take it over or it can be sold.

Another contingency that must be provided for is the possible incapacity of the sole proprietor. If she or he were badly hurt in an accident and unconscious for an extended period, the business could be ruined. A sole proprietor can guard against this danger by giving a competent person a legal power of attorney to carry on in such circumstances.

In some cases, the sole proprietorship option is virtually ruled out by circumstances. For example, if the nature of a business involves a high exposure to legal risks, as in the case of a manufacturer of a potentially hazardous product, a legal form that provides greater protection against personal liability will be required.

THE PARTNERSHIP OPTION

A **partnership** is a separate legal entity formed by two or more co-owners to operate a business for profit. Because of a partnership's voluntary nature, owners can set it up quickly, avoiding many of the legal requirements involved in creating a corporation. A partnership pools the managerial talents and capital of those joining together as business partners. As in a sole proprietorship, however, the owners share unlimited liability.

partnership
a legal entity based on the voluntary association of two or more persons to carry on, as co-owners, a business for profit

QUALIFICATIONS OF PARTNERS

Any person capable of contracting may legally become a business partner. Individuals may become partners without contributing capital or having a claim to assets at the time of dissolution; such persons are partners only in regard to management and profits. The formation of a partnership, however, involves consideration of not only legal issues but also personal and managerial factors. A strong partnership requires partners who are honest, healthy, capable, and compatible.

Operating a business as a partnership has benefits, but it is also fraught with problems. When *Inc.* magazine surveyed individuals about their opinions regarding the partnership form of ownership, almost 60 percent of the respondents considered a partnership to be a "bad way to run a business."[1] The respondents were also asked to identify what they believed to be good and bad qualities associated with the partnership form. Good qualities included spreading the workload and emotional and financial burden. Negatives associated with partnerships included personal conflicts between partners, partners not living up to expectations, and the lack of one clear leader. Interestingly, few of the perceived pros or cons are directly associated with financial matters. Those disliking partnerships focused on the deterioration of relationships. Many spoke of a partner's dishonesty, at worst, and differing priorities, at best. However, some of the respondents who considered a partnership a bad way to run a business did note some redeeming qualities. Similarly, advocates of the partnership form noted some inherently bad qualities. Thus, the issue is not black and white. The important point of these findings is that a partnership should be formed only if it is clearly the best option when *all* matters are considered.

Individuals contemplating forming a partnership should discuss the following questions. The objective of these questions is to clarify expectations before a partnership agreement is finalized.

- *What is our business concept?* This is a broad topic, and sometimes it helps to ask a third party to listen in, just to see if the partners are on each other's wavelength. First, the partners need to decide who will make the widgets and who will sell them. Then they need to talk about growth. Are they building the company to sell it, or are they after long-term growth? It's also important to discuss exactly how the business will be run. Do they want participative management, or will employees simply hunker down at machines and churn out parts? "If one guy is a fist pounder with a 'do-it-as-I-say' mentality, and the other believes that people ought to feel good about their jobs, that probably represents an irreconcilable difference," says Sam Lane, a consultant who works with partners.[2]

- *How are we going to structure ownership?* It sounds great for two people to write 50-50 on a cocktail napkin and leave it at that. But, in practice, splitting the company down the middle can paralyze the business. If neither is willing to settle for 49 percent, then the partners should build some arbitration into the partnership agreement.

- *Why do we need each other?* "I thought it would be much less scary with two of us," says Arthur Eisenberg, explaining his rationale for teaming up with his partner. That may be so, but bringing on a partner means sharing responsibility and authority. "If you are taking on a partner because you are afraid of going it alone, find some other way to handle the anxiety," advises Mardy Grothe, a psychologist.[3]

- *How do our lifestyles differ?* The fact that one partner is single and the other has a family, for example, can affect more than just the time each puts in. It may mean that one partner needs to pull more money out of the business. Or it may affect a partner's willingness to take risks with the company. "All of this stuff needs to get talked out," says Peter Wylie, a psychologist. "The implications are profound."[4]

As already suggested, failure to clarify expectations is a frequent deterrent to building an effective working relationship.

RIGHTS AND DUTIES OF PARTNERS

partnership agreement
a document that states explicitly the rights and duties of partners

Partners' rights and duties should be stated explicitly in writing in a **partnership agreement.** This document should be drawn up before the firm begins operating and, at the very least, should cover the following items:

1. Date of formation of the partnership
2. Names and addresses of partners
3. Statement of fact of partnership
4. Statement of business purpose(s)
5. Duration of the business
6. Name and location of the business
7. Amount invested by each partner
8. Sharing ratio for profits and losses
9. Partners' rights, if any, regarding withdrawal of funds for personal use
10. Provision for accounting records and their accessibility to partners
11. Specific duties of each partner
12. Provision for dissolution and sharing of the net assets

13. Restraint on partners' assumption of special obligations, such as endorsing a note of another

14. Provision for protection of surviving partners, decedent's estate, and so forth in the event of a partner's death

Unless the articles specify otherwise, a partner is generally recognized as having certain implicit rights. For example, partners share profits or losses equally, unless they have agreed to a different ratio.

In a partnership, each partner has **agency power,** which means that a business decision by one partner can bind all members of the firm. Good faith, together with reasonable care in the exercise of managerial duties, is required of all partners in a business. Since the partnership relationship is fiduciary in character, a partner cannot compete in another business and remain a partner. Nor can a partner use business information solely for personal gain.

agency power
the ability of any one partner to legally bind the other partners

TERMINATION OF A PARTNERSHIP

Death, incapacity, or withdrawal of any one of the partners ends a partnership and necessitates liquidation or reorganization of the business. While liquidation often results in substantial losses to all partners, it may be legally necessary, because a partnership represents a close personal relationship of the parties that cannot be maintained against the desire of any one of them.

This disadvantage may be partially overcome at the time a partnership is formed by stipulating in the articles that surviving partners can continue the business after buying the decedent's interest. This option can be facilitated by having each partner carry life insurance that names the other partners as beneficiaries.

THE LIMITED PARTNERSHIP

A small business sometimes finds it desirable to use a special form of partnership called the **limited partnership.** This form consists of at least one general partner and one or more limited partners. The **general partner** remains personally liable for the debts of the business; **limited partners** have limited personal liability as long as they do not take an active role in the management of the partnership. In other words, limited partners risk only the capital they invest in the business. An individual with substantial personal assets can, therefore, invest money in a limited partnership without exposing his or her personal estate to liability claims that might arise through activities of the business. If a limited partner becomes active in management, however, his or her limited liability is lost. As with general partnerships and corporations, a limited partnership must register with the appropriate provincial ministry.

limited partnership
a partnership with at least one general partner and one or more limited partners

general partner
a partner in a limited partnership who has unlimited personal liability

limited partner
a partner in a limited partnership who is not active in its management and has limited personal liability

THE CORPORATION OPTION

The origin of **corporations** in Canadian law comes from Canada's British heritage. In a ruling by the British House of Lords in 1896 (*Salomon vs. Salomon & Co.*), Lord Macnaghten confirmed the legal status of a corporation under the law, saying, "The company is at law a different person altogether from the subscribers to the memorandum [the shareholders]. Nor are the subscribers as members liable, in any shape or form." In Canada, the *Canada Business Corporations Act* and the various equivalent provincial statutes recognize the corporation as a **legal entity,** meaning that a corporation can sue and be sued, hold and sell property, engage in business operations that are stipulated in the articles of association, and pay taxes separately from the corporation's owners.

corporation
a business organization that exists as a legal entity and provides limited liability to its owners

legal entity
a business organization that is recognized by the law as having a separate legal existence

A corporation is chartered under either federal or provincial laws. The length of its life is independent of its owners' (shareholders') lives. The corporation, and not its owners, is liable for debts contracted by the business. The directors and officers serve as agents to bind the corporation.

ARTICLES OF ASSOCIATION

articles of association
the document that establishes a corporation's existence

To form a corporation, one or more people must apply to the appropriate federal or provincial ministry. After preliminary steps, including payment of an incorporation fee, have been completed, the written application (which is usually prepared by a lawyer) is approved by the government and becomes the corporation's articles of incorporation. In some provinces, documents showing that the corporation exists are called the *corporate charter* or *certificates of incorporation*. The **articles of association** typically provides the following information:

1. Name of the company
2. Restrictions, if any, on business the corporation may carry on
3. Location of principal office in the province of incorporation
4. Classes, voting privileges, and maximum number of shares the corporation is allowed to issue
5. Restrictions, if any, on share transfers
6. Names and addresses of incorporators and first year's directors

Articles of association should be brief, in accord with federal or provincial law, and broad in the statement of the firm's powers. Details should be left to the bylaws.

RIGHTS AND STATUS OF SHAREHOLDERS

share certificate
a document specifying the number of shares owned by a shareholder

pre-emptive right
the right of shareholders to buy new shares in the corporation before they are offered to the public

Ownership in a corporation is evidenced by **share certificates,** each of which stipulates the number of shares owned by a shareholder. An ownership interest does not confer a legal right to act for the firm or to share in its management. It does, however, provide the shareholder with the right to receive dividends in proportion to stockholdings—but only when the dividends are properly declared by the firm. Ownership of shares typically carries a **pre-emptive right,** or the right to buy new shares, in proportion to the number of shares already owned, before new shares are offered for public sale.

The legal status of shareholders is fundamental, of course, but it may be overemphasized. In many small corporations, the owners typically serve both as directors and as managing officers. The person who owns most or all of the shares can control a business as effectively as if it were a sole proprietorship. Thus, this form of organization works well for individual- and family-owned businesses, where maintaining control of the firm is important.

Major shareholders must be concerned about their working relationships, as well as their legal relationships, with other owners who are active in the business. Cooperation among all owners and managers of a new corporation is necessary for its success. Specifying legal technicalities is important, but it is an inadequate basis for successful collaboration. Owners and the members of the management team need to clarify their expectations of each other's roles as best they can. Failure to have clear expectations about working relationships can cause one or more persons to feel that others serving as managers or co-owners are not honouring their word.

LIMITED LIABILITY OF SHAREHOLDERS

For most shareholders, their limited liability is a major advantage of the corporate form of organization. Their financial liability is limited to the amount of money they invest in the business. Creditors cannot require them to sell personal assets to pay corporation debts. However, small corporations are often in a somewhat shaky financial condition during their early years of operation. As a result, a bank that makes a loan to a small firm may insist that the shareholders assume personal liability for the firm's debts, either by signing promissory notes not only as representatives of the firm but also personally, or by signing a separate personal guarantee of the company's debts. If the corporation is unable to repay the loan, the banker can then look to the owners' personal assets to recover the amount of the loan. In this case, the corporate advantage of limited liability is lost.

Why would owners agree to personally guarantee a firm's debt? Simply put, they may have no choice if they want the money. Most bankers are not willing to loan money to an entrepreneur who is not prepared to put his or her own personal assets at risk.

The courts may also override the concept of limited liability for shareholders and hold them personally liable in certain unusual cases—for example, if personal and corporate funds have been mixed together or if the corporation was formed to try to evade an existing obligation.

DEATH OR WITHDRAWAL OF SHAREHOLDERS

Unlike a partnership interest, ownership in a corporation is readily transferable. Exchange of shares is sufficient to convey an ownership interest to a different individual.

Shares of large corporations are exchanged constantly without noticeable effect on the operation of the business. For a small firm, however, a change of owners, though legally similar, can involve numerous complications. For example, finding a buyer for the shares of a small firm may prove difficult. Also, a minority shareholder in a small firm is vulnerable. If two of three equal shareholders in a small business sold their shares to an outsider, the remaining shareholder would then be at the mercy of that outsider. The minority shareholder might be removed from any managerial post she or he happened to hold or be legally ousted from the board of directors and no longer have a voice in the management of the business.

The death of a majority shareholder can have unfortunate repercussions in a small firm. An heir, the executor, or a purchaser of the shares might well insist on direct control, with possible adverse effects for other shareholders. To prevent problems of this nature, legal arrangements should be made at the outset to provide for management continuity by surviving shareholders and fair treatment of a shareholder's heirs. As in the case of a partnership, mutual insurance can ensure the ability to buy out a deceased shareholder's interest. This arrangement would require an option for the corporation or surviving shareholders to (1) purchase the decedent's shares before they are offered to outsiders and (2) specify the method for determining the price per share. A similar arrangement might be made to protect remaining shareholders in case one of the owners wished to retire from the business at any time.

CHOOSING AN ORGANIZATIONAL FORM

Identify factors to consider in choosing among the primary legal forms of organization.

2

Choosing a legal form for a new business deserves careful attention because of the various, sometimes conflicting, features of each organizational option. Depending on the particular circumstances of a specific business, the tax advantages of one form, for example, may offset the limited-liability advantages of another form. Some tradeoffs may be necessary. Ideally, an experienced lawyer should be consulted for aid in selecting the most appropriate form of organization.

Exhibit 10-2 summarizes the main considerations in selecting one of the three primary forms of ownership. A brief description of each factor follows.

- *Initial organizational requirements and costs:* Organizational requirements and costs increase as the formality of the organization increases. That is, a sole proprietorship is typically less complex and less expensive to form than a partnership, and a partnership is less complex and less expensive to form than a corporation. In view of the relatively modest costs, however, this consideration is of minimal importance in the long term. Incorporation can be done through a lawyer, generally for under $500, or by using a kit that walks you through the process for under $100. Kits are generally available in the "self-help" section of most bookstores. In either case fees charged by the province will be extra, generally in excess of $400.
- *Liability of owners:* A sole proprietorship and a general partnership have the inherent disadvantage of unlimited liability for the owners. With these forms of organization, there is no distinction between the firm's assets and the owners' personal assets. Creditors lending money to the business can require the owners to sell personal assets if the firm is financially unable to repay its loans. In contrast, the corporate form limits the owners' liability to their investment in the business. If a corporation is small, however, its owners are often required to guarantee a loan personally.
- *Continuity of business:* A sole proprietorship is immediately dissolved on the owner's death. Likewise, a general partnership is terminated on the death or withdrawal of a partner, unless the partnership agreement states otherwise. A corporation, on the other hand, offers continuity. The status of an individual investor does not affect the corporation's existence.
- *Transferability of ownership:* Ownership is transferred most easily in the corporation. The ability to transfer ownership, however, is intrinsically neither good nor bad. Its desirability depends largely on the owners' preferences. In certain businesses, owners may want the option of evaluating any prospective new investors. In other circumstances, unrestricted transferability may be preferred.
- *Management control:* A sole proprietor has absolute control of the firm. Control within a general partnership is normally based on the majority vote; an increase in the number of partners reduces each partner's voice in management. Within a corporation, control has two dimensions: (1) the formal control vested in the shareholders who own the majority of the voting common shares and (2) the functional control exercised by the corporate officers in conducting daily operations. In a small corporation, these two forms of control usually rest in the same individuals.
- *Attractiveness for raising capital:* A corporation has a distinct advantage when raising new equity capital, due to the ease of transferring ownership through the sale of common shares and the flexibility in distributing the shares. In contrast, the unlimited liability of a sole proprietorship and a general partnership discourages new investors.
- *Income taxes:* Income taxes frequently have a major effect on an owner's selection of a form of organization. Later in this chapter, we look more closely at federal tax laws as they relate to choosing a form of organization.

More information on the advantages and disadvantages of each form of organization can be found on the Canada Revenue Agency website at http://www.canadabusiness.ca

So is owning a minority share of a private company a good idea? As with many business questions, the answer can be only "it depends." If both management and employee are "above board" going into it, a fair and proper shareholder's agreement is in place, and

Form of Organization	Initial Organizational Requirements and Costs	Liability of Owners	Continuity of Business	Transferability of Ownership	Management Control	Attractiveness for Raising Capital	Income Taxes
Sole proprietorship	Minimum requirements; generally no registration or filing fee	Unlimited liability	Dissolved upon proprietor's death	May transfer ownership in company name and assets	Absolute management freedom	Limited to proprietor's personal capital	Income from the business is taxed as personal income to the proprietor
General partnership	Minimum requirements; generally no registration or filing fee; written partnership agreement not legally required but strongly suggested	Unlimited liability	Unless partnership agreement specifies differently, dissolved upon withdrawal or death of a partner	Requires the consent of all partners	Majority vote of partners required for control	Limited to partners' ability and desire to contribute capital	Income from the business is taxed as personal income to the partners
Corporation	Most expensive and greatest requirements; filing fees; compliance with federal or provincial regulations for corporations	Liability limited to investment in company	Continuity of business unaffected by shareholder withdrawal or death	Easily transferred by transferring shares	Shareholders have final control, but usually board of directors controls company policies	Usually the most attractive form for raising capital	The corporation is taxed on its income and the shareholder is taxed if and when dividends are received
Form of organization preferred	Proprietorship or general partnership	Corporation	Corporation	Depends on the circumstances	Depends on the circumstances	Corporation	Depends on the circumstances

EXHIBIT **10-2** *Comparison of Legal Forms of Organization*

IN THE TRENCHES

Confronting the Ethical Issues

The Not-So-Silent Minority

Minority shareholders in a corporation often complain of unfair treatment and lack of a say in the corporation's direction. A look through the business press for 2007 illustrates the perils of being a minority shareholder in public companies. Minority shareholders in Shell Canada strenuously objected to the initial share purchase price offered by Royal Dutch Shell for their shares; Magna International entered into a questionable deal with Russia's Oleg Deripaska that could affect the future value of the share price to the detriment of minority shareholders; St. Lawrence Cement minority shareholders also objected to the initial offer for their shares by Swiss company Holcim. These are but a few examples, and many in the legal and corporate governance arena suggest that Canada's laws do not protect minority shareholders of publicly traded companies sufficiently.

Minority shareholders in private companies face many of the same issues. Many private companies give or sell minority ownership to key employees as a way of incenting them to stay with the company—the proverbial "golden handcuffs." Owning a minority interest in the company you work for can be good for both the company and the employee. It is a source of motivation for the employee and enables the company to both retain and reward key employees. As long as everyone is happy with their treatment and both the company and employee are performing well, all is golden. It's when things go awry that problems arise. Management decisions and practices by the majority shareholders and the lack of a market for shares in private companies make the value of minority ownership questionable. It is common practice for owners of independent business to mix business and personal financial decisions. For example, many business owners have the business lease the expensive automobile they drive, pay for winter excursions to industry conventions in warmer climates, hire family members for sometimes "phantom" jobs, declare management bonuses, and so on. None of these actions are illegal and in fact are some of the benefits of owning a business. However, these also negatively impact the earnings and therefore the value of a business, and this is not good for minority shareholders.

Minority shareholders in private companies face many of the same issues. Many private companies give or sell minority ownership to key employees as a way of incenting them to stay with the company—the proverbial "golden handcuffs." Owning a minority interest in the company you work for can be good for both the company and the employee. It is a source of motivation for the employee and enables the company to both retain and reward key employees. As long as everyone is happy with their treatment and both the company and employee are performing well, all is golden. It's when things go awry that problems arise. Minority ownership does not guarantee a job, and in extreme circumstances a minority shareholder could not only lose their job but could see his or her equity become worthless if the company fails completely. Management decisions and practices by the majority shareholders and the lack of a market for shares in private companies make the value of minority ownership questionable. It is common practice for owners of independent business to mix business and personal financial decisions. For example, many business owners have the business lease the expensive automobile they drive, pay for winter excursions to industry conventions in warmer climates, hire family members at higher rates of pay than non-family employees might be paid for a similar job, declare management bonuses, and so on. None of these actions are illegal and in fact are some of the benefits of owning a business. However, these also negatively impact the earnings and therefore the value of a business, and this is not good for minority shareholders.

funds are set aside for the eventual repurchase of the share, then it can be a win-win. Unfortunately, this is rarely the case.

THE BOARD OF DIRECTORS

A common shareholder ordinarily casts one vote per share in shareholders' meetings. Thus, the shareholder indirectly participates in management by helping elect the directors. The **board of directors** is the governing body for corporate activity. It elects the firm's officers, who manage the enterprise with the help of management specialists. The directors also set or approve management policies, consider reports on operating results from the officers, and declare dividends (if any).

board of directors
the governing body of a corporation, elected by the shareholders

GROWING NEED FOR BOARDS OF DIRECTORS

All too often, the majority shareholder in a small corporation (the entrepreneur) appoints a board of directors only to fulfill a legal requirement. Such owners make little or no use of directors in managing their companies. In fact, the entrepreneur may actively resist efforts of these directors to provide managerial assistance. When appointing a board of directors, such an entrepreneur tends to select personal friends, relatives, or businesspeople who are too busy to analyze the firm's circumstances and are not inclined to argue. Board meetings may be mere formalities to satisfy legal requirements. Some entrepreneurs, however, have found an active board to be both practical and beneficial. Following several scandals in the early 2000s, such as Enron and WorldCom, the United States introduced legislation known as *Sarbanes-Oxley* to impose a higher standard of reporting, behaviour, and responsibility on officers and directors of publicly traded companies. Canada has followed suit with similar legislation. The Ontario Securities Commission has set out the conditions in Guideline OSC 58-201, first issued in 2005. Since virtually all publicly traded corporations are traded on the TSX, an Ontario stock exchange, these guidelines cover almost all such Canadian companies. Additional federal legislation covering both public and private corporations is pending.

The use of boards of directors is becoming increasingly attractive for a number of reasons. The growing complexity of small businesses—resulting from globalization and technological developments, for example—makes the expertise of well-chosen directors especially valuable. In a family business, outsiders can play a unique role in helping evaluate family talent and mediate differences among family members.

USE OF OUTSIDE DIRECTORS BY SMALL COMPANIES

Objectivity is a particularly valuable contribution of outside directors. They can look at issues more dispassionately than insiders who are involved in daily decision making. Outside directors, for example, are freer to scrutinize and to question a firm's ethical standards. Some operating executives, without the scrutiny of outside directors, may rationalize unethical or illegal behaviour as being in the best interest of the company.

In a family business, an outside board can help mediate and resolve issues related to leadership succession, in addition to providing more general direction. As outsiders, they bring to the business a measure of detachment from potentially explosive emotional differences.

CONTRIBUTIONS OF DIRECTORS

A properly assembled board of directors can bring supplementary knowledge and broad experience to corporate management. By virtue of their backgrounds, directors can fill

IN THE TRENCHES

Entrepreneurial Experiences

When Shareholders Disagree

When the shareholders of Takhini Hot Springs outside Whitehorse, Yukon, reached loggerheads over the future of the 100-year-old company, a battle for control threatened to break out. In 2005 the majority shareholders took control of the board of directors over dissatisfaction with management's actions. This led to bad blood and the threat of lawsuits over control of the business. After months of feuding, the group of majority shareholders and the minority shareholders reached an out-of-court settlement in July 2007 on a way forward: The eight majority shareholders would have 120 days to come up with a way to buy out the 23 minority shareholders. If that didn't happen, the majority shareholders agreed to give the minority shareholders 120 days to come up with the cash to buy them out. Time expired for the majority shareholders in late November.

Minority shareholder Carla Pitzel, one of the original investors in Takhini Hot Springs, leads the group hoping to take control of company. The majority shareholders failed to secure the financing and, in late November 2007, Pitzel stated the minority shareholders want to and will buy out all the shares of the majority group. "We want to own it all, just our small group," Pitzel said. "We have the financing in place, and we have the plans in place. It is really exciting, because we have had a vision for the place for nine years and finally we just feel like we are going to be able to do it." The group's plans include new pools, renovations to the main building, residential development, and a new hotel and spa.

After months of legal and financial wrangling, the minority shareholders succeeded in buying out majority shareholders and took control of business. "We are glad that we have been able to keep Takhini Hot Springs in the hands of Yukoners," says Tom Parlee, one of the new owners. "We will continue to operate the hot springs as a family-oriented resort. Renovating the existing building will give us a transitional facility until we develop new hot pools."

The renovated springs re-opened in July 2008, but more is in store. Shareholder Garry Umbrich says, "Our long-term vision is to develop an eco-resort using our geothermal resource to the fullest. Our team is working toward a carbon-neutral approach to development. Takhini Hot Springs will be in the forefront of putting the Yukon on the tourism map in terms of sustainable development."

Source: Chuck Tobin, "Changes Simmering for Hot Springs' Ownership," *Whitehorse Star*, November 23, 2007, p. 2; and "Springs Get New Owners, Changes," *Whitehorse Star*, April 4, 2008, p. 7.

gaps in the experience of a management team. The board should meet regularly to provide maximum assistance to the chief executive. In board meetings, ideas should be debated, strategies determined, and the pros and cons of policies explored. In this way, the chief executive is assisted by the experience of all the board members. Their combined knowledge makes possible more intelligent decisions on issues crucial to the firm.

By utilizing the experience of a board of directors, the chief executive of a small corporation is in no way abdicating active control of its operations. Instead, by consulting with and seeking the advice of the board's members, she or he is simply drawing on a larger pool of business knowledge. A group will typically make better decisions than a single individual working in isolation.

An active board of directors serves management in several important ways: by reviewing major policy decisions, advising on external business conditions and on proper reaction to the business cycle, and providing informal advice from time to time on specific problems that arise. With a strong board, a small firm may gain greater credibility with the public, as well as with the business and financial community.

SELECTION OF DIRECTORS

Many resources are available to an entrepreneur who is attempting to assemble a cooperative and experienced group of directors. The firm's lawyer, banker, accountant, other business executives, and local management consultants might all be considered as potential directors, but such individuals lack the independence needed to critically review an entrepreneur's plans. Also, the owner is already paying for their expertise. For this reason, the owner needs to consider the value of an outside board—one with members whose income does not depend on the firm.

The nature and needs of a business will help determine the qualifications required in its directors. For example, a firm that faces a marketing problem may benefit greatly from the counsel of a board member with a marketing background. Business prominence in the community is not essential, although it may help give the company credibility and enable it to attract other well-qualified directors.

After deciding on the qualifications to look for, a business owner must seek suitable candidates as board members. Suggestions may be obtained from the firm's accountant, lawyer, banker, and other associates in the business community. Owners or managers of other, noncompeting small companies, as well as second- and third-level executives in large companies, are often willing to accept such positions. Before offering candidates positions on the board, however, a business owner would be wise to do some discreet background checking, including whether there are any corporate or personal lawsuits against them as well as previous board experience.

COMPENSATION OF DIRECTORS

The amount of compensation paid to board members varies greatly, and some small firms pay no fees at all. It is not unusual, however, for a small firm to pay a director from $200 to $300 monthly or $1,000 or so for each of four quarterly meetings. A midsized company (with approximately 500 employees) might pay its board members somewhat higher amounts.

The relatively modest compensation offered for the services of well-qualified directors suggests that financial compensation is not their primary motivation for serving on a board. Directors serving on boards of large corporations are usually well compensated in the form of director fees and possibly stock options, partly to compensate for their increased potential liability.

AN ALTERNATIVE: AN ADVISORY COUNCIL

In recent years, increased attention has been directed to the legal responsibilities of directors. Because outside directors may be held responsible for illegal company actions, even though they are not directly involved in wrongdoing, some individuals are reluctant to accept directorships. Thus, some small companies use an **advisory council** as an alternative to a board of directors. Qualified outsiders are asked to serve on a council as advisers to the company. This group then functions in much the same way as a board of directors does, except that its actions are only advisory in nature.

advisory council a group that functions like a board of directors but acts only in an advisory capacity

The following account describes the potential value of an advisory council:

> *A seven-year-old diversified manufacturing company incurred its first deficit, which the owner-manager deemed an exception that further growth would rectify. Council members noted, however, that many distant operations were out of control and apparently unprofitable. They persuaded the owner to shrink his business by more than one-half. Almost immediately, the business began generating profits. From its reduced scale, growth resumed—this time soundly planned, financed, and controlled.*[5]

The legal liability of members of an advisory council is not completely clear.[6] However, a clear separation of the council from the board of directors is thought to lighten, if not eliminate, the personal liability of its members. Since it is advisory in nature, the council may pose less of a threat to the owner and possibly work more cooperatively than a conventional board.

Explain how different forms of organization are taxed by the federal government.

FEDERAL INCOME TAXES AND THE FORM OF ORGANIZATION

To help you understand the federal income tax system, we must answer the twofold question "Who is responsible for paying taxes," and "How is tax liability ascertained?" The following sections discuss how taxes are determined for the major forms of organization and the tax savings associated with corporations.

HOW BUSINESSES ARE TAXED

The three major forms of organization are taxed in the following ways:

- Self-employed individuals who operate a business as a sole proprietorship report income from the business on their individual federal income tax returns.

They are then taxed at the rates set by law for individuals. The federal tax rates for 2008 are as follows:

Range of Taxable Income	Tax Rate
$0–$37,885	15.0%
$37,885–$75,769	15.0% on the first $37,885; 22.0% on the second $37,884
$75,769–$123,184	26% on the amount over $75,769
$123,184 and over	29% on the amount over $120,887

For example, assume that a sole proprietor has taxable income of $150,000 from a business. The taxes owed on this income would be $34,121.77, computed as follows:

Income × Tax Rate = Taxes

First	$37,885	15%	$ 5,682.75
Next	37,884	22	8,334.48
Next	47,415	26	12,327.90
Remaining	26,816	29	7,776.64
Total			$34,121.77

- Provincial income tax rates vary, and are additional to federal taxes. These rates can be found on Canada Revenue Agency's website at http://www.cra-arc.gc.ca.
- A sole proprietor and partnership reports the income it earns to Canada Revenue Agency, but the partnership itself does not pay any taxes. The income is allocated to the partners according to their agreement. The partners each report their own shares of the partnership income on their personal tax returns and pay any taxes owed.
- The corporation, as a separate legal entity, reports its income and pays any taxes related to these profits. The owners (shareholders) of the corporation need report on their personal tax returns only any amounts paid to them by the corporation in the form of dividends. The current small business (taxable income under $400,000) federal corporate tax rate is 12 percent. For example, the tax liability for the business in the example for a sole proprietorship above, if it were a corporation that had $150,000 in taxable income, would be $150,000 × 12 percent or $18,000. Provincial taxes vary and are additional to federal taxes. Of course, the owner(s) of the business would then have to pay personal taxes on salaries or dividends paid by the business to them.

If the corporation paid a dividend to its owners in the amount of $40,000, the owners would need to report this dividend income when computing their personal income taxes. Thus, the $40,000 would be taxed twice, first as part of the corporation's income and then as part of the owners' personal income.

For tax purposes, **ordinary income** is income earned in the everyday course of business. Salary is considered ordinary income. **Capital gains and losses** are financial gains and losses incurred from the sale of property that is not a part of a firm's regular business operations, such as gains or losses from the sale of common shares.

Typically, capital losses may be deducted only from capital gains, not from ordinary income. However, there is a provision under the *Income Tax Act* to allow owners of businesses to convert losses from a failed business venture into an "Allowable Business Investment Loss," or ABIL. An ABIL claim may also be made when a guarantor of a corporate loan is compelled by the lender to pay on the guarantee. The ABIL thus allows the owner to realize some personal tax savings in the case of business failure.

ordinary income
income earned in the ordinary course of business, including any salary

capital gains and losses
gains and losses incurred from sales of property that are not a part of the firm's regular business operations

LAWS, REGULATION, AND LEGAL AGREEMENTS

Understand the major legal and regulatory issues businesses face. **5**

In addition to legal issues surrounding the form of ownership, businesses are subject to additional laws and regulations. Not all laws and regulations apply to all types of business, but some laws and regulations do. For example, a company would not have to be concerned with packaging regulations if it is not selling a product, nor would a company likely be concerned with intellectual property issues such as patents and copyrights if it is in most service businesses.

In addition to laws and regulations, businesses enter into legally binding agreements of various kinds. Examples of these would be lease agreements for space to operate, employment contracts with employees, and purchase agreements with suppliers. These contracts and agreements are enforceable through the civil court system. It should be noted that a business in one province will have no standing—not be recognized—by the court in another province. For example, an Ontario corporation trying to sue a customer in Manitoba for nonpayment of a debt would have to assign its claim to a person or corporation in Manitoba, who would then bring the matter to the Manitoba courts.

TYPES OF LAW AND REGULATION IN CANADA

REGULATING COMPETITION

Competition Act
federal antitrust
legislation designed
to maintain a
competitive
economy

In a fully competitive economic system consumers benefit by being able to buy products and services from those companies that best satisfy their needs. The principle law ensuring fair competition is the federal *Competition Act.* To some extent this protects small businesses from unscrupulous dealings with other corporations. For example, discounts and other forms of incentives must be offered to all customers. Discrimination is allowed only based on criteria such as volume of product purchased. Other provisions regulate the relationship between businesses and their suppliers and prohibit certain practices such as

- Tied selling, which is the requirement that a supplier will supply a required product only if the customer purchases another product.
- Refusal to deal, where a supplier refuses to sell to a willing customer.
- Exclusive dealing, where a supplier insists on being the exclusive supplier to a customer.

The *Competition Act* has other provisions to ensure that one or more companies do not dominate a particular market or industry to the extent that fair competition cannot happen.

PROTECTING CONSUMERS

In addition to protection under the *Competition Act,* other federal and provincial legislation protects consumers by ensuring such things as accurate labelling and the safety of food and drugs. Some examples of such laws are

- *Ontario Business Practices Act,* which prevents false, misleading, or deceptive claims to consumers
- *Canadian Consumer Packaging and Labelling Act,* which sets the requirements for product labels and for packaging certain products
- *Textile Labelling Act,* which sets out requirements for labelling clothing and other textiles.
- *Food and Drug Act,* which regulates the manufacture, production, transport, storage, and labelling of food and drugs.
- *Hazardous Product Act,* which regulates the manufacture of hazardous and potentially hazardous products. One example is the requirement that baby cribs be manufactured with no more than 10 cm between the rails.
- *Motor Vehicle Safety Act,* which is an example of a regulation affecting a particular industry.

**freedom of
information and
privacy legislation**
protects individuals
from having their
personal information
collected and used
by businesses and
other organizations
for any purpose to
which the individual
objects

One relatively new form of protection for consumers and individuals generally is **freedom of information and privacy legislation.** This legislation protects individuals from having their personal information collected and used by businesses and other organizations for any purpose to which the individual objects. For example, consumers' names, addresses, and other information cannot be sold by one company to another without the consent of the individual. Another example is that organizations—not just businesses—must obtain prior approval to put a consumer on a mail or email distribution list. Under FOIP legislation, organizations must take reasonable steps to ensure the security of information they need to collect on customers, users, or members. An example of the importance of this is the discovery of individuals' health records on the hard drives of old computers disposed of by a hospital.[7]

There are two sources of legislation: the federal *Personal Information Privacy and Electronic Documents Act* and the additional legislation of some provinces. For more information on this type of legislation and its implications for business, refer to the following sites:

> http://www.privacyforbusiness.ic.gc.ca
> http://www.foip.gov.ab.ca

PROTECTING INVESTORS

Provinces have **securities acts** to protect investors. These laws specify how businesses and individual investors must behave through the process of attracting investment. For example, the practice of insider trading—trades by the decision makers of a business using knowledge not available to the general public about the business—is not allowed and is closely monitored. Other provisions give some protection to the minority shareholders in corporations.

PROMOTING PUBLIC WELFARE

Many diverse kinds of law are designed to benefit the public welfare. Municipal health bylaws, for example, establish minimum standards of sanitation for restaurants to protect the health of patrons. Increasingly, environmental protection legislation such as the *Ontario Environmental Protection Act,* which has its counterpart in many provinces, ensures businesses do not do undue harm to the environment. For example, old service station sites must have any leakage from storage tanks remediated; another example is that oil companies must now do a pre-drilling site assessment and post-use remediation of sites before they can drill oil and gas wells.

Other legislation such as the *Canadian Human Rights Act* and similar provincial laws prevent discrimination based on age, gender, religion, and race. Other provisions set out the requirement for public facilities to be accessible to those in wheelchairs, for example.

PROTECTING EMPLOYEE RIGHTS

Employers are required to take reasonable steps to protect employees from robbery, assault, and other crimes at work. Other laws such as **occupational health and safety acts, employment standards codes,** and **workers' compensation acts** have been designed primarily for employees and potential employees. (See Chapter 9.)

PROTECTING A FIRM'S INTANGIBLE ASSETS

In addition to managing and protecting its physical assets, a firm must protect its intangible assets, which include trademarks, patents, copyrights, industrial designs, integrated circuit topography, and plant breeders' rights. The most common forms of protection are portrayed in Exhibit 10-3.

TRADEMARKS A **trademark** is a word, name, symbol, device, slogan, or any combination thereof used to distinguish a product sold by one manufacturer. Protection is given under the *Trade-Marks Act.* Examples of trademarks would be Nike's "swoosh" and Intel's "Intel Inside" sticker on computer equipment. Potential names for products or companies should be carefully investigated to ensure that they are not already in use. This can be done through the **Canadian Intellectual Property Office (CIPO),** which also publishes *A Guide to Trade-Marks.* CIPO's website is http://www.cipo.gc.ca.

Personal Information Privacy and Electronic Documents Act supports and promotes electronic commerce by protecting personal information that is collected, used, or disclosed by providing for the use of electronic means to communicate or record information or transactions

securities acts provincial legislation that regulates the advertisements, issuance, and public sales of securities

Ontario Environmental Protection Act provincial legislation that establishes procedures, standards, and liability to ensure environmental protection

Canadian Human Rights Act federal legislation that prohibits discrimination against people and guarantees basic human rights

occupational health and safety acts provincial legislation that regulates health and safety in the workplace to ensure safe workplaces and work practices

EXHIBIT **10-3**
*Most Common Forms
of Intangible Asset
Protection*

TRADEMARK
Examples: Sony, Acura, Pepsi, Xerox

PATENT
Examples: Post-It notes, coupon dispenser, zip fastener

COPYRIGHT
Examples: songs, books, designs

**employment
standards codes**
provincial legislation
regulating working
conditions, minimum
wages, and other
work-related issues

**workers'
compensation acts**
provincial legislation
that provides
employer-supported
insurance for workers
who become ill
or are injured in
the course of
employment

trademark
a word, name,
symbol, device,
slogan, or any
combination thereof
used to distinguish a
product sold by one
manufacturer

Trade-Marks Act
federal legislation
that regulates trade-
marks and provides
for their registration

**Canadian
Intellectual
Property Office
(CIPO)**
responsible for the
administration and
processing of intellec-
tual property (ideas,
designs, creativity)

patent
the registered,
exclusive rights of
an inventor to make,
use, or sell an
invention

PATENTS A **patent** is the registered, exclusive right of an inventor to make, use, or sell an invention (the latter is called licensing) for a 20-year period. This right is granted under the *Patent Act.* Patents must be applied for, and there are certain conditions an invention must fulfill before a patent application will be accepted by CIPO. A patent is good only in the country that grants the patent, so patenting an invention in many countries can be a very expensive and time-consuming effort.

COPYRIGHTS A **copyright** is the exclusive right of a creator (author, composer, designer, or artist) to reproduce, publish, perform, display, or sell work that is a product of his or her intelligence and skill. Copyright works in a similar manner to patents.

INDUSTRIAL DESIGN Industrial design is the protection afforded by the *Industrial Designs Act* to the original shape, pattern, or ornamentation applied to a manufactured article. It must be applied for prior to the design being made public and is granted for a five-year term, renewable on application for an additional five years.

INTEGRATED CIRCUIT TOPOGRAPHY The three-dimensional configuration of the electronic circuits used in microchips and semiconductor chips is protected for 10 years under the *Integrated Circuit Topography Act.*

PLANT BREEDERS' RIGHTS The ability to control the multiplication and sale of new varieties of plant seeds is protected for 18 years under the *Plant Breeders' Rights Act.*

TO PATENT OR NOT?

Obtaining intellectual property protection through a patent is not necessarily a smart business decision. Filing a patent puts the information about a technology in the public domain—that is, where other companies can see it. If a business is not ready to immediately capture a sizeable part of the market, either because the technology is not fully developed or it does not have the distribution channels or production capacity in place, filing a patent can give a larger competitor time to come up with their own version of the product and gain a "first to market" advantage. Many companies choose to try to keep their technology quiet until they are ready to launch the product into the market before filing a patent. Others launch their product, which precludes filing a patent, hoping to build market share while "flying under the radar" of the competition. In situations where some aspect of the design can be easily altered to get around the patent protection or if the technological life is relatively short, the first-to-market or under-the-radar-strategy may make better business sense. It should also be noted that protecting intellectual property through obtaining a patent is only as good as the owner's ability to defend the patent. Should another company infringe on the design, the most common

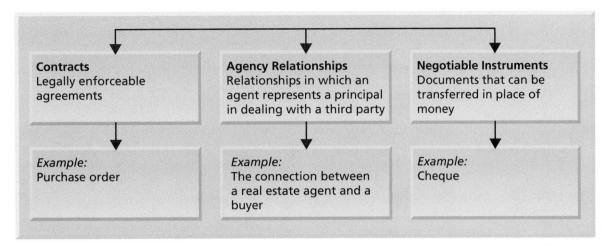

EXHIBIT **10-4** *Basic Elements of Law*

action is to have a lawyer send a "cease and desist" letter. If this is ignored however, very costly and lengthy legal action is often the result.

There are situations where protecting intellectual property is very important. Licensing a technology to another company normally requires protection of the property or there is nothing of value for the licensee to license. Another situation is where a company develops a technology with the hopes of being bought by a larger competitor. This is very common in high-technology businesses.

BUSINESS AGREEMENTS AND THE LAW

An entrepreneur should be careful in structuring agreements with individuals and other businesses. Because today's society seems to encourage lawsuits and legal action, entrepreneurs must understand such basic elements of law as contracts, agency relationships, and negotiable instruments, to name just a few (see Exhibit 10-4).

CONTRACTS

Businesses frequently make agreements with employees, customers, suppliers, and others. If the agreements are legally enforceable, they are called **contracts.** For a valid contract to exist, the following six requirements must be met:

1. *Offer:* A clear, genuine offer must be communicated. This offer must be free of mistakes or misrepresentations as to its essential terms, and both parties must be of like mind as to the terms.
2. *Voluntary agreement:* A genuine offer must be accepted unconditionally by the other party.
3. *Competent contracting parties:* Contracts with individuals who are under legal age, insane, seriously intoxicated, or otherwise unable to understand the nature of the transaction are typically voidable.
4. *Legal act:* The subject of the agreement must not be in conflict with public policy or law, as it would be in a contract to sell an illegal product.
5. *Consideration:* The parties must exchange something of value, such as money or time, known in legal terms as consideration.

Patent Act
federal legislation that gives a patent holder the exclusive right to construct, sell, manufacture, and use a patented invention for 20 years

copyright
the exclusive right of a creator to reproduce, publish, perform, display, or sell his or her own work

Industrial Designs Act
federal legislation that protects the original shape, pattern, or ornamentation applied to a manufactured article

Integrated Circuit Topography Act
federal legislation that protects the three-dimensional configuration of electronic circuits in microchips and semiconductor chips

Plant Breeders' Rights Act
federal legislation that protects the multiplication and sale of new varieties of plant seeds

contracts
agreements that are legally enforceable

Statute of Frauds
legislation enacted to prevent fraudulent lawsuits without proper evidence of a contract

agency relationship
an arrangement in which one party represents another party in dealing with a third party

6. *Form of contract consistent with content:* Contracts may be written or oral, but under the **Statute of Frauds,** contracts for the following must be in written form: sales transactions of $1000 or more, sale of real estate, and actions that cannot be performed within one year after the contract is made. The existence of an oral contract must be demonstrable in some way; otherwise it may be difficult to prove.

If one party to a contract fails to perform in accordance with the contract, the court will either require specific performance or, more likely, award money to the injured party to restore it to the condition it would have been in had the contract been performed. In other cases or in addition to damages, the injured party has the right to rescind (cancel) the contract.

AGENCY RELATIONSHIPS

An **agency relationship** is an arrangement whereby one party—the agent—represents another party—the principal—in contracting with a third party. Examples of agents are the manager of a branch office who acts as an agent of the business, a partner who acts as an agent for the other partner(s), and a real estate agent who represents a buyer or seller.

Agents differ in the scope of their authority. The manager of a branch office is a general agent with broad authority. A real estate agent is a special agent with authority to act only in a specific transaction.

The principal is liable to the third party for performance of contracts made by the agent acting within the scope of his or her authority. The principal is also liable for fraudulent, negligent, and other wrongful acts of an agent that are executed within the scope of the agency relationship, as the third party may rescind the contract and bring actions against the principal and agent.

An agent has certain obligations to the principal. In general, the agent must accept the orders and instructions of the principal, act in good faith, and use prudence and care in discharging agency duties. Moreover, the agent is liable if he or she exceeds stipulated authority and causes damage to the third party as a result. An exception occurs when the principal ratifies (approves) the act, whereupon the principal becomes liable.

It is apparent that the powers of agents can make the agency relationship a potentially dangerous one. For this reason, businesses should exercise care in selecting agents and clearly stipulate their authority and responsibility.

negotiable instruments
credit documents that are transferable from one party to another in place of money

Bills of Exchange Act
A federal law that sets out the requirements for negotiable financial instruments such as cheques and promissory notes

NEGOTIABLE INSTRUMENTS

Credit documents that can be transferred from one party to the other in place of money are known as **negotiable instruments.** The requirements for such documents are set out in the federal **Bills of Exchange Act.** Examples of negotiable instruments are promissory notes, bank drafts, trade acceptances, and ordinary cheques. In general, the requirements for a negotiable instrument are as follows:

1. There must be a written, signed, unconditional promise or order to pay.
2. The amount to be paid in money must be specified.
3. The instrument must provide for payment on demand at a definite time or at a determinable time.
4. The instrument must be payable to the bearer or to the order of someone.

LOOKING BACK

1 Identify the common forms of legal organization used by small businesses and describe the characteristics of each.

- The most common legal forms of organization used by small businesses are the sole proprietorship, the partnership, and the corporation.
- In a sole proprietorship, the owner receives all profits and bears all losses. The principal disadvantage of this form is the owner's unlimited liability.
- In a partnership, which should be established on the basis of a written partnership agreement, success depends on the partners' ability to build an effective working relationship.
- Corporations are particularly attractive because of their limited-liability feature. The fact that ownership is easily transferable makes them well suited for combining the capital of numerous owners.

2 Identify factors to consider in choosing among the primary legal forms of organization.

- The key factors in the choice among different legal forms of organization are organizational requirements and costs, liability of the owners, continuity of the business, transferability of ownership, management control, attractiveness for raising capital, and income taxes.

3 Describe the effective use of boards of directors and advisory councils.

- Boards of directors can assist small corporations by offering counsel and assistance to their chief executives.
- To be most effective, members of the board should be properly qualified, independent outsiders.
- One alternative to an active board of directors is an advisory council, whose members are not personally liable for the company's actions.

4 Explain how different forms of organization are taxed by the federal government.

- Self-employed individuals who operate businesses as sole proprietorships report income from the businesses on their individual tax returns.
- A partnership reports the income it earns to Canada Revenue Agency, but the partnership itself does not pay income taxes. The income is allocated to the owners according to their partnership agreement.
- A corporation reports its income and pays any taxes due on this corporate income. Individual shareholders must also pay personal income taxes on dividends paid to them by a corporation.

5 Understand the major legal and regulatory issues businesses face.

- The federal and provincial governments have legislation to regulate competition, protect consumers and investors, promote public welfare, protect employees' rights, and protect an individual's or business's intellectual property.
- Businesses and individuals enter into agreements with other businesses or individuals that are known as contracts.
- Agency relationships exist where an individual or business is appointed an agent of another party (the principal) to represent the principal to third parties.
- In the normal course of business, individuals and businesses use negotiable instruments such as cheques in place of cash.

KEY TERMS

advisory council, p. 279
agency power, p. 271
agency relationship, p. 286
articles of association, p. 272
Bills of Exchange Act, p. 286
board of directors, p. 277

Canadian Human Rights Act, p. 283
capital gains and losses, p. 281
CIPO (Canadian Intellectual Property Office), p. 284
Competition Act, p. 282
contracts, p. 286

copyright, p. 285
corporation, p. 271
employment standards codes, p. 284
freedom of information and privacy legislation, p. 282
general partner, p. 271

DISCUSSION QUESTIONS

1. Why would investors tend to favour a new business led by a management team over one headed by a lone entrepreneur? Is this preference justified? Why or why not?
2. Discuss the merits of the three major legal forms of organization.
3. Does the concept of limited liability apply to a sole proprietorship? Why or why not?
4. Suppose a partnership is set up and operated without a formal partnership agreement. What problems might arise? Explain.
5. Explain why the agency power of partners is of great importance.
6. Evaluate the three major forms of organization in terms of management control by the owner and sharing of the firm's profits.
7. How might a board of directors be of value to management in a small corporation? What qualifications are essential for a director? Is ownership of shares in the firm a prerequisite for being a director?
8. What may account for the failure of most small corporations to use boards of directors as more than rubber stamps?
9. How do advisory councils differ from boards of directors? Which would you recommend to a small company owner? Why?
10. How does the *Canadian Human Rights Act* affect hiring practices? Be specific.
11. Discuss the legal protection provided by patents. Does the granting of a patent guarantee no one else can use the design?

YOU MAKE THE CALL

SITUATION 1

Dennis Wong and Mark Stroder became close friends as 16-year-olds when both worked part-time for Wong's dad in his automotive parts store. After high school, Wong went to college, while Stroder got a job with a hardware retailer and devoted his weekends to auto racing. Wong continued his association with the automotive parts store by buying and managing two of his father's stores.

In 2005, Wong conceived the idea of starting a new business that would rebuild automobile starters, and he asked Stroder to be his partner in the venture. Originally, Stroder was somewhat concerned about working with Wong because their personalities are so different. Wong has been described as outgoing and enthusiastic, while Stroder is reserved and skeptical. However, Stroder is now out of work, and so he has agreed to the offer. They will set up a small shop behind one of Wong's automotive parts stores. Stroder will do all the work; Wong will supply the cash.

The "partners" have agreed to name the business Startover, and now they need to decide on a legal form of organization.

Question 1 How relevant are the individual personalities to the success of this entrepreneurial team? Do you think Wong and Stroder have a chance to survive their "partnership"? Why or why not?

Question 2 Do you consider it an advantage or a disadvantage that the members of this team are the same age?

Question 3 Which legal form of organization would you propose for Startover? Why?

Question 4 Would you recommend incorporation to Stroder and Wong? Why or why not?

SITUATION 2

Bob was the leading performer at a corporate design firm; Clarence was the leader at its competitor. Deciding to work together, they both quit their jobs and started a firm.

Clarence argued that, as the older and more experienced of the two, he was being exposed to greater risk than Bob. Therefore, Clarence negotiated to receive 51 percent of the firm and a compensation package based on each partner's own sales, net of expenses. As expected, Clarence earned more the first year. The next year, though, Bob unexpectedly sold more than Clarence and requested reconsideration of the terms: "I urged Clarence to regard me not as a risk anymore but as an asset." To which Clarence retorted "Well, no asset's going to make more than I do." He hired a support team—for himself, not for Bob—and stopped sending Bob the figures on which their take-home pay was based. Bob accessed the information on the accounting department's

computer and discovered that his partner had siphoned off more than $10,000. He confronted Clarence. "Okay, okay, I took it," his partner confessed. "But I deserved it; I had to manage the staff."

Source: Adapted from "Partner Wars," *Inc.*, vol. 16, no. 6 (June 1994), p. 40.

Question 1 What mistake was made in the formation of this partnership?

Question 2 Is Clarence right in claiming that he should receive more than Bob?

Question 3 Do you see an ethical problem in this situation?

Question 4 If you were Bob, what would you do?

SITUATION 3

For years, a small distributor of china had followed the practice of most small firms, treating the board of directors as merely a legal necessity. Composed of two co-owners and a retired steel company executive, the board was not a working board. But the company, run informally with traditional management methods, was profitable.

The majority owner, after attending a seminar, decided that a board might be useful for more than legal or cosmetic purposes. Thus, she invited two outsiders—both division heads of larger corporations—to join the board. This brought the membership of the board to five. The majority owner believed the new members would be helpful in opening up the business to new ideas.

Question 1 Can two outside members on a board of five make any real difference in the way the board operates?

Question 2 Evaluate the owner's choices for board members.

Question 3 What will determine the usefulness or effectiveness of this board? Do you predict that it will be useful? Why or why not?

EXPERIENTIAL EXERCISES

1. Interview a lawyer whose clients include small businesses. Inquire about the legal considerations involved in choosing the form of organization for a new business. Report your findings to the class.
2. Interview the partners of a local business. Inquire about the factors they considered when drawing up their partnership agreement. Report your findings to the class.
3. Discuss with a corporate director, lawyer, banker, or business owner the contributions of directors to small firms. Prepare a brief report on your findings. If you discover a particularly well-informed individual, suggest that person to your instructor as a possible speaker.
4. Interview a local lawyer and determine what areas of law he or she considers most vital to small business owners. Report your findings to the class
5. Interview a local business owner—preferably a manufacturer of a technology-based product—about his or her strategy to protect the intangible assets (intellectual property) of the business. Report your findings to the class.

EXPLORING THE WEB

1. You can find legal advice and information for small businesses on Western Economic Diversification's website at http://www.wd.gc.ca.
   a. Follow the link to "Just for You" to "Services for Business" and then "Business Tools & Guides." From there, view the "Business Start-up Assistant."
   b. Read brief descriptions of each type of business organization: sole proprietorships, partnerships, and corporations.
   c. According to this page, what are the key considerations in deciding whether or not to incorporate?

CHAPTER 11

Selecting a Location and Planning the Facilities

IN THE SPOTLIGHT

Scrapbooksbydesign.ca

Where should an entrepreneur locate a retail business to compete expand its market reach? Toronto's Scrapbooks by Design located online to grow beyond the limitations of its retail location. Even though only 19 percent of Canadian Federation of Independent Business members sell their products online, having a physical "bricks and mortar" location has become increasingly important in the world of Internet marketing.

Founded in 2003 in Toronto's Beach area, the scrapbooking store went online in 2006 to expand its market reach, and sales over the Internet are now larger than sales from the retail store. Within 18 months of opening, the store became so successful that founder Patrick Piette decided to give up his investment banking career and turn his full attention to the business. "I couldn't add value by giving craft advice," says Piette, who admittedly knows little about scrapbooking and crafts, so he decided to launch an e-commerce site to give the business an Internet presence. It took $80,000 and three significant software overhauls before he was satisfied but Piette says it was money well spent. Piette handles the online side himself, while five full-time and two part-time employees take care of the retail store.

Being online is not without its challenges. Canadian shoppers "are ruthless when they're buying online, says Ted Mallet, vice-president of research for the Canadian Federation of Independent Business. "If they run into the slightest glitch when they're buying, then they ditch whatever was in that shopping cart" and skip the purchase.

Piette says getting customers to feel comfortable is a challenge. "For a lot of older women, going online to shop is still new and unfamiliar," he says. But once shoppers have a good experience with that first purchase, they do come back, and spend three times more for each order than customers who come into the store, according to Piette. It's also important to make it easy for people to find the company on the web, so Piette spends about $3000 per month to advertise on search engines such as Google. Piette advises business owners considering an online presence to advertise and market it just "as you would a physical location." Spending the money on the site is important too. "I could have done for a few thousand dollars. It wouldn't be as flexible as it is and would have been a lot more labour intensive . . . but it's a good way to start out if you aren't sure," Piette says.

Anna G. Tufvesson/Nordic Photos/Getty Images

Despite the success of his online venture he has no plans to move his business completely online. He says the retail store keeps him in touch with customers, and by talking to them in person he keeps on top of trends.

Scrapbooksbydesign.ca is just one of thousands of successful companies for which the Internet has become an important part of their marketing strategy.

http://www.scrapbooksbydesign.ca

Source: Laura Ramsay, "Selling on the Web? Keep it Simple," *The Globe and Mail*, September 5, 2007, p. B6.

A business idea begins to take shape as an entrepreneur formulates a business plan. The idea becomes more tangible as the entrepreneur selects the resources needed to implement the plan, including the business site and any necessary facilities and equipment. For some entrepreneurial ventures, these resources may be limited to a briefcase, desk space at home, and a site on the Internet; for others, they may include a new building. Regardless of the specific resources needed, every sound location decision is founded on certain basic principles.

In this chapter we discuss three primary options for the initial location decision—a traditional physical building, the entrepreneur's home, and a website on the Internet, also known as *e-commerce*. Although we recognize that the Internet can be an integral part of operations for both traditional and home-based businesses, we treat e-commerce ventures in a separate category because of the Internet's significance as a sole sales outlet for these businesses.

LOCATING THE BRICKS-AND-MORTAR START-UP

Describe the factors affecting choice of a bricks-and-mortar business location.

In many cases the choice of a location for a business is often a one-time decision—made only when the business is first established or purchased. However, an entrepreneur must occasionally consider relocating the business to reduce operating costs, get closer to customers, or gain other advantages. Also, as a business grows, it is sometimes desirable to expand operations to other locations.[1]

THE IMPORTANCE OF THE LOCATION DECISION

bricks-and-mortar location
The traditional physical store or location from which businesses have historically operated

The importance of the initial location decision for a traditional physical building—a **bricks-and-mortar location**—is underscored by the costs and impracticality of pulling up stakes and moving an established business. Also, if the choice of site is particularly poor, the business may never be successful, even with adequate financing and superior managerial ability. This importance of location is so clearly recognized by national chains that they spend thousands of dollars investigating sites before establishing new stores. As noted in Chapter 4, one of the reasons franchising is so attractive is that franchisors typically assist the franchisee in site selection.

The choice of a good location is much more vital to some businesses than to others. For example, the site chosen for a dress shop can make or break the business because it must be convenient for customers. In contrast, the physical location of the office of a painting contractor is of less importance, since customers do not need frequent access to the facility. Even painting contractors, however, may suffer if their business site is poorly chosen. For example, some communities are more willing or able than others to invest resources to keep property in good condition, thereby providing greater opportunities for painting jobs.

KEY FACTORS IN SELECTING A GOOD LOCATION

Five key factors, shown in Exhibit 11-1, guide the location investigation process: customer accessibility, environmental business conditions, resource availability, personal preference, and site availability and costs. In a particular situation, one factor may carry more weight than others, but each always has an influence on the final location decision.

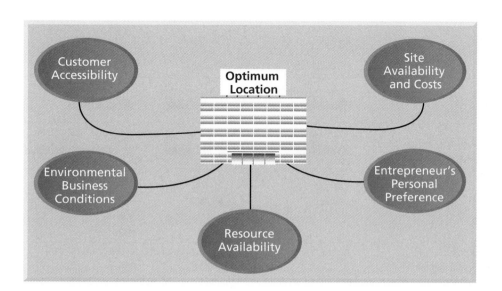

EXHIBIT **11-1**
*Five Key Factors in
Determining a Good
Business Location*

CUSTOMER ACCESSIBILITY

The foremost consideration in selecting a location should be customer accessibility. Retail outlets and service firms are typical examples of businesses that must be located so as to make access convenient for target customers. Rarely will customers be willing to regularly travel long distances to shop. Consider Brian Grant Duff, who moved his business from downtown Vancouver to the West Side in 2008. Grant Duff's All Nations Stamp and Coin had operated downtown for six years, but he became increasingly unhappy with the location. While Duff hadn't experienced skyrocketing rent increases like many small businesses in the downtown, core, the lack of parking and loss of transit due to construction of a rapid transit line drove him to move to a new location. His new location features free parking and, since All Nations Stamp and Coin has always been a destination, Grant Duff is sure long-time customers will check out the new store. "Most people living downtown don't have room to collect anything, but in Dunbar people not only have the room, but there's a bunch of private schools nearby and I might end up with a whole new generation of collectors," he says.[2]

Many products, such as snack foods and gasoline, are convenience goods, which require a retail location close to target customers; otherwise, consumers will substitute competitive brands. Services such as tire repair and hair styling are also classified as convenience items and require a location accessible to customers.

Customer accessibility is also vital in industries in which the cost of shipping the finished product is high relative to the product's value. For example, packaged ice and soft drinks must be produced near consuming markets, because transporting these products can be expensive.

Convenient access for customers is one reason small businesses have successfully created such a strong presence on the Internet. Using a computer with Internet access, customers can reach a small business's home page from anywhere in the world. (Locating a start-up on the Internet is discussed later in this chapter.)

Locating close to niche market customers often dictates a site that otherwise would be less than desirable. For example, Carey Vigneux located his gymnastics and exercise club inside an existing recreation centre in LaSalle, near Windsor, Ontario.[3] The business location is ideal according to Vigneux, because people who drop by the large recreation centre are already physically fit, "and you can tap into their relatives," Vigneux says.

	Retail	Wholesale	Manufacturing
Customer Accessibility			
Environmental Business Conditions			
Proximity to Raw Materials and Suppliers			
Suitability of Labour Supply			
Availability of Transportation			
Personal Preference of the Entrepreneur			

ENVIRONMENTAL BUSINESS CONDITIONS

A start-up business is affected in a number of ways by the environment within which it operates; environmental conditions can hinder or promote success. For example, weather is an important environmental factor influencing the demand for products such as air conditioners and swimming pools (see Exhibit 11-2). Competition, legal requirements, and the tax structure are a few of the many other critical environmental factors.

Every entrepreneur seeks profits; therefore, all factors affecting the financial picture are of great concern. Provincial and local governments can help or hinder a new business by forgiving or levying taxes. Considerable variation exists across Canada in provincial corporate income taxes and retail sales tax rates. Exhibit 11-3 shows the rates

	Sales Tax %	Corporate Tax (Small Business) %	Corporate Tax (General) %
Alberta	0	3.0	10.0
British Columbia	7.0	4.5	12.0
Manitoba	7.0	3.0	14.0
New Brunswick	8.0	5.0	13.0
Nova Scotia	8.0	5.0	16.0
Newfoundland	8.0	5.0	14.0
Ontario	8.0	5.5	14.0
Prince Edward Island	10.0	4.3	16.0
Quebec	7.5	8.0	9.9
Saskatchewan	5.0	4.5	13.0

Source: http//www.alberta-canada.com/investLocate/reasonsto_invest/provincialFederalTaxation.cfm, retrieved January 23, 2008.

IN THE TRENCHES

Exploring Global Opportunities

Mini-Mills from Prince Edward Island to *Where?*

Prince Edward Island seems like an unlikely home for a successful international exporter, but home it is for Belfast Mini-Mill Ltd., which makes miniature textile mills that can be used by small-scale manufacturers worldwide.

Founded in 1992 by Larry Sutherland after selling the family weaving-loom business in Vancouver, the company is representative of the diverse nature of businesses finding viable markets for their products and services worldwide. Belfast is now run by Sutherland's son-in-law Doug Nobles. "When we first started out we weren't looking for a global market," admits Nobles, "but after a few years we had customers coming out of the woodwork like Scotland, which was a complete surprise to us." The client in Scotland is a small village surrounding a lighthouse on a remote island of 2,500 sheep and less than 70 residents. The mill, which Belfast builds "cottage-industry" size for portability, enables the village to export luxurious textiles culled from the sheep's wool, creating a dependable livelihood.

Belfast has sold mills to villagers high in the Andes, the Falkland Islands, South Africa, New Zealand, Australia, England, and throughout North America. It is finalizing a new wind-powered design for a village in Mongolia. "A lot of cashmere and alpaca are in very remote areas that have no industry or power," says Nobles, "but they have lots of wind, so coupling our concept with a windmill goes so well for these small villages."

Perhaps most remarkable is how people located in such remote, distant communities hear about Belfast Mini-Mills. While some clients come across the website, most are drawn from simple advertisements in select textile magazines and by word of mouth. The global boutique textiles industry is pretty tight-knit, so word of mouth is a key promotional tool for the company as alpaca and llama farmers readily share their secrets. "All over the world it seems alpaca is the 'in' thing," Nobles says, "I would say 90 percent of our mills are producing alpaca fibre."

According to Nobles, "Our biggest attribute is our knowledge and our service, and it's pretty hard for someone to compete with that."

Source: Daryl-Lynn Carlson, "It's a Small World for Niche Players," *National Post,* April 23, 2007, p. EN1.

for the various provinces. Variation also exists in provincial personal tax rates, with Ontario and Alberta having the lowest rates and Saskatchewan and Manitoba the highest, depending on taxable income level.[4] Municipal taxes and levies, as well as cost of living differences, also influence the cost of locating in a particular town or city. KPMG's 2006 competitiveness study ranked Sherbrooke, Moncton, Charlottetown, Halifax, Quebec City, Saskatoon, Chilliwack, B.C., and St. John's, NF the lowest-cost Canadian cities in which to do business.[5] Obviously, the best time to evaluate environmental conditions is prior to making a location commitment.

RESOURCE AVAILABILITY

The availability of resources associated with producing a product and operating a business should also be considered in selecting a location. Raw materials, labour supply, and transportation are some of the factors that have a bearing on location. Proximity to raw materials and suitability of labour supply are particularly critical considerations in the location of a manufacturing business.

PROXIMITY TO RAW MATERIALS AND SUPPLIERS If required raw materials are not abundantly available in all areas, a region in which these materials abound offers special location advantages. For a business dependent on bulky or heavy raw materials that lose much of their bulk or weight in the manufacturing process, proximity to these materials is a powerful force driving the location decision. A sawmill is an example of a business that must stay close to its raw materials in order to operate economically.

Some companies buy components or materials in small amounts or have highly customized products requiring frequent purchases from suppliers. Proximity to suppliers allows these companies to save time and respond to customers' needs faster. A printing company would be an example of a business that benefits from being close to suppliers of paper, ink and other materials.

SUITABILITY OF LABOUR SUPPLY A manufacturer's labour requirements depend on the nature of its production process. Available supply of labour, wage rates, labour productivity, and a history of peaceful industrial relations are all particularly important considerations for labour-intensive firms. In some cases, the need for semi-skilled or unskilled labour justifies locating in an area with surplus labour. In other cases, firms find it desirable to seek a pool of highly skilled labour.

AVAILABILITY OF TRANSPORTATION Access to quality transportation is important to almost all firms. It permits customers to travel to retail stores and allows manufacturers to ship finished goods. In Canada, most of the population lives in a narrow band within 200 kilometres of the U.S. border. However, a great deal of business is done with the United States, making good north–south transportation critical.

PERSONAL PREFERENCE OF THE ENTREPRENEUR

As a practical matter, many entrepreneurs tend to discount customer accessibility, environmental business conditions, and resource availability and consider only their home community. The possibility of locating elsewhere never enters their minds. Just because an individual has always lived in a particular town, however, does not automatically make the town a satisfactory business location!

On the other hand, locating a business in one's home community is not necessarily illogical. In fact, there are certain advantages. From a personal standpoint, the entrepreneur generally appreciates and feels comfortable with the atmosphere of the home community, whether it is a small town or a large city. From a practical business standpoint, the entrepreneur can more easily establish credit. Hometown bankers can be dealt with more confidently, and other businesspeople may be of great service in helping evaluate a given opportunity. If potential customers are local residents, the prospective entrepreneur probably has a better idea of their tastes and preferences than an outsider would have. Relatives and friends may be the entrepreneur's first customers and may help advertise his or her products or services.

Nevertheless, personal preference does not always dictate a local site. Sometimes the choice is a location offering other advantages. Greg McFarland moved from the family farm to an acreage in the hamlet of Carroll, south of Brandon, Manitoba, where his small business manufactures walkers for people with leg problems. "It's home," says McFarland, and has the advantage of low overheads and a safe, healthy lifestyle for his family. "If I was in a situation where I needed fifty people to work here it might be different, but as long as I can get the people I need where I am, the buildings are paid for, so why move?"[6] Personal preference, however, should not be allowed to take priority over obvious location weaknesses.

SITE AVAILABILITY AND COSTS

Once an entrepreneur has settled on a certain area of the country, a specific site must still be chosen. The availability of potential sites and the costs associated with obtaining them must be investigated.

SITE AVAILABILITY An entrepreneur, evaluating a site for his new business, is said to have exclaimed "It must be a good site—I know of four businesses that were there in the last two years!" Fortunately, such a misguided approach to site evaluation is not typical of entrepreneurs, many of whom seek professional assistance in determining site availability and appropriateness. Local real estate agents are one good source.

If an entrepreneur's top choices are unavailable, other options must be considered. One choice is shared facilities. In recent years, business incubators have sprung up in all areas of the country. A **business incubator** is a facility that rents space to new businesses or to people wishing to start businesses. Incubators are often located in recycled buildings, such as abandoned warehouses or schools. They serve fledgling businesses by making space available, offering management advice, and providing clerical assistance, all of which help lower operating costs. An incubator tenant can be fully operational the day after moving in, without buying phones, renting a copier, or hiring office employees.

business incubator
a facility that provides shared space, services, and management assistance to new businesses

The purpose of business incubators is to see new businesses hatch, grow, and leave the incubator. Most incubators—though not all—have some type of government or university sponsorship and are motivated by a desire to stimulate economic development. Although the building space provided by incubators is significant, their greatest contribution is the business expertise and management assistance they provide. According to the Canadian Association of Business Incubation (http://www.cabi.ca), 80 percent of businesses started in an incubator survive past five years, compared to a survival rate of less than 50 percent for all start-ups.[7]

Executive suites are another form of a shared facility. These commercially owned offices provide tenants with an office, shared conference rooms, receptionists, and office equipment. Executive suites can be found in all major cities, and are a popular alternative to a home office.

SITE COSTS Ultimately, the site selection process must depend on evaluation of relevant costs. Unfortunately, an entrepreneur is frequently unable to afford the "best" site. The costs involved in building on a new site may be prohibitive, or the purchase price of an existing structure may exceed the entrepreneur's budget.

Assuming that a suitable building is available, the entrepreneur must decide whether to lease or buy. Although ownership confers greater freedom in the modification and use of a building, the advantages of leasing usually outweigh these benefits. We recommend that most new firms lease for two reasons:

1. A large cash outlay is avoided. This is important for a new small firm, which typically lacks adequate financial resources.
2. Risk is reduced by avoiding substantial investment and by postponing commitments for space until the success of the business is assured and the nature of building requirements is better known.

IN THE TRENCHES

Entrepreneurial Experiences

NIMBY

NIMBY (Not In My Back Yard) can be a major obstacle to locating a business. Public resistance to locating certain kinds of businesses close to their homes often makes the headlines of Canadian newspapers. One example is a proposed meat-packing operation on the northern edge of Calgary, Alberta. Another is Flamboro Springs, a water bottling company recently seeking a new location in Flamborough, Ontario. When the matter came before a committee of the Stoney Creek council, three neighbours of the location showed up to voice their concerns. Ron Leenders, who lives on an adjacent farm, said, "Industrial development is ruining the rural character of the area." Kevin King, who lives across the road from Flamboro Springs, objected to what he called "dismantling of the agricultural lands" in the area. Neighbour Tony Marriott says industrial uses have grown considerably on the site, part of which was zoned industrial several years ago "solely to allow the building of a storage shed," he protested.

The Flamborough Chamber of Commerce supported the application, noting the company employs 12–15 people depending on the season and contributes taxes to the community.

Debates of this kind are very common and highlight the conflict between economic development and incompatible land use.

Source: Dianne Cornish, "Flamboro Springs Expansion Gets Green Light from Committee," *Flamborough Post*, April 8, 2005, p. 1.

When entering into a leasing agreement, the entrepreneur should check the landlord's insurance policies to be sure there is proper coverage for various types of risks. If not, the lessee should seek coverage under his or her own policy. It is important to have the terms of the leasing agreement reviewed by a lawyer. Sometimes a lawyer can arrange for special clauses to be added to a lease, such as an escape clause that allows the lessee to exit the agreement under certain conditions. And a lawyer can ensure that an entrepreneur will not be unduly exposed to liability for damages caused by the gross negligence of others. Consider the experience of one firm that wished to rent 300 square feet of storage space in a large complex of offices and shops. On the sixth page of the landlord's standard lease, the firm's lawyer found language that could have made the firm responsible for the entire 30,000-square-foot complex if it burned down, regardless of blame!

LEASE TERMINOLOGY[8]

Lessor is the owner of the property who is leasing it to a tenant(s). Often the lessor is represented by an agent.

Lessee is the person or business leasing the space—the tenant

Square feet (sf) is the measurement of space you will occupy. Usable square feet is the actual space you will use; rentable square feet includes an allocation of a portion of the common areas (lobby, hallways, washrooms, for example)

to your space. Therefore 1,000 sf of usable square feet could become 1,100 sf of rentable space. You will pay for the 1,100 sf of rentable space.

Net rent (base rent) refers to the net cost to rent space in a building and may be expressed as a monthly or annual amount or as a dollar per square foot per year (psf) amount. Our 1,100 sf rent above could be expressed as $10 psf, $11,000 per year, or $916.67 per month.

Triple net rent refers to the practice of the tenant paying for the operating expenses such as taxes, insurance, common area maintenance, utilities, and janitorial services in addition to the monthly base rent. This amount is usually estimated at the beginning of the year, and tenants pay monthly. The landlord then reconciles the accounts at the end of the year when actual costs are known and either charges or refunds the tenant for the difference. In some retail leases there may be a requirement for the tenant to pay a percentage of revenues in addition to triple net rent. There may also be a requirement to pay into a cooperative advertising fund, for a major shopping mall, for example.

Realty taxes are property taxes charged to the property by the municipality. They may be included in the "triple net" charges or be charged separately in the same way as operating expenses.

Leasehold improvements are improvements or changes to the space to make it suitable to the tenant's purpose and taste. These can be considerable if walls and utilities must be moved, but at the very least will likely involve cosmetic changes such as new paint or wall and floor covering.

Inducements are such things as temporary reductions in rent, rent-free periods at the beginning of the lease term, and leasehold improvements paid for by the lessor. They are commonly used by lessors to entice you to lease the space.

ASSESSING SPACE NEEDS[9] While it may be helpful to use the services of a space planner, architect, or consultant, some of the things to think about in determining space requirements can be easily understood.

- The number of employees
- The split between offices and enclosed areas
- Size of offices and workstations
- Open layout versus individual offices
- "Overhead" space such as lobby, lunchroom, storage rooms, and meeting rooms
- Yard space and loading docks for industrial or warehousing businesses
- Parking requirements (employees and customers or visitors)
- Ceiling height for industrial or warehousing businesses
- Retail floor layout (see below for examples of typical layouts)
- Shop layout, equipment size, and surrounding space requirements

NEGOTIATING A LEASE[10]

It is highly recommended that professional advice is sought prior to signing a lease. An experienced lawyer can save you from not only onerous lease terms but also potential problems. It may also be a good idea to hire a broker to negotiate a lease on your behalf if you have leased before.

Most landlords will have what they claim to be a standard lease form. Don't be fooled by this: every paragraph is negotiable. The landlord will be more or less open to concessions depending on his of her appraisal of the value of the tenant. For example, a large department store in a suburban mall will likely pay less per square foot than smaller shops, as it is the "anchor tenant" that attracts other businesses and customers to the mall.

Of course, the major points in the negotiation will be the costs: the base rent, triple net amount, and inducements. Other points to consider are as follows:

- If the property is destroyed by fire or becomes unusable for any reason, you should be able to terminate the lease or have a provision that rebuilding, repairs, or restoration be done in a reasonable amount of time.
- The landlord should be responsible for personal injury claims by staff and visitors in the common areas of the building.
- Make sure the lease allows your business to install signage.
- Try to ensure the lease can be assigned or that the space can be subleased to another business. If this can't be done, the lessee will be responsible for all lease payments for the entire life of the lease, whether using the space or not.
- Most renewal periods are between three and five years. It is advisable to make sure there is a right to renew at the end of the first and succeeding lease terms.
- Be aware of any clause that gives the landlord the right to move a tenant from one location in the building to another, especially if location (such as in a shopping mall) is critical to the success of your business.

Once a suitable location has been found, the site must be properly laid out and equipped to effectively serve the business's needs.

DESIGNING AND EQUIPPING THE PHYSICAL FACILITIES

Discuss the challenges of designing and equipping a physical facility.

A business plan should describe the physical space in which the business will be housed. Although the plan may call for a new building or an existing structure, ordinarily a new business occupies an existing building, with minor or major remodelling. Therefore, the following discussion will focus on designs for existing facilities.

CHALLENGES IN DESIGNING THE PHYSICAL FACILITIES

When specifying building requirements, the entrepreneur must avoid committing to a space that is too large or too luxurious. At the same time, the space should not be too small or too austere for efficient operation. Buildings do not produce profits directly; they merely house the operations and personnel who do so. Therefore, the ideal building is practical, not pretentious.

The general suitability of a building for a given type of business operation depends on the functional requirements of the business. For example, a restaurant should ideally be on one level. Other important factors are the age and condition of the building, fire hazards, heating and air conditioning, lighting and restroom facilities, and entrances and exits. Obviously, these factors are weighted differently for a factory operation than for a wholesale or retail operation. But in any case, the comfort, convenience, and safety of the business's employees and customers must not be overlooked.

BUILDING LAYOUT

Achieving a good layout involves arranging physical facilities so that they contribute to efficient business operations. We will take a brief look at general layout problems common to manufacturers (whose primary concern is production) and retailers (whose primary concern is customer traffic).

FACTORY LAYOUT

Factory layout presents a three-dimensional space problem. Overhead space may be utilized for power conduits, pipelines for exhaust systems, and the like. In addition, proper design of storage areas and handling systems makes use of space near the ceiling. Space must also be allowed for the unobstructed movement of products from one location to another.

The ideal setup for a manufacturing process is to have a straight-line, forward movement of materials from receiving room to shipping room. If this ideal cannot be realized for a given process, backtracking, sidetracking, and long hauls of materials should at least be minimized, to reduce production delays.

Two contrasting types of layouts are used in industrial firms. A **process layout** (see Exhibit 11-4) groups similar machines together. Drill presses, for example, are separated from lathes in a machine shop using a process layout. The alternative, a **product layout,** arranges special-purpose equipment along a production line in the sequence in which it is used in processing. The product is moved progressively from one work station to the next, and the machines are located at the stations where they are needed for the various stages of production.

process layout
a factory design that groups similar machines together

product layout
a factory design that arranges machines according to their roles in the production process

EXHIBIT **11-4**
Typical Process Layout

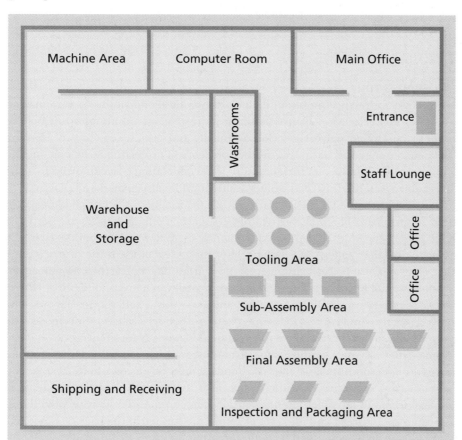

EXHIBIT **11-5**
Grocery Store Layout

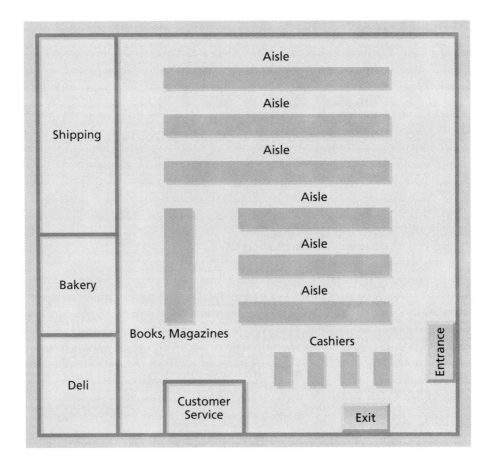

RETAIL STORE LAYOUT

The objectives for retail store layout include displaying merchandise so as to maximize sales and customer service. Convenient and attractive surroundings contribute to a customer's continued patronage. Colour, music, and even aroma are all important layout factors for a retail business. Another objective is protecting a store's equipment and merchandise. Finally, an efficient layout lowers operating costs. In order to achieve all these objectives, the flow of customer traffic must be anticipated and planned.

The grid pattern and the free-flow pattern are the two most widely used layouts. A **grid pattern** is the plain, block layout typical of supermarkets and hardware stores (see Exhibit 11-5). It provides maximum merchandise exposure and simplifies security and cleaning. A **free-flow pattern** (see Exhibit 11-6) makes less efficient use of space but has greater visual appeal and allows customers to move in any direction at their own speed. Free-flow patterns result in curving aisles and greater flexibility in merchandise presentation.

Most retailers, especially food merchandisers, use a **self-service layout,** which permits customers direct access to the merchandise. Self-service not only reduces selling expenses but also permits shoppers to examine the goods before buying.

Some types of merchandise—for example, magazines and candy—are often purchased on an impulse basis. Impulse goods should be placed where customers can see them easily; some are typically displayed near the cash register. Products that customers need and for which they specifically come to the store may be placed in less conspicuous spots. Bread and milk, for example, are located at the back of a food store, with the idea that customers will buy other items as they walk down the aisles.

grid pattern
a block-like retail store layout that provides for good merchandise exposure and simplifies security and cleaning

free-flow pattern
a flexible retail store layout that is visually appealing and gives customers freedom of movement

self-service layout
a type of retail store design that gives customers direct access to merchandise

EXHIBIT **11-6**
Retail Store Layout

Various areas of a retail store differ markedly in sales value. Certainly, the best space should be given to departments or merchandise producing the greatest sales and profits. Customers typically turn to the right on entering a store, and so the right front space is considered the most valuable. The second most valuable retail areas are the centre front and right middle spaces. Department stores often place high-margin giftware, cosmetics, and jewellery in these areas. The third most valuable areas are the left front and centre middle spaces; the left middle space is fourth in importance. Since the back areas are the least important as far as retail space value is concerned, service facilities and the general office are typically found in the rear of a store. Finally, the first floor has greater space value than a higher floor in a multistory building.

CHALLENGES IN EQUIPPING THE PHYSICAL FACILITIES

The final step in arranging for physical facilities is the purchase or lease of equipment and tools. The types of equipment and tools required obviously depend on the nature of the business. Even within the three areas discussed here—manufacturing, retailing, and office equipment—there is great variation in the need for tools and equipment.

MANUFACTURING EQUIPMENT

Machines used in a factory may be either general purpose or special purpose.

GENERAL-PURPOSE EQUIPMENT

general-purpose equipment
machines that serve many functions in the production process

General-purpose equipment requires a minimum investment and is easily adapted to varied types of operations. Small machine shops and cabinet shops, for example, utilize this type of equipment. General-purpose equipment for metalworking includes lathes, drill presses, and milling machines. In a woodworking plant, general-purpose machines include ripsaws, planing mills, and lathes. In each case, jigs, fixtures, and other tooling items set up on the basic machinery can be changed so that two or more shop operations can be accomplished using the same piece of equipment. General-purpose equipment contributes important flexibility in industries in which products are so new that the technology is not yet well developed or there are frequent design changes in the products.

SPECIAL-PURPOSE EQUIPMENT

special-purpose equipment
machines designed to serve specialized functions in the production process

Special-purpose equipment can reduce costs in industries in which the technology is fully established and capacity operation is more or less ensured by high sales volume. Bottling machines and automobile assembly-line machinery are examples of special-purpose equipment used in factories. A milking machine in a dairy is an example of special-purpose equipment used by small firms. A small firm cannot, however, use special-purpose equipment economically unless it makes a standardized product on a fairly large scale. Using special-purpose machines with specialized tooling results in greater output per machine-hour of operation. The labour cost per unit of product is, therefore, lower. However, the initial cost of such equipment is much higher, and it may have little or no resale value because of its highly specialized function.

RETAIL STORE EQUIPMENT

Small retailers need may merchandise display racks or counters, storage racks, shelving, mirrors, seats for customers, customer pushcarts, cash registers, and other items to facilitate selling. Such equipment may be costly, but it is usually less expensive than that necessary for a factory operation.

If a store is intended to serve a high-income market, its fixtures should display the elegance and style expected by such customers. For example, polished mahogany showcases with bronze fittings lend a richness to the atmosphere. Indirect lighting, thick rugs, and big easy chairs also contribute to an air of luxury. In contrast, a store that caters to lower-income customers should concentrate on simplicity, as luxurious fixtures create an atmosphere inconsistent with low prices.

OFFICE EQUIPMENT

Obviously, every business office needs furniture, storage cabinets, and other such items. The more challenging task is selecting office equipment—computers, fax machines, copiers, printers, and telephone systems—that reflects the latest advances in technology applicable to a particular business.

The business plan should list the major pieces of equipment needed to furnish a business office. Careful selection of equipment helps a business operate efficiently. Also, by identifying major equipment needs in this section of the business plan, the entrepreneur can ensure that the financial section of the plan includes funds for their purchase.

BUILDING IMAGE

All new ventures, whether retailers, wholesalers, manufacturers, or service businesses, should be concerned with projecting the appropriate image to customers and the public at large. The appearance of the workplace should create a favourable impression about the quality of a firm's product or service and, generally, about the way the business is operated. For firms that have many visitors, especially clients, the design of the facility should make a good impression. It is especially important for small businesses to create the impression of being a solid, professional company.

LOCATING THE START-UP IN THE ENTREPRENEUR'S HOME

Describe the attraction and challenges of a home-based business.   3

home-based business
a business that maintains its primary facility in the residence of its owner

Rather than lease or buy a commercial site, increasing numbers of entrepreneurs are electing to use their basement, garage, or spare room for their business operation, creating a **home-based business.** According to a 2005 Statistics Canada survey, over 1.3 million Canadians work from home.[11] In the past, a home location for a business was regarded as second-rate. "Ten years ago, if you were working out of your home, it was like you had some sort of disease," says Don Vlaek, a former employee at a pizza business who now works from his home as a consultant.[12] But times have changed, and home-based entrepreneurs no longer feel embarrassed about their location. The home office, once simply a stage in the growth of many businesses, is now a viable permanent option. At present, many entrepreneurs have no plans to ever move out of the home.

THE ATTRACTION OF HOME-BASED BUSINESSES

Why do many entrepreneurs find operating a business at home so attractive? Although motivations vary, the main attraction of a home-based business relates to financial and family lifestyle considerations.

FINANCIAL CONSIDERATIONS

Like most business ventures, a home-based business has an important goal—earning money—and locating at home helps increase profits by reducing costs. This was the motivation for Tricia Kell of Winnipeg, whose family had to come to grips with an accident that left her husband seriously injured and unable to work.[13] "We had to make ends meet," Kell said. "With that, came all the ideas for the business." Her business, Seek-in-Site, offers online resources for financial and home management and consumer information, based on the hard-won household and money management skills she acquired after her husband's accident.

Money was also the major motivation for Roland Glenn, who operates LemonBusters out of his Toronto home. LemonBusters offers used-car buyers pre-purchase assessments on used vehicles. Glenn left his job as a truck driver to become a stay-at-home dad for one year after the birth of his son, Lewis. At the end of that year he knew he couldn't return to the work force, but he and wife Donna needed some income to maintain their lifestyle, and LemonBusters was born. What began as a part-time business to supplement family income is now a thriving full-time business in southern Ontario.[14]

FAMILY LIFESTYLE CONSIDERATIONS

Many young entrepreneurs remain in a family business because of close family ties. Similarly, entrepreneurs who locate business operations in the home are frequently motivated by the desire to spend more time with family. Diane Huband of Lethbridge, Alberta, left her banking job to have children. Shortly after her return to work at the bank, she quit to become a distributor for Pampered Chef, a line of culinary convenience ware, taking these upscale products to Tupperware-style kitchen parties to sell them. "Most of my salary used to go to day care and parking," she said. With the advantage of running a home-based business, she can set her own schedule. "I can be at home with the kids when I want to." When she has an evening demonstration, husband Garth takes care of the children.[15]

Even couples with grown children enjoy the lifestyle afforded by a home business. Nancy Cole and John Perry of Schurman's Point, near Summerside. P.E.I., left their hectic long-time careers to establish Periwinkle bears, handcrafted stuffed bears. The slow pace of painstaking craftsmanship is a far cry from Cole's position with the Department of Veterans Affairs and Perry's 35-year radio broadcasting career. "It's the control and freedom. Just being able to have more of a hand in our destiny and where we want to go is wonderful," says Cole.[16]

CHALLENGES OF OPERATING A BUSINESS AT HOME

Just as most businesses located at commercial sites have their problems, home-based businesses face special challenges attributable to their location. We will look briefly at three of these challenges—family and business conflicts, business image, and legal considerations.

FAMILY AND BUSINESS CONFLICTS

For entrepreneurs who locate at home in order to be close to family members, business demands can conflict with parental responsibilities. In order to prevent the responsibilities of the home and of the business from interfering with each other, owners of home-based businesses need to establish both spatial and nonspatial boundaries between the business and the home. For example, the owner should set aside specific business space in the home and schedule definite hours for business matters. In fact, clients' calls may necessitate the observance of regular business hours. And just as the owner needs to protect the business from undue family or home interference, she or he also needs to protect the home from unreasonable encroachment by business matters. Since the owner never leaves the home to go to an office or place of business, he or she may find that either the business or the family absorbs every waking moment.

Entrepreneur Cheryl Stephenson, who operates Executive Perfection from her Burlington, Ontario home, tried to incorporate her children into as many aspects of her business support company as possible. But she recognizes the need for limits. At some point it became necessary to put her younger child in full-time daycare, while the older one is in school all day. She expresses the challenges and tradeoffs this way:

> *"You can't run a business and have kids calling for you. It's not fair. It's flexible as far as time goes. I can go on school field trips, and take the kids on special trips, but I get faxes and calls at all hours of the night. It's hard to get away.*[17]

BUSINESS IMAGE

Maintaining an image of professionalism when working at home is a major challenge to home-based entrepreneurs. Allowing young children to answer the telephone, for example, may dispel a professional image. Likewise, a baby crying or a dog barking in the background during a phone call can be distracting to a client.

If clients or salespeople visit the home-based business, it is critical that a professional office area be maintained. Space limitations sometimes make this difficult. Such was the experience of Scott Walker, owner of a family-owned firm that manufacturers the novelty party game Walla Balla. His office is located in the basement of his home. Walker recalls the day when a salesperson came to the office: "She came into the house and down the dark stairs to our dimly lit basement office. Throughout the entire meeting, I could tell she was uncomfortable about her surroundings."[18]

One way to avoid such awkwardness is to rent a boardroom at an executive centre. Another is to meet for coffee at a nearby coffee shop.

LEGAL CONSIDERATIONS

Some local laws pose a problem for home-based businesses. **Zoning ordinances,** or zoning bylaws, for example, regulate the types of enterprises permitted in various geographical areas. Most cities now require home-based businesses to be licensed and restrict the kind of business and amount of traffic allowed for a home-based business.

zoning ordinances
local laws regulating land use

David Hanania, founder and president of Home Business Institute, points out that many zoning laws, dating as far back as the 1930s, have never been updated. The intent of such laws is to protect a neighbourhood's residential quality by preventing commercial signs and parking problems. There is also an increasing trend to regulate home-based business by charging fees, similar to the business taxes levied by many municipalities on businesses operating within their limits. Manufacturer's agent Leo Kelsch of Winnipeg said he was forced to pay the $135 licence fee when the city found out his business phone was at his house. "I have no stock. I have no signage. I have no employees and I don't deal with the public," Lelsch said. "But because I have a phone, I'm liable."[19]

There are also tax issues related to a home-based business. Generally, a separate space must be clearly devoted to business activities in order for the entrepreneur to claim a tax deduction. An accountant can be helpful in explaining these tax regulations.

Insurance considerations may also affect a home-based business. An entrepreneur's homeowner's policy is not likely to cover business activities, liabilities, and equipment. The policy should be checked with the homeowner's agent. If the business is not covered, a special home-based business policy can be purchased for $300–$500 depending on the amount of coverage and replacement value of the equipment.

TECHNOLOGY AND HOME-BASED BUSINESSES

Advancements in business-application technology are a major catalyst in the rapid growth of home-based businesses. Personal computers, fax machines, voice mail, Internet access, and email are among the technological tools that help the home-based business compete effectively with commercial site businesses. Such technology makes it possible to open some types of businesses almost anywhere.

More recently, new technology has allowed long distance calls to be placed over the Internet through special computer software. Once a web phone is set up, dialing a call is much like surfing the Web. Voice over Internet Protocol (VoIP) is not being adopted

IN THE TRENCHES

Utilizing Technology

Bears on the Web

A conversation at a Christmas gathering around the kitchen table led the Clark family to develop a home-based business on the Internet. "None of this could have happened without it being a Web-based business," says Nick Clark, a managing partner of Black Bear.net Inc., an online retailer of smoked salmon, art, clothing, and hand-crafted gifts from the Queen Charlotte Islands off the coast of British Columbia. He says the website serves as a focal point for an operation that pools the talents of an extended family, draws upon the resources of the local community, and ships around the world.

The company, based on Bowen Island, B.C., is run by three brothers and their wives. Nick, who lives in Kelowna and also runs a software company in Calgary, is the technology guru and communicates regularly by email or phone with his brothers Jim and Bob, who live on the island. "At first, just a few orders trickled in but now our revenues are up in the six digits," says Nick. "And it's all run online out of our homes." According to the company's website, it currently ships to only Canadian addresses. While this strategy keeps the business a manageable size for the family, it also limits its ability to grow. This is an example of a trade-offs entrepreneurs must make.

Sources: Kevin Marron, "Web the Great Leveller for homebiz.com," *The Globe and Mail Report on Business*—Special Report, July 31, 2000, p. W1. Reprinted by permission of Kevin Marron, courtesy of the *Globe and Mail Report on Business;* and http://www.blackbear.net/home/order.asp (accessed January 23, 2008).

as fast as providers first hoped nor traditional telcos feared, but for businesses that are dependent of long distance services it can be a real money saver. Chris Groot, vice president of Marketing and Sales for IT Sportsnet says the company's phone capacity went from a receptionist and three lines to an automated attendant and unlimited lines by installing VoIP. "It's a much more efficient use of our support people," says Groot. VoIP has also reduced the long distance charges for the company, which has a customer support centre and deals with programmers in remote locations.[20]

Banking via computer also supports home-based businesses. Electronic banking is expanding each year, as customers come to expect more convenience and time-saving services from financial institutions.

Check out http://www.homebusinessreport.com or http://www.cbsc.org for more information on home-based business in Canada.

LOCATING ON THE WEB

4 Understand the potential benefits of locating a start-up on the Internet.

We live in a digital economy fuelled by the tremendous growth of the Internet. Access to the Internet continues to transform the way we live and the way business is conducted. It is important for aspiring entrepreneurs to learn as much as they can about cyberspace because there's opportunity online.

What is e-commerce? What benefits does e-commerce offer the start-up? What business models reflect an e-commerce strategy? These are the primary questions we address in this section of the chapter. We hope that our discussion will help you understand both the opportunities and the limitations associated with today's digital economy. Additional e-commerce topics are discussed in other chapters.

WHAT IS E-COMMERCE?

What does the term e-commerce really describe? **E-commerce** means electronic commerce or paperless exchange of business information via the Internet. It is an alternative means of conducting business transactions that traditionally have been carried by telephone, by mail, or face to face in bricks-and-mortar stores. Internet businesses continue to grow in number. While virtually all companies use the Internet in some way, such as a web page or e-mail, according to Statistics Canada, 16 percent of larger companies and 7 percent of small and medium companies (SMEs) sell over the Internet. The number is expected to continue to grow. The kinds of businesses most likely to use e-commerce are retail, wholesale, transportation and warehousing, and manufacturing.[21]

> **e-commerce**
> the paperless exchange of business information via the Internet.

Although the Internet, like the telephone, is basically a tool that parties use to communicate with each other, it is a communication medium unlike any previously available to companies. A Web location reshapes the way small firms conduct business, while also providing an alternative to the bricks-and-mortar store.

BENEFITS OF E-COMMERCE TO START-UPS

Electronic commerce benefits a start-up in a number of ways. It offers the new firm the opportunity to compete with bigger businesses on a more level playing field. Limited resources frequently restrict the ability of small firms to reach beyond local markets. Confined to their bricks-and-mortar world, small firms typically serve a restricted geographic area. But the Internet blurs geographic boundaries. E-commerce allows any business access to customers anywhere. The Internet is proving to be a great equalizer, giving small firms a presence comparable to that of the giants in the marketplace. Companies like Scrapbooksbydesign.ca and Black Bear.net Inc, featured earlier in this chapter are good examples of small Canadian companies using e-commerce as either the only way of selling or as a way of expanding their market reach.

An e-commerce operation can help the start-up with early cash flow problems by compressing the sales cycle—that is, reducing the time between receiving an order and converting the sale to cash. E-commerce systems can be designed to generate an order, authorize a credit card purchase, and contact a supplier and shipper in a matter of minutes, all without human assistance. The shorter cycle translates into quicker payments from customers and improved cash flows to the business.

E-commerce also enables small firms to build on one of their greatest strengths—customer relationships. The Internet has brought new life and technology to bear on the old-fashioned notion of customer service. **Electronic Customer Relationship Marketing (eCRM)** is an electronically based system that emphasizes customer relationships. At the heart of eCRM is a customer-centric data warehouse. A typical eCRM system allows an e-commerce firm to integrate data from websites, call centres, sales force reports, and other customer contact points, with the goal of building customer loyalty. There are, of course, innumerable other benefits that small firms can reap from e-commerce; space does not allow us to discuss them all here.

> **electronic Customer Relationship Marketing (eCRM)**
> an electronically based system that emphasizes customer relationships

E-commerce has several limitations that also need to be considered when you are deciding where to locate and how to operate your business. These potential limitations fall into two categories: technical limitations and nontechnical limitations. Technical limitations include the cost of developing and maintaining a website, insufficient telecommunications bandwidth, constantly changing software, the need to integrate digital and nondigital sales and production information, and access limitations of dial-up, cable, and wireless, as well as the fact that not all of your potential customers will have Internet access. Nontechnical limitations include customer concern over privacy issues, the security and privacy of your Web operations, customers' inability to touch products, employees' lack of technical knowledge, and the challenges of dealing with global cultures and languages.[22]

E-COMMERCE BUSINESS MODELS

The Merriam Webster dictionary defines an opportunity as "a favourable juncture of circumstances" or "a good chance for advancement or progress." Thus, it is logical to study the circumstances surrounding e-commerce in order to uncover the opportunities the Internet offers as a start-up location. Let's begin by examining some existing e-commerce business models.

business model
a group of shared characteristics, behaviours, and goals that a firm follows in a particular business situation

The term *business model* describes a group of shared characteristics, behaviours, and goals that a firm follows in a particular business situation. Online business firms differ in their decisions concerning which customers to serve, how best to become profitable, and what to include on their websites. Exhibit 11-7 shows some possible alternatives for business models. None of these models can currently be considered dominant, and some Internet businesses cannot be described by any single model. The real world of e-commerce contains endless combinations of business models. However, it is important to keep in mind that a poorly devised business model can be a major factor in business failure.

TYPE OF CUSTOMERS SERVED Marketing theory classifies traditional bricks-and-mortar firms as manufacturers, wholesalers, or retailers, depending on the customers they serve. E-commerce businesses also are commonly distinguished according to customer focus. There are three major categories of e-commerce business models: business-to-business (B2B), business-to-consumer (B2C), and auction sites. In this section, we examine some strategies used by e-commerce firms within these three categories.

EXHIBIT **11-7**

E-commerce Business Models

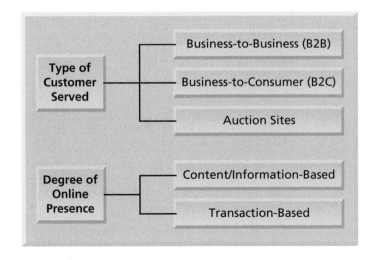

BUSINESS-TO-BUSINESS MODELS The dollar amounts generated by firms using a **business-to-business (B2B) model** (selling to business customers) are significantly greater than those for firms with a business-to-consumer (B2C) model (selling to final consumers). Because B2B success stories generally receive less publicity than B2C ventures do, the potential of a B2B opportunity may be overlooked. Aspiring entrepreneurs should be sure to consider the B2B model.

All B2B firms do not look alike. One form of B2B strategy emphasizes sales transactions. By using online capabilities, a B2B firm can achieve greater efficiency in its selling and buying. International Business Machines (IBM) is a good example. By dealing directly with its corporate customers online, it is able to build its computer systems and related products to meet the specific needs of its customers. As much as IBM relies on the Internet to deliver its business solution, it also has an extensive sales force and consulting services to deliver value to its many customers worldwide.

As B2B e-commerce models continue to develop and evolve, new versions will emerge. The wise entrepreneur will continue to monitor these changes to learn where opportunities lie.

BUSINESS-TO-CONSUMER MODELS In contrast to a B2B model, a **business-to-consumer (B2C) model** has final consumers as customers. In the traditional retail setting, customers generally approach a business location (a bricks-and-mortar store) with the intent of shopping or purchasing. Alternatively, customers might purchase via telephone or mail order, using a printed catalogue. The B2C model introduces another alternative for consumers—buying online.

Amazon.com represents the classic B2C firm, which is directly focused on individual final consumers. B2C ventures are extremely diverse in the products they sell, with offerings ranging from clothing to pet items, computer software, toys, and groceries. The B2C model offers three main advantages over bricks-and-mortar retailing: speed of access, speed of transaction, and round-the-clock access to products and services, often referred to as **24/7 e-tailing.**

It is true that many final consumers avoid online shopping for several reasons, the primary ones being reluctance to send credit card data electronically and to purchase a product without first seeing it. However, B2C e-commerce businesses have many advantages, including the ability to quickly change merchandise mixes and prices, as well as the appearance of the "store" (the website). Traditional merchants located in bricks-and-mortar stores find such changes very costly and time consuming.

AUCTION SITE MODELS Some entrepreneurs sell their wares over the Internet without either a website or a storefront, by means of e-commerce sites based on the auction site model. Internet **auction sites** are web-based businesses offering participants—final consumers and businesses—the ability to list products for bidding by potential buyers. Revenues to the auction site are derived from listing fees and commissions on sales.

Online auctions have become one of the real success stories on the Web. And, as you might have guessed, eBay, founded in 1995 by computer programmer Pierre Omidyar, is the 900-pound gorilla of auction sites. "I got it on eBay" is quickly becoming part of our collective vocabulary. You can buy or sell nearly anything on eBay—and it is incredibly easy. eBay consultants abound; for a fee, they will coach you on how to be a successful seller. Or you can "attend" eBay University to learn the ins and outs of operating an eBay business. Exhibit 11-8 provides a simple five-step procedure for selling items on eBay.

As easy as it is to sell a few items on eBay, it is a very different matter to actually make money as an ongoing business on the site. As in the more conventional forms of

business-to-business (B2B) model
a business model based on selling to business customers electronically

business-to-consumer (B2C) model
a business model based on selling to business to final customers electronically

24/7 e-tailing
electronic retailing providing round-the-clock access to products and services

auction sites
web-based businesses offering participants the ability to list products for bidding

EXHIBIT **11-8**

Selling Your Item on eBay

Step 1: Register as an eBay member, then click the "Sell" link at the top of any page.
Step 2: Gather information and digital pictures for your item description.
Step 3: Write your title and item description.
Step 4: Pre-pack your item to determine its shipping weight (but don't seal it yet).
Step 5: Choose the methods of payment you will accept; PayPal is the fastest and safest.

Source: "Selling Your Item," eBay, at http://pages.ebay.com/education/selling (accessed August 31, 2008).

retailing, a well-thought-out business plan is helpful in turning your business idea (or hobby) into a money-making proposition. Here are a few statistics about eBay that you might find interesting:[23]

1. There are 212 million registered eBay users worldwide.
2. Roughly $1,590 worth of goods are sold on eBay every second.
3. eBay has approximately 1.3 million sellers around the world.
4. AuctionsatOverstock.com
5. Amazon.com Auctions
6. Online Auction
7. WeBidz
8. Auction-warehouse
9. ePier
10. It's Gotta Go

As mentioned earlier, eBay generates much of its revenue through listing fees and advertising. To continue its rapid growth, eBay is expanding its services and entering new markets across the globe—most recently, in China, India, South Korea, Spain, Switzerland, and Taiwan—through new sites, acquisitions, and co-ventures. Overall, eBay does business in more than 20 countries. PayPal, eBay's global payments platform, has nearly 100 million accounts. No longer the only show in town, however, eBay faces marketing competition from the likes of Amazon.com and smaller competitors such as Overstock.com. Exhibit 11-9 contains a list of the top ten auction sites. How many have you visited?

In mid-2006, eBay took the bold step of opening eBay Express, a site dedicated to selling new merchandise at set prices. This site allows eBay to target consumers who are

EXHIBIT **11-9**

Top 10 Online Auction Sites

1. e-Bay
2. Ubid
3. Bidz.com
4. Yahoo auctions
5. MSN auctions
6. Amazon.com
7. Auctionweiser
8. Auction Addict
9. Auction-warehouse
10. Auctonet.com[24]

looking for bargains and don't like the auction format. Pierre Omidyar, eBay chairman and founder, owns approximately 14 percent of the online behemoth.[25]

DEGREE OF ONLINE PRESENCE A second broad way of categorizing e-commerce models relates to the firm's intended level of online presence. The role of a website can range from merely offering content and information to enabling complex business transactions.

CONTENT/INFORMATION-BASED MODEL In a **content/information-based model** of e-commerce, a website provides access but not the ability to buy or sell products and services. During the early days of e-commerce, the content model was the model of choice. For example, America Online (AOL) began with this model. Originally, revenue for AOL came from fees paid by users for the privilege of connecting and gaining access to its content. Today, many content models are still found, mostly in countries where Internet usage by small firms is less developed.

A slight variation of the content model is the *information-based model.* A website built on this model contains information about the business, its products, and other related matters but doesn't charge for its use. It is typically just a complement to an existing bricks-and-mortar store. Many small businesses use this model for their online operations. Your dentist or plumber may have a website that simply describes the services offered but requires a phone call to set up an appointment.

TRANSACTION-BASED MODEL In a **transaction-based model** of e-commerce, a website provides a mechanism for buying or selling products or services. The transaction-based model, which is at the very heart of e-commerce, calls for websites to be online stores where visitors go to shop, click, and buy.

Clearly, the location decision is complicated, but it is vital to a successful venture. Take your time, do your research, and make a wise choice.

content/ information- based model
a business model in which the website provides information but not the ability to buy or sell products

transaction-based model
a business model in which the website provides a mecha- nism for buying or selling products or services

LOOKING BACK

1 **Describe the factors affecting choice of a bricks-and-mortar business location.**

- Customer accessibility is a key factor in the location decision of retail and service businesses.
- Climate, competition, legal requirements, and the tax structure are types of environmental factors affecting the location decision.
- Availability of resources, such as raw materials, labour supply, and transportation, is important to location decisions.
- The entrepreneur's personal preference is a practical consideration in selecting a location.
- An appropriate site must be available and within the entrepreneur's budget.
- Lease terms and the negotiation process must be understood prior to entering into discussions about leasing space for the business.

2 **Discuss the challenges of designing and equip- ping a physical facility.**

- The ideal building is practical, not pretentious.
- The general suitability of a building depends on the functional requirements of the business.
- The comfort, convenience, and safety of the business's employees and customers must not be overlooked.
- Leasing space doesn't require a large cash outlay, but buying increases freedom in modifying and using space.
- Good layout emphasizes productivity for manufac- turers and customer accessibility for retailers.
- Most small manufacturing firms must use general-purpose equipment, although some can use special-purpose equipment for standardized operations.

- The cost of special-purpose equipment is high and it often has little or no resale value because of its highly specialized function.
- Small retailers may require merchandise display racks and counters, mirrors, and other equipment that facilitates selling.
- Display counters and other retailing equipment should create an atmosphere appropriate for the customers in the retail target market.
- Entrepreneurs must select office equipment that reflects the latest advances in technology applicable to a particular business.

3 Describe the attraction and challenges of a home-based business.

- Home-based businesses are started to both make money and incorporate family lifestyle considerations.
- Operating a business at home can create conflicts with family members and pose business image and legal challenges.
- Technology has helped entrepreneurs start home-based businesses.

4 Understand the potential benefits of locating a start-up on the Internet.

- E-commerce offers small firms the opportunity to compete with bigger companies on a more level playing field.
- Internet operations can help small firms with cash flow problems by compressing sales cycles.
- E-commerce enables small firms to build stronger customer relationships.
- New versions of the business-to-business (B2B) model continue to develop and evolve.
- The three main advantages of online business-to-consumer (B2C) firms are speed of access, speed of transaction, and continuous access to products and services, often referred to as 24/7 e-tailing.
- Auction sites are online firms that bring buyers and sellers together.
- The role of a website can range from merely offering content and information to permitting the buying and selling of products and services online.

KEY TERMS

auction sites, p. 313
bricks-and-mortar location, p. 294
business incubator, p. 299
business model, p. 312
business-to-business (B2B) model, p. 313
business-to-consumer (B2C) model, p. 313

content/information-based model, p. 315
e-commerce, p. 311
electronic Customer Relationship Marketing (eCRM), p. 311
free-flow pattern, p. 304
general-purpose equipment, p. 306
grid pattern, p. 304

home-based business, p. 307
process layout, p. 303
product layout, p. 303
self-service layout, p. 304
special-purpose equipment, p. 306
transaction-based model, p. 315
24/7 e-tailing, p. 313
zoning ordinances, p. 309

DISCUSSION QUESTIONS

1. What are the key attributes of a good business location? Which of these would probably be most important for a retail location? Why?
2. Which resource factors might be most vital to a new manufacturing venture that produces residential home furniture? Why?
3. Is the hometown of the business owner likely to be a good location? Is it logical for an owner to allow personal preferences to influence a decision about business location? Explain your answers.

4. Under what conditions would it be most appropriate for a new firm to buy rather than rent a building for the business?
5. Explain the issues an entrepreneur should be aware of in negotiating a lease.
6. What factors should an entrepreneur evaluate when considering a home-based business? Be specific.
7. In a home-based business, there is typically some competition, if not conflict, between the interests of the home and those of the

business. What factors determine whether the risk is greater for the home or the business?

8. What legal issues should one consider before starting a home-based business?

9. When should a small manufacturer utilize (a) a process layout and (b) a product layout? Explain.

10. Discuss the conditions under which a new small manufacturer should buy

a. general-purpose equipment

b. special-purpose equipment.

11. Discuss the two different ways of categorizing business models used for e-commerce.

12. Contrast B2B and B2C businesses. Identify some of the reasons final consumers give for not using online shopping.

YOU MAKE THE CALL

SITUATION 1

A husband and wife operate small department stores in two prairie towns with populations of about 2,000 each. Their clientele consists of the primarily blue-collar and rural populations of those two areas. After several years of successful operation, they have decided to open a third store in a town of 5,000 people. Most of the businesses in this larger town are located along a six-block strip—an area commonly referred to as "downtown." One attractive site for the store is in the middle of the business district, but the rental fee for that location is very high. Another available building, vacated several years earlier by Woolworths, is located on a block at one end of the business district. Other businesses on the same block include an electronics store and some service businesses. Two clothing stores are located in the next block—closer to the centre of town. The rent for the former Woolworths store is much more reasonable than that for the downtown site, a three-year lease is possible, and a local bank is willing to loan sufficient funds to accomplish the necessary remodelling.

Question 1 Does the location in the middle of the business district seem to be substantially better than the other site?

Question 2 How might these owners evaluate the relative attractiveness of the two sites?

Question 3 To what extent would the department store benefit from having the service businesses and the electronics business in the same block?

Question 4 What other market or demographic factors, if any, should the owners consider before opening a store in this town?

SITUATION 2

A business incubator rents space to a number of small firms that are just beginning operations or are fairly new. In addition to supplying space, the incubator provides a receptionist, computer, conference room, fax machine, and copy machine. In addition, it offers management counselling and assists new businesses in getting reduced advertising rates and reduced legal fees. One client of the incubator is a jewellery repair, cleaning, and remounting service that does work on a contract basis for pawn shops and jewellery stores. Another is a home health care company that employs a staff of nurses to visit the homes of elderly people who need daily care but who cannot afford or are not yet ready to go to a nursing home.

Question 1 Evaluate each of the services offered by the incubator in terms of its usefulness to these two businesses. Which of the two businesses seems to be a better fit for the incubator? Why?

Question 2 If rental costs for incubator space were similar to rental costs for space outside the incubator, would the benefits of the services offered seem to favour location in the incubator? Why or why not?

SITUATION 3

Entrepreneur Karen Moore wants to start a catering and decorating business to bring in money to help support her two young children. Moore is a single parent; she works in the banking industry but has always had the desire to start a business. She enjoys decorating for friends' parties and is frequently told "You should do this professionally. You have such good taste, and you are so nice to people."

Moore has decided to take this advice but is unsure whether she should locate in a commercial site or in her home, which is in rural Ontario. She is leaning toward locating at home because she wants more time with her children. However, she is concerned that the home-based location is too far away from the city, where most of her potential customers live.

Initially, her services would include planning for wedding receptions and other special events, designing flower arrangements, decorating the sites, and even cooking and serving meals.

Question 1 What do you see as potential problems with locating Moore's new business at home?
Question 2 What do you see as the major benefits for Moore of a home-based business?
Question 3 How could Moore use technology to help her operate a home-based business?

EXPERIENTIAL EXERCISES

1. Search for articles in business periodicals that provide rankings of provinces or cities as business sites. Report on your findings.
2. Identify and evaluate a local site that is now vacant because of a business closure. Point out the strengths and weaknesses of that location for the former business, and comment on the part location may have played in the closure.
3. Interview a small business owner concerning the strengths and weaknesses of that

business's location. Prepare a brief report summarizing your findings.
4. Visit three local retail stores and observe the differences in their layouts and flow of customer traffic. Prepare a report describing the various patterns used and explaining the advantages of what you consider to be the best pattern.

EXPLORING THE WEB

1. Do a word search on the Web for "home-based business Canada." Report on five of the references you find in your search.
2. Access two of the Web addresses provided in this chapter. Report on your findings.

3. Go to http://www.investbc.com and, from the information provided, profile British Columbia as a possible site for a business. Be specific about the types of information contained on the website.

THE BUSINESS PLAN: LAYING THE FOUNDATION

ASKING THE RIGHT QUESTIONS

As part of laying the foundation for preparing your own business plan, respond to the following questions regarding location.

BRICKS-AND-MORTAR START-UP LOCATION QUESTIONS

1. How important are your personal reasons for choosing a location?
2. What business environment factors will influence your location decision?

3. What resources are most critical to your location decision?
4. How important is customer accessibility to your location decision?
5. What special resources do you need?
6. How will the formal site evaluation be conducted?
7. What laws and tax policies of municipal and provincial governments have been considered?
8. What is the cost of the proposed site?

PHYSICAL FACILITY QUESTIONS

1. What are the major considerations in choosing between a new and an existing building?
2. What is the possibility of leasing a building or equipment?
3. How feasible is it to locate in a business incubator?
4. What is the major objective of your building design?
5. What types of equipment do you need for your business?

HOME-BASED START-UP LOCATION QUESTIONS

1. Will a home-based business be a possibility for you?
2. What are the advantages and disadvantages of a home-based business?
3. Have you given consideration to family lifestyle issues?
4. Will your home project the appropriate image for the business?
5. What zoning ordinances, if any, regulate the type of home-based business you want to start?

INTERNET START-UP QUESTIONS

1. What type of customers will be served by the Internet start-up?
2. What degree of online presence will you strive for?

Operations Management and Control Systems

IN THE SPOTLIGHT

Orphan Industries: BDC's 2007 Canadian Innovation Award Winner for Productivity Improvement

Improving productivity and efficiency are among the keys to success in manufacturing in the global economy. Orphan Industries, part of St. John's Newfoundland's D. F. Barnes Group of Companies, applied the LEAN Manufacturing principles to achieve outstanding cost reductions, making the company more competitive and winning the BDC award in the process. The five LEAN principles, discussed later in this chapter, are (1) defining value from a customer perspective; (2) identifying and mapping the value system; (3) reducing waste and improving work flow; (4) manufacturing according to customer demand; and (5) pursuing perfection by repeating the cycle in pursuit of continuous improvement.

The D. F. Barnes group's main business is contract manufacturing serving the Atlantic offshore, marine, and industrial markets. It boasts a long list of prominent Canadian and international customers including Fisheries and Oceans Canada, Maersk, Petro-Canada, Sea Systems, Schlumberger, and Atlantic Towing. One of its companies is Orphan Industries, an ISO 9001:2000 certified manufacturer. Orphan undertook a one-year pilot project examining the production of its Launch and Recovery System (LARS), a system used for sub-sea service and repair mainly in offshore oil and gas activities. Other uses include marine salvage research and exploration. Orphan's approach involves three critical elements: (1) using LEAN techniques such as work flow analysis, supplier development, improved measurement of results at different stages in the manufacturing process, standardizing work processes, and working with suppliers to reduce costs and improve quality; (2) improving information flow and shop floor communication and; (3) adopting new manufacturing and information technology. This three-pronged approach yielded a reduction in labour hours for the LARS unit by 35–40 percent. This provided cost reductions that have allowed the company to be both more competitive and more profitable. In turn, Orphan was able to secure long-term contracts for

Photo courtesy of D. F. Barnes Limited

LARS in Canada and the United States. The company has also increased its market reach into other contract manufacturing opportunities at home and abroad.

In a world of low-cost manufacturing competition in developing nations, Canadian manufacturers like Orphan must constantly strive to improve their operations processes and quality to be able to effectively compete. Orphan Industries is a great example of the kinds of results that can be achieved through effective management of manufacturing operations. This outstanding productivity improvement earned Orphan BDC's 2007 Canadian Innovation Award for Productivity Improvement.

http://www.dfbarnes.com

Sources: "BDC's Canadian Innovation Award for Productivity Improvement" at http://www.cme-mec.ca/pdf/DFBarnes.pdf, accessed March 20, 2008 and Sean McCarthy, Director of Continuous Improvement, D.F. Barnes.

All firms have an **operations process,** or **production process,** consisting of the set of activities that produce goods and services for customers. In a manufacturing business, this process begins with the purchase of raw materials and includes all the steps required to create the products desired by customers.

THE OPERATIONS PROCESS

Discuss the nature of the operations process for both products and services.

1

The operations, or production, process is necessary to get the job done—that is, to perform the work and create the quality expected by customers. It is central to having a sustainable, profitable business.

THE NATURE OF THE OPERATIONS PROCESS

operations process (production process)
the activities that produce a firm's goods and services

operations management
the planning and control of the operations process

Operations management involves the planning and control of a conversion process. It includes acquiring inputs and then overseeing their transformation into products and services desired by customers. An operations process is required whether a firm produces a tangible product, such as clothing or bread, or an intangible service, such as dry-cleaning or entertainment. The production process in clothing manufacturing, the baking process in a bakery, the cleaning process in dry-cleaning, and the performance process in entertainment are all examples of an operations process. Operations processes differ in general for products and services, and they also differ from one type of product or service to another.

Despite their differences, all operations processes are similar in that they change inputs into outputs. Inputs include money, raw materials, labour, equipment, information, and energy—all of which are combined in varying proportions, depending on the nature of the finished product or service. Outputs are the products and/or services that a business provides to its customers. Thus, the operations process may be described as a conversion or transformation process. As Exhibit 12-1 shows, the operations process

EXHIBIT **12-1**
The Operations Process

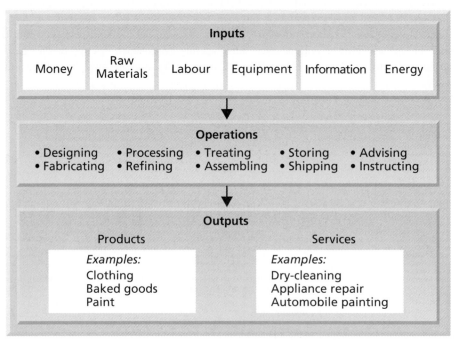

converts inputs of various kinds into products, such as baked goods, or services, such as dry-cleaning. A printing plant, for example, uses inputs such as paper, ink, the work of employees, printing presses, and electric power to produce printed material. Car wash facilities and motor freight firms, which are service businesses, also use operating systems to transform inputs into car-cleaning and freight-transporting services.

MANUFACTURING VERSUS SERVICE OPERATIONS

The operations of product- and service-producing firms differ in a number of ways. One of the most obvious differences is that greater customer contact typically occurs in a service firm. In a beauty shop, for example, the customer is a participant in the operations process as well as a user of the service. James B. Dilworth has identified and summarized four areas of difference:

1. Productivity generally is more easily measured in manufacturing operations than in service operations because the former provides tangible products, whereas the products of service operations are generally intangible. A factory that produces automobile tires can readily count the number of tires produced in a day. Repair service operations may repair or replace portions of a tangible product, but their major service is the application of knowledge and skilled labour. Advisory services may provide only spoken words, an entirely intangible product and one that is very difficult to measure.

2. Quality standards are more difficult to establish, and product quality is more difficult to evaluate, in service operations. This difference is directly related to the previous one. Intangible products are more difficult to evaluate because they cannot be held, weighed, or measured. We can evaluate a repair to a tangible product by comparing the product's performance after the repair with its performance before the repair. It is more difficult to know the worth of such a service as a legal defence. No one knows for certain how the judge would have ruled had the attorney performed in some different manner.

3. Individuals who provide services generally have contact with customers, whereas people who perform manufacturing operations seldom see the consumer of the product. The marketing and customer relations aspects of a service often overlap the operations function. The doctor–patient relationship, for example, is often considered to be a very important component of the physician's services. In the service of hair care, the hairdresser–patron contact is necessary. Therefore, the impact of discourteous salespersons or restaurant employees is of great concern in many establishments.

4. Manufacturing operations can accumulate or decrease inventory of finished products, particularly in standard product, repetitive production operations. A barber, in contrast, cannot store up haircuts during slack times so that he or she can provide service at an extremely high rate during peak demand time. Providers of services often try to overcome this limitation by levelling out the demand process. Telephone systems, for example, offer discount rates during certain hours to encourage a shift in the timing of calls that can be delayed.[1]

TYPES OF MANUFACTURING OPERATIONS

Manufacturing operations differ in the degree to which they are repetitive. Some factories produce the same product day after day and week after week. Other production

job shops
a type of manufacturing operation in which short production runs are used to produce small quantities of unique items

repetitive manufacturing
a type of manufacturing operation in which long production runs are used to produce a large quantity of a standardized product

batch manufacturing
a type of manufacturing operation that is intermediate (between job shops and repetitive manufacturing) in volume and variety of products

facilities have great flexibility and often change the products they produce. There are three types of manufacturing operations—job shops, repetitive manufacturing, and batch manufacturing.

Job shops are characterized by short production runs. Only one or a few products are produced before the general-purpose machines are shifted to a different production setup. Each job may be unique, requiring a special set of production steps to complete the finished item. Machine shops exemplify this type of operation.

Firms that produce one or relatively few standardized products use **repetitive manufacturing,** which is considered mass production as it involves long production runs. Repetitive manufacturing is associated with the assembly-line production of automobiles and other high-volume products. Highly specialized equipment can be employed, because it is used over and over again in manufacturing the same item. Few small business firms engage in repetitive manufacturing.

An intermediate type of production is called **batch manufacturing.** Batch manufacturing involves more variety (and less volume) than repetitive manufacturing but less variety (and more volume) than job shops. In batch manufacturing, one production run of 100 standardized units may be followed by a second production run of 100 units of another type of standardized product. A bottling plant that fills bottles with several varieties of soft drinks is engaging in batch manufacturing.

OPERATIONS PLANNING AND SCHEDULING

In manufacturing, production planning and scheduling procedures are designed to achieve the orderly, sequential flow of products through a plant at a rate commensurate with scheduled deliveries to customers. In order for this objective to be reached, it is essential to avoid production bottlenecks and to utilize machines and personnel efficiently. Simple, informal control procedures are often used in small plants. If a procedure is simple and the output small, a manager can keep things moving smoothly with a minimum of paperwork. Eventually, however, any manufacturing organization experiencing growth will have to establish formal procedures to ensure production efficiency.

Because service firms are so closely tied to their customers, they are limited in their ability to produce services and hold them in inventory for customers. An automobile repair shop must wait until a car arrives, and a beauty shop cannot function until a customer is available. A retail store can perform some of its services, such as transportation and storage, but it, too, must wait until the customer arrives to perform other services.

Part of the scheduling task for service firms relates to planning employees' working hours. Restaurants, for example, schedule the work of servers to coincide with variations in customer traffic. In a similar way, stores and medical clinics increase their staff to meet times of peak demand. Other strategies of service firms focus on scheduling customers. Appointment systems are used by many automobile repair shops and beauty shops, for example. Service firms such as dry-cleaners and plumbers take requests for service and delay delivery until the work can be scheduled. Still other firms, such as banks and movie theatres, maintain a fixed schedule of services and tolerate some idle capacity. Some businesses attempt to spread out customer demand by offering incentives to use services at off-peak hours—examples include early-bird dinner specials at a restaurant and lower-price tickets for afternoon movies.

PLANT MAINTENANCE

Murphy's Law states that if anything can go wrong, it will. In operating systems that use tools and equipment, there is indeed much that can go wrong. The maintenance function is intended to correct malfunctions of equipment and, as far as possible, prevent breakdowns from occurring.

THE ROLE OF MAINTENANCE

Effective maintenance contributes directly to product and service quality and thus to customer satisfaction. Poor maintenance often creates problems for customers. A faulty shower or a reading lamp that doesn't work, for example, makes a motel stay less enjoyable for a traveller.

Equipment malfunctions and breakdowns not only cause problems for customers but also increase costs for the producing firm. Employees may be unproductive while repairs are being made, and expensive manufacturing equipment may stand idle when it should be producing. Furthermore, improperly maintained equipment wears out more rapidly and requires early replacement, thus adding to the overall costs of operation.

The nature of maintenance work obviously depends on the type of operations process and the type of equipment being used. In an office, for example, machines that require maintenance include computers, fax machines, printers, copiers, and related office equipment. Maintenance services are usually obtained on a contract basis—either by calling for repair personnel when a breakdown occurs and/or by scheduling periodic servicing. In manufacturing firms that use more complex and specialized equipment, plant maintenance is much more difficult and clearly requires the close attention of management. In small plants, maintenance work is often performed by regular production employees. As a firm expands its facilities, it may add specialized maintenance personnel and eventually create a maintenance department.

TYPES OF MAINTENANCE

Plant maintenance activities fall into two categories. **Preventive maintenance** consists of inspections and other activities intended to prevent machine breakdowns and damage to people and buildings. **Corrective maintenance** comprises both the major and the minor repairs necessary to restore equipment or a facility to good condition.

A small firm can ill afford to neglect preventive maintenance. A machine that is highly critical to the overall operation must be inspected and serviced regularly to preclude costly breakdowns.

Major repairs, which are a part of corrective maintenance, are unpredictable as to time of occurrence, repair time required, loss of output, and cost of downtime. Because of this unpredictability, some small manufacturers contract with outside service firms for major repair work.

THE NEED FOR MANAGEMENT CONTROL SYSTEMS

Management controls are not glamorous, but they can make the difference between success and failure for a small firm. When we think about management controls, we usually think about financial controls, such as budgets for various activities the business undertakes. These kinds of controls will be discussed further in Chapter 13. From an

preventive maintenance activities intended to prevent machine breakdowns, injuries to people, and damage to facilities

corrective maintenance repairs necessary to restore equipment or a facility to good condition

Describe the need for management control systems.   2

operations point of view, management controls are critical to efficiency and effectiveness. Businesses must monitor, manage, and control such things as quality, production schedules, productivity, waste, rework, and inventory to ensure customers are kept happy and that operations are performed in such a way that the firm performs its operations function at a profit. It is true that what gets measured gets paid attention to, and managers can use control systems to signal to employees what is important by determining what gets measured.

THE CONTROL CYCLE

control cycle
a period of time over which an activity is planned, measured, corrected, and replanned

variance
the difference between planned or forecast activity and actual activity

The concept of the **control cycle** in operations begins with objectives being set at the beginning of a period of activity, usually a day, a week, a month, a quarter, or a year. For example, output of the operations process for a manufacturer could be forecast as so many units per day, week, or month. As the activity takes place, results are measured and compared to objectives set at the beginning, and corrective actions take place if there is a large enough **variance** from the objectives. Such actions could be adding staff or working overtime to increase output, for example. At the end of the period of activity, new objectives may be set and the cycle begins again. Exhibit 12-2 illustrates the control cycle.

Some critical questions that must be answered are

- What to measure?
- How to measure?
- How often to measure?
- What is unacceptable variance from plan?
- What actions can be taken to correct the variance?

For each kind of business, different aspects of the operations process will be more important to measure. For some, such as manufacturing, output, rework or warranty work, wastage, productivity, quality, and inventory may all be important. For a service business, employee work scheduling or on-time provision of the service may be most

EXHIBIT **12-2**
The Control Cycle

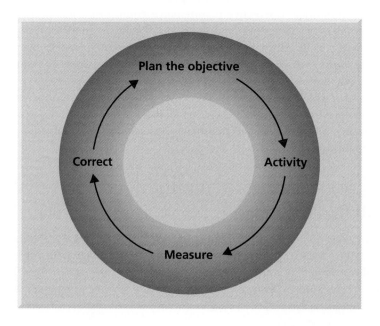

important. The answers to the other questions depend on the length of time the cycle spans. If the operations cycle is very short, as in the case of a fast-food restaurant for example, output may be measured in terms of number of customers served every 15 minutes, or how many hamburgers are ordered in the same period. Major fast-food franchises such as McDonald's and KFC have honed their control systems to a science, ensuring a ready supply of food items to minimize waiting time and increase the number of customers that can be served in a given amount of time. In a longer cycle, such as house construction, output or number of customers served are not relevant measures. The company may measure employee hours and materials usage for each house under construction on a weekly or monthly basis instead.

TYPICAL MANAGEMENT CONTROL SYSTEMS

In today's competitive marketplace, most customers place a high premium on quality. Whether a business is producing products, services, or some combination of the two, achievement of an appropriate level of quality is an important factor in business success and survival.

QUALITY GOALS OF OPERATIONS MANAGEMENT

Explain the key elements of total quality management (TQM) programs.

3

Quality must be more than a slogan. Owners of successful small firms realize that quality management is serious business and that a strong commitment is essential for realization of quality goals. Incorporating quality management is really a process that begins with the firm's mission and objectives. There is a basic paradox in business where firms that focus on making money at all costs usually are less financially successful than those that focus on providing a quality product or service experience to the customer. Consequently most mission statements make no reference to profit but instead contain such terms as "the best," "most respected," "superior," in relation to the customer and the market. The mission statement and the firm's objectives should reflect commitments and these should then be linked through to the set of activities and product/service features that ensure quality is managed for the benefit of the customer.

One definition of **quality** is "the totality of features and characteristics of a product or service that bears on its ability to satisfy stated or implied needs."[2] Quality has many different aspects. For example, a restaurant's customers base their perceptions of its quality on the taste of the food, the attractiveness of the décor, the friendliness and promptness of the servers, the cleanliness of the silverware, the type of background music, and numerous other factors. The operations process establishes a level of quality as a product is produced or as a service is provided. Although costs and other considerations cannot be ignored, quality must constitute a primary focus of a firm's operations. It is important to understand that "quality" is determined by the customer, and entrepreneurs must understand their customers' definition of quality.

International competition is increasingly turning on quality differences. Automobile manufacturers in Canada and the United States, for example, now place greater emphasis on quality in their attempts to compete effectively with foreign producers. However, it is not solely big business that needs to make quality a major concern; the operations process of a small firm also deserves careful scrutiny. Many small firms have been slow to give adequate attention to the achievement of high quality. In examining the operations process, therefore, small business managers must direct special attention to achieving superior product or service quality.

quality
the features of a product or service that enable it to satisfy customers' needs

total quality management (TQM)

an all-encompassing management approach to providing high-quality products and services

An aggressive effort by a firm to achieve superior quality is often termed **total quality management (TQM).** Total quality management implies an all-encompassing, quality-focused management approach to providing products and services that satisfy customer requirements. Firms that implement TQM programs are making quality a major goal.

THE CUSTOMER FOCUS OF QUALITY MANAGEMENT

A firm's quality management efforts should begin with a focus on the customers who purchase its products or services. A concrete customer focus is the driving force behind successful quality programs. Without such a focus, the quest for quality easily degenerates into an aimless search for some abstract, elusive ideal.

CUSTOMER EXPECTATIONS

Quality is ultimately determined by the extent to which a product or service satisfies customers' needs and expectations. Customers have expectations regarding the quality of both products (durability and attractiveness, for example) and services (speed and accuracy, for example). A customer is concerned with *product quality* when purchasing a camera or a loaf of bread; the customer's primary concern is *service quality* when having an automobile repaired or tailoring done. Frequently, a customer expects some combination of product *and* service quality—when buying a lawnmower, a customer may be concerned with the performance of the lawnmower, knowledge and courtesy of the salesperson, credit terms offered, and terms of the warranty.

Customers often have in mind specific standards that are relevant to a product or service. In the following comments, customers revealed their expectations regarding three types of service businesses:

AUTOMOBILE REPAIR CUSTOMERS
- Be competent. ("Fix it right the first time.")
- Explain things. ("Explain why I need the suggested repairs—provide an itemized list.")
- Be respectful. ("Don't treat me like I'm stupid.")

HOTEL CUSTOMERS
- Provide a clean room. ("Don't have a deep-pile carpet that can't be completely cleaned . . . You can literally see germs down there.")
- Provide a secure room. ("Have good bolts and a peephole on the door.")
- Treat me like a guest. ("It is almost like they're looking me over to decide whether they're going to let me have a room.")
- Keep your promises. ("They said the room would be ready, but it wasn't at the promised time.")

EQUIPMENT REPAIR CUSTOMERS
- Share my sense of urgency. ("Speed of response is important. One time I had to buy a second piece of equipment because of the huge downtime with the first piece.")
- Be competent. ("Sometimes I'm quoting stuff from their instruction manuals to their own people, and they don't even know what it means.")
- Be prepared. ("Have all the parts ready.")[3]

A genuine concern for customer needs and customer satisfaction is a powerful force that energizes the total quality management effort of a business. When customer

IN THE TRENCHES

Entrepreneurial Experiences

Trucking Air

Trucking a load of air makes no sense, but that's just what happens every day across North America when trucks "deadhead" on the return from a delivery for want of a load. In today's era of high fuel costs, this is both a high cost and foregone opportunity for revenues. It can also be frustrating for shippers who may be looking for a truck going in a particular direction and unable to find one.

Brent Moore from Grande Prairie, Alberta, experienced this frustration first hand when looking for a truck to haul some equipment for his oilfield equipment rental business. Watching empty trucks go by on the highway and being unable to communicate his need, Moore came up with the idea for a web-based solution using global positioning system technology (GPS). In January 2007 he teamed up with long-time friend and computer science expert Duncan Ford to create Canhaul.com, an online service that enables truckers to advertise their location and availability in a way that makes it easy for shippers to find a match. Their solution combines a call centre with the online presence to deliver first-class customer service to truckers and shippers. The company plots every load on a Google map so customers can see exactly where their shipment is. The service was an instant hit. Within four months of launch listings reached over 300 per month and won Canhaul the 2007 Canadian Information Productivity Gold Award for excellence.

But the story doesn't end there: while developing the business concept, the company arranged to be a reseller of GPS-based systems for Florida-based TransMobile. The relationship led to TransMobile buying an interest in the company late in 2007 and moving Moore and Ford to its Florida offices to work on new projects. While Canhaul operates in Canada, Moore and Ford are developing Emission Critical, a system that allows trucking companies to monitor everything from tire pressure to maintenance needs of their fleets, and document fuel savings from this and route optimization to gain "carbon credits." Moore believes the focus on helping the needs of truckers will make the company the preferred solution in the industry, while helping reduce the environmental impact of the trucking industry.

Sources: http://www.cipa.com/award_winners_07/canhaul (accessed March 25, 2008); interview with Brent Moore.

satisfaction is seen merely as a means of increasing profits, its effect on quality is negligible. When the customer becomes the focal point in quality efforts, however, real quality improvement occurs, and profits tend to grow as a result.

CUSTOMER FEEDBACK

Attentive listening to customers' opinions can often provide information about their level of satisfaction. Employees having direct contact with customers can serve as the eyes and ears of the business in evaluating existing quality levels and customer needs. Unfortunately, many managers are oblivious to the often subtle feedback from customers. Preoccupied with operating details, managers may not listen to, let alone solicit, customers' opinions. Employees having direct contact with customers—servers in a restaurant, for example—are seldom trained or expected to obtain information about customers' quality expectations.

Experts now recommend that firms make aggressive efforts to involve and empower customers in efforts to improve quality.[4] The marketing research methods of observation, interviews, and customer surveys, as described in Chapter 6, can be used to investigate customers' views regarding quality. Some businesses, for example, provide comment cards for their customers to use in evaluating service or product quality.

One method of comparing how a firm performs on the dimension of quality (or others, for that matter), is **benchmarking,** which is the process of identifying the best products, services, and practices of other businesses, carefully studying those examples, and using any insights gained to improve one's own operations. A simple type of benchmarking occurs as owner-managers eat in competitors' restaurants or shop in competitors' stores and then use what they learn to make improvements in their own businesses.

TOOLS AND TECHNIQUES OF QUALITY MANAGEMENT AND CONTROL

Effective quality management requires the use of various tools, techniques, and procedures needed to ensure high-quality products and services. Once the focus is on the customer and the entire organization is committed to providing top-quality products and services, operating methodology becomes important. Implementing a quality management program requires developing practical procedures for training employees, inspecting products, and measuring progress toward quality goals. We will discuss three important areas—employee participation, the inspection processes, and the use of statistical methods of quality control.

EMPLOYEE PARTICIPATION

In most organizations, employee performance is a critical quality variable. Obviously, employees who work carefully produce better-quality products than those who work carelessly. The admonition "Never buy a car that was produced on a Friday or a Monday!" conveys the popular notion that workers lack commitment to their work and are especially careless prior to and immediately after a weekend away from work. The vital role of personnel in producing a high-quality product or service has led managers to seek ways to actively involve employees in quality management efforts.

Many businesses have implemented work teams and empowerment of employees as approaches to building employee involvement in the workplace. Japanese firms are particularly noted for their use of work teams. Many self-managed work teams, both in Japan and in Canada, monitor the quality level of their work and take any steps necessary to continue operating at the proper quality level.

The quality circle is another technique that utilizes the contributions of employees in improving the quality of products and services. Originated by the Japanese, it is widely used by small firms around the world. A **quality circle** consists of a group of employees, usually a dozen or fewer. They meet on company time, typically about once a week, to identify, analyze, and solve work-related problems, particularly those involving product or service quality. Quality circles can tap employees' potential to make enthusiastic and valuable contributions.

THE INSPECTION PROCESS

Management's traditional method of maintaining product quality has been **inspection,** which consists of scrutinizing a part or a product to determine whether or not it is

benchmarking
the process of studying the products, services, and practices of other firms, and using the insights gained to improve quality internally

quality circle
a group of employees who meet regularly to discuss quality-related problems

inspection
an examination of a product to determine whether it meets quality standards

acceptable. An inspector typically uses gauges to evaluate important quality variables. For effective quality control, the inspector must be honest, objective, and capable of resisting pressure from shop personnel to pass borderline cases.

Although the inspection process is usually discussed with reference to *product* quality, comparable steps can be used to evaluate *service* quality. Follow-up calls to customers of an auto repair shop, for example, might be used to measure the quality of the firm's repair services. Customers can be asked whether recent repairs were performed in a timely and satisfactory manner.

In manufacturing, **inspection standards** consist of design tolerances that are set for every important quality variable. These tolerances indicate, in discrete terms, the variation allowable above and below the desired level of quality. Inspection standards must satisfy customer requirements for quality in finished products. Traditionally, inspection begins in the receiving room, where the condition and quantity of materials received from suppliers are checked. Inspection is also customary at critical processing points—for example, *before* any operation that might conceal existing defects and *after* any operation that might produce an excessive amount of defects. Of course, final inspection of finished products is of utmost importance.

Inspecting each item in every lot processed, called *100 percent inspection,* theoretically could be used to ensure the elimination of all bad materials and all defective products prior to shipment to customers. Such inspection goals are seldom reached, however, as this method of inspection is not only time consuming, but also costly. Furthermore, inspectors often make honest errors in judgment, both in rejecting good items and in accepting bad items. Also, some types of inspection, such as opening a can of vegetables, destroy the product, making 100 percent inspection impractical.

In an inspection, either attributes or variables may be measured. **Attribute inspection** determines quality acceptability based on attributes that can be evaluated as being either present or absent. For example, a light bulb either lights or doesn't light; similarly, a water hose either leaks or doesn't leak.

Variable inspection, in contrast, determines quality acceptability based on where variables (such as weight) fall on a scale or continuum. For example, if a box of candy is to be sold as containing a minimum of 1 kg of candy, an inspector may judge the product acceptable if its weight falls within the range of 1 kg to 1.05 kg.

STATISTICAL METHODS OF QUALITY CONTROL

The use of statistical methods can often make controlling product and service quality easier, less expensive, and more effective. As some knowledge of quantitative methods is necessary to develop a quality control method using statistical analysis, a properly qualified employee or outside consultant must be available. The savings made possible by use of an efficient statistical method can often justify the consulting fees required to devise a sound plan.

Acceptance sampling involves taking random samples of products and measuring them against predetermined standards. Suppose, for example, that a small firm receives a shipment of 10,000 parts from a supplier. Rather than evaluate all 10,000 parts, the purchasing firm might check the acceptability of a small sample of parts and generalize about the acceptability of the entire order. The size of the sample affects the discriminating power of a sampling plan. The smaller the sample, the greater the risk of either accepting a defective lot or rejecting a good lot due to sampling error. A larger sample reduces this risk but increases the cost of inspection. A well-designed plan strikes a

inspection standard
a specification of a desired quality level and allowable tolerances

attribute inspection
the determination of product acceptability based on whether it will or will not work

variable inspection
the determination of product acceptability based on a variable such as weight or length

acceptance sampling
the use of a random, representative portion to determine the acceptability of an entire lot

balance, simultaneously avoiding excessive inspection costs and minimizing the risk of accepting a bad lot or rejecting a good lot.

statistical process control

the use of statistical methods to assess quality during the operations process

Statistical process control involves applying statistical techniques to control work processes. Items produced in a manufacturing process are not completely identical, although the variations are sometimes very small and the items may seem to be exactly alike. Careful measurement, however, can pinpoint differences. Usually, these differences can be plotted in the form of a normal curve, which aids in the application of statistical control techniques.

The use of statistical analysis makes it possible to establish tolerance limits that allow for inherent variation due to chance. When measurements fall outside these tolerance limits, however, the quality controller knows that there is a problem and must then search for the cause. The problem might be caused by variations in raw materials, machine wear, or changes in employees' work practices. Consider, for example, a candy maker that is producing 500 g boxes of candy. Though the weight may vary slightly, each box must weigh at least 500 g. A study of the operations process has determined that the actual target weight must be 550 g, to allow for the normal variation between 500 and 600 grams. During the production process, a box is weighed every 15 or 20 minutes. If the weight of a box falls outside the tolerance limits—below 500 or above 600 g—the quality controller must immediately try to find the problem and correct it. Continuing improvements in computer-based technology have advanced the use of statistical control processes in small firms.

control chart

a graphic illustration of the limits used in statistical process control

A **control chart** graphically shows the limits for the process being controlled. As current data are entered, it is possible to tell whether a process is under control or out of control. Control charts may be used for either variable or attribute inspections.

INTERNATIONAL CERTIFICATION FOR QUALITY MANAGEMENT

A firm can obtain international recognition of its quality management and environmental management programs by meeting a series of standards, known as **ISO 9000** and **ISO 14000,** respectively, developed by the International Organization for Standardization in Geneva, Switzerland.

ISO 9000

the standards governing international certification of a firm's quality management procedures

The certification process requires full documentation of a firm's quality management procedures, as well as an audit to ensure that the firm is operating in accordance with those procedures. In other words, the firm must show that it does what it says it does.

ISO 9000 certification is primarily concerned with "quality management," which means what the organization does to fulfill the customer's quality requirements and applicable regulatory requirements while aiming to enhance customer satisfaction and achieve continual improvement of its performance in pursuit of these objectives. ISO 9000 certification can give a business credibility with purchasers in other countries and thereby ease its entry into export markets. However, substantial costs are involved in obtaining certification.

ISO 14000

the standards governing responsible environmental management

ISO 9000 certification is particularly valuable for small firms, because they usually lack a global image as producers of high-quality products. Buyers in other countries, especially in Europe, view this certification as an indicator of supplier reliability. Many large corporations, such as automobile makers, require their domestic suppliers to conform to these standards. Small firms, therefore, may need ISO 9000 certification either to sell more easily in international markets or to meet the demands of their domestic customers.

IN THE TRENCHES

Exploring Global Opportunities

ISO 9000 Brings the World to Small and Medium Enterprise

As part of their competitive strategy, some small firms seek the international certification known as ISO 9000. Such certification provides a competitive edge, because the rating assures customers and suppliers worldwide that the firm has achieved high quality standards.

A key element of the strategy of Calgary-based Inventronics Ltd. is the ISO 9001–2000 certification of its Brandon, Manitoba, manufacturing facility. Inventronics designs and manufactures custom enclosures and other products for sophisticated equipment in both indoor and outdoor applications. The company's main market is the telecommunications equipment business, with subsidiary markets in the electronics, utilities, and computer services industries.

A worldwide downturn in telecom spending in the early 2000s resulted in the company spinning off its United Kingdom–based European unit to focus on the North American market. While spending in the telecom sector is slowly recovering, company president Dan Stearne credits the company's Brandon employees with minimizing the impact on the bottom line. "Our Brandon employees found ways to achieve essential cost efficiencies while also maintaining stringent quality standards," says Stearne.

The ISO 9000 certification gives Inventronics credibility in the U.S. market, according to Alan Kurtz, director of Marketing and Sales. "For a small company relative to the size of many of our customers, the ISO certification tells the market we are a serious player. It gives our customers a comfort that we can be trusted as a supplier," says Kurtz.

With the telecom industry and the U.S. economy strengthening, a move back into the international arena is not too far in the future for Inventronics.

Sources: http://www.inventronics.com/html/corporate/corporate_overview.htm (accessed March 29, 2008) personal communication with the company, and "City Workforce Key to Firm's Success," *Brandon Sun*, May 28, 2004.

ISO 9000 is based on eight quality management principles:

1. Customer focus
2. Leadership
3. Involvement of people in the organization
4. A process approach to quality management
5. A systems approach to quality management
6. Continual improvement
7. A factual approach to decision making
8. Mutually beneficial supplier relationships

ISO 14000 is a set of generic management standards for responsible environmental management. The standards apply to what the organization does to

- Minimize harmful effects on the environment caused by its activities
- Achieve continual improvements of its environmental management performance

According to the International Organization for Standardization, ISO 14001 benefits organizations as a clear signal to its customers of its environmental concern and stewardship as well as a method of moving beyond regulatory compliance to a position of improved productivity and enhanced competitive advantage.

ISO 9000 and 14000 standards are currently implemented by over 1 million organizations in 161 countries worldwide.[5] More information on ISO 9000 and ISO 14000 can be found at http://www.iso.org.

QUALITY MANAGEMENT IN SERVICE BUSINESSES

As discussed earlier, maintaining and improving quality are no less important for service businesses, such as motels, dry-cleaners, accounting firms, and automobile repair shops, than for manufacturers. In fact, many firms offer a combination of tangible products and intangible services, and effectively manage quality in both areas. Six factors positively influence customers' perception of service quality:

1. *Being on target:* Set and meet the customer's expectations. Do what was promised, when and where it was promised. Heighten the customer's awareness of the service provider's actions.
2. *Care and concern:* Be empathetic. Tune in to the customer's situation, frame of mind, and needs. Be attentive and willing to help.
3. *Spontaneity:* Empower service providers to think and respond quickly. Allow them to use their discretion and bend, rather than quote, procedures.
4. *Problem solving:* Train and encourage service providers to be problem solvers. Service providers have the customer's undivided attention when that person is experiencing a problem. A positive response to a problem will stick in the customer's mind. Capitalize on this opportunity to show the organization's capabilities.
5. *Follow-up:* Follow-up captures customers' attention and is often sincerely appreciated. It is associated with caring and professionalism, so follow up with flair and create a reputation for legendary service quality.
6. *Recovery:* Customers experiencing problems often have low expectations for their resolution; thus, they are exceedingly mindful and appreciative of speedy solutions. Making things right quickly is a powerful factor in creating an enduring image of high-quality service.[6]

COMPETITIVE STRENGTH THROUGH IMPROVED PRODUCTIVITY

Explain how reengineering and other methods of work improvement can increase productivity and make a firm more competitive.

productivity
the efficiency with which inputs are transformed into outputs

A society's standard of living depends, to some extent, on its **productivity**—the efficiency with which inputs are transformed into outputs. Similarly, the competitive strength of a particular business depends on its productivity. This section discusses approaches that can be used by small businesses to become more competitive through improved productivity.

THE IMPORTANCE OF IMPROVING PRODUCTIVITY

To remain competitive, a firm should continually try to improve its productivity. Improvement efforts vary greatly. Some involve major reorganizations or changes in technology, while others merely upgrade existing operations.

A business firm's productivity may be expressed in the following way:

$$Productivity = \frac{Outputs}{Inputs} = \frac{Products\ and/or\ services}{Labour\ +\ Energy\ +\ Money\ +\ Raw\ materials\ +\ Information}$$

A firm improves its productivity by doing more with less—increasing outputs and/or decreasing inputs. This can be accomplished in many different ways. For example, a small restaurant may improve the pastry making of its chef by sending the chef to cooking school, buying better ingredients, getting a better oven, or redesigning the kitchen.

At one time, productivity and quality were viewed as competitive, if not conflicting. However, production at a high quality level reduces scrap and rework. Therefore, quality improvements, automation, and other improvements in operations methods are all routes to better productivity.

Improving productivity in the labour-intensive service sector is especially difficult, since managers have less opportunity to take advantage of automation.

Measurement problems are always an issue in assessing the quality of a service. It is easier to measure the length of a piece of wood than the quality of motel accommodations. As noted earlier, however, methods can be devised for measuring the quality of services. For example, a motel manager might maintain a record of the number of problems with travellers' reservations, complaints about the cleanliness of rooms, and so on.

For many types of service firms, quality control constitutes the most important managerial responsibility. All that such firms sell is service, and their future success rests on customers' perceptions of the quality of that service.

Nevertheless, small service firms can find ways to become more efficient. At one time, for example, customers in barber shops wasted time waiting for barbers who took them on a first-come, first-served basis. To improve the system, many shops started using an appointment schedule. A drop-in customer can still get service immediately if a barber isn't busy or else sign up for the first convenient appointment. Such a system provides continuity in the barber's work schedule, and reduces delays and frustration for customers.

REENGINEERING FOR IMPROVED PRODUCTIVITY

In the early 1990s, Michael Hammer and James Champy described a method for restructuring corporations to provide better service for customers. In their best-selling book, *Reengineering the Corporation*, Hammer and Champy defined **reengineering** as "the fundamental rethinking and radical redesign of business processes to achieve dramatic improvements in critical, contemporary measures of performance, such as cost, quality, service, and speed."[7]

reengineering
a fundamental
restructuring
to improve the
operations process

Reengineering is concerned with improving the way in which a business operates, whether that business is large or small. Hammer and Champy concentrated their early analysis on large corporations such as Wal-Mart, Taco Bell, and Bell Atlantic, which redesigned their rigid bureaucratic structures to become more efficient. Firms that engage in reengineering seek fundamental improvements by asking questions about why they perform certain functions the way they do. They expect to make dramatic, radical changes rather than minimal adjustments to traditional operating methods. Reengineering involves careful analysis of the basic processes followed by a firm in creating goods and services for customers.

Proponents of reengineering recommend evaluating a firm's business operations at the most basic level. By emphasizing thoroughness in the analysis of the firm's operations, such broad-based assessment alerts a firm's management to the danger of making small improvements in an inherently weak or outmoded operating system.

Reengineering's emphasis on basic processes is crucial and holds the potential for substantial improvements in operations. Like effective quality control efforts, it directs attention to activities that create value for the customer. Essentially, reengineering asks how the operations process can be better managed, even if it means eliminating traditional departmental lines and specialized job descriptions.

THE DOWNSIDE OF REENGINEERING

The fundamental assumption about reengineering is "if it isn't broken, take it apart and fix it anyway." This can be a risky assumption. While it is true that processes in place are sometimes reexamined only infrequently, it may also be true that a process in place is the best way to do things. Careful thought should go into the decision to reengineer a process. If the process is critical to the firm's operations, the risks associated with reengineering may simply be not worth it.

According to expert Hugh Alley, 70 percent of information technology development projects fail to deliver promised functionality on time and on budget. He goes on to say that 30 percent to 50 percent of reengineering efforts and 75 percent to 80 percent of TQI initiatives fail. Alley outlines six key reasons process improvement initiatives fail:

1. Many efforts take on the whole business at once. This has two flaws: (a) not every effort will have the same impact and (b) it simply takes too long and costs too much in time, attention, and money. It's simply too risky.
2. Fixing one department or process without considering the preceding or downstream processes or departments affected is futile. The improvement might not only result in any significant results, but also negatively impact the performance of other processes or departments.
3. Bringing in outside experts is fraught with danger. The expert, or even the manager, may have assumptions that "there is only one best way to organize your work," "I can easily understand how you do your work today," "I can design work better than you can," "There is little about your work now worth saving," and "You will do your work the way I specify." The people doing the work must be involved if the change is to be successful.
4. Many improvement efforts consume too much employee time. Since production always trumps projects, improvement efforts tend to get drawn out over time, and enthusiasm is lost.
5. Many improvement projects run out of steam as management time and attention is taken up by new or emergency issues. Projects need a champion.
6. As Bill Cosby said in one of his stand-up comedy sketches, "Don't like surprises." Surprising employees reduces their comfort level and willingness to participate. The second kind of surprise is the unforeseen glitch—technical or otherwise.

Alley suggests five tools to help avoid unsuccessful efforts:

1. Be customer focused. If the customer needs next-day delivery, then prioritize projects based on which ones will achieve this.
2. Phase in improvements. Measurable improvements in one area in a month are better than a dozen projects underway with no tangible results.
3. Involve the employees. They know the work better than anyone.

4. Divide the project up into manageable, scheduled packages of work that can be assigned to individuals or groups
5. Communicate. Make sure there are no surprises and employees know what to expect.[8]

REENGINEERING COMPARED TO CONTINUOUS QUALITY IMPROVEMENT

Continuous quality improvement programs emphasize doing things better from an operations standpoint to increase quality, increase throughput, or reduce costs. As stated earlier, continuous improvement involves such things as training for personnel and replacing old equipment with newer, faster equipment. Continuous improvement is about *incremental* improvements to *existing* processes. Reengineering, on the other hand, requires a much more radical change in the way operations processes work. As opposed to the incremental improvements continuous improvement seeks to make in existing processes, reengineering involves a *discontinuous* change in the way an organization works by changing the processes themselves. This often involves changes to not only processes but also the management structure, control systems, and reporting lines between people in the process and those who manage it.

continuous quality improvement
a constant and dedicated effort to improve quality

OPERATIONS ANALYSIS

Improving productivity for an overall operation involves analyses of work flow, equipment, tooling, layout, working conditions, and individual jobs. For a specific manufacturing process, it means finding answers to questions such as these:

- Are the right machines being used?
- Can one employee operate two or more machines?
- Can automatic feeders or ejectors be used?
- Can power tools replace hand tools?
- Can the jigs and fixtures be improved?
- Is the workplace properly arranged?
- Is each operator's motion sequence effective?

Work methods can be analyzed for service or merchandising firms as well as for manufacturers. For example, a small plumbing company serving residential customers might examine its service vehicles to ensure they are equipped with the best possible assortment and arrangement of parts, tools, and supplies. In addition, the company might analyze the planning and routing of repair assignments to minimize unnecessary backtracking and wasting of time.

LEAN MANUFACTURING

One modern method of analyzing and improving operations for manufacturing and service companies is

LEAN MANUFACTURING

It gets its name because it is just that: lean. It uses less of everything compared with mass manufacturing: space, labour, tools, inventory and generally results in fewer defects. Lean organizations apply a three-pronged approach to

- Eliminate waste
- Ensure quality
- Involve employees in designing and managing their work

LEAN manufacturing involves five key principles.

1. Define value from the customer's perspective by
   a. Identifying value-added (from the customer's point of view) product features and eliminating features that do not add customer value
   b. Manufacturing to customer need instead of manufacturing an inventory of finished goods
2. Identify and map the value stream by
   a. Identifying material and information flows in the manufacturing process
   b. Highlighting bottlenecks, hand-offs from one operation to the next, where inventory is stored, and how it moves and is used

   The result is a picture or diagram of current processes from start to finish, allowing a focus on non-value-added activities.
3. Reduce or eliminate waste and improve flow by
   a. Eliminating all activities that consume resources but do not create value
   b. Performing only activities that add value in the eyes of the customer

   In LEAN manufacturing, waste is any activity for which the customer is not willing to pay, since that activity adds no value and often consumes resources. Waste exists in all parts of the business, from the front office to the shipping dock. This analysis results in redefining the value stream to one that includes only value-added activities.
4. Pull from customers, using their information and demand to establish production levels rather than being based on arbitrary or predefined inventory levels
5. Pursue perfection by returning to step one and repeating this process periodically in an effort to achieve continuous improvement

While the largest benefits of applying the LEAN principles are found in manufacturing, they can be applied to virtually any kind of service operation, from warehousing and transportation to accounting services.

REDUCING OR ELIMINATING WASTE

LEAN manufacturing
a system of techniques designed to eliminate waste, ensure quality, and involve employees in designing and managing their work

From a **LEAN manufacturing** perspective there are seven types of waste that can be reduced or eliminated to increase efficiency and thereby increase profits:

1. Stop overproduction for building inventory, and eliminate products no longer in demand or that are redundant to the product being produced.
2. Manage inventory to prevent holding or buying unnecessary raw materials or performing unnecessary work-in-progress.
3. Streamline transportation of materials to reduce or eliminate multiple handling or delays in handling.
4. Optimize motion and actions of personnel. For example, storing parts closer to where employees work will reduce the amount of time they spend retrieving parts.
5. Reduce waiting times for parts or previous stages in the manufacturing process: idle time is wasted time.
6. Reduce or eliminate defects. Defective units either cannot be sold or require rework to make them saleable. Either way, this is not a value-added activity.
7. Reduce or stop overprocessing by eliminating unnecessary steps or product features that customers do not value.

LEAN MANUFACTURING AND THE WORKFORCE

Employees are generally affected in very positive ways in LEAN manufacturing and service operations. Employees are involved in forming teams, training ensuring quality, performing basic maintenance, and so on. They are empowered to fix quality problems or stop production if a major problem occurs so only quality product goes out the door. Employees are cross-trained to acquire new skills and be able to perform multiple jobs in the manufacturing process.

BENEFITS OF "BEING LEAN"

Among the benefits of implementing LEAN principles are

- Creating a culture of continuous improvement
- Decreasing manufacturing cycle times—the time it takes to manufacture an order
- Reducing waste
- Empowering employees
- Increasing profits and cash flow
- Increasing production capacity
- Increasing customer satisfaction
- Reducing costs[9]

IN THE TRENCHES

Utilizing Technology

A Food Safety Award Winner

Some operations processes can be improved by applying new technology. Viau Foods of Laval is the largest independent producer of pepperoni in Canada. It has experienced rapid growth, and it's paper-based tracking system simply couldn't keep track of all of the production batches, a key requirement for both food safety regulations and ensuring quality.

Working with Sologlobe Inc. of Montreal, the company decided to pursue a more all-encompassing solution that, in addition to tracing batches, optimized logistics, manufacturing, and quality management. The results were gains in efficiencies, lower costs, and increased customer satisfaction. It now has a state-of-the-art traceability system that has become a competitive advantage and a product differentiator.

Regulation is forcing many companies to a technology solution. Companies like Viau Foods that export to the United States will become subject to that country's *Bioterrorism Act,* which requires food processors to document all suppliers and have the information available 24/7 to provide to government agencies. With its new system, Viau can demonstrate compliance, keeping access to this important market.

Viau's implementation of the new system won it the 2007 Canadian Information Productivity Awards Silver Award of Excellence in the Efficiency and Operational Improvements category.

Source: http://www.cipa.com/award_winners_07/viau (accessed March 3, 2008).

LAWS OF MOTION ECONOMY

The **laws of motion economy** underlie any work improvement program—whether it is aimed at the overall operation of a plant or at a single task. These laws concern work arrangement, the use of the human hands and body, and the design and use of tools. Here's an example of one of these laws: If a worker makes motions simultaneously in opposite directions over similar paths, automaticity and rhythm develop naturally, and less fatigue is experienced.

METHODS OF WORK MEASUREMENT

There are several ways to measure work in order to establish a performance standard. **Motion study** consists of detailed observation of all the actual movements a worker makes to complete a job under a given set of physical conditions. From this study, a skilled observer should be able to detect any wasted movements, which can then be corrected or eliminated. **Time study,** which follows motion study, typically involves use of a stopwatch to determine an average time for performing a given task.

PURCHASING POLICIES AND PRACTICES

Although its importance varies with the type of business, **purchasing** constitutes a key part of operations management for most small businesses, as purchasing activities are used to obtain materials, merchandise, equipment, and services to meet production and marketing goals. Through purchasing, a firm secures all production factors except labour. For example, manufacturing firms buy raw materials, merchandising firms purchase goods to be sold, and all types of firms obtain supplies.

THE IMPORTANCE OF PURCHASING

The quality of a finished product depends on the quality of the raw materials used. If tight tolerances are imposed on a product by design requirements, the manufacturer must acquire high-quality materials and component parts. Then, if the manufacturer uses a well-managed production process, excellent products will result. Similarly, the acquisition of high-quality merchandise makes a retailer's sales to customers easier and reduces the number of necessary markdowns and merchandise returns.

Purchasing also contributes to profitable operations by ensuring that goods are delivered when they are needed. In a small factory, failure to receive materials, parts, or equipment on schedule can cause costly interruptions in production operations. In a retail business, failure to receive merchandise on schedule may mean a loss of sales and, possibly, a permanent loss of customers who were disappointed.

Another aspect of effective purchasing is securing the best possible price. Cost savings go directly to the bottom line, and purchasing practices that seek out the best prices can have a major impact on the financial health of a business.

Note, however, that the importance of the purchasing function varies according to the type of business. In a small, labour-intensive service business—such as an accounting firm—purchases of supplies are responsible for a very small part of the total operating costs. Such businesses are more concerned with labour costs than with the cost of supplies or other materials they may require in their operations process.

PURCHASING POLICIES AND COST CONTROL

A small firm can increase the cost-effectiveness of its purchasing activities by adopting appropriate purchasing policies and practices. Through decisions related to making or buying, outsourcing, and diversifying or concentrating sources of supply, the firm's management can optimize both present and future earnings.

MAKING OR BUYING

Many firms face **make-or-buy decisions.** Such decisions are especially important for small manufacturing firms that have the option of making or buying component parts for the products they produce. A less obvious make-or-buy choice exists with respect to certain services—for example, purchasing janitorial or car rental services versus providing for those needs internally. Some reasons for making component parts, rather than buying them, follow:

make-or-buy decision
a firm's choice between producing and purchasing component parts for its products

- More complete utilization of plant capacity permits more economical production.
- Supplies are assured, with fewer delays caused by design changes or difficulties with outside suppliers.
- A secret design may be protected.
- Expenses are reduced by an amount equivalent to transportation costs and the outside supplier's selling expense and profit.
- Closer coordination and control of the total production process may facilitate operations scheduling and control.
- Products produced may be higher quality than those available from outside suppliers.

Some reasons for buying component parts, rather than making them, follow:

- An outside supplier's part may be cheaper because of the supplier's concentration on production of the part.
- Additional space, equipment, personnel skills, and working capital are unnecessary.
- Less diversified managerial experience and skills are required.
- Greater flexibility is provided, especially in the manufacture of a seasonal item.
- In-plant operations can concentrate on the firm's specialty—finished products and services.
- The risk of equipment obsolescence is transferred to outsiders.

When considering the decision to make or buy the financial factors to consider are the incremental costs to make purchase plus any opportunity costs the company might incur. Opportunity costs for making a component would be any higher-value component or item that could be made with the freed-up capacity from buying instead of making. For example, ABC Company now makes a component for its final product Annual requirements are 10,000 units and costs of producing them are as follows:

Materials	$ 20,000
Direct Labour	50,000
Variable Overhead	100,000
Fixed Overhead	40,000
Total Costs	$210,000

An outside supplier has offered a price of $16 per unit for 10,000 units for a total of $160,000. To compare the two, not considering opportunity costs for the sake of simplicity:

Buy		Make
Purchase Price	$160,000	$ 0
Materials		20,000
Direct Labour		50,000
Variable Overhead		100,000
Total Costs	$160,000	$170,000

Fixed overhead is not considered since the company would have to pay for it whether it makes or buys the component. In this case the company would save $10,000 per year by buying the component.

The decision to make or buy should be based on long-run cost and profit optimization, as it may be expensive to reverse. Other factors might include quality control, reliability of the supplier, and shipping costs. Underlying cost differences need to be analyzed carefully, since small savings from either buying or making may greatly affect profit margins.

OUTSOURCING

outsourcing

purchasing products or services that are outside the firm's area of competitive advantage

Buying products or services from other business firms is known as **outsourcing.** Although the preceding discussion of making or buying component parts related specifically to manufacturing, the concept can also be extended to procurement of services. A small company, for example, may contract with outside suppliers to provide accounting services, payroll services, janitorial services, equipment repair services, and so on. A firm can often reduce costs by taking advantage of the economies of scale and the expertise of outside service providers, rather than trying to provide all such services in-house. Also, outside firms that specialize in specific areas usually provide better service in those areas.

For small businesses, the main reasons to outsource are usually lack of skills to do certain tasks, or not enough work of certain kinds to justify having an employee responsible for doing the activity. For most businesses, for example, services such as delivery services are contracted out. The costs of acquiring a vehicle through lease or purchase, the cost of operating and maintaining the vehicle, and the cost of a driver could be in excess of $2500 per month, whereas the cost of paying a courier company to do the deliveries is generally substantially less. There is the additional benefit of a courier service having multiple vehicles and drivers available so that pickups can be made as needed compared to a business's own courier who would typically follow a preplanned route and is thus less able to respond to the need for an "emergency" delivery request. Typical services outsourced by small businesses include bookkeeping and accounting, janitorial service, and payroll preparation.

THE DANGERS OF OUTSOURCING Outsourcing is typically done only for noncore activities of a firm. The critical operations processes are kept firmly in control by hiring employees to do the work and managing the process internally. When a business outsources an activity, it loses some control over it. In the example above, a grumpy courier driver from an outside courier service may make a bad impression, which in turn reflects badly on the shipper's business. The business can complain to the courier company about its grumpy employee, but it has no ability to discipline the employee, as it could if it had its own vehicle and driver. Keeping internal control of key processes is also important for quality control, maintaining production schedules, and, in some cases, keeping costs under control. The decision to outsource should be made only after careful analysis of the costs and benefits, both monetary and qualitative. Businesses should also be very wary of losing the ability to be creative and innovative in certain areas of their business by giving up some activities.

DIVERSIFYING SOURCES OF SUPPLY

Small firms often must decide whether it is desirable to use more than one supplier when purchasing a given item. The somewhat frustrating answer is, "It all depends." For example, a business would rarely need more than one supplier when buying a few rolls of tape. However, several suppliers might be involved when a firm was buying a component part to be used in hundreds of products.

A small firm might prefer to concentrate purchases with one supplier for any of the following reasons:

- A particular supplier may be outstanding in its product quality.
- Concentrating purchases may lead to quantity discounts.
- Orders may be so small that it is impractical to divide them among several suppliers.
- The purchasing firm may, as a good customer, qualify for prompt treatment of rush orders and receive management advice, market information, and financial leniency in times of crisis.
- A small firm may be linked to a specific supplier by the very nature of its business—if it is a franchisee, for example.

The following reasons favour diversifying rather than concentrating sources of supply:

- Shopping among suppliers enables the purchasing firm to locate the best source in terms of price, quality, and service.
- A supplier, knowing that competitors are getting some of its business, may try to provide better prices and service in order to obtain a larger piece of the purchasing pie.
- Diversifying supply sources for key products provides insurance against interruptions caused by strikes, fires, or similar problems with sole suppliers.

Some firms compromise by following a purchasing policy of concentrating enough purchases with a single supplier to justify special treatment and, at the same time, diversifying purchases sufficiently to maintain alternative sources of supply.

RELATIONSHIPS WITH SUPPLIERS

Before choosing a supplier, a purchaser should be thoroughly familiar with the characteristics of the materials or merchandise to be purchased, including details of construction, quality and grade desired, intended use, maintenance or care required, and the importance of style features. In manufacturing, the purchaser must especially focus on how different grades and qualities of raw materials affect various manufacturing processes. Firms purchasing services are concerned about the qualifications of the personnel conducting the service and the ability to meet schedules.

IN THE TRENCHES

Exploring Global Opportunities

Outsourcing Comes with Challenges

Many businesses use outsourcing to accomplish tasks that are too costly or impractical for them to perform in-house. Most commonly, this involves large companies outsourcing noncore activities such as information technology support, back-office data processing, and perhaps even billing to smaller companies that specialize in those functions. One popular trend has been for Canadian software companies to outsource the code writing for new applications to companies in India, China, and other countries in the Far East. While this can save companies a lot of money, it is not without its problems.

ARSystems International is a small Toronto-based company that sells web-based software applications and services to the tradeshow industry, mainly for easing registration for events. In 2004 CIO Michael Morton was curious about "offshoring" to supplement his small team of 11 developers. Through Google he came across Shinetech Software Inc, a Beijing software developer. Morton took the company up on an offer of 40 free hours of development to put together an inventory software project, a low-priority and low-risk project his own developers wouldn't get around to for months.

The two-week pilot project ran smoothly: Shinetech hit every deadline, and Morton had to field only the occasional question. Shinetech charged US$1300 based on rates of $10–$12 per hour, compared to US$110–$150 per hour in North America. "It blew me away," says Morton, who has since done two more successful projects with Shinetech. However, Morton is not sure how much more offshoring ARSystems will do.

"We had a hard time keeping up with them," according to Morton. "It's like having a dream development partner at a tenth of the cost." But there are difficulties. The 12-hour time difference means questions take a day to answer, and many times Morton's own team were forced to stay as late as 11 P.M. to solve crises. Morton also found more complex projects required more documentation and explanation, which further complicated the process. A strategy that was supposed to improve the efficiency of his department ended up causing headaches and extra work.

Morton isn't completely soured on offshoring, but cautions it has to be the right project. For ARSSystems that would be one that didn't involve core applications that require a lot of handholding.

Source: Adapted from Andrew Wahl, "Offshoring: A Cautionary Tale," *Canadian Business,* vol. 78, iss. 12, June 6–19, 2005, p. 15. Used by permission.

SELECTING SUPPLIERS

A number of factors are relevant in deciding which suppliers to use on a continuing basis. Perhaps the most significant of these factors are price and quality. Price differences are clearly important to a firm's bottom line, if not offset by quality issues or other factors.

Quality differences are sometimes difficult to detect. For some types of materials, statistical controls can be applied to evaluate vendors' shipments. In this way, the purchaser can obtain an overall quality rating for various suppliers. The purchaser can often work with a supplier to upgrade quality. If satisfactory quality cannot be achieved, the purchaser clearly has a reason for dropping the supplier.

Supplier location becomes an especially important factor if a firm tries to keep inventory levels low, depending instead on rapid delivery of purchased items when they are needed. A supplier's overall reliability in providing goods and services is also significant. The purchaser must be able to depend on the supplier to meet delivery schedules and to respond promptly when emergency situations arise.

The services offered by a supplier must also be considered during the selection process. The extension of credit by suppliers provides a major portion of the working capital of many small firms. Some suppliers plan sales promotions, provide merchandising aids, and furnish management advice. During recessions, some small retailers have even received direct financial assistance from long-standing suppliers. The provision of repair work for some types of products is another useful service offered by certain suppliers. A small industrial firm, for example, may select a particular supplier of a truck or diesel engine in large part because the supplier has a reliable service department.

BUILDING GOOD RELATIONSHIPS WITH SUPPLIERS

Good relationships with suppliers are essential for firms of any size, but they are particularly important for small businesses. The small firm is only one among dozens, hundreds, or perhaps thousands buying from that supplier. And because the small firm's purchases are often small in volume, they may not be of concern to the supplier.

To implement a policy of fair play and to cultivate good relations with suppliers, a small firm should try to observe the following purchasing practices:

- Give sales representatives a prompt, courteous hearing.
- Avoid abrupt cancellation of orders merely to gain a temporary advantage.
- Avoid attempts to browbeat the supplier into special concessions and/or unusual discounts.
- Cooperate with the supplier by making suggestions for product improvement and/or cost reduction, whenever possible.
- **Provide courteous, reasonable explanations when rejecting bids, and make fair adjustments in the case of disputes.**

Although price can never be completely ignored, the development of cooperative relationships with qualified suppliers can pay substantial dividends to many small firms. Small business buyers should remember that, although it takes a long time to build good relationships with suppliers, those relationships can be damaged by one ill-timed, tactless act.

Increasingly in the 2000s there is a trend to closer linkages between suppliers and customers. Some of the drivers of this are the torrid pace of business activity, the need for flexibility in a time of rapid technological change, and the application of technology to the exchange of data between firms. In many instances the use of Electronic Data Interchange (EDI) has taken the place of traditional paper-based systems, and in fact many larger companies refuse to do business with smaller companies that cannot communicate using EDI. In an EDI environment orders are placed and tracked via electronic communications, received by the customer and logged into the computer, which then approves the transfer of funds electronically from the customer to the supplier in payment. EDI eliminates the need to reenter order and billing data, and speeds the information exchange between companies.

Getting smaller suppliers to adopt EDI can be a problem. Quebec-based Rona stores adopted EDI in the mid-1990s, but by 2001 only 7 percent of the company's 3,200 suppliers were connected. Fortunately new inexpensive Internet-based solutions have become available to smaller suppliers that make EDI almost painless to adopt. Rona had another 1000 suppliers on board within a year.[10]

DEVELOPING STRATEGIC ALLIANCES

Some small firms have found it advantageous to develop **strategic alliances** with suppliers. This form of partnering enables the buying and selling firms to work much more closely together than is customary in a simple contractual arrangement.

M2M International Ltd. of Wallaceburg, Ontario, is a supplier of automotive moulds, and has a number of strategic alliances with mouldmakers and service providers in Taiwan, Singapore, the United States, and Germany. Y. C. Lin, general manager of Hon Yi Steel Mold Co., Ltd., one of M2M's Taiwanese partners says, "Undoubtedly, labour is cheaper in Taiwan, and that is an advantage. But the lifestyle is also different. Our people are willing and able to work overtime when needed, and we have a culture of continuous learning." While the Taiwanese firm brings concrete cost savings and reduced delivery times to the table, companies such as M2M offer intangible benefits such as proximity to and familiarity with large North American original equipment manufacturers (OEMs).[11]

MANAGING INVENTORY

Inventory management can make the difference between success and failure for a small firm. The larger the inventory investment, the more vital proper inventory management is. Inventory management is particularly important in small retail or wholesale firms, as inventory typically represents a major financial investment by these firms. The importance of managing working capital, including inventory, will be discussed in greater detail in Chapter 13. Suffice it to say here that businesses must be careful not to tie up too much of their working capital—the cash and near-cash assets needed to operate the business—in inventory. The fewer times inventory "turns" in a year (see Chapter 13) the more risky to have too much inventory. The impact on cash flow can be fatal.

OBJECTIVES OF INVENTORY MANAGEMENT

Both purchasing and inventory management share the same objective: to have the right goods in the right quantities at the right time and place. Achieving this general objective requires pursuing more specific subgoals of inventory control: ensuring continuous operations, maximizing sales, protecting assets, and minimizing inventory investment.

Ensuring continuous operations is particularly important in manufacturing, as delays caused by lack of materials or parts can be costly. Furthermore, sales can be maximized by completing production in a timely manner and by stocking an appropriate assortment of merchandise in retail stores and wholesale establishments. Protecting inventory against theft, shrinkage, and deterioration, and minimizing investment costs likewise contribute to operational efficiency and business profits.

INVENTORY COST CONTROL

Maintaining inventory at an optimum level—the level that minimizes stockouts and eliminates excess inventory—saves money and contributes to operating profits. To determine the optimum level, managers must pay close attention to purchase quantities, because those quantities affect inventory levels. The ideal quantity of an item to purchase (at least some of which will be carried in inventory) is the number of items that minimizes total inventory costs, or the **economic order quantity (EOQ).**

If a firm could order merchandise or raw materials and carry inventory with no expenses other than the cost of the items, management could be less concerned about what quantity to order at any given time. However, inventory costs are affected by both the costs of purchasing and the costs of carrying inventory—that is,

Total inventory costs = Total carrying costs + Total ordering costs

As noted earlier, carrying costs include storage costs, insurance premiums, the cost of money tied up in inventory, and losses due to spoilage or obsolescence. Carrying costs increase as inventories increase in size. Ordering costs, on the other hand, include expenses associated with preparing and processing purchase orders, and expenses related to receiving and inspecting the purchased items. The cost of placing an order is a fixed cost; therefore, total ordering costs increase as a firm purchases smaller quantities more frequently. Quantity discounts, if available, favour the placement of larger orders.

The point labelled EOQ in Exhibit 12-3 is the lowest point on the total costs curve; it coincides with the intersection of the carrying costs and ordering costs curves. In cases in which sufficient information on costs is available, this point can be calculated with some precision.[12] Even when the economic order quantity cannot be calculated with precision, a firm's goal must be to minimize both ordering costs and carrying costs.

ABC INVENTORY ANALYSIS

Some inventory items are more valuable or more critical to a firm's operations than others. Therefore, those items have a greater effect on costs and profits. As a general rule, managers should attend most carefully to those inventory items entailing the largest investment.

economic order quantity (EOQ)
the quantity to purchase in order to minimize total inventory costs

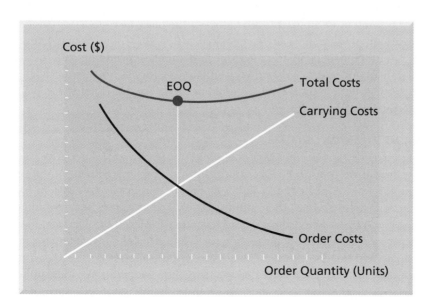

EXHIBIT **12-3**
Graphic Portrayal of the Economic Order Quantity

EXHIBIT **12-4**
Example of ABC Inventory Method

Part Number	Price (Cost)	Annual Demand	Dollar Volume	Cumulative Dollar Volume	Inventory Category
S 479	$19.50	225	$4387.50	$ 4387.50	A
P 360	6.90	450	3105.00	7492.50	A
Q 112	4.10	420	1722.00	9214.50	B
S 480	1.65	500	825.00	10,039.50	B
P 361	3.10	155	480.50	10,520.00	C
Q 113	0.75	475	356.25	10,876.25	C
S 450	26.00	10	260.00	11,136.25	C
S 410	.25	115	28.75	11,165.00	C
P 330	8.50	30	255.00	11,390.00	C
Q 108	.78	85	66.30	11,456.30	C

ABC method
a system of classifying items in inventory by relative value

One approach to inventory analysis, the **ABC method,** classifies inventory items into three categories based on value. The purpose of the ABC method is to focus managerial attention on the most important items. The number of categories could easily be expanded to four or more, if that seemed more appropriate for a particular firm.

In the A category are a few high-value inventory items that account for the largest percentage of total dollars or are otherwise critical in the production process and, therefore, deserve close control. They might be monitored, for example, by an inventory system that keeps a running record of receipts, withdrawals, and balances of each such item. In this way, a firm can avoid an unnecessarily heavy investment in costly inventory items. Category B items are less costly but deserve moderate managerial attention because they still make up a significant share of the firm's total inventory investment. Category C contains low-cost or noncritical items, such as paperclips in an office or nuts and bolts in a repair shop. The carrying costs of such items are not large enough to justify close control. These items might simply be checked periodically to ensure that a sufficient supply is available.

As can be seen in Exhibit 12-4, the highest-value inventory items are categorized as A, the next highest-value items are categorized as B, and the lowest-value items as C. In terms of inventory management, more time and attention would be paid to category A items, slightly less to category B, and very little to category C. Some experts suggest the top 20 percent of items by dollar value should be categorized as A items, the next 30 percent as B, and the remaining items as C.

JUST-IN-TIME INVENTORY SYSTEM

just-in-time inventory system
a method of reducing inventory levels to an absolute minimum

Reducing inventory levels remains a goal of all operations managers. The **just-in-time inventory system** attempts to cut inventory carrying costs by reducing inventory to an absolute minimum. Popularized in Japan as *kanban,* the just-in-time system has led to cost reductions there and in other countries. New items are received, presumably, just as the last item of that type from existing inventory is placed into service. Many large North American firms have adopted some form of the just-in-time system for inventory management, and small businesses can also benefit from its use.

Adoption of a just-in-time system necessitates close cooperation with suppliers. Supplier locations, production schedules, and transportation schedules must be carefully considered, as they all affect a firm's ability to obtain materials quickly and in a predictable manner—a necessary condition for using a just-in-time inventory system.

The potential for failures is high in the just-in-time system. Out-of-stock situations, which arise when delays or mistakes occur, may result in interrupted production or unhappy customers. Most firms using the just-in-time inventory system maintain some safety stock (a reserve amount for use in emergency) to minimize difficulties of this type. Although safety stock represents a compromise of the just-in-time philosophy, it protects a firm against large or unexpected withdrawals from inventory and delays in delivery of replacement items.

It is important to recognize that just-in-time will not work for all types of businesses, such as specialty retail outlets. Some of these retailers order seasonal products with long lead times. For example, ski/snowboard shops order in bulk months in advance. Special orders can be accommodated, but manufacturers are generally very slow in delivering them, since the cost of producing small or "one-off" orders is very high compared to the longer production runs they normally have. In general, just-in-time inventory works well for businesses that have predictable, ongoing demand for inventory items and where there are backup suppliers that can be called upon if supply problems are encountered. Most manufacturers with assembly-line-type manufacturing have adopted just-in-time. The most obvious example of this is automobile and other machinery manufacturers.

INVENTORY RECORD-KEEPING SYSTEMS

The larger the business, the greater the need for record keeping, but even a very small business needs a system for keeping tabs on its inventory. Because manufacturers are concerned with three broad categories of inventory (raw materials and supplies, work-in-process, and finished goods), their inventory records are more complex than those of wholesalers and retailers. Small firms should emphasize simplicity in their control methods. Too much control is as wasteful as it is unnecessary.

In most small businesses, inventory records are computerized. A large variety of software programs are available for this purpose; the manager, in consultation with the firm's accounting advisers, can select the software best suited for the particular business.

A **physical inventory system** depends on an actual count of items on hand. The counting is done in physical units such as pieces, gallons, and boxes. By using this method, a firm presumably gains an accurate record of its inventory level at a given point in time. Some businesses have an annual shutdown to count everything—a complete physical inventory. Others use **cycle counting,** scheduling different segments of the inventory for counting at different times during the year. This simplifies the inventorying process and makes it less of an ordeal for the business as a whole.

A **perpetual inventory system** provides an ongoing, current record of inventory items. It does not require a physical count. However, a physical count of inventory should be made periodically to ensure the accuracy of the system and to make adjustments for such factors as theft.

physical inventory system
a method that provides for periodic counting of items in inventory

cycle counting
a system of counting different segments of the physical inventory at different times during the year

perpetual inventory system
a method for keeping a running record of inventory

LOOKING BACK

1 Discuss the nature of the operations process for both products and services.

- Service and manufacturing operations typically differ in the extent of their contact with customers and the level of difficulty in establishing quality standards.
- The three types of manufacturing operations are job shops, repetitive manufacturing, and batch manufacturing.
- Operations management involves planning and scheduling activities that transform inputs into products or services.
- Proper plant maintenance is necessary for efficient operation and achievement of quality performance.
- Preventive maintenance is needed to minimize breakdowns in machinery; corrective maintenance is used to restore equipment to good condition.

2 Describe the need for management control systems.

- Several aspects of operations must be managed through management controls.
- Firms use management controls to monitor and manage such aspects as quality, productivity, output, waste, rework, and inventory.
- The control cycle is a period of time over which an activity is planned, measured, corrected, and replanned.
- A large-enough variance from the planned activity triggers management action to correct the problem.

3 Explain the key elements of total quality management (TQM) programs.

- Quality of products or services is a primary goal of the operations process.
- Quality management efforts are focused on meeting customer needs.
- Effective quality management requires an organizational culture that places a high value on quality.
- Quality management tools and techniques include employee involvement, quality circles, inspections, and statistical analysis.
- Service businesses can benefit from use of quality management programs.

4 Explain how reengineering and other methods of work improvement can increase productivity and make a firm more competitive.

- The competitive strength of a business depends on its level of productivity.
- Reengineering involves restructuring firms by redesigning their basic work processes.
- Laws of motion economy can be applied to make work easier and more efficient.
- Work may be analyzed through use of motion study and time study.

5 Discuss the importance of purchasing and the nature of key purchasing policies.

- Purchasing is important because it affects quality and profitability.
- A key decision for manufacturers is whether to make or buy components.
- In outsourcing, a small firm contracts with outside suppliers for accounting, repair, or other services and products.
- Decisions concerning diversifying sources of supply must take into account both the advantages and the disadvantages of having multiple suppliers.
- Purchasing policies may relate to concentrating or diversifying sources of supply.
- Careful selection of suppliers will identify those offering the best price, quality, and services.
- Paying bills promptly and dealing professionally with suppliers will help build good relationships, which in turn can bring benefits, such as training provided by a supplier.
- Strategic alliances enable small firms to work closely with their suppliers.

6 Describe ways to control inventory and minimize inventory costs.

- The calculation of economic order quantities, ABC inventory analysis, and the just-in-time inventory system can all help minimize inventory costs.
- Inventory record-keeping systems include the physical inventory method and the perpetual inventory method.

KEY TERMS

ABC method, p. 348
acceptance sampling, p. 331
attribute inspection, p. 331
batch manufacturing, p. 324
benchmarking, p. 330
continuous quality
    improvement, p. 337
control chart, p. 332
control cycle, p. 326
corrective maintenance, p. 325
cycle counting, p. 349
economic order quantity (EOQ),
    p. 347
inspection, p. 330
inspection standard, p. 331

ISO 9000, p. 332
ISO 14000, p. 332
job shops, p. 324
just-in-time inventory system, p. 348
laws of motion economy, p. 340
LEAN manufacturing, p. 338
make-or-buy decision, p. 341
motion study, p. 340
operations management, p. 322
operations process (production
    process), p. 322
outsourcing, p. 342
perpetual inventory system,
    p. 349
physical inventory system, p. 349

preventive maintenance, p. 325
production process, p. 322
productivity, p. 334
purchasing, p. 340
quality, p. 327
quality circle, p. 330
reengineering, p. 335
repetitive manufacturing, p. 324
statistical process control, p. 332
strategic alliance, p. 346
time study, p. 340
total quality management
    (TQM), p. 328
variable inspection, p. 331
variance, p. 326

DISCUSSION QUESTIONS

1. Defend the customer focus of quality management.
2. Describe the control cycle.
3. Explain why management control systems are important.
4. Explain what is meant by total quality management.
5. A small manufacturer does not believe that statistical quality control charts and sampling plans are useful. Can traditional methods suffice? Can 100 percent inspection by final inspectors eliminate all defective products? Why or why not?
6. How do operations processes differ for manufacturing firms and service firms?
7. Customer demand for services is generally not uniform during a day, week, or other period of time. What strategies can be used by service firms to better match a firm's capacity to perform services to customer demand for services?
8. Explain the purpose and nature of reengineering.
9. Doing something rapidly and doing it well are often incompatible. How can quality improvement possibly contribute to productivity improvement?
10. What conditions make purchasing a particularly vital function in a small business? Can the owner-manager of a small firm safely delegate purchasing authority to a subordinate? Explain.
11. Under what conditions should a small manufacturer either make component parts or buy them from others?
12. Explain the basic concept underlying the calculation of an economic order quantity.

YOU MAKE THE CALL

SITUATION 1

A college professor opened a furniture shop in Ontario and has watched it grow to 85 employees and $5 million in annual sales volume. The firm pro-duces high-quality chairs, tables, and other items for the contract furniture market. Each piece is sanded and polished, sealed with linseed oil, and finished with paste wax. No stain, colour, or varnish is added, and the furniture never needs refinishing.

As the firm has grown larger, it has begun to use the equivalent of mass production. Many of the original craftspeople have moved on and have been replaced by production workers. The founder is seeking to maintain quality through employee participation at all levels. He believes that quality can be maintained indefinitely if the company doesn't get too greedy. He has expressed his philosophy as follows:

> *We're still not driven by profit but by meaningful relationships among employees and between the producer and the user. It's a way of life. We throw out a lot of good stuff. If we had to produce something just to make a buck, I'd go back to teaching school.*

Question 1 How has this firm's growth made quality management easier or more difficult?

Question 2 The founder recognizes that people and relationships have a bearing on quality. What can he do to persuade or enable production employees to have the right attitude toward quality?

Question 3 The founder's comments suggest that profits and quality may be incompatible. When does making a profit lead to lower quality? Can or should this firm use financial incentives?

SITUATION 2

Derek Dilworth, owner of a small manufacturing firm, is trying to rectify the firm's thin working capital situation by carefully managing payments to major suppliers. These suppliers extend credit for 30 days, and customers are expected to pay within that time period. However, the suppliers do not automatically refuse subsequent orders when a payment is a few days late. Dilworth's strategy is to delay payment of most invoices for 10 to 15 days beyond the due date. Although he is not meeting the "letter of the law," he believes that the suppliers will go along with him rather than lose future sales. This practice enables Dilworth's firm to operate with sufficient inventory, avoid costly interruptions in production, and reduce the likelihood of an overdraft at the bank.

Question 1 What are the ethical implications of Dilworth's payment practices?

Question 2 What impact, if any, might these practices have on the firm's supplier relationships? How serious would this impact be?

SITUATION 3

The owner of a small food products company was confronted with an inventory control problem involving differences of opinion among his subordinates. His accountant, with the concurrence of his general manager, had decided to "put some teeth" into the inventory control system by deducting inventory shortages from the pay of route drivers who distributed the firm's products to stores in their respective territories. Each driver was considered responsible for the inventory on his or her truck.

When the first "short" paycheques arrived, drivers were angry. Sharing their concern, their immediate supervisor, the regional manager, first went to the general manager and then, getting no satisfaction there, appealed to the owner. The regional manager argued that there was no question about the honesty of the drivers. He said that he personally had created the inventory control system the company was using, and he admitted that the system was complicated and susceptible to clerical mistakes by the driver and by the office. He pointed out that the system had never been studied by the general manager or the accountant, and he maintained that it was ethically wrong to make deductions from the small salaries of honest drivers for simple record-keeping errors.

Question 1 What, if anything, is wrong with the general manager's approach to making sure that drivers do not steal or act carelessly? Is some method of enforcement necessary to ensure careful adherence to the inventory control system?

Question 2 Is it wrong to deduct from drivers' paycheques shortages documented by inventory records?

Question 3 How should the owner resolve this dispute?

EXPERIENTIAL EXERCISES

1. Outline the operations process involved in your present educational program. Be sure to identify inputs, operations, and outputs.
2. Outline, in as much detail as possible, your customary practices in studying for a specific course. Evaluate the methods you use, and specify changes that might improve your productivity.
3. Using the ABC inventory analysis method, classify some of your personal possessions into three categories. Include at least two items in each category.
4. Interview the manager of a bookstore about the type of inventory control system used in the store. Write a report in which you explain the methods used to avoid buildup of excessive inventory and any use made of inventory turnover ratios (ratios that relate the dollar value of inventory to the volume of sales).

EXPLORING THE WEB

1. To answer the following questions, consult the website of the American Society for Quality at http://www.asq.org.
   a. Choose the link for "Organization-Wide Approaches" under "Learn About Quality." What is the nature of ISO 9000 international certification for a small manufacturing company, and what organization sets the standards for such certification?
   b. Choose the link "Tools & Resources" under "Knowledge Centre" and select "Quality Tools" Summarize two quality management techniques used by professionals.
   c. Identify three other sites listed and describe the types of quality information available at those sites.
2. To answer the following questions, examine the website for the National Quality Institute at http://www.nqi.ca.
   a. Look at the requirements for PEP certification and show how it is related to quality performance.
   b. Find the home page of one of the winners and describe the information presented there.
3. To locate suppliers, you may search the Internet rather than consult the Yellow Pages.
   a. Examine the online version of Thomas Register at http://www.thomasnetr.com. Look under "Thomas Global" and explain how many companies are included, what countries are represented, and how many different languages present the information.
   b. Track down and list suppliers for a product of your choice, using Yahoo! at this time. For example, to find a source of frozen dough you could click on "Other Services," "Business, and Economy," "Business to Business," "Food and Beverage," "Baked Goods," "Manufacturing and Processing," "Manufacturers," then choose "Frozen Dough."

CHAPTER 13

Evaluating and Managing Financial Performance

IN THE SPOTLIGHT

The Turnaround Pros

After every wild party someone has to clean up the mess. Ian McKinnon has a reputation for turning around failing technology companies. His latest project is Mississauga, Ontario's Certicom Corp, a wireless encryption company that very nearly didn't survive the technology-sector meltdown.

What is McKinnon's turnaround philosophy? "We're business operators, not stock promoters or financial engineers. A lot of it is just focusing on the details of managing your expenses, making sure your revenues are growing and keeping your expenses less than your revenues," says McKinnon.

Less than three years after Certicom went public on the Toronto Stock Exchange in 1997, its share price was $250 per share. Buoyed by the tech-sector euphoria, management moved the head office to Silicon Valley, hired an expensive but inexperienced executive team, and leased enough space for 1000 people, even though it never employed more than 450. In 2001 the company reported a loss of over US$40 million on revenues of only $26.6 million. "They overhired, they overcommitted," says McKinnon, who blames Certicom's downfall on both the market pressure to spend all the easy capital and on executives' visions of grandeur. "For a while there was a corporate jet being rented periodically," he says. "They just went nuts."

When McKinnon joined Certicom in 2002, drastic measures were necessary. He moved the company back to Mississauga and abandoned a NASDAQ listing, a move that saved the company about $750,000 (US) per year. Three rounds of layoffs reduced the staff to 115, including all but eight of the underperforming 32-person sales force. McKinnon then rebuilt the management team, keeping only one of the cofounders of Certicom. The company slowly recovered and moved into the black, but probably not as fast as shareholders would have liked. "The focus is on customers and employees," says McKinnon, "and my view is that if you take care of those two interest groups, shareholders are going to benefit."

Certicom's story illustrates the need for companies to act quickly to reduce costs in response to changing business conditions. Axing staff may sound cruel, but it's like losing a limb to save the body. If the company is unable to survive the downturn in business, all 450 employees would be out of a job. This drastic action not only saved the company but also allowed Certicom to become an industry leader in encryption technology and a winner of the 2006 Canadian Advanced Technology Alliance Leadership Award for Advanced Technology for its elliptic curve cryptography (ECC) innovation.

http://www.certicom.com

© Arcaid/Alamy

Sources: Adapted from Andrew Wahl, "Bring in the Cleanup Crew," *Canadian Business,* vol. 75, iss. 21, November 11, 2002, p. 47. Used by permission; and http://www.certicom.com, accessed March 27, 2008.

Managers must have accurate, meaningful, and timely information if they are to make good decisions. This is particularly true of financial information about a firm's operations. An inadequate accounting system is a primary factor in small business failures. Owner-managers of small firms sometimes believe that they have less need for financial information because of their personal involvement in day-to-day operations, but they are deceiving only themselves.

Rarely are small business owner-managers expert accountants—nor should they expect to be *or even want to be.* But every one of them should know enough about the accounting process, including developing and interpreting financial statements, to recognize which accounting methods are best for their company.

This chapter examines the basic elements of an effective accounting system. Then suggestions are presented on how to use accounting data to draw conclusions about and manage a firm's financial performance.

financial statements (accounting statements)
reports of a firm's financial performance and resources, including an income statement, a balance sheet, and a statement of cash flows

1 **Describe the purpose and content of financial statements.**

ACCOUNTING STATEMENTS: TOOLS FOR DETERMINING FINANCING NEEDS

Financial statements, also called **accounting statements,** provide important information about a firm's performance and financial resources. Key financial statements are the income statement, the balance sheet, and the cash flow statement. Understanding the purpose and content of each of these financial statements is essential if an entrepreneur is to determine the start-up's financial requirements and assess the financial implications of the business plan.

THE INCOME STATEMENT

income statement (profit and loss statement)
a financial report showing the profit or loss from a firm's operations over a given period of time

An **income statement,** or **profit and loss statement,** indicates the amount of profits generated by a firm over a given time period, often a year. In its most basic form, the income statement may be represented by the following equation:

Sales − Expenses = Profits

cost of goods sold
the cost of producing or acquiring goods or services to be sold by a firm

Thus, the income statement answers the question "How profitable is the business?" In providing the answer, the statement reports financial information related to five broad areas of business activity:

gross profit
sales less the cost of goods sold

1. Revenue derived from selling the company's product or service
2. Costs of producing or acquiring the goods or services to be sold
3. Operating expenses related to both marketing and distributing the product or service to the customer and administering the business
4. Financing costs of doing business—specifically, the interest paid to the firm's creditors
5. Tax payments

operating expenses
costs related to general administrative expenses and selling and marketing a firm's product or service

As Exhibit 13-1 shows, the income statement begins with sales revenue, from which is subtracted the **cost of goods sold,** or the cost of producing or acquiring the product or service, to yield the firm's **gross profit.** Next, **operating expenses,** consisting of both selling and marketing expenses and administrative expenses, are deducted, to determine **operating income** (that is, earnings before interest and taxes). To this point, the firm's income has been affected solely by the activities involved in selling the company's

operating income
earnings before interest and taxes are paid

product or service, producing or acquiring the goods or service, and running the business, which are considered the firm's operating activities. Note that no financing costs have been subtracted to this point.

Earnings before taxes are found by deducting from the firm's operating income its **financing costs**—the firm's interest expense on its debt. Next, the firm's income taxes are calculated, based on its earnings before taxes and the applicable tax rate for the amount of income reported. For instance, if a firm had earnings before taxes of $100,000 and its tax rate was 28 percent, it would owe $28,000 in taxes ($0.28 \times \$100,000 = \$28,000$). When small firms sell their products or services on a cash-only basis, some business owners are tempted *not* to report all income for tax purposes. It is important to note that such an action is neither legal nor ethical.

The resulting figure is the **net income available to owners** (frequently called *net income*), which represents income that may be reinvested in the firm or distributed to its owners—provided, of course, cash is available to do so. As you will come to understand after you read the discussion of cash flow later in this chapter, a positive net income on an income statement does not necessarily mean that a firm has any cash.

Exhibit 13-1 is the 2008 income statement for Computer World Ltd., a fictional computer and software retailing company. The company had sales of $830,000 for the 12-month period ending December 31, 2008. The cost of goods sold was $540,000, resulting in a gross profit of $290,000. The company had $190,000 in operating expenses, which included marketing expenses, general and administrative expenses, and depreciation. After total operating expenses were subtracted, the company's operating income (earnings before interest and taxes) amounted to $100,000. To this point, we have calculated the profits based only on operating activities rather than financing decisions, such as how much debt or equity was used to finance the company's operations. The figure for operating income represents the income Computer World would generate if it were an all-equity company—that is, a business without any debt. The figure for operating income is important to the owners because it best measures a company's profitability on its asset investment before any money is distributed to investors and creditors. That is, it measures the financial attractiveness of a business opportunity.

Computer World's interest expense of $20,000 (the liability it incurred by using debt financing) is then deducted to arrive at the company's earnings (profits) before taxes: $80,000. If we assume a 25 percent tax rate, the company will incur $20,000 in income tax liability, leaving a net income of $60,000. The net income of $60,000 represents the "bottom line" of the income statement. This amount is the profit that was earned for the firm's owners on their investment. However, as shown at the bottom of Exhibit 13-1, dividends in the amount of $15,000 were paid to Computer World's owners; the remaining $45,000 ($60,000 net income less $15,000 in dividends) was retained by the firm and will appear as an increase in retained earnings on the balance sheet.

THE BALANCE SHEET

While an income statement reports the financial results of business operations over a period of time, a **balance sheet** provides a snapshot of a business's financial position at a specific point in time. Thus, a balance sheet captures the cumulative effects of all earlier financial decisions. At the given point in time, the balance sheet shows the assets a firm owns, the liabilities (or debt) outstanding or owed, and the amount the owners

financing costs
the amount of interest owed to lenders on borrowed money

net income available to owners (net income)
income that may be distributed to the owners or reinvested in the company

balance sheet
a financial report that shows a firm's assets, liabilities, and owners' equity capital at a specific point in time

Sales revenue		$830,000
Cost of goods sold	540,000	
Gross profit		$290,000
Operating expenses:		
Marketing expenses	$ 90000	
General and administrative expenses	72,000	
Depreciation	28,000	
Total operating expenses	$190,000	
Operating income	$100,000	
Interest expense	20,000	
Earnings before taxes	$ 80,000	
Income tax (25%)	20,000	
Net income		$60,000
Dividends paid	15,000	
Change in retained earnings	$ 45,000	

have invested in the business (their equity). In its simplest form, a balance sheet follows this formula:

Outstanding debt + Owners' equity = Total assets

Exhibit 13-2 illustrates representative elements in the balance sheet of a typical small firm, Computer World. Each of the three main components of the balance sheet—assets, debt capital, and owners' equity capital—will be discussed in the following sections.

TYPES OF ASSETS

A company's assets, shown on the top half of Exhibit 13-2, fall into three categories: (1) current assets, (2) fixed assets, and (3) other assets.

current assets (working capital)
liquid assets that can be converted into cash within a company's operating cycle

Current assets, or **working capital,** comprise those assets that are relatively liquid; that is, they can be converted into cash within a given operating cycle. Current assets include cash, accounts receivable, inventories, and prepaid expenses. Ineffective management of current assets is a prime cause of financial problems in small companies. (We will discuss this issue more thoroughly later in the chapter.)

- *Cash:* Every firm must have cash for current business operations. Also, a reservoir of cash is needed to compensate for the unequal flow of funds into the business (cash receipts) and out of the business (cash expenditures). The size of a firm's cash reservoir is determined not only by the volume of sales but also by the predictability of cash receipts and cash payments.

accounts receivable
the amount of credit extended to customers that is currently outstanding

- *Accounts receivable:* The firm's accounts receivable consists of payments due from its customers from previous credit sales. **Accounts receivable** can become a significant asset for firms that sell on a credit basis.
- *Inventories:* The raw materials and products held by the firm for eventual sale constitute the inventory. Although their relative importance differs from one type of business to another, inventories often account for a major part of a firm's working capital. Seasonality of sales and production levels affect the size of inventories. Retail

EXHIBIT **13-2**
Balance Sheets for Computer World Ltd. for December 31, 2007 and 2008

	2007	2008	Change
Assets			
Current assets:			
Cash	$ 38,000	$ 43,000	$ 5000
Accounts receivable	70,000	78,000	8000
Inventories	175,000	210,000	35,000
Prepaid expenses	12,000	14,000	2000
Total current assets	$295,000	$345,000	$ 50,000
Fixed assets:			
Gross plant and equipment	$760,000	$838,000	$ 78,000
Accumulated depreciation	355,000	383,000	28,000
Net plant and equipment	$405,000	$455,000	$ 50,000
Land	70,000	70,000	0
Total fixed assets	$475,000	$525,000	$ 50,000
Goodwill and patents	30,000	50,000	20,000
Total assets	$800,000	$920,000	$120,000
Debt (Liabilities) and Equity (Net Worth)			
Current liabilities:			
Accounts payable	$ 61,000	$ 76,000	$ 15,000
Income tax payable	12,000	15,000	3000
Accrued wages and salaries	4000	5000	1000
Interest payable	2000	4000	2000
Total current liabilities	$ 79,000	$100,000	$ 21,000
Long-term notes payable	146,000	200,000	54,000
Total liabilities	$225,000	$300,000	$ 75,000
Common shares	$300,000	$300,000	$ 0
Retained earnings	275,000	320,000	45,000
Total shareholders' equity	$575,000	$620,000	$ 45,000
Total debt and equity	$800,000	$920,000	$120,000

stores, for example, may find it desirable to carry a larger-than-normal inventory during the pre-Christmas season.

- *Prepaid expenses:* A company often needs to prepay expenses. For example, insurance premiums may be due before coverage begins, or rent may have to be paid in advance. For accounting purposes, prepaid expenses are recorded on the balance sheet as current assets and, then, as they are used, shown on the income statement as operating expenses.

Fixed assets are the more permanent assets in a business. They might include machinery and equipment, buildings, and land. Some businesses are more capital intensive than others—for example, a motel is more capital intensive than a gift store—and, therefore, have more fixed assets.

fixed assets relatively permanent resources intended for use in the business

Intangible assets the third category includes such intangible assets as patents, copyrights, and goodwill. For a start-up company, organizational costs—costs incurred in organizing and promoting the business—may also be included in this category.

intangible assets assets that have no physical form but still provide value to the business

TYPES OF FINANCING

The bottom half of the balance sheet in Exhibit 13-2, Debt (Liabilities) and Equity (Net Worth), indicates how the firm is financing its assets. Financing comes from two main sources: debt capital (liabilities) and ownership equity. Debt capital is money that has been borrowed and must be repaid at some predetermined date. Ownership equity, on the other hand, represents the owners' investment in the company—money they have personally put into the firm without any specific date for repayment. Owners recover their investment by withdrawing money from the firm or by selling their interest in it.

Debt capital is financing provided by a creditor. As shown in Figure 13-2, it is divided into (1) current, or short-term, debt and (2) long-term debt. Current debt, or short-term liabilities, includes borrowed money that must be repaid within the next 12 months. Sources of current debt may be classified as follows:

accounts payable (trade credit)
outstanding credit payable to suppliers

- **Accounts payable** represents the credit extended by suppliers to a firm when it purchases inventories. The purchasing firm usually is given 30 or 60 days to pay for the inventory. This form of credit is also called **trade credit**.

  Other payables include interest expenses and income taxes that are owed and will come due within the year.

accrued expenses
short-term liabilities that have been incurred but not paid

- **Accrued expenses** are short-term liabilities that have been incurred but not yet paid. For example, employees may have performed work for which they will not be paid until the following week or month.
- Short-term notes represent cash amounts borrowed from a bank or other lending source for a short period of time, such as 90 days. Short-term notes are a primary source of financing for most small businesses, as these businesses have access to fewer sources of long-term capital than their larger counterparts.

long-term debt
loans from banks or other sources with repayment terms of more than 12 months

Long-term debt includes loans from banks or other sources that lend money for longer than 12 months. When a firm borrows money for five years to buy equipment, it signs an agreement—a long-term note—promising to repay the money in five years. When a firm borrows money for 30 years to purchase real estate, such as a warehouse or office building, the real estate stands as collateral for the long-term loan, which is called a mortgage. If the borrower is unable to repay the loan, the lender can take the real estate in settlement.

Owners' equity capital is money that the owners invest in a business. Note that they are only *residual owners* of the business; that is, creditors must be paid before the owners can retrieve any of their equity capital from the business's income. Likewise, if the company is liquidated, creditors are always paid before the owners are paid.

The amount of ownership equity in a business is equal to (1) the total amount of the owners' investments in the business and (2) the cumulative profits (net of any losses) retained within the business from its beginning less any cash withdrawals by the owners.

retained earnings
profits that are reinvested in the business instead of being distributed to the owners

The second item (profits less withdrawals) is frequently called **retained earnings**—because these earnings have been reinvested in the business instead of being distributed to the owners. Thus, the basic formula for owners' equity capital is as follows:

$$\text{Owners' equity} = \text{Owners' investment} + \underbrace{\text{Cumulative profits} - \text{Owners' cash withdrawals}}$$

$$\text{or} \quad \text{Owners' equity} = \text{Owners' investment} + \text{Earnings retained within the firm}$$

In summary, financing for a new business derives from two sources: debt capital and ownership equity. Debt capital is money borrowed from financial institutions, suppliers, and other lenders. Owners' equity capital represents the owners' investment in the company, either through funds invested in the firm or through profits retained in the business.

DIFFERENCES IN FINANCIAL STATEMENTS BETWEEN CORPORATIONS AND SOLE PROPRIETORSHIPS OR PARTNERSHIPS

The principal differences between financial statements for corporations like Computer World and a sole proprietorship or partnership conducting the same kind of business are in the treatment of monies taken out of the firm by the owners, proprietor, or partners and in the treatment of retained earnings.

Recall from Chapter 10 that corporations exist as a separate legal entity from their owners (shareholders). In corporations, owners who work in the business are considered employees of the corporation and are paid a salary or other kind of income. They may also be paid dividends out of earnings of the corporation. The corporation files its own tax return with Canada Revenue Agency. In sole proprietorships and partnerships, the business does not have a separate legal existence. All of the profits of the business are considered to be distributed to the proprietor or partners at the end of each year and are claimed as business income on their personal income tax returns. During the year, the money taken out by the proprietor or partners—what would be considered a salary in a corporation—comes out in the form of a draw against anticipated profits. There are no income tax, Employment Insurance, or Canada Pension Plan deductions from drawings, nor are the drawings recorded as an expense of the business.

In a corporation the profits not distributed to owners in the form of dividends are retained in the business as retained earnings. These accumulate over time and are a part of the equity of the business as discussed above. Because the earnings of a proprietorship or partnership are considered to be the personal income of the proprietor or partners, there are no retained earnings in a proprietorship or partnership. It should be noted, however, that a sole proprietorship or partnership should still keep accurate financial statements just as a corporation does.

Exhibit 13-2 presents balance sheets for Computer World for December 31, 2007, and December 31, 2008, along with the change for each category. By referring to the columns representing the two balance sheets, you can see the financial position of the firm at the beginning *and* at the end of 2008.

The 2007 and 2008 balance sheets for Computer World show that the firm began 2008 (ended 2007) with $800,000 in total assets and ended 2008 with total assets of $920,000. These assets were financed 30 percent by debt and 70 percent by equity. About half of the equity came from investments made by the owners (common shares), and the other half came from reinvesting profits in the business (retained earnings). Referring back to the income statement in Exhibit 13-1, note that the $45,000 increase in retained earnings, shown in the Changes column in Exhibit 13-2, equals the firm's net income for the year less the dividends paid to the owners.

Let's consider how the income statement and the balance sheet complement each other. Because the balance sheet is a snapshot of a firm's financial condition at a point in time, and the income statement reports results over a given time period, both are required for a complete picture of a firm's financial position. Exhibit 13-3 shows how the income statement and the balance sheet fit together. To understand how a firm performed during 2008, you must know the firm's financial position at the beginning of the year (balance sheet on December 31, 2007), its financial performance during the

EXHIBIT **13-3**
*Income Statement
and Balance Sheet
Relationship*

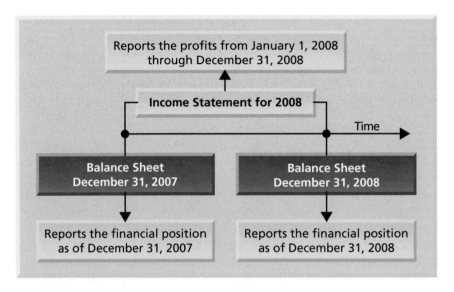

year (income statement for 2008), and its financial position at the end of the year (balance sheet on December 31, 2008).

CASH FLOW MEASUREMENT

It's important to note that, although a company's income statement may show profits, these profits are not necessarily represented by cash. Although accounting profits are the primary measure of a firm's performance, having actual cash in the firm's bank account is essential, too. Many entrepreneurs have been deceived by a good-looking income statement, only to discover that their companies are running out of cash. For this reason, the third financial statement used by businesses is the **statement of cash flows.** Most entrepreneurs find this statement to be difficult to understand and calculate, and therefore not useful in managing cash. As with all financial statements, the statement of cash flows is historical, and therefore of little use in anticipating cash needs. A more effective tool for this is the cash flow forecast, which will be explained in greater detail later in this chapter. In addition to having an up-to-date cash flow forecast, small businesses should keep a running total of cash in the bank—very much like knowing the balance in your personal bank accounts.

**statement of cash
flows**

a financial report
that shows changes
in a firm's cash posi-
tion over a given
period of time

2 **Identify the basic
requirements for an
accounting system.**

BASIC REQUIREMENTS FOR ACCOUNTING SYSTEMS

An accounting system structures the flow of financial information to provide a complete picture of a firm's financial activities. Conceivably, a few very small firms may not require formal financial statements. Most, however, need at least monthly financial statements, which should be computer generated. The benefits of using a computer in developing financial information are so great and the costs so low that it makes absolutely no sense to do otherwise.

Regardless of its level of sophistication, an accounting system for a small business should accomplish the following objectives:

- Provide an accurate, thorough picture of operating results
- Permit a quick comparison of current data with prior years' operating results and budgetary goals

- Offer financial statements for use by management, bankers, and prospective creditors
- Facilitate prompt filing of reports and tax returns to regulatory and tax-collecting government agencies
- Reveal employee fraud, theft, waste, and record-keeping errors

THE RECORD-KEEPING SYSTEM

An accounting system provides the framework for managerial control of a firm. Its effectiveness rests on a well-designed and well-managed record-keeping system. In addition to the financial statements intended for external use with bankers and investors (the balance sheet, the income statement, and the statement of cash flows), internal accounting records should be kept. The major types of internal accounting records are as follows:

- *Accounts receivable records:* Records of receivables are vital for not only making decisions on credit extension but also billing accurately and maintaining good customer relations. An analysis of these records will reveal the effectiveness of a firm's credit and collection policies.
- *Accounts payable records:* Records of liabilities show what the firm owes to suppliers, facilitate the taking of cash discounts, and allow payments to be made when due.
- *Inventory records:* Adequate records are essential for the control and security of inventory items. Inventory records supply information for use in making purchases, maintaining adequate stock levels, and computing turnover ratios.
- *Payroll records:* Payroll records show the total salaries paid to employees and provide a base for computing and paying payroll taxes.
- *GST and sales tax records:* All businesses are required to collect and remit Goods and Services Taxes and, except in Alberta, provincial sales taxes. There are substantial fines and penalties for late or incorrect payments, so correct records must be kept.
- *Cash records:* Carefully maintained records showing all receipts and disbursements are necessary to safeguard cash. They provide essential information about cash flows and cash balances.
- *Fixed asset records:* Fixed asset records show the original cost of each asset and the depreciation taken to date, along with other information such as the condition of the asset.
- *Other accounting records:* Among the other accounting records that are vital to the efficient operation of a small business are the insurance register (showing all policies in force), records of leaseholds, and records of the firm's investments outside its business.

COMPUTER SOFTWARE PACKAGES

Software packages can be used to generate the required accounting records. Most computer software packages include the following features:

- A chequebook that automatically calculates a firm's cash balance, prints cheques, and reconciles the account with the bank statement at month's end
- Automatic preparation of income statements, balance sheets, and statements of cash flows

- A cash budget or cash flow forecast that compares actual expenditures with budgeted expenditures
- Preparation of subsidiary journal accounts—accounts receivable, accounts payable, and other high-activity accounts

In addition, numerous software packages fulfill specialized accounting needs such as graphing, cash flow analysis, and tax preparation. Although the options are almost unlimited in terms of accounting software programs appropriate for use in a small firm, there are several leaders in the entry-level category. Ranging in cost from $100 to $500, they include Simply Accounting (http://simplyaccounting.com), DacEasy (http://daceasy.com), M.Y.O.B. (Mind Your Own Business—http://www.myob.com), QuickBooks (http://www.quickbooks.com), Peachtree by Sage (http://www.peachtree.com), and NetSuite (http://www.oraclesmallbusiness.com). Although all these programs have been well tested and widely used, the small business owner should carefully consider the appropriateness of computer software or hardware before purchasing it. The chance of acquiring computer equipment or programs that do not fit a firm's needs is still significant.

OUTSIDE ACCOUNTING SERVICES

Instead of having an employee or a member of the owner's family keep records, a firm may have its financial records kept by a chartered accountant, bookkeeping firm, or service bureau that caters to small businesses. Very small firms often find it convenient to have the same person or agency keep their books and prepare their financial statements and tax returns.

With improvements in Internet security, many businesses now transmit their accounting data to a bookkeeper via the Internet and receive their financial statements back the same way. This means that even businesses in remote areas can easily and securely have access to services to fill their accounting needs.

Numerous small public accounting firms offer complete accounting services to small businesses. Such accounting firms usually offer their services at a lower cost than larger accounting firms. However, larger accounting firms have begun paying closer attention to the accounting needs of small businesses, and, although their fees may be higher, discounts are usually available. Cost is, of course, an important consideration in selecting an accountant, but other major factors, such as whether the accountant has experience in the particular industry in which the entrepreneur is operating, should play a dominant role in this decision.

The importance of a good accountant to a small business cannot be overemphasized. Accountants, in addition to their training, have experience with a wide variety of businesses across many different industries. This makes them excellent advisers to business owners. Further, even though a small business might be incorporated, there is a great need for tax planning for both the owners and the business to minimize the taxes paid and to plan for the eventual harvest of the business (see Chapter 15 for a more in-depth discussion of harvesting a business). Many accountants specialize in family or owner-managed businesses and can arrange the affairs of both the business and its owners to achieve the short- and long-term financial objectives of the owners.

ALTERNATIVE ACCOUNTING OPTIONS

Accounting records can be kept in just about any form as long as they provide users with needed data and meet legal requirements. Very small firms have some options in selecting accounting systems and accounting methods. Two such options—cash versus accrual accounting and single-entry versus double-entry systems—reflect the most basic issues in an accounting system.

CASH VERSUS ACCRUAL ACCOUNTING

The major distinction between cash and accrual accounting is in the point at which a firm reports revenue and expenses. The **cash method of accounting** is easier to use; it reports revenue and expenses only when cash is received or a payment is made. In contrast, the **accrual method of accounting** reports revenue and expenses when they are incurred, regardless of when the cash is received or payment is made.

The accrual method, while involving more record keeping, is preferable because it provides a more realistic measure of profitability within an accounting period. Canada Revenue Agency requires almost all Canadian businesses to use accrual accounting (farmers and fishers are the main ones allowed to use the cash method of accounting).

SINGLE-ENTRY VERSUS DOUBLE-ENTRY SYSTEMS

A single-entry record-keeping system is occasionally still found in the very small business. It is not, however, a system recommended for firms that are striving to grow and achieve effective financial planning. A single-entry system neither incorporates a balance sheet nor directly generates an income statement. **A single-entry system** is basically a chequebook system of receipts and disbursements.

Most introductory accounting textbooks provide information on setting up a **double-entry system.**[1] This type of accounting system provides a self-balancing mechanism in the form of two counterbalancing entries for each transaction recorded. It can be done with the record-keeping journals and ledgers found in most office supply retail stores. However, the relatively simple accounting software programs designed for small firms are preferable.

INTERNAL ACCOUNTING CONTROLS

As already noted, an effective accounting system is vital to a firm's success. Without the information it provides, management cannot make informed decisions. However, the quality of a firm's accounting system is dependent on the effectiveness of the controls that exist within the firm. **Internal control** is a system of checks and balances that plays a key role in safeguarding a firm's assets and in enhancing the accuracy and reliability of its financial statements. The importance of internal control has long been recognized in large corporations. Some owners of smaller companies, concerned about the cost or appropriateness of a system of internal control for a small company, don't appreciate its value—but they should.

Building internal controls may be difficult within a small company, but it is no less important than for a large company. The absence of internal controls significantly increases the chances of not only fraud and theft but also bad decisions based on inaccurate and untimely accounting information. Effective internal controls are also

---

Explain two alternative accounting options. **3**

cash method of accounting
a method of accounting that reports transactions only when cash is received or a payment is made

accrual method of accounting
a method of accounting that matches revenues when they are earned against the expenses associated with those revenues

single-entry system
a chequebook system of accounting reflecting only receipts and disbursements

double-entry system
a self-balancing accounting system that uses journals and ledgers

Describe the purpose of and procedures related to internal control. **4**

internal control
a system of checks and balances that safeguards assets and enhances the accuracy and reliability of financial statements

necessary for an audit by independent accountants. Chartered accountants are unwilling to express an opinion about a firm's financial statements if the firm lacks adequate internal controls.

Although a complete description of an internal control system is beyond the scope of this textbook, it is important to understand the concept. An example of an internal control is separation of employees' duties, so that the individual maintaining control over an asset is not the same person recording transactions in the accounting ledgers. That is, the employee who collects cash from customers should not be allowed to reconcile the bank statement. Here are some other examples of internal control from one author's experience:

- Identifying the various types of transactions that require the owners' authorization
- Establishing a procedure to ensure that cheques presented for signature are accompanied by complete supporting documentation
- Limiting access to accounting records
- Sending bank statements directly to the owner or at least having a different employee responsible for reconciling the bank account than the one who prepares cheques and deposits
- Periodically reviewing all suppliers to ensure no fraudulent invoices are paid for goods or services not received
- Safeguarding blank cheques
- Requiring all employees to take regular vacations so that any irregularity is likely to be revealed
- Controlling access to the computer facilities

The importance of developing an effective system of internal control cannot be overemphasized. Extra effort may be needed to implement internal controls in a small company, in which business procedures may be informal and segregation of duties is difficult because of the limited number of employees. Even so, it is best to try to develop such controls. An accountant may be of assistance in minimizing the problems that can result from the absence of internal controls.

ASSESSMENT OF FINANCIAL PERFORMANCE

Once an effective accounting system is in place, a firm's owner must determine how to use the data it generates most productively. Mark Twain said, "He who does not read is no better off than he who cannot read." An owner who has a good accounting system but doesn't use it is in the same situation. This section provides a framework for interpreting financial statements, designed to clarify these statements for individuals who never took an accounting course or who had difficulty with such a course in college or university.

An owner needs to understand the financial effect—positive or negative—that management decisions may have. Ultimately, the results of operating decisions appear in a firm's financial statements.

It is important to understand that comparisons can be made in only two ways: with other firms in the industry of a similar size and with historical performance. The exact methods used to interpret financial statements can vary, with the perspective of the interpreter determining what areas are emphasized. For example, if a banker and an

IN THE TRENCHES

Entrepreneurial Experiences

Can Cost Control Specialists Help You?

Finding ways to save money has always been a key part of managing a business. One hundred years ago it was all about using people more efficiently; today the emphasis is on chopping unseen, often unnecessary, expenses. Firms that track down hidden costs are finding this pursuit to be very profitable, for themselves and for their clients. One such company is ERA Canada, formerly Expense Reduction Analysts Canada, which operates in 18 countries including Canada.

Canadian President Ross Pinkerton says it's not always easy for a company to take on the hard work of keeping expenses to a minimum. And face it, adds Pinkerton, reducing a business's expenses—especially everyday general operating or nonstrategic costs—"isn't exactly a sexy proposition compared to, say, launching a new marketing campaign or brainstorming for new ways to grow revenues." Focusing on "nonstrategic" cost, the company looks at everything from merchant card processing fees to office equipment, printing, stationery, advertising, and cleaning services and supplies.

How do companies lose control over spending? Senior management is more concerned with large-scale expenditures, and over time the day-to-day spending gets out of control. Management is busy and doesn't have the time to watch the nonstrategic expenses, according to Pinkerton. By providing additional resources ERA is able to do the research into costs and negotiate with suppliers, delivering cost savings of 15 to 20 percent on the areas it reviews for its clients.

ERA makes its money by taking a percentage of the savings, so one advantage to clients is that they don't pay for the service unless the consultants can actually reduce costs.

Sources: Zena Olijnyk, "Stretch Your Dollar," *Canadian Business,* Vol. 77, No. 16 (August 29, 2004), pp. 86–87; John Cooper, "Bottom Line Specialists," *CMA Management,* Vol. 74, Iss. 4, May 2000, pp. 22–25.

entrepreneur were analyzing the same financial statements, they might focus on different data. But whatever perspective is taken, the issues are fundamentally the same and are categorized into four areas:

1. *Liquidity:* does the firm have the capacity to meet its short-term (one year or less) financial commitments?
2. *Profitability:* is the firm producing adequate operating profits on its assets?
3. *Stability:* how is the firm financing its assets?
4. *Return to owners:* are the owners (shareholders) receiving an acceptable return on their equity investment?

Answering these questions requires restating the data from the income statement and the balance sheet in relative terms, or **financial ratios.** Only in this way can comparisons be made with other firms through industry averages, and across time. Typically, the industry averages or norms used for comparison purposes are those published by Industry Canada, Statistics Canada, or companies such as Dun & Bradstreet.

financial ratios
restatements of selected income statement and balance sheet data in relative terms

EXHIBIT **13-4**

*Financial Ratios for
Retail Electronics and
Appliance Stores
(Industry SIC Code
5731 and NAICS
Code 443)*

	Median Firms	**Top 25%**
Current ratio	1.6	2.5
Quick ratio	0.7	0.7
Accounts receivable collection period (days)	16.0	10.0
Inventory turnover*	3.77	1.3
Gross profit margin	33.7%	30.5%
Return on equity (before tax)	0.4%	47.4%
Net profit margin	1.2%	1.6%
Return on assets	−1.4%	−1.4%
Debt/equity	1.64	1.58
*Calculated from data from both sources		

Exhibit 13-4 shows the industry norms from Dun & Bradstreet for small personal computer stores, with selected data from Industry Canada's Performance Plus, available at http://www.sme.ic.gc.ca. One caution regarding using this data is that it is over two years old. Another is that the Dun & Bradstreet data are taken from the 2006 voluntary reporting by businesses in this category and represent data for the median firms and top 25 percent of firms by profitability. Performance Plus data is about two years older (i.e., 2004) than Dun & Bradstreet's, but is also taken from financial statements filed with corporate tax returns. Since Dun & Bradstreet's information is from voluntary submissions and Industry Canada's is from mandatory filings, there are a larger number of companies in the Performance Plus database, making the information potentially more accurate.

CAN THE FIRM MEET ITS FINANCIAL COMMITMENTS?

5 Evaluate a firm's liquidity.

liquidity
the ability of a firm
to meet maturing
debt obligations by
having adequate
working capital
available

A business—or a person, for that matter—that has a lot of money relative to the amount of debt owed is described as highly liquid. More accurately, the **liquidity** of a business is defined as the firm's ability to meet maturing debt obligations. That is, does a firm now have or will it have in the future the resources to pay creditors when debts come due?

This question can be answered in two ways: (1) by comparing the firm's assets that are relatively liquid in nature with the debt coming due in the near term or (2) by examining the timeliness with which liquid assets are being converted into cash.

MEASURES OF LIQUIDITY

The first measure of liquidity compares cash and the assets that should be converted into cash within the year against the debt (liabilities) that is coming due and will be payable within the year. The assets are the current assets, and the debt consists of the current liabilities in the balance sheet. The first measure is **working capital,** expressed simply as total current assets *minus* total current liabilities. For Computer World this is $345,000 − $100,000 = $245,000 (see Exhibit 13-2). Positive working capital therefore is the net short-term assets the company can use to operate. It is generally not possible to compare this to industry figures. We can, however compare the working capital to prior years to see the trend. Working capital in 2007 was $216,000, so Computer World has increased working capital compared to the previous year. A better measure of liquidity, and a relative one that can be compared to both historic performance and the industry, is the **current ratio:**

$$Current\ ratio = \frac{Current\ assets}{Current\ liabilities}$$

Since the three primary current assets are cash, accounts receivable, and inventories, this measure of liquidity can be made more restrictive by excluding inventories, the least liquid of the current assets, in the numerator. This revised ratio is called the **acid-test ratio,** or **quick ratio**:

$$Acid\text{-}test\ ratio = \frac{Current\ assets - Inventories}{Current\ liabilities}$$

Let's compute the current ratio and the acid-test ratio from the financial statements for Computer World Leasing Company, which were presented in Exhibit 13-2:

Calculations of the current ratio and the acid-test ratio for 2008 follow:

$$Current\ ratio = \frac{Current\ assets}{Current\ liabilities} = \frac{\$345{,}000}{\$100{,}000} = 3.45$$

$$Acid\text{-}test\ ratio = \frac{Current\ assets - Inventories}{Current\ liabilities}$$

$$= \frac{\$345{,}000 - \$210{,}000}{\$100{,}000} = 1.35$$

These figures are then compared with the prior year and with industry norms, or averages, reported by Performance Plus and Dun & Bradstreet:

2008 current ratio = 3.45

2008 acid test (quick) ratio = 1.35

Industry norm for current ratio = 1.6 (median firms)

In terms of the current ratio and the acid-test ratio, Computer World is more liquid than the average firm in its industry. Computer World has $3.45 in current assets for every $1 in current liabilities (debt), compared to $1.60 for a "typical" firm in the industry. The firm has $1.35 in current assets less inventories per $1 of current debt, compared to the industry norm of $0.90 (all firms). On both measures Computer World is outperforming the "average" firm in the industry. If the acid-test or quick ratio had been lower than the industry comparator it would indicate the firm had more inventories relative to current debt than most other firms. Which ratio should be given greater weight depends on the actual liquidity of the inventories. We'll return to this issue shortly.

We can see from the comparison of the ratios from 2007 to 2008 that both the current ratio and acid-test ratio in 2008 are lower than in 2007. This indicates that Computer World is carrying more inventory relative to current debt than in 2007, but is still less than other firms in the industry.

current ratio
a measure of a company's relative liquidity, determined by dividing current assets by current liabilities

acid-test ratio (quick ratio)
a measure of a company's liquidity that excludes inventories

Another measure of liquidity examines a firm's ability to convert accounts receivable and inventory into cash on a timely basis. The ability to convert accounts receivable into cash may be measured by computing how long it takes on average to collect the firm's receivables. In other words, how many days of sales are outstanding in the form of accounts receivable? This question can be answered by computing the **average collection period:**

average collection period
the average time it takes a firm to collect its accounts receivable

$$\text{Average collection period} = \frac{\text{Accounts receivable}}{\text{Daily credit sales}}$$

For purposes of illustration, if we assume that all sales are credit sales, as opposed to cash sales, the average collection period in 2008 for Computer World is 34.3 days:

$$\text{Average collection period} = \frac{\text{Accounts receivable}}{\text{Daily credit sales}}$$

$$= \frac{\$78,000}{\$830,000 \div 365} = 34.30 \text{ (rounded to 34)}$$

Industry norm for average collection period = 16 (median firms)

Comparing this value to the industry norm of 16 days, we find that Computer World collects its receivables about 18 days—about two and a half weeks—slower than the average firm in the industry. While Computer World is taking longer than most firms in the industry to collect from customers, meaning this trend should be watched in the future, it appears that the company's accounts receivable are of reasonable liquidity when viewed from the perspective of the length of time required to convert receivables into cash.

To gain some insight into the liquidity of Computer World's inventories, we now need to determine how many times the firm is turning over its inventories during the year. The **inventory turnover** is calculated as follows:

inventory turnover
the number of times inventories "roll over" during a year

$$\text{Inventory turnover} = \frac{\text{Cost of goods sold}}{\text{Inventory}}$$

Note that sales in this ratio are shown at the firm's cost, as opposed to the full market value when sold. Since the inventory (the denominator) is at cost, it is desirable to also measure sales (the numerator) on a cost basis in order to avoid a biased answer. As a practical matter, however, sales (at full-market value) are often used instead of cost of goods sold by suppliers of industry norm data. Thus, for consistency in comparisons, it may be necessary to use the sales figure in the numerator.

The inventory turnover for Computer World is calculated as follows:

$$\text{Inventory turnover} = \frac{\text{Cost of goods sold}}{\text{Inventory}}$$

$$= \frac{\$540,000}{\$210,000} = 2.57$$

Industry norm for inventory turnover = 3.77 (median firms)

This analysis reveals a significant problem for Computer World. The firm is carrying excessive inventory, possibly even some obsolete inventory. That is, it is generating only $2.57 in sales for every $1 of inventory held, compared to $3.77 in sales for the average firm. It is now more obvious why the current ratio made the firm look better than the acid-test ratio: Inventory is a larger component of current ratio for Computer World than for other firms. So, the current ratio for Computer World is not totally comparable with the industry norm.

IS THE FIRM PRODUCING ADEQUATE OPERATING PROFITS ON ITS ASSETS?

Another question that is vitally important to a firm's investors is whether operating profits—profits that will be available for distribution to all the firm's investors—are sufficient relative to the total amount of assets invested. Exhibit 13-5 provides an overview of the computation of the rate of return on all capital invested in a firm, both by creditors and by common stockholders. The total capital from various investors becomes the firm's total assets. These assets are invested for the express purpose of producing operating profits—profits that are then distributed to creditors and stockholders. A comparison of operating profits and total invested assets reveals the rate of return that is being earned on all the capital.

The profits—and, more importantly, cash flows—are then shared by each investor or investment group according to the terms of its investment agreement. Based on the amount of profits flowing to each investor, the rate of return on each investment can be computed.

MEASURING A FIRM'S RETURN ON INVESTMENT

The first step in analyzing a firm's return on investment is finding the rate of return on the total invested capital (capital from all investors)—a rate of return that is independent of how the company is financed (debt versus equity). The rate is arrived at by calculating the **operating income return on investment (OIROI),** which compares a firm's **operating income (earnings before interest and taxes)** to its total invested capital or total assets. The operating income return on investment is computed as follows:

$$Operating\ income\ return\ on\ investment = \frac{Operating\ income}{Total\ assets}$$

The operating income return on investment for Computer World for 2008 is as follows:

$$Operating\ income\ return\ on\ investment = \frac{Operating\ income}{Total\ assets}$$

$$= \frac{\$100,000}{\$920,000} = 0.1087, or\ 10.87\%$$

Industry norm for operating income return on investment = 3.0%

It is evident that the firm's return on total invested capital is much higher than the average rate of return for the industry. For some reason, Computer World is generating more operating income on each dollar of assets than its competitors.

Sidebar notes:

Assess a firm's operating profitability. **6**

operating income return on investment (OIROI)
a measure of operating profits relative to total assets

operating income (earnings before interest and taxes)
profits before interest and taxes are paid

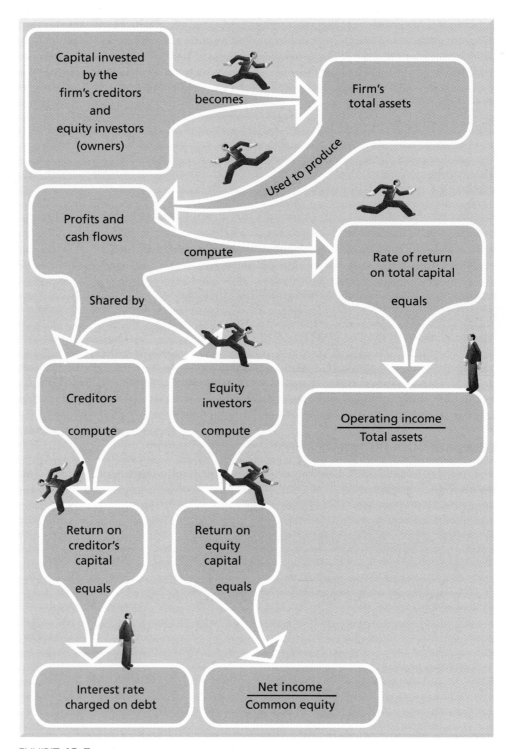

EXHIBIT **13-5** *Return on Invested Capital: An Overview*

UNDERSTANDING THE RETURN-ON-INVESTMENT RESULTS

The owners of Computer World should not be satisfied with merely knowing that they are earning a competitive return on the firm's assets. They should also want to know *why* the return is above average. To gain more understanding, the owners could separate the operating income return on investment into two important components: the operating profit margin and the total asset turnover.

The **operating profit margin** is calculated as follows:

$$Operating\ profit\ margin = \frac{Operating\ profits}{Sales}$$

operating profit margin
the ratio of operating profits to sales, showing how well a firm manages its income statement

The operating profit margin shows how well a firm is managing its income statement—that is, how well a firm is managing the activities that affect its income. There are five factors, or driving forces, that affect the operating profit margin and, in turn, the operating income return on investment:

1. The number of units of product or service sold (volume)
2. The average selling price for each product or service unit (sales price)
3. The cost of manufacturing or acquiring the firm's product (cost of goods sold)
4. The ability to control general and administrative expenses (operating expenses)
5. The ability to control expenses in marketing and distributing the firm's product (operating expenses)

These influences should be apparent from analysis of the income statement and consideration of what is involved in determining a firm's operating profits or income.

The second component of a firm's operating income return on investment is the **total asset turnover,** which is calculated as follows:

$$Total\ asset\ turnover = \frac{Sales}{Total\ assests}$$

total asset turnover
the ratio of sales to total assets, showing the efficiency with which a firm's assets are used to generate sales

This financial ratio indicates how efficiently management is using the firm's assets to generate sales—that is, how well the firm is managing its balance sheet. If Company A can generate $3 in sales with $1 in assets while Company B generates $2 in sales per asset dollar, then Company A is using its assets more efficiently in generating sales. This is a major determinant in the firm's return on investment.

By taking the product of the two foregoing financial ratios, we can restate the operating income return on investment:

$$Operating\ income\ return\ on\ investment = \frac{Operating\ profits}{Sales} \times \frac{Sales}{Total\ assets}$$

or

$$OIROI = Operating\ profit\ margin \times Total\ asset\ turnover$$

Separating the operating income return on investment into its two factors—the operating profit margin and total asset turnover—better isolates a firm's strengths and weaknesses when attempting to identify ways to earn a competitive rate of return on its total invested capital.

Computer World's operating profit margin and total asset turnover can be computed as follows:

$$Operating\ profit\ margin = \frac{Operating\ profits}{Sales}$$

$$= \frac{\$100,000}{\$830,000} = 0.1205,\ or\ 12.05\%$$

$$Total\ asset\ turnover = \frac{Sales}{Total\ assets}$$

$$= \frac{\$830,000}{\$920,000} = 0.90$$

From data on industry norms,

Industry norm for operating profit margin = 1.8%

Industry norm for total asset turnover = .74

Thus, for Computer World,[2]

Operating income return on investment = Operating profit margin $\times$ Total asset turnover

or

$$OIROI_{Computer\ World} = 0.1205 \times 0.90 = 0.1085,\ or\ 10.85\%$$

and for the industry,

$$OIROI_{Ind} = 0.018 \times 0.74 = .0133,\ or\ 1.33\%$$

Clearly, Computer World is very competitive when it comes to managing its income statement—keeping costs and expenses in line relative to sales—as reflected by the operating profit margin. In other words, its managers are performing very well in controlling the five driving forces of the operating profit margin. Computer World's total asset turnover shows why its managers are very competitive in terms of operating income return on investment. The firm is using its assets efficiently; the balance sheet is being managed well. Computer World's advantage is that it generates $0.90 in sales per dollar of assets, while the competition produces $0.74 in sales from every dollar in assets.

The analysis should not stop here, however. It is clear that Computer World's assets are not being used efficiently, but the next question should be "Which assets are the problem?" Is this firm overinvested in all assets or mainly in accounts receivable or inventory or fixed assets? To answer this question, we must examine the turnover ratio for each asset. The three ratios—**accounts receivable turnover,** inventory turnover, and **fixed asset turnover,** are calculated as follows:

accounts receivable turnover
the number of times accounts receivable "roll over" during a year

fixed asset turnover
a measure of the relationship of sales to fixed assets

Turnover Ratios		Computer World	Industry Norm
Accounts receivable turnover $= \dfrac{Credit\ sales}{Accounts\ receivable}$		$\dfrac{\$830,000}{\$78,000} = 10.64$	17
Inventory turnover $= \dfrac{Cost\ of\ goods\ sold}{Inventory}$		$\dfrac{\$540,000}{\$210,000} = 2.57$	3.77
Fixed asset turnover $= \dfrac{Sales}{Fixed\ assets}$		$\dfrac{\$830,000}{\$525,000} = 1.58$	3.7

DEBT OR EQUITY FINANCING?

Computer World's problems are now clearer. The firm has excessive inventories and accounts receivable, as was evident earlier. Also, it is too heavily invested in fixed assets for the sales being produced. It appears that these two asset categories are not being managed well. Consequently, Computer World is experiencing a lower than necessary operating income return on investment. One possible explanation of the discrepancy in fixed asset turnover is that Computer World owns its land and building, where the average firm in the industry does not. This was likely a conscious decision of the owners. It is also true that the land may be undervalued on the balance sheet, as the value is recorded at cost and the true value may be much higher.

We have shown how to analyze a firm's ability to earn a satisfactory rate of return on its total investment capital. To this point, we have ignored the firm's decisions as to whether to use debt or equity financing and the consequence of such decisions on the owners' return on the equity investment. The analysis must now move to how the firm finances its investments.

Measure a firm's use of debt or equity financing. 7

HOW IS THE FIRM FINANCING ITS ASSETS?

We'll return to the issue of profitability shortly. Now, however, let's consider how the firm is financed. Are the firm's assets financed to a greater extent by debt or by equity? Two ratios will be used to answer this question (although many others could be used). First, we must determine what percentage of the firm's assets are financed by debt—including both short-term and long-term debt. (The remaining percentage must be financed by equity.) As will be discussed in Chapter 14, the use of debt, or **financial leverage,** can increase a firm's return on equity, but with some risk involved. This is why these ratios are commonly referred to as measures of stability. The **debt ratio** is calculated as follows:

financial leverage
the use of debt in financing a firm's assets

debt ratio
the ratio of total debt to total assets

$$Debt\ ratio = \frac{Total\ debt}{Total\ assets}$$

The same relationship can be stated as the **debt-equity ratio,** which is total debt divided by total equity, rather than total debt divided by total assets. Either ratio leads to the same conclusion.

debt-equity ratio
the ratio of total debt to total equity

For Computer World in 2008 debt as a percentage of total assets is 33 percent, compared with an industry norm of 42 percent. The computation is as follows:

$$Debt\ ratio = \frac{Total\ debt}{Total\ assets}$$

$$= \frac{\$300,000}{\$920,000} = 0.33,\ or\ 33\%$$

Industry norm for debt ratio = 42%
(Calculated from additional data not included in Exhibit 13-1)

$$The\ debt\text{-}equity\ ratio = \frac{Total\ debt}{Total\ equity}$$

$$= \frac{\$300,000}{\$620,000} = .48$$

Industry norm for debt-equity ratio = 1.64 (median firms)

Thus, Computer World uses considerably less debt than the average firm in the industry, which means that it has less financial risk.

A second perspective on a firm's financing decisions can be gained by looking at the income statement. When a firm borrows money, it is required, at a minimum, to pay the interest on the debt. Thus, determining the amount of operating income available to pay the interest provides a firm with valuable information. Stated as a ratio, the computation shows the number of times the firm earns its interest. Thus, the **times interest earned ratio** is commonly used in examining debt position. This ratio is calculated as follows:

times interest earned ratio
the ratio of operating income to interest charges

$$Times\ interest\ earned\ ratio = \frac{Operating\ income}{Interest\ expense}$$

For Computer World, the times interest earned ratio is as follows:

$$Times\ interest\ earned\ ratio = \frac{Operating\ income}{Interest\ expense}$$

$$= \frac{\$100,000}{\$20,000} = 5.00$$

Industry norm for times interest earned ratio = 2.9

Computer World is better able to service its interest expense than most comparable firms. This is related to the low amount of debt: lower debt means less interest to pay. Remember, however, that interest is paid not with income but with cash. Also, the firm may be required to repay some of the debt principal as well as the interest. Thus, the times interest earned ratio is only a crude measure of a firm's capacity to service its debt. Nevertheless, it gives a general indication of the firm's debt capacity.

ARE THE OWNERS RECEIVING ADEQUATE RETURN ON THEIR INVESTMENT?

Evaluate the rate of return earned on the owners' investment. 8

The last question looks at the accounting return on the owners' investment, or **return on equity**. We must determine whether the earnings available to the firm's owners (or stockholders) are attractive when compared to the returns of owners of similar companies in the same industry. The return on the owners' equity capital can be measured as follows:

return on equity
the rate of return that owners earn on their investment

$$Return \ on \ equity = \frac{Net \ income}{Common \ equity}$$

The return on equity for Computer World in 2008 is as follows:

$$Return \ on \ equity = \frac{Net \ income}{Common \ equity}$$

$$= \frac{\$60,000}{\$300,000} = 0.2, \ or \ 20\%$$

Industry norm for return on equity = 0.4% for median firms and 47.4% for top 25% firms

It appears that the owners of Computer World are receiving a return on their investment superior to that of owners of most competing businesses, but not the leading ones in the industry. Why? To answer this question, we have to understand the following:

1. The return on equity (ROE) will increase as the difference between a firm's operating income return on investment (OIROI) and the interest rate paid for the use of debt financing (i) increases; that is, as (OIROI – i) increases, ROE increases.
2. As a firm's debt ratio (total debt ÷ total assets) increases, ROE will increase if OIROI is greater than i, but ROE will decrease if OIROI is less than i.

Computer World has a higher return on equity because it has a much higher profit margin than most competitors do. From the earlier calculation of industry OIROI we can see that these firms are earning a return on their investments much lower than the likely cost of debt (the interest rate). Computer World also uses much less debt, which would normally result in a lower ROE. However, we should recognize that the use of less debt does reduce Computer World's risk.[3]

SUMMARY OF FINANCIAL RATIO ANALYSIS

As a summary of financial ratios used in evaluating a firm's financial position, all ratios for Computer World for 2008 are presented in Exhibit 13-6. The ratios are grouped by the issue being addressed: liquidity, operating profitability, financing, and owners' return on equity. Recall that the turnover ratios for accounts receivable and inventories are used for more than one purpose. These ratios have implications for both the firm's liquidity and its profitability; thus, they are listed in both areas. Note also that the exhibit shows both average collection period and accounts receivable turnover. Typically, only one of these ratios is used in analysis, since each represents a different way to measure the same thing. Presenting the ratios together, however, provides an overview of our discussion.

ENTREPRENEUR

IN THE TRENCHES

Entrepreneurial Experiences

It Takes "Mental Headgear" to Use Financial Ratios

After graduating from college, Alan Wills and a friend established a firm to sell headgear and other accessories for winter sports. The idea originated from a class project they had worked on together. They first named the firm Do Rags, but then later changed the name to Mental Headgear. After several years of operations, Wills bought out his partner with the idea of aggressively growing the business. At the time of the sale, the firm's financial statements were as follows:

Balance Sheet

Current Assets		Current Liabilities	
Cash	$ 12,852	Accrued commissions payable	$ 20,176
Accounts receivable	272,706	Accounts payable	80,881
Sales rep receivables	2676	Current notes payable	11,128
Payroll tax refund	325	Payroll taxes payable	4919
Due from employees	1645	Federal income tax payable	2618
Bad cheques receivable	549	Total current liabilities	$119,722
Inventory	146,452	Long-term notes payable	206,969
Total current assets	$437,205	Total liabilities	$326,691
Total fixed assets	$ 12,977	Stockholders' equity	
Other assets:		Capital shares	$ 230
Other prepaid expenses	$ 12,867	Paid-in capital	145,590
Show exhibits	3039	Retained earnings	(51,825)
Noncompete agreement	15,631	Prior period adjustments	(35,163)
Notes receivable	12,131	Current earnings	108,327
Total other assets	$ 43,668	Total shareholders' equity	167,159
Total assets	$493,850	Total liabilities and equity	$493,850

Income Statement		Financial Ratios	
Sales revenue	$1 470,344	Current ratio	3.65
Cost of goods sold	812,205	Acid-test ratio	2.43
Gross profits on sales	$ 658,139	Average collection period	67.70
Operating expenses:		Inventory turnover	5.55
Marketing expenses	$ 275,999	Operating income return on investment	23.6%
General and administrative expenses	265,616	Operating profit margin	7.9%
Total operating expenses	$ 541,615	Total asset turnover	2.98

Income Statement		Financial Ratios	
Operating income	$ 116,524	Fixed asset turnover	113.30
Other income	18,638	Debt ratio	0.66
Interest expense	25,215	Times interest earned ratio	4.62
Earnings before taxes	$ 109,947	Before-tax return on equity	65.8%

What can be learned about Mental Headgear from the financial ratios?

1. The firm has $3.65 in current assets for every dollar in current debt, which means that the firm is relatively liquid by any standard.

2. Accounts receivable are collected every 68 days on average.

3. Inventory is turned over 5.55 times each year, or every 66 days.

4. The firm earns an operating income return on investment of about 24 percent by earning an 8 percent operating profit margin and by turning the firm's assets over almost three times per year. That is, for every $1 invested in the company, it earns $0.24—a relatively attractive return on investment but necessary to compensate Wills for the risk being taken.

5. The company is financed by about two-thirds debt and one-third owner's equity.

6. Wills's before-tax return on equity is almost 66 percent, which represents a very high return on the owner's investment. This return, however, is a result of being in a relatively risky business and using a lot of debt financing. (Note that we have calculated the firm's return on equity on a before-tax basis. The firm is a partnership, and taxable income is reported by the owners on their personal tax return.)

While there is considerable risk in any small business, we can conclude, based on one year's information, that Mental Headgear appears to be an attractive opportunity for Wills.

It is important to understand that ratios vary by type of industry and even by size of company within industries. For example, some industries are extremely **capital intensive,** meaning they require large investments in equipment and facilities. Other industries, such as power producers, have very predictable revenue and can therefore safely finance themselves with much higher levels of debt. Another example would be retail, where most firms have virtually no accounts receivable—all purchases are made with cash, credit cards, or debit cards. Select ratios for different industries are presented in Exhibit 13-7.

capital intensive industries that require large investments in equipment and facilities

THE WORKING-CAPITAL CYCLE

Describe the working-capital cycle of a small business. **9**

So far we have focused on managing a firm's income statement carefully—managing expenses relative to the firm's level of sales. Owners and managers must also effectively administer the firm's balance sheet by managing both investments in working capital and long-term investments. This chapter considers the investment decisions of a firm, discussing first the management of working capital—that is, the management of short-term assets and liabilities. The process for making decisions on long-term investments, such as those for equipment and buildings, is beyond the scope of this book.

EXHIBIT **13-6**
*Financial Ratio
Analysis for Computer
World*

Financial Ratios	Computer World	Industry Norm
1. Firm liquidity		
Current ratio $= \dfrac{\text{Current assets}}{\text{Current liabilities}}$	$= \dfrac{\$344{,}000}{\$100{,}000} = 3.45$	1.6
Acid-test ratio $= \dfrac{\text{Current assets} - \text{Inventories}}{\text{Current liabilities}}$	$= \dfrac{\$345{,}000 - \$210{,}000}{\$100{,}000} = 1.35$	0.7
Average collection period $= \dfrac{\text{Accounts receivable}}{\text{Daily credit sales}}$	$= \dfrac{\$78{,}000}{\$830{,}000} \div 365 = 34$	16
Accounts receivable turnover $= \dfrac{\text{Credit sales}}{\text{Accounts receivable}}$	$= \dfrac{\$830{,}000}{\$78{,}000} = 10.64$	17
Inventory turnover $= \dfrac{\text{Cost of goods sold}}{\text{Inventory}}$	$= \dfrac{\$540{,}000}{\$210{,}000} = 2.57$	3.77
2. Operating profitability		
Operating income return on investment $= \dfrac{\text{Operating income}}{\text{Total assets}}$	$= \dfrac{\$100{,}000}{\$920{,}000} = 10.87\%$	1.33%
Operating profit margin $= \dfrac{\text{Operating profits}}{\text{Sales}}$	$= \dfrac{\$100{,}000}{\$830{,}000} = 12.05\%$	1.2%
Total asset turnover $= \dfrac{\text{Sales}}{\text{Total assets}}$	$= \dfrac{\$830{,}000}{\$920{,}000} = 0.90$	3.7
Inventory turnover $= \dfrac{\text{Cost of goods sold}}{\text{Inventory}}$	$= \dfrac{\$540{,}000}{\$210{,}000} = 2.57$	3.77
Fixed asset turnover $= \dfrac{\text{Sales}}{\text{Fixed assets}}$	$= \dfrac{\$830{,}000}{\$525{,}000} = 1.58$	11.2
3. Financing		
Debt ratio $= \dfrac{\text{Total debt}}{\text{Total assets}}$	$= \dfrac{\$300{,}000}{\$920{,}000} = 33.0\%$	
Times interest earned ratio $= \dfrac{\text{Operating income}}{\text{Interest}}$	$= \dfrac{\$100{,}000}{\$20{,}000} = 5.00$	2.9
Debt–equity ratio $= \dfrac{\text{Total debt}}{\text{Total equity}}$	$= \dfrac{\$300{,}000}{\$620{,}000} = 0.48$	1.64
4. Return on equity		
Return on equity $= \dfrac{\text{Net income}}{\text{Common equity}}$	$= \dfrac{\$80{,}000}{\$300{,}000} = 26.7\%$	0.4%

working-capital management
the management of
current assets and
current liabilities

Ask the owner of a small business about financial management and you will hear about the joys and tribulations of managing cash, accounts receivable, inventories, and accounts payable. **Working-capital management**—managing short-term assets (current assets) and short-term sources of financing (current liabilities)—is extremely important to most small firms. In fact, there may be no financial discipline that is more important, and yet more misunderstood. Good business opportunities can be irreparably damaged by ineffective management of a firm's short-term assets and liabilities.

EXHIBIT **13-7**
Industry Ratios

	Construction	Wholesale Trade	Machinery Manufacturing	Performing Arts and Spectator Sports	Utilities	Mining
Current Ratio	1.5	1.5	1.6	1.3	1.7	1.4
Debt-equity ratio	2.5	2.0	1.7	2.3	1.3	1.6
Net margin	3.2%	1.8%	2.2%	4.4%	23.2%	0.9%
Return on assets	5.9%	4.9%	4.8%	7.6%	0	3.0%
Accounts receivable days	47.8	45.6	60	25.8	62.5	51.2

The key issue in working-capital management is to avoid running out of cash. And understanding how to manage cash effectively requires knowledge of the working-capital cycle. "Business owners should be thinking about this issue from day one," says Stephen King, president of Virtual Growth, a financial-consulting firm. Many entrepreneurs overlook effective cash management because they have other issues on their minds. "So long as more money seems to be coming into the business than going out, many company owners don't give cash management a second thought. And that leaves them vulnerable to all kinds of cash-flow dangers."[4]

Net working capital consists primarily of three assets: cash, accounts receivable, and inventories less current liabilities (short-term notes, accounts payable and accruals).[5] A firm's working-capital cycle is the flow of resources through these accounts as part of the firm's day-to-day operations. The steps in a firm's **working-capital cycle** are as follows:

Step 1 Purchase or produce inventory for sale, which increases accounts payable—assuming the purchase is a credit purchase—and increases inventories on hand.

Step 2 a. Sell the inventory for cash, which increases cash, or
b. Sell the inventory on credit, which increases accounts receivable.

Step 3 a. Pay the accounts payable, which decreases accounts payable and decreases cash.
b. Pay operating expenses and taxes, which decreases cash.

Step 4 Collect the accounts receivable when due, which decreases accounts receivable and increases cash.

Step 5 Begin the cycle again.

Exhibit 13-8 shows this cycle graphically.

Depending on the industry, the working-capital cycle may be long or short. For example, it is short and repeated quickly in the grocery business; it is longer and repeated more slowly in an automobile dealership. Whatever the industry, however, management should be working continuously to shorten the cycle.

THE TIMING AND SIZE OF WORKING-CAPITAL INVESTMENTS

It is imperative that owners of small companies understand the working-capital cycle, in terms of both the timing of investments and the size of the investment required (for example, the amounts necessary to maintain inventories and accounts receivable). The owner's failure to understand these relationships underlies many of the financial problems of small companies.

net working capital
the sum of a firm's current assets (cash, accounts receivable, and inventories) less current liabilities (short-term notes, accounts payable, and accruals)

working-capital cycle
the daily flow of resources through a firm's working-capital accounts

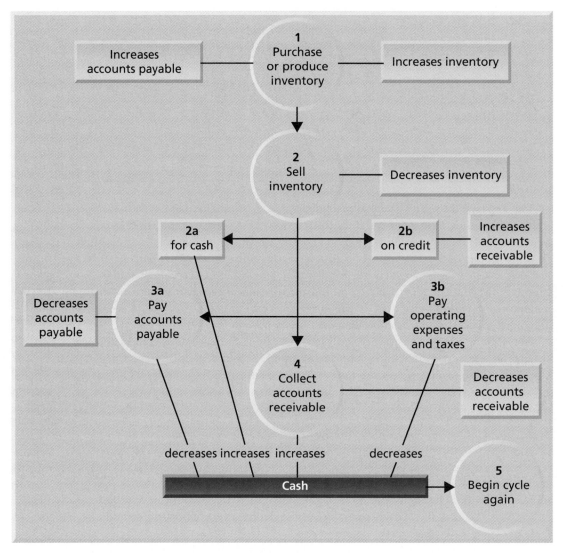

EXHIBIT **13-8** *Working-Capital Cycle*

Exhibit 13-9 shows the chronological sequence of a hypothetical working-capital cycle. The timeline reflects the order in which events unfold, beginning with an investment in inventory and ending with collection of accounts receivable. The key dates in the figure are as follows:

Day a Inventory is ordered in anticipation of future sales.
Day b **Inventory is received.**
Day c Inventory is sold on credit.
Day d Accounts payable come due and are paid.
Day e Accounts receivable are collected.

The investing and financing implications of the working-capital cycle reflected in Exhibit 13-9 are as follows:

• Money is invested in inventory from day *b* to day *c*.
• The supplier provides financing for the inventories from day *b* to day *d*.

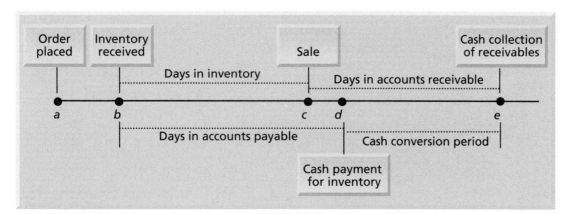

EXHIBIT **13-9** *Working-Capital Time Line*

- Money is invested in accounts receivable from day *c* to day *e*.
- Financing of the firm's investment in accounts receivable must be provided from day *d* to day *e*. This time span, called the **cash conversion period,** represents the number of days required to complete the working-capital cycle, which ends with the conversion of accounts receivable into cash. During this period, the firm no longer has the benefit of supplier financing (accounts payable). The longer this period lasts, the greater the potential cash flow problems for the firm.

cash conversion period
the time required to convert paid-for inventories and accounts receivable into cash

EXAMPLES OF WORKING-CAPITAL MANAGEMENT

Exhibit 13-10 offers two examples of working-capital management by firms with contrasting working-capital cycles: Pokey, Inc. and Quick Turn Company. On August 15, both firms buy inventory that they receive on August 31, but the similarity ends there. Pokey, Inc. must pay its supplier for the inventory on September 30, before eventually reselling it on October 15. It collects from its customers on November 30. As you can see, Pokey, Inc. must pay for the inventory two months prior to collecting from its customers. Its cash conversion period—the time required to convert the paid-for inventories and accounts receivable into cash—is 60 days. The firm's managers must find a way to finance this investment in inventories and accounts receivable, or else they will experience cash flow problems. Furthermore, although increased sales should produce higher profits, they will compound the cash flow problem.

Now consider Quick Turn Company's working-capital cycle, shown in the bottom portion of Exhibit 13-10. Compared to Pokey, Quick Turn Company has an enviable working-capital position. By the time Quick Turn must pay for its inventory purchases (October 31), it has sold its product (September 30) and collected from its customers (October 31). Thus, there is no cash conversion period because the supplier is essentially financing Quick Turn's working-capital needs.

To gain an even better understanding of the working-capital cycle, let's see what happens to Pokey's balance sheet and income statement. To do so, we will need more information about the firm's activities. A month-by-month listing of its activities and their effect on its balance sheet follow. Pay close attention to the firm's working capital, especially its cash balances.

July: Pokey, Inc. is a new company, having started operations in July with $1000, financed by $300 in long-term debt and $700 in common stock. At the outset, the owner

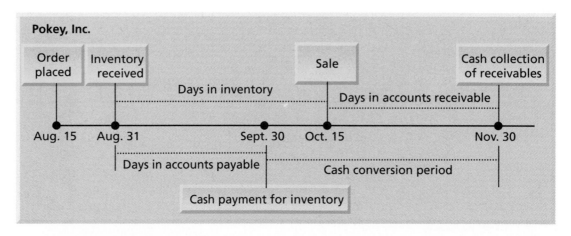

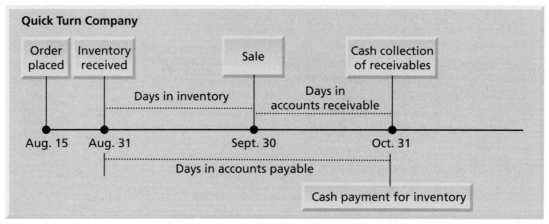

EXHIBIT **13-10** *Working-Capital Time Lines for Pokey, Inc. and Quick Turn Company*

purchased $600 in fixed assets, leaving the remaining $400 in cash. At this point, the balance sheet would appear as follows:

	July
Cash	$ 400
Accounts receivable	0
Inventory	0
Fixed assets	600
Accumulated depreciation	0
Total assets	$1000
Accounts payable	$ 0
Accrued operating expenses	0
Income tax payable	0
Long-term debt	300
Common stock	700
Retained earnings	0
Total debt and equity	$1000

August: On August 15, the firm's managers ordered $500 in inventory, which was received on August 31 (see Exhibit 13-10). The supplier allowed Pokey 30 days from the time the inventory was received to pay for the purchase; thus, inventories and accounts payable both increased by $500 when the inventory was received.

	July	August	Changes: July to August
Cash	$ 400	$ 400	
Accounts receivable	0	0	
Inventory	0	500	+$500
Fixed assets	600	600	
Accumulated depreciation	0	0	
Total assets	$1000	$1500	
Accounts payable	$ 0	$ 500	+$500
Accrued operating expenses	0	0	
Income tax payable	0	0	
Long-term debt	300	300	
Common shares	700	700	
Retained earnings		0	
Total debt and equity	$1000	$1500	

So far, so good—no cash problems yet.

September: On September 30, the firm paid for the inventory; both cash and accounts payable decreased by $500.

	July	August	September	Changes: August to September
Cash	$ 400	$ 400	$ (100)	−$500
Accounts receivable	0	0	0	
Inventory	0	500	500	
Fixed assets	600	600	600	
Accumulated depreciation	0	0	0	
Total assets	$1000	$1500	$1000	
Accounts payable	$ 0	$ 500	$ 0	−$500
Income tax payable	0	0	0	
Long-term debt	300	300	300	
Common shares	700	700	700	
Retained earnings	0	0	0	
Total debt and equity	$1000	$1500	$1000	

Now Pokey, Inc. has a cash flow problem in the form of a cash deficit of $100.

October: October was a busy month for Pokey. On October 15, merchandise was sold on credit for $900; sales (in the income statement) and accounts receivable increased by that amount. The firm incurred operating expenses (selling and administrative expenses) in the amount of $250, to be paid in early November; thus, operating expenses (in the income statement) and accrued operating expenses (liabilities in the balance sheet) increased by $250. (An additional $25 in accrued expenses resulted from accruing taxes that will be owed on the firm's earnings.) Finally, in October, the firm's accountants recorded $50 in depreciation expense (to be reported in the income statement), resulting in accumulated depreciation on the balance sheet of $50.

	July	August	September	October	Changes: September to October
Cash	$ 400	$ 400	$ (100)	$ (100)	
Accounts receivable	0	0	0	900	+$900
Inventory	0	500	500	0	−500
Fixed assets	600	600	600	600	
Accumulated depreciation	0	0	0	(50)	−50
Total assets	$1000	$1500	$1000	$1350	
Accounts payable	$ 0	$ 500	$ 0	$ 0	
Accrued operating expenses	0	0	0	250	+$250
Income tax payable	0	0	0	25	+25
Long-term debt	300	300	300	300	
Common shares	700	700	700	700	
Retained earnings	0	0	0	75	+75
Total debt and equity	$1000	$1500	$1000	$1350	

The October balance sheet shows all the activities just described, but there is one more change in the balance sheet: It now shows $75 in retained earnings, which had been $0 in the prior balance sheets. As you will see shortly, this amount represents the firm's income. Note also that Pokey, Inc. continues to be overdrawn by $100 on its cash. None of the events in October affected the firm's cash balance. All the transactions were the result of accruals recorded by the firm's accountant, offsetting entries to the income statement. The relationship between the balance sheet and the income statement is as follows:

Change in the Balance Sheet	Effect on Income Statement
Increase in accounts receivable of $900	Sales $900
Decrease in inventories of $500	Cost of goods sold $500
Increase in accrued operating expenses of $250	Operating expenses $250
Increase in accumulated depreciation of $50	Depreciation expense $50
Increase in accrued taxes of $25	Tax expense $25

November: In November, the accrued expenses were paid, which resulted in a $250 decrease in cash along with an equal decrease in accrued expenses. At the end of November, the accounts receivable were collected, yielding a $900 increase in cash and a $900 decrease in accounts receivable. Thus, net cash increased by $650. The final series of balance sheets is as follows:

	July	August	September	October	November	Change October to November
Cash	$ 400	$ 400	$ (100)	$ (100)	$ 550	+$650
Accounts receivable	0	0	0	900	0	−900
Inventory	0	500	500	0	0	
Fixed assets	600	600	600	600	600	
Accumulated depreciation	0	0	0	(50)	(50)	
TOTAL ASSETS	$1000	$1500	$1000	$1350	$1100	
Accounts payable	$ 0	$ 500	$ 0	$ 0	$ 0	
Accrued operating expenses	0	0	0	250	0	−$250
Income tax payable	0	0	0	25	25	
Long-term debt	300	300	300	300	300	
Common shares	700	700	700	700	700	
Retained earnings	0	0	0	75	75	
TOTAL DEBT AND EQUITY	$1000	$1500	$1000	$1350	$1100	

As a result of the firm's activities, Pokey, Inc. reported $75 in profits for the period. The income statement for the period ending November 30 is as follows:

Sales revenue		$900
Cost of goods sold		500
Gross profit		$400
Operating expenses:		
Cash	$250	
Depreciation	50	
Total operating expenses		$300
Operating income		$100
Income tax (25%)		25
Net income		$ 75

The $75 in profits is reflected as retained earnings on the balance sheet to make the numbers match.

The somewhat contrived example of Pokey, Inc. illustrates an important point that deserves repeating: An owner of a small firm must understand the working-capital cycle of his or her firm. Although the business was profitable, Pokey ran out of cash in September and October (−$100) and didn't recover until November, when the accounts receivable were collected. This 60-day cash conversion period represents a critical time when the firm must find another source of financing if it is to survive. Moreover, when sales are ongoing throughout the year, the problem can be an unending one, unless financing is found to support the firm's sales. Also, as much as possible, a firm should arrange for sooner payment by customers (preferably in advance) and negotiate longer payment schedules with suppliers (preferably over several months).

An understanding of the working-capital cycle provides a basis for examining the primary components of working-capital management: cash flows, accounts receivable, inventory, and accounts payable.

MANAGING CASH FLOWS

It should be clear to you by now that the core of working-capital management is monitoring cash flows. Cash is constantly moving through a business. It flows in as customers pay for products or services, and it flows out as payments are made to suppliers, employees, etc. The typically uneven nature of cash inflows and outflows makes it imperative that they be properly understood and regulated.

THE NATURE OF CASH FLOWS

A firm's net cash flow may be determined quite simply by examining its bank account. Monthly cash deposits less cheques written and pre-authorized withdrawals during the same period equal a firm's net cash flow. If deposits for a month add up to $100,000 and cheques total $80,000, the firm has a net positive cash flow of $20,000. The cash balance at the end of the month is $20,000 higher than it was at the beginning of the month. Exhibit 13-11 graphically represents the flow of cash through a business; it includes not only the cash flows that arise as part of the firm's working-capital cycle (shown in Exhibit 13-8), but other cash flows as well, such as those from purchasing fixed assets

EXHIBIT **13-11**
Short- and Long-Term Cash Flows

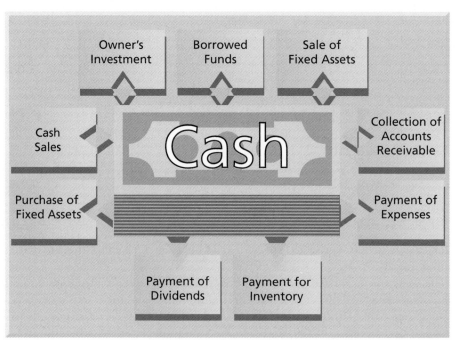

and issuing stock. More specifically, cash sales, collection of accounts receivable, payment of expenses, and payment for inventory reflect the inflows and outflows of cash that relate to the working-capital cycle, while the other items in Exhibit 13-11 represent other, longer-term cash flows.

In calculating net cash flows, it is necessary to distinguish between sales revenue and cash receipts—they are seldom the same. Revenue is recorded at the time a sale is made but does not affect cash flow at that time unless the sale is a cash sale. Cash receipts, on the other hand, are recorded when money actually flows into the firm, often a month or two after the sale. Similarly, it is necessary to distinguish between expenses and disbursements. Expenses occur when materials, labour, or other items are used. Payments (disbursements) for these expense items may be made later when cheques are issued.

NET CASH FLOW AND NET PROFIT

In view of the distinguishing characteristics just noted, it should come as no surprise that net cash flow and net profit are different. Net cash flow is the difference between cash inflows and outflows. Net profit, in contrast, is the difference between revenue and expenses. Failure to understand this distinction can play havoc with a small firm's financial well-being.

One reason for the difference is the uneven timing of cash disbursements and the expensing of those disbursements. For example, the merchandise purchased by a retail store may be paid for (a cash disbursement) before it is sold (when it becomes recognized as a cost of goods sold). On the other hand, labour may be used (an expense) before a paycheque is written (a cash disbursement). In the case of a major cash outlay for a building or equipment, the disbursement shows up immediately as a cash outflow. However, it is recognized as an expense only as the building or equipment is depreciated over a period of years.

Similarly, the uneven timing of sales revenue and cash receipts occurs because of the extension of credit. When a sale is made, the transaction is recorded as revenue; the cash receipt is recorded when payment for the account receivable is received, often 30 or 60 days later. We observed this fact earlier as part of our discussion of the working-capital cycle.

Furthermore, some cash receipts are not revenue and never become revenue. When a firm borrows money from a bank, for example, it receives cash without receiving revenue. When the principal is repaid to the bank some months later, cash is disbursed. However, no expense is recorded, because the firm is merely returning money that was borrowed. Any interest paid to the bank on the loan would, of course, constitute both an expense when owed and a cash disbursement when paid.

It is imperative that small firms manage cash flows as carefully as they manage revenue, expenses, and profits. Otherwise, they may find themselves insolvent, while showing handsome paper profits. More businesses fail because of lack of cash than because of lack of profits.

THE GROWTH TRAP

When a firm experiences rapid growth in sales volume, the firm's income statement may simultaneously reflect growing profits. However, rapid growth in sales and profits may be hazardous to the firm's cash. A **growth trap** can occur, because growth tends to soak up additional cash more rapidly than such cash can be generated in the form of additional profits.

growth trap
a cash shortage resulting from rapid growth

Inventory, for example, must be expanded as sales volume increases; additional dollars must be expended for merchandise or raw materials to accommodate the higher level of sales. Similarly, accounts receivable must be expanded proportionally to meet the increased sales volume. Obviously, a growing, profitable business can quickly find itself in a financial bind—growing profitably, while going broke at the bank.

The growth problem is particularly acute for small firms. Quite simply, it's easier to increase a small firm's sales by 50 percent than those of a very large firm. This fact, combined with the difficulty a small firm may have in obtaining funds externally, highlights the detrimental effect that too-rapid growth can have on small businesses if cash is not managed carefully.

In short, a high-growth firm's need for additional financing may exceed its available resources, even though the firm is profitable. Without additional resources, the firm's cash balances may decline sharply, leaving it in a precarious financial position.

CASH FLOW FORECAST

cash flow forecast (cash budget)
a planning document strictly concerned with the receipt and payment of dollars

Cash flow forecasts are tools for managing cash flows. These forecasts are concerned specifically with dollars received and paid out. In contrast, income statements take items into consideration before they affect cash—for example, expenses that have been incurred but not yet paid and income earned but not yet received.

By using a cash flow forecast, an entrepreneur can predict and plan the cash flows of a business. No single planning document is more important in the life of a small company, either for avoiding cash flow problems when cash runs short or for anticipating short-term investment opportunities if excess cash becomes available.

To better understand the process of preparing a cash flow forecast, consider the example of Candace Corporation, a manufacturer of containers. Its owner, Candace Lambert, wishes to develop a monthly cash flow forecast for the next quarter (July through September) and has made the following forecasts.

Historical and predicted sales:

Historical Sales		Predicted Sales	
April	$ 80,000	July	$130,000
May	100,000	August	130,000
June	120,000	September	120,000
		October	100,000

- Of the firm's sales dollars, 40 percent are collected the month of the sale, 30 percent one month after the sale, and the remaining 30 percent two months after the sale.
- Inventory is purchased one month before the sales month and is paid for in the month in which it is sold. Purchases equal 80 percent of projected sales for the next month.
- Cash expenses have been estimated for wages and salaries, rent, utilities, and tax payments, all of which are reflected in the cash budget.
- The firm's beginning cash balance for the budget period is $5000. This amount should be maintained as a minimum cash balance.

- The firm has a $20,000 line of credit with its bank at an interest rate of 12 percent annually (a 1 percent monthly rate). The interest owed is to be paid monthly.
- Interest on a $40,000 bank note (with the principal due in December) is payable at an 8 percent annual rate for the three-month period ending in September.

Based on this information, Candace has used a computer spreadsheet to prepare a monthly cash budget for the three-month period ending September 30. Exhibit 13-12 shows the results of her computations, which involved the following steps:

Step 1 Determine the amount of collections each month, based on the projected collection patterns.

Step 2 Estimate the amount and timing of the following cash disbursements:
  a. Inventory purchases and payments. The amount of the purchases is shown in the boxed area of the table, with payments made one month later.
  b. Rent, wages, taxes, utilities, and interest on the long-term note.
  c. Interest to be paid on any outstanding short-term borrowing. For example, the table shows that for the month of July Candace would need to borrow $10,600 to prevent the firm's cash balance from falling below the $5000 acceptable minimum. Assume that the money will be borrowed at the end of July and that the interest will be payable at the end of August. The amount of the interest in August is $106, or 1 percent of the $10,600 cumulative short-term debt outstanding at the end of July.

Step 3 Calculate the net change in cash (cash receipts less cash disbursements).

Step 4 Determine the beginning cash balance (ending cash balance from the prior month).

Step 5 Compute the cash balance before short-term borrowing (net change in cash for the month plus the cash balance at the beginning of the month).

Step 6 Calculate the short-term borrowing or repayment—the amount borrowed if there is a cash shortfall for the month or the amount repaid on any short-term debt outstanding.

Step 7 Compute the cumulative amount of short-term debt outstanding, which also determines the amount of interest to be paid in the following month.

As you can see in Exhibit 13-12, the firm does not achieve a positive cash flow until September. Short-term borrowing must be arranged, therefore, in both July and August. By preparing a cash budget, Candace can anticipate these needs and avoid the nasty surprises that might otherwise occur.

A cash budget should anticipate occasions when a small business has idle funds or has generated unexpected excess funds. Taking advantage of the many short-term investment opportunities that are available, including certificates of deposit and money market certificates, can put excess cash to work for a firm.

MANAGING ACCOUNTS RECEIVABLE

Chapter 7 discussed the extension of credit by small firms and the managing and collecting of accounts receivable. This section considers the impact of credit decisions on working capital and particularly on cash flow. The most important factor in managing cash well within a small firm is the ability to collect accounts receivable quickly.

Explain the key issues in managing accounts receivable, inventory, and accounts payable.

EXHIBIT **13-12**

*Three-Month Cash Flow
Forecast for Candace
Corporation for
July–September*

		May	June	July	August	September
Monthly sales		**$100,000**	**$100,000**	**$130,000**	**$130,000**	**$120,000**
	Cash receipts					
	Cash sales for month			$ 52,000	$ 52,000	$ 48,000
	1 month after sale			36,000	39,000	39,000
	2 months after sale			30,000	36,000	39,000
Step 1	Total collections			$118,000	$127,000	$126,000
	Purchases (80% of sales)		**$104,000**	**$104,000**	**$96,000**	**$80,000**
	Cash disbursements					
Step 2a	Payments on purchases			$104,000	$10,000	$ 9,000
	Rent			3,000	3,000	3,000
	Wages and salaries			18,000	18,000	16,000
Step 2b	Tax prepayment			1,000		
	Utilities (2% of sales)			2,600	2,600	2,400
Step 2c	Interest on long-term note)					800
	(1% of short-term debt)				106	113
	Total cash disbursements			$128,600	$127,706	$118,313
Step 3	Net change in cash			$ 10,600	$ 706	$ 7,87
Step 4	Beginning cash balance			5,000	5,000	5,000
Step 5	Cash balance before borrowing			$ 5,600	$ 4,294	$ 12,687
Step 6	Short-term borrowing (payments)			10,600	706	7,687
	Ending cash balance			$ 5,000	$ 5,000	$ 5,000
Step 7	Cumulative short-term debt outstanding			$ 10,600	$ 11,306	$ 3,619

HOW ACCOUNTS RECEIVABLE AFFECT CASH

Granting credit to customers, although primarily a marketing decision, directly affects a firm's cash account. By selling on credit and thus allowing customers to delay payment, the selling firm delays the inflow of cash.

The total amount of customers' credit balances is carried on the balance sheet as accounts receivable—one of the firm's current assets. Of all noncash assets, accounts receivable are closest to becoming cash. Sometimes called *near cash,* or *receivables,* accounts receivable typically are collected and become cash within 30 to 60 days following a sale.

THE LIFE CYCLE OF ACCOUNTS RECEIVABLE

The receivables cycle begins with a credit sale. In most businesses, an invoice is then prepared and mailed to the purchaser. When the invoice is received, the purchaser processes it, prepares a cheque, and mails the cheque in payment to the seller.

Under ideal circumstances, each of these steps is taken in a timely manner. Obviously, delays can occur at any stage of this process. One small business owner found that the shipping clerk was batching invoices before sending them to the office for processing, thus delaying the preparation and mailing of invoices to customers. Of course, this practice also postponed the day on which the customers' money was received and deposited in the bank so that it could be used to pay bills. John Convoy, a cash flow consultant and former treasurer of several small firms, explains, "Most overdue receivables are unpaid because of problems in a company's organization. Your cash flow system is vulnerable at points where information gets transferred—between salespeople, operations departments, accounting clerks—because errors disrupt your ability to get paid promptly."[6]

Credit management policies, practices, and procedures affect the life cycle of receivables and the flow of cash from them. When establishing credit policies, it is important for small business owners to consider cash flow requirements as well as the need to stimulate sales. A key goal of every business should be to minimize the average time it takes customers to pay their bills. By streamlining administrative procedures, a firm can facilitate the task of sending out bills, thereby generating cash more quickly. Here are some examples of credit-management practices that can have a positive effect on a **firm's cash flows:**

- Use the most effective methods for collecting overdue accounts. For example, prompt phone calls to overdue accounts can improve collections considerably.
- Minimize the time between shipping, invoicing, and sending notices on billings.
- Review previous credit experiences to determine impediments to cash flow, such as continued extension of credit to slow-paying or delinquent customers.
- Provide incentives for prompt payment by granting cash discounts or charging interest on delinquent accounts.
- Age accounts receivable on a monthly or even a weekly basis to identify quickly any delinquent accounts (see Exhibit 13-13).
- Use a **lock box**—a post-office box for receiving remittances. If the firm's bank maintains the lock box to which customers send their payments, it can empty the box frequently and immediately deposit any cheques received into the firm's account.

firm's cash flows
after-tax cash flows generated from operations less the firm's investments in assets

lock box
a post-office box for receiving remittances from customers

EXHIBIT **13-13**
An Example of an Accounts Receivable Aging Report as of September 30

Customer	Date	Inv #	Current	30–60 days	60–90 days	Over 90 days	Total
ABC Corp	Sept 1	1234	$ 344				
	Aug 31	2345	$ 699				
	Aug 15	3456		$ 995			
	July 10	4567			$ 1663		
	June 29	5678				$ 88	
Total for Customer			$1043	$ 995	$ 1663	$ 88	$ 3789
XYZ Ltd	Sept 5	1235	$ 26				
	Sept 6	1236	$1521				
	Aug 24	2447		$3995			
	Aug 24	3701		860			
	June 22	5622				$ 426	
Total for Customer			**$1547**	**$4855**	**$**	**$ 426**	**$ 6828**
Total for Report			**$2590**	**$5850**	**$1663**	**$ 514**	**$10,617**

ACCOUNTS RECEIVABLE FINANCING

Some small businesses speed the cash flow from accounts receivable by borrowing against them. By financing receivables, these firms can often secure the use of their money 30 to 60 days earlier than would be possible otherwise. Called "factoring" and discussed in more detail later in this chapter, this practice was once concentrated largely in the garment business, but has since expanded to many other types of small businesses, such as manufacturers, food processors, distributors, home building suppliers,

ENTREPRENEUR

IN THE TRENCHES

Entrepreneurial Experiences

The High Cost of Getting Paid

Many companies accept debit cards and credit cards as means of payment. While this is most prevalent in retail and consumer service businesses, other companies such as small manufacturers also accept payment in this manner for smaller purchases or low-volume and infrequent customers. Most consumers find this method of payment very convenient—but is certainly comes at a cost.

Every time someone swipes a bank card through the debit card machine at Knot Just Bagels in downtown Vancouver it costs owner Glenn Pepperell 10 cents, whether it's a couple of loonies for coffee and a bagel, or a much larger order. Multiply that by an average 1200 transactions a month and it adds $120 to the cost of doing business. Added to this is the cost to rent the equipment for $30 to $40 dollars per month plus the telephone lines. "The average consumer's view is that it's free," he said. "But there is a cost. We both pay. You pay for so many transactions on your bank account, or it's built into your bank membership."

The shift to plastic costs merchants varying rates depending on the products they sell and the volume of business they do, but most business people, like Pepperell, feel they have no choice but to offer the service. Others simply take cash and run the risk that cash-strapped customers may bypass them in favour of a plastic-accepting competitor. Still others put a minimum transaction amount, usually five dollars, for accepting debit or credit as payment or tack on an extra charge for customers who want to pay this way.

Fraud is another concern. We've all heard or read of stories of fraudsters stealing PIN pads or inserting a device to collect customer's PIN numbers. In 2007 this cost card issuers $107 million, and while this sounds like a lot of money, 99.99 percent of the 4 billion transactions in Canada go through without a hitch, according to Tina Romano, a spokesperson for Interac. Simple actions like locking up the machine when closed, making sure it is in a place where it can't be easily accessed when not being used and reminding customers to hide their PIN number when they put it in can go a long way to reducing this problem. Technology such as embedding microchips into cards to encrypt information is another solution under trial in Kitchener-Waterloo, Ontario.

Whatever decision business owners make, it will involve trade-offs between customer convenience and added costs.

Source: Adapted from Gillian Shaw, "Paying by Debit Involves Many Hidden Prices; Retailers and Customers Alike Pay for Use of Plastic," *The Vancouver Sun,* March 14, 2008, p. C3.

and temporary employment agencies. Such financing is provided by commercial finance companies and by some banks. One important consideration about selling accounts receivable to a factor is the potential impact it might have on the firm's customers. They may either believe the firm has resorted to this because it is in financial difficulty or be harassed by collection tactics of the factoring company, and blame the invoicing company for it. Either way, the firm runs the risk of alienating customers who may take their business elsewhere.

Two types of accounts receivable financing are available. The first type uses a firm's **pledged accounts receivable** as collateral for a loan. Payments received from customers are forwarded to the lending institution to pay off the loan. In the second type of financing, a business sells its accounts receivable to a finance company, a practice known as factoring. The finance company thereby assumes the bad-debt risk associated with receivables it buys.

pledged accounts receivable
accounts receivable used as collateral for a loan

The obvious advantage of accounts receivable financing is the immediate cash flow it provides for firms that have limited working capital. As a secondary benefit, the volume of borrowing can be quickly expanded proportionally in order to match a firm's growth in sales and accounts receivable.

A drawback to this type of financing is its high cost. Rates typically run several points above the prime interest rate, and factors charge a fee to compensate them for their credit-investigation activities and for the risk that customers may default in payment. Another weakness of accounts receivable financing is that pledging receivables may limit a firm's ability to borrow from a bank by removing a prime asset from its available collateral.

MANAGING INVENTORY

Inventory is a "necessary evil" in the financial management system. It is "necessary" because supply and demand cannot be managed to coincide precisely with day-to-day operations; it is an "evil" because it ties up funds that are not actively productive.

REDUCING INVENTORY TO FREE CASH

Inventory is a bigger problem for some small businesses than for others. The inventory of many service firms, for example, consists of only a few supplies. A manufacturer, on the other hand, has several inventories—raw materials, work in process, and finished goods. Also, retailers and wholesalers, especially those with high inventory turnover rates such as firms in grocery distribution, are continually involved in solving inventory-management problems.

Chapter 12 discussed several ideas related to purchasing and inventory management that are designed to minimize inventory-carrying costs and processing costs. The emphasis in this section is on practices that will minimize average inventory levels, thereby releasing funds for other applications. The correct minimum level of inventory is the level needed to maintain desired production schedules and/or a certain level of customer service. A concerted effort to manage inventory can trim inventory excess and pay handsome dividends.

MONITORING INVENTORY

One of the first steps in managing inventory is to discover what's in inventory and how long it's been there. Too often, items are purchased, warehoused, and essentially forgotten. A yearly inventory for accounting purposes is inadequate for good inventory control. Items that are slow movers may sit in a retailer's inventory beyond the time when markdowns should have been applied.

Computers can provide assistance in inventory identification and control. However, physical inventories are still required periodically to verify the computer-generated count. There are many reasons the physical count and reported count may be different. Inaccurate recording of inventory coming in and going out is one reason the actual count may differ from what the computer claims. Another is called **shrinkage.** In addition to recording errors, shrinkage occurs when inventory is damaged or stolen and is normally written off (i.e., the value of the inventory concerned is deducted from inventory on the balance sheet and added to an expense line on the income statement) as either spoilage or materials used under cost of goods sold. Improved record-keeping methods, better materials-handling methods, and increased security measures are all ways to reduce shrinkage.

shrinkage
the difference between physical inventory count and reported count, which is normally written off as spoilage or materials used under cost of goods sold

CONTROLLING STOCKPILES

Small business managers tend to overbuy inventory for several reasons. First, an entrepreneur's enthusiasm may lead him or her to forecast greater demand than is realistic. Second, the personalization of the business–customer relationship may motivate a manager to stock everything customers want. Third, a price-conscious manager may be overly susceptible to a vendor's appeal to "Buy now, prices are going up."

Managers must exercise restraint when stockpiling. Improperly managed and uncontrolled stockpiling may greatly increase inventory carrying costs and place a heavy drain on the funds of a small business.

MANAGING ACCOUNTS PAYABLE

Cash flow management and accounts payable management are intertwined. As long as a payable is outstanding, the buying firm can keep cash equal to that amount in its own chequing account. When payment is made, however, that firm's cash account is reduced accordingly.

Although payables are legal obligations, they can be paid at various times or even renegotiated in some cases. Therefore, financial management of accounts payable hinges on negotiation and timing.

NEGOTIATION

Any business is subject to emergency situations and may find it necessary to ask creditors to postpone its payable obligations. Usually, creditors will cooperate in working out a solution because it's in their best interest for a client firm to succeed.

TIMING

"Buy now, pay later" is the motto of many entrepreneurs. By buying on credit, a small business is using creditors' funds to supply short-term cash needs. The longer creditors' funds can be borrowed, the better—within reason. Payment, therefore, should be delayed as long as acceptable under the agreement.

Typically, accounts payable (trade credit) involve payment terms that include a cash discount. With trade-discount terms, paying later may be inappropriate. For example,

Timetable (days after invoice date)	Settlement Costs for a $20,000 Purchase (terms: 3/10, net 30)
Day 1 through 10	$19,400
Day 11 through 30	$20,000
Day 31 and thereafter	$20,000 + possible late penalty + deterioration in credit standing

EXHIBIT **13-14**

An Accounts Payable Timetable

terms of 3/10, net 30 offer a 3 percent potential discount. Exhibit 13-14 shows the possible settlement costs over the credit period of 30 days. Note that for a $20,000 purchase, a settlement of only $19,400 is required if payment is made within the first 10 days ($20,000 less the 3 percent discount of $600). Between day 11 and day 30, the full settlement of $20,000 is required. After 30 days, the settlement cost may exceed the original amount, as late-payment fees are added.

The timing question then becomes "Should the account be paid on day 10 or day 30?" There is little reason to pay $19,400 on days 1 through 9, when the same amount will settle the account on day 10. Likewise, if payment is to be made after day 10, it makes sense to wait until day 30 to pay the $20,000.

By paying on the last day of the discount period, the buyer saves the amount of the discount offered. The other alternative of paying on day 30 allows the buyer to use the seller's money for an additional 20 days by foregoing the discount. As Exhibit 13-14 shows, the buyer can use the seller's $19,400 for 20 days at a cost of $600. The annualized interest rate can be calculated as follows:

$$Annualized\ interest\ rate = \frac{Days\ in\ year}{Net\ period - Cash\ discount\ period} \times \frac{Cash\ discount\ \%}{100 - Cash\ discount\ \%}$$

$$= \frac{365}{30 - 10} \times \frac{3}{100 - 3}$$

$$= 18.25 \times 0.030928$$

$$= 0.564,\ or\ 56.4\%$$

By failing to take a discount, a business typically pays a high rate for use of a supplier's money—56.4 percent per annum in this case. Payment on day 10 appears to be the most logical choice. Recall, however, that payment also affects cash flow. If funds are extremely short, a small firm may have to wait to pay until the last possible day in order to avoid an overdraft at the bank.

LOOKING BACK

1 Describe the purpose and content of financial statements.

- An income statement presents the financial results of a firm's operations over a given time period in selling the product or service, in producing or acquiring the goods or services, in running the firm, in financing the firm, and in paying taxes.
- The income statement does not measure a firm's cash flows, because it is calculated on an accrual basis rather than on a cash basis.
- A balance sheet provides a snapshot of a firm's financial position at a specific point in time, showing the amount of assets the firm owns, the amount of outstanding debt, and the amount of owners' equity.
- A statement of cash flows presents the sources and uses of a firm's cash flow for a given period of time.
- Measuring a firm's cash flows involves calculating a firm's after-tax cash flows from operations and then subtracting investments in net operating working capital and investments in fixed and other assets.
- An investor's cash flow is equal to the interest and dividends received from the business, plus the firm's repayment of debt or repurchase of stock, less any additional financing (debt or equity) provided by the investor.

2 Identify the basic requirements for an accounting system.

- An accounting system structures the flow of financial information to provide a complete picture of financial activities.
- The system should be objective, follow generally accepted accounting principles, and supply information on a timely basis.
- In addition to the balance sheet, income statement, and statement of cash flows, an accounting system should provide internal records that account for accounts receivable, accounts payable, inventories, payroll, cash, and fixed assets, as well as insurance policies, leaseholds, and outside investments.

3 Explain two alternative accounting options.

- Accounting systems may use either cash or accrual methods and may be structured as either single-entry or double-entry systems.
- With the cash method of accounting, transactions are recorded only when cash is received or a payment is made; the accrual method of accounting matches revenue earned against expenses associated with it.

- A single-entry system is basically a chequebook system of receipts and disbursements; a double-entry system of accounting incorporates journals and ledgers and requires that each transaction be recorded twice.

4 Describe the purpose of and procedures related to internal control.

- Internal control refers to a system of checks and balances designed to safeguard a firm's assets and enhance the accuracy of financial statements.
- Some examples of internal control procedures are separation of employees' duties, limiting access to accounting records and computer facilities, and safeguarding blank cheques.
- Building internal controls within a small business is difficult but important.

5 Evaluate a firm's liquidity.

- Liquidity is a firm's capacity to meet its short-term obligations.
- One way of measuring a firm's liquidity is to compare its liquid assets (cash, accounts receivable, and inventories) and its short-term debt, using the current ratio or the acid-test ratio.
- A second way to measure liquidity is to determine the time it takes to convert accounts receivable and inventories into cash, by computing the accounts receivable turnover and the inventory turnover.

6 Assess a firm's operating profitability.

- Operating profitability is evaluated by determining if the firm is earning a good return on its total assets, through computation of the operating income return on investment.
- The operating income return on investment can be separated into two components—the operating profit margin and the total asset turnover— to gain more insight into the firm's operating profitability.

7 Measure a firm's use of debt or equity financing.

- Either the debt ratio or the debt-equity ratio can be used to measure how much debt a firm uses in its financing mix.
- A firm's ability to cover interest charges on its debt can be measured by the times interest earned ratio.

8 Evaluate the rate of return earned on the owners' investment.

- Owners' return on investment is measured by dividing net income by the common equity invested in the business.
- The return on equity is a function of (1) the firm's operating income return on investment less the interest paid and (2) the amount of debt used relative to the amount of equity financing.

9 Describe the working-capital cycle of a small business.

- The working-capital cycle begins with the purchase of inventory and ends with the collection of accounts receivable.
- The cash conversion period is critical because it is the time period during which cash flow problems can arise and a firm can become illiquid.

10 Identify the important issues in managing a firm's cash flows.

- A firm's cash flows consist of cash flowing into a business (through sales revenue, borrowing, and so on) and cash flowing out of the business (through purchases, operating expenses, and so on).
- Profitable small companies sometimes encounter cash flow problems by failing to understand the working-capital cycle or failing to anticipate the negative consequences of growth.
- Cash inflows and outflows are reconciled in the cash budget, which involves forecasts of cash receipts and expenditures.

11 Explain the key issues in managing accounts receivable, inventory, and accounts payable.

- Granting credit to customers, primarily a marketing decision, directly affects a firm's cash account.
- A firm can improve its cash flow by speeding collections from customers, minimizing inventories, and delaying payments to suppliers.
- Some small businesses speed the cash flow from receivables by borrowing against them.
- A concerted effort to manage inventory can trim excess inventory and free cash for other uses.
- Accounts payable, a primary source of financing for small firms, directly affects a firm's cash flow situation.

KEY TERMS

accounting statements (financial statements), p. 356

accounts payable (trade credit), p. 360

accounts receivable, p. 358

accounts receivable turnover, p. 374

accrual method of accounting, p. 365

accrued expenses, p. 360

acid-test ratio (quick ratio), p. 369

average collection period, p. 370

balance sheet, p. 357

capital intensive, p. 379

cash conversion period, p. 383

cash flow forecast (cash budget), p. 390

cash method of accounting, p. 365

cost of goods sold, p. 356

current assets (working capital), p. 358

current ratio, p. 369

debt ratio, p. 375

debt-equity ratio, p. 375

double-entry system, p. 365

financial leverage, p. 375

financial ratios, p. 367

financial statements (accounting statements), p. 356

financing costs, p. 357

firm's cash flows, p. 393

fixed asset turnover, p. 374

fixed assets, p. 359

gross profit, p. 356

growth trap, p. 389

income statement (profit and loss statement), p. 356

intangible assets, p. 359

internal control, p. 365

inventory turnover, p. 370

liquidity, p. 368

lock box, p. 393

long-term debt, p. 360

net income available to owners (net income), p. 357

net working capital, p. 381

operating expenses, p. 356

operating income, p. 356

operating income (earnings before interest and taxes), p. 371

operating income return on investment (OIROI), p. 371

operating profit margin, p. 373

pledged accounts receivable, p. 395

profit and loss statement (income statement), p. 356

quick ratio, p. 369

retained earnings, p. 360

return on equity, p. 377

shrinkage, p. 396

single-entry system, p. 365

statement of cash flows, p. 362

times interest earned ratio, p. 376

total asset turnover, p. 373

trade credit (accounts payable), p. 360

working capital (current assets), p. 358

working-capital cycle, p. 381

working-capital management, p. 380

DISCUSSION QUESTIONS

1. What is the relationship between an income statement and a balance sheet?
2. Explain the purposes of the income statement and balance sheet.
3. Distinguish among (a) gross profit, (b) operating income (earnings before interest and taxes), and (c) net income available to owners.
4. Explain the accounting concept that income is realized when earned, whether or not it has been received in cash.
5. What are the primary types of records required in a sound accounting system?
6. What is liquidity? Differentiate between the two approaches given in this chapter to measure liquidity.

7. Explain the following ratios:
   a. Operating profit margin
   b. Total asset turnover
   c. Times interest earned
8. What is financial leverage? When should it be used and when should it be avoided? Why?
9. a. List the events in the working-capital cycle that directly affect cash and those that do not.
   b. What determines the length of a firm's cash conversion period?
10. a. What are some examples of cash receipts that are not sales revenue?
    b. Explain how expenses and cash disbursements during a month may be different.

YOU MAKE THE CALL

SITUATION 1

In 2008, Carter Dalton purchased the Baugh Company. Although the firm has consistently earned profits, little cash has been available for other than business needs. Before purchasing Baugh, Dalton thought that cash flows were generally equal to profits plus depreciation. However, this does not seem to be the case. The industry norms for the financial ratios and the financial statements (in thousands) for the Baugh Company, 2007–2008, follow.

Balance Sheet (in thousands)

	2007	2008
Assets		
Current assets:		
Cash	$ 8	$ 10
Accounts receivable	15	20
Inventory	22	25
Total current assets	$ 45	$ 55
Fixed assets:		
Gross plant and equipment	$ 50	$ 55
Accumulated depreciation	15	20
Net fixed assets	$ 35	$ 35
Other assets	12	10
TOTAL ASSETS	$ 92	$ 100

	2007	**2008**
Debt (Liabilities) and Equity		
Current liability		
Accounts payable	$ 10	$ 12
Accruals	7	8
Short-term notes	5	5
Total current liabilities	$ 22	$ 25
Long-term liabilities	15	15
Total liabilities	$ 37	$ 40
Total stockholders' equity	55	60
TOTAL DEBT AND EQUITY	$ 92	$ 100

Income Statement, 2008 (in thousands)

Sales revenue	$175
Cost of goods sold	105
Gross profit on sales	$ 70
Operating expenses:	
Marketing expenses	$ 26
General and administrative expenses	20
Depreciation	5
Total operating expenses	$ 51
Operating income	$ 19
Interest expense	3
Earnings before taxes	$ 16
Income tax	8
Net income	$ 8

Financial Ratios	**Industry Norms**
Current ratio	2.50
Acid-test ratio	1.50
Average collection period	30.00
Inventory turnover	6.00
Debt-equity ratio	1.00
Operating income return on investment	16.0%
Operating profit margin	8.0%
Total asset turnover	2.00
Fixed asset turnover	7.00
Times interest earned ratio	5.00
Return on equity	14.0%

Question 1 Why doesn't Dalton have cash for personal needs? (As part of your analysis, measure cash flows.)

Question 2 Evaluate the Baugh Company's financial performance, given the financial ratios for the industry.

SITUATION 2

A small firm specializing in the sale and installation of swimming pools was profitable but devoted very little attention to management of its working capital. It had, for example, never prepared or used a cash budget.

To be sure that money was available for payments as needed, the firm kept a minimum of $25,000 in a chequing account. At times, this account grew larger; it totalled $43,000 at one time. The owner felt that this approach to cash management worked well for a small company because it eliminated all of the paperwork associated with cash budgeting. Moreover, it had enabled the firm to pay its bills in a timely manner.

Question 1 What are the advantages and weaknesses of the minimum-cash-balance practice?
Question 2 There is a saying "If it isn't broken, don't fix it." In view of the firm's present success in paying bills promptly, should it be encouraged to use a cash budget? Be prepared to support your answer.

SITUATION 3

Ruston Manufacturing Company is a small firm selling entirely on a credit basis. It has experienced success and earned modest profits.

Sales are made on the basis of net payment in 30 days. Collections from customers run approximately 70 percent in 30 days, 20 percent in 60 days, 7 percent in 90 days, and 3 percent bad debts.

The owner has considered the possibility of offering a cash discount for early payment. However, the practice seems costly and possibly unnecessary. As the owner puts it, "Why should I bribe customers to pay what they legally owe?"

Question 1 Is offering a cash discount the equivalent of a bribe?
Question 2 How would a cash discount policy relate to bad debts?
Question 3 What cash discount policy, if any, would you recommend?
Question 4 What other approaches might be used to improve cash flow from receivables?

EXPERIENTIAL EXERCISES

1. Interview a local chartered accountant (CA) who consults with small firms on small business accounting systems. Report to the class on the levels of accounting knowledge the CA's clients appear to possess.
2. Contact several very small businesses and explain your interest in their accounting systems. Report to the class on their level of sophistication—for example, whether they use a single-entry system, a computer, or an outside professional.
3. Interview an owner of a small firm about the financial statements she or he uses. Ask the owner how important financial data are to her or his decision making.
4. Acquire a public firm's financial statements. Review the statements and describe the firm's financial position. Find an investment analyst's report or an article about the firm from *The Globe and Mail or National Post* and see if the writer agrees with your conclusions.
5. Interview a small business owner or credit manager regarding the extension of credit and/or the collection of receivables in that firm. Summarize your findings in a report.

EXPLORING THE WEB

1. Access the Meyers Norris Penny website at http://www.mnp.ca. Click on "MNP Library" and, under "Assurance," look at "What Kind of Financial Reports Do You Need?"
   a. What are the types of financial reports accountants prepare for businesses?
   b. What is each type used for, and what activities does the accountant undertake for each?
   c. Which type costs the most? The least? Why?

2. Access Dun & Bradstreet's database at http://www.dnb.ca and read the article in its resource centre on managing credit.

3. Access http://www.investopedia.com, click on "Tutorials" at the top of the page and then, under "More Advanced Topics," select "Ratio Analysis."
   a. Complete the tutorial on the balance sheet and income statement (profit and loss statement). Many of the ratios are unique to publicly traded companies. Try to match the ratios there with the equivalent ratios you read in this chapter.

   b. Which ratios are the same for both private companies and public companies?
   c. Which ratios are different for private companies and public companies? Why do you think they differ?

4. Go to the website for Business Owner's Toolkit at http://www.toolkit.cch.com.
   a. Select "Small Business Guide and the click on "Managing Your Business Finances" and check out the tutorials. What topics are covered in these tutorials?
   b. Open the link on "Credit and Collections." Examine the links there to discover the issues in accepting credit cards. What is the percentage range the credit card agency charges businesses? What are some types of businesses that will probably not be able to get approval to accept credit cards?
   c. Return to "Managing Your Business Finances" and follow the link to "Your Basic Bookkeeping." What steps are involved in bookkeeping? What are the five basic parts of an accounting system?

THE BUSINESS PLAN: LAYING THE FOUNDATION

ASKING THE RIGHT QUESTIONS

As part of laying the foundation to prepare your own business plan, you will need to develop the following:

1. Historical financial statements (if applicable) and five years of *pro forma* financial statements, including balance sheets, income statements, and statements of cash flows.
2. Monthly cash budgets for the first year and quarterly cash budgets for the second year.
3. Financial resources required now and in the future, with details on the intended use of funds being requested.

4. Underlying assumptions for all *pro forma* statements.
5. Current and planned investments by the owners and other investors.

If you are using BizPlan*Builder*® Express, refer to Part 3 for financial planning information that should be included in the business plan. Then turn to Part 2 for instructions on using the BizPlan software to prepare *pro forma* financial statements.

Financing Requirements, Pro Forma Financial Statements, and Sources of Financing

IN THE SPOTLIGHT

Building a Building Business—One House at a Time

You always remember your first.

Whether it's from the vantage point of your second home or your final downsized condo, nothing equals the thrill of being a first-time homeowner. Now imagine owning a company that's just completed building its first house—one that's high quality and bristling with enough smart features to suggest big things to come.

Ojibwa brothers Chris and Trevor Trainor don't have to imagine: they're putting the finishing touches on their first in Grand Bend, Ontario. "What am I, the COO?" jokes Trevor, as he inspects the paint on his hands. Chris nods, adding that he's the CFO. Neither is sure whom to crown CEO of SmartCraft Homes.

To describe financing their startup the brothers often use the term "bootstrapping," which is starting a business with little cash and depending on revenues to fuel growth. However, it would be more accurate to describe the initial cash as personal sources. The brothers' own savings were used and additional cash came from topping up the mortgages on their homes. Regardless of how you define their approach to this homebuilding venture, it's still quite a risk. "We're gambling on ourselves," confirms Chris, "and we're bursting with ideas." Smart-Craft did get financial assistance after Aboriginal Business Canada put them in touch with Tecumseh Community Development Corp. in Muncey, Ont., which in turn helped them secure a construction mortgage.

The first house is proof of the ideas the brothers have: a handsome and masculine, 2,000 square-foot, Craftsman-style dwelling steps from Lake Huron. It was built on weekends and holidays by Trevor and a few local helpers. Trevor lives nearby and commutes to his job at General Motors in Detroit. Chris pitched in whenever he could get away from his teaching job in Orillia and classes in the

Photo: Dave LeBlanc

Queen's University MBA program taught in Toronto. He hopes the MBA will give him the tools to run the company—which he describes as "the ultimate case study"—as efficiently as possible.

Their first house is actually a little larger than what they'd like to do in the future. Fans of the Cottage Company, a Seattle-based builder of "pocket Neighbourhoods" (800–1,000 square-foot loft bungalows arranged around a common courtyard), they'd like to try their hands at similar projects. They're so serious about SmartCraft's future, Chris is giving up his teaching job in Orillia and Trevor is giving up his gig at GM.

But, first things first—they've got to sell this house.

http://www.smartcrafthomes.com

Sources: Adapted from Dave LeBlanc, "Budding Builders Cut Their Teeth on First House," *The Globe and Mail,* April 6, 2007, p. G.11 and http://www.smartcrafthomes.com (accessed June 2008).

Businesses need cash to buy assets and to operate. Assets such as equipment and beginning inventory of product or materials must be paid for, and the business will need to pay employees, utilities, the telephone company, and many other kinds of expenses. The cash needed for all these expenses must come from somewhere, and that somewhere is called "financing." Financing comes in two forms: investing in the business for a share of the ownership of the business or having the business borrow money from individuals or other businesses.

In this chapter, we will not be dealing with traditional accounting methods or financial statements. These were covered in detail in Chapter 13. However, we will be using some of the same terminology. We will be looking at various methods of determining how much cash or financing the business will need and at the sources from which it can be found.

Businesses need cash for three principal things: first, to purchase assets such as equipment and inventory; second, to pay for other costs incurred such as payroll, advertising, taxes, and so on; and third, to pay for costs incurred before they even start up, such as research and development, market research, and expert advice.

DETERMINING ASSET REQUIREMENTS

ASSETS

Estimate the amount of financing a new or existing business will need.

Assets are tangible or intangible property a business owns, and fall into three categories: (1) current assets, (2) fixed assets, and (3) other assets. These were discussed in greater detail in Chapter 13, but for our purposes here we will talk about inventory, prepaid expenses, land, buildings and equipment, and "other" assets.

Most businesses need space and equipment to operate. This may be very simple in the case of a small café for example, which may need only some basic commercial kitchen equipment (coolers, coffee makers, and the like) and some chairs and tables, or this can be very complex in the case of a manufacturing company, which may need highly technical and specialized equipment. Similarly, the café will usually require a small part of a larger building in which to operate, one with good pedestrian traffic and a prominent location so it can be seen by passersby. The café will usually lease this space from the building owner. In the case of the manufacturing company or a warehousing business, an entire building may be required, and this may be owned by the business or leased from another company. We discussed space requirements in Chapter 11.

In either case, the costs of space and equipment can be estimated with a high degree of precision. A leasing agent or real estate agent can tell you the cost of leasing or buying space, including an estimate of operating costs (property taxes, business taxes, utilities, and maintenance). If the space is being leased, the lease contract will usually require the business to pay either a security deposit or to pay the first and last month's lease payment in advance, or both. For purposes of determining the amount of cash the business will need, all of the above costs are known quite accurately in advance.

Equipment suppliers can both advise as to the type and quality of equipment needed and quote a price for it. However, the business owner must make two additional decisions: (1) whether to buy or lease the equipment and (2) whether to acquire new or used equipment.

Leasing equipment has two advantages: (1) it requires no up-front cash, freeing up the firm's cash for other purposes, and (2) it provides a hedge against equipment obsolescence. However, leasing does require the business to make regular, usually monthly, payments to the leasing company. In either case, it is up to the business to pay for insurance and maintenance on the equipment. It can also be expensive to get out of a lease if it turns out the business does not need the equipment or cannot afford to keep making lease payments. For most small businesses, equipment that is leased is limited to equipment like the telephone system, photocopiers, fax machines, and the like. Equipment that is essential to what the business does is usually not leased.

While leasing is certainly an option to be considered for financing the acquisition of needed equipment, an entrepreneur should not simply assume that leasing is always the right decision. Only by carefully comparing the interest charged on a loan to the cost of a lease, the tax consequences of leasing versus borrowing, and the significance of the obsolescence factor can an owner make a good choice. Also, the owner must be careful about contracting for so much equipment that it becomes difficult to meet installment or lease payments.

The Royal Bank of Canada website (http://www.rbc.com) and Industry Canada's website (http://www.ic.gc.ca), among others, have lease-versus-buy calculation programs online to help with this decision.

The decision to buy new or used equipment will depend on many things. For example, if the business is a professional one such as an insurance broker and requires customers to come to its location, used office furniture may convey the wrong image. If the business relies on state-of-the-art technology, used equipment is not an option. However, some types of businesses may be able to reduce the cost of equipment dramatically by purchasing used. When the owners of the Prairie Mill Bread Company were starting their artisan bakery in Calgary, they estimated the cost of the equipment they would need at over $70,000. Another local bakery had recently gone out of business, and the Prairie Mill was able to buy most of the equipment at the receivership auction for only about $25,000, a savings of over $45,000. This meant the owners could lower the amount of money they personally invested in the business and provide a "financial cushion" they could draw on if they needed cash later on.[1] As with the cost of the space the business will occupy, the cost of equipment needed can be determined quite accurately.

The other major asset some businesses will need to purchase is inventory, either an inventory of goods to sell when the business starts, in the case of a retail shop, or an inventory of materials and components in the case of a manufacturing business. As with equipment, suppliers can give very firm prices for the above.

The other assets a business may require are the costs of incorporation and protecting intellectual property such as patents. It may also be required to pre-pay some expenses such as insurance. In all of these cases the costs can be determined quite accurately.

PRE-START-UP EXPENSES

A business may have to spend cash on many kinds of activities and services before it starts operation, in addition to the assets discussed above: there may be costs to research the market and other critical aspects of the business; research and development on the product may have to be performed; professional advice may be needed from lawyers, accountants, and consultants; advertising and promotion may be done to build up to a grand opening of the business; business licenses and inspections may have to be paid for; and business cards and other supplies may have to be bought. Most of these costs can be determined accurately, but the cost of research and development can be much more difficult to estimate. There is also the risk of "overengineering" the product rather than making a decision to stop development and bring it to market.

WORKING CAPITAL OR OPERATING REQUIREMENTS

Once the business is in operation, it will need cash to operate. It must pay employees, pay for supplies and services, pay taxes, and so on. How much cash the business will need is determined by the difference between cash available and cash going out. Available cash consists of cash on hand and cash received from sales. Traditional financial statements do not reflect this, since they do not account for *timing* differences between when sales are recognized for accounting purposes and when the cash from those sales comes in, nor do they reflect when expenses are recognized for accounting purposes and when the cash has to be paid to the supplier. Traditional financial statements also do not forecast; they simply record history, or what has already happened. Does this mean financial statements are of little value to the business owner? No, it does not. As we saw in Chapter 11, financial statements are very important as a scorecard of how well the business is performing, as a picture of the business's financial health, and for diagnosing where the business could be performing better. For our purposes here, however, we need to determine how much cash the business will need to operate, and therefore how much financing it will need on an ongoing basis, and the tool we use to do this is the **cash budget** or **cash flow forecast.** The cash flow forecast is extremely important to include as part of the business plan for a new or growing venture, as it allows the entrepreneur to know not only how much is needed today, but also when additional cash will be required in the form of loans or additional investment to finance growth.

The cash flow forecast reflects the timing differences not achieved by traditional financial statements. Why would there be a timing difference? For revenues or sales, your business might have to give credit to customers, especially if the customers are other businesses. The sale is recorded for accounting purposes when you generate an invoice or a bill, but customers may not pay you the money for many days. There are industry statistics from Statistics Canada or Dun & Bradstreet that can give an average number of days it takes to get paid for most industries. For example, businesses in the commercial printing industry average about 70 days to get paid by their customers. This can have a dramatic effect on how much cash the business has to operate. Amounts owed to a business by its customers are called **accounts receivable.** Similarly, suppliers of goods and services to your business may extend credit to you, allowing you to pay them at some future point. This can reduce the amount of cash you need to operate. Amounts owed by your business to its suppliers are called **accounts payable.** Finally, the cash flow forecast accounts for the payment of amounts paid infrequently. For example, GST owing to the federal government may be paid by your business only every three months.

The cash flow forecast is usually broken down monthly for the first year, quarterly for the second and third year, and annually for the fourth and fifth years. It is broken down into four sections: cash incoming from operations, cash incoming from financing and other activities, cash outflow from operations, and cash outflow from nonoperating activities such as interest and tax payments. Exhibit 14-1 shows a simple monthly cash flow forecast.

A more detailed one-year spreadsheet can be found on the book's website at http://www.longenecker4e.nelson.com.

The forecast starts with how much cash is on hand at the beginning of the month. In the case of a new business like this one, that amount is zero. If your business receives cash (or debit card and credit card transactions), this is all or some of the amount of cash received from operations, net of credit card transaction fees. If it does

cash budget (cash flow forecast)
a planning document strictly concerned with the receipt and payment of dollars

accounts receivable
the amount of credit extended to customers that is currently outstanding

accounts payable (trade credit)
outstanding credit payable to suppliers

EXHIBIT **14-1**
*Typical Cash Flow
Forecast*

Cash Flow Forecast

	Month 1	Month 2	Month 3	Month 4	Month 5	Month 6
Opening Cash	0	58,200	9540	8230	7,452	5170.8
Cash Sales	0	4800	8000	10,000	12,000	10,000
A/R Opening	0	0	7200	14,160	19,248	25,699.2
Cr. Sales	0	7200	12,000	15,000	18,000	15,000
Collections	0	0	5040	9912	11,548.8	15,419.52
A/R Ending	0	7200	14,160	19,248	25,699	25280
Total Op Cash In	0	4800	13,040	19,912	23,549	25420
Start-up Capital	50,000	0	0	0	0	0
Financing	36,000	0	0	0	0	0
Other	0	0	0	0	0	0
Total Non-Op In	86,000	0	0	0	0	0
Total Cash Avail	86,000	63,000	22,580	28,142	31,001	30,590
Wages	2000	2640	4400	5500	6600	5500
Materials & Supp	800	1200	2000	2500	3000	2500
Lease/Rent	1500	750	750	750	750	750
G & A	1000	960	1600	2000	2400	2000
Ad & Promotion	10,000	1250	1250	1250	1250	1250
Selling Exp	0	1800	3000	3750	4500	3750
Taxes	0	0	0	0	0	0
Inventory Purch	0	30,000	0	3600	6000	7500
Total Op Cash Out	15,300	38,600	13,000	19,350	24,500	23,250
Interest	0	360	350	340	330	320
Loan Payments	0	1000	1000	1000	1000	1000
Equip Leases	0	0	0	0	0	0
Capital Expend	12,500	12,500	0	0	0	0
Incorp Cost	0	1000	0	0	0	0
Dividends	0	0	0	0	0	0
Total Non-Op Cash	12,500	14,860	1350	1340	1330	1320
Total Cash Out	27,800	53,460	14,350	20,690	25,830	24,570
Ending Cash	58,200	9540	8230	7452	5171	6020

all or some of its business by billing customers, the forecast requires you to estimate how long customers will take to pay, and thus how much cash will be collected from accounts receivable each month. The forecast in Exhibit 14-1 has a calculation for this built into it:

$$\begin{array}{ccccccc} \textit{Accounts} & & \textit{Credit} & & \textit{Collection} & & \textit{Accounts} \\ \textit{receivable} & + & \textit{Sales} & - & \textit{of Accounts} & = & \textit{receivable} \\ \textit{(beginning of month)} & & & & \textit{receivable} & & \textit{(end of month)} \end{array}$$

The accounts receivable (end of month) becomes the next month's accounts receivable (beginning of month). The total of cash sales plus collection of accounts receivable is the cash received from operations.

Cash incoming from financing and other activities is cash being invested in the business by its owners, cash from borrowing from a financial institution or other lender, or cash being generated by such things as selling equipment, which businesses sometimes do. You can see in the example that this business received cash from its owners and from a bank loan in the first month of operation.

Cash outflow from operations is cash paid to employees and suppliers of goods and services to the business. The example shows some typical categories of these. These can be very detailed, such as the "wages" category, or have some smaller categories aggregated together as in the case of "general & administrative," which is usually things like telephone service, office supplies, and so on that are very small amounts by themselves.

Cash outflow from nonoperating activities are things like loan payments, equipment lease payments, and taxes.

The difference between total cash available (beginning cash + cash incoming from operations + cash incoming from financing and other activities) and total cash outflow (cash outflow from operations + cash outflow from nonoperating activities) is the ending cash balance, which becomes the beginning cash balance for the next month. If this is a negative number, sufficient additional financing must be found to cover the shortfall, or the business will not be able to meet all its financial obligations and will be in danger of failing.

ESTIMATING REVENUES AND OUTFLOWS

The cash flow forecast is critical to new and growing businesses to see when additional cash will have to be found to help the business grow. However, it is just a forecast and therefore depends on your ability to estimate revenues and outflows in the future. For an existing business with a history to guide it, this is much easier to do; for a new business, this may be very difficult. The forecast starts with a sales forecast. We cannot overemphasize the need to create as accurate and believable forecast as possible. If the revenue numbers in the sales forecast are not accurate then all of the financial projections for the business will be wrong.

The various methods of generating a sales forecast are discussed in Chapter 5. The next important piece of information is how much of those sales will be cash sales and how much will be credit? If the business has credit sales, how much of the accounts receivable at the beginning of the month will be collected? Information from Industry Canada (Performance Plus http://sme.ic.gc.ca) or Dun & Bradstreet for your industry will help you answer these questions.

percentage of sales
method of forecasting asset investments and financing requirements

There are several methods of determining how much will be spent on the various operating outflow categories. One is **percentage of sales,** where industry averages (available from Industry Canada, Dun & Bradstreet, or some industry associations) are used. For example, companies in an industry may spend 3 percent of their sales on advertising and promotion. If you think your business will be typical, then this percentage of your forecast sales can be used. Keep in mind that you may spend more at certain times such as a grand opening or the Christmas season, and less at others, and this should be reflected in your forecast. For other categories, you may have a known amount (a maintenance contract for equipment, or the cost of leasing the space the business occupies, for example) or you can determine the amount by simple math. If you have four employees each paid $8 per hour for a 37.5 hour week, then the wages each month will be $5200.00 ($4 \times 8 \times 37.5 \times 52$ divided by 12 months).

There are several complications that can be built into or left out of the cash flow forecast, depending on how large they are in comparison to other items. In the wages example above, the business would normally be deducting income tax and other payroll deductions and not paying them to the government until the next month, for example. Calculating GST collected from customers and deducting GST paid to suppliers to determine a net GST payable is another complication that may not be worthwhile. In this case an estimate might be used in the cash flow forecast.

FINANCING REQUIREMENTS

As we have seen, determining the amount of financing a business needs is a combination of good research into costs for space, equipment, costs of various items, and careful thought about a sales forecast. Bringing all of this together in a cash flow forecast tells us how much the business will need to start and to grow. It also helps us deal with fluctuations in activity throughout the year. Almost every business has some seasons that are busier than others: most retailers do a large proportion of their business in the Christmas season; flower shops are much busier around special occasions such as Mother's Day; and golf courses do all of their business over a few months in most of Canada. Building this seasonality into the forecast allows the business owner to see when more cash will be needed so arrangements can be made in advance to have it available.

TYPES OF FINANCING

Financing comes from two main sources: debt capital (loans) and ownership equity. Debt capital is money that has been borrowed and must be repaid at some predetermined date. Ownership equity, on the other hand, represents the owners' investment in the company—money they have personally put into the firm without any specific date for repayment. Owners recover their investment by withdrawing money from the firm or by selling their interest in it.

Debt capital is financing provided by a creditor. It is divided into (1) current, or short-term, debt and (2) long-term debt. **Current debt,** or short-term liabilities, includes borrowed money that must be repaid within the next 12 months. Sources of current debt may be classified as follows:

- *Accounts payable* represent the credit extended by suppliers to a firm when it purchases inventories. The purchasing firm usually is given 30 or 60 days to pay for the inventory. This form of credit is also called *trade credit.*
- Other payables include interest expenses and income taxes that are owed and will come due within the year.
- **Accrued expenses** are short-term liabilities that have been incurred but not yet paid. For example, employees may have performed work for which they will not be paid until the following week or month.
- **Short-term notes** represent cash amounts borrowed from a bank or other lending source for a short period of time, such as 90 days. Short-term notes are a primary source of financing for most small businesses, as these businesses have access to fewer sources of long-term capital than their larger counterparts.
- **Long-term debt** includes loans from banks or other sources that lend money for longer than 12 months. When a firm borrows money for five years to buy

debt capital
business financing that was provided by creditors and must be repaid at some predetermined date

current debt (short-term liabilities)
borrowed money that must be repaid within 12 months

accrued expenses
short-term liabilities that have been incurred but not yet paid

short-term notes
cash amounts that were borrowed from a bank or another lending source and must be repaid within a short period of time

long-term debt
loans from banks or other sources with repayment terms of more than 12 months

mortgage
a long-term loan from a creditor for which real estate is pledged as collateral

owners' equity capital
owners' financial investments in a company, including profits retained in the firm

equipment, it signs an agreement—a long-term note—promising to repay the money in five years. When a firm borrows money for 30 years to purchase real estate, such as a warehouse or office building, the real estate stands as collateral for the long-term loan, which is called a **mortgage.** If the borrower is unable to repay the loan, the lender can take the real estate in settlement.

- **Owners' equity capital** is money that the owners invest in a business. Note that they are only residual owners of the business; that is, creditors must be paid before the owners can retrieve any of their equity capital from the business's income. Likewise, if the company is liquidated, creditors are always paid before the owners are paid.

In summary, financing for a new business derives from two sources: debt capital and ownership equity. Debt capital is money borrowed from financial institutions, suppliers, and other lenders. Owners' equity capital represents the owners' investment in the company, either through funds invested in the firm or through profits retained in the business.

We have discussed various ways of determining financing needs. Before we go on, it is important to reinforce the idea that all of the cash we need results in the creation of assets, whether in the form of accounts receivable; inventory; prepaid expenses; fixed assets such as land, buildings, and equipment; or "other assets." Now we consider the financing needed to purchase these assets. For every dollar of assets, there must be a corresponding dollar of financing. Certain principles govern the financing of firms:

1. The more assets a firm needs, the greater the firm's financial requirements. Thus, a firm experiencing rapid sales growth has greater asset requirements and, consequently, greater pressure to find financing.

spontaneous financing
short-term debts, such as accounts payable, that spontaneously increase in proportion to a firm's increasing sales

2. A firm should finance its growth in such a way as to maintain a proper degree of liquidity. Liquid assets are cash and assets that can be turned into cash fairly quickly, such as accounts receivable and inventory. Liquid assets are used to pay for short-term obligations such as payroll, accounts payable to suppliers, taxes payable, and loan payments. Liquidity is discussed in greater detail in Chapter 13.

3. The amount of total debt that can be used in financing a business is limited by the amount of equity provided by the owners. A bank will not provide all the financing for a firm; owners must put some of their own money into the venture. Thus, a business plan may specify that at least half of the firm's financing will come from equity and the rest will come from debt. In other words, management should limit the firm's debt ratio, which equals debt as a percentage of total assets (that is, total debt divided by total assets).

external equity
funds that derive initially from the owners' investment in a firm

profit retention
the reinvestment of profits in a firm

4. Some short-term debt arises spontaneously as the firm grows. Such **spontaneous financing** increases as a natural consequence of an increase in the firm's sales. For example, an increase in sales requires more inventories, causing accounts payable to increase. Typically, spontaneous sources of financing average a certain percentage of sales.

internal equity
funds that come from retaining profits within a firm

5. There are two sources of equity capital: external and internal. Initially, the equity in a company comes from the investment the owners make in the firm; these funds represent **external equity.** Once the company is in operation, additional equity may come from **profit retention,** as profits are retained within the company rather than distributed to the owners: These funds are called **internal equity.** For

the typical small firm, internal equity is the primary source of equity for financing growth. (Be careful not to think of retained profits as a big cash resource. As already noted, a firm may have significant earnings but no cash to reinvest. (This problem was discussed further in Chapter 13.)

In summary,

Total asset requirements	=	Total sources of financing	=	Spontaneous financing	+	External sources of financing	+	Profits retained within the business

This equation captures the essence of forecasting financial requirements. The entrepreneur who thoroughly understands these relationships will be able to forecast his or her firm's financial requirements.

CASH FLOW FORECASTS

Create pro forma (forecast) cash flows, income statements, and balance sheets. **2**

In the first section of this chapter we described how to construct a cash flow forecast. It is our belief that, while forecast income statements and balance sheets are important, the cash flow forecast is the most critical of the financial projections for a new or growing venture. Quite simply, if a business runs out of cash, it dies. The accountant's approach to creating pro forma financial statements would be to start with the income statement and balance sheet and then create a cash flow. We believe the reverse is true. Creating a cash flow brings together all of the elements of the income statement and balance sheet. It is a relatively simple thing to break a cash flow out into a balance sheet and income statement. We will illustrate this from the cash flow forecast example in Exhibit 14-1.

PRO FORMA INCOME STATEMENTS AND BALANCE SHEETS

While not as important as the cash flow forecast, the pro forma income statement is important for two reasons: first, it illustrates the cost structure of the business; second, and most importantly, it allows the entrepreneur to assess the likely profitability of the proposed venture. The pro forma balance sheet is important because it allows the entrepreneur to assess the effects of operations on critical ratios that may have to be kept at certain levels to please lenders (see the description of loan covenants later in this chapter) and to show when the company might be able to pay dividends to its shareholders. Let's now see how to break the cash flow in Exhibit 14-1 into these statements.

The first thing we need to do is identify which items belong on the income statement and which belong on the balance sheet. The balance sheet items in Exhibit 14-1 are cash, accounts receivable, inventory, prepaid expenses (represented by the prepaid lease amount in month 1), accounts payable (represented by inventory purchases and incorporation cost), start-up capital, financing, and capital expenditures. The other items are all income statement items.

The second thing we have to do is remind ourselves about the *timing* of inflows and outflows and our assumptions surrounding them. For example, inventory purchases in month 6 will be 30 percent of month 5's sales, but this figure ($30,000 \times 30\% = 9000$) does not show up on the six-month cash flow because the cash will not be paid out until month 7. Referring back to Exhibit 14-1, the pro forma income statements and balance sheets for months 1 and 6 can be constructed as follows:

Pro Forma Income Statement
For the months ended Months 1 and 6

Month 1		Month 6	
Sales	$0	$112,000	(the sum of cash and credit sales for months 1–6)
Cost of goods sold	0	33,600	(the inventory that was sold)
Gross margin	0	79,000	
Wages	2000	26,640	(the sum of wages for months 1–6)
Materials & supplies	800	12,000	
Lease	750	4500	(does not include the prepaid portion in month 1)
G & A	1000	9960	
Ad & promotion	10,000	16,250	
Selling expenses	0	16,800	
Interest expense	0	1700	
Net income	(14,550)	(9450)	

As we can see, while profitability is improving, the company was still in a loss position at the end of six months. Now let's look at the balance sheet.

Pro Forma Balance Sheet
As at the End of Months 1 and 6

Month 1		Month 6	
Current Assets			
Cash	$58,200	$ 6020	ending cash from Exhibit 14-1)
Accounts receivable	0	25,280	(ending A/R from Exhibit 14-1)
Inventory	30,000	22,500	(all of the inventory purchased—COGS)
Prepaid expenses	750	750	(prepaid lease—first and last month's due in month 1)
Total current assets	88,950	54,550	
Fixed Assets			
Capital expenditures	12,500	25,000	(for simplicity, we are ignoring depreciation)
Other Assets			
Incorporation costs	1000	1000	(for simplicity, we are ignoring amortization)
Total Assets	**102,450**	**80,550**	
Current Liabilities			
Accounts payable	31,000	9000	(assuming we pay in 30-day terms)
Current portion of long-term debt	12,000	12,000	(loan payments due within 12 months)
Total current liab.	43,000	21,000	

Long-Term Liabilities		
Bank loan	36,000	31,000
Less current portion	(12,000)	(12,000)
Total L.T. liab.	24,000	19,000
Total liabilities	67,000	40,000
Equity		
Common shares	50,000	50,000
Retained earnings	(14,550)	(9450)
Total equity	35,450	40,550
Total Liabilities & Equity	**102,450**	**80,550**

Doing this correctly takes practice and patience. The author was out by $2000 on the balance sheet and had trouble discovering why. Using a spreadsheet and filling in the months between 1 and 6 quickly showed where the problem was and the balance sheet balanced. Students are encouraged to set up a cash flow forecast and try breaking it into the pro forma financial statements. It's not as hard as it looks. The full six month financial statements can be found on the book's website at http://www.longenecker4e.nelson.com.

SOURCES OF FINANCING

The initial financing of a small business is often patterned after a typical personal financing plan. A prospective entrepreneur will first use personal savings and then attempt to gain access to the savings of family and friends. Only if these sources are inadequate will the entrepreneur turn to more formal channels of financing, such as banks and outside investors (see Exhibit 14-2).

Major sources of equity financing are personal savings, friends and relatives, private investors in the community, large corporations, venture capitalists, and sale of stock in public equity markets (going public). Major sources of debt financing are individual investors, business suppliers, asset-based lenders, commercial banks, government-sponsored programs, and community-based financial institutions. To gain insight into how start-ups are financed, consider the responses given by owners of the

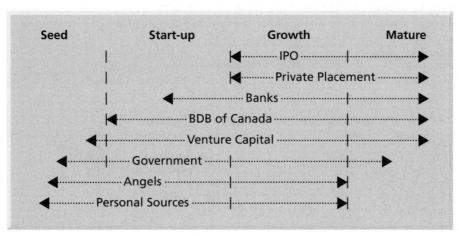

EXHIBIT **14-2**

Appropriate Sources of Financing

ETHICS

IN THE TRENCHES

Confronting the Ethical Issues

Playing with Payroll

When faced with a cash flow crisis, a business can encounter ethical questions. The following story illustrates the point.

The owner of a small manufacturing company in Vancouver was three days away from facing a payroll he knew he wouldn't be able to meet. Then a cheque from a customer for $9600 showed up on his desk. That amount was more than enough to cover the payroll, relieving him of a major worry and ensuring that his company would stay intact. Until the next payroll came due, anyway. The problem was, the cheque was clearly a duplicate payment for an invoice that had already been paid.

If there were compelling reasons not to use the money for payroll—such as overdue payments to suppliers—the owner chose to overlook them. It's understandable. Every growing business, no matter how successful, struggles with cash flow problems. But cash flow is not only a management issue of whom to pay what and how much to pay, and when to pay. It's also fraught with ethical implications—or it should be. Managing payroll, after all, also means making judgments about how other companies ought to be treated . . . aren't your suppliers as agonized about cash flow as you are? And while it may make for a sound management decision to spend money expanding operations—rather than pay vendors whose invoices are caked with dust—is it an honest way to deal with others?

But who has the time to spend fretting about right and wrong when what's at stake is a matter of life and death? Not the owner of the manufacturing company . . . even though the cheque was a duplicate payment from a customer due to an error in its accounting system. So what was our owner to do? On the one hand concerned about cash flow, he wanted to cash the cheque. On the other hand, if the customer caught the mistake it would likely take its business elsewhere. The reality is that returning the cheque was the ethical thing to do.

For the next three days, the owner aggressively went after every receivable. By the end of the week, it became clear that the efforts were paying off. The company had brought in enough money to cover payroll. "Exactly at the point where I knew we had managed through our cash-flow crisis," he says, "I went to the customer and returned the cheque, telling them they had made a mistake and paid me twice. They were so grateful for our honesty they have now given us all of their business."

What would you have done in this situation? In making your decision, remember that the consequences of whether—and how—you address such questions can have broader implications than you realize. Ultimately, bad ethics can cause bad business practices to become acceptable behaviour.

Source: Personal interview by the author, 1998.

PROFIT 100 firms—the 100 fastest-growing firms in Canada—when they were asked about the financing sources they used to finance their firms:[2]

Personal sources	60%	Venture capital	15%
Family and friends	21%	Private investors	15%
Chartered banks	46%	Government	13%
Other lenders	20%	Public stock	31%
Foreign lenders	8%	Other	19%

IN THE TRENCHES

Exploring Global Opportunities

Amanah Tech Consulting Inc.

The United Arab Emirates (U.A.E.) is not a market most young exporters would tackle first, but Saskatoon's Nezar Freeny is not your average young exporter. In the competitive world of web-based solutions, Freeny has carved out a definite niche for his company. He carefully chose the name (Amanah means "trust" in Arabic) because, as a young entrepreneur Freeny says his biggest challenge is building trust. "Most of the CEOs we deal with are twice my age and most older people are not quick to trust someone much younger, especially when it comes to signing a large business contract," says Freeny.

With seed capital from Canadian Youth Business Foundation and assistance from various Saskatchewan and federal government agencies and programs, Freeny attended trade shows in Dubai to build contacts and soon landed two major contracts for web-hosting services and another with the government of Qatar in late 2002. The key to success is offering reliability in an area of the world where the infrastructure is unreliable and Internet charges are very expensive.

Today export sales, primarily to countries in the Gulf of Arabia, account for 90 percent of Amana Tech's sales.

Source: "Canada's Young Entrepreneurs Take on the World," Department of Foreign Affairs and International Trade, September 2002, pp. 4–5, and http://www.cybf.ca, accessed May 10, 2005.

Though the pool of capital available for start-up companies is not any larger now than it was a decade ago, the variety of financing options is greater. The greater variety of financing sources makes it more likely that a venture will find money somewhere.

Let's now turn our attention to specific sources of financing and some of the conditions and terms that an entrepreneur must understand before obtaining financing. Exhibit 14-3 gives an overview of the financial sources discussed in this chapter. Keep in mind that the use of these and other sources of funds is not limited to initial financing. They are also frequently used to finance growing day-to-day operating requirements and business expansions.

INDIVIDUAL INVESTORS

The search for financial support usually begins close to home. As mentioned earlier, the aspiring entrepreneur frequently has three sources of early financing: (1) personal savings, (2) friends and relatives, and (3) other individual investors.

PERSONAL SAVINGS

It is imperative that the entrepreneur have some personal assets in the business, and these typically come from personal savings. Indeed, personal savings is the source of equity financing most frequently used in starting a new business. With few exceptions, the entrepreneur must provide an equity base. A new business needs equity to allow for

EXHIBIT **14-3**
Sources of Funds

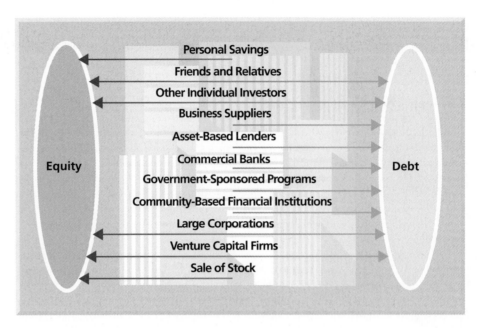

a margin of error. In its first few years, a firm can ill afford large fixed outlays for debt repayment. Also, a lender—or anyone else for that matter—is unlikely to loan a venture money if the entrepreneur does not have his or her own money at risk.

A problem for many people who want to start a business is lack of sufficient personal savings for this purpose. It can be very discouraging when the lender asks "How much will you be investing in the business?" or "What do you have for collateral to secure the bank loan you want?" There is no easy solution to this problem, which is faced by many entrepreneurs. Nonetheless, many individuals who lacked personal savings for a start-up have found a way to accomplish their goal of owning their own company. In most cases, it required creativity and some risk taking—as well as finding a partner who could provide the financing, or friends and relatives who were willing to help.

FRIENDS AND RELATIVES

At times, loans from friends or relatives may be the only available source of new financing. Such loans can often be obtained quickly, as this type of financing is based more on personal relationships than on financial analysis. However, friends and relatives who provide business loans sometimes feel that they have the right to offer suggestions concerning the management of the business. Also, hard business times may strain the bonds of friendship. But if relatives and friends are the only available source of financing, the entrepreneur has no alternative. To minimize the chance of damaging important personal relationships, however, the entrepreneur should plan for repayment of such loans as soon as possible. In addition, any agreements made should be put in writing, as memories tend to become fuzzy over time. It's best to clarify expectations up-front rather than be disappointed or angry later.

informal capital
funds provided by wealthy private individuals to high-risk ventures, such as start-ups

OTHER INDIVIDUAL INVESTORS

A large number of private individuals invest in others' entrepreneurial ventures. They are primarily people with moderate to significant business experience but may also be affluent professionals, such as lawyers and physicians. This type of financing has come to be known as **informal capital** because no established marketplace exists in which

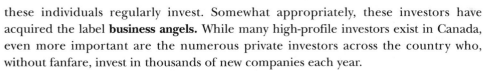

IN THE TRENCHES

Entrepreneurial Experiences

Try Bootstrapping It

Many entrepreneurs finance their firm in its early years in part by "bootstrapping"—that is, getting the money any way they can. Here are a few examples of successful bootstrappers:

- With few personal assets to back a loan guarantee, Natasha Betancor-Leon's Richmond B.C. company Amore Pet Services simply wasn't attractive to the banks. The company, which makes all-natural ingredient pet food, has had to finance with cash from customers.[3]
- The founder of MIPPS, Inc. of Thornhill, Ontario, Sharon Vinderine, financed her business from friends and family. Turned down repeatedly by conventional lenders, Vinderine had no choice but to focus on customers and build revenues. Now, with growing revenues and positive cash flow, the company may be more attractive to lenders.[4]

As highlighted at the beginning of the chapter Ojibwa brothers Chris and Trevor Trainor put up their personal savings and homes to get their home-buiding company off the ground. Once they secured their first client, the Tecumseh Community Development Corp. in Muncey, Ontario, provided a construction mortgage; however, the brothers' houses are still pledged as collateral.[5]

these individuals regularly invest. Somewhat appropriately, these investors have acquired the label **business angels.** While many high-profile investors exist in Canada, even more important are the numerous private investors across the country who, without fanfare, invest in thousands of new companies each year.

business angel
a private investor who finances new, risky small ventures

The total amount invested by business angels is not known with certainty; however, it is very large and some estimates suggest it is 8 to 10 times the amount invested by venture capital companies. Formal venture capital investment in Canada varies from year to year, depending on economic conditions. In 2006 $1.69 billion was invested by venture capital companies, about the same as in 2005 but less than one-third the $6.6 billion invested in 2000 before the technology sector "meltdown." It is interesting to note that over half the funds venture capital companies raise to invest comes from individual Canadians.[6]

The traditional path to informal investors is through contacts with business associates, accountants, and lawyers. Recently, more formal angel networks have taken shape. In forums across the country, entrepreneurs make presentations to groups of private investors gathered to hear about new ventures. For example, angel networks now operate in Ottawa, Calgary, Vancouver, and other Canadian cities that offer qualified entrepreneurs an opportunity to meet a group of private investors. Such networks can greatly increase the odds of finding an investor. Other entrepreneurs are also a primary source of help in identifying prospective informal or private investors.

In addition to providing needed money, private investors frequently contribute know-how to a business. Many of these individuals invest in the type of business in which they have had experience. Although angel financing is easier to acquire than some of the more formal types of financing, informal investors can be very demanding. Thus, the entrepreneur must be careful in structuring the terms of the investors' involvement. Freear, Sohl, and Wetzel investigated entrepreneurs' experiences with informal investors and summarized what the entrepreneurs would do differently:[7]

- Try to raise more external equity earlier
- Work to present their case for funding more effectively
- Try to find more investors and to develop a broader mix of investors, with each one investing smaller amounts
- Be more careful in defining their relationships with individual investors before finalizing the terms of the agreement

Just how demanding angels can be is expressed by Jeff Seglin, who offers these words of advice:

> *If you're auditioning for angel money, our advice is that you be terrifically smart, a brilliant manager, and facile in the intricacies of cash flow. It helps if you already know someone who is an angel investor. It wouldn't hurt if your business was built around some leading-edge proprietary technology in a market no other company dominates. And, of course, it's always nice if you can offer your prospective benefactors a clear exit strategy—since they'd like to cash in on their investments in, oh, say, five years.*[8]

While Seglin's tongue-in-cheek remarks are not fitting in many situations, his point is well taken. To raise equity capital from an angel, you'd best have a well-defined opportunity and know how to make an effective presentation.

VENTURE CAPITAL COMPANIES

venture capitalist
an investor or investment group that commits money to new business ventures

Corporations formed for the purpose of raising money to invest in high-potential growth companies are known as venture capital companies or VCs for short. While there are a few venture capital companies that offer early-stage or so-called "seed-capital" money to ventures still in development, most venture capital companies want to invest once there is more evidence of high growth potential. Such evidence could be in the form of sales to well-recognized companies or products in beta-test with potential customers. Venture capitalists generally want to fund companies that are entering a period of significant growth because they are looking for very high returns, which are a result of the value of the company increasing with that growth. In general, VCs are looking for a compound annual growth rate of 40 percent or more, and are looking for product or technology-based companies to invest in rather than service businesses.

As noted above, the amount of venture capital funding in Canada varies with business conditions and at $1.69 billion in 2006, it is not significant compared to the amounts estimated to have been invested by angel investors. Venture capital is seldom an option for a start-up small business but is often essential for a business with high growth potential, whose financing needs are too large for informal investors to fulfill. In their book *The Money of Invention: How Venture Capital Creates Wealth*, Paul Gompers and Josh Lerner state that 90 percent of all high-growth-potential companies do not attract venture capital fail within three years.[9]

The ideal candidate company for VC investment has the following attributes:

- A distinct technology, ideally with intellectual property protection
- A sustainable competitive advantage
- A comprehensive business plan

- A strong management team with start-up, industry, and technical experience
- Excellent market potential through targeting rapidly growing or global markets
- A credible exit strategy, usually through an initial public offering or being acquired

Specifically, venture capitalists are looking for

- People: a complete management team with compatible skills and unusual tenacity, integrity, imagination, and commitment
- Products: a significant lead over the competition with high value-added features that are legally protectable by patents or other intellectual property protection
- Markets: large and rapidly growing
- High margins: gross margins of 40–50 percent

Some aspects of how venture capitalists operate are the following:

- VCs perform detailed screens of investment opportunities and due diligence research based on knowledge of the industry of the potential investment candidate company.
- Investment is staged into multiple rounds tied to explicit performance milestones achieved by the company.
- Usually several venture capital companies will be involved, a concept known as "syndication."
- VCs want equity and incentive compensation given to the senior management team to link the interests of the VC and entrepreneurs.
- VCs will make selective use of covenants and restrictions in much the same way a bank will. These are discussed later in the chapter under bank financing.
- VCs want a strong board, often with a majority of directors appointed by themselves, to provide oversight, strategic advice, and credibility.

Venture capital companies receive hundreds, if not thousands, of business plans every year. Very few get past the initial screen, which is based on several criteria such as the VC's knowledge of the industry or technology, the amount available to invest, the growth potential of the venture, and the strength of the management team. Conventional wisdom is that a VC will invest in a "B" opportunity if the management team is an "A" team but not in an "A" opportunity if it comes with a "B" team. If you are approaching a venture capital company, send a brief summary in addition to the business plan. This summary should include:

- *Proposed financing:* the total amount of investment requested
- *Basic company demographics:* founding date, location(s), number of full- and part-time employees, background of the CEO and other senior management
- *Financing history:* current investors, amount raised, post-financing valuation, how many stock options are available, ownership percentage for major shareholders
- *Market opportunity:* target market description, size, location, growth rate, and growth drivers
- *Elevator pitch:* the 30-second description of what the company does, what the market opportunity is, and how the company will capitalize on it
- *Competition:* a brief description of major competitors or classes of competitors
- *Economics of the business:* what is the business model—that is, how does the business make money
- *Customers:* list key current customer or key potential customers

- *Development status:* what are the milestones that must be met to get to market
- *Revenue:* prior year's actual results, this year to date, and revenue and profit projections for each of the next five years

Note: the material above is adapted from a presentation made by former venture capitalist Brian Elder, currently an Executive-in-Residence at the Haskayne School of Business. Used with permission.

Is there a downside to attracting venture capital investment? Absolutely! If you look at the list of items above about how venture capitalists operate, you can see some of the pitfalls:

- *Control:* VCs can exert control in a number of ways. Depending on the amount invested and current value of the company, the venture capital company might own a majority of the shares in the company. Second, the VC will want representation on the board of directors, possibly even a majority of the seats including the chair's position. Since the board appoints the officers of the company, an entrepreneur could find him- or herself "fired" from the company he or she founded if there is a significant disagreement between what he or she wants to do and the VC thinks best. In fact, this is exactly what happened to Mark Blumes, founder of Mark's Work Warehouse. Third, the VC may put covenants on the company. These may be performance related in the form of milestones and financial performance that could see the VC able to take control out of the hands of the founders and management team, or they could be in the form of restrictions on what management can do without VC approval, such as borrowing or increasing management compensation.
- *Forced growth:* VCs gain a high return on their investment from high growth in the value of the company, which comes from (profitable) revenue growth. They may push the company to grow at a pace that is too fast for the capability of senior management, which may in turn cause the VC to replace the entrepreneurs and founders.
- *Forced-exit strategy:* VCs do not want to stay invested once growth starts to slow. They will invest only if there is a clear exit method such as an initial public offering (IPO) on a stock exchange or acquisition by a larger company. Either way, this may not be in accordance with the wishes of the founders, although either method would likely make them quite wealthy individuals.

As can be seen from the above discussion, venture capital is not a viable source of financing for most small businesses but can be very important to finance high-growth companies.

BUSINESS SUPPLIERS AND ASSET-BASED LENDERS

Companies with which a new firm will have business dealings can be primary sources of funds for inventories and equipment. Both wholesalers and equipment manufacturers/suppliers can provide trade credit (accounts payable) or equipment loans and leases.

TRADE CREDIT (ACCOUNTS PAYABLE)

Credit extended by suppliers is very important to a start-up. In fact, trade (or mercantile) credit is the source of short-term funds most widely used by small firms. Trade credit is of short duration; 30 days is the customary credit period. Most commonly, this type of credit involves an unsecured, open-book account. The supplier (seller) sends merchandise to the purchasing firm; the buyer then sets up an account payable for the amount of the purchase.

IN THE TRENCHES

Entrepreneurial Experiences

Top 10 Lies . . .

. . . Of Venture Capitalists	. . . Of Entrepreneurs
1. We can make a quick decision.	1. Our projections are conservative.
2. I like your company but my partners didn't.	2. Gartner (research) says our market will be $50 million by 2012.
3. If you get a lead investor, we'll follow.	3. "X" (very large client name) will sign our contract next week.
4. Show us some sales traction and we'll invest.	4. Key employees will join us just as soon as we get funded.
5. We have lots of cash available.	5. No one else is doing what we do (or: we have no competition).
6. We're investing in your team.	6. Several other VCs are doing due diligence as we speak.
7. We saw this coming so we didn't invest in B2B or B2C.	7. Google is too slow to be a threat.
8. This is a vanilla terms sheet.	8. Beta sites will pay us to test our software.
9. We can open the doors for you at major companies.	9. Patents make our business defensible.
10. We like early-stage investing.	10. All we have to do is get 1 percent of the market.

Source: Adapted from Lori Bamber, "A Private Matter," *The Money Book 2006,* Alberta Venture, pp. 12–13.

The amount of trade credit available to a new company depends on the type of business and the supplier's confidence in the firm. For example, wholesale distributors of sunglasses—a very seasonal product line—often provide business capital to retailers by granting extended payment terms on sales made at the start of a season. The sunglass retailers, in turn, sell to their customers during the season and make the bulk of their payments to the wholesalers after they have sold and collected the cash for the sunglasses. Thus, the retailer obtains cash from sales before paying the supplier. More often, however, a firm has to pay its suppliers prior to receiving cash from its customers. In fact, this can be a serious problem for many small firms that sell to large companies.

EQUIPMENT LOANS AND LEASES

Some small businesses, such as restaurants, use equipment that is purchased on an installment basis through an **equipment loan.** A down payment of 25 to 35 percent is usually required, and the contract period normally runs from three to five years. The equipment manufacturer or supplier typically extends credit on the basis of a conditional sales contract (or mortgage) on the equipment. During the loan period, the equipment cannot serve as collateral for another loan.

equipment loan
an installment loan from a seller of machinery used by a business

Of the several categories of asset-based loans, the most frequently used is factoring. As mentioned in Chapter 13, factoring is an option that makes cash available to a business before accounts receivable payments are received from customers. Under this option, a factor (often owned by a bank-holding company) purchases the accounts receivable, advancing to the business from 70 to 90 percent of the amount of an invoice. The factor, however, does have the option of refusing to advance cash on any invoice considered questionable. The factor charges a servicing fee, usually 2 percent of the value of the receivables, and an interest charge on the money advanced prior to collection of the receivables. The interest charge may range from 2 to 3 percent above the prime rate. Jennifer Barclay, the founder of a profitable apparel business with sales of $5 million, was struggling to pay the firm's suppliers on time. The reason for the problem, according to Barclay, was that, "our customers weren't paying us fast enough." Her solution was to sell the firm's accounts receivables to a factor.[10]

In asset-based lending in which non-leased equipment is used as collateral for an asset-based loan, the loan amount will likely be between 50 and 100 percent of the equipment value.

BANK FINANCING: CHARTERED BANKS AND CREDIT UNIONS

Commercial banks and credit unions are the primary providers of debt capital to small companies. Typically, lenders will finance a percentage of the purchase of fixed assets and provide working capital loans to finance inventory and accounts receivable.

ENTREPRENEUR

IN THE TRENCHES

Entrepreneurial Experiences

Touched by an Angel

Angels are a diverse group of wealthy individuals who play a key role in the origination of new businesses. Here are a few Canadian companies started with investment from business angels:

- Vancouver-based ActiveState Corp, growth capital came from several local angel investors led by the "Dean" of Vancouver's angel community, Haig Farris.[11]
- Sheila James and Marwan Forzley started their Ottawa-based Internet-payment software company using personal sources and angel investments from larger technology companies in the Ottawa area. MODASolutions Corp.'s product makes it possible to pay over the Internet with most of the same options as conventional retail such as direct debit from the purchaser's bank account, not just with credit cards.[12]
- Another Ottawa start-up, Liquid Computing, received a total of $2 million to fund the development of a server aimed at the high-end technical market. By 2008 the company had developed an industry-leading set of software products for data centre management and has a client list that includes many of North America's major corporations and government agencies.[13]
- Byron Osing of Calgary created Telebackup Systems Inc., a vendor of systems for remote backups of PCs. Osing sold the business to Veritas, using the proceeds to create Launchworks Inc., a company that invests in early-stage technology companies.[14]

Credit unions, as opposed to banks, have become an increasingly popular source of loans for small business. Many small business owners view credit unions as easier to deal with and more flexible than banks for a number of reasons. Chief among them is that the credit union is member owned, often within a smaller community, and is thus seen as more interested in community development and service to its members. According to Statistics Canada, credit unions and other non–chartered bank institutions held about 11 percent of the short-term business loans in Canada in 2004 and about 2 percent of long-term loans.[15] While small business loan statistics are not broken out, small businesses are more likely to seek loans from credit unions and the above statistics may under-reflect the use of credit unions by SMEs.

TYPES OF LOANS

Four ways lenders tend to make business loans are through lines of credit, term loans, mortgages, and corporate credit cards.

LINES OF CREDIT A **line of credit** is an agreement between the borrower and the lender as to the maximum amount of credit the lender will provide the borrower at any one time. Under this type of agreement, the lender has an obligation to provide the stated capital. The entrepreneur should arrange for a line of credit in advance of actual need because lenders extend credit only in situations about which they are well informed. Attempts to obtain a loan on a spur-of-the-moment basis are generally ineffective. Lines of credit are generally backed by accounts receivable and/or inventory. Pledging these assets as collateral for the line of credit means that if the company gets into financial difficulty, the lender can seize the inventory and sell it, and direct the company's customers to pay the lender rather than the company. The amount lenders will lend on a line of credit is calculated by a formula called a margin formula. It is generally 50 to 80 percent of the value of accounts receivable plus 50 percent of the value of inventory.

line of credit
a legal commitment by a lender to lend up to a maximum amount

TERM LOANS Given certain circumstances, lenders will loan money on a 5- to 10-year term. Such **term loans** are generally used to finance equipment with an economically useful life corresponding to the loan's term. Since the economic benefits of investing in such equipment extend beyond a single year, lenders can be persuaded to lend on terms that more closely match the cash flows to be received from the investment. For example, it would be a mistake for a firm to borrow money for a short term, such as six months, when the money is to be used to buy equipment that is expected to last for five years. Failure to match the loan's payment terms with the expected cash inflows from the investment is a frequent cause of financial problems for small firms. The importance of synchronizing cash inflows with cash outflows when structuring the terms of a loan cannot be overemphasized.

term loan
money loaned for a 5- to 10-year term, corresponding to the length of time the investment will bring in profits

MORTGAGES Mortgages, which represent a long-term source of debt capital, are of two types: chattel mortgages and real estate mortgages. A **chattel mortgage** is a loan for which certain movable property, such as major pieces of equipment, serves as collateral. The borrower retains title to the equipment but cannot sell it without the lender's consent. A **real estate mortgage** is a loan for which real property, such as land or a building, provides the collateral. Typically, these mortgages extend over 25 or 30 years.

chattel mortgage
a loan for which equipment or other moveable property serve as collateral

real estate mortgage
a long-term loan with real property held as collateral

CORPORATE CREDIT CARDS A recent trend by the major Canadian lenders has been to offer small businesses financing in the form of a corporate Visa or other credit card. This achieves several things from the bank's perspective, not least of which is moving the financing from the branch to the credit card division. The card does offer the business a level of convenience in making purchases, not having to establish trade credit, and still delaying when the goods have to be paid for. There are a couple of cautions, however: first, while the card may be in the business's name, the terms normally state that the business owner(s) are liable for any indebtedness; second, the spending limits on the card may be inadequate to support the needs of the business and thus will either have to be raised or a different form of loan soon sought. Interest rates on corporate credit cards are lower than for personal credit cards and are generally comparable to the interest rate on a small business loan. Corporate credit cards can be very useful, but a growing business will soon find it requires other sources of finance.

UNDERSTANDING A LENDER'S PERSPECTIVE

To be effective in acquiring a loan, an entrepreneur needs to understand a lender's perspective about making loans. All lenders have two fundamental concerns when they make a loan: (1) how much income the loan will provide the lender, either in interest income or in other forms of income, and (2) the likelihood that the borrower will default on the loan. A lender is not interested in taking large amounts of risk and will, therefore, design loan agreements so as to reduce the risk to the bank.

In making a loan decision, a lender looks at the proverbial "five C's of credit": (1) the borrower's *character*, (2) the borrower's *capacity* to repay the loan, (3) the *capital* being invested in the venture by the borrower, (4) the *conditions* of the industry and economy, and (5) the *collateral* available to secure the loan.

It is imperative that the borrower's character be above reproach. A bad credit record or any indication of unethical behaviour will make getting a loan extremely difficult. The borrower's capacity is measured by the lender's confidence in the firm's ability to generate the cash flows necessary to repay the loan. In the lender's mind, the firm's cash flows represent the primary source for repaying the loan. To evaluate capital, the lender looks at the equity investment of the owners in the business—the more equity, the better. Although they are completely outside the control of the entrepreneur, the

IN THE TRENCHES

Entrepreneurial Experiences

Innovative Ways to Finance a Business

Razor Suleman estimates that 15 to 10 percent of sales by Snap Promotions, his Toronto-based promotional products distribution company, are in exchange for goods and services. Working through a barter network that keeps track of the "credit" and "payments" in the form of goods and services, Suleman and other members of the network are able to move excess inventories and "buy" goods and services with little or no cash. Preserving cash reduces the amount of financing a business needs to operate and, while barter may not be the principal method of financing, it can reduce conventional sources of finance to more manageable levels. How big is bartering? One Toronto-based network facilitated trades worth $453 million in 2003 and has over 1,400 members.

Source: Glenn Wilkins, "Barter Gets Better," *PROFIT,* vol. 23, no. 4 (September 2004), p. 91.

current economic conditions may be a big factor in the receptivity of lenders to loan requests. Finally, collateral is of key importance to lenders as a secondary source for repaying the loan in case the firm's cash flows are insufficient.

Obtaining a bank loan requires cultivation of a lender and personal selling. Although a lender's review of a loan request certainly includes analysis of economic and financial considerations, this analysis is best complemented by a personal relationship between lender and entrepreneur. This is not to say that a lender would allow personal feelings to override the facts provided by a careful loan analysis. But, after all, a lender's decision as to whether to make a loan is driven in part by the lender's confidence in the entrepreneur as a person and a professional. Intuition and subjective opinion based on past experience often play a role here. In view of this mixture of impersonal analysis and personal relationship, there are several things to remember when requesting a loan:

- Before calling on a lender for a business loan, obtain an introduction from someone who already has a good relationship with the lender. Cold-calling is not appropriate under these circumstances.
- Do not wait until there is a dire need for money. Such lack of planning is not perceived favourably by prospective lenders.
- Do not expect a lender to show the same enthusiasm you have for your venture. A lender is not an entrepreneur or a venture capitalist.
- Develop alternative sources of debt capital; that is, visit with several lenders. However, be sensitive to how a lender might feel about your courting more than one bank.

A lender needs certain key questions answered before a loan will be made:

- What are the strengths and qualities of the management team?
- How has the firm performed financially?
- What will the venture do with the money?
- How much money is needed?
- When is the money needed?
- When and how will the money be paid back?
- Does the borrower have a good public accountant and attorney?
- Does the borrower already have a banking relationship?

A well-prepared written presentation—something like a shortened version of a business plan—is helpful, if not necessary. Capturing the firm's history and future in writing suggests that the entrepreneur has given thought to where the firm has been and is going. As part of this presentation, a lender expects a prospective borrower to provide the following detailed financial information:

- Three years of the firm's historical financial statements, if available, including balance sheets, income statements, and statements of cash flow
- The firm's pro forma financial statements (balance sheets, income statements, and statements of cash flow), in which the timing and amounts of the debt repayment are included as part of the forecasts
- Personal financial statements, showing the borrower's personal net worth (net worth–assets–debt) and estimated annual income

FORMULA LENDING

Major Canadian banks have increasingly turned to ways to reduce the administrative burden of small business loans. This includes the loan application and processing process.

Today, most loans under $200,000 will be assessed using a credit scoring system based not on the business merits but on the credit history and creditworthiness of the owners of the business. Research sponsored by the banks suggests that if the owners of the business have been good credit risks and responsible with their personal finances then they are very likely to be so with their small business loans.

The bank will do a credit check on the owners and require a personal statement of net worth—like a personal balance sheet—detailing the owners' assets and liabilities in detail. This includes assets such as land and real estate, vehicles, personal property such as furniture, investments, and the corresponding liabilities such as mortgages on property, loans for vehicles, credit card balances, etc. The bank will also require independent verification of earnings, likely for the last several years. This may require a response from an employer, which could be a problem if the employer doesn't know her or his employee may be leaving to start a business, or it could require submission of personal income tax returns.

SELECTING A LENDER

The wide variety of services provided by lenders makes choosing a bank a critical decision. For a typical small firm, the provision of chequing account facilities and the extension of short-term (and possibly long-term) loans are the two most important services of a bank. Normally, loans are negotiated with the same bank in which the firm maintains its chequing account. In addition, the firm may use the bank's safety deposit vault or its services in collecting notes or securing credit information. An experienced lender can also provide management advice, particularly in financial matters, to a new entrepreneur.

The location factor limits the range of possible choices of lenders. For convenience in making deposits and conferring about loans and other matters, a bank should be located in the same general vicinity as the firm. All lenders are interested in their home communities and, therefore, tend to be sympathetic to the needs of local business firms. Except in very small communities, two or more local lenders are usually available, thus permitting some freedom of choice.

Lenders' lending policies are not uniform. Some lenders are extremely conservative, while others are more willing to accept risks. If a small firm's loan application is neither obviously strong nor patently weak, its prospects for approval depend heavily on the bank's approach to small business accounts. Differences in willingness to lend have been clearly established by research studies, as well as by the practical experience of many business borrowers.

NEGOTIATING THE LOAN

In negotiating a bank loan, four important issues must be resolved: (1) the interest rate, (2) the loan maturity date, (3) the repayment schedule if payment is required over time, and (4) loan covenants.

prime rate
the interest rate charged by a commercial lender on loans to its most creditworthy customers

INTEREST RATE The interest rate charged by lenders is usually stated in terms of the prime rate. The **prime rate** is the rate of interest charged by lenders on loans to their most creditworthy customers. This rate is published each day in the business section of most local newspapers, and in *The Globe and Mail* and the *National Post*.

If a lender quotes a rate of "prime plus three" and the prime rate is 5 percent, the interest rate for the loan will be 8 percent. The interest rate can be a floating rate that varies over the loan's life—that is, as the prime rate changes, the interest rate on the loan changes—or it can be fixed for the duration of the loan. Although a small firm should always seek a competitive interest rate, concern about the interest rate should not override consideration of the loan's maturity date, its repayment schedule, and any loan covenants.

LOAN MATURITY DATE As already noted, a loan's term should coincide with the use of the money—short-term needs require short-term financing, while long-term needs demand long-term financing. For example, since a line of credit is intended only to help a firm with its short-term needs, it is generally limited to one year. However, some lenders require that a firm "clean up" a line of credit one month each year. Because such a loan can be outstanding for only 11 months, the borrower can use the money to finance seasonal needs but cannot use it to provide permanent increases in working capital.

REPAYMENT SCHEDULE With a term loan, the schedule for repayment is generally arranged in one of two ways. The loan can be repaid in (1) *equal* monthly or annual payments that cover both interest on the remaining balance and payment on the principal or (2) *decreasing* monthly or annual payments that cover both equal payments on the principal and interest on the remaining balance.

For example, assume that a firm is negotiating a $250,000 term loan, at an interest rate of 10 percent, to be repaid in five equal annual payments. Entering into a financial calculator (or a computer spreadsheet) the values

PV (present value) = $250,000
N (number of payments) = 5
I/YR (interest rate per year) = 10
FV (future value in 5 years) = 0

we find that the equal annual payment, or PMT, is $65,949.37.

Once we know the amount of the annual payment required to repay the loan in five years, we can develop this repayment schedule, as shown on a spreadsheet:

End of Year	Annual Payment[a]	Interest Payment[b]	Payment on Principal[c]	Loan Balance
				$250,000
1	$65,949	$25,000	$40,949	209,051
2	65,949	20,905	45,044	164,006
3	65,949	16,401	49,549	114,458
4	65,949	11,446	54,504	59,954
5	65,949	5995	59,954	0

[a]Equal payments that exactly repay the loan in 5 years
[b]10% × remaining loan balance
[c]Annual payment – interest charge
[d]Prior loan balance – payment on principal

At the end of the first year, when the first $65,949 ($65,949.37 rounded to the nearest dollar) payment is made, $25,000 is applied to interest (10% interest rate × $250 000 beginning loan balance), and the other $40,949 is used to reduce loan principal. Once this payment is made, $209,051 is owed in year 2 ($250,000 − $40,949). At the end of the second year, the process is repeated. The payment of $65,949 includes

NEL

$20,905 for interest (10% interest rate × $209,051 loan balance) and $45,044 ($65,949 − $20,905) for principal reduction. This process is continued over five years, until the loan is paid off.

If, on the other hand, we calculate payments so that each yearly payment covers repayment of one-fifth of the principal plus the amount of interest owed on the remaining principal, we have the following repayment schedule:

End of Year	Loan Balance[a]	Payment on Principal[b]	Interest Payment[c]	Annual Payment[d]
				$250,000
1	200,000	$50,000	$25,000	$75,000
2	150,000	50,000	20,000	70,000
3	100,000	50,000	15,000	65,000
4	50,000	50,000	10,000	60,000
5	0	50,000	5000	55,000

[a]Prior loan balance − payment on principal
[b]$250,000/5
[c]10% × remaining loan balance
[d]Payment on principal + interest payment

Now the payment in the first year is $75,000, consisting of a $50,000 payment on principal ($250,000/5 years) and a $25,000 interest payment (10% × $250,000). The amount of the annual payment declines each year as the principal balance is paid down, decreasing interest expense.

Which repayment plan is preferable? A lender will typically prefer the decreasing payments approach, in which a firm repays equal amounts of principal plus interest, because the loan principal will be reduced more quickly in the early years. For an entrepreneur, which plan is preferable depends on the firm's ability to service the repayment of the debt over time. The equal payments approach requires less cash outflow in the early years, when a new business usually cannot afford large payments. On the other hand, if in the early years a firm can make the larger payments required by the decreasing payments approach, the firm will pay out less over the life of the loan. The Industry Canada website (http://www.ic.gc.ca), as well as most lenders' websites, contains loan calculator programs.

LOAN COVENANTS In addition to setting the interest rate and specifying when and how the loan is to be repaid, a bank normally imposes other restrictions on the borrower. **Loan covenants** restrict borrowers from certain activities that might lessen their ability to repay the loan. Following are some types of loan covenants a borrower might encounter:

loan covenants bank-imposed restrictions on a borrower that enhance the chances of timely repayment

1. *Provision of timely and complete information:* A bank will usually require that the business provide financial statements on a monthly basis or, at the very least, quarterly. In some cases, the bank will require that the statements be audited by a public accounting firm. Other covenants may require the business to notify the bank of any significant changes, such as loss of a major customer.
2. *Salary limitations:* As a way to restrict a firm's management from siphoning cash out of the business, the bank may limit managers' salaries. It also may not allow any personal loans from the business to the owners.

3. *Key ratios:* A bank may put limits on various financial ratios to make certain that a firm can handle its loan payments. For example, to ensure sufficient liquidity, the bank may require the borrower to maintain a current ratio (current assets/current liabilities) of at least 2. Or the bank might limit the amount of debt the firm can borrow until the loan is paid, as measured by the debt ratio (debt/total assets).

4. *Personal guarantee:* The borrower will normally be required to personally guarantee the loan. A lender wants the right to look at both the firm's assets and the owner's personal assets before making a loan. If a business is structured as a corporation, the owner and the corporation are separate legal entities and the owner can escape personal liability for the firm's debts—that is, the owner has **limited liability.** However, most lenders are not willing to lend money to any small business without the owner's personal guarantee as well. If the entrepreneur is not confident enough about the business to put personal assets at risk, then most lenders will not be willing to assume the risk either. Only after years of an ongoing relationship with a lender might an owner be exempt from personally guaranteeing a loan.

limited liability
the restriction of an owner's legal financial responsibilities to the amount invested in the business

A common question about loan covenants is "Are they negotiable?" If a lender includes loan covenants that you believe are unreasonable, can you question them? The answer is a qualified *yes*. Some things may not be negotiable, such as a personal guarantee, but other provisions that might hurt the firm can certainly be discussed.

Regarding loan covenants, Jill Andresky Fraser, finance editor for *Inc.* magazine, offers this advice:[16]

1. Ask to see a sample list of the covenants before the closing date so that you can avoid a situation in which desperation for funds—or a lack of careful analysis—persuades you to simply sign anything. Make certain that you can live with the bank's terms about the consequences of being out of compliance.

2. To see if you could have complied with all loan covenants, especially key ratios, if your loan had been in place during the most recent one-, two-, and three-year periods, analyze your company's past performance over these periods.

3. If results indicate possible future problems, schedule a visit with your lender and suggest more realistic covenants.

In conclusion, here are some of the primary reasons lenders give for denying an application for a business loan:[17]

- Bank's lack of familiarity with the business and its owners, or with the industry in which the business operates
- Excessive business losses by the applicant
- Unwillingness on the part of the owners to guarantee the loan personally
- Insufficient collateral
- Inadequate preparation by the owners
- Past personal credit problems of the owners
- Government regulations that restrict certain types of lending
- Poor regional or national economic conditions

GOVERNMENT-SPONSORED PROGRAMS AND AGENCIES

There are still a few government programs that provide financing to small businesses, although the number of such programs is shrinking in this era of fiscal restraint. Even though some funds are available, however, they are not always easy to acquire. Time and patience on the part of the entrepreneur are required.

FEDERAL ASSISTANCE TO SMALL BUSINESSES

The federal government has a long history of helping new businesses get started, primarily through programs aimed at assisting in research and development, exporting, and regional development, and those intended to assist specific groups. As mentioned earlier, the main federal program aimed at supporting new and small business is the **Canada Small Business Financing Program (CSBFP).**

Canada Small Business Financing Program
a federal government program that provides financing to small businesses through private lenders, for which the federal government guarantees repayment

SMALL BUSINESS FINANCING These loans are made by private lenders, usually commercial banks, for amounts up to $250,000. The federal government guarantees up to 90 percent of the value of the loan. Loan proceeds must be used to acquire new or used machinery, commercial vehicles, computer or telecommunications equipment, leasehold improvements, land, or buildings. To obtain a loan under the program, the borrower applies through a bank and pays an up-front fee of 2 percent of the value of the loan, which can be financed as part of the loan, and goes to the government. The bank makes the credit decision to lend or not, and can normally release the loan proceeds as promptly as it would with a nonguaranteed loan. Under the program, the loan can have a fixed or floating rate of interest. The floating rate is set at the bank's prime rate plus a premium of three percentage points, effectively making the rate "prime plus three." The fixed rate is set at the bank's conventional residential mortgage rate for the term of the loan plus the same premium of three percentage points.

BUSINESS DEVELOPMENT BANK (BDC) The BDC is a federal Crown corporation that provides a number of services for entrepreneurs, as well as innovative lending/investing programs. For most of its history, the BDC was considered a "lender of last resort"; conventional sources of funds had to be sought first. Today it is much more aggressive in working with other lenders and investors or on its own to support new and small businesses. One of the innovative services it offers is CASE, or Counselling Assistance to Small Enterprise, which uses retired executives and business owners as consultants to new and small businesses. As a source of funds, the BDC offers conventional lending as well as "venture loans," which combine some features of loans with the advantages of equity. This results in lower interest costs, but requires some return in the form of a royalty on future sales or options to buy stock in the business.

INDUSTRIAL RESEARCH ASSISTANCE PROGRAM (IRAP) Part of the National Research Council, IRAP helps smaller firms improve their technological capacity through financial assistance for research and development and expert advice. More than 200 industry technical advisers (ITAs) are available to assist companies in areas such as plant layout, productivity, cost control, production process improvement, and assessment of new manufacturing technology.

TAX INCENTIVES Some tax write-offs and rebates are available for certain kinds of activities, such as research and development (or, in official terminology, "scientific research and experimental development").

PROGRAM FOR EXPORT MARKET DEVELOPMENT (PEMD) Since 1971 this program has assisted Canadian businesses in marketing their products abroad through financial assistance to visit foreign markets or attend international trade shows.

FEDERAL AND PROVINCIAL ASSISTANCE There are a large number of other federal and provincial assistance programs including many grants, which don't have to be paid back. For example, most provinces have wage-subsidy programs either for specific industry sectors or for targeted groups of potential employees. Most provinces also have their

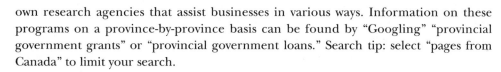

IN THE TRENCHES

Entrepreneurial Experiences

Financing for Young Entrepreneurs

A few programs exist to offer loans to young Canadian entrepreneurs—generally in the age range of 15 to 30 or 35 years of age. The Business Development Bank of Canada (BDC) offers a financing program (for 18- to 35-year-olds), with flexible payment options available. The program also gives the option of 50 hours of mentoring support.

The Canadian Youth Business Foundation also offers loans to young entrepreneurs aged 18 to 34. This is a "last resort" source—you must have been turned down by the banks and credit unions. The loan must be for a new, full-time business and is limited to $15,000, although the Foundation rarely loans more than $10,000. Entrepreneurs need to have a business plan, and the program includes mentoring support.

These programs are listed on the BDC and CYBF websites. Some of the loans can be applied for online.

Source: http://www.bdc.ca/en/i_am/young_entrepreneur/default.htm and http://www.cybf.ca/ entrepreneurs (accessed September 3, 2008)

own research agencies that assist businesses in various ways. Information on these programs on a province-by-province basis can be found by "Googling" "provincial government grants" or "provincial government loans." Search tip: select "pages from Canada" to limit your search.

OTHER SOURCES OF FINANCING The sources of financing that have been described thus far represent the primary avenues for obtaining money for small firms. The remaining sources are generally of less importance but should not be ignored by an entrepreneur in search of financing.

LARGE CORPORATIONS In the past, large corporations have made a limited amount of funds available for investing in smaller companies when it is in their self-interest to maintain a close relationship with such companies. Larger firms are now becoming more involved in providing financing and technical assistance for smaller businesses. As businesses divest noncore divisions or departments, they often finance the purchase by the employees of the division. When the technology-sector meltdown occurred in 2000–01, thousands of technology-company employees lost their jobs. Many decided to start their own businesses. Thirteen Nortel engineers started Seaway Networks after discovering their project was about to be cut. The engineers quit their jobs to pursue the project, and Nortel signed over the intellectual property rights in exchange for equity in the company. Other Nortel employees created new ventures as a result of similar circumstances.[18]

STOCK SALES Another way to obtain capital is by selling stock (shares in the company) to outside individual investors through either private placement or public sale. However, finding outside stockholders can be difficult when a new firm is not known and has no ready market for its securities. In most cases, a business must have some history of profitability before its stock can be sold successfully.

IN THE TRENCHES

Entrepreneurial Experiences

Looking Beyond the Banks: A Cautionary Tale

Yve's Creations Ltd., an Edmonton, Alberta, company that designs, manufactures, and sells adaptive clothing for elderly people and those who are physically challenged, was originally financed by a loan from the Royal Bank of Canada when it was started in 1998 by Yvette, who uses only her first name. In October 2001, three and a half years into the five-year term and with only $40,000 remaining outstanding, the bank demanded repayment of the loan, even though it admitted "Since inception both accounts and loans have operated within the terms and conditions agreed upon." Yve's had never missed a loan payment or even had a returned cheque, but the bank held firm, citing lack of profits and a high debt-to-equity ratio. Yvette had personally covered all of the company's losses and says the bank had personal guarantees worth twice the outstanding amount of the loan.

Her story illustrates the dangers of bank financing for small businesses. Yvette had assumed a five-year loan was a five-year loan. Unaware that virtually all bank loans to small business are "demand" loans, which the bank can ask to be repaid anytime without reason, she was stunned to receive the letter from the bank. What made the bank's action more ironic is that in 1998, at the time the loan was made, it had used Yvette and her business in an advertising campaign to highlight the bank's commitment to women entrepreneurs.

Fortunately, Yvette's story has a happy ending: she found a "white knight" to rescue her business from likely bankruptcy. According to Yvette, "A customer and his wife came into my store a year and a half ago to purchase garments for his mother and were so impressed by the product and service that they handed me their card and told me to call them if I ever needed money. So when the bank said they were pulling my loan, first, I shed tears of frustration, then I called these people. When I described my situation, they offered to help me." Within 24 hours the couple loaned Yvette sufficient money to pay off the bank.

Yvette learned some hard lessons from the experience. Her advice? Be cautious, get everything in writing, and make sure the bank can't pull the loan before the term is up unless you are in default. She says that she hopes to finance growth with personal sources in the future, but if she has to borrow from a financial institution again, it would be from a credit union. Yvette believes credit unions are a better place for small businesses to borrow from because "they are more people-oriented, more community-oriented, and they have policies not to call loans unless they are actually in default. You may pay a bit more, but it's worth it."

Source: Personal interview by the author, June 2002.

Whether it is best to raise outside equity financing depends on the firm's long-range prospects. If there is opportunity for substantial expansion on a continuing basis and if other sources are inadequate, the owner may logically decide to bring in other owners. Owning part of a larger business may be more profitable than owning all of a smaller business.

PRIVATE PLACEMENT One way to sell common stock is through **private placement,** in which the firm's stock is sold to selected individuals—usually the firm's employees, the owner's acquaintances, members of the local community, customers, and suppliers. When a stock sale is restricted to private placement, an entrepreneur can avoid many requirements of the securities laws.

PUBLIC SALE When small firms—typically, larger small firms—make their stock available to the general public, this is called going public, or making an **initial public offering (IPO).** The reason often cited for a public sale is the need for additional working capital.

In undertaking a public sale of its stock, a small firm subjects itself to greater regulation. Each province has a securities commission to watch over the publicly traded stock. The commission is responsible for regulating the trade of public shares, and companies must report financial results and other activities to it on a quarterly basis. Among other things, the commission looks for "insider trading," where the officers and directors of a company make trades for personal gain based on advance knowledge of events, results, or plans not available to the outside investor. Publicly traded companies also have to abide by the regulations of the stock exchange they trade on, whether the TSX Venture Exchange, the Toronto Stock Exchange, or U.S. exchanges such as the NASDAQ.

Common stock may also be sold to underwriters, which guarantee the sale of securities. Compensation and fees paid to underwriters typically make the sale of securities in this manner expensive. Fees may range from 10 to 30 percent of the sale, with 18 to 25 percent being typical. Options and other fees may cause the actual costs to run even higher. The reason for the high costs are, of course, the elements of uncertainty and risk associated with public offerings of the stock of small, relatively unknown firms.

A further consideration affecting the decision to "go public" is the extraordinary legislation and reporting requirements imposed on publicly traded companies in the wake of various corporate scandals in the early 2000s. Responding to the Enron, WorldCom, and Tyco International frauds among others, which cost shareholders millions, employees their jobs, and some executives jail time, legislators in the United States introduced the *Sarbanes-Oxley* Act (SOX). Under this act, public corporations must have a much higher level of internal controls to make fraudulent activity difficult. The act also holds officers and directors of public companies more directly responsible for their actions and enforces a much more transparent and complete results-reporting requirement.

The practice of corporate governance, a term used to describe the manner in which the directors of a corporation must conduct oversight on the business, has become crucial for public companies on both sides of the border. In Canada, where most public companies are traded on either the Toronto Stock Exchange (TSX) or the TSX Venture Exchange, the Ontario Securities Commission Guideline OSC 58-201 determine the makeup and responsibilities of the board of directors of public companies. In addition Canadian securities administrators are developing Multilateral Instruments 52-109 and 52-316, expected to be enacted in 2008 or 2009. These instruments make up C-SOX, mirroring SOX, and are primarily designed to ensure the effectiveness of internal controls that relate to financial reporting. Many Canadian public corporations trade their shares on both the TSX and U.S. exchanges, so they have had to comply with the U.S. legislation since it was brought in several years ago.

private placement
the sale of a firm's capital stock to selected individuals

initial public offering (IPO)
the issuance of stock that is to be traded in public financial markets

Describe the appropriateness of types of financing at various stages of a venture's life.

Not all sources of finance are appropriate or even available to companies at different stages of growth or development. Before a business is launched, it may have great difficulty in borrowing from conventional lenders. Usually the cash required at this pre-start-up phase is supplied from personal sources of the entrepreneur, "love money" from family and friends, or from business angel investors. Only once the business has a track record of sales and profits will lenders be interested in extending loans to it. Companies that have very high growth potential may be attractive to venture capital companies. The business press focuses a great deal on large, public companies, but fewer than 1 percent of all Canadian companies finance themselves by "going public." However, companies that require large amounts of financing for growth or research and development, such as biotechnology companies, cannot generally obtain sufficient financing unless they do offer shares to the public. Exhibit 14-2 (on page 415) illustrates sources of financing available at various stages of development. These sources will be discussed below in greater detail.

FINDING SOURCES OF FINANCING

Earlier in this chapter we addressed two questions about financing a small company, especially a start-up firm: *How much* financing will be needed? *What type* of financing might be available? Three basic types of financing were identified: (1) spontaneous financing, which comes from sources that automatically increase with increases in sales (such as accounts payable and accrued expenses), (2) profit retention, which requires owners to forego taking cash out of the business to allow it to remain within the firm to finance growth, and (3) **external financing,** which comes from outside investors. But before looking at specific sources, the entrepreneur must ask "Should I use debt or equity financing?" Most capital sources specialize in providing one or the other, but generally not both.

external financing
financing from outside investors

DEBT OR EQUITY FINANCING?

Evaluate the choice between debt financing and equity financing.

Assume that a firm needs $100,000 in outside financing. The firm can borrow the money (debt financing), issue common shares (equity financing), or use some combination of the two. The decision as to whether to use debt or equity financing depends to a large extent on the type of business, the firm's financial strength, and the current economic environment—that is, whether lenders and investors are optimistic or pessimistic about the future. It also depends on the owner's personal feelings about debt and equity. Given identical conditions, one entrepreneur will choose debt and another equity—and both can be right.

POTENTIAL PROFITABILITY

Choosing between debt and equity involves tradeoffs for owners with regard to potential profitability, financial risk, and voting control. Borrowing money (debt) rather than issuing common shares (owner's equity) increases the potential for higher rates of return to the owners. Borrowing also allows the owners to retain voting control of the company. Such debt, however, exposes them to greater financial risk. If, on the other hand, the owners choose to issue shares (rather than increase debt) in order to reduce risk, they limit their potential rate of return and give up some voting control.

The following discussion will consider each of these factors—potential profitability, financial risk, and voting control.

To see how the choice between debt and equity affects potential profitability, let's consider some facts about the Levine Company, a new firm that's still in the process of raising needed capital:

- The owners have already invested $100,000 of their own money in the new business. To complete the financing, they need another $100,000.
- If the owners raise the money needed by issuing common shares, new outside investors will hold 30 percent of the outstanding shares. (Even though these new investors will have contributed half the money required, they will not necessarily expect half the shares, because they will recognize the value of the original owners' "sweat equity"—that is, the time and effort they contributed in starting the business.)
- If Levine borrows the money, the interest rate on the debt will be 10 percent, so the interest expense each year will be $10,000 (0.10 × $100,000).
- Estimates suggest that the firm will earn $28,000 in operating profits (earnings before interest and taxes) each year, representing a 14 percent return on the firm's assets of $200,000 (0.14 × $200,000 = $28,000).

If the firm issues shares, its balance sheet will read as follows:

Total assets	$200,000
Debt	$ 0
Equity	200,000
Total debt and equity	$200,000

But if the firm borrows money, the balance sheet will appear as follows:

Total assets	$200,000
Debt (10% interest rate)	$100,000
Equity	100,000
Total debt and equity	$200,000

Given the above information and assuming no taxes (just to keep things simple), the firm's income statement under the two financing plans will be as follows:

	Equity	**Debt**	
Operating income	$28,000		$28,000
Interest expense	0	10,000 (0.10 × $100,000)	
Net income	$28,000		$18,000

As the income statement reveals, net income is greater if the firm finances with equity rather than with debt. However, the rate of return on the owners' investment, which is more important than the absolute dollar number for net income, is greater if the firm finances with debt. Since

$$Owners'\ return\ on\ equity\ investment = \frac{Net\ income}{Owners'\ investment}$$

issuing equity yields

$$Owners'\ return\ on\ equity\ investment = \frac{\$28,000}{\$200,000} = 0.14,\ or\ 14\%$$

whereas issuing debt yields

$$Owners'\ return\ on\ equity\ investment = \frac{\$18,000}{\$100,000} = 0.18,\ or\ 18\%$$

Thus, the owners' return on the equity investment is 18 percent if debt is issued—and only 14 percent if equity is issued. In other words, if equity financing is used, the owners will earn $14 for every $100 invested; if debt is used, however, the owners will earn $18 for every $100 invested. Thus, in terms of the rate of return on their investment, the owners are better off borrowing money at a 10 percent interest rate than issuing stock to new owners who will share in the profits.

As a general rule, as long as a firm's operating income return on its assets (operating income ÷ total assets) is greater than the cost of the debt (interest rate), the owners' return on equity investment will increase as the firm uses more debt. Levine hopes to earn 14 percent on its assets but pay only 10 percent in interest for the debt financing. Using debt, therefore, increases the owners' opportunity to enhance the rate of return on their investment.

FINANCIAL RISK

If debt is so beneficial to the rate of return, why wouldn't Levine's owners use even more debt and less equity? Then the rate of return on the owners' investment would be even higher. For example, if the Levine Company financed with 90 percent debt and 10 percent equity—$180,000 in debt and $20,000 in equity—the firm's net income would be $10,000, computed as follows:

Operating income	$28,000	
Interest expense	18,000	(0.10 × $180,000)
Net income	$10,000	

With $10,000 in net income and an owners' investment of only $20,000, the return on the equity investment would be 50 percent ($10,000 net income / $20,000 owner's investment).

Despite this higher expected rate of return for the owners, there is a good reason to limit the amount of debt: *Debt is risky.* If the firm fails to earn profits, creditors will still insist on their interest payments. In an extreme case, creditors can force a firm into bankruptcy if it fails to honour its financial obligations.

Equity, on the other hand, is less demanding. If a firm does not reach its goal for profits, an equity investor must accept the disappointing results and hope for better results next year. Equity investors cannot demand more than what is earned.

While Levine's owners would prefer debt if the firm did well, if the firm has poor financial results they would be better off with equity. Thus, although the use of debt financing increases potential returns when a company is performing well, it also increases the possibility of lower—even negative—returns if the company doesn't attain its goals in a given year. Debt is a two-edged sword; if debt financing is used and things go well, they will go *very* well—but if things go badly, they will go *very* badly. In short, debt financing makes doing business more risky.

VOTING CONTROL

The third issue in choosing between debt and equity is the degree of control retained by owners. Most owners of small firms resist giving up control to outsiders.

For the Levine Company, raising new capital through equity financing meant giving up 30 percent of the firm's ownership, with the original owners still controlling 70 percent of the stock. However, many small firm owners are reluctant to give away any of the company's stock. They do not want to be accountable in any way to minority owners, much less take a chance of eventually losing control of the business.

Given this aversion to losing control, many small business owners choose to finance with debt rather than with equity. They realize that debt increases risk, but it also permits them to retain all the stock and full ownership.

KEEPING THE RIGHT PERSPECTIVE

The nature and maturity of the business affect which financing sources are available for starting and running smaller companies. An entrepreneurial firm that has high growth potential and significant opportunity to capture large profits for investors has many more possible sources of financing than a firm that provides a good lifestyle for the

Discuss the most important factors in the process of obtaining start-up financing.

6

ENTREPRENEUR

IN THE TRENCHES

Entrepreneurial Experiences

Alternative Financing

When we think of sources of financing for small firms, we usually think of banks, private investors, and nonbank lenders. But with a little creativity, an entrepreneur may be able to find some other sources that are not so conventional.

Mohamed Rahman, an unemployed immigrant from Bangladesh with training as a systems engineer, with no business experience and no money to invest, started a business providing network assistance in Ottawa in 2001. With a $9500 loan from the Ottawa Community Loan Fund, a micro-lending fund for small businesses the banks won't touch, Rahman turned his business into a lighting company when the tech sector meltdown occurred later in 2001. By 2003 he had sales of $78,000 and continued growth has enabled him to buy a home for his family and a car.

With no experience and no collateral, the banks were not interested in financing his small start-up requirements. "Before OCLF, nobody wanted to give me a single dollar because I didn't have anything," said Mr. Rahman. Micro-lending programs began in the developing world and have been copied in several places in Canada since the mid-1990s. The Mennonite Central Committee runs several such programs from Vancouver to Calgary to Nova Scotia. The programs provide peer support, and in some programs the other borrowers in the program form a "lending circle" that co-signs each other's loans, leading to an almost perfect record of repayment.

Source: Adapted from Kristin Goff, "Micro Loans, Macro Goals," *Ottawa Citizen,* June 16, 2004, p. C1. Used by permission.

owner but nothing in the way of attractive returns to investors. Another concern of investors is whether the business is a start-up with no track record or a firm that has a proven record of profits.

Three-quarters of the financing for start-ups comes from personal savings, with the remainder coming primarily from family, friends, or partners. The latter sources typically provide funds in the form of loans. For some "bootstrappers," credit cards can be a significant source of financing in the early years of the business. It is only after the business has become established that bank loans, finance company loans, and trade credit (accounts payable) become significant sources of financing. Venture capitalists and business angels mostly limit themselves to investing in firms that offer potentially high returns to their investors within a 5- to 10-year period.

Amar Bhide, a professor at Harvard University who spent extensive time interviewing owners of some of the high-growth companies in the United States, learned that few of these companies had access to venture capital markets. Instead, they were most often required to bootstrap their financing—that is, to get it any way they could. Based on many interviews, Bhide warns of the real danger of becoming unduly focused on getting financing. While locating financial sources is certainly a critical issue, an entrepreneur should avoid losing sight of other matters important to business operations. Bhide offers the following recommendations to any aspiring entrepreneur who wants to start a business:

- Get operational. At some point, it is time to stop planning and just make things happen.
- Go for quick break-even and high cash flow–generating projects whenever possible.
- Fit growth goals to available personal resources.
- Have a preference for high-ticket, high-profit-margin products and services that can sustain direct personal selling.
- Start up with only a single product or service that satisfies a clear need.
- Forget about needing a crack management team with textbook credentials. The team can be developed as the venture develops.
- Focus on cash, rather than profits, market share, or anything else.
- Cultivate the lender.[19]

We believe Bhide's advice is worth consideration by anyone beginning the start-up process.

LOOKING BACK

1 Estimate the amount of financing a new or existing business will need.
- A direct relationship exists between sales growth and asset needs; as sales increase, more assets and more financing are required.
- The two basic types of capital used in financing a company are debt financing and ownership equity.

2 Create pro forma (forecast) cash flows, income statements, and balance sheets.
- While all types of financial projections are critical, the cash flow forecast is arguably the most important.
- The pro forma income statement and balance sheet can be constructed from the cash flow forecast simply and easily with a little practice.

3 Describe the types and sources of financing available.

- Three sources of early financing for an entrepreneur are personal savings, friends and relatives, and other individual investors.
- Business suppliers, a major source of financing for the small firm, can offer trade credit (accounts payable) and equipment loans and leases.
- Asset-based lending is financing secured by working-capital assets, such as accounts receivable and inventory.
- Commercial banks are the primary providers of debt financing to small companies, offering lines of credit, term loans, and mortgages.
- Government-sponsored programs and agencies at the federal, provincial, and local levels provide financing to small businesses.
- Community-based financial institutions, large corporations, venture capitalists, and stock sales represent other sources of financing for the small firm.

4 Describe the appropriateness of types of financing at various stages of a venture's life.

- Not all sources are appropriate or even available to companies at different stages of growth.
- Pre-start-up ventures are usually financed from personal sources, "love money," or angel investors.
- Lenders generally loan to businesses that have physical assets.
- Fast-growth companies may need to make a public offering of shares to finance growth.

5 Evaluate the choice between debt financing and equity financing.

- Choosing between debt and equity financing involves tradeoffs with regard to potential profitability, financial risk, and voting control.
- Borrowing money rather than issuing common stock (owners' equity) creates the potential for higher rates of return to the owners and allows the owners to retain voting control of the company, but it also exposes the owners to greater financial risk.
- Issuing common stock rather than borrowing money results in lower potential rates of return to the owners and the loss of some voting control, but it does reduce their financial risk.

6 Discuss the most important factors in the process of obtaining start-up financing.

- The entrepreneur should get operational as quickly as possible with a product or service that satisfies a clear need, even at the expense of raising capital.
- Quick break-even and high cash flow–generating projects should be chosen whenever possible, with a preference for high-ticket, high-profit-margin products and services.
- Growth goals must be tailored to available personal financial resources.
- The entrepreneur must focus on cash—not profits, market share, or anything else.

KEY TERMS

accounts payable (trade credit), p. 408

accounts receivable, p. 408

accrued expenses, p. 411

business angel, p. 419

Canada Small Business Financing Program (CSBFP), p. 432

cash budget (cash flow forecast), p. 408

cash flow forecast (cash budget), p. 408

chattel mortgage, p. 425

current debt (short-term liabilities), p. 411

debt capital, p. 411

equipment loan, p. 423

external equity, p. 412

external financing, p. 436

informal capital, p. 418

initial public offering (IPO), p. 435

internal equity, p. 412

limited liability, p. 431

line of credit, p. 425

loan covenants, p. 430

long-term debt, p. 411

mortgage, p. 412

owners' equity capital, p. 412

percentage of sales, p. 410

prime rate, p. 428

private placement, p. 435

profit retention, p. 412

real estate mortgage, p. 425

short-term notes, p. 411

spontaneous financing, p. 412

term loan, p. 425

venture capitalist, p. 420

DISCUSSION QUESTIONS

1. Describe the process for estimating the amount of assets required for a new venture.
2. Explain the three factors that guide the choice between debt financing and equity financing.
3. Assume that you are starting a business for the first time. What do you believe are the greatest personal obstacles to obtaining funds for the new venture? Why?
4. If you were starting a new business, where would you start looking for capital? Should your answer depend on the nature of your new business?
5. Explain how trade credit and equipment loans can provide initial capital funding.
6. Describe the different types of loans made by a commercial bank.
7. What does a lender need to know in order to decide whether to make a loan?
8. What are the usual forms of venture capital investments?
9. Why is venture capital an inappropriate type of financing for most small firms?
10. In what ways does the federal government help with initial financing for small businesses?
11. What personal sources of financing could you use to start a business?

YOU MAKE THE CALL

SITUATION 1

Richard Moller is well on his way to starting a new venture—Max, Inc. He has projected a need for $350,000 in initial capital. He plans to invest $150,000 himself and either borrow the additional $200,000 or find a partner who will buy shares in the company. If Moller borrows the money, the interest rate will be 12 percent. If, on the other hand, another equity investor is found, he expects to have to give up 60 percent of the company's shares. Moller has forecasted earnings of about 18 percent in operating income on the firm's total assets.

Question 1 Compare the two financing options in terms of projected return on the owner's equity investment. Ignore any effect from income taxes.
Question 2 What will happen if Moller is wrong and the company earns only 5 percent in operating income on total assets?
Question 3 What must Moller consider in choosing a source of financing?

SITUATION 2

James Ridings's firm, Craftmade International, Inc., sells ceiling fans. Originally, Ridings was a sales representative for a company that sold plumbing supplies. When the company added ceiling fans to its line, Ridings developed a number of customers who bought the fans. Some time later, when the firm eliminated the ceiling fans, Ridings had customers and nothing to sell them. Consequently, in 1997, he became partners with James Ivins, a sales representative for a firm that imported ceiling fans. They scraped together $30,000 and bought 800 fans from Taiwan, which quickly sold. Encouraged, Ridings raised $45,000 to buy more fans. Again, they sold quickly. By the end of the first year, Ridings and Ivins had put together a sales force of 15 and were selling 3,000 fans per month. By 1999, the two men had started designing their own high-quality and high-profit-margin fans. Sales had grown to $10 million, and the firm was profitable. However, while the firm's sales were increasing at 50 percent per year, a problem developed: The firm ran into cash problems. At one critical point, Ridings had to persuade a supplier to accept shares in lieu of payment on a $224,000 order. Another time, Ridings and Ivins had to approach 16 bankers within a matter of a few days before finding someone who would loan them $100,000 to pay their bills.

Question 1 Craftmade International, Inc. is a successful firm when it comes to growing, but what are its owners overlooking?
Question 2 What steps would you suggest to Ridings and Ivins to solve their problems?

SITUATION 3

Too little working capital had been a constant problem at Industrial Robotics (IR), a designer of automated manufacturing equipment. But, in 2007, with 47 employees and seven offices across North America, IR faced a cash shortage that threatened to hit $1 million. Founder Jack Miller wasn't concerned. But his banker, Mario Sarducci, thought that amount was too much for a company barely doing $5 million in sales. Sarducci had worked on the IR file for the previous decade and wanted Miller to reduce his travelling expenses, shrink overhead, maximize profits, and give the bank good financial information. "You're not running a profitable operation," Sarducci lectured, "and your balance sheet doesn't support your credit. My bank has gone as far as it will go." Indeed, the bank had gone even further. At the end of 2007, IR had overdrawn its $800,000 line of credit by $300,000. If Sarducci had refused to honour those cheques, he would have forced the company to close. But Miller wasn't alarmed: "Entrepreneurs come up against barriers. They're walls to some; to others, they're only hurdles."

Question 1 Miller and Sarducci clearly have a different perspective about what needs to happen at IR. Do you think this situation is common between an entrepreneur and a banker?

Question 2 Why do you think Miller and Sarducci have such different views on the company's needs?

Question 3 What suggestions would you give Miller?

EXPERIENTIAL EXERCISES

1. Interview a local small business owner to determine how funds were obtained to start the business. Be sure you phrase questions so that they are not overly personal, and do not ask for specific dollar amounts. Write a brief report on your findings.

2. Interview a local lender about lending policies for small business loans. Ask the lender to comment on the importance of a business plan to the bank's decision to loan money to a small business. Write a brief report on your findings.

3. Review recent issues of *PROFIT* or *Canadian Business*, and report to the class on the financing arrangements of firms featured in these magazines.

4. Interview a stockbroker or investment analyst on his or her views regarding the sale of common stock by a small business. Write a brief report on your findings.

EXPLORING THE WEB

1. Go to the Industry Canada website at http://www.ic.gc.ca.
   a. Select "By Subject" under "Programs and Services" on the left of the page and click on "Finding Financing" and then "Sources of Financing" at the bottom of the page. Select two different sources from your area and link to their sites to see how they differ.
   b. Go back to the "Finding Financing" page and click on "Canada Small Business Financing Program." Prepare a summary of the program including what can be financed and what cannot.

2. Go to Business Owner's Toolkit at http://www.toolkit.com.
   a. From the menu under "Small Business Guide, select "Getting Financing for Your Business." Search for information on sources of debt financing, the types of loans available, and what lenders look for when making a loan.
   b. *Inc.*'s web site at http://www.inc.com provides many examples of specific start-up companies using private-equity financing. Taking the perspective of a private investor, go to http://www.inc.com and find a venture you would want to finance. Explain why.

THE BUSINESS PLAN: LAYING THE FOUNDATION

ASKING THE RIGHT QUESTIONS

As part of laying the foundation for your own business plan, respond to the following questions regarding the financing of your venture:

1. What is the total financing required to start up the business?
2. How much money do you plan to invest in the venture? What is the source of this money?
3. Will you need financing beyond what you personally plan to invest?
4. If additional financing is needed for the start-up, how will you raise it? How will the financing be structured—debt or equity? What will the terms be for the investors?
5. Based on your pro forma financial statements, will there be a need for future financing within the first five years of the firm's life? If so, where will it come from?
6. How and when will you arrange for investors to cash out of their investment?

THE FINANCIAL PLAN SECTION OF THE BUSINESS PLAN

Most business plans are written for the purpose of requesting financing. The financial plan section should include answers to the following:

1. How much financing is being requested and from what source(s)?
2. What will the money raised be used for (working capital, purchase of fixed assets, acquisition, etc.)?
3. How does the new financing relate to current financing and to what you have already put into the business (i.e., how it affects the balance sheet and the resulting leverage and stability of the company; see Chapter 13)?
4. How does the financing affect ownership of the business, if it is equity being sought?

5. How will the financing will be repaid or, if it is equity, how and when will the investors receive their returns?
6. What additional future financing is anticipated?
7. What returns might an investor anticipate over the life of the investment until his or her exit from the company?

THE FINANCIAL PROJECTIONS

Financial projections are required to support the business plan in general and the financing request in particular. Conventional wisdom is that a business plan should include

- **Cash flow forecasts monthly for the first year, quarterly for the second and third years, and annually for the fourth and fifth years.**
- **Pro forma (forecast) income statements monthly for the first year, quarterly for the second and third years, and annually for the fourth and fifth years.**
- **Pro forma balance sheets annually for the first five years.**

A sensitivity analysis (expected, best, and worst cases) should be done on each of the statements to show how much variation from the expected case will result in changes being made to the plan or the need for additional funds. This is a measure of the riskiness of the venture.

USING BIZPLANBUILDER® EXPRESS

If you are using BizPlan*Builder*® Express, refer to Part 3 for information on what should be included in the business plan relating to sources of financing. Then turn to Part 2 for instructions on using the software to prepare a brief version of the business plan for submission to potential investors.

PART 4

Growth

AND EXIT

15 Managing Growing Firms and Exit Strategies

CHAPTER 15

Managing Growing Firms and Exit Strategies

LOOKING AHEAD

After studying this chapter, you should be able to

1 Describe managing for growth.

2 Explain the various types of outside management assistance.

3 Explain the importance of having an exit strategy.

4 Describe succession planning.

5 Describe serial entrepreneurs.

6 Describe harvesting options and effective harvesting strategies.

7 Discuss issues in preparing for life after the harvest.

IN THE SPOTLIGHT

Full Steam Ahead

Kaboose Inc. is riding the exploding demand for Web content aimed at children and families, growing from a bare-bones start-up in 1999 to North America's largest independent online media company in the kids-and-family market. With a Web portfolio including popular sites like Babyzone, ParentZone, Birthday in a Box, Two Peas in a Bucket, Kaboose's 120,000 pages of content attracted 12 million unique visitors a month in 2007, and its family of sites have more than 2 million registered users—a fact that brought advertisers knocking. In 2007 it recorded its first profit of $500,000, a $1 million turnaround from 2005. It is a Canadian success story.

Chairman and Chief Executive Jason DeZwirek and vice-president Eric Yuzpe had no idea Kaboose would travel so far so fast when they started the company. With $250,000 seed money from a venture capital fund, the pair formed Kaboose. By 2000, when many high-tech companies had collapsed, Kaboose had about 20 online games at its site and 15,000 to 20,000 regular users a month. Using a combination of Kaboose cash flow and Mr. Yuzpe's trust fund, the company went on a buying spree. It picked up Zeeks.com, a popular site for teens and "tweens" in September 2001, KidsDomain.com in November, and Funschool.com in February 2002. "Kids-Domain shares had traded as high as US$180 a share. We bought it when it had sunk to $0.25," Mr. DeZwirek says. "Between the three sites, investors had poured in more than US$60 million by then, and we got them for pennies on the dollar." What they got for their money was a treasure trove of games and applications, and a trio of sites already drawing 1.2 million viewers a month.

The pair also demonstrated good management skills. "Together the three sites had about 200 staff; we didn't keep any of them," Mr. DeZwirek says. "We handled everything with the eight people we already had in Canada. The two biggest challenges facing a company like ours are content and distribution, and we had both. I think we had sort of the Holy Grail for dot-coms." They avoided one of the pitfalls that traps many entrepreneurs. "They knew what they didn't know and they brought in professionals to fill the gaps."

The new senior managers include Jonathan Graff, who joined the company as a consultant and became chief operating officer and president in June 2003. Previously, he had worked as a business development manager for HomeStore.com in Los Angeles, New York, and Toronto. He has also known Mr. DeZwirek since they met at camp at age nine. As Kaboose expanded, it brought an infusion of industry talent including a former director of interactive marketing with Publisher's Clearinghouse, and a new chief revenue office who had worked on sales and marketing at Time Warner Inc.'s AOL. "The continued addition of top-tier industry talent supports our strategy of increasing our share of the family Internet market," says Graff.

In late 2007 Kaboose paid $141 million in cash and stock for Bounty Group Ltd., Britain's largest parenting club and leading online family destination.

http://www.kaboose.ca

Photo by Carlos Osorio

Sources: Adapted from "Full Steam Ahead" by Terrence Belford, *Financial Post*, October 25, 2004, p. FE1, used by permission; http://www.kaboose.ca accessed April 10, 2008; and "Kaboose Grabs Bounty for $141 Million," *The Globe and Mail*, November 16, 2007.

In this chapter we examine the aspects of transitioning a small firm successfully through the growth process. The transition to more professional management that becomes necessary in a growing firm is highlighted by Kaboose Inc., featured "In the Spotlight," an example of a three-person firm that has grown strategically with the assistance of skilled managers and adequate financing. As part of the product life cycle, many entrepreneurs ultimately "harvest" or sell their venture, and this chapter describes several aspects of the succession and harvesting process.

MANAGING FOR GROWTH

1 **Describe managing for growth.**

An owner-manager of a successful small business has overcome the initial hurdles regarding financing and securing a client base. However, continuing to expand the business, either through opening additional sites or by expanding product or service lines, requires continued focus. Managing the challenges and transitions from start-up through successive growth stages is critical to a new company's eventual success. A study by the Queen's School of Business, sponsored by the Royal Bank of Canada and the Canadian Manufacturers and Exporters Association, identified many barriers to success and implications for growth for Canadian SMEs (small and medium-sized enterprises). Entitled *Managing for Growth; Enabling Sustainable Success in Canadian SMEs,* the study of over 800 Canadian firms identified nine broad areas of challenge for businesses as they transition from start-up through fast growth to sustainability. The report suggests

> *Managers of Canadian SMEs that have the capacity for profitable growth but fail to achieve commercial success often lack the necessary organizational and leadership skills to respond to business challenges. Although external challenges can be considerable, good managers work around them. They don't blame government or investors for their difficulties. Nor do they look to government to solve all their problems. Instead they improve the way they manage problems.*[1]

The study identified the following areas in which successful SMEs must perform well:

1. Strategy for growth

   * Many SMEs have strategic business plans but too little attention is paid to execution of the plan.

   * Plans are often not updated as internal or external variables change.

   * Plans are not the same as action: management that is preoccupied with planning ignores the most important part of the plan—the action that results from it.

   * Strategic plans need to be flexible enough to leave room for innovation and new ideas.

   * SME managers promote their companies to lenders and investors from their own perspective rather than the financier's. Consequently, they often fail to communicate the investment potential of their company.

   * Managers can improve their chances of finding financing by learning the language of finance, using advisers to help plan their presentations, and writing business plans that target the financier's interests.

- SMEs need to consider a wider spectrum of financing options, from family and personal sources to angels and venture capital.

- When approaching investors, SMEs should consider compatibility of objectives, particularly when the entrepreneur is trading some control of the company for capital to finance survival or growth.

- SME managers need to show through action that their company is a high-quality, growth-oriented, and professional investment opportunity.

2. Creating external networks and market connectivity

- Entrepreneurs need a tight network of good relationships with customers and markets, suppliers, financiers, competitors, advisers, and colleagues to gain the momentum to propel a young company through the growth stages.

- Being part of an industry cluster encourages innovation and collaboration, draws customers, and creates confidence in the company.

- Collaboration and alliances with colleagues and competitors can help small companies compete with larger, well-established companies for the same market.

3. Upgrading management skills and capabilities

- Turnover of some key personnel during transition from one growth stage to another can be a sign of good management: key personnel from one growth stage may not be suited to the working environment of the next.

- Key personnel retained from one growth stage to another—including the entrepreneur-owner—need to retrain to learn the management skills required for the next growth stage.

- Managers need to think ahead in order to draw the company forward. This means finding and hiring personnel with experience in the next growth stage.

4. Challenging the leader's assumptions

- Entrepreneurs can become too focused on the needs of their present growth stage and be unable to step back to see where they are headed. The perspective of outside advisers is critical for successful transitions from one growth stage to another.

- Multiple sources of advice should be sought: family, lawyers, accountants, boards, employees, and consultants.

- SME managers need to consider the expertise and objectivity of advisers when choosing an advisory team.

5. Managing succession and exits

- Successful succession means passing the company to the next generation, selling it, or delegating and letting go of responsibility and authority. Well-managed exits ensure the investors get their capital out at a fair value and the entrepreneur is fairly compensated for the time and effort spent building the business.

- Both succession and exits require considerable planning. Entrepreneurs who enjoy being the manager and cornerstone of the company during the excitement of start-up need to envision their role once the company becomes sustainable. Moreover, leaders who don't think ahead may not be adequately prepared to avoid unpleasant takeover attempts.

- Managers need to examine their satisfaction with their own leadership role as well as the needs of the company when deciding how and when to let go of authority.

6. Growth and organizational change

- Managers need to deal with organizational inertia or resistance to change in the face of a rapidly changing environment, yet many companies are unable to cope.

- Clear plans for the change process, communication, and allocation of adequate time and resources are necessary to ensure efficient change without reducing productivity.

7. Professionalizing the business infrastructure

- SMEs tend to operate with informal structures that may be suitable for start-up but become a drain on resources as the company moves into fast-growth and sustainability stages.

- Once in the fast-growth stage a company needs to formalize its operations, including human resource practices, accounting and control systems, performance measures, and formal boards of directors and/or advisers.

8. Maintaining organizational culture and values

- In the start-up stage the values of the company are those of the founder. As a firm grows, the values become those of the entire staff.

- Companies with a positive organizational culture tend to have more loyal and dedicated employees, resulting in higher productivity.

- Successful managers create desirable organizational culture by hiring based on company values, compensating and rewarding employees for behaviour consistent with those values, and constantly re-evaluating the appropriateness of the culture and values for the current stage of growth.

- A company's values need to be communicated consistently to all levels of staff.

The study concludes with some recommended actions to help entrepreneurs manage transitions from start-up through high growth to sustainability:

1. Set time aside every year for an annual planning review to assess current performance and plan for the next growth stage.
2. Anticipate and be prepared for growth challenges all companies experience rather than allowing crises to dictate actions.
3. Change the company's course and direction if that is what is required to meet these challenges.
4. Groom leadership at all levels of the company. Provide opportunities for professional upgrading and development for all managers on a yearly basis.
5. Encourage managers to step back from the day-to-day operations to assess the company from a broader perspective.

6. Set aside resources for professional advice at critical transitions between growth stages.
7. Learn about best practices in organizational development through case studies and advisory groups.
8. Promote, communicate, and manage change throughout the organization.
9. Open communication lines with all levels of staff to promote discussion about the evolution and growth of the company.

The preceding viewpoint presumes that the goal is to grow—and grow quickly. As was suggested earlier, however, growth has its good and bad sides. Many firms have encountered severe, if not fatal, consequences from growing too quickly. Refer to "In the Trenches" for Rob Feenie's experience, which highlights the potential of a founder being forced out of the business. The renowned chef turned to investors for funding when the expansion of this famed restaurant went over budget.

Some entrepreneurs prefer not to grow too large or too quickly. They prefer to remain small or at least to control the level of growth at what for them is a manageable rate when everything is considered, including priorities for their personal lives. SPUD, a Vancouver-based organic food delivery firm, highlighted below "In the Trenches," has

IN THE TRENCHES

Entrepreneurial Experiences

Chef Breaks Ties—Life after the Pot Boils Dry

In November, following a spat with investors, Rob Feenie walked away from Lumiere, the five-star Vancouver restaurant he founded, and Feenie's, its laid-back sidekick. His abrupt departure was front-page news and sent shock waves through the culinary community. "I didn't want to leave," shrugs Mr. Feenie, 43. "But it was out of my control. I had turned to the wrong people for help. It was the biggest mistake of my life. I had the wool pulled over my eyes."

He claims he was stripped of his duties and effectively terminated by his former partners, husband and wife duo David and Manjy Sidoo. Ironically, they had come to his rescue two ago when payment obligations on Lumiere's new $1.2 million kitchen threatened to bring down the entire enterprise. He signed over majority ownership of the restaurants because he was $350,000 in the red after buying out his original partner Ken Lei, and paying for the upgrade.

Feenie is a star, a giant in the Vancouver culinary scene, whose credentials include winning an Iron Chef America competition in 2005. He has had his own television cooking show, and under him Lumiere, which opened in 1995 with an initial investment of $500,000, was distinguished with the prestigious Relais Gourmand and Tradition et Qualité awards.

When asked what brought him to the point of bankruptcy two years ago, Feenie said, "I'm a chef. I'm not an accountant or bookkeeper. It's not my thing. I put the wrong people in the wrong places to be accountable. It's been 12 fabulous years." In early 2008 Feenie started over as executive chef and "food concept architect" for the Cactus Club Café, a B.C.–based restaurant chain.

Sources: Brian Hutchinson, "A Chef's Life after the Pot Boils Dry," *National Post,* April 5, 2008, and Mia Stainsby, "Chef Breaks Ties," *Vancouver Sun,* November 2, 2007.

IN THE TRENCHES

Entrepreneurial Experiences

SPUD Sinks Its Roots into San Francisco

Vancouver organic grocery delivery firm Small Potatoes Urban Delivery (SPUD) has acquired two San Francisco–based food delivery companies, Organic Express and Westside Organics. Organic Express delivers groceries to about 5000 customers in San Francisco and Los Angeles. The company, founded in 1995, has grocery warehouses in both California cities and generates about $6 million in annual revenues. Westside Organics was founded in 2001 and serves about 1000 customers in San Francisco. The company employs 10 people and has annual revenues of $1 million. "This takes us to six North American cities now and we're very much on track with our five-year plan [to expand to 20 cities throughout the continent]," SPUD founder and chief executive officer David Van Seters said in an interview.

SPUD began operations in Vancouver in 1998 with four employees, and has since expanded to Victoria, Calgary, and Seattle. Van Seters said the Organic Express and Westside Organics acquisitions will push annual SPUD revenues to about $18 million, with a base of more than 11,000 customers. The combined organization will employ about 160 people and have a fleet of 44 vehicles.

Van Seters said the purchase will give SPUD more buying power and create economies of scale, although there are no plans to close Organic Express offices or reduce staff. A Westside Organics warehouse will close and merge with the Organic Express facility. "We plan to take their average order size of $33 and boost it to well over $55, so we expect to add new staff," he said. "We did that in Calgary because our website is so much more sophisticated and offers more products, so the average order size goes up." SPUD espouses environmental values, with a focus on buying local, eco-friendly products.

Most customers place their orders online, and Van Seters feels it's a more sustainable way to shop because it eases pollution by reducing car trips to the supermarket. He said Organic Express and Westside Organics have similar values. "We are maybe more passionate about buying locally so we will try to find more new local suppliers in each of those two California markets," Van Seters said. "We will continue our practice of calculating and publishing the distance all of our products travel from where they're grown or produced." He said the average food product travels about 2,500 kilometres from where it is grown to where it is sold, but SPUD has reduced that to 800 kilometres, as more than 50 percent of its products are locally grown or produced.

Van Seters said SPUD's next expansion targets might include Edmonton and Portland. "We're following the MBA 101 strategy of expanding in concentric circles from your home base and staying in your time zone as long as possible," he said. Van Seters said the company will launch a new website in a month that will reposition SPUD as more of a "lifestyle" brand, focusing on people who want to experiment with new recipes and gourmet food. "We will promote the whole philosophy of being able to shop fast so you can dine slow and take time and use quality ingredients to make great meals with your family and friends," he said.

Source: Adapted from Bruce Constantineau, "SPUD Sinks Its Roots into San Francisco," *Vancouver Sun,* March 17, 2008.

pursued a logical and sustainable expansion plan, following the kinds of practices described in the *Managing for Growth* study.[2] SPUD has developed efficient systems, entailing purchasing, logistics, warehousing, and quality controls that contribute to cost-effectiveness and enhanced profitability.

OUTSIDE MANAGEMENT ASSISTANCE

Explain the various types of outside management assistance.

2

Given the potential for managerial deficiencies, as was highlighted earlier in this chapter, many entrepreneurs should consider using outside management assistance. Such assistance can supplement the manager's personal knowledge and the expertise of the few staff specialists on the company's payroll.

THE NEED FOR OUTSIDE ASSISTANCE

The typical entrepreneur is not only deficient in managerial skills but also lacks the opportunity to share ideas with peers. Although entrepreneurs can confide, to some extent, in subordinates, many experience loneliness. A survey of 210 owners revealed that 52 percent "frequently felt a sense of loneliness.[3] Moreover, this group reported a much higher incidence of stress symptoms than those who said they did not feel lonely.

By using consultants, entrepreneurs can overcome some of their managerial deficiencies and reduce their sense of isolation. Furthermore, an insider directly involved in a business problem often cannot see the forest for the trees. In contrast, an outside consultant brings an objective point of view and new ideas, supported by a broad knowledge of proven, successful, cost-saving methods. The consultant can also help the manager to improve decision making by better organizing fact gathering and introducing scientific techniques of analysis.

SOURCES OF MANAGEMENT ASSISTANCE

Entrepreneurs who seek management assistance can turn to any of a number of sources, including business incubators, government programs, and management consultants. There are numerous other sources of knowledge and approaches to seeking needed management help. For example, owner-managers may increase their own skills by consulting public and university libraries, attending evening classes at local colleges and universities, and considering the suggestions of friends and customers.

BUSINESS INCUBATORS

As we discussed in Chapter 11, a business incubator is an organization that offers both space and managerial and clerical services to new businesses. There are many incubators in Canada, some of them involving governmental agencies and/or universities. The primary motivation in establishing incubators has been a desire to encourage entrepreneurship and thereby contribute to economic development.

Incubators offer new entrepreneurs on-site business expertise. Often, individuals who wish to start businesses are deficient in pertinent knowledge and lacking in appropriate experience. In many cases, they need practical guidance in marketing,

EXHIBIT **15-1**
*Services Provided by
Business Incubators
to New Firms*

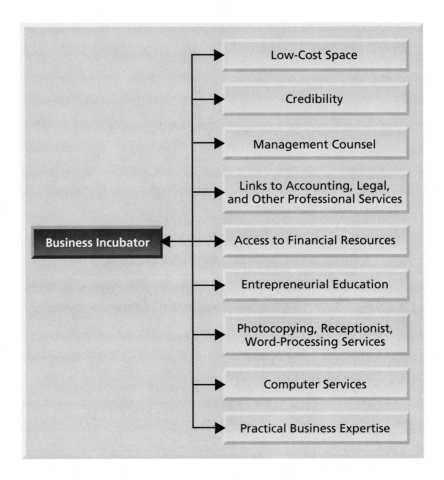

record keeping, managing, and preparing business plans. Exhibit 15-1 shows the services available in a business incubator.

An incubator provides a supportive atmosphere for a business during the early months of its existence when it is most fragile and vulnerable to external dangers and internal errors. If the incubator works as it should, the fledgling business gains strength quickly and, within a year or so, leaves the incubator. Information pertaining to incubators located at college or universities can be obtained from http://www.ic.gc.ca, or from the Canadian Association of Business Incubation at http://www.cabi.ca.

CANADIAN YOUTH BUSINESS FOUNDATION (CYBF)

Founded by CIBC and the Royal Bank in 1996, the Canadian Youth Business Foundation (CYBF), the organization has helped thousands of young Canadians pursue self-employment or launch a venture. The CYBF offers support through the following:

- *Mentorship:* An experienced businessperson will provide advice during the start-up phase of a new business.
- *Loan program:* Those aged 18 to 29 with a sound business plan can obtain up to $15,000 in capital.

Obtain more information on CYBF from its website: http://www.cybf.ca.

INDUSTRY CANADA

Through its Industrial Research Assistance Program (NRC-IRAP), Industry Canada offers technical assistance and research funding for businesses. Through its Field Advisory Service, firms can access the expertise of industry technical advisers (ITAs) to assist a firm to define its technical needs, identify technical opportunities, solve product and production problems, access or acquire technology and expertise from Canadian or foreign sources, access financial assistance programs, and obtain referrals to other available assistance.

Small and medium-sized firms (up to 500 employees) may be eligible for 75 percent of funding up to $15,000 to assist with projects in the areas of technical feasibility studies, small-scale R&D, external technical assistance, or problem solving using a university or college engineering or science student. More substantial funding may be granted to high-potential industrial R&D projects where there is a high likelihood of the project profitably improving the technology base of the business, leading to industrial development and commercial exploitation of the technology in Canada, and assisting the business in international markets. The program is delivered by an extensive integrated network of 260 professionals in 100 communities across Canada. Refer to the website at http://www.nrc-cnrc.gc.ca/doingbusiness/irap_e.html.

Another initiative of Industry Canada is the Canadian Technology Network. The CTN is a network of industry, provincial, and federal government groups that offer various kinds of assistance and information to businesses. The network includes trade and industry associations, provincial and federal research bodies, universities, and private research laboratories that cross-refer clients to each other to provide businesses with an efficient means of finding the right kind of assistance. Refer to the network's website at http://www.ctn-rct.ca/en.

COUNSELLING ASSISTANCE TO SMALL ENTERPRISE (CASE)

The Business Development Bank (BDC) offers many consulting and training services in addition to providing loans and other financial services. The most prominent is CASE, or Counselling Assistance for Small Enterprise, which uses industry-experienced counsellors to assist new and existing businesses with management support and mentoring. Since its inception, CASE has helped more than 100,000 Canadian entrepreneurs and businesses to start, expand, or professionalize.

UNIVERSITIES AND COLLEGES

Business, science, engineering, law, and other faculties of many universities and colleges have programs to assist businesses in a variety of ways, from technical support to student consulting and advice. Other programs use projects for course credit, using undergraduate and masters students to do market research, business plans, and feasibility studies. Several universities, such as Mt. Mary's University and Acadia, offer consulting services to small business owners from street-front locations.

MANAGEMENT CONSULTANTS

Management consultants serve small businesses as well as large corporations. The entrepreneur should regard the services of a competent management consultant as an investment in improved decision making or cost reduction; many small firms could save as much as 10 to 20 percent of annual operating costs. The inherent advantage in using such consultants is suggested by the existence of thousands of consulting firms. They range from large, well-established firms to small one- or two-person operations. Two broad areas of services are rendered by management consultants:

1. Helping improve productivity and/or prevent trouble by anticipating and eliminating its causes
2. Helping a client get out of trouble

Business firms have traditionally used consultants to help solve problems they could not handle alone. A consultant may be used, for example, to aid in designing a new computer-based management information system. An even greater service that management consultants provide is periodic observation and analysis, which keeps small problems from becoming large ones. This role of consultants greatly expands their potential usefulness. Outside professionals typically charge by the hour, so an owner should prepare as completely as possible before a consulting session or visit begins.

The "In the Trenches" illustrates the type of an analysis that a management consultant would assist a founder or manager with when assessing the implications of expanding a business.

NETWORKS OF ENTREPRENEURS

networking
the process of developing and engaging in mutually beneficial business relationships

Entrepreneurs also gain informal management assistance through **networking**—the process of developing and engaging in mutually beneficial business relationships with peers. As business owners meet other business owners, they discover a commonality of interests that leads to an exchange of ideas and experiences. The settings for such meetings may be trade associations, civic clubs, networking groups, or any situation that brings businesspeople into contact with one another. Of course, the personal network of an entrepreneur is not limited to other entrepreneurs, but those individuals may be the most significant part of that network. Numerous support networks have developed in recent years, including Business Partnerships Canada, a small business networking site located at http://businesspartnerships.ca.

OTHER BUSINESS AND PROFESSIONAL SERVICES

A variety of business and professional groups such as bankers, chartered accountants, lawyers, insurance agents, suppliers, trade associations, and chambers of commerce provide management assistance.

IN THE TRENCHES

Entrepreneurial Experiences

How Do I Know I'm Ready for a Second Location?

Regardless of the business you're in, a second location is one of the most critical decisions you'll make in your company's lifetime, says Richard Carson, partner, Deloitte, responsible for the Canadian customer and market strategy practice from his office in Toronto. "In some ways it's like the decision to have a second child. You absolutely need to make sure your business model is working financially, operationally and in terms of lifestyle." To do that, you will have to drill down and take a laser-like look at what you're doing right and whether or not you can replicate that success.

There are 2.5 million small business owners in Canada, 90% of which are under $1,000,000 in sales, says Taunya Woods Richardson, president and CEO of Powerhouse International Inc. in Calgary, a firm that helps build peer advisory boards for small business owners, offers mentorship programs and takes on advocacy initiatives. "I guarantee 90% of that 90% don't drill down through their numbers," she says. "Most business owners are optimists operating on hope and prayers every month. Many don't truly understand the numbers behind their business, and that's what's getting them into trouble. If your existing business doesn't work there is no reason to layer on a second problem. It's only going to compound the issue."

How do you know if your business model is working? "You want to make sure your net profit is healthy and it's the right net profit," Ms. Woods Richardson says. In other words, find out how your profits and costs compare to the industry's. Then go further and break down profitability per product/service. Understand what really sells. The deeper you go, the better. "You have to be strategic when you are planning to move forward with a second location," Ms. Woods Richardson says. "Growth, as much as lack of growth, can compromise a business." We've had a number of members who have tried to move to a second location but it hasn't worked because they've taken too much on, too quickly, and as a result, put the entire business at risk."

Part of the strategy should include optimizing existing operations. "Further investment in an existing location sometimes provides a greater return than establishing a new business," says University of Alberta's Lloyd Steier. "Have you optimized returns on your existing business?" A second location is an expensive proposition. You are guaranteed to double your operating expenses but you are not guaranteed to double your revenues. So explore all opportunities for your existing business before making that investment. "Often the better approach is to try and expand the physical size of your first location, or take the infrastructure and use it for a different use," Mr. Carson says. "For example, if you have a restaurant, you could move into catering. Could you do more business via Web-based sales?"

Companies are often surprised at how far they can push the productivity in one location, whether it's by merchandising improvements, service, or staff improvements. Still think you should pursue a second location? Now, it's time to get reflective on your own role in the company. "Business success is often attributable to the hard work and hands-on skills of the founder," Mr. Steier says. "Are you able to clone yourself and/or do you have systems in place wherein the organization or at least of the locations can function without you?" Also step back and look at the bigger picture. What's happening around you in terms of market trends? Is this the best time to secure a lease or buy a property? What's happening with the economy, client spending, the labour situation, and the competition?

"You have to take all that into consideration, otherwise you are just hoping things are going to work out versus knowing it's going to work," Ms. Woods Richardson says. Is the right location available? Successful businesses such as Crate & Barrel wait years for the ideal location before expanding. And, what will that second location mean to your first? "Many people don't think about the degree to which the second location will have synergy or cannibalization with the first," Mr. Carson says. "Often, you get the elements of both. The synergy might be in terms of efficiencies, but cannibalization can occur when customers choose the second location over the first.

Finally, do you have an exit strategy if the second location isn't working?

Source: "How Do I Know I'm Ready for a Second Location?" Business Solutions, Special Feature to the *National Post,* March 10, 2008, page FP9.

It takes initiative to draw on the management assistance available from such groups. For example, it is easy to confine a business relationship with a CA to audits and financial statements, but the CA can advise on a much broader range of subjects.

Besides offering advice on tax matters, a good accountant can help in a variety of situations. When you hire or fire, what benefits or severance package should you offer? When you're planning to open a new branch, will your cash flow support it? When you embark on a new sideline, will the margins be adequate? When you reduce insurance, what's the risk? When you factor receivables, how will it affect the balance sheet? When you take on a big account, what's the downside if you lose the account? Or when you cut expenses, how will the cuts affect the bottom line?[4]

As you can see from the examples given, potential management assistance often comes disguised as professionals and firms encountered in the normal course of business activity. By staying alert for and taking advantage of such opportunities, a small firm can strengthen its management and improve its operations with little, if any, additional cost.

3 **Explain the importance of having an exit strategy.**

harvesting

the exit process used by entrepreneurs and investors to unlock the value of a business

THE IMPORTANCE OF THE HARVEST

Thus far, the first two phases of the entrepreneurial process—starting a company and managing its growth—have been presented. But that's not the end of the story. **Harvesting** is the method entrepreneurs and investors use to exit a business and, ideally, reap the value of their investment in the firm. Many entrepreneurs successfully grow their businesses but fail to develop effective exit strategies. As a result, they are unable to capture the full value of the business that they have worked so hard to create.

According to a national survey conducted by CIBC, over 500,000 small businesses will change hands before 2010 (see "In the Trenches"). Many entrepreneurs who founded companies in the 1950s and 1960s are—or soon will be—engaged in a harvest strategy. They will be transferring ownership either to the next generation of family members or to other individuals and investors who have an interest in the business. Most entrepreneurs do not like to think about the harvest, even though few events in the life of an entrepreneur, and of the firm itself, are more significant. Consequently, the decision to harvest is frequently the result of an unexpected event, possibly a crisis, rather than a well-conceived strategy.

An entrepreneur needs to understand that harvesting encompasses more than merely selling and leaving a business; it involves capturing value (cash flows), reducing risk, and creating future options. In addition, for the entrepreneur, there are personal and nonfinancial considerations. An owner may receive a lot of money for the firm but still be disappointed with the decision to exit the business if he or she is not prepared for a change in lifestyle. Thus, carefully designing an intentional harvest strategy is as essential to an entrepreneur's personal success as it is to his or her financial success.

The harvest is vitally important to a firm's investors as well. Investors who provide high-risk capital—particularly venture capitalists—generally insist on a well-thought-out exit strategy. Investors realize that it is easy to put money into a business but difficult to get it out. As a result, a firm's appeal to investors is driven by the availability of harvest options. If investors are not convinced that opportunities will exist for exiting the investment, there will be no investment.

IN THE TRENCHES

Entrepreneurial Experiences

Exodus of Entrepreneurs "Staggering"

Canadian businesses are facing a retirement crisis that could cripple the nation's economy if the necessary preparations aren't made, industry experts say. One of the most susceptible groups is the small business sector, which according to a recently released CIBC study stands to lose half a million owners by 2010. By 2020, about half of the 2.5 million active entrepreneurs in Canada will have been put out to pasture—a figure called "staggering" by Rob Paterson, senior vice-president of CIBC Small Business Banking.

The Canadian Federation of Independent Business (CFIB), a voice for many small and medium-sized enterprises across the country, echoed those concerns. The CFIB is wrapping up its own detailed study on the same issue—to be released within the next few months—and says its findings correspond with those of the bank. "It is quite alarming what we're seeing . . . it is fast approaching, probably a lot faster than a lot of people think, and the (retirement) issue is going to be quite big," says Doug Bruce, director of research for the CFIB. "I think now is the time to get business owners preparing for their own succession, because it not only has implications for each individual small business, but also for the overall economy," because independent companies account for almost half of Canada's economic activity.

The question of how business owners ready themselves for successions is vital, says Gord Wusyk, principal of Predictable Futures—The Family Business Centre, which specializes in succession planning for family businesses in Western Canada. Wusyk says his Edmonton-based company attempts to get entrepreneurs thinking about succession when they're still in their 50s. This is especially important if they hope to pass the business to the kids. "Start early rather than late, because then you can prepare people for leadership or get your son or daughter to work for four or five years outside the business to get independent experience before they take over the company," he says.

After more than 30 years of owning and operating Davey Fabrics, Edmonton entrepreneurs Al Davey and wife Jan called it quits. Luckily family members were waiting in the wings. Son Grant, childhood friend Dan King, and his cousin Jim Davey took over the business in 2001. "I guess the day Grant joined the business is when we first thought about it . . . You don't ask your son or daughter into the business, you let him ask, and let them ask and ask and ask and ask some more," Al says.

Grant began with the company in 1989. Al says the moment he passed through the door was when the first seeds of succession were planted, although formal planning didn't actually start until 1996. The new owners are stretching their legs and looking for new opportunities, such as dealing more with fire-retardant fabrics for Alberta's thriving oil industry. "It's good to see that they're thinking and taking the business in new directions," Al says, adding that both he and his wife remain connected to the operation, not in the day-to-day workings but rather in an advisory role as directors.

Such stories are rare today because most business owners end up selling outside the family; only about 25 or 30 percent of small firms are passed from one generation to the next, Wusyk says. Another concern is the lack of preparation for the inevitable day the small business owners will retire, CIBC says. On the financial security side, the bank notes that only one in five small business proprietors maximized their RRSP contribution in 2003. Even among entrepreneurs closest to retirement, less than one-third maximized their 2003 RRSP contributions.

(Continued)

According to the CIBC report, the impact on Ontario's small business community shouldn't be as bad elsewhere in the country. In the next decade, roughly 21 percent of owners plan to retire, compared with 26 percent in Alberta. Some in Toronto's business scene believe the city's small business community will continue to thrive, largely due to the influx of immigrants with an entrepreneurial spirit who arrive in the city in droves each year.

An issue facing potential suitors of existing businesses is access to capital. The CFIB's Bruce wonders who will buy the hundreds of thousands of businesses placed on the market in the coming years—and more to the point, how they're going to afford it. His organization has studied the problem of access to capital for years and has found that the small business sector always has a tougher time than the larger companies securing the financing to start or purchase a business. He insists that financial institutions must play a greater role if the small business sector is to survive, "by not only providing information to clients, but also providing the needed financing for the successors."

Source: John Ludwick, "Exodus of Entrepreneurs 'Staggering,' Small-Business Sector Faces Biggest Shock in Retirement Crisis," *Business Edge,* Vol. 1, No. 3, February 17, 2005. Used by permission.

SUCCESSION PLANNING

4 Describe succession planning.

Small business owners choosing to retire or slow down may not want to sell the business, but pass it on to the next generation, or even just hire managers to reduce the time and work commitment for a period of time prior to ultimately selling the venture. In either event, a well-managed succession plan provides the benefits of securing the owner's financial future, and maintaining relationships with investors, lenders, and customers.

Creating a written succession plan addresses several key issues, including identifying future managers and leaders, how to assess potential candidates, the monitoring process, the training and declaration of a successor, and the timeline for succession. Concrete operational and tax issues will be addressed. The *Managing for Growth* study has several recommendations:

- Owners should not look for a clone of themselves but select someone with the right mix of skills and leadership qualities to continue expanding the business.
- Training candidates in the corporate culture will enhance the probability of employee and customer acceptance.
- Ownership should not be passed to the next generation until they have worked outside the family business, allowing them to build credibility and gain a broader knowledge of the competitive marketplace and alternative best practices.
- Establish clear guidelines and expectations for performance for a two-to-three-year period after succession; ensure controls are in place before the transfer.

While many founders will retain ownership in the venture after they "retire," many others will sell the business in order to "harvest" their profits to secure a sound financial retirement.

IN THE TRENCHES

Entrepreneurial Experiences

Passing the Keys to Key Staff

In 1948, when Ernie Poole sold Edmonton-based Poole Construction Ltd. to his sons, George and John, he handwrote a list of business guidelines for them, hoping it would help them continue the family tradition. The brothers ran the business for nearly 30 years, keeping the family tradition alive. But by 1977, it was their turn to pass on the business to a new leader. It seemed tradition would come to an end: They sold the company to its management and a group of 25 employees and the company continued to offer shares to its employees every year thereafter. Their decision led to the success story of the company now known as PCL, a $5-billion construction firm that employs more than 8,500 people and has locations across North America and in the Bahamas. It also set PCL on a path toward becoming 100% employee-owned.

The Poole name continues to be closely associated with PCL, which is proud of its family heritage and Ernie Poole's handwritten paper with his business guidelines still hangs in its North American headquarters. What's more, PCL might not be a family business any more but it has grown into the PCL family of companies. "Management buyout can be a terrific strategy but it takes some time to implement," says Edmonton-based Carole Spooner, a partner at Meyers Norris Penny LLP. For a management buyout to be successful, "typically you have to make sure you have a strong management team," she says. The problem in many small businesses is the owner often is, for all practical purposes, the manager—and many tend to keep a tight control over information, says Michael Naprawa, a British Columbia–based broker for international brokerage firm Sunbelt.

That leaves his or her key employees with a limited opportunity to develop the information and experience needed to own and run the business. "Typically, most managers only manage a certain scope of the business, so they might not be broad enough to run it all. What's more, relationships can change between managers and employees once they become the owners," he says. Mr. Naprawa cites the example of a company sold by a woman to three key employees after her husband passed away. The employees, he says, had great technical expertise, and they all got along as employees—because they had to. "As owners, they couldn't," he says. This is why succession-planning consultants such as Ruth Steverlynck, director of PricewaterhouseCoopers' Centre for Entrepreneurs and Family Business in B.C., and Janice Kelner, director for its counterpart in Alberta, recommend business owners who want to sell their company to management begin the process long in advance of the actual transfer date—years in advance, in fact.

This allows the owner to assess management's weaknesses and strengths, and to put together a strategy to ensure the skills and strengths needed to run the company successfully are in place. As well, it allows for formal transition strategies to be set up. For example, an interim management that includes the original owner can be put together to help through the adjustment period. Employees, clients, suppliers and the new owners will thus have an opportunity to ease into the new relationship structure. Just as with the option of leaving a company to a family member, many of the potential problems in a management buyout can often be addressed effectively if dealt with early enough.

Source: Alexandra Lopez-Pacheco, "Passing the Keys to Key Staff," *Financial Post,* November 5, 2007.

serial entrepreneurs innovative and creative people who are more interested in starting new businesses than running them

SERIAL ENTREPRENEURS

Dr. Walter Good is a professor and marketing department head at the I.H. Asper School of Business at the University of Manitoba. He says serial entrepreneurs are innovative and creative people who are generally more interested in starting new businesses than running them. "Serial entrepreneurs tend to be strongly focused. They'll start a venture and develop it to a certain stage. Then they'll lose interest in it, the challenge runs out or, in some cases, they get shoved aside by the investment capital that's come into the business, and they move on. Next thing you know, they've started another venture."

Good believes that while most of us rarely look beyond the edges of our desk, serial entrepreneurs are visionaries. "I typically associate four characteristics with them: Determination, commitment, perseverance and vision," he says. "They have a vision. They see something else no one else does and set out a path to get there." Good says "They're never really satisfied. They're always trying to analyze systems, dissect them, and understand them. They reflect on mistakes as a learning experience because everything is part of the process."[5]

ENTREPRENEUR

IN THE TRENCHES

Entrepreneurial Experiences

Serial Entrepreneurs Are Driven to Create

Larry Finnson is hoping that success is even sweeter the second time around. Best known as the president and co-founder of Krave's Candy Co., which has manufactured and marketed Clodhoppers fudge-clustered candy in Winnipeg since 1996, Finnson stepped down in October to concentrate on a new endeavour—24K Water Co. "I figured that I took Clodhoppers as far as I could," he says. "To be honest, after 10 years, I was burning out of passion. It was time to do something else." This is not about clodhoppers it is about the organization one of the founders started after he left clodhoppers.

Finnson, 36, initially became interested in the beverage industry in 2004, learning more about the business through food and confection trade shows he attended. Once he discovered that he could combine bottled water with zeal for his Nordic roots, it was impossible to keep a cap on his enthusiasm. "I'm 100 per cent Icelandic," Finnson says. "I always thought if I could find bottled water from Iceland, the cleanest country in the world—that would be ideal." Internet research led Finnson to Icelandic Glacial, a premium bottled–mineral water company. Demonstrating his guerrilla marketing knack, which made Clodhoppers a household name and earned it shelf space in Wal-Marts around North America, Finnson sent an introductory email with a photo of himself posed beside the famous 15-foot-tall Viking statue in Gimli, Manitoba. "They said: 'We like your style. Let's meet!'" he recalls. Following a meeting in Minneapolis, Finnson was made Canada's exclusive distributor of Icelandic Glacial.

His 24K Water Co. will launch Icelandic Glacial in Winnipeg Wal-Mart locations in April and plans to expand into other markets shortly afterward.

"It's been a natural transition for me," he says. "I went to the school of hard knocks and worked my butt off for 10 years to learn the industry and build relationships. Now I'm taking those contacts and springboarding onto the next [challenge]." Finnson says that for entrepreneurs such as him, the excitement is in seeing a vision unfold and the fun is in overcoming the fears that come with taking a new risk. "I would say it's like building a three-headed Frankenstein, then trying to figure out how to control it," he says. "There's a little bit of madness in great entrepreneurship."

According to a study of entrepreneurship by CIBC World Markets, 33 percent of Canada's 2.5 million small business owners have owned or currently own more than one business, classifying them as "serial entrepreneurs." One quarter of these entrepreneurs have owned a business that is no longer in operation, and 22 percent of those with one business say they are seriously considering starting another venture in addition to their current enterprise.

Tony Lourakis, president and CEO of Complete Innovations Inc., falls into both categories. "Thinking big is always exciting to me," says Lourakis, whose company, based in Richmond Hill, Ontario, provides mission-critical operations and management software for more than 350 courier, mobile workforce, and transportation-related companies. It's the 26-year-old's second company, although as he puts it, "I've been running businesses from a very young age." The son of a Greek immigrant property and real estate entrepreneur, Lourakis says self-employment comes naturally. "From the time I could walk, my father had me working for him. By the time I had my driver's licence, he would go to Greece in the summer and leave me to run his business."

Lourakis started his first company, an IT consulting firm, while still in college. "I always had an interest in computer technology and knew I wanted to be in business for myself, but didn't know what it would be until I took my interest and recognized there might be something there." In 1997, a friend in the courier business asked Lourakis and his partner to build an affordable software system that would give smaller operations the same dispatch and tracking abilities that big players such as UPS and Fed-Ex had.

"We weren't the first company to come up with courier software, but we came up with a Windows-based system that was priced so that small and medium-sized businesses could afford it," he says, adding that innovation continues to inspire him. "Doing something new, something cool, something that will help—that's exciting. You might do something that's been done before, but you'll put a different twist on it and find a better way to deliver it." In addition to Complete Innovations, Lourakis is a shareholder and consultant in a couple of his friends' ventures—just another side effect of being a serial entrepreneur—and says that he's toying with importing extra virgin olive oil from his family's olive groves in Greece. "I'm constantly thinking up new business ideas and concepts. It's the only way I know how to live."

When asked if he can imagine going through the start-up process again, Larry Finnson affirms that he is an entrepreneur for life. "I'm not quite exhausted yet. I'm a little more exhausted than I was 10 years ago, but I know 10 times as much, so I think I probably have another one in me," he says.

"I'll always have my fingers in something—I wouldn't be happy without it."

Sources: Adapted from Barbara Chabai, "Serial Entrepreneurs are Driven to Create," *Business Edge,* February 16, 2006, Vol. 6, No. 4; "The Candy Man Can," *Canadian Business Online,* October 2006; and http://www.clodhoppers.tv/about.html.

METHODS OF HARVESTING

The five basic ways to harvest an investment in a privately owned company are (1) selling the firm, (2) releasing the firm's free cash flows to its owners, (3) offering stock to the public through an initial public offering, (4) issuing a private placement of the stock, or (5) liquidation.

Describe harvesting options and effective harvesting strategies. **6**

SELLING THE FIRM

As in any harvest strategy, the financial issues arising from the sale of a firm include questions of how to value the firm as well as how to structure the sale. Most frequently, an entrepreneur's motivation for selling a company relates to estate planning and the opportunity to diversify her or his portfolio of investments.

Sale transactions can, for all practical purposes, be reduced to three types, based on the motives of the buyers: strategic acquisitions, financial acquisitions, and employee acquisitions. A strategic buyer is interested in synergies that can be gained from the acquisition; a financial buyer is more often interested in the firm as a stand-alone business; and an employee buyer is primarily interested in preserving employment. Let's consider each type of transaction in more detail.

STRATEGIC ACQUISITIONS

strategic acquisition
a purchase in which the value of the business is based on both the firm's stand-alone characteristics and the synergies that the buyer thinks can be created

From the seller's perspective, the key point in a **strategic acquisition** is that the value buyers place on the business depends on the synergies they think they can create. Since the value of a business to a buyer is derived from both its stand-alone characteristics and its synergies, strategic buyers often will pay a higher price than financial buyers, who value the business only as a stand-alone entity. Thus, in strategic acquisitions, the critical issue is the degree of strategic fit between the firm to be harvested and a potential buyer. If the potential buyer is a current rival, and if the acquisition would provide long-term, sustainable competitive advantages (such as lower cost of production or superior product quality), the buyer may be willing to pay a premium for the firm.

FINANCIAL ACQUISITIONS

financial acquisition
a purchase in which the value of the business is based on the stand-alone cash-generating potential of the firm being acquired

Buyers in **financial acquisitions,** unlike strategic buyers, look primarily to a firm's stand-alone cash-generating potential as its source of value. Often, the value a financial buyer hopes to tap relates to stimulating future sales growth, reducing costs, or both. This fact has an important implication for the owner of the firm being purchased. The buyer often will make changes in the firm's operations that translate into higher pressures on the firm's personnel, resulting in layoffs that the current owner might find objectionable. As a result, financial acquisitions have garnered an unfavourable reputation among many small business owners.

leveraged buyout (LBO)
a purchase heavily financed with debt, where the potential cash flow of the target company is expected to be sufficient to meet debt repayments

During the past decade, the **leveraged buyout (LBO),** a financial acquisition involving a very high level of debt financing, became synonymous with the bust-up LBO, in which the new owners pay the debt down rapidly by selling off the acquired firm's assets. Frequently, acquisitions were financed with $9 in debt for every $1 in equity—thus the name *leveraged* buyout.

management buyout (MBO)
leveraged buyout that includes the firm's top management as significant shareholders in the acquired firm

Buildup LBOs have occurred in a number of industries where smaller companies frequently operate, such as funeral services and automobile dealerships. Such LBOs frequently include the firm's top management as significant shareholders in the acquired firm—in which case the arrangement is referred to as a **management buyout (MBO).** There is evidence that MBOs can contribute significantly to a firm's operating performance by increasing management's focus and intensity. In view of this evidence, an MBO is a potentially viable means of transferring firm ownership for both large and small businesses. In many entrepreneurial businesses, managers have a strong incentive to become owners, but they often lack the financial capacity to acquire the firm. An MBO can solve this problem through the use of debt financing, which is often underwritten by the firm's owner.

IN THE TRENCHES

Entrepreneurial Experiences

A Seller's Motto: "Do As I Say, Not as I Do"

A new survey of entrepreneurs confirms that most business sales are mismanaged by the owners from the start. Newport Partners, a Toronto-based firm specializing in personal and business-financing services for entrepreneurs, released a survey of 100 Canadians who have sold businesses in the past five years. The poll reveals some disturbing trends: Business owners are waiting till they get an offer before they address key issues in selling a business, which means they're not negotiating from strength, and are leaving money on the table.

The survey shows a surprising amount of sellers' remorse, as the former owners regret their failure to get the best deal not only for themselves, but also for their management staff and customers. While most entrepreneurs were pleased with the results of their sale, "The process was often lonely, emotional and conducted without proper planning," Newport founding partner David Lloyd noted.

Key findings of the report include 26 percent of the respondents claiming the most common reason for selling was "I received an attractive offer." Coming in second at 14 precent was "I needed more capital or strategic support," and at 13 percent "the sale was motivated by partners or shareholders." Eighty-one percent of the respondents turned to lawyers for advice on selling, and 68 percent to an accountant. Only 40 percent used an additional advisor experienced in selling businesses. These entrepreneurs did not approach the sale of their businesses with the same rigour they bring to other business dealings. Only 23 percent said they had "methodically planned" the sale two or three years in advance. Only 33 percent obtained a professional valuation of their business, which might have given them more negotiating power. Mr. Lloyd said in an interview that while only 17 percent had access to a trusted friend or personal advisor during the sale, 53 percent recommend it. "They would have liked to have someone in their corner helping them with this roller-coaster process."

What happens after the sale? The surveyed entrepreneurs reported feeling at loose ends after selling their business. Some had nothing to do, while others felt bad for not doing more to secure agreements with the purchasers that would preserve people's jobs. Nearly half of the sellers signed a management contract to continue working for or advising the company for a period of time. In hindsight, only 6 percent "strongly advise" other entrepreneurs to do so. Hanging around what used to be your baby—and over which you now have only limited control—isn't fun.

Source: Adapted from Rick Spence, "A Seller's Motto," *Financial Post,* February 4, 2008, accessed online April 10, 2008.

EMPLOYEE ACQUISITIONS

Employee acquisitions provide another way for a business's founder to cash out, and for the employees to acquire an ownership interest in their company. In some cases, long-term employees purchase the business in stages, sometimes over several years, as the owner-founder prepares for retirement.

Employee ownership is not a panacea. Selling all or part of a firm to employees works only when the sale resolves existing conflicts in such a way that both the owner and the employees are better off. While advocates maintain that employee ownership improves

employee ownership
a method by which a firm is sold either in part or in total to its employees

motivation, leading to greater effort and reduced waste, the value of any greater employee effort resulting from improved motivation will vary significantly from firm to firm.

RELEASING THE FIRM'S FREE CASH FLOWS

The second harvesting strategy involves the orderly withdrawal of the owners' investment in the form of the firm's free cash flows. The withdrawal process could be immediate if the owners simply sold off the assets of the firm and ceased business operations. However, for a value-creating firm—one that earns attractive rates of return for its investors—this does not make economic sense. The mere fact that a firm is earning rates of return that exceed the investors' opportunity cost of funds indicates that the firm is worth more as a going concern than a dead one. Thus, downsizing the company is not a viable option. Instead, the owners might simply stop growing the business; by doing so, they increase the free cash flows that can be returned to the investors.

free cash flow
operating profits plus depreciation less cash taxes and less the investments required to grow the firm

Free cash flow represents the amount of cash that can be distributed to investors after all operating needs have been met. Specifically,

$$\begin{array}{c} \textit{Free cash} \\ \textit{flow} \end{array} = \begin{array}{c} \textit{Operating} \\ \textit{profits} \\ \textit{(after taxes)} \end{array} + \textit{Depreciation} - \textit{Taxes} - \begin{array}{c} \textit{Investments} \\ \textit{required to} \\ \textit{grow the firm} \end{array}$$

In a firm's early years, all its cash flow is usually devoted to growing the business. Thus, the firm's free cash flow during this period is zero—or, more likely, negative—requiring its owners to seek outside cash to finance future growth. As the firm matures and opportunities to grow the business decline, sizable free cash flows frequently become available to its owners. Rather than reinvest all the cash flows in the firm, the owners can begin to withdraw the cash, thus harvesting their investment. If they decide to do so, only the amount of cash necessary to maintain current markets is retained and reinvested; there is little, if any, effort to grow the present markets or expand into new markets.

Harvesting by withdrawing a firm's cash from the business has two important advantages: The owners can retain control of the firm while they harvest their investment, and they do not have to seek out a buyer or incur the expenses associated with consummating a sale. There are disadvantages, however. Reducing reinvestment when the firm faces valuable growth opportunities results in lost value creation and could leave a firm unable to sustain its competitive advantage. The end result may be an unintended reduction in harvestable value below the potential value of the firm as a long-term going concern. Also, there may be tax disadvantages to an orderly liquidation, compared with other harvest methods. For example, if a firm simply distributes the cash flows as dividends, the income may be taxed both as corporate income and as personal dividend income to the stockholders. (Of course, this would not be a problem for a sole proprietorship or partnership.)

Finally, for the entrepreneur who is simply tired of day-to-day operations, siphoning off the free cash flows over time may require too much patience. Unless other people in the firm are qualified to manage it, this strategy may be destined to fail.

GOING PUBLIC

The third method of harvesting is going public. Many entrepreneurs consider the prospect of an initial public offering (IPO) as the "holy grail" of their career, as firms involved in an IPO are generally star performers. However, most entrepreneurs do not really understand the IPO process. This section considers two issues relating to an IPO: (1) how going public relates to the harvest and (2) the process by which a firm goes public.

THE IPO AS A HARVEST STRATEGY

An **initial public offering (IPO)** is used primarily as a way to raise additional equity capital to finance company growth, and only secondarily as a way to harvest the owner's investment. Lisa D. Stein, vice president of Salomon Smith Barney, offers the following reasons for going public:[6]

- To raise capital to repay certain outstanding debt
- To strengthen the company's balance sheet to support future growth
- To create a source of capital that can be selectively accessed in the future to fund the company's continuing growth
- To create a liquid currency to fund future acquisitions
- To create a liquid market for the company's stock
- To broaden the company's shareholder base
- To create ongoing interest in the company and its continued development

initial public offering (IPO)
the first sale of shares of a company's stock to the public

Similar conclusions were reached in a study in which the CEOs of firms that had gone public were asked to indicate the level of importance of 17 different possible motivations. The following motivations received the highest percentage of "very important" ratings:[7]

Raise capital for growth	85%
Raise capital to increase working capital	65%
Facilitate acquiring another firm	40%
Establish a market value for the firm	35%
Enhance the firm's ability to raise capital	35%

CEOs clearly consider financing future growth to be the primary objective of going public.

Having publicly traded stock can be beneficial to owners in that a public market offers greater liquidity and facilitates the eventual harvest of their investment. In fact, there is evidence that IPOs eventually lead to a harvest. While start-up firms tend to go public in order to finance expansion, established companies go public in order to liquidate the shareholdings of owners. It has been shown that the median percentage of ownership by a firm's officers and directors declines from 68 percent to 18 percent in the 10 years following an IPO.[8] Thus, although an IPO is not primarily a harvest mechanism, going public does provide the owners with increased liquidity—which facilitates their eventual exit.

THE IPO PROCESS

The IPO process may be one of the most exhilarating—but frustrating and exhausting—experiences of an entrepreneur's life. Owner-managers frequently discover that they do not like being exposed to the variability of public capital markets and to the prying questions of public-market investors. In a survey of the Inc. 100 companies, CEOs who had participated in public offerings indicated that they had spent on average 33 hours per week for four and a half months on the offering.[9] To many, the cost of the IPO process seemed exorbitant. They found themselves being misunderstood and having little influence on the decisions being made, and they were frequently disillusioned with investment bankers and the entire process. At some point, they wondered where they had lost control of the process—a feeling shared by many entrepreneurs involved in a public offering.

To understand an IPO, you must consider the shift in power that occurs during the process. When the chain of events begins, the firm's managers are in control. They dictate whether or not to go public and who the investment banker will be. After the prospectus has been prepared and the road show is under way, however, the firm's managers, including the entrepreneur, are no longer the primary decision makers. The investment banker is now in control. Finally, the marketplace, in concert with the investment banker, begins to take over. Ultimately, it is the market that dictates the final outcome.

Information on the IPO process can be accessed at http://www.sedar.com, the System for Electronic Document Analysis and Retrieval for the disclosure of documents for public companies and investment funds across Canada.

ISSUING A PRIVATE PLACEMENT OF THE STOCK

With an IPO, a portion of the firm's equity is sold in *public* equity markets. There is, however, an alternative form of equity, in which *private* equity capital, through venture capital firms or private investors, is infused to help founder-controlled firms grow. Trying to finance liquidity and growth while retaining control is perhaps the most difficult task facing founders. In a survey of entrepreneurs who had transferred or were planning to transfer ownership of their businesses, 85 percent of the respondents stated that maintaining control of the firm was "very important."[10] About 45 percent also considered providing capital for the firm's future growth and meeting the personal liquidity needs of family members "very important."

Recognizing the need for creativity in this area, some venture capital groups have developed financing approaches that more fully recognize the needs of exiting owners whose firms have significant growth potential. Let's consider a company that could be sold for $50 million as an LBO. The sale would most likely be financed through 80 percent debt, comprising $28 million in debt having first claim on the assets in the event of liquidation (senior debt) and $12 million in debt that is subordinated debt, and 20 percent equity ($10 million). Even though they would have cashed out, many entrepreneurs would find such an arrangement intolerable; they simply would not want their firm subjected to this kind of high-leverage transaction.

An alternative approach provides less cash but allows the initial owner to retain control.[11] In this case, the firm just described would be sold for $45 million—10 percent less than the LBO price assumed above. However, the sellers would receive only $38 million in cash, with the remaining $7 million being reinvested in the firm. In return, they would retain 51 percent of the ownership. The $38 million would be financed from two sources: $24 million in senior debt and $14 million provided by a private investor ($7 million in common equity for 49 percent of the firm's ownership and $7 million in preferred stock). The preferred stock would have an annual dividend (to be paid in additional shares of stock in the first years of the transaction), as well as warrants for additional common stock to bring the private investor's economic—not voting—ownership up to 65 percent, but only if management did not make its projections. For instance, current management

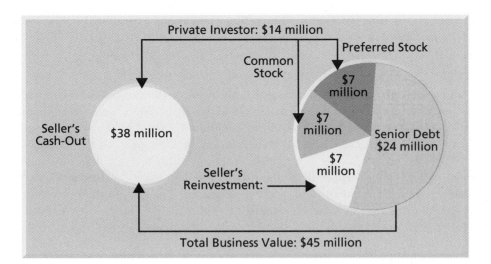

EXHIBIT **15-2**
*Illustration of Private
Equity Placement*

might predict that current earnings would increase 60 percent over the next five years. If this goal was realized, then the family or initial owners would keep the 51 percent economic share of the firm when the eventual exit occurred. If the goal was not realized, however, the seller's economic ownership would be scaled down based on how far results were from the target, but not below 35 percent. This arrangement is depicted graphically in Exhibit 15-2.

This financial arrangement has potential advantages over an LBO for firms with continued growth potential. First, the lower debt ratio allows for a lower interest rate on the debt than does an LBO, and thus the firm's cash flows can be used to grow the firm rather than just pay down debt. Second, the arrangement allows the senior owners to cash out while the firm retains the control and cash necessary to grow the firm. The investors also have the potential to realize significant economic gains if the firm performs well.

LIQUIDATION

A founder or manager would not typically choose to liquidate his or her business, as the harvest value will be less. However, some businesses, such as one-person consulting firms, cannot effectively operate without the owner, and as such offer limited value to potential buyers. Other firms may not be attractive due to deterioration of their customer base, a leveraged financial position, or aging and unproductive equipment.

When an owner is forced to harvest, and selling the firm as an ongoing operation is not possible, the only solution may be to sell assets at the market rate and pay any outstanding debts to bankers, suppliers, and other creditors.

LIFE AFTER THE HARVEST

There are really two key questions that an entrepreneur must address in anticipation of post-harvest life:

- Will I experience serious regrets over the decision to harvest my investment in a company?
- What will become my passion after I have become more than contented with the "easy life," where I have the option to play golf every day if I choose or to travel to my heart's content?

Discuss issues in
preparing for life after   **7**
the harvest.

The answers to these questions might seem apparent before the fact but become less so with the passage of time.

WILL I MISS THE JOURNEY?

For an entrepreneur, exiting a business that has been an integral part of life for some time can be a very emotional experience. When an entrepreneur invests a substantial part of his or her working life in growing a business, a real sense of loss may accompany the harvest. *Thus, entrepreneurs should think very carefully about their motives for exiting and what they plan to do after the harvest.* Entrepreneurs who harvest their investment frequently have great expectations about what life is going to be like with a lot of liquidity, something many of them have never known. The harvest does provide the long-sought liquidity, but some entrepreneurs find managing money—in contrast to operating their own company—less rewarding than they had expected.

WHAT'S NEXT?

Entrepreneurs by their very nature are purpose-driven people. So, after the harvest, an entrepreneur who has been driven to build a profitable business will need something larger than the individual to bring meaning to his or her life.

Many entrepreneurs have a sense of gratitude for the benefits they have received from living in a capitalist system. As a result, they want to give back, both with their time and with their money. The good news is that there is no limit to the number of worthy charitable causes, including universities and civic organizations. And, it may be that the call to help others with a new venture may be too strong for an individual with an entrepreneurial mind-set to resist. But whatever you decide to do, do it with passion.

LOOKING BACK

1 Describe managing for growth.

- Managing challenges and transitions from start-up through successive growth stages is critical to a new company's eventual success.
- A Queens School of Business study, sponsored by the Royal Bank of Canada and the Canadian Manufacturers and Exporters Association, identified many barriers to success and implications for growth for Canadian SMEs.

2 Explain the various types of outside management assistance.

- Outside management assistance can be used to remedy staff limitations.
- Business incubators provide guidance as well as space for beginning businesses.
- Three government-sponsored sources of assistance are the Industrial Research Assistance Program, the

Canadian Technology Network, and Counselling Assistance for Small Enterprise.
- Management assistance may also be obtained by engaging management consultants and by networking with other entrepreneurs.
- Business and professional groups such as bankers and CAs also provide management assistance.

3 Explain the importance of having an exit strategy.

- Harvesting is the means entrepreneurs and investors use to exit a business and, ideally, unlock the value of their investment in the firm.
- Harvesting is about more than merely selling and leaving a business. It involves capturing value (cash flows), reducing risk, and creating future options.
- A firm's accessibility to investors is driven by the availability of harvest options.

4 Describe succession planning.

- A well-managed succession plan provides the benefits of securing the owner's financial future, and maintaining relationships with investors, lenders, and customers.
- Written succession plans address key issues, including identifying future managers and leaders, how to assess potential candidates, the monitoring process, the training and declaration of a successor, and the timeline for succession.

5 Describe serial entrepreneurs.

- Serial entrepreneurs are more interested in starting new businesses than running them.

6 Describe harvesting options and effective harvesting strategies.

- The five ways to harvest an investment in a privately owned company are (1) selling the firm, (2) releasing the firm's free cash flows to its owners, (3) offering stock to the public through an initial public offering, (4) issuing a private placement of the stock, or (5) liquidation.
- In a strategic acquisition, the value placed on a business depends on the synergies that the buyer believes can be created.
- Financial buyers look primarily to a firm's stand-alone cash-generating potential as the source of its value.

- In leveraged buyouts (LBOs), high levels of debt financing are used to acquire a firm.
- A management buyout (MBO) is an LBO in which management is part of the group buying the company.
- The orderly withdrawal of an owner's investment in the form of the firm's free cash flows is one harvesting method.
- An initial public offering (IPO) is used primarily as a way to raise additional equity capital to finance company growth, and only secondarily as a way to harvest the owner's investment.
- Private equity capital is a way to acquire outside financing, which can allow the original owners to cash out.

7 Discuss issues in preparing for life after the harvest.

- For an entrepreneur, exiting the business that has been an integral part of life for some time can be a very emotional experience.
- Entrepreneurs should think very carefully about their motives for exiting and what they plan to do after the harvest.
- An entrepreneur who has been driven to build a profitable business will need something larger than the individual to bring meaning to his or her life.

KEY TERMS

employee ownership, p. 465
financial acquisition, p. 464
free cash flow, p. 466
harvesting, p. 458

initial public offering (IPO), p. 467
leveraged buyout (LBO), p. 464
management buyout (MBO), p. 464
networking, p. 456

serial entrepreneur, p. 462
strategic acquisition, p. 464

DISCUSSION QUESTIONS

1. What are some of the factors that should be consider when expanding a business?
2. What are the characteristics of a serial entrepreneur?
3. What are some advantages and drawbacks of a business incubator location for a start-up retail firm?
4. Explain what is meant by the term *harvesting*. What is involved in harvesting an investment in a privately held firm?

5. What is the primary purpose of an initial public offering (IPO)? How does an IPO relate to a harvest?
6. What advice would you give to an entrepreneur who was planning to exit his or her firm?
7. What emotions might an entrepreneur experience after leaving a firm that had been an integral part of his or her life?

YOU MAKE THE CALL

SITUATION 1

Austin and Francis Waugh founded Casa Bonita 15 years ago. They started with a single fast-food Mexican restaurant and they both worked seven days a week. From that small beginning, they expanded to 84 profitable restaurants. Over the years, other restaurant owners expressed an interest in buying the firm; however, the Waughs were not interested in selling. Then an English firm, Unigate Limited, offered them $32 million for the business and said Austin could remain the firm's CEO. The Waughs were attracted by the idea of having $32 million in liquid assets. They flew to London to close the deal. On the flight home, however, Austin began having doubts about their decision to sell the business. He thought, "We spent 15 years of our lives getting the business where we wanted it, and we've lost it." After their plane landed, they spent the night in Toronto and then flew back to London the next day. They offered the buyers $1 million to cancel the contract, but Unigate's management declined the offer. The Waughs flew home disappointed.

Question 1 How could the Waughs be disappointed with $32 million?
Question 2 What should the Waughs have done to avoid this situation?
Question 3 What advice would you offer Austin about continuing to work for the business under the new owners?

SITUATION 2

Ed and Barbara Bonneau started their wholesale sunglasses distribution firm 30 years ago with $1000 of their own money and $5000 borrowed from a banker in Ed's hometown. The firm grew quickly, selling sunglasses and reading glasses to companies such as Wal-Mart and other big-box retailers. Although the company had done well, the market had matured recently and profit margins narrowed significantly. Wal-Mart, for example, was insisting on better terms, which meant significantly lower profits for the Bonneaus. Previously, Ed had set the prices that he needed to make a good return on his investment. Now, the buyers had consolidated, and they had the power. Ed didn't enjoy running the company as much as he had in the past, and he was finding greater pleasure in other activities; for instance, he served on a local hospital board.

Just as Ed and Barbara began to think about selling the company, they were contacted by a financial buyer, who wanted to use their firm as a platform and then buy up several sunglass companies. After negotiations, the Bonneaus sold their firm for about $20 million. In addition, Ed received a retainer fee for serving as a consultant to the buyer. Also, the Bonneau's son-in-law, who was part of the company's management team, was named the new chief operating officer.

Question 1 Do you agree with the Bonneaus' decision to sell? Why or why not?
Question 2 Why did the buyers retain Ed as a consultant?
Question 3 Do you see any problem with having the Bonneau's son-in-law become the new chief operating officer?

EXPERIENTIAL EXERCISES

1. Interview a management consultant, CASE counsellor, or representative of a CA firm to discuss small business management weaknesses and the willingness or reluctance of small firms to use consultants. Prepare a report on your findings.
2. Referencing search engines, your local newspaper, or business owners you know,

identify a serial entrepreneur. Identify how long he or she usually operated a business before moving on to another venture. Determine if the ventures had a common theme or competitive orientation.

3. Identify a Canadian company that has expanded in the past year. Has the expansion enhanced its competitive position and financial performance, or caused performance issues?

4. Check your local newspaper for a week or so to find a privately held company that has been sold recently. Try to determine the motivation for the sale. Did it have anything to do with the prior owners' desire to cash out of the business? If so, try to find out what happened.

5. Ask a local family business owner about future plans to exit the business. Has the owner ever been involved in an exit strategy? If so, ask the owner to describe what happened and how it all worked out, as well as what he or she learned from the experience. If not, ask if the owner is aware of any company whose owners cashed out. Visit that company owner to inquire about the exit event.

6. Refer to some of the entrepreneurs and companies cited in this chapter. Have they moved on, and, if so, why? Did their next venture build on their previous venture?

EXPLORING THE WEB

Consult the home page of the Canadian Technology Network on the Web at http://ctn.nrc.ca. Prepare a one-page report summarizing the types of organizations available to assist businesses and identifying the services they provide.

Search for Canadian firms that have "gone public" recently. Determine what precipitated the expansion. Did the founder sell the organization? Were funds required for expansion?

CASES

	CASE TITLE	Entrepreneurial and Start-Up	Business Plan	Franchising or Family Business	Market Research Strategy	Pricing, Promotion, Distribution	Financial Performance and Requirements	Operations and Legal Control	Human Resources	Chapters
1	Printing Express							⚖	🚶	9,10,12
2	Industrial Hose Headquarters						🏛			13
3	The Ultimate Garage			📊	✉	🌐				4,6,7
4	Cardio-Core Boot Camp			📊						4
5	G.A.P Adventures Inc.				✉	🌐				6,7,8
6	Prestige Dance Academy	🔥	✏		✉		🏛			1,2,5
7	Smitty's Li'l Haulers	🔥		📊	✉		🏛			1,2,3,14
8	Calvert Toyota						🏛	⚖		10,13,14

Printing Express

Using Financial and Accounting Information for Decisions

Sitting at her desk in the small office just off the Printing Express customer service counter, Marika Cooper pondered the current state of and future prospects for her company. Commercial printing is a tough business, and it had been particularly tough for the Printing Express owner. Cooper had seen sales fall 12 percent from 2007 to 2008, but, more significantly, her net profit had "fallen through the floor," declining by 18 percent over the same period. Cooper had spent every available working hour serving clients, appealing to suppliers to extend additional credit, and expediting the production of customers' orders through the various production operations. At the same time, she was trying to assist her husband in making a success of his small courier-delivery business.

Industry experts had long been saying the industry had a very good future, but not for all segments and sizes of business. They preached a gospel of "specialize, differentiate, and focus on the customer." Customers were still buying printing, but were simply being more selective about matching their needs to different printing companies' capabilities. In order to attract customers, experts advised smaller companies like Cooper's to select a niche and focus on being the best at customer service (quality had become a given). Trying to be all things to all customers was the recipe for disaster.

"Am I on the road to disaster?" Cooper asked herself. "Am I watching my business cycle down to oblivion, or can I restructure my company to become one of those successful 'niche' players?"

LOCATION AND BACKGROUND

Printing Express opened its doors in Markham, Ontario, on September 11, 1995. It was located in a mall, just off Highway 7, surrounded by a few office buildings. The rapid pace of office-building construction in the area seemed to provide a built-in growth opportunity. Cooper believed that, by providing a broad base of services, Printing Express would become the obvious choice for printing services for the businesses locating in these office buildings. Their geographic proximity also meant more convenience and better customer service. After some investigation, she determined there was enough business available within a 15-minute radius of her location to make the business viable immediately and expected growth could result in Printing Express becoming a sizeable competitor in the "small company" segment of the industry.

Cooper started Printing Express in 1995 after a successful five-year sales career with a major printing company located closer to downtown Toronto. Frustrated with the sometimes snail-like pace of that company's production processes, she began to think about starting her own business. She was confident that she had the skills to attract customers and believed she could set up operations to run much more efficiently than her employer's. This would result in quicker delivery times and overall increased customer satisfaction. After losing "one more" customer due to production's inability to meet the customer's deadlines, she actively began researching her idea, and Printing Express was launched.

THE COMPANY IN 2008

Management and Staff

Printing Express employed six people plus Cooper: a full-time customer service representative to staff the desk and answer the phones; a production supervisor who ran production operations and was responsible for purchasing materials, supplies, and services; and four production personnel (a graphic designer, a photocopy operator, a press operator, and a bindery/shipping person). Cooper was the outside sales representative and general manager of the business. A list of part-time employees, including several relatives of Cooper and others working for Printing Express, was kept on call to handle the frequent peak activity periods.

Jack Donald was the production supervisor. He had been a production coordinator for Cooper's previous employer and had joined Cooper when she opened Printing Express. He had 12 years' experience as a pressman and foreman prior to becoming production coordinator, a position he held for two years prior to joining Printing Express. He initially was the company's sole production employee until volume increased to allow hiring additional staff. Donald rarely had an active role in operating equipment by 2008; his time was occupied almost completely with purchasing, supervising, and backing up Cooper and the customer service representative with customer inquiries.

The other employees had been added as volume grew, and Cooper was quite pleased with her current crew. Most had experience in similar capacities within the industry but came to Printing Express because it was located much closer to where they lived.

Policies

Printing Express operated with few formal, and no written, policies. Wages were comparable to competitors in similar capacities. Cooper had instituted a policy of paying a commission to any employee who "sold" a job for the company and, consequently, Printing Express did business with community associations, sports organizations, church groups, and service clubs to which its employees belonged, as well as for a number of businesses solicited by this informal sales force.

Competition

In 1995 there was little competition in the immediate area of Printing Express's location. Offering a broad base of capability meant that Cooper had in-house desktop capability, high-speed photocopiers, small offset printing equipment (up to 12- × 18-inch sheets), and various bindery equipment (cutting machines, folders, paper drills, and so on). By 2008 competition had become quite intense.

Several franchise and nonfranchise copy centres had opened within a few blocks of Printing Express, and a new full-service, modern printing company (which did not offer photocopying service) opened about one kilometre away. In spite of having had a few years lead getting into the market, Printing Express found itself being squeezed by the photocopy shops on one end and by the new full-service printing company at the other. The result was intense price competition, especially on the printing end of the business. Margins on photocopy work had not been affected, however.

Equipment Needs

Printing equipment generally has a 10- to 20-year useful life if maintained properly, but the rapid pace of technological change means that some of it now becomes outdated and uneconomical much more quickly. Printing Express needed to make an investment of about $100,000 to update its graphic design software and hardware. Photocopy equipment is usually replaced every five years, but Cooper had delayed this in 2007 by not wanting to incur any extra debt. The situation was now critical: she needed to either lease (an operating expense) or buy a new copier at a cost of about $75,000.

Financial Position

Financial data on small, owner-managed firms is often difficult to evaluate due to the measures allowed or tolerated in accounting practices to structure both business and personal affairs to the greatest advantage of the owner(s). This becomes evident in looking at Printing Express's summary income statements and balance sheets (Exhibits 1 and 2) and the 2007 detailed income statement and balance sheet (Exhibits 3 and 4). Industry standard cost percentages and key business ratios are given in Exhibit 5.

The long-term debt was incurred when Printing Express was started and consisted of a loan under the *Canada Small Business Financing Program* (CSBFP). The working-capital loan (line of credit) was also opened in 1995, and the limit had been increased as sales increased. Due to the intense competition since 1999, and the consequent squeeze on profits, Printing Express had been forced to increase its utilization of the line of credit and is currently near its maximum.

EXHIBIT **1**
*Printing Express's
Summary Income
Statement*

	2002	2003	2004	2005	2006
Sales	459,645	601,988	841,634	1,039,188	1,288,722
Cost of Goods	351,379	448,855	620,760	763,764	946,051
Gross Margin	108,266	153,133	220,874	275,424	342,671
Selling, General and Administrative	96,544	112,040	161,036	198,971	246,275
Operating Income	11,722	41,093	59,838	76,453	96,396
Interest Expense	53,067	50,879	47,656	44,057	48,554
Net Income before Tax	−41,345	−9786	12,182	32,396	47,842

	2002	2003	2004	2005	2006
Current Assets					
Cash	27,395	22,633	100	100	150
Accounts Receivable	111,867	156,452	166,735	201,366	222,684
Inventories	22,024	37,990	62,935	88,969	97,255
Prepaid Expenses	9893	4561	13,298	15,381	7219
TOTAL CURRENT ASSETS	171,179	221,636	243,068	305,816	327,308
Fixed Assets Net of Accum. Deprec.	202,658	250,517	299,775	348,876	397,978
Other Assets	69,500	69,850	69,850	70,032	70,441
TOTAL ASSETS	443,337	542,003	612,693	724,724	795,727
Current Liabilities					
Bank Line of Credit	25,495	104,444	143,903	195,847	211,805
Accounts Payable	54,877	66,399	75,208	90,741	115,870
Wages Payable	1401	4337	10,287	6555	4339
Current Portion of Long-Term Debt	35,710	35,710	35,710	35,710	35,710
TOTAL CURRENT LIABILITIES	117,483	210,890	265,108	328,853	367,724
Long-Term Debt	214,290	178,580	142,870	107,160	71,450
Notes Payable	62,400	92,400	132,400	184,000	204,000
Due to Shareholders	28,409	49,164	49,164	49,164	49,164
	305,099	320,144	324,434	340,324	324,614
Common Equity	62,100	62,100	62,100	62,100	62,100
Retained Earnings	−41,345	−51,131	−38,949	−6,553	41,289
TOTAL EQUITY	20,755	10,969	23,151	55,547	103,389
TOTAL LIABILITIES AND EQUITY	443,337	542,003	612,693	724,724	795,727

EXHIBIT **2** *Printing Express's Summary Balance Sheet*

EXHIBIT **3**
*Printing Express's
Detailed 2007 Income
Statement*

Sales	1,134,075
Materials	324,119
Direct Labour	327,634
Other Direct Costs	201,352
Cost of Goods Sold	853,105
Gross Margin	280,970
Administrative Expenses	171,384
Selling Expenses	51,487
Operating Margin	58,099
Interest Expense	32,978
Net Income before Taxes	25,121

EXHIBIT **4**
*Printing Express's
Detailed 2007 Balance
Sheet*

Current Assets	
Cash	150
Accounts Receivable	297,361
Inventories	98,442
Prepaid Expenses	19,055
TOTAL CURRENT ASSETS	415,008
Fixed Assets (Net)	375,602
Other Assets	70,441
TOTAL ASSETS	861,051
Current Liabilities	
Bank Line of Credit	177,141
Accounts Payable	225,046
Wages Payable	5740
Current Portion of Long-Term Debt	35,710
TOTAL CURRENT LIABILITIES	443,637
Long-Term Debt	35,740
Notes Payable	204,000
Due to Shareholders	49,164
	288,904
TOTAL LIABILITIES	732,541
Common Equity	62,100
Retained Earnings	66,410
TOTAL EQUITY	128,510
TOTAL LIABILITIES & EQUITY	861,051

PRINTING EXPRESS, 2008

"We certainly can't continue on as we have been," muses Cooper. "The economic growth in Markham shows no sign of slowing. Yet I'm being picked away at from both ends of my business." She believes her options are to (1) sell off the printing equipment and focus her business on photocopying, where margins have remained stable but where there are more competitors; (2) add larger and more sophisticated printing equipment and compete for more complicated and therefore more profitable

EXHIBIT **5**

Industry Comparison Ratios

Income Statement		Financial Ratios	
Sales	100%	Current Ratio:	1.67:1
COGS	76.30%	Quick Ratio:	1.17:1
Gross Margin	23.70%	Debt/Equity:	1.69:1
		Average Collection Period	58.2
Admin Expenses	10.44%	Return on Equity:	37.15%
Selling Expenses	8.25%	Interest Coverage:	2.51:1
		Average Payment Period:	68.6
Interest Expense	1.97%		
Income Before Tax	5.05%		

Balance Sheet

Assets		Liabilities	
Cash	5.96%	Notes Payable	9.66%
Accounts Receivable	33.04%	Accounts Payable	14.41%
Inventories	12.95%	Other Current	9.24%
Other Current	3.80%	TOTAL CURRENT	33.31%
TOTAL CURRENT	55.75%		
		Long-Term Debt	29.55%
Net Fixed Assets	39.90%		
Other Assets	4.35%	TOTAL LIABILITIES	62.86%
TOTAL ASSETS	100.00%	Equity	37.14%
		TOTAL LIABILITIES AND EQUITY	100.00%

printing jobs; (3) form an alliance with a larger company located closer to downtown that wants access to the Markham-area business but could also send photocopy and small printing orders to Printing Express; (4) ride out the current situation and see if she could survive it; or (5) sell off the business and work on making her husband's business a success.

Questions

1. Using Printing Express's financial information, evaluate the following:
    - The firm's liquidity
    - The firm's profitability
    - The firm's use of debt financing
    - The return on equity

2. Identify any reasons that you can't use the "four-question approach" of assessing the liquidity, profitability, stability, and growth to assess a firm's financial performance exactly as suggested in Chapter 13. What modifications are required?

3. Should Cooper keep the business or sell it? If she keeps it, what should she do? What are the primary factors to be considered in reaching such a decision?

Industrial Hose Headquarters, located in New Westminster, British Columbia, a city adjacent to Vancouver, is owned by Bill Reinboldt and Bob Kingston. Bill serves as the general manager and is responsible for sales. Industrial Hose sells and stocks custom-made hose and coupling products for industrial applications such as air hoses, hydraulic lines, and so on. The market has several segments including marine, automotive and trucking, and general industrial and manufacturing. Reinboldt and Kingston both worked for another hose distributor prior to starting Industrial Hose.

INDUSTRIAL HOSE'S FINANCIAL SITUATION

Industrial Hose had been quite profitable in most years since it was started. Profits for 2008 were the strongest; however, Bill had concerns as to whether demand would suffer with the downswing in the local economy. Exhibit 1 shows the income statement for 2008. The balance sheet as of October 31, 2008 Industrial Hose's fiscal year-end, is shown in Exhibit 2. Notice the large balances in accounts receivable and inventories and the relatively low cash balance compared to current liabilities. This was of some concern to Bill, who preferred to work with sufficient cash balances to ensure bills and other obligations, such as taxes and loan payments, could be made on time. He was particularly sensitive to paying his primary suppliers on time to maintain the discounts that contributed to Industrial Hose's bottom line.

INDUSTRIAL HOSE'S ACCOUNTS RECEIVABLE

Accounts receivable were $763,704 in October 2005. This was considerably better than the situation at other times of the year. Peak sales activity usually happened from June through September,

resulting in high accounts receivable through most of this period and for some time after. It was normal for the receivables to reach over $1.0 million by the end of September and gradually decline to about half that amount by the end of December. Industrial Hose did not age its accounts receivable, so Bill had no detail on overdue accounts. Fortunately, the firm had never had a serious bad-debt problem, and, consequently, the accounts were assumed to be relatively current on an overall basis.

Normal credit terms extended to clients were net due in 30 days from the invoice date. Bill had been giving some thought to offering a 2 percent discount if the invoice was paid in 10 days. He thought this might improve Industrial Hose's cash position. Monthly statements were sent to all outstanding accounts, with an interest charge of 1.5 percent applied to any overdue balance. Most customers ignored the interest charge, and Bill had never enforced its payment.

Industrial Hose was located in the heart of a light industrial manufacturing area, and about 25 percent of its business was done with "walk-in" customers. Not all of these had bothered to establish credit with the company. About 60 percent of these customers either paid by cash or, more frequently, credit card at the time of purchase, which helped the firm's cash flow considerably. Almost all of the remaining business was done on a trade-credit basis.

INDUSTRIAL HOSE'S INVENTORY

As mentioned above, Industrial Hose carried a large amount of inventory, consisting mainly of standard and bulk hoses and couplings. Industrial Hose's inventory was about 31 percent higher than industry standards. Both Bill and Bob considered the high inventory necessary in order to offer customers a "guaranteed availability" for immediate delivery. Bill thought that the inventory

EXHIBIT **1**

*Industrial Hose
Headquarters*

Income Statement for the Year Ending October 31, 2008	
Sales	$3,753,935
Cost of Goods Sold	2,644,018
Gross Margin	$1,109,917
Selling General, and Administrative Expenses (including management salaries)	916,096
Net Income before Taxes	193,821
Income Tax	34,658
Net Income	$ 159,163

EXHIBIT **2**

*Industrial Hose
Headquarters*

Balance Sheet as of October 31, 2008	
Assets	
Current Assets:	
Cash	$ 158,395
Accounts Receivable	763,704
Inventory	1,151,270
Prepaid Expenses	46,315
Total Current Assets	$2,119,684
Fixed Assets	427,666
TOTAL ASSETS	$2,547,350
Liabilities	
Current Liabilities	
Bank Line of Credit	$ 422,052
Accounts Payable	864,756
Income, Payroll, and GST Taxes Payable	75,480
Total Current Liabilities	$1,362,288
Long-Term Debt	314,785
Shareholders' Equity and Retained Earnings	$ 870,277
TOTAL LIABILITIES AND EQUITY	$2,547,350

might be reduced by installing a more sophisticated inventory control and tracking system to reduce the inventory of slow-moving items. Bill thought this might reduce the overall inventory by about 20 percent. Bob was not sure this was possible, insisting that the current system was adequate for tracking inventory.

Currently, inventory was physically counted twice per year: at year-end and at six months. Through the rest of the year, the warehouse manager "eyeballed" the inventory on a weekly basis

and ordered what he thought needed to be ordered. Since the inventory was counted only twice per year, accurate financial statements could be prepared only twice per year. Monthly statements were prepared using a "best guess" of the inventory value, which meant both the balance sheet and the cost of goods sold on the income statement were suspect.

Bill had done some investigation into inventory control systems and thought that a computerized perpetual inventory system using bar-code scanners was the way to go. The cost of the software was not a problem, but the ongoing costs to maintain the system and generate the various reports would likely mean the addition of one more clerk. However, the cost of this was only a fraction of the over $200,000 in initial cash recovery from reducing the inventory and the ongoing savings from more efficient purchasing and reduced carrying charges the system should allow.

BANK DEBT

Industrial Hose carried two forms of bank debt. The operating line of credit was authorized to $1.5 million, secured by the accounts receivable, inventory, and personal guarantees given by Bill and Bob. Margin maximums of 75 percent of accounts receivable under 90 days and 50 percent of inventory were used to establish the maximum amount that could be borrowed. Assuming all accounts receivable were under 90 days, the above formula would allow maximum credit line usage of $572,778 based on the accounts receivable plus $575 635 based on the inventory, for a total of $1,148 413. The amount actually being used was $422,052 on October 31. The bank has been hinting more and more strongly that it would like better information and control systems in place for the inventory and accounts receivable. The bank is uncomfortable with the inventory estimates for 10 of 12 months of the year, and believes that without better information on the accounts receivable it is only a matter of time until Industrial Hose suffers a major bad-debt problem.

Long-term debt carried by the company consisted of the mortgage on the current land and buildings, purchased in 1997, when the lease on the company's first location expired. Bill and Bob were sufficiently confident in the business's future at the time to buy a building. Industrial Hose occupies two bays and leases out the remaining three to other businesses. The mortgage was amortized over 25 years and will be paid off in 2018. Bill thought that it would be nice to free up some cash to pay the mortgage off a little sooner, but so far this has not been possible. The security for the loan is the property itself, although both Bill and Bob had been required to sign personal guarantees for the

mortgage as well. Both would like to be in a position to negotiate the return of their guarantees when the mortgage comes up for renewal in 2011.

ACCOUNTS PAYABLE

As with accounts receivable, trade credit provided a large amount of working capital for Industrial Hose. Total accounts payable on October 31, 2005, were $864,756. Similar to accounts receivable, accounts payable tracked the sales cycle: inventories were increased in May and were maintained at high levels into September. As accounts receivable were collected, the trade payables were paid off. This resulted in a large variation in how long Industrial Hose took to pay its suppliers through the year. The smaller companies normally took this in stride, but at least one major hose supplier, Goodyear Tire and Rubber, was quite strict about payment terms. If payments were not received by the end of the month following invoice (an average of 45 days), the company was put on C.O.D. terms. From time to time, this had caused a problem for Industrial Hose, and various techniques had been used to avoid delaying payments to Goodyear. These included delaying payments to other suppliers and negotiating (at great cost) short-term extensions of the line of credit with the bank. Industrial Hose simply could not afford to lose Goodyear as a supplier.

Smaller suppliers and those of lesser importance normally were more patient with Industrial Hose's account. However, even these had their limits, and Bill was reluctant to stretch them much beyond 60 days because they would begin requesting payment.

PROFITABILITY

Industrial Hose's net profit for the fiscal year 2008 was about 25 percent higher than the average of the best-performing firms in the industry. While Bill was pleased with that, he wondered if the profit could be raised even further, and whether liquidity could be increased as well. The economic boom experienced in the late 1990s by the Greater Vancouver area was fading, due partially to the decline in the lumber market caused by export duties to the U.S. market and partially by depressed commodity prices. Bill wanted to make sure the company was in a position to weather the downturn for however long it lasted.

Questions

1. Evaluate the overall performance and financial structure of Industrial Hose Headquarters.

2. What are the strengths and weaknesses of the firm's management of accounts receivable and inventory?

3. Should the firm reduce or expand its bank borrowing?

4. Evaluate Industrial Hose's management of accounts payable.

5. Calculate Industrial Hose's cash conversion period. Interpret your calculation.

6. How can Industrial Hose improve its working-capital situation?

The Ultimate Garage

Market Research, Strategy, and Promotion

Ultimate Garage has been providing discerning residential garage owners with custom, high-end storage and organizational solutions since 2003. When Hutton attended the Bachelor of Applied Entrepreneurship program at Mount Royal College, he had a very clear concept for his business plan class. He envisioned incorporating the latest computer-generated interior design software, top-of-the line storage and organizational systems, and expert professional craftsmen in its residential and commercial garage projects. Following extensive research, including demographic analysis of garage owners in the Calgary area, and home renovation analysis, the venture was launched.

Extensive costing had been prepared, and promotional venues, such as trade shows, were booked. Clients followed. It is now trendy in Alberta to "gussy up your garage" according to Jamie Hutton, co-owner of Ultimate Garage, a successful Calgary-based company that builds custom, high-end storage and organizational solutions for discerning residential garage owners. "The garage is really the last frontier in home renovations," says Hutton. "Homeowners are buying into the fact that an eye-appealing garage that is clean, well organized, and functional is going to add value to their property and enhance their quality of life." Hutton says garages are no longer the place to dump stuff that does not fit elsewhere in a house. "Homeowners are taking real pride in having a garage that is a visual showcase and an expression of their lifestyle."

Hutton was also quick to point out that it is not just the car collector or carpenter hobbyist leading the charge in remodelling garages. "There are a wide range of renovators from the family that wants a visually appealing and clutter-free garage, to the ultimate gardener, the sports enthusiast, the fitness buff, the wine collector, the games room player, and, increasingly, the home-based business."

The array of top-of-the-line garage products and services available can be mind-boggling to the average homeowner, who in a fast-paced Alberta economy does not have the time and patience required to do it himself, preferring instead to rely on experts such as Ultimate Garage. "We make this process as painless as possible," says Hutton. "Initially, we meet with the homeowners, determine their specific needs, select products to achieve their objectives, and then create a computer-generated drawing of what the garage will look like when done. From that point forward, modifications can be made and the garage transformation is ready to start."

Communication is key to any successful renovation. It is important for the homeowners to know what products are available and best suited to their specific needs. "We work from the floor up," explains Hutton. "Our clientele are educated about the types of floor coverings and floor mat systems, storage cabinets, shelving, wall brackets, work stations, ceiling storage racks, lift system (for automobiles, motorcycles, and garden tractors) and lighting. We provide a complete wall-to-wall package."

A new garage and workplace floor covering with a 20-year limited guarantee is also available.

"Our new resin-based flooring system is ideal for those that want a new garage floor in a day," says Hutton. "Previously, resurfacing an existing garage floor took several days. For a typical two-car garage, we are able to install and cure the floor on the same day. This allows homeowners to leave for work in the morning and come home in the evening to a brand new garage floor."

Hutton pointed to several features that make this system the ultimate long-term garage floor solution for Albertans:

- One-hour cure time for liquid applied resin-base flooring
- Installers are trained and approved contractors

Sources: http://www.ultimategarageinc.com (accessed on May 1, 2008) and author's memory of class discussions with J. Hutton.

- One application, seamless system
- 100% reactive resin; solvent-free
- Available in a variety of colours incorporating pigmented, quartz, and flake systems
- Waterproof and stain resistant
- Superior UV resistance
- Resistant to chemical attack, mechanical abuse, and abrasions
- Different levels of slip resistance are possible
- Easy to clean and maintain.

Some clientele want a specific look and feel to their garage. "Themed garages are growing in popularity," says Hutton. "As an example, for the ultimate garage mechanic, we offer a complete line of 'automobilia' products such as vintage signage and electric wall signs. When it is done, people will literally stop their cars in the middle of the street to gawk at your new garage."

"Our business has been growing steadily," says Hutton. "Anyone can mount a bracket on a wall. What makes Ultimate Garage different—and one of the main reasons for our success is because we work very hard at creating the right lifestyle enhancements for our discerning customers that ultimately improves the value of their property—we take the extra time to educate them en route to designing and delivering a sophisticated storage and organizational solution that is right for their needs."

Questions

1. Describe the marketing strategy pursued by Ultimate Garage, and identify the target markets you think the company is pursuing.
2. Visit Ultimate Garage's website, and analyze its effectiveness. Consider alternative promotional venues and create a recommendation.
3. Evaluate your local market to determine if a similar service is available. If so, compare the advertising communication and identify which firm is more effective.
4. Identify how Ultimate Garage could expand its services.
5. Assess the franchising potential for the venture. Would you recommend that Ultimate Garage expand through franchising?
6. Design a CRM process for the company. Identify the benefits a CRM system would provide.

Cardio-Core Boot Camp

Franchising

It's not quite 6 a.m., and the faces of the people arriving outside Burnaby Village Museum are still showing signs of sleep. But even before the first streaks of light appear in the morning sky, a cheerful voice is cutting through the grey morning.

"We're going to run!" It's Leslie Newbery, an instructor with Cardio-Core Boot Camp. And the workout is on. Despite its somewhat intimidating name, there's little of the "military" about this early-morning workout. Rather, it's an inclusive approach to fitness that's designed to get everyone, from the complete beginner to the advanced workout addict, outdoors and working out.

Today's workout starts with a run, followed by circuit training. Short sessions of strength training, focusing on core stability and strength, are interspersed with two minutes of cardio in the form of running a hill circuit, doing lunges, skipping rope, jogging, or doing step-ups. At every stage, Newbery offers options to challenge the various levels of the participants. Everyone moves at his or her own speed, and everyone is offered encouragement and personalized support.

It's all part of the philosophy of inclusiveness that's espoused by the company's founders, Jen Hamilton and Karen Harmon. Both women have extensive backgrounds in fitness—Harmon boasts 26 years of experience and Hamilton 16—and decided to pool their talents to offer something different. In an interview, Harmon explained the line of thought that led to the boot camp as being one simple question: "Why can't we do what we do inside, outside?"

It turned out there was no reason why not—and the boot camp idea took off quickly. The two started out in Pitt Meadows more than two years ago, then opened an operation in the Tri-Cities.

Burnaby was recently added to the list, and New Westminster is set to open April 3. Today there are 10 locations around the Lower Mainland.

Both women are raising children and trying hard to achieve balance in their own lives. Which is why, as demand grew, they saw an opportunity to branch out and offer franchises. "Being mothers of three, and busy, we wanted to create opportunities for people to run their own business," Hamilton explained. Each franchise is individually owned and operated, but Harmon and Hamilton take operators through a one-month training program to ensure the program is carried through as they envision it. "It's a lot of fun. We're growing so quickly, and it's an amazing feeling," Hamilton said.

They see many reasons for the success of the boot camp philosophy. For starters, they're both big believers in the concept of outdoor fitness. "Being outdoors is amazing. When you're breathing in the fresh air, it's healing," Harmon said. Participants are asked to bring yoga mats, an exercise ball, and hand weights but, for the most part, any apparatus needed is whatever's available in the location at hand. In Burnaby, for instance, the stairs outside Shadbolt Centre are incorporated into the workout, the railing along the deck overlooking Deer Lake becomes a handy spot for push-ups, and an old stone wall along Deer Lake Parkway can be just the ticket for tricep dips.

It's all part of the philosophy that fitness needn't be complicated. Tying in to that is a focus on making the camps accessible to everyone, of any level. "We get everyone from jocks to people that haven't exercised in 20 years," Harmon said. Each participant is given an assessment prior to the boot camp, providing their measurements and going through endurance testing. Then, at the end of the camp, they're tested again to measure progress. "Everyone sees results," Hamilton said, noting those results involve better endurance, fewer inches, and an improved emotional state.

Sources: http://www.corebootcamp.com, accessed April 28, 2008, and Julie MacLellan, *Burnaby Now*, March 8, 2006.

Along the way, everyone gets the help they need to make progress.

Hamilton notes that, with two instructors, they're able to offer more nurturing and instruction for those who need it. The focus is, as she puts it, on "getting back to the basics" of working out: cardio and core work. "When people have a strong core, it allows them to excel in many areas," she pointed out. For participants, the boot camp is kept interesting by the fact that no two workouts are the same. "It's fresh every time they come," Harmon noted. "We want people to stay interested."

Put it all together and both women note that the atmosphere created is one of teamwork. "It's the camaraderie. People really encourage one another," Harmon said. "Everyone comes together as a team, supporting one another," added Hamilton. And they're quick to note the weather never seems to matter.

Sessions go rain or shine, warm or cold—though Newbery will be the first to point out that her Burnaby sessions have never yet seen rain—and participants simply dress for the weather.

"There have been times when we have had rain, but people end up laughing," Harmon said. The sessions are open to everyone. Participants so far have ranged in age from 11 to 72, and both men and women are encouraged to take part. All participants can choose how often they'd like to work out. Each boot camp runs in a four-week segment, and people can choose to work out three or five days a week, mornings or evenings—paying for either 12 or 20 sessions altogether.

With an initial investment of just $10,000, and over 50 locations, including 11 in Ontario, by 2008 Cardio Core has steadily expanded its franchising operations.

It offers the following to franchisees:

- A 30-day training period, and support during the first year
- CC lifestyle clothing line
- Training for staff at Cardio-Core Headquarters
- A franchise advisory committee
- Franchise quarterly meetings and retreats
- An operations and marketing manual
- Computer software

Questions

1. What competitive advantages has Cardio-Core developed for its service? Who is the company's target market?

2. Using the franchise assessment factors listed in Chapter 4, evaluate the attractiveness of the franchise opportunity offered by Cardio-Core. Visit the company website and source articles to add material for your analysis. State whether or not the franchise is an attractive investment and provide your reasoning.

3. Given your analysis, what recommendations would you make to the founders to ensure the success of their franchise expansion across Canada?

G.A.P Adventures Inc.

Pricing and Promotion Strategies

Bruce Poon Tip tapped into a new industry, adventure tourism, in 1990 when he founded G.A.P Adventures Inc. (G.A.P) based on the reasoning that there had to be people who wanted "real" travel adventure. Recognized as an industry leader, G.A.P offers over 1000 different tour packages to more than 100 countries, with Peru, Kenya, and Thailand as its top destinations.

The Toronto-based company has over 200 employees with three offices in North America and 17 other international offices. As the only Canadian operator invited to attend the United Nations Launch of the year of Eco Tourism in New York in January 2002, Bruce explained his business philosophy.

> While ecotourism currently accounts for only 10 percent of all travel, the mainstream market is starting to crave adventure travel. Ecotourism tends to involve smaller groups with an interest in experiencing the reality of another country. As well, there is an awareness that to really stretch and expand their horizons people have to get off the allinclusive beaches and massive cruise ships." At 21, Bruce founded his concept when he travelled Thailand for $10 a day and stayed with the hill tribes. "It wasn't my first visit, but it was my most genuine," says Bruce who recently consulted on *Survivor*. "See, study, and understand the country and its people in their natural, day-to-day state without disturbing or changing them."

While most tourists assume it involves untamed wilderness, arduous physical activity, risk, and discomfort in the form of heat, cold, or lumpy beds, that's not necessarily true. It's up to the traveller to choose a more rustic or comfortable trip. Bigger in Australia and Europe than in North America,

Source: http://www.gapadventures.com, used by permission of G.A.P Adventures.

ecotourism offers both prosperity to the locals and a cultural exchange between the travellers and inhabitants. Bruce's belief is so strong he spearheaded a post-graduate diploma in ecotourism and adventure travel at Humber College, and has hired several grads.

G.A.P continues to evolve. In 2004 the popularity of the Antarctica program prompted the purchase of their own vessel, which will also be used to expand their explorer expeditions to new areas, including the Amazon river.

G.A.P has also expanded their tour line by creating "Comfort Class Journeys" to target an older, but still adventurous demographic. The comfort class tours will increase the level of comfort without compromising the grassroots Latin American experience. The Comfort Class tours will favour small hotels and inns of slightly higher caliber compared to the accommodation used in the regular adventure programs. They will also organize private transportation for those that want increased flexibility.

GAP has also set new viewership records for reality TV through the series "Great Adventure People," a documentary-styled adventure travel show that follows real travellers on a real G.A.P Adventures trip. The first set of episodes featured Peru, Ecuador, and the Galapagos. The second series, being filmed in Italy, Vietnam, and Morocco, will be released in late 2005.

Here are some highlights from the G.A.P website.

SMALL IS BEAUTIFUL

At G.A.P we travel in small groups, with most of our trips having a maximum of 12 travellers. This small size is a very important aspect of our concept of travel. It provides the group the advantage of security and intimacy while still allowing us to be flexible. It allows us to travel like a group of friends and less like a tour group. More importantly, it means we are more sensitive to the fragile local cultures we travel within and can access places and events not available to larger groups.

GETTING THERE IS HALF THE FUN

We utilize a combination of local and private transportation that varies according to the area. All of our adventures use an array of transport that is both flexible and exciting. The various modes of transport used on every trip make our adventures more interesting than a traditional bus tour. You may be on a vintage bus, a train, a native canoe, a rickshaw, or even an elephant back.

YOUR HOME AWAY FROM HOME

The ideal accommodation captures the magic of the areas we visit. Five-star hotels are not suitable as it creates a western environment. What we offer is clean, simple hotels and *hosterias* that are unintrusive. You may stay on a farm, in a converted monastery, or a quaint bed and breakfast.

INCREDIBLE VALUE

One of the first things many travellers note is the price of our adventures. While it is true our prices are low, more important is the value for the money we provide. If you look closely, many items, such as local guides, entrance fees, and sightseeing, are included. We also give you an indication before you leave home of any extra anticipated daily expenditures. We negotiate directly with our guesthouses, guides, and transportation to enable our prices to remain low.

MISSION STATEMENT

Our priority is to satisfy every customer, every time, through outstanding personalized service. We are dedicated to the customer experience and are constantly evaluating how we can improve this experience.

VISION

We are the Great Adventure People, and we are a company of travellers. Through a dedicated group of travellers an exciting company was born, with a vision of travelling while respecting the land and her people. While others focus on attractions and creating a western environment, our vision is face to face travel at a grassroots level.

INNOVATION

We were the first, and we continue to innovate. By doing this, we stay ahead of companies that have since followed our path. Our travellers know that by travelling with G.A.P they are travelling with leaders who set the path and don't follow it.

Besides receiving an award as one of Canada's top 40 entrepreneurs under 40, Bruce has been honoured as one of Canada's top five entrepreneurs by *Canadian Business*, and has won the Global Traders Leadership award.

Questions

1. Which marketing strategies has G.A.P Adventures adopted? Do you think the strategies fit its target markets? Why or why not?
2. Do you think the promotional activities of G.A.P Adventures could be improved and/or extended? Explain.
3. What kind of forecasting method do you believe would be most appropriate to estimate G.A.P Adventure's market?
4. Do you think the mission statement is effective?

Prestige Dance Academy

Entrepreneurial Passion

Picture a group of children pretending to be butterflies twirling and leaping around a calming blue room. Their teacher is enthusiastic and encourages them to be creative and carefree. The children are smiling and having the time of their lives. This is much more than a dance lesson for their teacher, Amanda Harburn; it is the realization of a life-long dream.

Amanda, who graduated in December 2004 from the Applied Business and Entrepreneurship degree program at Mount Royal College (MRC) in Calgary, has combined her passion for dance and her drive for success to open Prestige Dance Academy. The studio offers a wide range of ballet, music theatre, hip-hop, preschool, Mom & Me, and private dance lessons.

Her business idea came at a young age. She started dancing when she was three, and always imagined that she would become a dance teacher. As a teenager she worked at a local dance studio where she had the chance to try almost every job—from caretaker to secretary to instructor—and realized she wanted to do it all.

One summer she and another youthful instructor opened a holiday dance camp. Things worked out well. "I had a business mind and once I realized I loved working with kids, I just put them together." She pursued her dream in a logical manner, starting by working one night a week in an office to acquaint herself with basic accounting and administrative process while in high school. The business program courses were geared toward entrepreneurship and prepared her for all aspects of starting the business.

However, being a true entrepreneur, she launched her venture at age 19 prior to starting her degree. It was not easy. "At times it's been hard to make people believe in me," says Amanda. The

Source: Adapted from Tom Keyser, *Business Edge,* Vol. 4, No. 37, October 21, 2004; author discussions with Amanda Harburn. Used by permisssion.

bankers didn't. She had neither a track record nor a credit rating when she asked for a start-up loan. They showed her the door. The contractors who installed her sprung (and costly) dance floor didn't show much respect either. Soon after she opened, one of her retail neighbours caught her by surprise. "We all have bets on how long you'll survive," revealed her fellow entrepreneur. "Well, I hope you're betting I will be here for a long time," was Amanda's cheerful rejoinder. "Nope," said the man from a few doors down. "I bet against you."

The doubter did not collect on his wager. In less than three years, the studio went from zero students to over 400. Amanda is also debt free, is turning a respectable profit, and has recently added a second dance floor. In 2004 Amanda was selected as the CIBC Student Entrepreneur of the Year winner over more than 200 students representing universities and colleges across Canada. She dazzled the judges with her airtight business plan, her presentation, and her encouraging revenues.

While her current concern is how to expand the business to a second location while maintaining her standards, the process has not been easy. After researching her competition throughout the city, a statistical analysis indicated that the booming Westhills area of Calgary's southwest quadrant was the place to set up. There were expanding communities, young upscale families, high disposable income, and a gap in competition. In 2002, with $20,000, and large amounts of volunteer elbow grease, including drywalling duties free of charge by Amanda's father, she transformed an ordinary storefront into a professional studio.

Amanda acknowledges she made a serious mistake when she spent her entire promotional budget the wrong way, hiring a marketing firm that failed to drum up results. "You learn and you fail and you try again," she shrugged. "I was devastated." Now her marketing cash goes to Canada Post, which twice a year delivers Prestige Dance

Academy flyers to homes in her target neighbourhoods. After examining a city map detailing traffic flow, she placed a sign for four months a year on a major road leading into the area. Returns have been encouraging; enrolment has quadrupled in less than three years.

Like all small business operators she has had to learn how to deal with the occasional disappointed customer, as well as with the odd NSF cheque. The advice of her instructors at MRC has proven invaluable on a dozen occasions.

In the main, though, her instincts have carried Amanda through. She sticks to high standards, limiting class size to 10 pupils. Meanwhile, she appreciates that her business doesn't require an expensive inventory. The fact that students usually commit to a 10-month course allows her to plan for financial contingencies.

Having completed an undergraduate degree, Amanda is working full time with the studio. She is juggling her upcoming marriage, expansion, volunteer work at such programs as "Inn from the Cold," as well as day-to-day operations and teaching. It's hard to imagine anyone betting against her now.

Questions

1. Referring to the theories of entrepreneurship character, describe whether Amanda's experience and character fits the models.
2. What type of research did Amanda conduct that contributed to the success of her venture? What did she fail to research properly?
3. What issues will Amanda encounter as a second site is opened?
4. What strategy did she pursue to create service differentiation?
5. Evaluate Amanda's preparation for entrepreneurship. How did it affect the process of her starting a venture?

Smitty's Li'l Haulers

Start-up versus Buyout

It was October 1998 and Jeff Malott, a young, aspiring entrepreneur, had just toured the rustic factory and retail store of Smitty's Li'l Haulers, a Shedden, Ontario–based manufacturer of children's toy wagons. Jeff was very impressed with what he had seen. Smitty's was for sale and Jeff wondered if this was the right opportunity for him.

Jeff Malott was a native of London, Ontario. Following high school, he apprenticed as an automotive mechanic specializing in European automobiles. Before he completed his apprenticeship Jeff realized he had a strong desire to pursue his own business. Jeff began his entrepreneurial pursuit by enrolling in business classes at local colleges. One of the ideas he was interested in exploring was a nightclub and bar concept. The lifestyle attracted him and he thought he had some ideas that would make the business a success. Jeff took a part-time job working for UPS while he pursued his education. His exploration led him to London's Small Business Centre in 1998 for some assistance in writing the business plan for the proposed bar. They in turn referred him to George Lightfoot, a retired commercial banker who had started a private entrepreneurship training school.

Jeff and George discussed Jeff's ideas at length. This led to Jeff enrolling in courses at the school to acquire additional business skills needed to run a small business and to finalize the business plan for the bar. In September 1998 George approached Jeff to take a look at Smitty's Li'l Haulers as a possible alternative to starting the bar and nightclub.

George was acquainted with the owner of Smitty's and had been approached to assist in finding a buyer for the company. Initially, Jeff was surprised by the idea of buying a business. He had simply never considered it.

JEFF'S SUPPORT NETWORK

Jeff was fortunate in having a strong support network. His parents were very pleased with his entrepreneurial aspirations, although Jeff's father was not in favour of the bar idea. Jeff had been exposed to entrepreneurship from a very early age. His mother had run a successful restaurant in London while Jeff was growing up. She sold the business in 1986 and immediately started a second business in executive transportation, which she sold and retired from in 1993. Jeff's girlfriend Sharlene was very encouraging of his aspirations, and Jeff also had a network of family members and friends to discuss his ideas with and on whom he could call on to help start up a business.

SMITTY'S LI'L HAULERS

Smitty's had been founded in 1986 in the small town of Shedden, Ontario, about 35 kilometres southwest of London, by John Smith and his family. The business made a line of rugged, high-quality toy wagons that could also be used for chores around the home and garden. (See Exhibit 1 for details on the product line.) The parts for the wagons were purchased from various suppliers and assembled in a made-over barn on the farm of one of John's friends. (See Exhibit 2 for photo.) They were sold through a retail store in Shedden and through a network of farm implement distributors and other select retailers in the southwestern Ontario region. About 65 percent of sales were through the Shedden store. Sales through these channels had grown to 400–500 units per year by 1978.

Richard Ivey School of Business
The University of Western Ontario

This case was written by Leo Donlevy at the 2004 Case Writing Workshop under the supervision of Professors James A. Erskine and Michiel R. Leenders. It was prepared solely to provide material for class discussion. The author does not intend to illustrate either effective or ineffective handling of a managerial situation. The author may have disguised certain names and other identifying information to protect confidentiality.

Product Line Details			
Model	**Deck Size**	**Features**	**Retail Price**
100	16″ × 32″	Solid rubber wheels; 2-board rails	$109.95
150	16″ × 32″	Solid rubber wheels; 3-board rails	$159.95
200	16″ × 32″	10″ × 4″ pneumatic wheels; 3-board rails	$199.95
300	20″ × 36″	10″ × 4″ pneumatic wheels; 3-board rails	$229.95
400	22″ × 44″	4″ × 6″ pneumatic wheels; 3-board rails	$279.95
450	22″ × 44″	10″ × 4″ pneumatic, knobby all-terrain tires; front swivel suspension	$309.95
450 Green	22″ × 44″	Same as 450 but in olive drab green and includes camouflage canopy and pad	$379.95
Flatbed	22″ × 44″	Front swivel suspension	$179.95
"Smitty's Super" Trikes			$149.95
Custom Rocking Horse			$189.95
Wagon Canopies and Pad			$69.95 (100–300 models)
			$79.95 (400 & 450 models)
Sleigh Conversion Kits			$69.95 (100–200 models only)

EXHIBIT **1** *Smitty's Li'l Haulers*

Smitty's had also ventured into the retail furniture business. John had created a division called "Once a Tree" to retail hand-crafted fine furniture made by regional craftsmen. They supplied the store in Shedden with china cabinets, tables, chairs, and shelving units, which sold at a premium price compared to the volume-manufactured items sold in urban furniture stores. This division accounted for about 30 percent of Smitty's sales volume by 1998.

In the mid-1990s Smitty's was able to secure two large orders for wagons: a 3000-unit order from a major tool distributor and a 600-unit order from a chain of independent retail hardware stores. The tool company used the wagons as part of a promotion to its dealers, and the wagons were branded with the company name and logo rather than the traditional Smitty's brand. The hardware stores sold the wagons through their network in southwestern Ontario. Smitty's had also entered into negotiations with Canadian Tire to distribute their wagons but were unable to come to a deal. These orders had been completed by the time Jeff first met John.

The size of the two large orders strained Smitty's assembly and financial capacity and the stress took its toll on John Smith. According to Jeff, the strain nearly killed John. Faced with serious health problems, John approached his friend George Lightfoot to help him find a buyer for

EXHIBIT **2**
Photo of Model 400

▲ Courtesy of Smitty's Wagon Co.

Smitty's. John was not interested in just any buyer, however. He wanted someone who would "take care of the business," according to Jeff. John wanted a buyer who would leave the business in Shedden and who had the same small-town values of quality and good value for the customer.

JEFF'S IMPRESSIONS OF SMITTY'S AND THE PROPOSED DEAL

Jeff's was very excited by his visit to the Smitty's assembly plant. His mechanical background told him this was a quality product, if a bit rough. He saw lots of opportunities to improve the design, the quality, and the operation of the business. For example, Smitty's had a paper-based, somewhat loose accounting system in place. The books were put in order only at the end of every year by the accountant. Smitty's also had no presence on the Internet. In fact, the business did not even own a computer. Jeff also thought there were opportunities to grow the business, either by pursuing additional large orders or by expanding the distribution network. He also thought the business would eventually have to leave Shedden in order to achieve this growth, and this would likely be a deal-killer for John.

Jeff and John talked at length about the business during Jeff's visit. "John liked me," according to Jeff and, "he liked my youthful enthusiasm." John shared some financial statements with Jeff and was very proud to point out the huge impact the two large orders had on the company's results. John wanted $100,000 for Smitty's, which included the inventory of parts and finished goods, all tools and equipment, goodwill, and the "Once a Tree" furniture division. Jeff was not really interested in "Once a Tree," but John insisted it had to be part of any eventual deal.

JEFF'S ALTERNATIVES

Following his visit to Shedden, Jeff pondered his alternatives. There was the possibility of going full time with UPS and trying to climb the ladder there, but that really didn't appeal to him. He was sure his future was in owning his own business and had become quite focused on the bar and nightclub idea. In fact, he had a virtually complete business plan. Now the Smitty's option presented itself and, while he had been impressed by his visit to Shedden, the notion of buying a business left him asking if there might be other, even more attractive businesses for sale in the area.

THE RIGHT OPPORTUNITY?

If buying Smitty's was the right opportunity for him, Jeff had first to answer several questions. Did buying make more sense than starting his own busi-

ness? How should he assess the Smitty's opportunity? Were there better opportunities out there? If he did decide to pursue Smitty's, how should he finance it? He had some money saved up, but nowhere near the $100,000 John wanted. What was a fair price for Smitty's? Jeff realized he had some soul-searching to do—not to mention a lot of work over the next several weeks.

Calvert Toyota

Structuring Financing for a Car Dealership

Mike Calvert has worked for the Metro Toyota dealership in Saskatoon as the general manager for the past several years. The present owner, Tom Gray, is interested in selling the dealership. While Calvert would like to buy the dealership, he does not have the necessary personal financing. As a result, he has approached a number of bankers to see if he could borrow the money for the purchase price. His only personal assets are shares of stock that he already owns in the dealership and some stock in a Chevrolet dealership where he had previously worked.

In an effort to secure financing to acquire the dealership, Calvert approached a banker with the following items: (1) the agreement between the seller and Calvert, the prospective buyer (Exhibit 1) and (2) the pro forma financial statements for the first year of operation if he acquires the business (Exhibits 2 and 3).

In order to understand how Calvert is proposing to structure the financing, you should be aware of the following:

1. There are two entities: the dealership and a real estate partnership. The dealership is the entity that will transact the day-to-day operations. The real estate partnership is a separate entity that will own the land and building associated with the business. Thus the rent expense in the dealerships' income statement (Exhibit 3) is actually the note payment to the real estate partnership. In turn, this rent income received by the partnership will be used to pay the note payments to the bank.
2. The income statement does not include a salary for Calvert.
3. Calvert will also be purchasing an insurance agency, which is not included in the financial statements. This agency will offer insurance coverage to customers. Historically, this operation has been very profitable.

EXHIBIT **1**
Legal Description of the Agreement

SALES AGREEMENT

This Agreement is entered into the day and year herein below set forth by and between METRO TOYOTA, INC., hereinafter referred to as "Seller," and MIKE CALVERT TOYOTA, INC., hereinafter referred to as "Purchaser."

WHEREAS, Seller is the owner of certain assets in connection with its business in Saskatoon, Saskatchewan; and

WHEREAS, Purchaser desires to acquire such assets from Seller upon and pursuant to the terms and conditions set forth herein;

Source: Interview with Mike Calvert, September 24, 2002.

NOW, THEREFORE, in consideration of the mutual promises, covenants, and agreements of Purchaser and Seller herein, Purchaser and Seller agree hereby as follows:

1. Purchase and Sale
Seller hereby sells to the Purchaser and Purchaser hereby purchases from Seller the following assets at the purchase price indicated:

Asset	Purchase Price
Accounts Receivable	$ 104,000
Financing company receivables	$ 110,000
Inventory	$ 126,000
Parts	$ 360,000
Prepaid items	$ 25,000
Fixed assets	$ 475,000
TOTAL	$1 200,000

PURCHASE PRICE
The purchase price for the assets set forth in Paragraph 1 shall be ONE MILLION TWO HUNDRED THOUSAND AND NO/100 DOLLARS ($1,200,000), which shall be allocated among the respective assets as set forth in Paragraph 1. The purchase price shall be payable as follows:

a. At the closing, Purchaser shall pay to Seller, by cashier's or certified cheque, the sum of $600,000.00; and
b. The balance of the purchase price shall be fully satisfied by Purchaser's endorsement of and delivery to Seller at the closing of the following stock certificates:

    i. One hundred thirty thousand (130,000) shares of the common stock of Gray Taylor, Inc. evidenced by certificate number 1472.
    ii. Sixty-five thousand (65,000) shares of the preferred stock of Gray Taylor, Inc., evidenced by certificate number 423.
    iii. Seventy-five thousand five hundred (75,500) shares of the common stock of Metro Toyota, Inc. evidenced by certificate number 10333.
    iv. Two hundred fifty (250) shares of the common stock of Tom Gray Management Co., Inc., evidenced by certificate number 67230.

AGREEMENT FOR PURCHASE AND SALE OF REAL PROPERTY

The Province of Saskatchewan

City of Saskatoon
This agreement for Purchase and sale of Real Property made the day and year herein below set forth by and between GC, LTD., a Limited Partnership, whose sole General Partner is TOM GRAY, hereinafter referred to as "Seller," and MICHAEL R. CALVERT, TRUSTEE, hereinafter referred to as "Purchaser."

1. Legal Description
1.01   The property consists of that one (1) certain 4.721 acre tract of land out of the J. Walters Survey, more particularly described by metes and bounds in the attached Exhibit "A," incorporated herein for all purposes, together with all of Seller's right, title,

and interest in and to adjacent street, alleys, rights-of-way, accessions, or reversion and all improvements located therein which, together, are herein designated as the "Property."

2. Purchase and Sale

2.01 The purchase price for the property shall be the sum of THREE MILLION AND NO/ 100 DOLLARS ($3,000,000.00)

2.02 Seller and Purchaser hereby agree that the purchase price shall be allocated among the land and improvements as follows:

Item	Amount
Land	$ 500,000
Buildings	1,850,000
Fences	30,000
Outdoor Lighting Fixtures	20,000
Lifts	75,000
8000 litre underground storage tank	10,000
Air compressor system	15,000
Concrete paving and parking areas	500,000
TOTAL:	$3,000,000

3. Payment of Purchase Price

3.01 The sum of TWO MILLION TWO HUNDRED THOUSAND AND NO/100 DOLLARS ($2,200,000.00) shall be payable in cash at time of closing.

3.02 The balance of the purchase price shall be evidenced by a Promissory Note executed by Purchaser and payable to the order of Seller, contain the following provision:

a. Interest, at the same rate charged by the Bank of Montreal on the notes to be executed by Purchaser described in Paragraph 3.03 hereof.

b. Installments of principal and interest shall be due and payable monthly based upon a fifteen (15) year amortization with the principal balance of the Note, together with all accrued and unpaid interest thereon, being due and payable on or before the third anniversary date of the Note.

c. Maker shall reserve the right to prepay all or any portion of the principal balance due, at any time, and from time to time, without penalty or fee.

d. Such Note shall be secured by a Second Lien Deed of Trust to a Trustee ("Trustee") designated by Seller and shall be on Saskatchewan Bar form or other form mutually acceptable to Seller and Purchaser. Such Note shall be secondary, inferior, and subordinate to the First Lien Note and Deed of Trust described in Paragraph 3.03 hereof.

3.03 A portion of the cash payable at closing shall be obtained by Purchaser through a loan from the Bank of Montreal, which shall be secured by the vendor's lien to be retained by Seller in the Deed to Purchaser and assigned to the Bank of Montreal together with a First Lien Deed of Trust on the Property.

Calvert-Davis Real Estate Partnership Pro Forma Balance Shteet

Assets

Land	$ 500,000
Buildings	1,850,000
Improvements	650,000
TOTAL ASSETS	$3,000,000

Liabilities

Note payable—Bank of Montreal	$2,000,000
Note payable—GC, LTD.	800,000
Note payable—Calvert Toyota	200,000
	$3,000,000
Net worth	0
TOTAL LIABILITIES:	$3,000,000

Assets

Cash		$ 200,000
Accounts Receivable:		
Service and Parts	$ 95,000	
Warranty claims	7000	
PDS	2000	
Finance co. receivable—Current	335,000	
Total Receivables		$ 439,000

Inventories

New vehicles—Toyota	$1,500,000	
Used vehicles	200,000	
Parts and accessories	**360,000**	
Gas, oil, and grease	15,000	
Body shop materials	5000	
Sublet repairs	5000	
Work in process—labour	26,000	
Total inventories		$2,111,000
Prepaid expenses		25,000
Total current assets		$2,775,000
Fixed assets		515,000
Other assets		200,000
TOTAL ASSETS		$3,490,000

EXHIBIT **2**
Pro Forma Balance Sheet

Debt (Liabilities) and Equity

Reserve for repossession losses	$ 225,000	
Vehicle inventory financing	1,625,000	
Current portion of long-term debt	155,000	
Total current liabilities		$2,005,000
Notes payable—capital loans	$ 860,000	
Other notes and contracts	25,000	
Total long-term debt		$ 885,000
Total Liabilities		$2,890 000
NET WORTH		
Capital Stock		600,000
TOTAL LIABILITIES AND EQUITY		$3,490,000

EXHIBIT **3**

Calvert Toyota Pro Forma Income Statement

Total gross profit		$3,717,000
Departmental selling expenses:		
Sales commissions and incentives	$550,000	
Delivery expense	36,000	
Total selling expenses		$ 586,000
Departmental operating expenses:		
Advertising	$240,000	
Policy adjustments	20,000	
Floor plan interest	220,000	
Demos and company vehicles	50,000	
Personnel training	3000	
Freight	3000	
Supplies and small tools	30 000	
Laundry and uniforms	15,000	
Depreciation—equipment and vehicles	100,000	
Maintenance, repair, and rental equipment	10,000	
Miscellaneous expense	10,000	
Supervision salaries	478,000	
Salaries and wages	300,000	
Clerical salaries	180,000	
Vacation and time-off pay—production personnel		10,000
Total operating expenses		$1,669,000
Total selling and operating expenses		2,255,000
Department profit (loss)		1,462,000
Overhead expenses:		
Rent and equipment	$420,000	
Payroll taxes	115,000	

Employee benefits	60,000	
Stationery and office supplies	30,000	
Data processing services	25,000	
Outside services	60,000	
Dues and subscriptions	12,000	
Telephone	32,000	
Legal and auditing	20,000	
Postage	3000	
Travel and entertainment	12,000	
Heat, light, power, and water	50,000	
Other insurance	50,000	
Other taxes	25,000	
Total overhead expenses		$ 964,000
Total expenses		$3,219,000
Net profit before bonuses		$ 498,000

Questions

1. Explain how the proposed financing for the dealership is to be structured as represented in the agreement.
2. Is buying the dealership a good investment for Calvert? Explain.
3. If you were the banker, would you make the loan? Why or why not?
4. As the banker, how would you want to structure the loan? (Consider any problems with making the loan and how the loan could be structured to compensate for these deficiencies—if any.)
5. The pro forma statements prepared by Calvert assume that the note payments to the bank are amortized (equal payments each month). What changes should be made to the statements if the bank requires equal principal payments plus interest? (Assume a 12 percent interest rate.)

Appendix A

Venture Feasibility and Business Plan Checklist

The following extended checklist includes the type of questions a founder should be able to answer when evaluating the feasibility of her or his venture. The information should be clearly stated in a business plan for investors and lenders to evaluate. The checklist also includes questions pertaining to expansion, and should be reviewed to ensure the expansion strategy is both logical and feasible. Not all questions will apply to all ventures.

MARKETING RESEARCH AND PRODUCT STRATEGY

- Have the industry and economic trends that contribute to creating an opportunity for the venture been identified? Are they realistic? Do they include a long-term analysis?
- Have the key differentiating factors for the venture been identified? Are those factors important to the target markets that have been identified?
- Does the competitive analysis address the core service and product factors? Is the research detailed?
- Has a detailed analysis of the target markets been prepared? For consumer products: does the demographic/psychographic/usage pattern analysis indicate a need for the venture? Does the trend analysis indicate long-term need? For business-to-business ventures: has the specific market niche been identified and the purchasing patterns analyzed? Are the assumptions pertaining to potential need realistic?
- Have specific niche strategies been developed? Is the strategy easy to duplicate by competitors?
- What specific strategies have been developed to ensure continued competitive advantage?
- Has a CRM system been developed/designed?
- Is there potential for growth in other geographic areas or industries?
- Could the concept be franchised?

- Are there any costing/production efficiencies created by the venture? Is technology utilized in creating a differentiation or costing benefit? Is the benefit long term or short term?
- Has the venture benchmarked the best practices and products from the competition?

MARKETING STRATEGY

- Is the marketing philosophy logical and clearly stated?
- Has a detailed sales forecast been prepared? Is it realistic? What percentage of the market is required to make the venture feasible?
- Is the communications strategy effective in reaching the target markets? Is the budget comparable to the industry (have the FPIs been referred to)? Have a range of advertising and promotional venues been evaluated and a detailed, costed, and multi-streamed campaign been developed? Has a contingency promotional strategy been developed if sales fail to reach the forecast?
- Is the web-based communication effective?
- Has the product been test-marketed?
- Has a customer survey or feedback process been developed?
- Have sample advertisements been developed and costing quotes received?
- Have appropriate packaging and delivery strategies been developed?
- Does the price/quality grid indicate the venture's product is correctly priced?
- Does the pricing strategy fit the target markets, the competitive environment, and profit goals?
- Has future product development been identified, and is it adequate to maintain the venture's competitive position?

THE MANAGEMENT TEAM AND HUMAN RESOURCE PLANNING

- Has the founding management team been identified, and their roles, compensation, and authority been stated? Do they have the skills to launch and grow the business? If not, has the training they need been identified? Are managers committed emotionally and financially to the success of the venture?
- Have the jobs required to operate the business been identified, job descriptions been developed, and compensation been clarified? Are skilled staff available to fill the positions? Have the labour laws for the province of operation been checked, and standards, such as overtime payment, been clarified?
- Has payroll been created, or contracted out?
- Has a mission statement been developed? Have SMART short-term and long-term goals been stated?
- While the disciplinary, feedback, and training processes may not have been developed, have they been identified as required and a management person assigned to develop them in the first few months of operation?
- Has the management team discussed how it will communicate, and how decisions will be made?

- Has the management team discussed the leadership style it will employ, and the motivational techniques that could be implemented articulated? Is the role of staff with regards to serving the client clearly understood?
- Has the founding team identified what professionals are required to guide the venture? Has an accountant been identified to participate in tax planning and preparation of financial statements?
- Has a mentor with industry experience been identified?
- Has a clear and detailed GANTT chart or timeline been developed to identify milestones and deadlines?
- Has harvesting and exit potential been discussed?
- Has a board of directors been created?

LEGAL AND RISK MANAGEMENT

- Has the legal structure been created? Has a minute book been created if the venture is incorporated?
- Has a partnership or shareholder agreement been created and signed?
- Is the ownership clearly stated, and future profit sharing outlined so that conflict will be avoided?
- Has insurance been obtained?
- Have quality control processes been identified to reduce operational risks?
- Have licenses and local permits been obtained?
- Has a BIN/GST number been secured, and filing for employees established with Canada Revenue Agency?
- If patents or copyright are required, have they been secured?
- Has a secure place been obtained to store records (such as HR files, agreements)?
- Have contracts been developed if necessary?
- Have municipal, provincial, and federal requirements been identified and addressed?

OPERATIONS

- If manufacturing: has the location been accessed according to proximity to customers, human resources, costing, size etc?
- If product/technology: has a prototype been developed? What are the major barriers that could arise in getting the product to market from a production viewpoint?
- Have suppliers been identified and an accurate costing developed?
- Is the facility layout efficient? Is storage available?
- Have the operating costs been identified?
- Has a quality control process been identified? How will quality be ensured?
- Have production schedules been developed? Are they reasonable?
- What is the expansion capability of the location?
- Has the costing of the product or service been compared to industry data? Is it reasonable?
- Have renovation or maintenance costs been identified?

FINANCIAL AND ACCOUNTING

- Has an accounting system been established? Does it provide the detail necessary to control costs? Who will input data and maintain the books?
- Are the pro forma financial statements and the cash flow detailed and realistic? Have costs on the income statement been compared to industry for reasonableness? Are assumptions clearly stated? Have contingency statements been prepared?
- Have fixed costs and variable costs been clearly identified? Is the break-even reasonable? What percentage of capacity is required to break even? Is it realistic?
- Has a point-of-sale system been purchased? Have credit terms for customers been established? Have bank accounts been created? Who has signing authority? Is it clear?
- How will inventory be tracked? Has a system or process been identified?
- Has a detailed start-up cost chart been created?
- Has the operating capital required been clearly identified?
- Does the financing proposal, for investors or lenders, make sense given the industry, the type of venture, the opportunity for harvesting, and the industry risk? Is the funding clarified for both short-term (such as inventory) and long-term (product development, leasehold improvements, equipment purchase) requirements? Is the venture profitable?
- Has a repayment or harvest strategy been clearly stated? Is it realistic (i.e, is the debt repayment feasible)?
- Are the accounting, inventory, production, and other systems integrated and compatible?
- Is collateral available for lenders?

Sample Business Plan

Pulse Dance Inc.
Confidentiality Agreement

This business plan has been submitted on a confidential basis solely for the benefit of selected individuals and is not for use by any other persons. Neither may it be reproduced, stored, or copied in any form.

By accepting delivery of this plan, the recipient agrees to return this copy to the address listed above. This plan is not to be copied, faxed, reproduced, or distributed without express written permission.

Signature

Name (typed or printed)

Date

EXECUTIVE SUMMARY

Pulse Dance Inc. provides advanced-level dance classes for non-professional adult dancers, specializing exclusively in jazz, ballet, hip hop, and lyrical. The Studio will offer an opportunity for 20– to 34-year-old adults with previous dance experience to continue dancing at a level that challenges them, thus providing a service unique to the city of Calgary. Located at 4th St SW and 23rd Ave SW, in the centre of Mission and Cliff Bungalow, PDS is perfectly situated in the city to cater to this particular demographic. PDS will offer a flexible schedule, competitive rates, high quality instruction and performance opportunities for its members, ensuring an experience that adheres to the needs of many female adult professionals, students, and parents, who love to dance.

Courtesy of Lauren Round and Meghan Hicks

VENTURE FACTS

Type of business:	Dance Studio
Services:	Advanced level, adult dance classes—jazz, hip hop, ballet, lyrical, breakdance, acro, and stretch and strength
Legal structure:	Incorporating the business in order to ensure legal protection, financial security and asset security. Share structure includes f common shares for 2 principles who invested $11,200; preferred shares for angel investors who invested $16,600.
Location:	Retail location—320 23rd Ave SW, Calgary AB, main floor unit; 1674 square feet, rental rate—$25 per sq ft; operating costs—$11.00 per sq ft
Name of founders:	Lauren Round and Meghan Hicks
Experience:	Lauren—16 years of competitive dance experience and 4 years teaching experience, Meghan—15 years of dance experience and 5 years teaching experience
Key milestone dates:	Investments secured by May 1, 2008 Studio opening August 15, 2008 Classes to begin September 21, 2008
Primary target market:	Women with previous advanced-level dance experience, aged 20–34
Goals:	Number of clients year 1—200 Retention of clients in year 2—60% Number of clients year 2—260 (30% growth)
Capital requirement:	$25,738.45 leasehold improvements $10,588.70 equipment and furniture $5,08.00 initial marketing $41,335.15
Investment structure:	$10,600 common shares—founders $16,600 class A preferred shares—investors $27,201.40 operating line of credit @ prime + 3% (rate guaranteed for 5 years) $54,401.40 total initial financing
Terms and payback period:	Anticipated date for total loan repayment—January 31, 2010

A lump sum payment of $15,000 will be applied during the first year, with the remainder paid off in year 2 of operations. Anticipated date for repayment to investors—July 31, 2011 (3 year term with buy-back provision)

Terms—10% ROI received as a balloon payment (principal + interest) at the repayment

Legal and accounting council: Legal—Don Osmond

Accounting—Meghan Hicks
and Lauren Round

Mentor or Advisors:	Nathan Atkin of New Groove Dance Lisa Matthews of Precision Dance Co.

TABLE OF CONTENTS

THE OPPORTUNITY

Pulse Dance Studio Inc. (PDS) is a dance studio that specializes in advanced-level jazz, hip hop, ballet, and lyrical classes on a weekly basis. The service will be intended for those individuals who have been dancing for a number of years at a higher level of instruction and who therefore look to continue doing so at a level that challenges them.

PDS is geared toward women who are looking to continue dancing at an advanced level that is both challenging and fun. The desired target market will consist primarily of women aged 20–34 living in the downtown and southern Calgary core.

There are a number of dance studios and dance programs offered throughout the city, including private professional dance schools, which are most often audition based; however, very few schools and studios cater to those interested in advanced-level classes for non-professionals. PDS will therefore position itself as Calgary's first dance studio specializing exclusively in advanced adult-level jazz, hip hop, ballet, and lyrical classes for non-professional dancers.

Other core features will include

- Two newly renovated dance studios with reinforced hardwood flooring, wall-to-wall mirrors, ventilation system
- Viewing area comprising smaller couches and chairs provided for guests of dancers during classes
- Additional advanced classes such as acro, breakdance, and stretch and strength

Operations

PDS operates on a fixed weekly schedule catering to individuals interested in advanced-level dance classes during lunch hours and evenings on weekdays and throughout the

*This information is provided on the book's companion site at www.longenecker4e.nelson.com

day on weekends. The Studio will provide many opportunities for interested dancers to enrol in various classes when it is most convenient for them. The studio

- Operates from Monday to Saturday during the fall session, Monday–Sunday during the winter session and Monday–Saturday, with reduced hours, in the spring session (expectation of expanding hours and classes in successive years)
- Offers Moms and Tots classes on Mondays and Saturdays
- Provides opportunities for community performances throughout Calgary's communities in conjunction with Latin Corner Dance Studio[1]
- Has payment periods occurring on a drop-in basis or by session
- Offers shared discounts with Starbucks at 23rd Ave SW, Lululemon at 4th St and 17th Ave SW, and Yoga Santosha on 4th St SW

Layout

Pulse Dance will be located in the heart of Mission and Cliff Bungalow, a trend-setting community just south of downtown. The 1674 sq. ft. space is a main floor unit at the front of the building with a full window display facing 23rd Avenue.[2] Pale yellow walls and white and light blue accents will be used throughout the space. To the right of the main entrance, a reception desk will sit perpendicular to the window, beside which an entrance to change rooms will be constructed running length-wise toward the back of the space. To the left, two studios will also be constructed within the space, one at the front facing 23rd Avenue, and approximately 800 sq. ft. in size, and the second in back with a size of approximately 500 sq. ft. Couches and chairs will be placed along the side wall of the studio for guests to use. The mirrors will be placed along the dividing wall between opposite studios, and portable ballet bars will be moved onto the floor when needed. The complex provides a common bathroom for its tenants that will be accessible through the rear doors of the space. A proper ventilation system will be installed to keep air flowing through the studios; reinforced hardwood flooring will be used in each of the two studios; and daily, thorough cleans will be done to ensure cleanliness.

Staff

Pulse Dance will initially hire four part-time staff members who can teach multiple disciplines as follows:

- One certified ballet instructor who holds accreditation from the Royal Academy of Dance Canada (RAD)[3] and if possible the PAEC (Performing Arts Educators of Canada)[4]
- One stretch and strength, jazz, and acro instructor
- One hip hop and breakdance instructor
- Occasional guest teacher (once a week)

Founders Lauren Round and Meghan Hicks will assume the following positions:

- Financial adviser/accountant—Meghan
- Managerial work/administrative aspects of business—organizing and conducting registration, answering and returning phone calls, email, mailing lists, advertising promotions, etc.—conducted by both Lauren and Meghan
- Meghan and Lauren will teach 46% of classes in the fall session, 45% of classes in the winter session and 53% of classes during the spring session

At PDS it will not be made mandatory that all instructors, with the exception of the ballet teacher, have certification or accreditation in the specified area of dance they instruct. Instead, an audition component will be included in all interviews for prospective instructors, after which a decision will be made by the owners, with regards to the candidate's dance creativity, capability, communication and teaching ability, individual style, and level of instruction. Depending on the demand for each class offered, more or fewer teachers may be required for each style of dance offered.[5]

Hours of Operation

Fall Session:	Monday–Thursday	5:00 pm–10:00 pm
Fridays	5:00 pm–9:30 pm	
Saturday	10:00 am–6:00 pm	
Winter Session only:	Sunday	10:00 am–5:00 pm

TARGET MARKET

Pulse is specifically targeting adults with a dance background, who want to dance at an intermediate or advanced level. The clients will be primarily female, aged 20–34, who participate in dance as a recreational activity to stay active and healthy, while continuing to develop their technique. Pulse is focusing on those who work and live in the downtown and uptown neighbourhoods.

Secondary Target Market

The secondary market is males aged 20–34 with dance experience, as well as those who reside in other suburban neighbourhoods of the city, and frequent the area.

Demographics

The Nexus generation represents 33% of Canada's population.[6] In Calgary, the target age group is prominent in and around 17th Avenue SW, 4th Street SW, and the downtown core areas—making up 40.49–54.25% of the population.[7] Females represent over 50% of the population, the majority has a post-secondary education, and there is only a 4.8% unemployment rate for the area.[8] Best Customers Demographics states that "college graduates spend more than twice the average on fees for recreational lessons."[9] The per capita income projections for Calgary are $41,800 for 2008, $44,700 for 2010,

Area	Population	Ages 20–34	Females	Household Income	Tenants
Mission	4488	36.7%	36.36–45.36%	$37,040	48.71–71.42%
Cliff Bungalow	1845	40.9%	45.36–57.08%	$35,576	71.42–100%
Lower Mount Royal	3254	52.9%	45.36–57.08%	$35,570	71.42–100%
Downtown Core	7523	45.5%	36.36–45.36%	$28,658	71.42–100%
Sunalta	3241	52.3%	45.36–57.08%	$32,409	71.42–100%
Beltline	17794	—	45.36–57.08%	—	71.42–100%
Ward 8	71259	39.1%	—	—	68.8%

and $49,200 for 2013; representing an estimated growth of 17.7% in the next 5 years; meaning growth and prosperity are evident in Calgary's future.[10]

The City of Calgary 2006 Census determined that there are 240,506 20–34 year olds in Calgary. Females aged 20–24 make up 38 307, and ages 25–34 account for 82,002; meaning that females hold a slight majority advantage for the age range.[11]

Psychographics

The target market is made up of two psychographic clusters; Urban Young, and Urban Downscale. Within these are the following sub-clusters that apply to the concept:

- Young Digerati—young, well-off urban trendsetters
- Electric Avenues—young, upper-middle-class urban singles
- Grads & Pads—young, midscale urban singles
- Daytrippers & Nightowls—young, lower-middle-class urban singles and couples
- Rooms with a View—young, multi-ethnic singles in downscale urban high-rises[12]

These groups have greater spending capacity, mostly due to the fact that the majority do not have children. They are tech-savvy, educated, and heavy consumers. They have relatively high amounts of disposable income and are notorious for spending freely on products and services including entertainment and fashion. They frequent health clubs and have active lifestyles.[13]

In Calgary, these clusters are most prominent in the communities of 17th Avenue SW, 4th Street SW, and the Downtown Core—accounting for over 50% of the population

Trends

Individuals are becoming increasingly aware of the benefits of living a healthy and active lifestyle; including dancing. Euromonitor states that "the fitness industry is set to grow strongly as people undertake sports and exercise for longer."[14] The data supports Pulse's focus on adults continuing their dance practice. The benefits of dance are also becoming increasingly known; a study showed that people who did exercise that followed a rhythmic pattern lowered their risk of heart disease. The targeted generation has heard about healthy eating and exercise in a way that older generations have not. It is their nature, and part of their social scene, to be active and exercise.[15]

Research shows that the Generation Y group often stays longer in the family home, which gives them a higher level of discretionary income. The group is also known for its high spending and confidence in the future (willingness to incur debt).[16] Females' average disposable income level is on the rise. The increase of participation of females in the workforce has given women more discretionary income to spend on non-essential items.[17]

Usage Patterns and Opportunity

Statistics Canada states that only 38.4% of Albertan females, aged 20–34, are physically inactive; 27% are moderately active, 33.4% are physically active, with 60.4 falling between the two; illustrating the large market size of potential users.[18]

The average Alberta household spends $7156 on recreation and education. Average expenditure by females aged 20–34 in urban areas of Alberta is $511.80–527.14 per year, on sports fees including dance. Also, in the last three months, 30% of the target market participated in dance. The Alberta Recreation Survey (2004) states that 29% of households in Calgary have taken part in dance within the past 12-month period, 57.5% of individuals take part in recreation for the purpose of health and exercise, and 56.3% participate for pleasure. The most common barriers to entry were the cost of equipment and fees. Since taking classes at a dance studio omits the potentially expensive membership fee at recreation facilities, a dance option may be more attractive to our target market. The equipment required for dance is also minimal and infrequently purchased, therefore less expensive than alternative recreational activities.[19]

The employment rate in Calgary rose almost 3% from 2001 to 2006. According to the most recent *Consumer Trends Report*, consumption is forecasted to continue to rise, along with personal disposable income. From 1992 to 2002 disposable income rose 3.7% and the average credit limit rose 10.2%.[20] An exponential growth in credit limit is important for the target market because the psychographic characteristics of Generation Y individuals include not being afraid to spend on credit. Credit increases one's disposable income, which the identified psychographic clusters would partially use toward an active lifestyle.

Based on the fact that there are 120 309 females aged 20–34 in Calgary and that 29% of households participate in dance, Pulse can anticipate a potential market size of 34 889.

COMPETITIVE ANALYSIS

The Industry

The Dance industry in Canada is growing. From the 1970s until the end of the 1990s, the number of dancers across Canada increased from 40% to 70%. By 2001, 80% of dancers were under the age of 45, 63% of dancers were under the age of 35, and 85% of dancers were female. In 2004, more than 1 million Canadian adults were taking dance classes or performing dances themselves,[21] and the most recent data shows that over the past three months, 31.22% of women aged 20–34 participated in dance in Canada.

In Alberta, a 2005 survey determined that social dancing was the third most popular activity in the province, with 49% of Albertans participating.[22] Within the last three months, 21.2%–30.0% of women aged 20–34 participated in dancing. The province is one of just two in Canada with an average expenditure by females aged 20–34 on sports fees including dance, of $511.80–$527.14, the highest in Canada.

The dance industry in Calgary currently comprises 87 registered dance schools and studios. The majority of these businesses are classified as medium-sized dance studios experiencing sales volumes of more than $200 000 annually and less than $500 000, with just less than 10 studios in the upper bracket experiencing a sales volume of $500 000 or greater.[23] The 2004 Alberta Recreation survey shows that 29% of households participated in dance, with an average number of participating members exceeding 445).

Trends

Many adults "devote a great deal of their free time to perfecting their dancing skills, enter competitions, perform before audiences and reach "professional" levels of expertise," if they had taken lessons since they were children.[24] Susan Kramer adds that dance is important for adults because it provides much needed meditation by getting the body to move aerobically.[25] Recent dance trends in Calgary include the movement toward young-adult and adult instruction. The YWCA, in conjunction with the University of Calgary, provides an example of this. It has launched a Dance Pilot Project aimed at involving advanced adult dancers, beginner adult dancers, and seniors in a combined dance program to "bridge the connections between University of Calgary dance and the community."[26] Newer styles of dance such as the West Coast Swing,[27] Afro-Brazilian dances, and hip hop, have also increased in popularity among adults in Calgary.[28] There are no licenses or registration given by any governing body for dance studios to exist in Alberta, (however, studios are required to have a SOCAN license—a flat fee paid annually to ensure that musicians are paid accordingly), which allows for the proliferation of dance studios targeting various markets and teaching various styles of dance.[29]

Direct Competition

Currently in Calgary, there are five direct competitors of PDS Inc. The industry leader in the city, operating since 1982, is Decidedly Jazz Danceworks (DJD). It is a large studio with a sales volume between $1,000,000 and $2,500,000. The studio has over 1000 registered students and offers more than 75 classes weekly.[30] Free House Dance Plus Ltd. (FHDP) follows close behind with a sales volume between $500,000 and $1,000,000. The studio also offers an adult dance component comparable in quality to that of DJD.[31] Latin Corner Dance Studio (LCD) focuses primarily on Latin dance forms but targets primarily men and women over the age of 25, comprising a portion of Pulse Dance's target market. The studio is recognized for its high-quality classes and middle-range prices. The YWCA[32] and the City of Calgary[33] also offer beginner adult dance classes including hip hop, at very affordable prices. The quality of the classes offered is minimal compared to that of the above mentioned studios however.

Indirect Competition

There are also a number of indirect competitors in located near PDS. Yoga Santosha, on 4th St SW and 16th Ave SW, offers a variety of yoga classes, from beginner to advanced, seven days a week, targeting primarily women aged 20 and older.[34] Also located in the downtown area, at 11th Ave SW, is Core Yoga and Pilates. Classes run Monday to Saturday throughout the year at very affordable rates intended for adult women (and men).[35] Alive Personal Training is located at 2nd St. SW and 21st Ave SW and offers a variety of fitness programs for adult women and men on a weekly basis.[36] Curves Fitness for women is located in the same building as PDS; however, it does not offer any dance classes and could therefore be seen as a strategic partner, given that it targets a similar audience.

Competitive Status

The opportunity for PDS therefore exists in the absence of more advanced level classes in jazz, hip hop, ballet and lyrical offered at these studios (See Exhibit 1). There is also an opportunity to offer these classes at prices competitive to that of DJD and FHDP, the top two direct competitors, while still maintaining high-quality instruction; a convenient; accessible location; newly renovated facilities; various styles of dance classes; and various class times. PDS will be offering classes Friday evenings, unlike FHDP, and Sundays, beginning in the winter session, unlike DJD, in an attempt to earn a share of the market not currently being engaged. From Wednesday to Friday, classes will be offered in the early evening for those working downtown or close to the studio, rather than late at night like its competitors. PDS also recognizes the opportunity to provide its members with performance opportunities, which are currently not offered by all competitors, including DJD.

EXHIBIT **1**

Number of Studios Offering Adult Jazz, Hip Hop, Ballet and Lyrical classes in the City of Calgary within Target Market

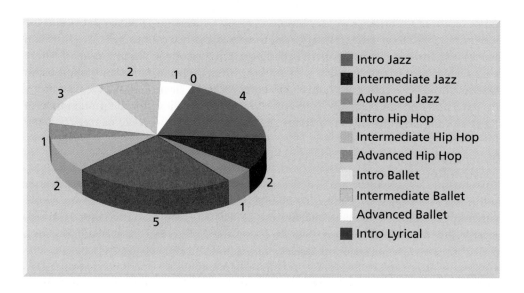

Competitive Matrix of Direct Competitors

This matrix is available at *www.longenecker4e.nelson.com.*

LOCATION ANALYSIS

Pulse will be located in the Alberta Professional Centre at 100, 320–23rd Avenue SW, in the Mission/Cliff Bungalow area, half a block west of the intersection of 23rd Avenue and 4th Street SW. The location was chosen based on its uptown, trendy position in the city, as well as its accessibility, safety, size, and relevance to the target market.

Characteristics

The four-storey building is designed for retail and office space. The space available for Pulse is 1674 square feet, located on the main floor on the building, facing the street, with external access (24 hours per day, 7 days a week).[37] There are large glass doors and a window at the front, allowing for a lot of natural light. The building has recently undergone complete renovations and upgrading of the electrical, mechanical, and structural components of the building.[38]

The main building entrance doors are locked at 6 pm daily. The only way into the building is through the occupant spaces on the main floor that operate into the evenings. The parking lots and adjacent street are well lit, ensuring the safety of the area for females attending evening classes.

The building is surrounded by low-rise apartment buildings. The intersection is busy with vehicles and pedestrians, with an estimated flow of 16,000 vehicles per day on 4th Street,[39] which is a major artery connecting the downtown core with Mission. The neighbourhood is established with minimal development; therefore, the present image is expected to remain.

The lease will be a three-to-five-year term, with a rate of $25 per square foot (psf) including taxes. Operating costs are estimated at $11 psf per annum. Renovations are allowed and must be approved by the owner, who offers a 50/50 split on the costs. Refer to Start-Up Costs for an explicit breakdown of costs and lease terms.

Pulse will incur an annual rent expenditure of $41,850 (1674 sq. ft.× $25). When compared to the average industry expenditure in Alberta of $30 500 per year, Pulse is approximately 37% above average. The Calgary commercial retail space vacancy is very low, with a rate of 1.5%; lease rates are at a premium because of demand.[40] In addition, Pulse is in a trendy neighbourhood, occupying a larger space in order to accommodate two studios.

Location Requirements

The space requires renovations. Two studios will be constructed, mirrors and sprung hardwood floors will be installed, and walls will be put up to create a change room and front reception area. The renovations will be submitted for approval from the building owner, and Pulse will obtain the required City of Calgary permits to proceed.[41]

According to the City of Calgary, Pulse qualifies as a C2 commercial school, which is permitted to operate at this location. An application for tenancy change will have to be formally submitted, and a municipal business license is required. A business sign is allowed on the exterior of the space, and Pulse will also require a municipal signage permit (see Start-Up Costs for additional details).[42]

Transportation and Parking

Pulse is located in a very accessible area for pedestrians, transit commuters, and drivers, attracting those who live and commute to work in the area. According to a recent article, this target market "tends to be younger and fairly new to the living-on-your-own scene, which means convenience is important to them." There is a parking lot on the west side of the building, where Pulse could rent one parking stall for $160/month. On the east side of the building, there is a visitor parking lot with 2-hour free parking and 14 stalls. There is also ample metered street parking along 23rd Avenue, as well as additional street parking on 4th Street and 2nd Street. There are three bus routes that run along 4th Street. The 3, 419, and 433 have stops less than a block away. These routes connect Mission with the downtown core, Elbow Drive, and suburban neighbourhoods to the south.[43]

Competition

There are no direct competitors in the area of Mission. The closest is the primary competitor, Decidedly Jazz Danceworks, approximately six blocks north, providing an opportunity for Pulse to attract some of its clients with our competitive advantage of lower-cost classes, and Sunday scheduling (see Competitive Analysis section). There is a Curves for Women directly above Pulse's space in the building. Curves targets a different target market so it will not be a competitor, but could potentially bring in additional clients who hear about Pulse through users of Curves.

Target Market

The location is ideal for Pulse because of the target-market density and future growth potential. According to the City of Calgary & Neighbourhood Services, Mission has had a population increase of 18.7% from 2002 to 2007. The median household income in 2000 was $37,040 and the age distribution has a 36.7% representation of 20–34-year-olds, with the highest density of age being 25–34. The proportion of single individuals represents 58.6% and females represent 45.36–57.08% of this figure. Those who have a college-or university-level post-secondary education represent 69.8% of the population.

Amenities

Fourth Street is known as "restaurant row" due to the existence of more than three dozen restaurants, bars, and coffee shops covering a wide variety of cultures. Leaseco Realty Inc. boasts that "shopping, entertainment, art, medical services, business services, retail stores, and a hip young exciting energy are evident. Making the area a popular place to work, live, and play." The area is unique because it incorporates historical buildings with new urban development.

The location is very effective because of its match to the studio's target market. The high density of females aged 20–34, who fall within the required psychographic clusters, will find Pulse to be conveniently situated. In addition, the proximity of our competitors means that there is a demand for Pulse's services in the area, without being too close to the competition.

PRICING STRATEGY

PDS will be employing a follow-the-leader pricing strategy in line with that of FHDP Exhibit 2, Price Comparison Chart, depicts the difference in prices offered at various studios for various classes, including those studios that offer additional membership fees. Prices will be set for middle-level income earners, considerably lower than prices offered by the industry leader DJD. The target age of PDS is females aged 20 to 34 who, for the most part, will be finishing school, beginning careers, or further establishing careers. Because the studio will be located in the middle-upper income neighbourhood of Mission and Cliff Bungalow, where the percentage of 20–34 year old women living in the neighbourhood is 40.49%–54.25%, PDS has appropriately positioned itself to capture its particular market. Pulse Dance Inc. will be a high-quality, higher-price studio in line with Free House Dance Pulse Ltd.

FHDP, as mentioned previously, is listed as a large dance studio with an annual sales volume of $500,000 to $1,000,000. DJD, also a large dance studio, is earning $1,000,000 to $2,500,000 annually. PDS will ensure that the quality of dance facilities, the quality of the dance instructors, the quality of varying levels of dance, and the overall quality of the experience will be competitive with both of the above-mentioned studios. In comparison however, PDS will offer lower prices. It will provide an extra week of classes per session. It will base the hiring of jazz, hip hop, lyrical, breakdance, acro, and guest teachers on their level of creativity and ability, not necessarily according to certification or accreditation, to ensure that the most innovative and/or contemporary styles are being taught. It will allow its members to select from a varied schedule of available class times weekly to best suit their needs, and, finally, PDS will ensure that the studio itself is properly constructed and designed with dancers in mind and maintained for their continued comfort. It therefore intends to position itself only slightly above FHDP— primarily due to its more marketable location in the current market situation, and will thus provide a competitive alternative for an advanced-level adult dance studio. Figure 3, Prince Quality Grid, illustrates the range in price and quality of each of the direct competitors for the dance classes they offer.

According to the Financial Performance Indicator (FPI) for the industry, the average total revenue for dance studios is $249,400 per year. Operating expenses are on average $182,800 and total expenses amount to $233,400, thus, net profit is generally $16,000 per operating year. The FPI also provides that, on average, 64% of dance studios are in fact profitable with net profits of approximately $30,300.[44] PDS has structured its pricing strategy in compliance with the FPI in order to provide accurate prices for participants, and therefore appropriately compares to competitors in the market.

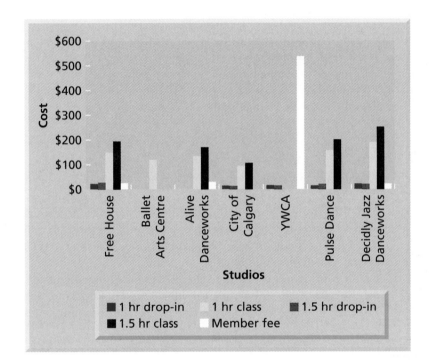

EXHIBIT **2**
Price Comparison Chart

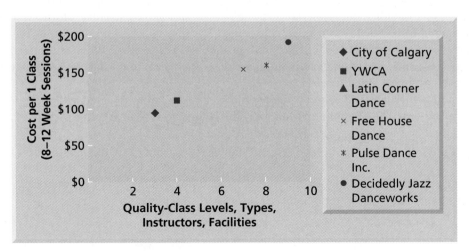

EXHIBIT **3**
Price Quality Grid

PROMOTIONAL ANALYSIS

Objective

As discussed in the Target Market section, 30% of females aged 20–34 participated in dance in the last three months. With 120,309 females aged 20–34 in Calgary, the total number of potential clients for Pulse is 36,093. In order to reach the maximum amount of clients in the most effective way, Pulse will implement a strategic advertising and promotional strategy over the course of 12 months.

Budget

The industry average annual expenditure on advertising and promotion is $6000. Because Pulse is a start-up business, however, located on a secondary street, the budget will be significantly higher to compete in an already competitive industry. Pulse is anticipating a $18,600 budget for the first 12 months, $15,000 for the following 12 months, and will then meet the industry average in the third year of operations.

Strategy

A relatively constant and moderate level of advertising will be used since the target market refuses a "hard sell," and advertising managers have learned that "you have to get the merchandise in front of them without being in their face."[45] Timing will be scheduled carefully to ensure minimum overlap of advertising methods to avoid deterring our target market. The modes of advertising are selected according to their fit with the target market and pre-determined budget.

There will be initial promotions to attract clients, as well as ongoing promotions to achieve a competitive advantage. Advertising will include radio, magazine, online, and public transit. Pulse will also be an exhibitor at trade shows and community festivals.

Promotions

Upon opening, Pulse will host a promotional open house for clients to come and try out classes at the new studio. The promotion will take place approximately two to three weeks after opening, once other advertising modes have started. Feedback forms will be requested to be filled out by those who attend in order to determine how they found out about Pulse and what they liked and/or didn't like; providing Pulse with information as to which advertising techniques are the most efficient and what can be done differently at the studio, if need be.

Temporary signs will be put up along 4th Street since Pulse is located on a secondary street. Signage will be submitted for approval to the City of Calgary, and will therefore adhere to the temporary-signs bylaw.[46]

Pulse will implement a "first time" promotion, in which the client pays full price for the initial drop-in class and gets a second drop-in class free if he or she returns within a week. In addition, when a client refers a friend to the studio, the client receives his or her class for free. Package rates and class cards are also available.

Advertising

Pulse will broadcast advertisements over two radio stations. The target market has a strong interest in music and it is important to cover more than one station since Nexus consumers are prone to "cluster loyalty"; as opposed to having one favourite radio station, they will have several. The stations are selected based on their listener profiles and suitability to Pulse.

Online advertising is important for the target group, who are tech-savvy and use technology as a major part of their lives. Email and online promotions effectively reach these consumers. Pulse will advertise on the radio station's website in addition to on-air. The website will have a "sign up for news" function where clients can provide their email address and receive information on upcoming events, promotions, and other news about Pulse. With the popularity of social networking and Facebook among the generation, a social page can be created that would be tailored specifically to the appropriate gender, age, location, and user interests. Facebook will not be utilized in the initial 12-month period, but may be used in the second year, for additional advertising. Pulse's website will be permanent and will start up just prior to opening.[47]

Fast Forward Weekly magazine will be utilized since the majority of readers are 18–35 years of age, and 44% are females.[48] Pulse's primary competitor, Decidedly Jazz Danceworks, also uses the magazine to advertise. In addition, it advertises in the Yellow Pages, which is something Pulse will consider for future advertising at a later date.

Pulse will be an exhibitor at the Calgary Women's Show due to its strong focus on the target market. Females are the focus and 44% of attendees are 18–35 years old. The full-time workforce represents 57% of visitors to the show, and 75% have a college/university level education.[49] The Lilac Festival brings in approximately 100,000 people with a 60% representation of the target age group, and the majority of attendees being those who live in the immediate area. The average income of attendees is $75,000 and 68% said they would make future purchases from the exhibitors they visited.[50]

Calgary Transit will be used to attract those commuting to downtown Calgary and the 4th street area. Stats Canada shows that there are 37,690 females who use public transit as their commuting method to work; representing 17%, and is the second most popular transportation method among females.[51]

Exhibit 4 outlines the initial advertising schedule for Pulse Dance Inc.

The poster for the 28" LRT advertisement is bright, eye catching, and to the point, and will be representative of all visual advertisements that Pulse will create. Promotional items will be used for the shows/festivals. The item for the Women's Show will be a tote bag for carrying dance shoes that will display the Pulse logo in large print on the outside. Water bottles will be distributed at the Lilac Festival, which will be bright yellow, and again display the Pulse logo.

Strategic Alliances will be developed with neighbouring product/service providers in the area. Both Lululemon and Starbucks will be approached to set up an alliance where they would both advertise Pulse within their locations, and Pulse would advertise for them as well as offer promotional discounts for clients who hear about Pulse through these alliances.

Type	Company	Frequency	Price	Details	Total Price
Magazine					
	Fast Forward Weekly	4 weeks online and 4 weeks in weekly magazine—Aug 18–24, advertise registration; Sept 15–21, Jan 12–18, May 3–8, to advertise beginning of classes	$20 per thousand hits online (leader board) $309 for ⅛ pg. ad. (4-week package)	Estimating 1000 hits online	$ 2236
Radio					
	Vibe 98.5	1 wk. on-air—Sept 15–21; 2 wks online—Sept 15–21, Jan 12–18, to advertise beginning of classes	$175/ad (on-air) $200/wk (banner)	20 ads per week, one banner per week	$ 4100
	CJay 92	1 wk. on-air —Jan 12–18; 1wk online—May 3–8, to advertise beginning of classes	$175/ad (on-air) $150/wk (banner)	20 ads per week, one banner per week	$3650
Events					
	Women's Show	2 × annually	$1400/show	One show only	$ 1400
	Lilac Festival	1 day annually	$450/booth	2 booths	$ 900
Transit					
	LRT	4 weeks—Nov 15–22 and Apr 3–9 (registration), Jan 12–18 and May 3–8 to advertise beginning of classes	$85 (×2) and $120 × 2	Approx. 8 trains and 12 stations.	$ 4240
	Bus	4 weeks—Aug 18–24 (registration); Sept 15–21, Jan 12–18, May 3–8 to advertise beginning of classes	$22 (×2)	Approx. 20 bus routes	$ 880
Website					
	Serverside Studios	Permanent	—	Maintenance additional $200/yr	$ 60
TOTAL					$18,600

LEGAL STRUCTURE

Capital Requirements

The start-up cost for the studio is $66,258.56. The owners are investing $27,200 worth of cash and assets into the business. The building owner has agreed to provide a leasehold improvement subsidy amounting to $11,857.46, and both Meghan Hicks' and Lauren Round's relatives have provided love money for the business, totalling $16,600.

The remaining amount of $27,201.40 will be funded by an operating line of credit with an interest rate of prime + 3% (8.75%), and will be paid off by the end of the first year of operations (see Start-Up Costs).

Share Structure

Lauren Round is the Principle and Secretary, and Meghan Hicks is the Principle and Treasurer. They are the only two common shareholders, with a 50/50 ownership split. The initial investment is $27 200 with 2000 common shares issued, and 1000 preferred shares. The preferred shares are non-transferable and have buy-back provisions with a three-year term and 10% rate of return. Pulse will pay the investors a balloon payment at the end of year 3 in the amount of $16,600 plus 10% interest.

Name	Type of Shares	Number Issued	Equity Contributed (FMV)
Meghan Hicks	Common	1000	$ 5600
Lauren Round	Common	1000	$ 5600
Jo-Anne & Dan Campbell	Preferred Class A	500	$ 8600
Bonnie & Ron Freisen	Preferred Class A	500	$ 8000
Total Equity			$27,200

Insurance

Due to the nature of the business, Pulse is viewed by insurance companies as a relatively safe business. The insurance that has been recommended is General Commercial Liability coverage. The coverage covers tenant's legal liability, bodily injury (to both employees and clients), fire, burglary, theft, and vandalism. The plan will cost $2500 per year.

MANAGEMENT TEAM

The management team at Pulse will consist of two owners; Lauren Round and Meghan Hicks. Both will be fully involved in the operations of the studio and will oversee various tasks. Based on Lauren's marketing education and experience, she will be in charge of managing the advertising and promotion, as well as instructor scheduling and student registration for all classes. Meghan will be in charge of the accounting and finance for the business, based on her accounting and business education and experience.

Both owners have a strong dance background and will be involved in the interviewing and hiring of teachers and staff for the studio. They will also teach classes and share the responsibility of all human resource tasks. After three months of operations, the owners will each receive a $35,000 annual salary.

Dance instructors with advanced-level dance experience and instructor experience will be hired on a part-time basis. Instructors who can teach more than one discipline will be given preference, with a total of three regular instructors being hired, and one guest instructor, who will change throughout the year. The studio will have two mentors; Nino Acosta of Latin Corner Dance Studio has strong industry experience and will assist with

EXHIBIT **5**
*Management Team
Tasks, Titles, and
Salary and Benefits*

Team Member	Skills	Tasks and Duties	Ownership and Title	Salary and Benefits
Lauren Round	General business, entrepreneurship, marketing, dance experience (able to teach several disciplines)	Marketing, scheduling, HR, and online registration. Also teaching part-time (14–17hrs/week)	Principle with 50% ownership	Salary of $35,000/yr beginning 3 months after opening. Health and dental coverage is included.
Meghan Hicks	Accounting, tax, finance, entrepreneurship, dance experience (able to teach several disciplines)	Accounting, finance, HR, and online registration. Also teaching part-time (10–15hrs/week)	Principle with 50% ownership	Salary of $35,000/yr beginning 3 months after opening. Health and dental coverage is included.
Instructors (×4)	All will have 5+ years of advanced dance experience, 2+ years of instructor experience. Ballet instructor will have RAD certification. Guest instructor will be booked bi-weekly.	1—hip hop/break dance 2—acro, lyrical, stretch and strength 3—ballet 4—guest	Instructors No ownership	Salary of $22/hr for all except guest instructor, who receives $25/hr.

marketing strategies for Pulse; Lorna Thackrey of Definitive Dance Inc. has experience and knowledge with studio start-up and operation and will provide guidance in these areas. For additional details, a GANTT chart is available at www.longenecker4e.nelson.com.

MISSION STATEMENT

Pulse Dance Inc. strives to enrich the lives of adult dancers by providing both challenging and exciting dance classes to those specializing exclusively in jazz, ballet, hip hop, and lyrical. PDS prides itself on its high-quality instruction, flexible schedules, competitive rates, performance opportunities, and a positive and energetic atmosphere.

FUNDING

Type of Financing

As advised by ATB Financial, an operating line of credit will be used to fund Pulse's cash shortfalls. Because Pulse qualifies for more than is required (based on collateral), a line of credit for $29,500 will be issued. Having the excess means that Pulse will have it available for use if needed, but will pay for only what is used.

The operating line of credit must be paid back in full, with interest, within 10 years. The interest rate is guaranteed for a five-year term and is set at prime + 3%; prime is currently 5.75% so the rate would be 8.75%.

A summary of the start-up costs for PDS is shown in Exhibit 6.

EXHIBIT **6**
*Start-Up Costs for Pulse
Dance Inc.*

Leasehold Improvements

Hardwood flooring (1300 sq. ft.)	
Installation of floors and baseboards	6500.00
Materials	6354.00
Foam underlay	1027.00
Drywall (300 ft)	16000.00
Wall-to-wall mirrors (60 ft)	6122.00
Studio doors (2)	171.94
Changeroom door	85.97
Ventilation upgrades	750.00
Paint (4 18.9L cans)	516.00
Paint supplies	68.32
Leasehold subsidy	(11857.46)
Total leasehold improvements	25738.45

Equipment and furniture

Office Desk (for reception area only)	500.00
Office Chair	39.00
Office supplies (pens, highlighters, stapler, hole-punch, scissors, white out)	28.58
Paper (1 box)	34.99
White board and markers	16.49
Cork board and tacks	44.95
Book shelf (3)	80.97
Filing cabinet	159.00
Printer/fax machine combo	199.00
Phone	69.99
Clocks (4)	39.96
Wooden Coat hangers	39.99
Wooden benches (changeroom)	91.98
Lockers (8 18")	628.00
Couch	199.99
Sitting chairs (4)	180.00
Stereo systems (2)	179.98
Speaker system (2)	2499.88
Garbage bins (3)	8.97
Ballet bars (2 double-sided 10 ft bars)	826.00
Ballet bars (2 double-sided 8 ft bars)	660.00
Studio Signage	2100.00
Web Designer–student	400.00
Merchant services equipment	1450.00
Cleaning Supplies	110.00
Total equipment and furniture	10588.70

Operating Costs

Rent/Utilities (month of August and September)	10044.00
Insurance	416.00
Incorporation Licences (package 3)	325.00
Municipal Business Licence	236.00
Salaries (August-training and September)	1462.00
Advertising	5008.00
Phone and Internet (57.90/month)	115.80
Alarm system	176.98
Merchant Services (1.59%)	290.46
Total operating costs	18074.24
Total Start-up Costs	**54401.40**

EXHIBIT **6**
Start-Up Costs for Pulse Dance Inc. (Continued)

Financing	
Lauren Round	
Cash	5000.00
Love money	8600.00
Total	13,600.00
Meghan Hicks	
Cash	5000.00
Love money	8000.00
Computer	600.00
Total	13,600.00
Total Financing	27,200.00
Loan	27,201.40

Pulse Dance Inc.'s income statement and balance sheet can be found in Exhibits 7 and 8. The sales forecast and cash flow statement are available on the book's companion site at www.longenecker4e.nelson.com

EXHIBIT **7**
Income Statement for Pulse Dance Inc.

Pulse Dance Inc.
Income Statement

		Year Ended July 31, 2009		Year Ended July 31, 2010
Revenue				
Revenue from Sub-Contracting Studios:				
Summer Camps		16,898.00		16,898.00
Daily Use During the Year		22,200.74		22,200.74
Revenue from Sales				
Drop In Classes		56,420.00		67,704.00
Drop In Packages		30,750.00		36,900.00
Session Packages		65,175.00		78,210.00
Total Revenue		191,443.74		221,912.74
Operating Expenses:				
Lease & Utility Costs	60,264.00		60,264.00	
Amortization Expense	1016.21		1784.19	
Owner's Salaries	52,500.00		70,000.00	
Wages	23,701.50		23,701.50	
Benefits *(see appendix 58)*	1920.00		1920.00	
CPP & EI	984.10		984.10	
Worker's Compensation *(see appendix 61)*	75.85		75.85	
Advertising & Promotion	18,600.00		15,000.00	
Alarm	566.88		467.88	
Phone & Internet	694.80		694.80	
Merchant Services	3872.29		2906.74	
Office Supplies	192.00		192.00	
Cleaning Supplies	110.00		75.00	
Municipal License	236.00		97.00	
Legal Fees	500.00		500.00	
Interest Expense (Operating Line)	1,723.87		533.81	
Insurance	2500.00		2500.00	

Total Expenses	169,457.50	181,696.87
Income from Operations	21,986.24	40,215.87
Pay down of Operating Line of Credit	15,000.00	12,201.40
Income before Taxes	6986.24	28,014.47
Tax Expense (16.12%)	1126.18	4515.93
Net Income	5860.06	23,498.54

EXHIBIT **7**
(Continued)

Pulse Dance Inc.
Balance Sheet

EXHIBIT **8**
Balance for Pulse Dance Inc.

	Year Ended July 31, 2009	Year Ended July 31, 2010
ASSETS		
Current Assets		
Cash	$ 5180.45	$ 30,431.75
Office Supplies	63.57	63.57
Cleaning Supplies	110.00	75.00
Property, Plant & Equipment		
Dance Floor	13,881.00	13,881.00
Stereo System	179.98	179.98
Speaker System	2499.88	2499.88
Furniture	1627.96	1627.96
Furnishings & Accessories	4256.33	4256.33
Leasehold Improvements	7714.23	7714.23
Computer	600.00	600.00
Less: Accumulated Amortization—Equipment		
(see appendix 62)	−1016.21	−2800.40
	35,097.19	58,529.30
Other Assets	14,980.46	2845.49
Total Assets	$ 50,077.65	$ 61,374.79
LIABILITIES & OWNER'S EQUITY		
Current Liabilities		
Accounts Payable	$ 5416.19	$ 5416.19
Long-Term Liabilities		
Operating Line of Credit	12,201.40	—
Shareholder's Equity		
Common Shares	10,000.00	10,000.00
Preferred Shares	16,600.00	16,600.00
Retained Earnings	5860.06	29,358.60
Total Liabilities & Owner's Equity	$ 50,077.65	$ 61,374.79

BREAK-EVEN ANALYSIS

Calculations revealed that PDS would be required to sell 490 session packages throughout its first operating year in order to achieve a break-even status. When our profit goal of 10% was added to the equation, it was determined that 539 packages would need to be sold to break-even and earn 10% profit. In terms of viability, PDS projects that it will sell 219 session packages, 410 drop-in packages, and 3177 drop-in classes totalling $152,345 in revenue. This amount alone is not enough to break even; however, PDS will also be sub-contracting the space to increase total revenue to $191,443.74, which exceeds the revenue generated from the sale of 539 session packages, totalling $185 146.50. It is therefore viable for PDS to break even and earn a 10% profit in year 1.

LIQUIDITY			Year 1		Year 2	FPI Ratio
Current	Total Current Assets/ Current Liabilities	5354.02/ 5416.19	0.989	30,570.32/ 5416.19	5.640	0.917
PROFITABILITY						
Operating Expenses to Sales	Operating Expenses/ Net Sales	169,457.50/ 191,443.74	0.885	181,696.87/ 221,912.74	0.819	0.936
Income to Sales	Net Income/ Net Sales	5860.06/ 191,443.74	0.031	23,498.54/ 221,912.74	0.106	0.064
Rent to Sales	Rent Expense/ Net Sales	60,264/ 191,443.74	0.317	60,264/ 221,912.74	0.272	0.122
Promotion to Sales	Advertising Expense/ Net Sales	18,600/ 191,443.74	0.097	15,000/ 221,912.74	0.067	0.024
Return on Investment	Net Income/ Average Equity	5860.06/ (10,000 + 16,600 + 5860.06)	0.184	23,498.54/ (10,000 + 16,600 + 29,358.60)	0.420	0.171
STABILITY						
Leverage	Total Debt/Equity	(5416.19 + 12,201.40)/ (10,000 + 16,600 + 5860.06)	0.167	(5416.19)/ (10,000 + 16,600 + 29,358.60)	0.097	0.100
Interest Coverage	Net Profit before tax and interest/ interest expense	8710.11/ 1723.87	5.052	28,548.28/ 533.81	53.480	4.400
GROWTH						
Sales	(Year 2 − Year 1)/ Year 1 × 100%	(221,912.74 − 191,443.74)/ 191,443.74 × 100%	15.915%			
Profit	(Year 2 − Year 1)/ Year 1 × 100%	(23,498.54 − 5860.06)/ 5860.06 × 100%	3.000%			

RATIO ANALYSIS

The ratios representing the first operating year of PDS indicate that the liquidity ratio is slightly lower than 1 but in keeping with industry average. The rent–sales ratio is considerably higher for PDS due to inflated rent costs in Calgary versus other areas, and PDS's promotion-sales ratio is higher than the industry average because it is a start-up venture unlike the ones listed. It will, however, reach industry average by year 3. By year 2, our current assets are projected to be greater than our current liabilities because of the amount of loan repaid at the end of the first year. This is also reflected in the interest coverage ratio, as well as in the income–sales ratio, both of which are much higher than industry average. The ROI for investors is also significant as a result of loan repayments by year 2. The leverage ratio is fairly high in year 1; however, it begins to decline by year 2, and thus measures accurately against the standard. Therefore, with only some exceptions, PDS's financial forecast is in keeping with industry standards. See ratio chart below.

ENDNOTES

1. Nino Acosta. *Latin Corner Dance Studio,* April 2007, www.latincorner.ca/bio-nino.html
2. Leaseco Realty Inc., "Main Floor Retail and Office Space Available," 2008.
3. "Royal Academy of Dance Canada," 2008, www.radcanada.ca
4. "Performing Arts Educators of Canada," 2005, www.paec.ca
5. Class Schedules—Fall 2008, Winter 2009, Spring 2009
6. Andrew Clark. "Young, impatient and empowered," *Maclean's*: Toronto, May 17, 1999, 112(20), A3
7. NAICS and ArcIMS Maps
8. City of Calgary—Community Social Statistics Profiles
9. Best Customers—Demographics of Consumer Demand
10. *Financial Post* Canadian Demographics 2008
11. City of Calgary phone interview
12. Environics Analytics
13. Euromonitor, "New Aesthetes," 2008
14. "Find your rhythm," *Woodland Hills*: Feb 2008 27(6), 240
15. Antoinette Alexander, "Tech-savvy young shoppers may be untapped market," *Drug Store News*: New York, Jun 2004, 26(8), 97
16. Euromonitor, "Generation Y: Marketing to the Young Ones (18–26s)," 2008
17. Euromonitor, "Girl Power: Marketing to Today's Woman," 2008
18. Statistics Canada—Leisure-time physical activity by health region, 2005.
19. Alberta Recreation Survey—Calgary (2004)
20. Consumer Trends Report.
21. T.J. Cheney Research Inc., prepared for Canada Council for the Arts, "Facts of Dance: Then and No—and Now What?" April 2004, www.canadacouncil.ca
22. Canadian Fitness and Lifestyle Research Institute, 2005, http://www.cflri.ca/eng/
23. Canadian Business Index, 2007.
24. Dianne Milligan, "Dance, Recreational," *The Canadian Encyclopedia*, 2008, www.thecanadianencyclopedia.com
25. Susan Kramer, "Dance Meditation for Adults," 2007, www.bellaonline.com
26. Jill Wyatt and Anne Flynn , "YWCA Calgary— Dance Pilot Project," September 2005, www.calgaryurbancampus.ucalgary.ca/ywca
27. Cindy Stephen, "West Coast Swing steps," *Calgary Herald*, 2008, www.canada.com
28. "Genre Busting," November, 2007, www.ffwdweekly.com
29. Kealy Litun, interview by Lauren Round, *Alberta Dance Association*, February 11, 2008.
30. *Decidedly Jazz Danceworks*, January 2008, www.decidedlyjazz.com
31. *Free House Dance Plus Ltd.*, January 2008, www.freehousedance.com
32. YWCA, January 2008, www.fitnessonfifth.com

33. City of Calgary, January 2008, http://rec-econnect.gov.calgary.ab.ca/ econnect/activities

34. Yoga Santosha, www.yogasantosha.com

35. Core Yoga and Pilates, www.coreyogapilates.com

36. Alive Personal Training, http://alivepersonaltraining.com

37. Photos of Location—100, 320 23rd Avenue SW

38. Leasco Agent Location Meeting

39. City of Calgary—Traffic Maps

40. Calgary Commercial Real Estate Vacancy Rates

41. City of Calgary—Permits

42. City of Calgary—Business License Phone Interview

43 Calgary Transit Route Maps

44. SME and FPI

45. "Targeting Generation Y" by Linda P. Morton (ProQuest)

46. City of Calgary—Temporary Signs Bylaw

47. "Facebook Zombies—Marketing to Gen Y" by Lee Odden (TopRank Online Marketing)

48. Advertising—Phone Interviews

49. Calgary Women's Show

50. Lilac Festival

51. Statistics Canada—2001 Census Metropolitan Area, Mode of transportation

Endnotes

Chapter 1

1. "One Size Does Not Fit All Canadian Entrepreneurs, According to Annual RBC Survey," (September 28, 2007) at http://www.rbc.com/newsroom/20070928sme.html (accessed July 18, 2008).

2. Statistics Canada, *Market Research Handbook 2007*, 63–224.

3. *A Portrait of Small Business Growth and Employment in Western Canada*, Western Centre for Economic Research, School of Business, University of Alberta, Number 63–2001 (see http://www.wd.gc.ca/rpts/research/portrait/6_e.asp?printVersion=1 for further clarification).

4. "Poll: Most Like Being Own Boss," *USA Today*, May 6, 1991. For a scholarly study confirming the importance of a quest for independence as a motivational factor, see Marco Virarelli, "The Birth of New Enterprises," *Small Business Economics*, vol. 3, no. 3 (September 1991), pp. 215–23.

5. Aneliese Debus, "Small Business, Big Value," Canadian Federation of Independent Business (October 2007) at http://www.cfib.ca.

6. "Bankruptcies and Proposals Reported for 2003 by Major Urban Centres," at http://www.strategis.gc.ca (accessed May 2005).

7. Stewart Thornhill and Raphael Amit, *Learning about Failure: Bankruptcy, Firm Age and the Resource-based View* (Richard Ivey School of Business/The Wharton School, University of Pennsylvania, n.d.).

8. Steve Bareham, "Planning to Fail Can Spell Success," at http://www.Canadaone.com (accessed September 1999).

9. "Entrepreneurs' Start-up Cognitions and Behaviours: Dreams, Surprises, Shortages, and Fast Zigzags," http://www.babson.edu/entr/fer (accessed January 10, 2005).

10. Amar V. Bhide, *The Origin and Evolution of New Businesses* (New York: Oxford University Press, 2000), Chapter 1.

11. Norman R. Smith, *The Entrepreneur and His Firm: The Relationship between Type of Man and Type of Company* (East Lansing: Bureau of Business and Economic Research, Michigan State University, 1967). Also see Norman R. Smith and John B. Miner, "Type of Entrepreneur, Type of Firm, and Managerial Motivation: Implications for Organizational Life Cycle Theory," *Strategic Management Journal*, vol. 4, no. 4 (October–December 1983), pp. 325–40; and Carolyn Y. Woo, Arnold C. Cooper, and William C. Dunkelberg, "The Development and Interpretation of Entrepreneurial Typologies," *Journal of Business Venturing*, vol. 6, no. 2 (March 1991), pp. 93–114.

12. Cited in Gary M. Stern, "Young Entrepreneurs Make Their Mark," Nation's Business, vol. 84, no. 8 (August 1996), pp. 49–51.

13. Russell M. Knight, "Entrepreneurship in Canada," paper presented at the annual conference of the International Council for Small Business, Asilomar, California, June 22–25, 1980.

14. Sarah Dougherty for CanWest News Service, Montreal, "Young Entrepreneurs Quit Corporate Uncertainty," Calgary Herald, October 15, 2001, p. B6.

15. J. B. Rotter, "Generalized Expectancies for Internal versus External Control of Reinforcement," *Psychological Monographs,* 1966. A more recent review is given in Robert H. Brockhaus, Sr., and Pamela S. Horwitz, "The Psychology of the Entrepreneur," in Donald L. Sexton and Raymond W. Smilor (eds.), *The Art and Science of Entrepreneurship* (Cambridge, MA: Ballinger, 1986), pp. 25–48.

16. Jeffry A. Timmons and Stephen Spinelli, *New Venture Creation: Entrepreneurship for the 21st Century* (New York: McGraw-Hill/Irwin, 2007), pp. 249–55.

Chapter 2

1. Burke Campbell, "Getting Laid Off Supplied the Motivation," *Financial Post,* November 12, 2007.

2. http://www.eyesistant.com/news_pr-eywinner.html and http://www.mediclink.ca.

3. Leslie Brokaw, "How to Start an Inc. 500 Company," *Inc. 500* (Special Issue) 1994, p. 52.

4. http://www.orthosoft.ca (accessed June 2005).

5. http://www.taskperformance.ca.

6. Burke Campbell, "Storm's Fallen Trees Inspired Carpenter's Business," *National Post,* November 10, 2007.

7. Michael E. Porter, *Competitive Advantage* (New York: Free Press, 1985), p. 5, 18.

8. Gary Hamel, "Strategy as Revolution," *Harvard Business Review,* vol. 74, no. 4 (July–August 1996), p. 80.

9. See http://www.rutter.ca/rutinc_abt_profile.asp, http://www.rutter.ca/11_14-2007.asp, and PROFIT 100 "19th Annual Ranking of Canada's Fastest Growing Companies" (n.d.) at http://www.canadian business.com/rankings/profit100/list.jsp?pageID= list&type=p100&listType=&year=2007&page=1& content.

10. Gary Hamel, "Strategy as Revolution," *Harvard Business Review,* vol. 74, no. 4 (July–August 1996), p. 80.

11. From an unpublished manuscript "Feasibility Template" by Leo Donlevy, Dalton Hearding, and Dr. Peter Robinson.

12. Saul Chernos, "Teamwork Helps Firms Hear Customer's Voice," *Financial Post,* vol. 91, no. 29 (July 18–20, 1998) p. IT4.

13. Liz Katynski, "Big Box, Small Box: Superior Service Gives Small Retailers an Edge," *Manitoba Business,* vol. 21, no. 3 (April 1999), pp. 5–6.

14. http://www.upsidesoft.com (accessed January 29, 2008).

15. Susanne Baillie, "Tips from the Masters," *PROFIT: The Magazine for Canadian Entrepreneurs,* vol. 20, no. 2 (April 2001), p. 19.

16. Kali Pearson, "Canucks Who Make the Grade," *PROFIT: The Magazine for Canadian Entrepreneurs,* vol. 20, no. 2 (April 2001), p. 21.

17. Bruce Livesey, "Great Moments in Marketing," *PROFIT: The Magazine for Canadian Entrepreneurs,* vol. 17, no. 1 (February–March, 1998), pp. 34–40.

18. Karl H. Vesper, *New Venture Strategies,* rev. ed. (Englewood Cliffs, NJ: Prentice Hall, 1990), p. 192.

19. Kara Kuryllowicz, "Canada's Hottest IPOs: Westjet Airlines Ltd.," *PROFIT: The Magazine for Canadian Entrepreneurs,* vol. 19, no. 1 (February–March 2000), p. 34, and http://www.westjet.com (accessed June 2005).

20. Sean Silcoff, "Dutch (re)treat," *Canadian Business,* vol. 73, no. 15 (August 2000), pp. 42–45.

21. Sheldon Gordon, "Shakin' up Main Street," *PROFIT: The Magazine for Canadian Entrepreneurs,* vol. 19, no. 5 (September 2000), pp. 59–66.

22. Harvey Schachter, "Who Wants to be an Internet Tycoon," *PROFIT: The Magazine for Canadian Entrepreneurs,* vol. 19, no. 3 (May 2000), p. 36.

23. For example, see Richard Hall, "A Framework Linking Intangible Resources and Capabilities to Sustainable Competitive Advantage," *Strategic Management Journal,* vol. 14, no. 8 (November 1993), pp. 607–18; Steven Maijoor and Arjen van Witteloostujin, "An Empirical Test of the Resource-Based Theory: Strategic Regulation in the Dutch Audit Industry," *Strategic Management Journal,* vol. 17, no. 7 (July 1996), pp. 549–69; Christine Oliver, "Sustainable Competitive Advantage: Combining Institutional and Resource-Based Views," *Strategic Management Journal,* vol. 18, no. 9 (October 1997), pp. 697–713; and Thomas C. Powell and Anne Dent-Micallef, "Information Technology as Competitive Advantage," *Strategic Management Journal,* vol. 18, no. 5 (May 1997), pp. 375–405.

24. David J. Collis, "How Valuable Are Organizational Capabilities?" *Strategic Management Journal* (Special Issue), Winter 1994, pp. 143–52.

25. Ian C. MacMillan, "Controlling Competitive Dynamics by Taking Strategic Initiative," *Academy of Management Executive,* vol. 2, no. 2 (May 1988), pp. 111–12.

26. Chris Daniels, "Pearls to the Orient: Land of the Rising Sun Lucrative Market for BC Oyster Entrepreneurs," *Food in Canada,* vol. 60, no. 9 (November–December, 2000), pp. 20–21.

27. See http://www.bdc.ca/en/about/mediaroom/ news_releases/2007/2007101605.htm and http://www.iloverewards.com

28. Michael Barrier, "A Global Reach for Small Firms," *Nation's Business*, vol. 82, no. 4 (April 1994), p. 66.

29. See Canadian Youth Business Foundation (http://www.cybf.ca), "Kerri'd Treasures Unique Gifts, 2007 Business Award Winner" at http://www.kerridtreasures.com.

30. Amar Bhide, "How Entrepreneurs Craft Strategies That Work," *Harvard Business Review*, vol. 72, no. 2 (March–April 1992), p. 154.

31. Michael E. Porter, *Competitive Advantage* (New York: Free Press, 1985), p. 5.

32. Kim Hanson, "Small Business Blues: The Closing of Whitby Dominion Hardware Highlights Some of the Built-in Constraints Grinding away at Canada's Engine of Growth," *Financial Post—National Post*), vol. 1, no. 285 (September 25, 1999), p. D4.

Chapter 3

1. Lowell J. Spirer, "The Human Factor in Starting Your Own Business," e-book.

2. Darcy Nybo, "Family Fortunes and Friction—Sorting It All Out," *Business Examiner* (Thompson Okanagan ed.), July 4, 2007, p. 22.

3. Daniel L. McConaughy, "Family CEOs vs. Non-Family CEOs in the Family Controlled Firm: An Examination of the Level of Pay to Performance," *Family Business Review*, vol. 13, no. 2 (June 2000), pp. 121–31; and Simon Bartholomeusz and George A Tanewski, "The Relationship Between Family Firms and Corporate Governance," *Journal of Small Business Management*, vol. 44, no. 2 (April 2006), pp. 245–67.

4. David G. Sirmon and Michael A. Hitt, "Managing Resources: Linking Unique Resources, Management and Wealth Creation in Family Firms," *Entrepreneurship Theory and Practice*, vol. 27, no. 4 (Summer 2003), pp. 341–44.

5. John L. Ward, "New Research on Family Business Culture," proceedings of the Fifth Annual Kellogg Family Business Invitational Conference, Evanston IL, May 16–17, 2006, pp. 51–65.

6. Phyllis Cowan, "Halifax Seed Is Canada's Oldest Continuously Operating Seed Company," *CAFEpresse*, Summer 1997, p. 11.

7. A description of these bases of commitment and an extensive discussion of the theory and analysis that support these conclusions can be found in Pramodita Sharma and P. Gregory Irving, "Four Bases of Family Business Successor Commitment: Antecedents and Consequences," *Entrepreneurship*

Theory and Practice, vol. 29, no. 1 (January 2005), pp. 13–33.

8. Ibid.

9. Ibid.

10. Ibid., pp. 25–26.

11. Quoted in Jeff D. Opdyke, "Readers' Views on Family, Feuds and Quality of Life," CareerJournal .com (April 25, 2005), http://www.careerjournal.com (accessed December 13, 2006).

12. Darcy Nybo, "Family Fortunes and Friction—Sorting It All Out," *Business Examiner* (Thompson Okanagan ed.), July 4, 2007, p. 22.

13. Sue Birley, "Attitudes of Owner-Managers' Children Toward Family and Business Issues," *Entrepreneurship Theory and Practice*, vol. 26, no. 3 (Summer 2002), pp. 5–19.

14. Jonathan Black, "How to Raise an Entrepreneur," *Inc.*, vol. 27, no. 8 (August 2005), pp. 81–85.

15. Teo Paul Lin, "Spilling the Beans," *The Straits Times*, July 16, 2006, http://www.stomp.com. sg (accessed December 20, 2006).

16. John L. Ward, "Family Humor," proceedings of the Fifth Annual Kellogg Family Business Invitational Conference, Evanston, IL, May 16–17, 2006, p. 45.

17. Ibid.

18. Darren Dahl, "Was Firing Him Too Drastic?" *Inc*, vol. 28, no. 10 (October 2006), pp. 51–54.

19. Jeff Dennis, "Your Not-So-Silent Partner," *Profit*, vol. 24, no. 2 (May 2005), pp. 21–22.

20. John L. Ward, quoted in Margaret Steen, "The Decision Tree of Family Business," *Stanford Business* (August 2006) at http://www.gsb.stanford.edu/ news/bmag./sbsm0608/feature_familybiz.html (accessed September 4, 2008).

21. Cited in Kenneth Meeks, "Family Business," *Black Enterprise*, vol. 31, no. 1 (August 2003), p. 91.

22. Matthew Fogel, "A More Perfect Business," *Inc.*, vol. 25, no. 8 (August 2003), p. 44.

23. Ibid.

24. John L. Ward, "Family Humor," proceedings of the Fifth Annual Kellogg Family Business Invitational Conference, Evanston, IL, May 16–17, 2006, p. 45. Anonymous, "Keeping It in the Family: Roy Rump and Sons Tire and Auto Takes Success to the Third Generation," *Service Station & Garage Management* (Don Mills), vol. 34, Iss. 12 (December 2004), p. 33.

25. Ibid.

26. Austin Ramirez, quoted in Margaret Steen, "The Decision Tree of Family Business," *Stanford Business*, (August 2006) at http://www.gsb.stanford.edu/news/ bmag./sbsm0608/feature_familybiz.html (accessed September 4, 2008).

Chapter 4

1. http://www.canamfranchise.com (accessed January 2008).

2. http://www.cfa.ca (accessed May 11, 2005).

3. As reported in Jeffrey A. Tannenbaum, "Chain Reactions," *Wall Street Journal*, October 15, 1993, p. R6.

4. Erika Kotite, "Is Franchising for You?" Franchise & Business Opportunities 1995, *Entrepreneur* (Special Issue), p. 17.

5. http://www.canamfranchise.com (accessed January 2008).

6. Ibid.

7. http://www.yogenfruz.co.uk (accessed May 10, 2005).

8. Cynthia E. Griffen, "Global Warning," *Entrepreneur*, vol. 23, no. 1 (January 1995), p. 118.

9. James H. Amos, Jr., "Trends and Developments in International Franchising," *The Franchising Handbook* (American Management Association, 1993), p. 463.

10. See Jeffrey A. Tannenbaum, "More Franchisers Include Profit Claims in Pitches," *Wall Street Journal*, August 20, 1991, p. B1.

Chapter 5

1. Personal communication with the author, November 2001.

2. Mark Stevens, "Seven Steps to a Well-Prepared Business Plan," Executive *Female*, vol. 18, no. 2 (March 1995), p. 30.

3. William Sahlman, "How to Write a Great Business Plan," *Harvard Business Review*, vol. 75, no. 4 (July–August 1997), pp. 98–108.

4. Kenneth Blanchard and Spencer Johnson, *The One-Minute Manager* (New York: William Morrow, 1982).

5. John Southherst, "The Start-up Star Who Bats .900," *Canadian Business*, vol. 66, no. 3 (March 1993), pp. 66–72.

6. Stanley R. Rich and David Gumpert, *Business Plans That Win $$$: Lessons from the MIT Forums* (New York: Harper & Row, 1985), p. 22.

7. Arthur Andersen and Company, *An Entrepreneur's Guide to Developing a Business Plan* (Chicago: Author, 1990).

8. Matthew Stark, "What Do Investors Look for in a Business Plan? A Comparison of the Investment Criterion of Bankers, Venture Capitalists and Business Angels," *International Small Business Journal*, June 1, 2004.

9. Adapted from Phillip Thurston, "Should Smaller Companies Make Formal Plans?" *Harvard Business Review* (September–October 1983), p. 163.

10. Arthur Andersen and Company, *An Entrepreneur's Guide to Developing a Business Plan* (Chicago: Author, 1990).

11. William Sahlman, "How to Write a Great Business Plan."

12. Adapted from Rhonda M. Abrams, The Successful Business Plan: Secrets and Strategies, 2nd ed. (Grants Pass, OR: Oasis Press, 1993).

13. Fraser Institute, Complementary and Alternative Medicine in Canada: Trends in Use and Public Attitudes, 1997–2006, May 2007.

Chapter 6

1. Cheryl Abrams, "The Quick 'N Natural Soup Entrepreneur," *Business*, vol. 20, no. 3 (May–June 1998), pp. 32–33.

2. Gayle Sato Strodder, "Right off Target," *Entrepreneur*, vol. 22, no. 10 (October 1994), p. 56.

3. See *Inc.*'s website at http://www.inc.com.

4. See, for example, the website of the Research Institute of the University of Dayton at http://www.udri .udayton.edu/webcenter/wwwsurveys.htm.

5. Charles W. Lamb, Joseph F. Hair, and Carl McDaniel, *Marketing*, 9th ed. (Cincinnati: Thomson-Southwestern, 2008), p. 602.

6. Brian Vellmure, "Let's Start with Customer Retention," http://www.initiumtech.com/newsletter_120602.htm, September 4, 2004.

7. Thomas O. Jones and W. Earl Sasser, Jr., "Why Satisfied Customers Defect," *Harvard Business Review*, vol. 73, no. 6 (November–December 1995), p. 90.

8. Jerry Fisher, "The Secret's Out," http://www. entrepreneur.com/mag/article/0,1539,228496.html, June 8, 2004.

9. Bruce Horovitz, "Whatever Happened to Customer Service?" *USAToday*, September 26, 2003, pp. 1A–2A.

10. Dionne Searcey, "For Better or Worse," *Wall Street Journal*, October 30, 2006, p. R5.

11. See, for example, Del I. Hawkings, David L. Mothersbaugh, and Roger J. Best, *Consumer Behavior: Building Marketing Strategy,* 10th ed. (New York: McGraw-Hill Irwin, 2007), Chapter 17.

12. Ibid.

Chapter 7

1. http://www.iabcanada.com (accessed January 2008).

2. Melissa Campanelli, "Sharing the Wealth," *Entrepreneur*, February 2005, p. 40.

3. Jennifer Gill, "Attention Shoppers," Inc.com (accessed April 2006).

4. Shannon Scully, "Go Fetch More Money!" *My Business*, June–July 2003, p. 41.

5. http://www.webwasher.com (accessed February 5, 2007).

6. For more details regarding domain name rules, see http://www.register.com/domain-rules.cgi.

7. http://www.dnjournal.com/ytd.-sales-charts.htm (accessed February 1, 2007).

8. Chris Kivelhan, "Improve Your Website's Performance," (May 3, 2006) at http://www .entrepreneur.com/ebusiness/operations/ article159400.html (accessed July 30, 2007).

9. Corey Rudl, "4 Fatal Website Design Mistakes," at http://www.entrepreneur.com (accessed January 29, 2007).

10. Adapted from Janet Attard, "Trade Show Dos and Don'ts," http://www.businessknowhow.com/ tips/tradesho.htm (accessed February 5, 2007).

11. For a more detailed discussion of prospecting, see Lawrence B. Chonko and Ben M. Enis, *Professional Selling* (Boston: Allyn and Bacon, 1993), Chapter 9.

12. Stephanie Clifford, "Putting the Performance in Sales Performance," *Inc.*, February 2007, pp. 87–95.

13. Shane McLaughlin, "Paying Cash for Contacts," *Inc.*, vol. 20, no. 11 (November 1998), p. 107.

14. For an excellent discussion of price setting, see Charles W. Lamb, Jr., Joseph F. Hair, Jr., and Carl McDaniel, *Principles of Marketing* (Cincinnati: South-Western, 2008), Chapter 18.

15. Bob Weinstein, "Price Pointers," *Entrepreneur*, vol. 23, no. 2 (Feb. 1995), p. 50.

16. Robert J. Calvin, "The Price Is Right," *Small Business Reports*, vol. 19, no. 6 (June 1994), p. 13.

Chapter 8

1. A good discussion of modes of transportation is found in Charles W. Lamb, Jr., Joseph F. Hair, Jr., and Carl McDaniel, *Principles of Marketing* (Cincinnati, OH: South-Western, 1998), Chapter 14.

2. James F. Foley, *The Global Entrepreneur: Taking Your Business International* (Chicago: Dearborn Financial Publishing, 1999), p. 5.

3. Svante Andersson, "Internationalization in Different Industrial Contexts," *Journal of Business Venturing*, vol. 19, no. 6 (2004), pp. 851–75; "Don't Laugh at Gilded Butterflies," *The Economist*, vol. 371, no. 8372 (April 22, 2004), pp. 71–73; and Oliver Burgel, Andreas Fier, Georg Licht, and Gordon C. Murray, "The Effect of Internationalization on Rate of Growth of High-Tech Start-Ups—Evidence for UK and Germany," in Paul D. Reynolds et al. (eds,), *Frontiers for Entrepreneurship Research*, proceedings of the 20th Annual Entrepreneurship Research Conference, Babson College, June 2002.

4. "Profile of Canadian Exporters," *The Daily*, http://www.statcan.ca/Daily (accessed February 21, 2005).

5. Raymond Vernon, "International Investment and International Trade in the Product Cycle," *Quarterly Journal of Economics*, vol. 80, no. 2 (May 1966), pp. 190–207.

6. Rodney C. Shrader, Benjamin M. Oviatt, and Patricia Phillips McDougall, "How New Ventures Exploit Trade-Offs Among International Risk Factors: Lessons for the Accelerated Internationalization of the 21st Century," *Academy of Management Journal*, vol. 43, no. 6 (December 2000), pp. 1227–47.

7. Roger E. Axtell, "International Trade: A Small Business Primer," *Small Business*, vol. 10, no 1.

8. Stuart Laidlaw, "Exporting: Most Businesses Haven't Tapped Foreign Markets," *Financial Post Weekly* (July 22, 1995), p. 11.

9. http://www.psdglobal.com/servies/partners-in-security-2008-trade-mission.php (accessed March 12, 2008).

10. An interesting analysis of firm size and exporting behaviour is found in Abbas Ali and Paul M. Swiercz, "Firm Size and Export Behavior: Lessons from the Midwest," *Journal of Small Business Management*, vol. 29, no. 2 (April 1991), pp. 71–78.

11. Julie Amparano Lopez, "Going Global," *Wall Street Journal*, October 16, 1992, p. R20.

12. Charles F. Valentine, "Blunders Abroad," *Nation's Business*, vol. 44, no. 3 (March 1989), p. 54.

13. Roger Thompson, "EC92," *Nation's Business*, vol. 77, no. 6 (June 1989), p. 18.

14. A more detailed analysis of the FTA is found in "The Canada–United States Free Trade Agreement and Its Implication for Small Business," *Journal of Small Business Management*, vol. 28, no. 2 (April 1990), pp. 64–69.

15. An analysis of NAFTA is presented in the Government of Canada publication *The North American Free Trade Agreement (NAFTA): At a Glance* (Ottawa: Government of Canada, 1993).

16. Department of Foreign Affairs, http://www .dfait-maeci. gc.ca.

17. Anne Crawford, "Alberta's Strategy Focuses on Asia," *Calgary Herald*, October 4, 1995, p. D3.

18. Jill Andresky Fraser, "Structuring a Global Licensing Deal," *Inc.,* vol. 14, no. 11 (November 1992), p. 45.

19. http://www.arcticspas.com (accessed March 20, 2008).

20. Lopez, "Going Global," p. R20.

21. U. S. Department of Commerce, *A Basic Guide to Exporting* (Washington, DC: U. S. Government Printing Office, 1992), p. 13–2.

22. Personal discussion by the author with company officials.

23. For further discussion of factoring, see R. Michael Rice, "Four Ways to Finance Your Exports," *The Journal of Business Strategy* (July–August 1988), pp. 30–31.

Chapter 9

1. Jim Schell, "In Defense of the Entrepreneur," *Inc.,* vol. 13, no. 5 (May 1991), p. 30.

2. The best-known model is found in Neil C. Churchill and Virginia L. Lewis, "The Five Stages of Small Business Growth," *Harvard Business Review* (May–June 1983), pp. 3–12. A more recent study was conducted by Kathleen M. Watson and Gerhard R. Plaschka, "Entrepreneurial Firms: An Examination of Organizational Structure and Management Roles across Life Cycle Stages," Proceedings, United States Association for Small Business and Entrepreneurship, Baltimore, Maryland, October 13–16, 1993.

3. Stephen R. Covey, *The 7 Habits of Highly Effective People* (New York: Simon and Schuster, 1990), pp. 173–79.

4. Ellyn E. Spragins, "Hiring without the Guesswork," *Inc.,* vol. 14, no. 2 (February 1992), p. 81.

5. Robert Melnbardis, "A Factory Takes Off," *Canadian Business*, Productivity Supplement (November 1994), p. 45.

6. Diane P. Burley, "Making Job Descriptions Pay," *Independent Business*, vol. 5, no. 2 (March–April 1994), pp. 54–56.

7. Personal communication with the author, February 2004,

8. Doug Burn, "On-Site Training," *Canadian Plastics*, vol. 52, no. 2 (February 1994), pp. 29–30.

9. Ibid, pp. 29-30.

10. "Bonus Pay: Buzzword or Bonanza?" *BusinessWeek* (November 14, 1994), pp. 62–63.

11. Roger Thompson, "Switching to Flexible Benefits," *Nation's Business*, vol. 79, no. 7 (July 1991), pp. 16–23.

12. Joan C. Szabo, "Using ESOPs to Sell Your Firm," *Nation's Business*, vol. 79, no. 1 (January 1991), pp. 59–60.

13. Diana McLaren, "When the Union Comes Calling; It's Common for Small Business Owners and Managers to be Wary of Unionization," *The Globe and Mail*, October 17, 2007, p. E1.

14. Ibid. p. E1.

15. "Do You Need an Employee Policy Manual?" *Business*, vol. 10, no. 4 (July–August 1988), p. 48.

Chapter 10

1. "The Inc. FaxPoll: Are Partners Bad for Business?" *Inc.,* vol. 15, no. 2 (February 1992), p. 24.

2. Joshua Hyatt, "Reconcilable Differences," *Inc.,* vol. 13, no. 4 (April 1991).

3. Ibid.

4. Ibid.

5. Harold W. Fox, "Growing Concerns: Quasi-Boards—Useful Small Business Confidants," *Harvard Business Review*, vol. 60, no. 1 (January–February 1982), p. 164.

6. Fred A Tillman, "Commentary on Legal Liability: Organizing the Advisory Council," *Family Business Review*, vol. 1, no. 3 (Fall 1988), pp. 287–88.

7. Brown, S., "Cuts Leave Patient Privacy in Critical Condition," *Richmond News*, April 30, 2005, p. 10.

Chapter 11

1. For a more comprehensive treatment of relocation issues, see Rick Mullin, "Site Selection," *Journal of Business Strategy*, May–June 1996, pp. 26–39.

2. Sandra Thomas, "Lack of Parking Licks Stamp Shop," *Vancouver Courier*, January 9, 2008, Final Edition, p. 13.

3. Carey Vigneault, "Timing Proves Major Asset for LaSalle Venture," *The Windsor Star*, December 9, 2004, p. C2.

4. "Alberta Tax Advantage," at http://www.finance.alberta.ca/publications/budget/budget2008/tax.pdf (accessed September 4, 2008), p. 160.

5. http://www.competitivealternatives.com/highlights/cities/html (accessed September 4, 2008).

6. Angela Lovell, "Going to the Country," *Manitoba Business*, vol. 29, Iss. 2 (March 2007), p. 22.

7. http://www.cabi.ca (accessed January 2008).

8. Todd Bechard, "Getting Space," *CMA Management*, vol. 75, Iss. 3 (May 2001), pp. 14–15.

9. Ibid., p. 15.

10. Manfred Purtzki, "Negotiating a Lease," *Medical Post*, vol. 39, Iss. 27 (July 15, 2003), p. 41.

11. Ernest B Akyeampong, "Working at Home: An Update," *Perspectives*, Statistics Canada Catalogue no. 75-001-XIE, June 2007, p. 16.

12. Kevin Marron, "Web the Great Leveler for Home biz.com," *The Globe and Mail*, Report on Business, July 31, 2000, p. W1

13. "Small Businesses Launch Projects in Cyber Village IT Incubator Planned for Downtown," *Winnipeg Free Press*, March 16, 2001, p. B5.

14. "Minding Your Own Business . . . While Minding Your Children. Sidelines for at-Home Parents," *Today's Parent*, vol. 17, no. 7 (August 2000), pp. 68–69.

15. Dave Mabell, "Pampered Chef Cooks up New Form of Kitchen Party," *The Lethbridge Herald*, October 28, 2000.

16. Mary MacKay, "Bears in Mind: P.E.I. Couple Gives up Careers to Create Unique Periwinkle Bears from Exotic Fibres Woven at Their Home-Based Business in Schurman's Point," *The Guardian* (Charlottetown), February 21, 2001, Final Edition, p. D20.

17. Stephanie Henderson, "Home Ventures Take on Life of Their Own: Answering a Growing Demand," *The Spectator* (Hamilton), March 4, 1998, Final Edition, p. N8.

18. Cynthia E. Griffin, "Home Improvement," *Entrepreneur*, vol. 24, no. 9 (September 1996), pp. 106–07.

19. Bruce Owen, "City Expects Extra $2 Million from Home-Based Business Fees," *Winnipeg Free Press*, December 11, 2000, p. A3.

20. Grant Buckler, "Report on Small Business: Internet Phones. Is VoIP Ready for Your Company?" *The Globe and Mail*, March 17, 2005, p. C7.

21. "Electronic Commerce and Technology," *The Daily* (April 20, 2006) at http://www.statcan.ca/Daily/English/060420/d060420b.htm (accessed September 2, 2008).

22. http://www.witiger.com/ecommerce/benefits-limitations.htm (accessed September 4, 2008).

23. Perri Capell, "How to Make Money on eBay," *Wall Street Journal*, December 20, 2006, p. R5.

24. http://www.auctions. nettop20.com (accessed March 17, 2008).

25. http://www.premium. hoovers.com (accessed December 2006).

Chapter 12

1. American Society of Quality, http://www.asq.org/glossary/q.html (accessed September 4, 2008).

2. American Society of Quality, http://www.asq.org (accessed June 2005).

3. Adapted from Leonard L. Berry, A. Parasuraman, and Valarie A. Zeithaml, "Improving Service Quality in America: Lessons Learned," *Academy of Management Executive*, vol. 8, no. 2 (May 1994), p. 36.

4. Cynthia A. Lengnick-Hall, "Customer Contributions to Quality," *Academy of Management Review*, vol. 21, no. 3 (July 1996), p. 791.

5. http://iso.org/iso/iso_catalogue/management_standards/is0_9000_iso_14000.htm (accessed September 4, 2008).

6. Ken Myers and Jim Buckman, "Beyond the Smile: Improving Service Quality at the Roots," *Quality Progress*, vol. 25, no. 12 (December 1992), p. 57.

7. Michael Hammer and James Champy, *Reengineering the Corporation* (New York: HarperCollins, 1994), p. 32.

8. Hugh Alley, "Improving Your Process Improvement Efforts," *Plant*, vol. 62, Iss. 10 (July 14, 2003), p. 22.

9. Adapted from http://www.alberta-canada.com/productivity/lean/index.html, (accessed September 4, 2008).

10. Michelle Douglas, "Drawing Out the Benefits of EDI," *Computer Dealer News*, vol. 18. Iss. 11 (June 14, 2002), pp. 19–20.

11. Roberta Maynard, "Striking the Right Match," *Nation's Business*, vol. 84, no. 5 (May 1996), p. 19.

12. For formulas and calculations related to determining the economic order quantity, see an operations management textbook, such as James B. Dilworth, Operations *Management: Design, Planning, and Control for Manufacturing and Services* (New York: McGraw-Hill, 1992), pp. 375–79.

Chapter 13

1. See, for example, Michael Gibbins, *Financial Accounting: An Integrated Approach*, 5th ed. (Toronto: Thomson Nelson, 2003).

2. When we computed Computer World's operating income return on investment earlier, we found it to be 10.87 percent. Now it is 10.85 percent. The difference is the result of rounding.

3. The relationship of a firm's return on equity to its operating profitability and the use of debt will be explained in detail in Chapter 13.

4. Jill Andresky Fraser, "The Art of Cash Management," *Inc.*, vol. 20, no. 14 (October 1998), p. 124.

5. Accruals are not considered in terms of managing working capital. Accrued expenses, although shown as a short-term liability, primarily result from the

accountant's effort to match revenues and expenses. There is little that could be done to "manage accruals."

6. "Cash Flow: Who's in Charge," *Inc.,* vol. 15, no. 11 (November 1993), p. 140.

Chapter 14

1. Personal communication with the author, 1996.

2. "Canada's Fastest-Growing Companies," *PROFIT: The Magazine for Canadian Entrepreneurs,* vol. 24, no. 4 (June 2005), pp. 32–41.

3. "Big Bank Loans Decline," *Times-Colonist* (Victoria), October 19, 2004, p. D3.

4. http://www.PROFITguide.com (accessed May 11, 2005).

5. Dave LeBlanc, "Budding Builders Cut Their Teeth on First House," *The Globe and Mail,* April 6, 2007, p. G11.

6. "Venture Capital Investment Up 21% Across Canada in 2007" (February 12, 2008) at http://www.cvca .ca/files/NEWS/CVCA_Q4_2007_VC_Press_Release _Final.pdf (accessed September 4, 2008).

7. J. Freear, J. E. Sohl, and W. E. Wetzel, "The Private Investor Market for Venture Capital," *The Financier,* vol. 1, no. 2 (May 1994), pp. 7–15.

8. Jeffrey L. Seglin, "What Angels Want," *Inc.,* vol. 20, no. 7 (July 1998), p. 43.

9. Paul Gompers and Josh Lerner, *The Money of Invention: How Venture Capital Creates Wealth* (Harvard Business School Press, 2001).

10. Bruce Posner, "How to Pick a Factor," *Inc.,* vol. 14, no. 2 (February, 1992), p. 89.

11. Tony Wanless, "Dick Hardt's Angels," *BC Business,* vol. 32, no. 3 (March 2004), p. 28.

12. Robert Thompson, "NB Software Manufacturer Bucks Trend in Tech Sector: $5m in Financing," *Financial Post—National Post,* August 14, 2001, p. C6.

13. Jeff Buckstein, "Ottawa Startup Secures Trust for Online Payment," *Ottawa Citizen,* March 10, 2005, p. G4; and http://liquidcomputing.com/home/ home.php (accessed September 3, 2008).

14. Personal communication with the author, 2000.

15. http://www.40statcan.ca (accessed May 14, 2005).

16. Jill Andresky Fraser, "The Art of the Covenant," *Inc.,* vol. 19, no. 8 (August 1997), p. 99.

17. Robert Thompson, "VC Investment Slides More in U.S. than in Canada," *Financial Post—National Post,* February 26, 2002, p. FP8.

18. Peter Hum, "Safe Landing," *Ottawa Citizen,* March 10, 2005, p. E4.

19. Amar Bhide, "Bootstrap Finance: The Art of Startups," *Harvard Business Review,* vol. 70, no. 6 (November–December 1992), pp. 117–48.

Chapter 15

1. "Definitive Guide to Managing for Growth" at http://www.rbroyalbank.com/business/definitive guide/ecommerce.html (accessed September 4, 2008).

2. Ibid.

3. David E. Gumpert and David P. Boyd, "The Loneliness of the Small Business Owner," *Harvard Business Review,* vol. 62, no. 6 (November–December 1984), p. 19.

4. Howard Scott, "Getting Help from Your Accountant," *IB Magazine,* vol. 3, no. 3 (May–June 1992), p. 38.

5. Barbara Chabai, "Serial Entrepreneurs are Driven to Create," *Business Edge,* vol. 6, no. 4 (February 16, 2006).

6. Lisa D. Stein, presentation at the National Forum for Women in Finance, sponsored by the Financial Women's Association of New York, *Fortune,* and the Financial Executive Institute, New York, September 16–17, 1998.

7. S. R. Holmburg, "Value Creation and Capture: Entrepreneurship Harvest and IPO Strategies," in N. C. Churchill, W. D. Bygrave, J. C. Covin, D. L. Sexton, D. P. Slevin, K. H. Vesper, and W. E. Wetzel, Jr. (eds,), *Frontiers of Entrepreneurship Research* (Wellesley, MA: Babson College, 1991), pp. 191–204.

8. Wayne H. Mikkelson, Megan Partch, and Ken Shah, "Ownership and Operating Performance of Companies That Go Public," *Journal of Financial Economics,* vol. 44, pp. 281–308.

9. L. Brokaw, "The First Day of the Rest of Your Life," *Inc.,* vol. 15, no. 5 (May 1993), p. 144.

10. Nancy B. Upton and J. William Petty, "Funding Options for Transferring the Family-Held Firm: A Comparative Analysis," Working Paper, Baylor University, Waco, TX, 1998.

11. The source of this example is Heritage Partners, a Boston venture capital firm, which obtained a registered trademark for a process it calls the "Private IPO."

Glossary

(Numbers in parentheses refer to the chapter(s) containing the main discussion of the term.)

24/7 e-tailing electronic retailing providing round-the-clock access to products and services (11)

A

ABC method a system of classifying items in inventory by relative value (12))

acceptance sampling the use of a random, representative portion to determine the acceptability of an entire lot (12)

accounts payable (trade credit) outstanding credit payable to suppliers (13, 14)

accounts receivable the amount of credit extended to customers that is currently outstanding (14)

accounts receivable turnover the number of times accounts receivable "roll over" during a year (13)

accrual method of accounting a method of accounting that matches revenues when they are earned against the expenses associated with those revenues (13)

accrued expenses short-term liabilities that have been incurred but not yet paid (13, 14)

acid-test ratio (quick ratio) a measure of a company's liquidity that excludes inventories (13)

advertising the impersonal presentation of a business idea through mass media (7)

advisory council a group that functions like a board of directors but acts only in an advisory capacity (10)

agency power the ability of any one partner to legally bind the other partners (10)

agency relationship an arrangement in which one party represents another party in dealing with a third party (10)

agents and brokers intermediaries that do not take title to the goods they distribute (8)

area developers individuals or firms that obtain the legal right to open several franchised outlets in a given area (4)

articles of association the document that establishes a corporation's existence (10)

artisan entrepreneur a person with primarily technical skills and little business knowledge who starts a business (1)

asset-based valuation approach determination of the value of a business by estimating the value of its assets (16)

assorting bringing together homogeneous lines of goods into a heterogeneous assortment (8)

attitude an enduring opinion based on knowledge, feeling, and behavioural tendency (6)

attractive small firm a small firm that provides substantial profits to its owner (1)

attribute inspection the determination of product acceptability based on whether it will or will not work (12)

auction sites web-based businesses offering participants the ability to list products for bidding (11)

average collection period the average time it takes a firm to collect its accounts receivable (13)

average pricing an approach in which total cost for a given period is divided by quantity sold in that period to set a price (7)

B

balance sheet a financial report that shows a firm's assets, liabilities, and owners' equity capital at a specific point in time (13)

banner ads advertisements that appear across a web page, most often as moving rectangular strips (7)

batch manufacturing a type of manufacturing operation that is intermediate (between job shops and repetitive manufacturing) in volume and variety of products (12)

benchmarking the process of studying the products, services, and practices of other firms, and using the insights gained to improve quality internally (12)

benefit variables specific characteristics that distinguish market segments according to the benefits sought by customers (6)

Bills of Exchange Act A federal law that sets out the requirements for negotiable financial instruments such as cheques and promissory notes (10)

board of directors the governing body of a corporation, elected by the shareholders (10)

brand a verbal and/or symbolic means of identifying a product (6)

break-even point sales volume at which total sales revenue equals total costs (7)

breaking bulk an intermediary process that makes large quantities of product available in smaller amounts (8)

bricks-and-mortar location The traditional physical store or location from which businesses have historically operated (11)

budget a document that expresses future plans in monetary terms (6)

buildup process a forecasting method in which all potential buyers in the various submarkets are identified; then the estimated demand is totalled and a market share estimate applied (6)

business angel a private investor who finances new, risky small ventures (14)

business incubator a facility that provides shared space, services, and management assistance to new businesses (11)

business model a group of shared characteristics, behaviours, and goals that a firm follows in a particular business situation (11)

business plan a document that sets out the basic idea underlying a business and related start-up considerations (5)

business policies basic statements that serve as guides for managerial decision making (9)

business-format franchising an agreement whereby the franchisee obtains an entire marketing system and ongoing guidance from the franchisor (4)

business-to-business (B2B) model a business model based on selling to business customers electronically (11)

business-to-consumer (B2C) model a business model based on selling to business to final customers electronically (11)

buyout purchasing an existing business (2)

C

cafeteria plans (or flexible benefits programs) plans that allow staff to choose their benefits within a set budget (9)

Canada Small Business Financing Program (CSBFP) a federal government program that provides financing to small businesses through private lenders, for which the federal government guarantees repayment (14)

Canadian Human Rights Act federal legislation that prohibits discrimination against people and guarantees basic human rights (10)

Canadian Intellectual Property Office (CIPO) responsible for the administration and processing of intellectual property (ideas, designs, creativity) (10)

capital gains and losses gains and losses incurred from sales of property that are not a part of the firm's regular business operations (10)

capital intensive industries that require large investments in equipment and facilities (13)

capitalization rate a figure, determined by the riskiness of current earnings and the expected growth rate of future earnings, that is used to assess the earnings-based value of a business (16)

cash budget (cash flow forecast) a planning document strictly concerned with the receipt and payment of dollars (14)

cash conversion period the time required to convert paid-for inventories and accounts receivable into cash (13)

cash flow forecast (cash budget) a planning document strictly concerned with the receipt and payment of dollars (13, 14)

cash flow–based valuation approach determination of the value of a business by comparing the expected and required rates of return on the investment (16)

cash method of accounting a method of accounting that reports transactions only when cash is received or a payment is made (13)

channel of distribution a system of intermediaries that distribute a product (8)

chattel mortgage a loan for which equipment or other moveable property serve as collateral (14)

cognitive dissonance the anxiety that occurs when a customer has second thoughts immediately following a purchase (6)

common carriers transportation intermediaries available for hire to the general public (8)

Competition Act federal antitrust legislation designed to maintain a competitive economy (10)

competitive advantage a benefit that exists when a firm has a product or service that is seen by its target market as better than those of competitors (2)

confidentiality agreement a document used to ensure investors keep information confidential (5)

content/information-based model a business model in which the website provides information but not the ability to buy or sell products and services (11)

continuous quality improvement a constant and dedicated effort to improve quality (12)

contract carriers transportation intermediaries that contract with individual shippers (8)

contract employees independent contractors hired for fixed periods of time or for specific projects (9)

contracts agreements that are legally enforceable (10)

control chart a graphic illustration of the limits used in statistical process control (12)

control cycle a period of time over which an activity is planned, measured, corrected, and replanned (12)

copyright the exclusive right of a creator to reproduce, publish, perform, display, or sell his or her own work (10)

core competencies value-creating organizational capabilities that are unique to a firm

corporate refugee a person who leaves big business to go into business for him- or herself (1)

corporation a business organization that exists as a legal entity and provides limited liability to its owners (10)

corrective maintenance repairs necessary to restore equipment or a facility to good condition (12)

cost of goods sold the cost of producing or acquiring goods or services to be sold by a firm (13)

cost-advantage strategy a plan of action that requires a firm to be the lowest-cost producer within its market

cost-based commitment commitment based on the belief that the opportunity for gain from joining a business is too great to pass up (3)

credit an agreement between a buyer and seller that provides for a delayed payment for a product or service (7)

culture behavioural patterns and values that characterize a group of consumers in a target market (6)

current assets (working capital) liquid assets that can be converted into cash within a company's operating cycle (13)

current ratio a measure of a company's relative liquidity, determined by dividing current assets by current liabilities (13)

customer profile a description of potential customers in a target market (6)

customer relationship management (CRM) a company-wide business strategy designed to optimize profitability and customer satisfaction by focusing on highly defined and precise customer groups (6)

cycle counting a system of counting different segments of the physical inventory at different times during the year (12)

D

daywork a compensation system based on increments of time (9)

debt capital business financing that was provided by creditors and must be repaid at some predetermined date (14)

debt ratio the ratio of total debt to total assets (13)

debt-equity ratio the ratio of total debt to total equity (13)

demographic variables specific characteristics that describe customers and their purchasing power (6)

desire-based commitment commitment based on a belief in the purpose of a business and a desire to contribute to it (3)

direct channel a distribution channel without intermediaries (8)

disclosure document a detailed statement of information such as the franchisor's finances, experience, size, and involvement in litigation (4)

distribution physically moving products and establishing intermediary channels to support such movement (8)

double-entry system a self-balancing accounting system that uses journals and ledgers (13)

dual distribution a distribution system that involves more than one channel (8)

E

earnings-based valuation approach determination of the value of a business based on its potential future earnings (16)

economic order quantity (EOQ) the quantity to purchase in order to minimize total inventory costs (12)

electronic Customer Relationship Marketing (eCRM) an electronically based system that emphasizes customer relationships (11)

email promotion advertising delivered by means of electronic mail (7)

employee ownership a method by which a firm is sold either in part or in total to its employees (15)

employee stock ownership plans (ESOPs) plans that give employees a share of ownership in the business (9)

Employment Insurance (EI) benefits paid to workers who become unemployed provided they meet certain requirements, such as having been employed for a minimum number of weeks (9)

employment standards codes provincial legislation regulating working conditions, minimum wages, and other work-related issues (10)

empowerment increasing employees' authority to take action on their own or make decisions (9)

entrepreneur a person who launches, builds, and/or operates a business (1)

entrepreneurial opportunity an economically attractive and timely opportunity that creates value (1)

entrepreneurial team two or more people who work together as entrepreneurs (1)

equipment loan an installment loan from a seller of machinery used by a business (14)

evaluative criteria the features of a product that customers use to compare brands (6)

evoked set a group of brands that a customer is both aware of and willing to consider as a solution to a purchase problem (6)

executive summary a section of the business plan that conveys a clear and concise overall picture of the proposed venture (5)

external equity funds that derive initially from the owners' investment in a firm (14)

external financing financing from outside investors (14)

F

family business a company that two or more members of the same family own or operate together or in succession (3)

family business constitution a statement of principles intended to guide a family firm through times of crisis and change (3)

family council an organized group of family members who gather periodically to discuss family-related business issues (3)

family council an organized group of family members who gather periodically to discuss family-related business issues (3)

family retreat a gathering of family members, usually at a remote location, to discuss family business matters (3)

financial acquisition a purchase in which the value of the business is based on the stand-alone cash-generating potential of the firm being acquired

financial leverage the use of debt in financing a firm's assets (13)

financial plan a section of the business plan that provides an account of the new firm's financial needs and sources of financing as well as a projection of its revenues, costs, and profits (5)

financial ratios restatements of selected income statement and balance sheet data in relative terms (13)

financial statements (accounting statements) reports of a firm's financial performance and resources, including an income statement, a balance sheet, and a statement of cash flows (13)

financing costs the amount of interest owed to lenders on borrowed money (13)

firm's cash flows after-tax cash flows generated from operations less the firm's investments in assets (13)

fixed asset turnover a measure of the relationship of sales to fixed assets (13)

fixed assets relatively permanent resources intended for use in the business (13)

flexible pricing strategy a marketing approach that offers different prices to reflect differences in customer demand (7)

follow-the-leader pricing strategy a marketing approach that uses a particular competitor as a model in setting prices (7)

foreign refugee a person who leaves his or her native country and becomes an entrepreneur in the new country (1)

founder an entrepreneur who brings a new firm into existence (1)

franchise contract the legal agreement between franchisor and franchisee (4)

franchise the privileges in a franchise contract (4)

franchisee an entrepreneur whose power is limited by a contractual relationship with a franchising organization (1)

franchising a marketing system revolving around a two-party legal agreement, whereby the franchisee conducts business according to terms specified by the franchisor (4)

franchisor the party in a franchise contract who specifies the methods to be followed and the terms to be met by the other party (4)

free cash flow operating profits plus depreciation less cash taxes and less the investments required to grow the firm (15)

Free Trade Agreement (FTA) an accord that eases trade restrictions between Canada and the United States (8)

freedom of information and privacy legislation protects individuals from having their personal information collected and used by businesses and other organizations for any purpose to which the individual objects (10)

free-flow pattern a flexible retail store layout that is visually appealing and gives customers freedom of movement (11)

fringe benefits supplements to compensation, designed to be attractive and beneficial to employees (9)

G

General Agreement on Tariffs and Trade (GATT) an international agreement that aims to reduce tariffs and other trade barriers among countries (8)

general partner a partner in a limited partnership who has unlimited personal liability (101)

general-purpose equipment machines that serve many functions in the production process (11)

geographic variables defining a market by its location, size, or extent (6)

grid pattern a block-like retail store layout that provides for good merchandise exposure and simplifies security and cleaning (11)

gross profit sales less the cost of goods sold (13)

growth trap a cash shortage resulting from rapid growth (13)

H

harassment policies policies that ensure all employees are treated equitably (9)

harvesting the exit process used by entrepreneurs and investors to unlock the value of a business (15)

headhunter a search firm that locates qualified candidates for executive positions (9)

high-potential venture (gazelle) a small firm that has great prospects for growth (1)

home-based business a business that maintains its primary facility in the residence of its owner (11)

I

income statement (profit and loss statement) a financial report showing the profit or loss from a firm's operations over a given period of time (13)

indirect channel a distribution channel with one or more intermediaries (8)

Industrial Designs Act federal legislation that protects the original shape, pattern, or ornamentation applied to a manufactured article (10)

industry environment the combined forces that directly affect a given firm and all of its relevant competitors (2)

informal capital funds provided by wealthy private individuals to high-risk ventures, such as start-ups (14)

initial public offering (IPO) the first sale of shares of a company's stock to the public (14, 15)

inspection an examination of a product to determine whether it meets quality standards (12)

inspection standard a specification of a desired quality level and allowable tolerances (12)

institutional advertising the presentation of information about a particular firm, designed to enhance the firm's image (7)

intangible assets assets that have no physical form but still provide value to the business (13)

intangible resources organizational resources that are invisible and difficult to quantify

Integrated Circuit Topography Act federal legislation that protects the three-dimensional configuration of electronic circuits in microchips and semiconductor chips (10)

internal control a system of checks and balances that safeguards assets and enhances the accuracy and reliability of financial statements (13)

internal equity funds that come from retaining profits within a firm (14)

inventory turnover the number of times inventories "roll over" during a year (14)

ISO 14000 the standards governing responsible environmental management (12)

ISO 9000 the standards governing international certification of a firm's quality management procedures (12)

J

job description a written summary of duties required by a specific job (9)

job shops a type of manufacturing operation in which short production runs are used to produce small quantities of unique items (12)

job specification a list of knowledge, skills, abilities, or other characteristics needed by a job applicant to perform a specific job (9)

just-in-time inventory system a method of reducing inventory levels to an absolute minimum (12)

L

laws of motion economy guidelines for increasing the efficiency of human movement and tool design (12)

LEAN manufacturing a system of techniques designed to eliminate waste, ensure quality, and involve employees in designing and managing their work (12)

legal entity a business organization that is recognized by the law as having a separate legal existence (10)

letter of credit an agreement to honour a demand for payment under certain conditions (8)

leveraged buyout (LBO) a purchase heavily financed with debt, where the potential cash flow of the target company is expected to be sufficient to meet debt repayments (15)

licensing legal arrangement allowing another manufacturer to use the property of the licenser in return for royalties (8)

lifestyle business a microbusiness that permits the owner to follow a desired pattern of living (1)

limited liability the restriction of an owner's legal financial responsibilities to the amount invested in the business (14)

limited partner a partner in a limited partnership who is not active in its management and has limited personal liability (10)

limited partnership a partnership with at least one general partner and one or more limited partners (10)

line of credit a legal commitment by a lender to lend up to a maximum amount (14)

linkage a type of advertising agreement in which one firm pays another to include a click-on link on its site (7)

liquidation-value approach determination of the value of a business based on the money available if the firm were to liquidate its assets (16)

liquidity the ability of a firm to meet maturing debt obligations by having adequate working capital available (13)

loan covenants bank-imposed restrictions on a borrower that enhance the chances of timely repayment (14)

lock box a post-office box for receiving remittances from customers (13)

long-range plan (strategic plan) a firm's overall plan for the future (9)

long-term debt loans from banks or other sources with repayment terms of more than 12 months (13, 14)

M

macroenvironment the broad environment with its multiple factors that affect most businesses in a society (2)

make-or-buy decision a firm's choice between producing and purchasing component parts for its products (12)

management buyout (MBO) leveraged buyout that includes the firm's top management as significant shareholders in the acquired firm (15)

management functions the activities of planning, leading, organizing, and controlling (9)

management plan a section of the business plan that describes a new firm's organizational structure and the backgrounds of its key players (5)

management team managers and other key persons who give a company its general direction (9)

market a group of customers or potential customers who have purchasing power and unsatisfied needs (6)

market analysis an evaluation process that encompasses market segmentation, marketing research, and sales forecasting (6)

market-based valuation approach determination of the value of a business based on the sale prices of comparable firms (16)

market segmentation the division of a market into several smaller groups with similar needs or buying behaviour (2)

marketing mix the combination of product, pricing, promotion, and distribution activities (6)

marketing-advantage strategy a plan of action designed to provide a product or service with unique attributes that are valued by consumers (2)

marketing plan a section of the business plan that describes the user benefits of the product or service (5)

master licensee a firm or individual acting as a sales agent with the responsibility for finding new franchisees within a specified territory (4)

matchmakers specialized brokers who bring together buyers and sellers of businesses (16)

mentoring guiding and supporting the work and development of a new or less-experienced organization (3)

merchant middlemen intermediaries that take title to the goods they distribute (8)

microbusiness a small firm that provides minimal profits to its owner (1)

mission statement a concise written description of a firm's philosophy (5)

modified-book-value approach determination of the value of a business by adjusting book value to reflect differences between the historical cost and the current value of the assets (16)

mortgage a long-term loan from a creditor for which real estate is pledged as collateral (14)

motion study an analysis of all the motions a worker makes to complete a given job (12)

motivations forces that organize and give direction to the tension caused by unsatisfied needs (6)

multiple-unit ownership a situation in which a franchisee owns more than one franchise from the same company (4)

multisegmentation strategy a strategy that recognizes different preferences of individual market segments and develops a unique marketing mix for each (2)

N

need-based commitment commitment based on an individual's self-doubt and belief that he or she lacks career options outside the current business (3)

needs the starting point for all behaviour (6)

negotiable instruments credit documents that are transferable from one party to another in place of money (10)

net income available to owners (net income) income that may be distributed to the owners or reinvested in the company (13)

net working capital the sum of a firm's current assets (cash, accounts receivable, and inventories) less current liabilities (short-term notes, accounts payable, and accruals) (13)

networking the process of developing and engaging in mutually beneficial business relationships (15)

niche marketing choosing market segments not adequately serviced by competitors (2)

normalized earnings earnings that have been adjusted for unusual items, such as fire damage (16)

North American Free Trade Agreement (NAFTA) an accord that eases trade restrictions among Canada, the United States, and Mexico (8)

O

obligation-based commitment commitment that results from a sense of duty or expectation (3)

occupational health and safety acts provincial legislation that regulates health and safety in the workplace to ensure safe workplaces and work practices (10)

Ontario Environmental Protection Act provincial legislation that establishes procedures, standards, and liability to ensure environmental protection (10)

operating expenses costs related to general administrative expenses and selling and marketing a firm's product or service (13)

operating income (earnings before interest and taxes) profits before interest and taxes are paid (13)

operating income earnings before interest and taxes are paid (13)

operating income return on investment (OIROI) a measure of operating profits relative to total assets (13)

operating plan a section of the business plan that offers information on how a product will be produced or a service provided, including descriptions of the firm's facilities, labour, raw materials, and processing requirements (5)

operating profit margin the ratio of operating profits to sales, showing how well a firm manages its income statement (13)

operations management the planning and control of the operations process (12)

operations process (production process) the activities that produce a firm's goods and services (12)

opinion leader a group leader who plays a key communications role (6)

opportunistic entrepreneur a person with both sophisticated managerial skills and technical knowledge who starts a business (1)

ordinary income income earned in the ordinary course of business, including any salary (10)

organizational capabilities the integration of several organizational resources that are deployed together to the firm's advantage (2)

organizational culture patterns of behaviours and beliefs that characterize a specific firm (3)

organizational resources basic inputs that a firm uses to conduct its business (2)

outsourcing purchasing products or services that are outside the firm's area of competitive advantage (12)

owners' equity capital owners' financial investments in a company, including profits retained in the firm (14)

P

partnership a legal entity based on the voluntary association of two or more persons to carry on, as co-owners, a business for profit (10)

partnership agreement a document that states explicitly the rights and duties of partners (10)

Patent Act federal legislation that gives a patent holder the exclusive right to construct, sell, manufacture, and use a patented invention for 20 years (10)

patent the registered, exclusive rights of an inventor to make, use, or sell an invention (10)

penetration pricing strategy a marketing approach that sets lower than normal prices to hasten market acceptance of a product or service, or to increase market share (7)

percentage of sales method of forecasting asset investments and financing requirements (14)

perception the individual processes that give meaning to the stimuli confronting consumers (6)

perceptual categorization the process of grouping similar things so as to manage huge quantities of incoming stimuli (6)

perpetual inventory system a method for keeping a running record of inventory (12)

Personal Information Privacy and Electronic Documents Act supports and promotes electronic commerce by protecting personal information that is collected, used, or disclosed by providing for the use of electronic means to communicate or record information or transactions (10)

personal selling a sales presentation delivered in a one-on-one manner (7)

physical distribution (logistics) the activities involved in the physical movement of products (8)

physical inventory system a method that provides for periodic counting of items in inventory (12)

piggyback franchising the operation of a retail franchise within the physical facilities of a host store (4)

Plant Breeders' Rights Act federal legislation that protects the multiplication and sale of new varieties of plant seeds (10)

pledged accounts receivable accounts receivable used as collateral for a loan (13)

pop-up ads advertisements that burst open on computer screens (7)

precipitating event an event, such as losing a job, that moves an individual to become an entrepreneur (1)

pre-emptive right the right of shareholders to buy new shares in the corporation before they are offered to the public (10)

prestige pricing setting a high price to convey an image of high quality or uniqueness (7)

preventive maintenance activities intended to prevent machine breakdowns, injuries to people, and damage to facilities (12)

price a specification of what a seller requires in exchange for transferring ownership or use of a product or service (7)

price quality grid a grid that displays the relative positions of competitive products and the value they deliver (7)

price-lining strategy a marketing approach that sets a range of several distinct merchandise price levels (7)

primary data new market information that is gathered by the firm conducting the research (6)

prime rate the interest rate charged by a commercial lender on loans to its most creditworthy customers (14)

private carriers shippers that own their means of transport (8)

private placement the sale of a firm's capital stock to selected individuals (14)

pro forma statements reports that project a firm's financial condition (5)

procedures specific methods followed in business activities (9)

process layout a factory design that groups similar machines together (11)

product a total bundle of satisfaction—including a service, a good, or both—offered to consumers in an exchange transaction (6)

product advertising the presentation of a business idea designed to make potential customers aware of a specific product or service and their need for it (7)

product and trade name franchising a franchise relationship granting the right to use a widely recognized product or name (4)

product item the lowest common denominator in a product mix—the individual item (6)

product layout a factory design that arranges machines according to their roles in the production process (11)

product line the sum of related individual product items (6)

product mix consistency the similarity of product lines in a product mix (6)

product mix the collection of a firm's total product lines (6)

product strategy the way the product component of the marketing mix is used to achieve a firm's objectives (6)

productivity the efficiency with which inputs are transformed into outputs (12)

products and/or services plan a section of the business plan that describes the product and/or service to be provided and explains the merits of the product and/or service (5)

professional manager a manager who uses systematic, analytical methods of management (9)

profit retention the reinvestment of profits in a firm (14)

profit-sharing plans a percentage of profits is distributed to employees (9)

promotion marketing communications that inform and persuade consumers (7)

promotional mix a blend of selling, advertising, and promotional tools aimed at a target market (7)

prospecting a systematic process of continually looking for new customers (7)

psychographic variables variables related to how people think and behave (6)

publicity information about a firm and its products or services that appears as a news item, free of charge (7)

purchasing the process of obtaining materials, equipment, and services from outside suppliers (12)

Q

quality circle a group of employees who meet regularly to discuss quality-related problems (12)

quality the features of a product or service that enable it to satisfy customers' needs (12)

R

real estate mortgage a long-term loan with real property held as collateral (14)

reengineering a fundamental restructuring to improve the operations process (12)

reference groups groups that an individual allows to influence his or her behaviour (6)

refugee a person who becomes an entrepreneur to escape an undesirable situation (1)

reliability the extent to which a test is consistent in measuring job performance ability (9)

repetitive manufacturing a type of manufacturing operation in which long production runs are used to produce a large quantity of a standardized product (12)

replacement-value approach determination of the value of a business based on the cost necessary to replace the firm's assets (6)

retained earnings profits that are reinvested in the business instead of being distributed to the owners (13)

return on equity the rate of return that owners earn on their investment (13)

risk premium the difference between the required rate of return on a given investment and the risk-free rate of return (16)

S

sales forecast a prediction of how much of a product or service will be purchased within a market during a specified time period (6)

sales promotion an inclusive term for any promotional techniques that are neither personal selling nor advertising (7)

secondary data market information that has been previously compiled (6)

securities acts provincial legislation that regulates the advertisements, issuance, and public sales of securities (10)

segmentation variables The parameters used to distinguish one form of market behaviour from another (6)

self-service layout a type of retail store design that gives customers direct access to merchandise (11)

serendipity the phenomenon of making desirable discoveries by accident (2)

serial entrepreneurs innovative and creative people who are more interested in starting new businesses than running them (15)

service mark a legal term indicating the exclusive right to use a brand to identify a service (6)

share certificate a document specifying the number of shares owned by a shareholder (10)

short-range plans plans that govern a firm's operations for one year or less (9)

short-term notes cash amounts that were borrowed from a bank or another lending source and must be repaid within a short period of time (14)

shrinkage the difference between physical inventory count and reported count, which is normally written off as spoilage or materials used under cost of goods sold (13)

single-entry system a chequebook system of accounting reflecting only receipts and disbursements (13)

single-segmentation strategy a strategy that recognizes the existence of several distinct market segments but focuses on only the most profitable segment (2)

skimming price strategy a marketing approach that sets very high prices for a limited period before reducing them to more competitive levels (7)

small business marketing those business activities that identify a target market; determine that market's potential; and prepare, communicate, and deliver a bundle of satisfaction to that market (6)

sole proprietorship a business owned and operated by one person (10)

special-purpose equipment machines designed to serve specialized functions in the production process (11)

spontaneous financing short-term debts, such as accounts payable, that spontaneously increase in proportion to a firm's increasing sales (14)

stages in succession phases in the process of transferring leadership of a family business from parent to child (3)

standard operating procedure an established method of conducting a business activity (9)

start-up creating a new business from scratch (2)

statement of cash flows a financial report that shows changes in a firm's cash position over a given period of time (13)

statistical process control the use of statistical methods to assess quality during the operations process (12)

Statute of Frauds legislation enacted to prevent fraudulent lawsuits without proper evidence of a contract (10)

strategic acquisition a purchase in which the value of the business is based on both the firm's stand-alone characteristics and the synergies that the buyer thinks can be created (15)

strategic alliance an organizational relationship that links two independent business entities in a common endeavour (12)

strategic decision a decision regarding the direction a firm will take in relating to its customers and competitors (2)

strategy an action plan that guides resource investments to capitalize on business opportunities (2)

sustainable competitive advantage an established, value-creating industry position that is likely to endure over time (2)

T

tangible resources organizational resources that are visible and easy to measure (2)

time study the determination of the average time it takes a worker to complete a given task (12)

times interest earned ratio the ratio of operating income to interest charges (13)

total asset turnover the ratio of sales to total assets, showing the efficiency with which a firm's assets are used to generate sales (13)

total cost the sum of cost of goods sold, selling expenses, and overhead costs (7)

total fixed costs costs that remain constant as the quantity produced or sold varies (7)

total quality management (TQM) an all-encompassing management approach to providing high-quality products and services (12)

total variable costs costs that vary with the quantity produced or sold (7)

trademark a word, name, symbol, device, slogan, or any combination thereof used to distinguish a product sold by one manufacturer (6, 10)

Trade-Marks Act federal legislation that regulates trademarks and provides for their registration (10)

transaction-based model a business model in which the website provides a mechanism for buying or selling products or services (11)

transfer of ownership passing ownership of a family business to the next generation (3)

type A ideas start-up ideas concerned with providing customers with an existing product not available in their market (2)

type B ideas start-up ideas concerned with providing customers with a new product (2)

type C ideas start-up ideas to provide customers with an improved product (2)

U

unlimited liability liability on the part of an owner that extends beyond the owner's investment in the business (10)

V

validity the extent to which a test assesses true job performance ability (9)

variable inspection the determination of product acceptability based on a variable such as weight or length (12)

variable pricing strategy a marketing approach that sets more than one price for a good or service in order to offer price concessions to certain customers (7)

variance the difference between planned or forecast activity and actual activity (12)

venture capitalist an investor or investment group that commits money to new business ventures (14)

W

warranty a promise that a product will perform at a certain level or meet certain standards (6)

Web sponsorship a type of advertising in which a firm pays another organization for the right to be part of that organization's web page (7))

work team employee team managing a task without direct supervision (9)

workers' compensation acts provincial legislation that provides employer-supported insurance for workers who become ill or are injured in the course of employment (10)

working-capital cycle the daily flow of resources through a firm's working-capital accounts (13)

working-capital management the management of current assets and current liabilities (13)

World Trade Organization (WTO) an international organization that administers GATT and works to lower tariffs and trade barriers worldwide (8)

zoning ordinances local laws regulating land use (11)

Index

553